NAZISM 1919–1945

VOLUME 3

FOREIGN POLICY, WAR AND RACIAL EXTERMINATION

EXETER STUDIES IN HISTORY

General Editors: Jonathan Barry, Tim Rees and T.P. Wiseman

Other titles in this series include:

Government, Party and People in Nazi Germany
edited by Jeremy Noakes

Nazism 1919–1945 A Documentary Reader
edited by J. Noakes and G. Pridham

Vol. 1: The Rise to Power 1919–1934
Vol. 2: State, Economy and Society 1933–1939
Vol. 3: Foreign Policy, War and Racial Extermination

Intelligence and International Relations 1900–1945
edited by Christopher Andrew and Jeremy Noakes

The American Constitution:
The First Two Hundred Years 1787–1987
edited by Joseph Smith

The Failure of Political Extremism in Inter-War Britain
edited by Andrew Thorpe

The Last Years of Austria-Hungary:
Essays in Political and Military History 1908–1918
edited by Mark Cornwall

The Origins of NATO
edited by Joseph Smith

The Civilian in War
edited by Jeremy Noakes

Exeter Studies in History No. 13

NAZISM 1919–1945

VOLUME 3
FOREIGN POLICY, WAR AND RACIAL EXTERMINATION
A Documentary Reader

EDITED BY

J. NOAKES

AND

G. PRIDHAM

UNIVERSITY
of
EXETER
PRESS

First published in 1988 by
University of Exeter Press
Reed Hall, Streatham Drive
Exeter, Devon EX4 4QR
UK

Reprinted 1991 and 1995
Reprinted with updated bibliography 1997

This book is available in the USA and Canada
through Northwestern University Press, 625 Colfax Street,
Evanston, IL 60208–4210, USA.

British Library Cataloguing in Publication Data
A catalogue record of this book is available
from the British Library

ISBN 0 85989 474 6
ISSN 0260–8628

Printed in Great Britain
by Short Run Press Ltd, Exeter

Contents

List of Maps

Preface

This is the third volume of what will be a four-volume collection of documents on Nazism 1919–1945. Originally, the authors intended to cover Nazi foreign policy and the history of the regime during the war years 1939–1945 in this third volume. However, in order to devote adequate space to Nazi racial policies, we decided to postpone dealing with the German home front, i.e. the political system, economy, society, and the Resistance to a fourth volume.

This volume begins, therefore, with an account of German foreign policy 1933–1939. This section is loosely based on Part V of *Documents on Nazism 1919–1945* (J. Cape London 1974), now out of print. The commentary has been substantially revised, however, and much of the documentation is new, including an analysis of the development of military and naval policy in relation to German diplomacy. This leads into an account of German strategy during the Second World War, which is a much revised and expanded version of chapters 19 and 20 of *Documents of Nazism*.

The book continues with a general account of the Nazi empire, including an analysis of the development of German occupation policies and focusing on the various plans for and techniques of economic exploitation. This is followed by a detailed case study of the occupation of Poland in which Nazi racial policies found perhaps their most ruthless expression. It was, for example, in Poland that the first mentally ill and handicapped patients were killed, thereby in effect inaugurating the 'euthanasia' programme which forms the subject of the next section of the book. It was also in Poland that the gassing techniques developed for the 'euthanasia' programme were later applied to exterminate the Jews in the death camps. The book concludes with the most systematic documentation of the Holocaust available in English. As with the previous volumes, this book contains material from a wide range of sources both published and unpublished: State and Party documents, newspapers, speeches, memoirs, letters, diaries and post-war trial records.

We would like to thank Professor Ian Kershaw for helpful suggestions on much of the manuscript, Dr Lesley Sharpe for advice on some of the translations, Seán Goddard who drew the maps, Mike Rouillard who designed the cover, and Barbara Mennell whose role as copy editor went far beyond the call of duty.

November 1987 J. NOAKES AND G. PRIDHAM

PREFACE TO THE FOURTH IMPRESSION

As with the previous reprint, we have again taken the opportunity to update the bibliography.

January 1997 J. NOAKES AND G. PRIDHAM

ACKNOWLEDGEMENTS

Extracts from *Documents on British Foreign Policy 1919–1939*, third series, Vol. VII, and extracts from *Documents on German Foreign Policy 1919–1945* Series D are reproduced with permission of the Controller of Her Majesty's Stationery Office.

Every effort has been made to trace the copyright holders of the extracts reprinted in this edition. The publishers apologise for any inadvertent omission, which can be rectified in a subsequent reprint.

CHAPTER 25

Hitler's Foreign Policy 'Programme'

Hitler first formulated a coherent foreign policy programme in his book *Mein Kampf*, written during 1924–5; it was a programme designed to secure German hegemony over Europe and to provide the basis for establishing world supremacy. It was shaped by a combination of ideological tenets, some of which were already fixed in his mind before he embarked on his political career in 1919, and conclusions drawn from his assessment of European political and diplomatic developments in the early 1920s, conclusions which subsequently had to be modified in the light of developments after 1933.

To begin with, Hitler's foreign policy objectives were quite conventional. In 1919, he shared the goals of the Pan-Germans, focusing on the revision of the Versailles treaty and in particular the reacquisition of Germany's lost colonies and the creation of a Greater Germany unifying all Germans in one Reich. This is clear from the first three points in the Nazi Party programme of February 1920, which were probably inserted by Hitler himself.[1] Moreover, like the Pan-Germans, Hitler at this time regarded Britain and France, not Russia, as Germany's main enemies. Something of Hitler's outlook can be gauged from a speech he made in Munich on 10 December 1919, of which two rather garbled police reports have survived. They show his hostility to Britain and France and the significance he attached to the loss of the German colonies:

[1] Cf. Vol. 1 p. 14.

467

(a) . . . Let us look at our enemies! We can divide them into two groups: one group includes the absolute opponents: England and America;[2] the second group: nations which became our opponents as a result of their unfortunate situation or as a result of their circumstances. Russia was always looking for an outlet to the sea and comes in too. We have been pursuing a Polish policy since Bismarck's time. The so-called Reinsurance Treaty[3] came to an end in 1892 and was not renewed. As a result Bismarck was bitterly attacked [*sic*]. In 1893 Alexander, the Tsar of Russia, went to Paris. He was applauded and the friendship was forged. And the Germans—well they are no good at politics: if they don't like something, the State can go to the devil. Italy too originally had nothing against Austria. Men like Holtzendorf [*sic*], Bismarck, and Ludendorff saw long ago that Italy was not in favour of Germany, it was more likely to take an active part in the war. Serbia and Romania were trying to become Great Powers. Japan had no direct hatred against Germany, it was pursuing world policy.

A count (*a shout*: 'Bothmer'[4]) said recently: France is pursuing a Continental policy. In fact the French statesmen were pursuing world policy and will continue to do so under our glorious government. In the course of 300 years France has declared war on Germany twenty-seven times. . . .

(b) . . . If whole areas of the world mobilize, one cannot apportion war guilt to a single country. In earlier times English diplomacy has understood how to estrange all the nations from one another in order to secure advantages for itself. The removal of our colonies represents an irreparable loss for us. We are compelled to secure our raw materials from the Allies and at such an expense that we will be excluded from the world market as effective competitors. . . .

During the next five years, Hitler moved away from the conventional revisionist position and developed his own foreign policy programme which he formulated in *Mein Kampf*. It reflected both ideological principles and his experience of European politics.

Hitler's ideology was formed from a number of theories current in the early twentieth century. From Social Darwinism he derived the notion that human life like animal life was a struggle for the survival of the fittest. Moreover, he adopted a version of this theory in which it was applied to social groups as well as to individuals. And, since he followed the German disciples of Gobineau in seeing race as the primary factor in history, he

[2] Although France is not included here as an 'absolute' opponent, it is clear from the rest of the speech that Hitler regarded it as such (eds).

[3] The treaty concluded by Bismarck with Russia on 18 June 1887, whereby, having already made an alliance with Austria in 1879, he hoped to avoid a one-sided commitment. The treaty was not renewed by his successor, General Caprivi (eds).

[4] A Bavarian federalist (eds).

came to regard history as essentially a struggle for survival among the various races.[5] These races differed in cultural quality with the Aryans, of whom the Germans represented the most significant component, forming the only true creative element, while the Jews were purely parasitic. However, in his view, the outcome of this racial struggle would be determined not by their inherent cultural potential but rather by the physical health and the morale of the respective races. This in turn depended on a proper relationship between their numbers and the territory and natural resources—above all agricultural land—available to them, which in Hitler's view Germany in the 1920s lacked.

Hitler shared a widespread view that, compared with the other great powers—Russia, the United States, Britain, and France—Germany was 'a nation without space' (the title of a popular contemporary novel). Moreover, with the loss of her colonies and of parts of her own territory in 1919 under the Versailles treaty this problem had been exacerbated. Hitler rejected the adoption of birth control and internal colonization as a solution since in his view they would weaken the race both in numbers and quality and encourage excessive urbanization. Hitler shared a view, common among the German Right, which attributed to big cities many of the ills of modern civilization, in particular the emergence of a decadent 'asphalt culture' and of 'rootless masses' which were prey to Marxism. He insisted that the only viable solution was the acquisition of more territory or 'living space' (*Lebensraum*). Moreover, this must be agricultural land in Europe, which could support a fecund German peasantry, rather than overseas colonies. Hitler's preoccupation with 'living space' and the extension of German resources was reinforced by the experience of the effective Allied blockade in the First World War and by German success in carving out a large empire in the East under the Treaty of Brest-Litovsk of March 1918.

Hitler appreciated that before Germany could be in a position to conquer new territory her first priority must be to free herself from the restraints of the Versailles treaty and build up her strength. To achieve this she would need allies, particularly against the power which he came to regard as having a vested interest in frustrating German expansion—France. In his choice of allies, as well as in his selection of territory most suitable for German expansion, Hitler was greatly influenced by political developments during the early 1920s and by Baltic German refugees in Munich.

The first of these developments was the occupation of Fiume by the Italian nationalist D'Annunzio, on 12 September 1919, contrary to the terms of the Versailles treaty. This event caused growing tension between

[5] See Vol. 1 p. 3.

Italy and France. By the summer of 1920, Hitler had become convinced that the clash of interests between France and Italy in the Balkans and the Mediterranean would eventually lead to war. Germany should therefore exploit this situation and on 1 August 1920 he asserted: 'The basic demand is "Away with the Peace Treaty!" We must use all possible means to achieve this, primarily the clash of interests between France and Italy so that we can win Italy for ourselves.'[6] The problem was, however, that under the Versailles treaty Italy had acquired the German-speaking territory of South Tirol. If Germany were to insist on the unification of all German-speaking people within the Reich as demanded by Point 1 of the Nazi Programme of 1920, a German–Italian alliance would be out of the question. This contradiction was only resolved two years later when, at the time of Mussolini's rise to power, Hitler offered to sacrifice the South Tiroleans in return for Italian friendship. This was an important decision, for it represented the first occasion on which Hitler sacrificed a vital element of the revisionist programme in the interest of power politics. He justified his decision with the claim that 'in politics there is no room for sentiment, only for cold-bloodedness'.[7]

Hitler, then, was aware of the fact that if Germany was to revise Versailles and to acquire land in the form of colonies, she would need powerful allies to enable her to take on both Britain and France. Italy alone, however, would not be sufficient. Since the Austrian empire had now collapsed, the only other major power left was Russia. Initially, Hitler had not been opposed in principle to an alliance with Russia. Indeed, he made it clear in his early speeches that in his view this should have been the policy of the pre-war German Government. After 1919, however, Hitler came increasingly under the influence of a group of Baltic German refugees from the Russian Revolution who had joined the Nazi Party, notably Alfred Rosenberg, a refugee from Reval in Estonia. Rosenberg convinced Hitler that the Bolshevik revolution was the work of Jews, indeed that the Bosheviks were all Jews. In a speech on 27 July 1920, Hitler asserted that 'an alliance between Russia and Germany can only come about if the Jews are overthrown'.[8] To start with, therefore, he did not entirely rule out the idea of an alliance with Russia because for some time it was not clear whether or not the Bolshevik regime would survive. By 1922, however, he was adopting a firm anti-Russian stance.

This orientation was confirmed by another diplomatic development which had a significant impact on his foreign policy: the occupation of the

---

[6] Quoted in Axel Kuhn, *Hitlers aussenpolitisches Programm* (Stuttgart 1970) p. 42. This section owes much to this work.

[7] Speech by Hitler, 14.xi.22, quoted ibid., p. 73.

[8] Quoted ibid., p. 53.

Ruhr by France in 1923.[9] This created a new situation in which Hitler feared that France was bent on the immediate dismemberment of Germany. Furthermore, he became aware of the strength of British opposition to French policy. He became convinced that this represented a basic shift in British policy towards France deriving from fear of French hegemony on the Continent. In the light of this development Hitler came to conceive of the possibility of an alliance between Germany and Britain against France. It is clear that he now regarded France as the greater enemy both because of her immediate threat to Germany's territorial integrity and because, since France was in his view bent on Continental hegemony, she would never allow Germany to regain her lost territory in Eastern Europe, which would be the prerequisite for the attempt to achieve world power status.

An alliance with Britain, however, posed problems similar to those raised by an alliance with Italy. It would be impossible to seek an alliance with Britain while simultaneously trying to win colonies. Yet, if Germany were not to seek colonies, where could she acquire the necessary territory and resources for her surplus population? For even the old boundaries of 1914 had, he believed, been inadequate. In fact, in the meantime, he had already found a solution which would reconcile Germany's need for what he now called 'living space' (*Lebensraum*) with the renunciation of colonies in the interests of an alliance with Britain. Germany must seek living space in Russia where the Bolshevik regime was now clearly established. In this way, he believed, Germany would avoid the First World War position of having to fight against both Britain and Russia, a situation which, he argued, had resulted from the prewar German Government's attempt simultaneously to pursue a colonial policy against Britain and a Continental policy against France and Russia. It was a solution which carried overwhelming conviction as far as he was concerned, because it reflected both of the elements which shaped his strategy—considerations of power politics and ideology. This programme was elaborated for the first time in his autobiography, *Mein Kampf*, from which the following extracts are taken:

468

A clear analysis of the premises for German diplomacy inevitably led to the following conviction:

Germany has an annual increase in population of nearly 900,000. The difficulty of feeding this army of new citizens must increase from year to year and ultimately

[9] See Vol. 1 p. 26.

end in catastrophe, unless ways and means are found to forestall the danger of starvation and misery in time . . .

At the present time, there are on this earth immense areas of unused soil only waiting for the men to till them. However, it is equally true that Nature as such has not reserved this soil for the future possession of any particular nation or race; on the contrary, this soil exists for the people which possesses the force to take it and the industry to cultivate it.

Nature knows no political boundaries. First she puts living creatures on the globe and watches the free play of forces. She then confers the master's right on her favourite child, the strongest in courage and industry . . .

None can doubt that one day this world will be faced with the severest struggles for the existence of mankind. In the end, only the urge for self-preservation can conquer. Beneath it so-called humanity, the expression of a mixture of stupidity, cowardice, and know-it-all conceit, will melt like snow in the March sun. Mankind has grown great in eternal struggle, and only in eternal peace does it perish . . .

The acquisition of new soil for the settlement of our surplus population has an infinite number of advantages, particularly if we turn from the present to the future.

For one thing, the possibility of preserving a healthy peasant class as a foundation for a whole nation can never be valued highly enough. Many of our current ills are solely the result of the unhealthy relationship between rural and city population. A solid stock of small and middle peasants has always been the best defence against social ills such as plague us today . . .

The foreign policy of a völkisch State must first of all bear in mind the obligation to secure the existence of the race incorporated in this State. This must be done by establishing a healthy and natural relationship between the number and growth of the population, on the one hand, and the extent and quality of its soil on the other. That relationship must be such that it accords with the vital necessities of the nation.

What I call a healthy relationship is one in which a nation is sustained by its own soil. Any situation which falls short of this condition is unhealthy even though it may endure for centuries or even millennia. Sooner or later this imbalance must of necessity lead to the decline or even annihilation of the nation concerned. *Only a sufficiently large space on this earth can ensure the independent existence of a nation.*

The extent of the territorial expansion that may be necessary for the settlement of the national population must not be determined by present exigencies nor even on the basis of the extent of its agricultural productivity in relation to the size of the population. In the first volume, under the heading 'German Alliance Policy before the War', I have already explained *that the geographical dimensions of a State are of importance not only as a source of the nation's foodstuffs and raw materials, but also from the political and military standpoints.* Once a nation is assured of being able to maintain itself from the resources of its national territory, it must reflect on how this national territory can be defended. National security depends on the political strength of a State and this strength, in turn, depends to a considerable extent on the military possibilities inherent in its geographical situation. Thus, the German nation can assure its own future only as a World Power . . . *Germany today is not a world power . . .*

The National Socialist movement must seek to eliminate the present disastrous imbalance between our population and the area of our national territory, regarding the latter as the source of our food and the basis of our political power. And it ought to strive to eliminate the contrast between our past history and the hopelessness of our present political impotence. In striving for this it must bear in mind the fact that, as members of the highest species of humanity on this earth, we have a correspondingly high obligation and that we shall fulfil this obligation only if we inspire the German people with the racial idea, so that in addition to breeding good dogs and horses and cats, they will also care for the purity of their own blood . . .

We National Socialists must never allow ourselves to join in the hurrah patriotism of our contemporary bourgeois circles. It would be fatal for us to regard the immediate pre-war developments as a binding precedent in choosing our own way even in the slightest degree. We can recognize no obligation devolving on us which may have its historical roots in any part of the nineteenth century. In contrast to the policy of the representatives of that period, we must take our stand on the principles already mentioned in regard to foreign policy: namely, *the necessity of bringing our territorial area into a proper relationship with our population.* From the past we can learn only one lesson, namely, that the aim of our political activity must be twofold: (i) *The acquisition of land and soil as the objective of our foreign policy* and (ii) *the establishment of a new and uniform foundation as the objective of our domestic policy in accordance with our völkisch doctrine . . .*

The demand for the restoration of the frontiers of 1914 is a political absurdity of such proportions and implications as to make it appear a crime. Apart from anything else, the Reich's frontiers in 1914 were anything but logical. In reality they were neither final in the sense of embracing all ethnic Germans, nor sensible with regard to geo-military considerations . . .

Thus, we National Socialists have intentionally drawn a line under the foreign policy of pre-war Germany. We are taking up where we left off six hundred years ago. We are putting an end to the perpetual German march towards the South and West of Europe and turning our eyes towards the land in the East. We are finally putting a stop to the colonial and trade policy of the pre-war period and passing over to the territorial policy of the future.

However, when we speak of new land in Europe today we must principally bear in mind *Russia* and the border states subject to her. Destiny itself seems to wish to point the way for us here. In delivering Russia over to Bolshevism, fate robbed the Russian people of that intelligentsia which created the Russian State and was the guarantee of its existence. For the Russian State was not organized by the constructive political talent of the Slav element in Russia but was rather a marvellous example of the capacity for State-building possessed by the Germanic element in a race of inferior worth. Many powerful empires have been created in this way all over the earth. On more than one occasion, inferior races with Germanic organizers and rulers as their leaders have become formidable States and continued to exist as long as the racial nucleus which orginally created these states remained. For centuries Russia drew nourishment as a State from the Germanic nucleus of its governing classes. But this nucleus has now been almost completely exterminated and destroyed. It has been replaced by the Jew. Just as it is impossible for the Russian to shake off the Jewish yoke by exerting his own powers, so too is it impossible for the Jew to keep this formidable State in existence for any length of time. He himself is by no means an element of organization but rather a ferment of decomposition. The colossal empire in the East is ripe for dissolution. And the end of the Jewish domination in Russia will also be the end of Russia as a State. We have been chosen by destiny to be the witnesses of a catastrophe which will afford the strongest confirmation of the soundness of the völkisch theory of race.

England does not want Germany to be a world power, but France does not want Germany to exist at all; quite a vital difference after all! Today we are not struggling to achieve a position as a world power; we must fight for the existence of our fatherland, for the unity of our nation and the daily bread of our children. If we look round for European allies from this point of view, only two states remain: England and Italy.

England does not want a France whose military fist, unobstructed by the rest of Europe, can undertake a policy which one way or the other, must one day cut across English interests . . .

And Italy too cannot and will not want a further reinforcement of France's position of superior power in Europe.

On the coldest and soberest reflection it is at the present time primarily these two States, *England and Italy*, whose most natural selfish interests are not, at any rate essentially, opposed to the German people's requirements for existence and are indeed to some extent identified with them.

After he had written *Mein Kampf*, Hitler's basic foreign policy objectives did not change. The main purpose of his so-called 'Second Book', written in 1928 but not published until 1962, was to justify his assertion of the need to sacrifice German-speaking South Tirol in the interests of the Italian alliance at a time when the South Tirol problem was a subject of intense public debate and his own position was under attack. The book was essentially a restatement of the policy set out in *Mein Kampf*, though it did introduce one or two new perspectives.

In the first place, while re-emphasizing that 'in any conflict involving Germany, regardless on what grounds, regardless for what reasons, France will always be our adversary' (p. 128),[10] he now referred for the first time to the strategic threat posed by France's system of alliances in Eastern Europe. Referring specifically to Czechoslovakia and Poland, he pointed out that thanks to these alliances France was 'in a position to be able to threaten almost the whole of Germany with aircraft even an hour after the outbreak of a conflict' (p. 127).

Secondly he dealt with the argument that Britain would oppose German hegemony on the Continent because of traditional British balance of power policy (pp. 149f.). This he claimed was 'not correct'. For 'England actually concerned herself very little with European conditions as long as no threatening world competitor arose from them, so that she always viewed

[10] Quotations from *Hitler's Secret Book*, ed. Telford Taylor (New York 1962).

the threat as lying in a development which must one day cut across her dominion over the seas and colonies'. He cited Britain's attitude to Prussia in the eighteenth century as proof of this. Since Germany did not propose to challenge the British Empire, he argued that Britain would not fear Germany: 'If England remains true to her great world-political aims, her potential opponents will be France and Russia in Europe [since they challenged Britain's imperial position], and in other parts of the world especially the American Union in the future'. This reference to America was not the only one in the book. Indeed, for the first time Hitler devoted some attention to the United States. He praised Americans as a 'young, racially select people' (p. 100), but hinted at the need 'in the far future to think of a new association of nations consisting of individual States with a high national value, which could then stand up to the threatening overwhelming of the world by the American Union. For it seems to me that the existence of English world rule inflicts fewer hardships on present-day nations than the emergence of an American world rule' (p. 209).

Finally, Hitler now spelled out even more explicitly than in *Mein Kampf* the logical conclusion of the Social Darwinist position by pointing out that there was no limit to the expansion of a nation which proved itself racially superior: 'For this earth is not allotted to anyone nor is it presented to anyone as a gift. It is awarded by providence to people who in their hearts have the courage to conquer it, the strength to preserve it, and the industry to put it to the plough. . . . The present distribution of possessions has not been designed by a higher power but by man himself. . . . No. The primary right of this world is the right to life, so far as one possesses the strength for this. Hence on the basis of this right a vigorous nation will always find ways of adapting its territory to its population size' (pp. 15–16).

From the comments and arguments contained in *Mein Kampf* and the 'Second Book', both explicit and implicit, one can construct a foreign policy programme which consisted essentially of five stages. The first stage was the removal of the restrictions on German armaments imposed by the Treaty of Versailles and the remilitarization of the Rhineland. This was clearly essential if Germany was to operate from a position of military strength. The second stage was the destruction of France's system of alliances in Estern Europe through which she encircled Germany and the transformation of Austria (probably through *Anschluss*), Czechoslovakia, and Poland into German satellites. This would open the way to the third stage—the confrontation with France. The defeat of France, or its neutralization through the British alliance, would in turn secure Germany's western frontier so that she could move on to the conquest of *Lebensraum* in the East. The conquest of Russia was the crucial stage in Hitler's strategy because it involved the winning of the 'living space' which Hitler regarded as essential to Germany's future. The final stage was, at any rate at this time, only a vague idea in Hitler's mind, a logical inference from the Social Darwinist premises of his thought. The Germans, having proved themselves the superior racial group, should dominate the world, possibly through a confrontation with Britain, but preferably in association with her as a junior partner against the United States.

Hitler believed that the key to the implementation of his foreign policy programme lay in a transformation of Germany's domestic political situation and in this he found himself in agreement with much military thinking of the period. The First World War had shown that modern industrial warfare involved not just the professionals, but required the harnessing of the economy and society as a whole. Moreover, under the 'stab in the back' formula the German defeat in 1918 was interpreted in terms of a crisis of morale rather than a conventional military defeat, a crisis induced partly by enemy propaganda and partly by internal agitation. Thus, in their war memoirs which appeared in 1919, both General Ludendorff and Admiral Tirpitz concluded that the main reason for their defeat had been the failure of the German government to arouse a German will to victory and to produce effective propaganda with which to counter that of the Allies. From now onwards, questions of propaganda and morale acquired considerable significance in military thinking. Reflecting upon their experience, some military theorists, and notably Ludendorff himself, concluded that this new kind of 'total war' required 'total mobilization' of the population and for this a 'total state' geared to the militarization of society appeared necessary. Certainly, by 1932, the majority of officers had become convinced that, under the democratic system of Weimar, even in its post-1930 authoritarian version, Germany was incapable of effective rearmament, and that the unity of the nation was being undermined by 'selfish and divisive' party politics, its martial spirit sapped by the pacifism and soft humanitarian values of the new cultural establishment, and rearmament threatened by unstable government and anti-militarist elements in the Reichstag.

To some extent, Hitler was himself a product of Army indoctrination and it seems plausible that his views on the importance of morale and his own programme of political mobilization as the precondition for effective rearmament were as much the result of the post-war lectures and discussions in his 1919 indoctrination classes, and of reading military pamphlets and memoirs, as they were the product of his own personal experience of Allied propaganda at the front as he claimed in *Mein Kampf*.

Hitler envisaged a relationship between his regime and the Army in which the military would be relieved of any domestic political role and confined to its professional functions. He had enormous respect for the military expertise of the Army High Command and was anxious to provide them with optimum conditons in which to use it. He would provide the

Army with the best weapons, the best 'human material' in terms of physique and morale, a sympathetic climate at home and a favourable diplomatic situation abroad. They in turn would use their professional skills first to prepare, and then to deploy Germany's military strength with maximum effectiveness in the service of goals which he would define.

On 4 December 1932, Hitler spelled out his ideas in a letter to Colonel Walther von Reichenau, the Chief of Staff of the Commander of the military district of East Prussia, General Werner von Blomberg. Both Blomberg and Reichenau were already sympathetic to the Nazis and Reichenau had asked for Hitler's cooperation in ensuring peace and stability in East Prussia to strengthen the province against the potential threat from Poland. Hitler agreed in principle but declared that this was largely irrelevant to the main problems of German defence. Seizing this opportunity to try and win the support of a senior Reichswehr officer whom he knew to be already sympathetic, Hitler expounded his views on Germany's international position and the policies necessary to improve it, thereby providing us with valuable insights into his thinking on the eve of his take-over of power:

469

. . . The question of the territorial security of East Prussia is intimately connected to the whole foreign and domestic position of the Reich. I would like to sketch this briefly as follows:

The World War ended in such a way that France was unable to achieve all her aims. In particular, her hopes of a general internal collapse of the Reich were not realized. The peace treaty of Versailles was thus dictated by France's attempt to maintain as broad as possible a community of interest of states hostile to Germany. This aim was to be secured in the first place through the territorial truncation of the Reich. By handing over German territory to almost all of the surrounding states, it was hoped to forge a ring of nations bound together by common interests. In the East, Russia, which at the time was of no consequence (and whose development furthermore was unpredictable) was to be replaced by Poland, which was dependent on France. The fact that East Prussia was separated off by the Polish corridor inevitably led to the strong desire to incorporate this province into Poland, which in any case surrounded most of it. And, in fact, the propaganda for a greater Poland began to press for this immediately after the signing of the Versailles treaty.

Presumably out of fear of the danger which was clearly looming, German foreign policy endeavoured to relieve the pressure in the East by establishing a close relationship with Russia. While appreciating the political and military reasons for this approach, I have always considered it dubious and opposed it. The reasons for my attitude, of which General von Hammerstein, in particular, has been aware for many years, were and still are as follows:

1. Russia is not a state but an ideology which at the moment is restricted to this territory, or rather dominates it, but which maintains sections in all other countries which not only pursue the same revolutionary goal, but are also organisationally subordinate to the Moscow headquarters. A victory for these ideas in Germany must have incalculable consequences. However, the more one cooperates with the headquarters of this poisonous agency for diplomatic reasons, the more difficult it becomes to struggle against these poisonous tendencies. The German people are no more immune against Communism now than they were immune to the ideas of revolution in 1917 and 1918. Officers and statesmen can only assess this problem if they understand national psychologies. Experience shows that this is rarely the case.
2. For this reason I regard Soviet diplomacy not only as unreliable but as not comparable with the diplomatic leadership of other nations and, therefore, as ineligible to undertake negotiations and sign treaties. 'Treaties' can only be signed with combatants who are on the same ideological plane.
3. However, were we—which God forbid—to be saved by Soviet aid on some occasion, this would clearly imply the planting of the red flag in Germany.
4. In so far as the growth in Russia's military strength reduces the value to France of her Polish ally to the extent that French intentions towards Germany in the East are seriously jeopardized, France will either endeavour to draw Russia away from Poland or, in the event of the failure of such an action, drop Poland and replace her with Russia.
5. Germany's political cooperation with Russia produces an adverse response from the rest of the world. Economic cooperation will destroy our German export industry in the future.

It is for these reasons that for the past twelve years or so I have consistently proposed a closer relationship with Italy on the one hand and England on the other as the most desirable diplomatic goal.

Following the noticeable reduction in the value of her Polish ally, France has endeavoured—and in my view successfully—to involve Russia in the Far East in order to relieve pressure on the Polish border. This far-reaching French action may be regarded as in essence successfully accomplished in the non-aggression pact between Russia and Poland which has now been signed.[11]

The moment that a particular domestic political situation creates an international atmosphere hostile to Germany, Poland will seize the opportunity to attack and East Prussia will be lost. The declaration of a monarchy, for example, or any plan to restore the House of Hohenzollern—in whatever form—may immediately provoke this response.

The military means and possibilities open to East Prussia are, in my view, inadequate for a lengthy resistance with any prospect of success. Moreover, on the basis of the present political situation there will in my view be no military support from the Reich. I consider the impression of a speeding-up of German rearmament as the most serious danger. It is conceivable that France is no longer in a position

---

[11] On 25 July 1932 (eds).

to sabotage the granting of a theoretical equality of rights to Germany. In this case the succeeding period will be the most dangerous epoch in German history because the practical, technical, and organizational rearmament will have to follow on from the granting of theoretical equality. If ever there was a reason for a preventive war then it would be in this case for an attack by France on Germany. Such a military act alone would create the new facts which are desired and the same world, which today bestows its theoretical benevolence upon us, would be wary of trying to correct the fait accompli by force of arms.

France cannot wish for anything better than to leave the first step in this new measure to a third party. It can devise reasons and pretexts for it at any time.

Thus, as I have already emphasized, I consider the threat of this attack to be acute and believe that it would be advisable to reckon with its onset at any moment!

However at present there is no possibility of Germany intervening in such a conflict. The reason for this does not lie in the lack of the necessary armaments but much more in the total unsuitability of the German people for such a task thanks to its intellectual, moral, and political decline.

The German nation at the present time consists of two ideological camps of which one must be excluded from any military service for the present state. According to the last Reichstag elections [6.11.1932], the ideological breakdown of our people is as follows:

Communists	6 million
Social Democrats	7·4 million
Centre	4 million
State Party etc.	1 million
National Socialists	12 million
German National People's Party + Stahlhelm	3 million
German People's Party	1 million

That is to say: In the event of a war being forced on Germany, more than half of the population consists of people who are either more or less pacifist or else consciously hostile to defence and military matters. The opinion of some generals that military training (in a sudden war it could only be very brief) would eradicate ideological indoctrination by political parties is positively puerile. Even the two years military service [before 1914] in peacetime did not damage the SPD. To say that the SPD workers nevertheless did their duty in 1914 is wrong. For it was not the convinced Marxist who did his duty but the German in the Marxist who was stirred enough temporarily to renounce Marxism. The convinced Marxist leadership was already beginning to fight back in 1915 and, after remarkable and splendid resistance on the part of the population, finally in 1918 provoked a revolution and thereby caused the collapse of the Reich.

The Social Democracy of those days cannot be remotely compared with the KPD of today. In 1914 Marxism was a theory; today it dominates in practice an enormous part of the world. A war fought by Germany in its present state would from the start subject the whole nation to a test of nerves which, as far as the home front is concerned at any rate, would bear no comparison with similar events in the World War.

The idea that in this case one can fall back on the nationalist leagues is very flattering for these organizations which nowadays suffer such abuse and persecution, but is likely to be not only of no practical significance, but rather produce fearful consequences. For, if the nationalist elements are called up and moved to the front as more or less untrained cannon fodder, the homeland would then be simultaneously delivered into the hands of the red mob. The year 1918 was child's play compared with what would happen then.

Thus, while our political and military strategists regard German rearmament as a technical or organizational matter, I see the precondition for any rearmament as the creation of a new German national unity of mind and of will. Without the solution of this problem all talk of 'equality of rights' and 'rearmament' is superficial and idle chatter.

This creation of a unity of ideology, mind, and will among our people is the task which I set myself fourteen years ago and which I have struggled to achieve ever since. I am not surprised that our official civil and military agencies treat this problem with a total lack of understanding not to say stupidity. It has always been thus throughout history. No great ideas and reforms of humanity have ever come from the professionals. Why should it be any different today. However, recognition of this historical truth does not relieve the person who has taken the measure of this question in all its enormous significance from the duty of working to resolve it. I must, therefore, however regretfully, make a stand against, indeed must combat, any German government which is not ready and determined to carry out this inward rearmament of the German nation. All other measures follow from it.

I consider the present cabinet of General von Schleicher to be particularly unfortunate because through the person of its leader alone it must show even less appreciation of this question than any other would do. This time, as ever in history, this problem of the intellectual rearmament of the nation cannot be solved by an army but only by an ideology. To involve the Army in the matter makes it appear prejudiced in many people's eyes just as such an involvement thereby compromises the task itself in the eyes of the masses. For, neither the police nor the military have ever destroyed ideologies even less have they been able to construct them. However, no human structure can survive in the long term without an ideology. Ideologies are the social contracts and bases on which substantial human organizations have to be built. Thus, in contrast to our present statesmen I see Germany's tasks for the future as follows:

1. Overcoming Marxism and its consequences until they have been completely exterminated. The creation of a new unity of mind and will for our people.
2. A general intellectual and moral rearmament of the nation on the basis of this new ideological unity.
3. Technical rearmament.
4. The organizational mobilization of the national resources for the purpose of national defence.
5. Once this has been achieved, the securing of the legal recognition of the new situation by the rest of the world.

Only a deep-rooted process of regeneration instead of the present experimentation and continual seeking after new and petty palliatives can bring about a final and clear-cut solution to the German crisis. I would be grateful, Colonel, if you would judge my behaviour in the light of this view.

On coming to power in January 1933, Hitler had no clear idea how to achieve his foreign policy programme beyond his suggestion of German alliances with Britain and Italy. In any case, he had to adjust its implementation to the realities of power. His freedom of action was circumscribed in various ways both diplomatically and within the government itself. He had come to power through an alliance with the traditional elites, and Reich President von Hindenburg had insisted on selecting a general (von Blomberg) as the new Reich Defence Minister and on confirming the previous Foreign Minister, a diplomat (von Neurath), in office. Hitler was therefore obliged to establish a working relationship with the organizations which would be responsible for implementing his programme—the Armed Forces, especially the Army, and the Foreign Ministry—both of which had their own views and priorities.

CHAPTER 26

The Regime and the Armed Forces 1933–1936

Relations between the Nazi regime and the armed forces (*Wehrmacht*) during this period were determined above all by the fact that they shared the goal of German rearmament and also the conviction that the Weimar Republic had proved incapable of realizing this goal. The failure of General von Schleicher's efforts between 1930 and 1932 to secure a regime congenial to the Army (*Reichswehr*), which also possessed mass support in the country and, in particular, his inability to harness the Nazi movement had represented the bankruptcy of the *Reichswehr's* attempt to manipulate the political situation and create a new political basis for rearmament. Moreover, the political machinations of the Defence Ministry had begun to alienate a significant section of the officer corps. On the one hand, there was a growing feeling that the prestige of the Army, as the key symbol of national unity, was being jeopardized by such a close involvement in day-to-day politics, a feeling shared by the Reich President. On the other hand, a growing number of officers, particularly in the junior ranks, were becoming attracted to Nazism. This desire on the part of the Army to escape from the political arena coincided with the policy which Hitler had been urging since 1930 that it should renounce its former role of maintaining domestic order and concentrate on purely military matters.

(i) The Role of the Army in the Nazi Take-over of Power and the Struggle with the SA

Since Germany had been banned from maintaining an Air Force by the Versailles treaty and the Navy was restricted to only 15,000 men, it was the Army which presented the biggest potential challenge from the armed forces to the consolidation of a Nazi regime. Hitler was greatly assisted in his cultivation of the Army after 1933 by the fact that the new Minister of Defence, General Werner von Blomberg, and the new head of the *Ministeramt*, Colonel Walther von Reichenau, were already sympathetic to the regime. Blomberg had had a brilliant career as a staff officer and had proved less hidebound than most in coming to terms with the post-war order. However, the negative aspect of this adaptability was a tendency to allow romantic enthusiasm to overwhelm his critical faculties. A visit to the Soviet Union during 1928 had impressed him with the possibilities of social mobilization and control through Communist indoctrination and he appeared to envisage Nazism performing a similar role in Germany. Nevertheless, his support for Hitler was not primarily a matter of calculation, it had rather the force of a religious conversion. Blomberg soon became convinced that the Army should not adopt a non-commital attitude to the new regime. This 'reactionary' policy should be replaced by loyal support.

While Blomberg committed himself to the new regime with a rather naive enthusiasm, Reichenau's approach was more cool and calculating. He too had concluded that it was undesirable for the Army to sit on the sidelines. This was partly because he was impressed by Hitler's programme of national mobilization and partly because he believed that the Army could only secure influence through cooperation. Reflecting on the experience of the first months of the regime, he summed up his view of the situation in the following comments to a colleague made in the summer of 1933:

470

. . . The old Conservatives will be dealt with very differently. They are not the only ones who imagine that we just need to blink and all the fuss will be over. What an idea! What are we these days? A well-disciplined survival of past greatness which sits sulkily in the corner and which events have passed by. At the moment we are still just about in a position to have a patron [*i.e.* Hindenburg] who sits in his palace with Oskar and the other keepers of the grail or in peaceful Neudeck with his disillusioned neighbours and who doesn't realize that a lot has happened in the meantime. But one day it will be all up with the patron.

If we wish to do justice to our historic task, there is only one way: to establish contact with the place where all power is now in fact concentrated and yet to remain ourselves. One doesn't gain influence by sitting on the sidelines.

Our troops and also the nation, a section of which still regards us as the source of order, can legitimately demand that we do not allow ourselves to be pushed to one side. But even the most blinkered reactionary cannot seriously expect that we can reverse the wheel of history. I would like to know what with and above all where we would go. Our path goes forwards and that means we should go into the new state and maintain the position due to us. Otherwise we shall only benefit our competitors.

Our most dangerous enemy at the moment is the SA and above all its leadership who have been rendered superfluous by the ending of the revolution and who see their new task as taking over from us. Based on the organized mass, who have been aroused by military slogans, in pathetic naivety they see themselves as the coming rulers. If Heines[1] shoots the chandelier in the Breslau 'Monopol' to pieces, it need not bother us. There is no military ambition in that. I know Herr Röhm and his backers only too well, some of them come from our outfit. And we shouldn't forget that it is those who have failed, when their moral or other defects are combined with ambition and ability, who fight most fanatically to achieve their goal, namely, a triumphant return to the place from which they were not exactly honourably dismissed.

All power is now concentrated in one person and he will know how to underpin it still further. The masses applaud him like no one else. What was left of the parties has melted away like snow in the sun. The trade unions have been smashed, the Communists driven into a corner and provisionally neutralized, the Reichstag has surrendered its rights with the Enabling Law. The workers are keeping their heads down and, after the previous slump, their wage packets will be more important to them than any politics. The whole state apparatus with the police, the civil service concerned about their due rights, the communications media which gave Herr von Schleicher so many sleepless nights, press, radio, in short, everything through which the public can be kept on a lead is under firm control and is doing what it is told. And then we are supposed to come along with our seven decrepit divisions scattered over the whole of the Reich and be the only ones to dance out of line. Only fools can imagine that.

We are used to dealing soberly with the facts. Wishful thinking belongs in literature but not in our profession. The only path open to us is to draw the conclusions from the situation which we did not create.

The Colonel-General [Reichenau waved his hand in the direction of Blomberg's offices] has meanwhile gained Hitler's confidence, but his position is not easy. In practice, he sits between two stools, the new boss and the presidential palace, where he is regarded with suspicion. I regard it all the more as my task to keep in close personal contact which in a dictatorship is more vital than all the work of the ministries. And I am certain that this remarkable man, despite all the blemishes which his movement understandably still has, is following a clear path towards the goal of creating a state which can once more respect itself and also be respected by its neighbours, who have caused enough trouble for us in recent years. One must not forget that among all the negative impressions which go against the grain.

In this task I expect sympathetic cooperation. [He stuck in his monocle.] I recently made the same point to the district commanders and their chiefs of staff in the presence of the Colonel-General. I think they got the message.

---

[1] Edmund Heines, SA leader in Silesia.

Thus, although Blomberg and Reichenau were both sympathetic to Nazism in varying degrees, at the same time they were anxious to maintain the independence and strengthen the position of the Army within the state and both could see the threat posed by the Nazi Party, and, in particular, the SA, to the Army's independence. They concluded, however, that the best way to meet this threat was to cooperate with the regime and with Hitler in particular and thereby establish a special relationship. Moreover, they assumed that as the rearmament programme got under way so the size and importance of the armed forces would be bound to grow, ensuring them a permanent and if anything increasing role within the state. They believed, therefore, that they had little to fear and everything to gain by cooperating with a regime which would provide both financial and popular support for rearmament and, in any case, they had concluded that there was little alternative. The commitment of the new *Reichswehr* leadership to the regime took various forms: first, an opting out of the sphere of domestic politics, which in fact implied an acceptance of the changes which were taking place; secondly, public statements and gestures of identification with the new order; and finally, and most significantly, a form of 'self-coordination' involving the encouragement of Nazi indoctrination within the Armed Forces and concessions on matters of ideology and personnel.

Firstly, then, the Army ceased to interfere in domestic politics. At the first cabinet meeting on 30 January 1933, Blomberg supported Hitler's unwillingness to commit the Army against a possible general strike and added 'that the soldier is accustomed to regard an external enemy as his sole conceivable opponent'. This was an ominous statement, for it appeared to undermine the constitutional right of the President under Article 48 to declare martial law. And since Hindenburg's control over the Army was the trump card held by the Conservatives in their strategy of containing the Nazis, the fact that the Minister of Defence was unwilling for it to be used in the domestic context represented a lethal blow to this whole strategy. For, if the Army was unwilling to act against the Left, it would be even less willing to act against the SA.

Four days later, on 3 February 1933, Blomberg issued a briefing at a meeting of Group and District Commanders in the Defence Ministry from which the following notes have survived:

471

Present Situation

Cabinet is expression of broadly-based national will and realization of what many people have been seeking for years. Although it only represents a minority of the population, it is a united minority of millions which is determined to live and—if necessary—to die for its ideals. This provides great opportunities if the leading figures show firmness and skill.

Formation of the Cabinet
The question of the Defence Minister played the main role. The entry of the Nazis into the Government was decided when a general on the active list agreed to cooperate with Hitler (another solution put forward by Hitler of having a leading Nazi as Defence Minister presumably unacceptable to R.Pres.). After agreement Hitler-Blomberg—Monday 8 o'clock—question was decided and oath already taken at 11.30 am.

Tasks of Defence Minister
The 3 mentioned in his proclamation to the Wehrmacht:
1. Maintenance of the Wehrmacht as a power which should be above party.
2. Underpinning of the Wehrmacht by mobilizing the population.
3. Building up the Wehrmacht into an effective instrument for the maintenance of national security.
Re: 1. Above party in *politics*—Support for the militarization programme. 2 tasks: The first is no less important than the second. To sink into the role of a Party army would undermine the basis on which we stand.
Re: 2. The strengthening and spreading of military activities throughout the nation. The man in the Cabinet for this is Seldte[2] (Min Port(folio) only temporary). Hitler's and Seldte's ideas and aims coincide in the desire for the militarization of the nation. Seldte is the Minister most suitable to carry out this task alongside us soldiers.

On the evening of the same day, 3 February, at a dinner at the house of the Commander-in-Chief, General Kunrat von Hammerstein-Equord, attended by the district Army commanders, Hitler defined the role which he envisaged for the Armed Forces within the new regime and explained his goals. General Liebmann, an infantry commander who was present made the following notes:

472

The sole aim of general policy: *the regaining of political power*. The whole State administration must be geared to this end (all departments!).

1. *Domestic policy*: Complete reversal of the present domestic political situation in Germany. Refusal to tolerate any attitude contrary to this aim (pacifism!). Those who will not be converted must be broken. Extermination of Marxism root and

[2] Franz Seldte was the leader of the paramilitary ex-servicemen's organization, the *Stahlhelm*, and had been appointed Minister of Labour, see Vol. 1 pp. 121–2 (eds).

branch. Adjustment of youth and of the whole people to the idea that only a struggle can save us and that everything else must be subordinated to this idea. (Realized in the millions of the Nazi movement. It will grow.) Training of youth and strengthening of the will to fight with all means. Death penalty for high treason. Tightest authoritarian State leadership. Removal of the cancer of Democracy!

2. *Foreign policy*: Battle against Versailles. Equality of rights in Geneva; but useless if people do not have the will to fight. Concern for allies.

3. *Economics*: The farmer must be saved! Settlement policy! Further increase of exports useless. The capacity of the world is limited and production is forced up everywhere. The only possibility of re-employing part of the army of unemployed lies in settlement. But time is needed and radical improvement not to be expected since living space too small for German people.

4. *Building up of the armed forces*: Most important prerequisite for achieving the goal of regaining political power. National Service must be reintroduced. But beforehand the State leadership must ensure that the men subject to military service are not, even before their entry, poisoned by pacifism, Marxism, Bolshevism or do not fall victim to this poison after their service.

How should political power be used when it has been gained? That is impossible to say yet. Perhaps fighting for new export possibilities, perhaps—and probably better—the conquest of new living space in the east and its ruthless Germanization. Certain that only through political power and struggle can the present economic circumstances be changed. The only things that can happen now—settlement—stopgap measures.

Armed forces most important and most Socialist institution of the State. They must stay unpolitical and impartial. The internal struggle not their affair but that of the Nazi organizations. As opposed to Italy no fusion of Army and SA intended—most dangerous time is during the reconstruction of the Army. It will show whether or not France has *statesmen*: if so, she will not leave us time but will attack us (presumably with eastern satellites).

Although Blomberg had insisted in his 3 February briefing that the Army should be 'above party', his unwillingness for the Army to be used as a domestic weapon implied a willingness to condone action being undertaken by others which, in the circumstances of 1933, meant the Nazi paramilitary forces whether or not acting in the guise of 'auxiliary police'. That this was in fact the case was confirmed later in the month when Colonel Reichenau informed a meeting of the regional Army commanders: 'It is necessary to recognize that we are in a revolution. All that is rotten in the State must fall and that can only happen through terror. The Party will act ruthlessly against Marxism. The role of the Army is to stand at ease. No support for any of those being persecuted who seek refuge with the troops.'[3] The

[3] Cf. W. Sauer, Die Mobilmachung der Gewalt, in K. D. Bracher, W. Sauer, G. Schulz, *Die nationalsozialistische Machtergreifung* (Cologne Opladen 1960) p. 729.

reaction of the generals was apparently one of shock and they allegedly passed on the order in a modified form. However, there was only one protest—by one of Schleicher's former aides, Lieutenant Colonel Ott. During negotiations with Göring two months previously, Ott had already rejected his request to give the SA the freedom of the streets in the event of a Nazi government coming to power. Ott's protest cost him his job.

This tolerance by the *Wehrmacht* leadership of the crushing of the Left by the SA was followed in March by their acceptance of the 'coordination' of the states and, in particular, their rejection of specific request for assistance against the Nazi take-over by the Bavarian government.[4] Perhaps most striking of all, however, was their attitude to the political representatives of the traditional Right. From the point of view of tradition and social background, the German Nationalists (DNVP) and the officer corps were natural allies. Moreover, if the Conservatives were to have any hope of resisting the Nazi claims to total power, they would need the support of the Army. Yet the Army leadership showed no sympathy whatsoever for the plight of the DNVP in the summer of 1933. Blomberg bluntly told the regional commanders on 1 June 1933 that the Party had no claim to equal rights since the Nazis alone bore the credit for the revolution: 'It will be a good thing', he continued, when this movement achieves the total power which it seeks and the German Nationalists and the Centre Party disappear.'[5] Blomberg did not want a totalitarian dictatorship by the Nazi party but an end to what he saw as party divisiveness, and unity behind the new regime which, as a 'patriotic', i.e. right-wing nationalist, government was deserving of every German's support.

In his comments on the situation in the summer of 1933 Reichenau had referred to the SA as 'our most dangerous enemy'. Whereas the Army contained only just over 100,000 men, the SA now contained over two million after its amalgamation with the right-wing veterans' organization, the *Stahlhelm*. Moreover, the SA was effectively the army of the new governing party. Finally, the question of the SA also raised difficult questions in relation to the development of German rearmament, which had begun to acquire its own momentum during the previous five years.

Shortly before the departure of the International Military Control Commission in 1926, the Reich Defence Ministry had begun to make secret plans for German rearmament. In the autumn of 1928, the Defence Ministry had inaugurated a rearmament programme which envisaged the provision of initial equipment for a field army of 16 divisions to be achieved

[4] On the 'coordination' of the states see Vol. 1 pp. 144–46.

[5] Cf. K-J. Müller, *Das Heer und Hitler* (Stuttgart 1969) p. 65. This section owes much to this work.

by 1932. At the beginning of 1932, this was replaced by a second rearmament programme which envisaged the provision of initial equipment and six weeks of supplies for a 21 division field army (300,000 men) to be achieved by 1938. During the summer of 1932, the new Defence Minister, von Schleicher, began to press vigorously and publicly for German rearmament. This was partly for domestic political reasons and partly from a growing sense of concern at the parlous state of Germany's defences, both in terms of men and material. He regarded the situation as particularly acute because of the danger of a preventive attack by Poland, possibly supported, by France. Schleicher had long taken the view that effective rearmament required a mobilization of German society and he therefore determined to launch a major initiative, utilizing the right-wing paramilitary leagues to train a militia-type force to supplement the regular army. Thus, in November 1932, he introduced a new programme to create a peace-time army of 144,000 professionals and a militia consisting of short-service so-called 'E-units', with 85,000 men being given three months training each year. This would provide a 21 division field army by spring 1938.

This new initiative had serious implications for German domestic policy. For a crash programme to train a militia made the Army heavily dependent on the Nazi SA, which alone had the requisite personnel and organization. Initially Blomberg was happy for the Army to cooperate with the SA, since such cooperation also fitted into his general view of the desirability of a close relationship between the Army and the new regime. During 1933, the Army seconded a significant proportion of its officers to the SA to assist with its military training programme to the detriment of its own training. However, the problem was that the leader of the SA, Ernst Röhm, wished to reverse the relationship between the Army and the SA by reducing the professional army to the role of training the cadres of a new militia army dominated by the SA. In other words, through Schleicher's programme of using the SA to train a militia the *Reichswehr* was in danger of cutting its own throat. The only alternative was to abandon the idea of a militia and instead expand the conventional army through the traditional method of conscription. On 18 December 1933, therefore, the Defence Ministry rushed through a new programme which envisaged a peacetime army of 300,000 men (21 divisions) and a field army of 63 divisions with the built-in assumption that conscription would be introduced at the earliest diplomatically feasible moment.

The evidence suggests that the initiative for this massive expansion of the Army came from the Defence Ministry rather than from Hitler, who approved it because it fitted in which his long-term plans for German rearmament. In doing so, however, he had implicitly—explicitly according to Blomberg—supported the Army's position against the SA. At a series of meetings held at the Defence Ministry on 20–21 December, Blomberg and the Army chiefs determined the basis of the new programme. The following is an excerpt from a memorandum of these meetings:

473

Part I

Exposition of the Reich Defence Minister

It is unlikely that agreement will be reached over disarmament:[6] if not, we must act independently.

It is all the more important that every effort is made to ensure secrecy and camouflage: officer corps etc. must be trained in discretion.

If we prove capable of the measures to be initiated on 1 April 1934, it will show that we have made effective use of the past years. This is not an improvisation; from the start, all measures must have a firm foundation.

Thus:

1. Only one year's service.
2. For 1934 on a voluntary basis; but the next goal is conscription.
3. Immediate transition to a 21 division army with 300,000 men within four years.

It is expressly forbidden to mention a 21 division army: all such references must be particularly avoided in correspondence . . .

Initially, there are two main difficulties as regards defence matters:

a) The regulation of the border defences.
b) The attempts by the SA to establish its own Wehrmacht.

The Reich Chancellor agrees with the Reich Defence Minister that, apart from *pre-military training*, responsibility for everything else (direction and preparation of the deployment, mil. training etc.) lies with the *Reichswehr*. Leadership in war can also only lie with the Wehrmacht. It is not up to people at the lower levels to fight for these principles. In the event of friction, the Reich Defence Minister should be informed briefly and objectively . . . These things have to be fought out at the top. Such difficulties must not be allowed to affect the relationship with the SA and its leaders.

Officer requirements:

1. Shortening of training. Among other things, school leavers' certificate (*Abitur*) should not be required as a matter of principle.
2. Re-appointment of former officers up to age 40 (from L.O., police, SA, and from those in private employment).
3. Officers from the ranks of the NCOs.
4. Transfer of officers from staffs . . .

[6] At the disarmament conference in Geneva (eds).

5. Withdrawal of the officers seconded to the SA by 1 March 1934. In future, no more long-term secondments to the SA. The R. Def. Min. reserves the right to make such secondments in individual cases. Officers who are or wish to be employed by the SA on a long-term basis should transfer to the SA.

Details

(a) Recently various officers have been granted the right to wear the SA uniform; the R. Def. Min. will keep this under review. Initially, nothing is to be done to prevent it.

(b) The Aryan Clause must be observed in the case of the appointment of officer cadets; how far further changes will be introduced for the officer corps in this sphere remains to be seen . . .

In fact, there was already an implicit, if not explicit, bargain involved in the relations between the regime and the Army. In his speech to the generals, on 3 February 1933, Hitler had promised that in return for its cooperation 'no fusion of the Army and SA intended'. He was anxious to retain the *Reichswehr* as the professional core of the new enlarged conscripted *Wehrmacht* which he intended to create, and also he was concerned not to alienate the Army which might persuade the Reich President to intervene and impose martial law. On 30 January 1934, in a major speech to celebrate the first anniversary of his appointment as Chancellor, he included the following passage to reassure the Army:

474

. . . The fact that between the forces of the Revolution and the responsible leaders of a highly disciplined *Wehrmacht* such friendly collaboration in the service of the nation emerged, as in the case of the NS Party and myself as its leader on the one side and the officers and soldiers of the German Army on the other, represents a unique historical event. If, on the one hand, the Stahlhelm, during these past twelve months, moved more and more towards National Socialism and gave the finest expression to this alliance in the shape of an amalgamation [with the SA], then during the same period, the Army and its leadership stood by the new State in absolute loyalty and obedience and thereby, as history will recall, provided the prerequisite for our work.

Röhm, however, remained determined to secure his and the SA's dominance over the *Reichswehr* and, on 1 February 1934, expounded his plans in a memorandum to Blomberg which caused consternation among the Army leadership. Pressed by Blomberg, Hitler had to make his decision clear to the SA.

On 28 February 1934, at a meeting attended by the Army, SA, and SS leaders, Hitler rejected Röhm's idea of absorbing the *Reichswehr* into an SA-dominated militia and forced him to agree to the following 'Proposal for Cooperation with the SA' put forward by the Defence Ministry. This agreement signed by both sides represented a complete victory for the Army:

475

Fundamental principles:

1. Reich Defence Minister bears *sole* responsibility for the preparation of the defence of the Reich, mobilization, leadership in war.
2. *Task of the Wehrmacht*: Military preparation of the defence of the Reich, mobilization, leadership in war.
3. *Task of the SA*: (*a*) Pre-military training following on from youth training. (*b*) Training of those eligible for military service who have not been called up into the Wehrmacht. (*c*) Maintenance of the military effectiveness of former soldiers and of those who have not served but have undergone SA sports training.

District commanders as well as Border Guard section commanders must keep a check on the state of military training in association with the appropriate offices of the SA.

(*d*) Support for the measures taken for special border protection. (*e*) Participation in preparations for mobilization.

Re (*d*) and (*e*), it is the duty of the SA to obey the directives of the Reich Defence Minister and the local District Commanders and Section Commanders of the Border Guards . . .

Nevertheless, Hitler's decision proved unacceptable to Röhm who continued to assert his and the SA's claim to the dominant role in military affairs. On 30 June 1934, Hitler finally checked the SA with a purge of its leadership including Röhm in the notorious 'Night of the Long Knives'.[7] Among those murdered in the course of the purge were General von Schleicher and his wife and his former close associate, General von Bredow. Neither Blomberg and Reichenau in the Defence Ministry nor the Chief of the Army leadership, General Werner von Fritsch, made any attempt to defend or rehabilitate these generals. Indeed, Blomberg blocked any investigation by releasing the following statement to all officers of the Wehrmacht on 2 April 1935, which had already been issued to the members of the Schlieffen Association (for retired officers):

[7] See Vol. I pp. 167 ff.

476

As far as the death of the two generals is concerned, the personal honour of the two officers was not affected by the purely political power struggles in which they were involved. However, they followed paths which were regarded as hostile to the Government and which, therefore, led to the fatal consequences.

I cannot permit any discussion of the question, since the Reich Government has declared through a legislative act that the death of those involved in the events of 30 June and 1 July must be regarded as in the interests of the State.[8] Further investigation of the matter would take us into the political sphere which is barred according to the statutes of the Count Schlieffen Association.

Shortly after the purge Blomberg informed senior officers about its background. A departmental head at the Defence Ministry took down his speech in note form:

477

SA 1933 most faithful fighters. We incorporated them in defence organizations without prejudice. Most of those shot former officers. Disgrace! New political leadership [for SA] necessary. Führer has been informed for months. Wehrmacht went to the furthest limits in its cooperation. Führer's speech [presumably on 28 Feb] moving. On same day Röhm and SA leaders broke their word. Abuse of Führer. From 30 January 1933 onwards Röhm has spoken of continuing the rev. and replacement of Hitler by him. Flattery and sums of money have completely turned his head. French have wound him up still further. Meanwhile, SA has moved further and further away from Defence Ministry. Order on 23 May to collect arms in order to be able to press interests of SA against Wehrmacht and to get SA formations into the Wehrmacht as fully formed units. Hitler's decision to act made long ago. During the leave [of the SA] disturbances to be created, then SA would be summoned. Then Röhm wanted to calm things down and become [Defence] Minister. In addition, special plans for disarmament of the Wehrmacht. Staff guards created to use to get rid of undesirables. Gangs of criminals [organized within them]. Contact with Schleicher established by Röhm. Schleicher to become Vice-Chancellor, Röhm dictator. Contact established with France, Bredow. French toleration of new Cabinet in event of civil war. Gregor Strasser involved as well. Hitler to stay with illusion of power. Restructuring of Cabinet under pressure of disturbances. Disturbances to be set off by list of those to be dealt with, e.g. Wehrmacht Office. Hitler made his decision last week. He wanted to summon Röhm to a meeting and arrest him. Concern about how that would work. Since the SA learned of Wehrmacht countermeasures, it [SA] acted. SA wanted to carry out march on

[8] See Vol. I p. 182.

Munich and Berlin. Saturday afternoon was the time of departure. Munich lost its nerve and acted too soon. Toughness of intervention [necessary]: for the nation, against perversion, asocial characters. Hitler has complete faith in Wehrmacht. Loyal devotion. Intervention against Reaction. Foreign opinions [distort] change in relationship of Wehrmacht to Hitler. Beginning of a process of recovery. Disarming of the SA: transfer weapons to Wehrmacht. SS receives weapons sufficient for a division. NSKK [Nazi Motor Transport Corps] is being subordinated directly to Hitler, as are the Krüger camps [SA military training camps]. Troops did not show attitudes one should expect. Not done to rejoice about those killed and to discuss it in the mess. Death is something one should treat with respect. One officer [was] a member of the SA. Two other officers to face a case of high treason. People's Court. Death. [Actions of Führer] largely done for Wehrmacht. Demand for reciprocal attitude of Wehrmacht to Führer.

On 20 August 1934, Blomberg and Reichenau in effect rewarded Hitler for his support of the Army against the SA by ordering the armed forces to take a new oath of loyalty to the Führer.[9] Previously, the oath had been to the Weimar Constitution, which was still in theory in operation. Moreover, the new oath demanded 'unconditional obedience', a phrase which was new. The motives of the Defence Ministry in taking this step were, first, to bind the officer corps closer to the regime by reviving the old oath of loyalty to the person of the ruler, and secondly, in a continuation of the policy of establishing a special relationship with Hitler, to try and bind Hitler closer to the Wehrmacht. Blomberg interpreted the oath as made to Hitler as head of State and Führer of the German people rather than as leader of the Nazi movement, an interpretation which undoubtedly reflected the general attitude within the officer corps. He failed to realize that Hitler did not recognize such a distinction. The oath caused uneasiness among some officers at the time and was to have serious repercussions in the future. For, many officers either felt bound by their oath, even if they deplored certain actions of the regime, or were able to rationalize their inaction by reference to the oath.

(ii) The 'Co-ordination' of the armed forces and tension with the SS

The decision of the Defence Ministry to introduce a new oath of loyalty to Hitler was part of a consistent policy of trying to identify the armed forces as far as possible with the regime, while retaining its organizational independence. In fact, from the very beginning, the new Government could count on a good deal of sympathy and support from the officer corps.

---

[9] See Vol. I p. 186.

Suspicion and hostility came primarily from individual officers who through particular qualities of character or intellect, or through career experience, had acquired wider horizons, a deeper understanding of political matters, or a different moral perspective than their fellow officers. In this broadly positive response officers expressed attitudes similar to those of their class and generation in other professions with, in particular, the older and more senior officers tending to adopt a more calculating and less commited approach than younger colleagues. On the whole, the older generation of the upper and middle classes were not Nazis so much as Nationalists, in the sense that they would have preferred a return to some version of the pre-November 1918 regime and were disturbed by the radical style of Nazism. Yet the majority concluded that the negative features of the movement were largely outweighed by its positive ones: it promised to eliminate the Communist threat, to overcome class conflict, to reaffirm the traditional values of 'order' and 'decency', and above all to restore national pride. They welcomed the nationalist dynamic within the Nazi movement and saw it primarily as a counter-revolutionary force. It would provide an authoritarian state in which the friction and vacillation of party government would be replaced through the *Führerprinzip* by strong and vigorous leadership such as they—erroneously—believed had characterized Imperial Germany. As General von Einem put it: 'We have got a Chancellor again'.[10] It was as if the Weimar Chancellors, including even General von Schleicher, had not been legitimate figures of authority because they had been prepared to operate within the framework of the democratic Weimar Constitution. Hitler, on the other hand, by his open contempt for Weimar democracy gained legitimacy in the eyes of many Conservatives. His government appeared unequivocally *national* i.e. nationalist and anti-democratic. Hitherto, most officers had felt an inner conflict about committing themselves to the Weimar governments; now this conflict was resolved and it was with relief that they could leave politics to the Government and concentrate on their military activities. General Beck, Chief of the General Staff from 1933–1938 and a future leader of the resistance movement, wrote to a friend in March 1933 welcoming the 'political transformation' wrought by the Nazis: I have longed for it for years and I am pleased that my hope was not deceptive: it is the first glimpse of light since 1918.'[11] Hitler encouraged this development by consciously projecting an image of himself as a responsible statesman—in contrast to the radicalism of his Party. He thereby encouraged the German elites to cooperate with him and put their faith in the 'positive' aspects of Nazism, and with considerable

[10] Cf. W. Sauer op. cit., p. 735.

[11] Cf. K-J. Müller, *General Ludwig Beck* (Boppard 1980) p. 339.

success as far as the Army leadership was concerned. Thus, in 1934, Beck's successor as Chief of the General Staff, General Halder, wrote to him contrasting 'the pure and idealistic intentions of the Chancellor' with 'the majority of completely inadequate, to some extent really inferior, executive organs, which in practice pervert Hitler's noble nationalist intentions into a distortion, indeed to some extent the opposite, of what the Chancellor desires'.[12] Whereas the Weimar Chancellors were damned along with their parties, an anti-democratic and ultra-nationalist Chancellor could be excused the behaviour of his Party, which tended to be excused as 'signs of immaturity'.

Younger officers tended to welcome the Nazi take-over with less calculation and more enthusiasm than their seniors and they included some of the most idealistic members of their generation. Claus Schenk von Stauffenberg and Henning von Tresckow, both of whom were to end up as leading members of the Resistance, were just two of the most important examples of such misguided idealism. Their outlook had been shaped not by the reactionary ideas of pre-war Germany but by the ideas of 'conservative revolution' of the post-war era, a period when traditional values had been drastically called in question. Among the younger generation of the educated middle class there was a yearning for a radical transformation of society: the creation of new social forms, new political structures, and a new spirit of national solidarity. Many of these young officers were critical of the hidebound traditionalism and the social exclusiveness of some of their senior colleagues. Like many middle-class students, they saw in Nazism a movement which would break down class barriers and win the working class for the nation. In particular, some viewed the SA, in whose ranks it was claimed all classes marched side by side, as an alternative to the 'reactionary' professional army. Significantly, after the Nazi take-over a small number of young officers sought to join the SA.

Clearly, however, while idealism was an important motivation and accounts for the degree of enthusiasm for the new regime among many officers, no less important were motives of professional and self interest. And while both older and younger officers shared many of the differing attitudes of their class and of their respective generations towards the Nazi movement, there were also common motives which were specific to their own professional group. The new regime offered the prospects of a rapid expansion of the armed forces, which would break the serious promotion blockage in the officer corps; its economic policies would give priority to the material requirements of the armed forces after years of restraint; its foreign policy promised to secure freedom from the fetters of Versailles;

[12] Cf. K-J. Müller, *Das Heer und Hitler* op. cit., p. 40.

and last, but not least, it would provide a social climate in which the armed forces would regain the prestige which they had largely lost in the post-war years. Above all, the Nazis promised to reestablish the links between the armed forces and the nation and to do so without the Army having to involve itself in domestic politics. These were prospects which must have proved attractive to officers with ambition and with a serious commitment to their profession. In this situation it was obviously tempting to 'get on with the job' and leave politics to the politicians, particularly in a professional climate which was becoming increasingly technocratically oriented.

As part of its policy of identification with the new regime, the Defence Ministry introduced a number of measures designed to 'coordinate' the Army, deriving satisfaction from the fact that it was carrying them out on its own initiative and that it alone among the major institutions of the State had avoided direct Party interference. First, there were symbolic gestures. For example, Blomberg persuaded the Reich President to issue an order on 19 February 1934 that the Nazi Party's emblem of the swastika carried by an eagle with outstretched wings was to be worn on the uniforms of all members of the armed forces.

Secondly, the Defence Ministry adopted a policy of systematic political indoctrination. Thus, on 4 April 1934, Blomberg announced the following secret directive for the 'Permeation of the armed forces with the central idea of the National Socialist State':

478

. . . The first year of National Socialist leadership has laid the foundations for the political and economic reconstruction of the nation. The second year requires us to place the emphasis on the intellectual permeation of the nation with the basic ideas of the National Socialist state. Appropriate political instruction is thus an important task for all organizations supporting the new State. This is particularly the case for the Wehrmacht which is the protector and defender of the external security of National Socialist Germany and its living space.

I decree, therefore, that in future instruction in political questions will be treated with greater importance and given more emphasis. To ensure a uniform implementation of instruction in current political questions, from 1 April the Ministry of Defence will publish once or twice a month 'Directives for instruction in current political issues'.

A significant factor in the Army's attempt to demonstrate its loyalty to the regime was the fact that during this period it felt itself threatened by the paramilitary forces of the Party, first the SA and then the SS. Thus, on 21 April 1934, under pressure from the ambition of the SA, Blomberg issued the following directive concerning Wehrmacht propaganda:

479

The current situation urgently demands more vigorous propaganda for the Wehrmacht among the German public,

The Wehrmacht must appear in public more often as the *sole* bearer of arms in the nation,

as *absolutely reliable* as regards the Hitler Government

as *systematically trained* in National Socialist ideas.

I request commanding officers to pay particular attention to this question in the coming months and to exploit every possible opportunity to strengthen Wehrmacht propaganda.

Furthermore on 15 June 1934, Blomberg issued the following directive on 'National Socialist thought and Wehrmacht. Cultivation of Sociability in the officer corps. Breaking away from traditional social attitudes':

480

Since January 1933, the Wehrmacht has managed to preserve in the National Socialist State as well the position which it deserves in view of the steadfastness, unshakeable discipline, and the nationalist attitude it has adopted since the creation of the State. The recognition which the Führer, Adolf Hitler, has repeatedly granted to the Wehrmacht and the respect which the Wehrmacht receives from all sensible sections of the German people provide confirmation for this statement. We should be proud of that.

A commitment to nationalism is the clear basis of all military activity. We must not forget, however, that the ideology which shapes the new State is not only nationalist but national *socialist*. National Socialism derives the basis for its actions from the vital necessities of the whole nation and from the duty of working together for the totality of the nation. It is founded on the idea of the community of blood and fate of all Germans. There is no dispute about the fact that this law is and must remain the basis for the service of the German soldier. For, our military corpus of ideas and that of National Socialism derive from the same heritage of the Great War.

This law must not only inform our service on duty but must also dominate our private and social lives. I desire that the officer corps of the Wehrmacht should maintain the leading social position which it established for itself in the pre-War period and maintained in the difficult post-War years, especially in the small garrisons. However, today new forms are required for our social life and a broader section of the community should be involved than hitherto.

Prestigious social occasions are justified and necessary when they serve to establish closer official and comradely contacts with important representatives of the new Germany, particularly the Government agencies and the Leagues [SA and SS]. They should be kept simple and demonstrate a particular Wehrmacht style which combines tradition with progress. Nowadays, it can no longer be the task of an officer corps to encourage social relations within a particular social class as in the past. The concept of the national community [*Volksgemeinschaft*] must permeate our social activities as well. Prejudices based solely on social background and education are not justified. The fact that we may alienate some people who cannot throw off traditional social attitudes may be hard for those affected but is necessary. Anyone who today has not inwardly embraced the concept of the national community thereby excludes himself. The Wehrmacht has no reason to make allowances for him. It is not intended to lay down strict criteria for those who are to be invited or to establish blueprints for social events. Indeed it is impossible. I expect commanding officers to follow the right path by observing the points made . . .

On 30 January 1936, on the third anniversary of the Nazi take-over, Blomberg issued the following directive, which was intended to ensure uniformity in the political instruction of all three services:

481

The officer corps of the Wehrmacht can only fulfil its task of leadership in the nation and State if it adopts the National Socialist ideology which gives direction to the life of the German nation and State and appropriates it intellectually totally and with conviction. Thus, I consider the uniform political education and instruction of the officer corps of all three sections of the Wehrmacht to be particularly important.

To ensure that it is carried out I hereby issue the following regulation for the implementation of political instruction:

(a) In the War Colleges of the Army, the Air Force Colleges, and the Naval College at least two hours per month will be devoted to political instruction within the context of the part of the course dealing with defence organization (Army organization, service matters). Furthermore, every opportunity which occurs in the course of duty or instruction must be seized to deal with the interrelationships between people, State and [the Nazi] movement.

Those officers detailed to carry out political instruction will be sent on short combined courses for the three sections of the Wehrmacht at suitable moments (during breaks in the instruction) and will receive regular guidance on course structure and literature.

As a supplement to this instruction there will be special political lectures by outside personalities . . .

In addition to its programme of indoctrination, the Defence Ministry also pursued a personnel policy designed to ensure the coordination of the Wehrmacht with the regime. In addition to the rapid removal of Schleicher's aides within the first week, on 10 October 1933, a number of key figures who were known to be unsympathetic to the regime were retired: the chief of the Army's personnel office, General von dem Bussche-Ippenburg, the Chief of the General Staff (*Truppenamt*) General Adam, and the Commander-in-Chief, General von Hammerstein. Reichenau had hoped to replace Hammerstein and had the support of both Blomberg and Hitler. However, those who opposed him within the senior ranks of the Army, largely on personal and professional rather than political grounds, succeeded in gaining the ear of the Reich President and in pushing through a compromise candidate, General Werner von Fritsch. Fritsch, a brilliant unpolitical soldier, though sympathetic to the regime, was determined to maintain the Army's relative autonomy.

Perhaps the most significant of the concessions to the regime made by the Defence Ministry in its personnel policy was the following decree issued by Blomberg on 28 February 1934:

482

The regulations of the Law for the Restoration of a Professional Civil Service of 7 April 1933 § 3 (Aryan descent)[13] are to be applied to officers, deck officers, NCOs and other ranks . . .

The checking of Aryan descent must be carried out with despatch.

Officers, deck officers, NCOs, and other ranks who do not meet the requirements of § 3 of the Law for the Restoration of a Professional Civil Service cannot be retained in the Wehrmacht . . .

Since under the regulations of § 3 of the Civil Service Law, those who had fought at the front were excluded from the provisions of the decree, the Army and Navy only demanded proof of Aryan descent from those who had not done so. The Air Force, however, insisted that all its personnel should provide evidence of Aryan descent. In the event, it turned out that only seventy individuals in the Army and Navy were affected by this order: 7 officers, 8 officer cadets, 13 NCOs, and 28 privates in the Army, and 3 officers, 4 officer cadets, 3 NCOs, and 4 seamen in the Navy. There are no figures available for the Air Force. After the Nuremberg Laws of September 1935, a clause was inserted in the Defence Law excluding all Jews from the *Wehrmacht* irrespective of whether or not they had fought at the front. The acceptance by the *Wehrmacht* of this key element in Nazi ideology represented not only a serious blow to its independence but also an ominous surrender of basic moral principles. Significantly, there were

[13] Cf. Vol. 2 pp. 223 ff (eds).

very few protests from within the *Wehrmacht* and they focused on concern about its independence rather than the moral issue.

Growing concern about Party interference in the Wehrmacht was partially allayed by § 26 of the new Defence Law of 21 May 1935:

483

(i) Soldiers are not permitted to be politically active. Membership of the NSDAP or of one of its organizations or affiliates is suspended during the period of active service.
(ii) The right to vote and to take part in plebiscites is suspended for soldiers.
(iii) Soldiers require permission from their superiors to acquire membership of associations of all kinds and to establish associations both within and outside the Wehrmacht.

Blomberg, however, remained determined to ensure that the Army supported National Socialism, as is clear from the following directive, dated 22 July 1935, concerning 'Selection of officers of the reserve on the basis of their attitude to National Socialism':

484

For the Wehrmacht it is a matter of course that it is loyal to the National Socialist view of the State. For that reason it is necessary to select officers of the reserve according to the same principle. Thus, only such persons can be appointed and trained as officers of the reserve who declare their loyalty to the National Socialist State, outwardly support it, and do not behave indifferently let alone hostilely towards it.

I therefore request that the officer corps of the reserve shall be selected and constructed on the basis of these principles.

On 13 May 1936, Hitler issued the following secret directive to the *Wehrmacht*:

485

The National Socialist view of the State requires the encouragement of the racial idea and the selection of leaders from people with German or related blood.

The Wehrmacht has thus a clear duty to select its professional soldiers, and therefore its leaders and sub-leaders, according to the strictest racial criteria going beyond the legal regulations and, as educators in the military school of the nation, thereby to maintain a selection of the best Germans.

I expect the Wehrmacht to be conscious of this responsibility to the nation and fatherland. The Reich Minister of War will ensure the uniform application of this directive within the Wehrmacht.

The importance of emphasizing 'the racial idea' was taken seriously by the *Wehrmacht* leadership as is clear from the following excerpt taken from the draft curriculum for the Academy of Naval Administration of 1938:

486

Introduction to Nationalist Politics:

(a) People and Race

Concepts of 'race' and 'people'. Bases of the theory of heredity. Genetic lines. Relationship (species and groups). Appearance and hereditary profile.

General racial theory—the main human races: European, mongoloid, negroid, the sub-European races.

Racial theory of the German people—racial roots: nordic, falian, dinarian, alpine, Mediterranean, Eastern Baltic races.

Racial history of the German people—West germanic tribes (without Anglo-Saxons and Lombards) as basis of German nation. Mixture with Romano-Celts in South and West, Letts-Slavs and Illyrians in the East. The Jews. Racial policy and racial law, in particular, the National Socialist racial legislation.

With Hitler's purge of the SA leadership in the so-called 'Night of the Long Knives' of 30 June 1934, the Army believed it had secured a major victory over the SA. The Army had indeed played an important role in the affair providing substantial logistical and back-up support including arms for the SS units which carried out the arrests and executions. In his speech to the Reichstag justifying the affair on 13 July Hitler had reiterated his promise: 'In the State there is only one bearer of arms—the Army'. In fact, on 30 June, the very day of the purge, he had ordered that his SS boydguard unit, the *SS Leibstandarte*, should be set up as a fully equipped regiment independent of the *Wehrmacht*. Despite protests from Army district commanders, Blomberg not only agreed to this but offered to provide sufficient arms for the equipment of a division. The Army leadership (*Heeresleitung*) still hoped to restrict the role of this new *SS Verfügungstruppe* to internal police duties, which was the pretext for its creation, and that in time of war its members would be called up into the Army as individuals. However, on 2 February 1935, Hitler ordered that while the *SS Verfügungstruppe* should be subordinate to the Defence

Minister as far as its preparation for war was concerned, and that it should not be formed into a division in peacetime, with the outbreak of war it should function as a separate and fully equipped division under its own officers, though subordinate to the overall command of the Army for its deployment in battle. As a result of these decisions, the Army had not only lost its position as the sole bearer of arms but from now onwards had to confront the determined ambition of the SS to expand its military role. Indeed, this conflict with the SS was the most striking example of continuing friction between the Army and Party agencies, which were suspicious of its commitment to the regime and resentful of its relative independence.

The Defence Ministry and the Army leadership responded in different ways to this friction. Whereas Blomberg tended to regard it as the result of the Army's failure to integrate itself sufficiently into the new regime, its tendency to cling to traditional Prussian military and social values, which he saw as reactionary and out of tune with the new era, Werner von Fritsch, the Army commander, saw things rather differently. He was completely loyal to Hitler as head of state, whom he erroneously believed to be sympathetic to the Army's position, and also a supporter of what he believed Nazism stood for, i.e. a populist form of nationalism and the values of the front line soldier in the World War. However Fritsch was determined to resist Party interference in Army matters and to maintain as far as possible the Army's special position and its traditional values.

On 1 February 1938, two days before his resignation after being falsely denounced as a homosexual, Fritsch noted down his experiences as Commander-in-Chief of the Army over the previous four years:

487

On 3 January 1934, I was appointed Commander-in-Chief with effect from 1 February against the Führer's wishes, against Blomberg's wishes, but under the strongest pressure from Field-Marshal von Hindenburg.

I found a heap of ruins, in particular a severe crisis of confidence within the High Command.

Reichenau's and the Party's struggle against me began on the day of my appointment in so far as it had not already begun.

Reichenau's opposition is understandable, for he wanted to take over command of the Army and still does.

The Party sees in me not only the man who opposed the ambitions of the SA but also the man who tried to block the influx of party-political maxims into the Army.

Apart from the fact that the basis of our present Army is National Socialist and must be so, the infiltration of party-political influences into the Army cannot be tolerated since such influences can lead only to fragmentation and dissolution.

The task given me by the Führer when I reported to him on 1 February 1934 was: 'Create an army as strong and united as possible and with the best conceivable training'. I have followed these instructions ever since.

Reichenau's machinations meant that my relationship with Blomberg was continually troubled. Throughout these years I have never succeeded in establishing a relationship with Blomberg based on trust as should have been the case . . .

In the autumn of 1934, there was great agitation as a result of the machinations of the SS. The SS maintained the Army was preparing a *putsch*, and reports came in from all the military districts that the SS was planning a big coup. Then, the Führer decided to order the leading figures in the Party and many senior officers to a meeting in the Opera House. The Führer made a speech which was a clear statement of loyalty to the Army and its leader [i.e. Fritsch]. After the Führer's speech, the SS agitation decreased somewhat. But from the summer of 1935 it increased again. The behaviour of the *SS-Verfügungstruppen* at the military training establishment at Altengrabow, where for no reason at all they indulged in vicious abuse of the Army and myself, threw a significant light on the situation.

While during the subsequent phase, we managed to establish a good, in many cases intimate relationship with all Party agencies, this was not true of the SS. As far as our side was concerned, this may have derived from the fact that there was hardly a single senior officer who did not feel that the SS were spying on him. It is continually coming to light that, contrary to express instructions from the Führer's Deputy, SS people serving in the Army have received orders to provide reports on their superiors. Unfortunately, these matters come to my attention in such a form that I cannot pursue them.

Finally, the *SS Verfügungstruppe*, which is continually being expanded, must create conflict with the Army through its very existence. It is the living proof of mistrust towards the Army and its leadership.

Although the Army has a certain right to supervise the training of the *SS Verfügungstruppe*, this SS troop is developing completely separately and, as I see it, in conscious opposition to the Army. All units are unanimous in reporting that the relationship of the *SS-Verfügungstruppe* to the Army is very cold if not hostile. One cannot avoid the impression that the negative attitude towards the Army in the *SS Verfügungstruppe* is positively encouraged. This attitude finds external expression in the fact that only very rarely does an SS man salute an officer.

Attempts by the Army to retain its autonomy within the regime were undermined both by rivalry with the other two services, the Navy and the Luftwaffe, both of which were even more positively disposed towards the regime, and by rivalry between the Army leadership and the Ministry of Defence (after 1934 of War). The Ministry had established a *Wehrmacht* Office, which was intended to coordinate the three services. However, the Army leadership, and the Chief of the General Staff, General Beck, in particular, were determined to preserve their independence and their traditional superiority within the Armed Forces, especially since they had a low regard for the expertise of the *Wehrmacht* Office. These divisions within the Armed Forces enabled Hitler to play the various elements off one against the other and facilitated their subordination to the regime.

Despite these rivalries and tension between the Army and the Nazi organizations, especially the SS, the attitude of the armed forces to the regime during this period was in general very positive. For, above all, they found a sympathetic response to their plans for rearmament. However, in view of Germany's continuing subjection to the clauses of the Treaty of Versailles, any plans for German rearmament were bound to be closely interrelated with German foreign policy. It was part of the deal between Hitler and the Wehrmacht that he would create a favourable diplomatic and strategic situation for any commitment of the *Wehrmacht* to battle.

CHAPTER 27

German Foreign Policy 1933–1937

(i) The Background 1919–1932

The Nazis came to power at a time when German foreign and armaments policies were both in a state of flux. The signing of the Young Plan, on 7 June 1929, and the death of Stresemann, on 3 October 1929, had marked the end of an era, and the years 1930–33 were a period of transition to a new one, which represented the third major phase in German foreign policy since the War.

During the first phase, between 1919–23, France had endeavoured to compensate for her failure to impose harsher conditions on Germany during the treaty negotiations in 1919. Her aim was to destroy Germany's future potential as a great power by acquiring control of its main industrial centre, the Rhine-Ruhr region. This was to be achieved by encouraging separatist movements in the Rhineland and through the ruthless enforcement of the reparations agreements in the hope of provoking a German default on payments which would provide an excuse for invasion. Germany tried to resist these measures as best she could, partly by trying to exploit differences among the Allies, partly by cultivating a relationship with the other pariah state, the Soviet Union, and partly by a stubborn lack of cooperation. By the end of 1923, it had become clear that this policy of confrontation was proving counter-productive for both sides. The French occupation of the Ruhr in 1923 had proved very costly and it was evident that without the support of her allies France was not powerful enough to sustain a policy of crushing Germany over the long term. On the other hand, Germany's passive resistance had imposed intolerable strains on her political, economic, and social structures. In 1924 both sides drew back from the brink. Concerned about damage to its foreign trade, the United States intervened to shore up the international order established at Versailles. Exploiting its powerful economic position, and with the help of mediation from Britain, in 1924 America in effect imposed a new regulation for German reparations, the Dawes Plan, which prevented France from exploiting them in the future as a political weapon. This development initiated a new phase of economic stability and international reconciliaton.

The new German Foreign Minister, Gustav Stresemann, aimed to restore Germany's position as a major power by persuading the other powers, particularly France, of her peaceful intentions. By demonstrating Germany's willingness to fulfil her obligations under the Versailles treaty as far as possible, by participating fully in multilateral agreements such as the Locarno Pact of 1925, guaranteeing Germany's Western frontiers, and by joining the League of Nations in 1926, Stresemann endeavoured successfully to win recognition for Germany as a full and equal partner in the European Concert of nations. He intended that her complete integration into the international economic and political arrangements would develop a set of relationships and mutual dependencies between Germany and the other powers, which would persuade them of her peaceful intentions and also that the harsh provisions of Versailles were not only no longer relevant but were in fact counter-productive and, as a source of tension, should be removed. In short, a situation would be created in which a gradual and peaceful revision of Versailles would be possible. Finally, his policy would also facilitate a revival of the German economy and if necessary he was prepared to use German economic strength as a lever to secure revision of Versailles.

By 1928, this policy had achieved some success. Germany was once more treated as a more or less equal partner in the international community and relations with France had improved enormously by comparison with 1923. However, the concrete gains in terms of a substantial revision of Versailles had been small. Closer cooperation between Germany and France had been hampered to some extent by American pressure stemming from concern about the emergence of a European block which would have adverse effects on American foreign trade. However, it was also prevented by a growing French concern at Germany's increasing relative strength, coupled with their awareness that Stresemann's conciliatory policy did not have the overwhelming support of the German people. There were in fact powerful currents of opinion on the German Right, which regarded Stresemann's 'fulfilment' policy as a sell-out to the Allies and wished Germany to adopt a more intransigent line. The *Reichswehr*, in particular, was pressing for priority to be given to the ending of the disarmament clauses. Moreover, during 1928, there were signs, such as the take-over of the DNVP by Hugenberg and the Pan-Germans,[1] that this attitude was gaining ground. The problem was that by delaying rewards for Stresemann's policy of reconciliation, notably an evacuation of the Rhineland, the French were in effect discrediting it and thereby fanning the flames of German nationalism and helping to undermine German democracy.

Stresemann's policy was, however, also the victim of the world economic crisis which began in 1929. His policy required above all a long period of international peace and stability and a sense of confidence about the future. The great depression encouraged an atmosphere of 'catch as catch can' among the nations which took the form of protectionist tendencies undermining international cooperation and destroying confidence. It also increased domestic political tensions encouraging the growth of extremist movements and reducing governments' room for manoeuvre both at home and abroad.

The death of Stresemann on 3 October 1939 was followed in March 1930 by the collapse of the Grand Coalition between the Liberals, Catholic Centre Party, and Social Democrats which had provided the domestic political base for his foreign policy. The new right-wing presidential government under Chancellor Brüning decided to pursue a new course. Already, during the negotiations over the Young Plan, voices had begun to make themselves heard, both within the Foreign Ministry and among the representatives of the various interests and the economic experts involved, pressing for a tougher line. Now, with the Brüning government these views gained the upper hand. Brüning declared that the Locarno policy had failed, and significantly, on 13 June 1930, Stresemann's faithful and creative aide, Carl von Schubert, was replaced as State Secretary in the Foreign Ministry by Bernhard von Bülow, a critic of the Stresemann line.

The foreign policy of the new era was marked by both a new content and a new style. Ernst von Weizsäcker, a senior Foreign Ministry official and critic of Stresemann, described it on 26 December 1930 as a 'transition from fulfilment policy to a revisionist policy'.[2] The new government aimed to exploit the collapse of the old international order to secure the complete revision of Versailles, which had largely eluded Stresemann, and thereby neutralize the nationalist opposition at home and establish a solid domestic political base. The new government shifted the emphasis away from the multilateral political and economic arrangements characteristic of the Stresemann era, towards bilateral agreements, protectionist economic policies, and in general a far more pronounced assertion of German

[1] For the political background see Vol. I pp. 63 ff.

[2] Cf. P. Krüger, *Die Aussenpolitik der Republik von Weimar* (Darmstadt 1985) p. 521. This section owes a good deal to this book.

interests. In particular, it concentrated its attention on South-Eastern Europe, with the aim of securing a German sphere of economic influence through bilateral agreements with the countries of the Danube basin, exploiting their desperate need for markets for their agricultural produce to tie their economies to Germany. In 1931, the Foreign Ministry cooperated with Austria on a project to establish a joint Customs Union in the hope of paving the way for *Anschluss*. The Union was also intended in the future to include the states of South-East Europe and eventually the Baltic States, thereby virtually surrounding Poland with an economic cordon and enabling Germany to press her to agree to a revision of Germany's eastern frontiers. According to Brüning, Germany needed 'its adequate, natural living space'.[3] This would be achieved by establishing an indirect form of German hegemony in Eastern Europe, thereby realizing the old concept which had surfaced in the First World War of a *Mitteleuropa* under German control.

The Customs Union project represented a direct challenge to French influence in South-East Europe, while the idea of *Anschluß* was anathema to the Allies. Since Germany did not have the power to push through the project against Allied opposition the result was a débacle, in which France retaliated with economic sanctions thereby greatly increasing Germany's economic difficulties.

Brüning's government adopted the same hard line over reparations. Brüning regarded the Young Plan as a '*diktat*' and determined to destroy it. Instead of seeking relief from the Allies, he decided to pursue the fulfilment policy to absurdity. Through a tough deflationary policy at home involving sharp cuts in government expenditure, he intended to demonstrate, even at the cost of deepening the economic crisis, the impossibility of Germany fulfilling the terms of the plan. The policy was eventually successful in the sense that reparations were officially ended by the Allies at the Lausanne Conference in July 1932. However, Brüning was no longer there to reap the benefits and the cost in terms of increased political radicalization at home and the alienation of Germany's neighbours abroad was high.

It was not only the content of German foreign policy which changed after 1930 but also its style. German diplomacy abandoned the conciliatory tone of the Stresemann era and adopted a new style of confrontation and public polemics. To some extent, this reflected domestic political pressures. For both Brüning and Papen were endeavouring to shore up their position at home by heading off nationalist pressures through quick successes abroad. These nationalist pressures were building up an explosive head of

---

[3] Ibid. p. 529.

steam since the economic crisis was being blamed on the Versailles treaty in general and the Young Plan in particular. On the other hand, the Government made no effort to resist these pressures or to try and educate the public in the realities of the situation. Indeed nationalist propaganda provided welcome ammunition for the governments of Brüning and Papen in trying to persuade the Allies to grant concessions. It is clear that Brüning and Papen were happy to exploit pressure from the radical Right in order to achieve a revision of Versailles. In doing so they contributed to a dangerous process by which expectations were encouraged which the Government came under increasing pressure to fulfil.

The governments of Papen and Schleicher (1 June 1932–28 January 1933) were too brief to have any significant impact on German foreign policy. Both favoured a rapprochement with France, while Papen advocated closer relations with Poland and Schleicher preferred closer links with Russia.

(ii) The Diplomacy of Rearmament: The Wooing of England 1933–35

In retrospect, the years 1930–33 may be seen as a period of transition in foreign policy as well as domestic politics, easing the passage from Weimar democracy to the Third Reich. Initially, however, it was not at all clear what effect, if any, the appointment of Hitler as Chancellor would have on the development of German foreign policy. Hitler had of course publicly stated his foreign policy 'programme' in his book *Mein Kampf*. It is doubtful, though, whether the officials in the German Foreign Ministry had even read, let alone taken seriously, what he had written. Konstantin Freiherr von Neurath, a professional diplomat, had been retained as Foreign Minister at the express wish of the Reich President and, in a Cabinet in which it was assumed that the Nazis would be 'tamed' by the Conservatives, it seemed likely that the Foreign Ministry would play the major role in formation of foreign policy. Bernhard von Bülow wrote to Herbert von Dirksen, the German ambassador in Moscow on 6 February 1933:

488

I think the people there [in Moscow] overestimate the diplomatic importance of the change of government. Now that they are in a position of responsibility the National Socialists are naturally different people and will follow different policies from those they have previously proclaimed. That has always been the case and is the same with all parties. The presence of von Neurath and von Blomberg guarantee the continuation of the previous political relationships. The Communist persecution in Germany also does not need to affect our relationship.

Dirksen clearly concurred with Bülow's view of the situation, adopting an attitude that was typical of the vast majority of the German diplomatic service. Thus, he wrote to a colleague on 14 March 1933:

489

At any rate we officials in particular have the task of facilitating as far as possible the initiation of the National Socialist movement into government. We need peace and stability in our domestic politics and the present combination—perhaps and ideally with the inclusion of the Centre party—is the only one which offers the prospect of permanence.

Soon, however, Bülow became concerned. Hitler had stated some general views on the future course of his government in his speech to the generals on 3 February.[4] Bülow learnt of Hitler's statements and became worried about the danger of Germany provoking foreign intervention, or at least her complete isolation, through adopting too aggressive a line. On 13 March 1933, he prepared a memorandum which he submitted first to Blomberg and Neurath and then circulated to the German ambassadors. It was used by the Foreign Minister as the basis for his first briefing of the Cabinet on the foreign policy situation on 7 April 1933. It provides a valuable insight into the views of the Conservative revisionists at the beginning of the Nazi regime:

490

I. General

The goals of German foreign policy are set first and foremost by the Versailles treaty. The revision of this treaty—Germany's most pressing concern — absorbs most of its available energies. The further task of exploiting opportunities which occur for Germany through the continuing changes in Europe and the world as a whole, has to take second place to the revision of Versailles.

Just as the goals of our foreign policy are determined to a large extent by the Versailles treaty so also is their realization, in the sense of its effects on Germany's general position of strength. The debilitating impact on Germany of the Versailles treaty is far more extensive and lasting than the German people have generally recognised. In the light of the growing importance of technical armaments (in comparison to size of population), our military weakness is such that we have no

[4] See above p. 629–30.

prospect of achieving parity with France in the foreseeable future through an armaments race. In view of our limited financial resources and the technical difficulties involved in an expansion of the Wehrmacht, we shall require approximately five years to achieve military parity even with Poland. In addition, there is the need to carry out the restructuring of German armaments fairly slowly and quietly in order to avoid interventions, preventive actions, and diplomatic crises. This applies to the Reichswehr, Navy and police, and in particular to the Air Force, which is regarded as extremely important abroad.

At the moment, our security vis-à-vis France depends in the first instance on the Locarno treaty with its Anglo-Italian guarantee, vis-à-vis Poland on our relationship with Russia, vis-à-vis all the other states almost entirely on the general treaty arrangements (League of Nations, Kellogg Pact etc.) and on the desire for peace of almost all nations which rests on economic considerations. In view of our interest in the Locarno treaty vis-à-vis France, we have for the time being postponed the revision of the demilitarisation conditions for the Rhineland. The situation in the east of Germany is particularly dangerous at the present time. The only prospect of a successful repulsion of a Polish attack is in the event of Russian support, at least in the form of a Russian mobilization on Poland's eastern frontier. Whether we can reckon with such support in a crisis is at the moment uncertain.

II. The Revision of Versailles

In past years revision of Versailles has taken the form of an attack on it point by point (French artichoke theory). One cannot in fact deny that the simultaneous pursuit of several goals, let alone the attempt at a total revision, would have involved the danger of a complete failure (Examples: the failure to achieve the immediate evacuation of the Rhineland at Locarno, or the liberation of the Saar at the Hague). In future too, at any rate for the time being, we shall have to follow the method of revising particular aspects unless unexpected circumstances open up another way. One must also consider that the plan of a total revision would increase the danger of a compromise with a less satisfactory final result. To achieve the best possible result with the least possible sacrifice we shall have to choose the most favourable moment for the revision of each particular part of the treaty . . .

It is inadvisable to broach the question of the territorial revision of frontiers just yet so long as Germany is not sufficiently secure militarily, financially, and economically, and, in particular, so long as the disarmament question has not yet been settled. Until then, the territorial revision will have to be prepared—as hitherto—through propaganda abroad (on the basis of the Wilson points, the deception of Versailles). Sticking to the Wilson points is vital because the counter-propaganda operates quite successfully with the allegedly limitless nature of our demands. In addition, we must maintain the political, economic, and cultural positions of the Germans in the ceded territories even if this requires great financial sacrifices. However, although waiting patiently, we must of course always be prepared for the territorial questions, above all the Eastern problem, to come to a head on their own one day through natural developments, such as, for example, serious complications between Danzig and Poland.

The main goal of the territorial revision remains the transformation of the Eastern frontier, whereby we must seek to acquire all the relevant Polish territories at the same time, and reject partial or intermediate solutions (only *one* more partition of Poland). Academic studies relating to questions of ethnography, geology, communications etc., relevant to the drawing up of the boundaries, are far advanced. On the other hand, the question of how we are to absorb the agricultural surplus of these territories in future is still unclear. . . .

Danzig poses only one aspect of the problem of the corridor as far as we are concerned. Any special solution which applies to Danzig alone must be rejected because it would compromise our overall objective.

III. The other foreign policy goals

The other foreign policy goals of Germany stem from the political and economic upheaval of Europe in particular, from our geographical position, our economic bases (over-population, narrow raw material base), from the necessity for the industry of all nations to open up new territories, the need to combat the industrialization of agrarian states etc. The most essential task is the strengthening of Germany in all spheres, while at the same time avoiding political and economic danger zones. The encouragement and support of the German minorities and the Germans abroad is particularly important in relation to this . . .

French and Italian policies vis-à-vis Austria coincide in the negative goal of preventing the Anschluss, but conflict in the positive goal of incorporating Austria into their respective spheres of influence. The Franco-Italian rivalry puts Austria in a state of suspended animation and we can only hope that this situation will continue until Austria can be incorporated into the Reich. The greatest danger for German unity would be a Franco/Italian agreement on the basis of the incorporation of Austria into one or other of their spheres of influence. The prospects of such an agreement are for the time being remote . . .

Our policy vis-à-vis the Little Entente must concentrate on trying to reduce its ties to France as far as possible and, in particular, on stopping Czechoslovakia from linking itself too closely to Poland.

The best method of achieving this would undoubtedly be an economic policy which opened the German market to the products of these lands. Above all, the direction of Yugoslavia's and Romania's foreign policy could be significantly influenced in this direction in view of their present catastrophic economic situation.

These political considerations form the basis for our policy of economic support for the states on the lower Danube (Hungary, Romania, Yugoslavia, Bulgaria), which found expression in our willingness to grant preferences for wheat and in the aid which we gave to these states at international conferences, most recently at the Stresa conference. A decisive factor in this was also the consideration that these markets, which show considerable potential for the future must be kept open for German exports. However, the effectiveness of this policy has been considerably reduced recently through the almost total curtailment of the agricultural exports of these states of Germany. At the moment, apart from our willingness to offer economic support, we have nothing with which to counteract the great political and financial pull of France. We must, therefore, continue the Stresa policy and pursue it more effectively by increasing the exchange of goods with the states on the lower Danube as far as possible.

As far as Russia is concerned, the most important point to make is that we cannot dispense with Russian support against Poland. In this connection our good relations with the Russian army are particularly important since they guarantee us information about the state of Russian armaments, which is indispensable if we are to avoid unpleasant surprises.

In addition, there are important economic factors which only partly derive from the present economic crisis. Through its substantial orders, Russia has gradually become the largest customer for German industrial goods.

The vigorous fight against the Communists and cultural Bolshevism in Germany does not need to damage German-Russian relationships in the long term as is demonstrated by the example of Italy. At the moment, one cannot deny that there has been a cooling off of these relations. In order to change this situation, we shall have to pay particular attention to our relations with Moscow and, without running after the Soviet Union, make it clear that, as far as we are concerned, we keep our domestic struggle against Communism strictly separate from our diplomatic attitude to the Soviet Union. For this reason the extension of the Berlin treaty should be ratified as soon as possible. A revival of German-Russian trade through an increase in the purchase of Russian products as far as possible is equally desirable.

An agreement with Poland is neither possible nor desirable. We must maintain a certain degree of tension for revision and to keep Poland down politically and economically. However, the situation is by no means without danger since the present Polish government, recognising that its prospects are deteriorating with the continuing strengthening of Germany and that France might become less keen on her alliance, is apparently toying with the idea of a preventive war. The most immediate cause for this is naturally our territorial demands. Thus we cannot avoid playing down public discussion of these to some extent for the time being. The maintenance of the German presence in Poland, and particularly in Upper Silesia and in Danzig, which is not financially viable, causes us particular concern and very considerable costs.

Conclusion

The present world situation is marked by political and economic tensions. The necessary economic solutions are in many cases delayed or prevented by the existing political conflicts. In Germany's particular situation it is necessary to avoid diplomatic conflicts for as long as possible until we have become stronger. The world economic crisis gives us the great opportunity, through careful planning, to weather the storm better than others and thereby to secure a reconstruction of the world economic situation to our advantage. This would enable us to achieve a more favourable balance of forces, at least in Europe. By excluding political conflicts and concentrating on economic questions, we would avoid military dangers which we are not at the moment equal to.

A precipitate assertion of foreign policy demands would probably mobilise the important powers against us and jeopardise the fulfilment of these demands for a long time to come. A period of complete tranquillity abroad for a few years would in fact be a natural counterpart to the four year programme for the reconstruction at home. A period of relative quiet in foreign affairs would allow us to recover our strength far more effectively than the launching of continual diplomatic conflicts which cannot lead to success. How far this is tolerable from the domestic political angle I will not go into. On the other hand, considerable disadvantages have to be weighed against the dual advantage of the period of tranquility and the maturing of all our diplomatic demands. In the first place, there is the danger that our opponents will try to secure a renewal of the period of tranquility and thereby a strengthening of the status quo. Furthermore, it will be difficult to realize the idea in a form which not only excludes any recognition of the present frontiers but also, which is desirable from our point of view, acknowledges the frontiers to be an open question. Finally, the concept of a period of tranquility is so vague and open to so many interpretations that one would have to reckon with an endless series of complaints about the failure to stick to agreements.

Perhaps the same goal could be achieved without bilateral or multilateral ties, for example, through a unilateral declaration or multilateral discussion without a formal agreement. We would not then be forced to steer clear of the great political questions. It would be sufficient for us to emphasize that, after the settlement of the disarmament question, we would concentrate on economic and financial tasks. That would then lead to the break-up of the opposition group into which most European states have formed in response to the new regime in Germany and through concern about the future.

The essential points would be a close cooperation with England and Italy, the greatest possible reassurance for the French government about these questions which particularly interest it (e.g. the German defence programme), a good relationship with Russia, relations with the United States based on trust, and active participation in all international questions. In addition, a precondition for this would be if the Government were to formulate all foreign policy statements in a way appropriate to this end, and if all demonstrations by groups and organizations closely associated with the Government which are calculated to provoke foreign opinion were to be prevented.

The main task of foreign policy during the first phase of the regime was to provide diplomatic cover for the consolidation of Nazi power at home and for an acceleration of the rearmament programme. The other powers were highly suspicious of the new regime in view of the extreme aggressiveness of previous Nazi propaganda. Hitler was aware of the need to move cautiously. In the spring of 1933, he remarked pointedly to Carl Krogmann, the Mayor of Hamburg, that in the circumstances Germany would have to conclude a truce with the European powers for at least six years and that the 'sabre-rattling' of some National Socialist circles was a mistake as Germany had no weapons. His immediate policy therefore was one of apparent conciliation. He protested his desire for peace in a series of speeches in 1933 and followed the same line in several interviews he gave to foreign correspondents. On the same day as his address to the generals, Hitler spoke with representatives of the Associated Press claiming that 'nobody wishes for peace more that I'. Hitler's first major 'peace speech' was on 17 May in which he disclaimed any wish to subject other nations to German rule. He said that one of the aims of the 'German Revolution' was

491

. . . to re-establish a stable and authoritative Government supported by the will and confidence of the nation which should make our great people an acceptable partner of the other states of the world.

Speaking deliberately as a German National Socialist, I desire to declare in the name of the National Government, and of the whole movement of national regeneration, that we in this new Germany are filled with deep understanding for the same feelings and opinions and for the rightful claims to life of the other nations. The present generation of this new Germany which so far has only experienced the poverty, misery and distress of its own people, has suffered too deeply from the madness of our time to be able to contemplate treating others in the same way. Our boundless love for and loyalty to our own national traditions makes us respect the national claims of others and makes us desire from the bottom of our hearts to live with them in peace and friendship. We therefore have no use for the idea of Germanization. The mentality of the past century which made people believe that they could make Germans out of Poles and Frenchmen is completely foreign to us; the more so as we are passionately opposed to any attempt on the part of others to alienate us from our German tradition. We look at the European nations objectively. The French, the Poles, etc. are our neighbours, and we know that through no possible development of history can this reality be altered.

It would have been better for the world if in Germany's case these realities had been appreciated in the treaty of Versailles. For the object of a really lasting Treaty should not be to cause new wounds and keep old ones open, but to close wounds and heal them. A thoughtful treatment of European problems at that time could certainly have produced a settlement in the east which would have met both the reasonable claims of Poland and the natural rights of Germany. The Treaty of Versailles did not provide this solution. Nevertheless, no German Government will of its own accord break an agreement unless its removal could lead to its replacement by a better one.

But the legal character of such a Treaty must be acknowledged by *all*. Not only the conqueror but also the conquered party can claim the rights accorded in the Treaty. And the right to demand a revision of the Treaty finds its foundation in the Treaty itself. The German Government, in stating the reasons for the extent of its claims, wishes for nothing more than the results of what previous experience and the incontestable consequences of critical and logical reasoning show to be necessary and just. The experience of the last fourteen years, however, is unambiguous from a political and economic point of view.

Apart from the need to reassure foreign opinion about the new regime, the main issue with which German diplomacy had to deal with during 1933 was disarmament. After the French evacuation of the Rhineland in 1930 and the ending of reparations in 1932, the armament restrictions had moved into centre stage as the main remaining legacy of Versailles apart from the territorial provisions. On 2 February 1932, a disarmament conference had opened in Geneva. Germany took the line that since she had obeyed the restrictions of Versailles and reduced her armed forces to the minimum required, it was now up to the other powers to respond by reducing their armaments and by permitting Germany to rearm until a rough equality of armaments had been achieved. During 1932, Germany pressed her demands to the point of temporarily pulling out of the conference on 23 July, a tactic which eventually achieved part of its aim in a five power declaration on 11 December 1932 accepting that an agreement on equality of armaments for Germany was a desirable goal.

Under the new Hitler government the initiative in this question was initially taken by the Defence and Foreign Ministries which took a hard line and gave direct instructions to their representatives in Geneva, bypassing Hitler who was adopting a more cautious approach. By the Autumn of 1933, the Defence Ministry felt under increasing pressure to outflank the SA by replacing Schleicher's militia plan of November 1932, which involved the danger of the eventual absorption of the *Reichswehr* into the SA, with a more conventional form of expansion of the armed forces through conscription.[5] This would, however, mean an overt breach of the disarmament clauses of Versailles. Matters finally came to a head when the British put forward a compromise proposal which would have continued to limit German armaments. Blomberg persuaded Hitler to use the excuse of the tough line taken by France to pull out of the conference altogether on 14 October. At the same time, he withdrew Germany from the League of Nations. Hitler calculated correctly that the other powers would not retaliate against Germany and cleverly bolstered his position by holding a plebiscite on the issue on 12 November which produced a positive vote of 95 per cent.

Hitler now sought to preempt hostility and secure Germany's position by making bilateral agreements with various powers. In particular, he tried to use the armaments issue as a first step towards the alliance with Britain envisaged in *Mein Kampf*. In November 1933, Hitler sent his 'representative for disarmament questions', Joachim von Ribbentrop as a personal emissary to London where, in conversations with a number of leading figures, Ribbentrop suggested an agreement between Britain and Germany in which Germany would guarantee the British Empire in return for a free hand in Eastern Europe. Specifically, he proposed a Non-Aggression Pact for which a naval agreement would provide the basis. A few days later,

---

[5] See above p. 631–4.

on 29 November, the Commander-in-Chief of the Navy, Admiral Raeder, made a similar proposal for a naval agreement to the British naval attaché. On 5 December, Hitler brought up the question of armaments himself in an interview with the British ambassador, Sir Eric Phipps. He complained that

492

. . . Germany's frontier was completely undefended and, as things were at present, the French could walk into the country whenever they liked. Indeed there was a very real danger of some future weak French Government deciding to embark on a policy of foreign adventure in order to divert attention from its weakness at home and to proceed to the occupation of the left bank of the Rhine. This was an intolerable situation for Germany, who was thereby placed in the position of being externally considered to be a second-class Power. She must also be in a position to throw her weight into the scales at some future time, and, in this connexion, might not Great Britain herself be glad of other alternatives to her present friendships? . . .

Hitler then tried to drive a wedge between Britain and France by offering to concede substantial rearmament to Britain, while suggesting that Britain and Italy should combine to force France to come to terms. Phipps continued:

. . .

6. I enquired what exactly the Chancellor had meant when he had suggested to me in my previous interview that the 'highly armed' Powers should be bound by a species of *Stillstand* agreement to their present armaments. Herr Hitler replied that he had only had in mind France, Poland and Czechoslovakia. So far as Britain was concerned, not only should she not be included in any such standstill agreement, but he would even welcome considerable additions to the British fleet and air force.

7. On the naval side, I remarked that we had often proposed the total abolition of submarines, to which Herr Hitler replied that Germany also would be delighted if submarines could be abolished. He then repeated what General von Blomberg had told me . . . that Germany would never dream of competing against England at sea, but would like a few [*ein paar*] big ships after 1935, until which date she would remain within the limits prescribed by the Treaty.

8. The Chancellor declared that he did not believe the present French Government was strong enough to reach any satisfactory comprehensive agreement with Germany. I thereupon asked what procedure he would favour in order to reach an agreement. He replied that if Great Britain and Italy would urge upon France the advisability of concluding an arrangement, at any rate on the basis outlined above, it might induce the French Government to take the necessary decision. . . .

Although Britain neglected to take up his proposals, Hitler did not abandon his endeavours to reach an agreement with Britain. In the meantime, however, he moved to isolate France from another direction by seeking an understanding with Poland. The prospects for such an agreement were better than for some time. After Hitler's appointment Poland had seriously contemplated a preventive attack on Germany, but, disillusioned by France's lack of support, she was increasingly impressed both by Hitler's assurances of his peaceful intentions towards Poland and also by the evident cooling of relations between Germany and the Soviet Union. Germany's departure from the Disarmament Conference and the League of Nations in November 1933 caused anxiety and, on 15 November, Marshal Piłsudski requested a guarantee of Germany's peaceful intentions. According to Lipski, the Polish ambassador in Berlin:

493

The Reich Chancellor declared that all forms of aggression were contrary to his policy and that a war would be a catastrophe for everybody. Any war would simply bring Communism, which represented a fearful threat, to Europe. Poland was a bulwark against Asia. The Reich Chancellor suggested that any possibility of war should be excluded from Polish-German relations and remarked that this idea could best be given expression in the form of a treaty.

On 26 January 1934, Germany concluded a ten-year Non-Aggression Pact with Poland. This was the first occasion on which Hitler pushed through his own policy against the views of the Foreign Ministry. For, whereas Neurath and Bülow were in full agreement with him over the need to cultivate good relations with Britain, although a good deal more sceptical about the prospects of such a policy, they regarded Poland as Germany's arch-enemy with whom no agreement was possible. Hitler's decision to move away from Russia and towards Poland partly reflected his anti-Communist domestic policy. But it was intended, above all, to damage France's system of security alliances in Eastern Europe. For France had concluded an alliance with Poland in 1921 with the object of containing Germany. Hitler was now exploiting Poland's growing uncertainty of the reliability of France and their common hostility toward the Soviet Union. The pact also had considerable propaganda value for Hitler, who used it as evidence of his peaceful intentions in speeches he made during 1934 and 1935. Sir Eric Phipps, for example, wrote in a report to London that the German agreement with Poland showed Hitler's statesmanlike qualities, since for its sake he was prepared to lose some popularity.

In June 1934, Hitler made his first trip abroad as German Chancellor—significantly to visit Mussolini in Venice. He clearly hoped to pave the way for an understanding with Italy which would lead to the alliance envisaged in his programme. His main task was to try to calm Mussolini's uneasiness about German intentions in Austria. In this he proved unsuccessful. After the war, the German Foreign Minister, von Neurath, who was present at the meeting, recalled that 'their minds didn't meet; they didn't understand each other'.[6] Moreover, after his return to Germany, his attempt to woo Italy and indeed his whole peace policy received a severe setback when Austrian Nazis attempted a *coup d'état* against the Dollfuss Government in Vienna, an attempt which resulted in the assassination of Dollfuss but not in the overthrow of the regime. This event produced serious diplomatic complications, above all with Italy. Indeed Mussolini, who at the time was host to Frau Dollfuss, ordered troops to the Austrian border at the Brenner Pass and relations with Germany became tense.

The Austrian incident came at a time of serious crisis for the Nazi regime. The Röhm 'putsch' had occurred only a few weeks before and had re-awakened international suspicion of Nazism. Furthermore, Germany was in the middle of a grave balance of payments crisis which made her extremely vulnerable to international pressure.[7] Von Bülow, stressed the vulnerability of Germany's international position in a memorandum to von Neurath in August 1934:

494

In judging the situation we should never overlook the fact that no kind of rearmament in the next few years could give us military security. Even apart from our isolation, we shall for a long time yet be hopelessly inferior to France in the military sphere. A particularly dangerous period will be 1934–35 on account of the reorganization of the Reichswehr. Our only security lies in a skilful foreign policy and in avoiding all provocation.

In so doing we must, of course, not only prevent the taking of military measures against Germany such as are being quite openly discussed in military circles abroad. In view of our isolation and our present weakness, economically and as regards foreign currency, our opponents need not even expose themselves to the hazards, the odium and the dangers of military measures. Without mobilizing a single man or firing a single shot, they can place us in the most difficult situation by setting up a financial and economic blockade against us, either covert or overt. In a few

---

[6] Interrogation of von Neurath at the Nuremberg Trials, *Nazi Conspiracy and Aggression*, Suppl. B (Washington 1948), p. 1492.

[7] See above, p. 389.

of the most important countries 'mobilization measures' for this purpose, within the framework of the economic sanctions in Article 16, have been in readiness for years. Nevertheless, in my view, we need not at the moment fear a preventive war. For France, Britain and others will first wait to see whether, and how, we shall deal with our economic and other difficulties. Their present restraint, however, must not make us think that they would still remain passive if they had nothing more to expect from German domestic difficulties and if we rearmed intensively. France and Britain also would then intervene, the more so as they could not permit an unlimited unilateral German rearmament. It would be wishful thinking to expect them to wait until we are strong enough to be a serious danger to them. They would probably demand guarantees regarding the extent and purpose of our armaments even before we had recovered economically.

The author of this memorandum represented the Foreign Ministry view, but Hitler himself was not so pessimistic. He had more insight into the weakness of the other powers and in the spring of 1935 he put them to the first major text.

By the beginning of 1935, the German armed forces were expanding and the Reich Air Ministry was speeding up aircraft production with the result that it was becoming increasingly difficult to disguise the progress of German rearmament. The Army leadership had envisaged military conscription as an essential part of its December 1933 rearmament programme which had planned for a peacetime army of 21 divisions as the basis of a war-time field army of 63 divisions. On 6 March 1935, they revised this target in the light of their assessment of the defence needs against France, demanding a peacetime army of 30–36 divisions making conscription even more essential.

On 4 March 1935, the British defence White Paper gave the increase in German arms as the reason for new rearmament plans and six days later the French Government declared that the period of military service would be extended. Hitler responded by cancelling a visit of British ministers to Berlin that week with the excuse of a diplomatic cold. He used the opportunity to announce on 11 March the existence of a German air force, and on 16 March a decree introducing general conscription to produce a peacetime army of 36 divisions, the figure requested by the Army. The decree was coupled with a declaration that Germany had no further intention of observing the defence limitations of the Versailles treaty.

The other powers attempted to meet the new threat with a concerted response. On 11 April, the prime ministers of Britain, France, and Italy met at Stresa in Italy and afterwards issued a declaration in which they reasserted their determination to protect the integrity of Austria. On 17 April, the League of Nations passed a motion of censure on Germany's action. Finally, on 2 May, France concluded a mutual assistance pact with the Soviet Union.

The formation of the 'Stresa Front' represented the high point of German isolation. It proved a hollow gesture; for within three months, Hitler's tactics of trying to win over Britain with concessions on the rearmament issue appeared to have succeeded. In November 1934, Hitler had once more put forward the idea of a naval agreement with Britain, which had been hinted at a year earlier by Ribbentrop and Raeder in conversations with British officials. This time, however, the offer came from him and it was specific—offering to limit the size of the German fleet to 35 per cent of the British. It was a proposal with which the German navy was not entirely happy.

The German navy had ambivalent attitudes towards Britain. On the one hand, it was keen for cooperation in the medium term, using Britain as a counter-balance to France and winning British acceptance for German naval rearmament beyond the limits of Versailles. It tried to do this by playing on British fears about the rise of American naval power, suggesting that the German navy would be a useful ally. On the other hand, over the longer term, it envisaged the possibility of a confrontation with Britain.

This view coincided in part at least with Hitler's. At an interview on 27 June 1934, Hitler told Raeder that a major development of the fleet would have to wait until later and that it might have to be used against Britain. At the same time, he pointed out that if Germany had had an agreement with Britain in 1899, there would have been no war with Britain in 1914. The implications of his comments were that for the time being it was necessary to limit the fleet in order to achieve the alliance with Britain which was vital for Germany's initial goal of continental hegemony. After that, however, a large fleet would be required to establish world supremacy either with Britain as a junior partner or if need be against her.

In practice, this limitation required little sacrifice from Germany—at any rate in the immediate future. For the Versailles treaty restricted the German navy to approximately 144,000 tons. A level of 35 per cent of the British navy was equivalent to 520,000 tons and thus represented a tripling of the existing level. On 2 November 1934, Hitler reassured Raeder that 'he regarded the rapid construction of the navy until 1938 according to the announced schedule as . . . vital, since a war could not be fought unless the supplies of iron ore from Scandinavia could be secured.'[8] In other words, Hitler envisaged Germany being ready for a continental war by 1938 in which the navy would play a vital role against France and/or the Soviet Union. Moreover, the assumption was that the agreement with Britain could be dropped after 1938, when the 35 per cent level had been reached, if the British alliance had been achieved. Despite the German

[8] Cf. J. Dülffer, *Weimar, Hitler und die Marine* (Düsseldorf 1973) p. 297. This section owes much to this work.

Navy's preference for a figure of 50 per cent, Hitler insisted on 35 per cent in his anxiety to win Britain over.

Negotiations continued in March 1935 when Sir John Simon, the British Foreign Secretary, and Mr Anthony Eden, the Under-Secretary, visited Berlin to discuss general issues. The meetings between Hitler, Simon and Eden, attended also by the German Foreign Minister and Joachim von Ribbentrop, Hitler's expert on British questions, illustrate well the tactics of the two governments. On the one hand, Britain was trying to tie Germany down by bringing her back into the League of Nations and into the European framework of multilateral agreements. Thus Simon began by stating:

495

It was the object of British policy to serve peace by securing cooperation amongst all European countries. They hoped Germany would cooperate with all the others. They believed that the future would take on one of two forms: it would either take the form of general cooperation, which Britain greatly desired, or the form of a division into two camps, resulting in isolation on the one side, and the formation of blocs, which might look like encirclement, on the other. He was convinced that the future would develop in one or other of these two ways.

But Hitler wished above all to avoid such multilateral entanglements and preferred the freedom of manoeuvre offered by bilateral agreements. Again he tried to win over Britain to such a bilateral arrangement. This time, however, instead of offering concessions, he applied some degree of pressure, first through colonial demands and later in the sphere of armaments. Thus, in reply to Simon's request that Germany should rejoin the League, he raised in intentionally vague terms the question of colonies:

. . . The Chancellor then showed his British visitors a diagram indicating the comparative sizes of the European metropolitan countries and their colonies, together with other possessions having economic potentialities. He demonstrated that Germany with her 68 million inhabitants in an area of 460,000 square kilometres, that is to say, with a population density of 137 inhabitants to the square kilometre, had by herself insufficient economic living space [*Wirtschaftsraum*]. It would not do to try to find a solution, only to have it again denounced shortly afterwards, but in the interests of a true peace a solution must be sought which would be permanently acceptable; Britain would thus have pledged herself to Germany and Germany would abide absolutely by her Treaty obligations. He was not asking for the impossible, but for what, in his view, constituted the necessary and reasonable minimum. He recalled that Germany also had made great renunciations. Britain had no interest in making Germany a pariah among the nations, but in bringing her into Britain's own sphere of interest. No one could tell how history might develop. But a time would come when the European nations would have to stand together, and when it would be specially important for Germany and Britain to be standing together. No one in Germany, and least of all the National Socialists, felt any hatred or enmity towards Britain. Nor had they any such feelings towards France, but in view of French complexes it was infinitely more difficult to get on better terms with France. Germany was aware that she could never defend any possible colonial possessions of hers single-handed. But it might also happen that Britain would require outside help to defend her possessions. Should it be possible to find a solution, this might lead not only to cooperation in Europe but to special relations of friendship between England and Germany.

Simon expressed his pleasure at the frank statements made by both sides. He wished to make two observations: The first was that the Chancellor had so expressed his thoughts that they seemed to require closer relations between Britain and Germany than between Britain and France. Britain wanted to be on good terms with Germany, but must not allow this to prejudice her friendship with France. They did not wish to substitute one friend for another. They did not wish to have special engagements with anyone; Britain was an entirely uncommitted member of the Society of Nations. It would not be 'fair' were he to allow the impression to be created that Britain was being disloyal to one friend while seeking another. His second point concerned the colonial question. This would be carefully studied. . . .

During the translation of Simon's remarks, the Chancellor expressed his agreement with the first point (relations with France); as regards the second point, he said that he had no intention of seizing foreign possessions. . . .

On the following day, the discussions concentrated on the armament issue. Hitler repeated his offer of an Anglo-German naval ratio of 100:35 and it was agreed that preliminary naval conversations should be held in London. When the discussions turned to the question of air armaments, Simon asked about the present strength of the German air force. To the astonishment of the British, Hitler replied (untruthfully) that Germany had reached air parity with Britain.

To sum up the significance of the conversations; Hitler had once more suggested Anglo-German cooperation, an offer which had once again been rejected. The British did not want a bilateral agreement with Germany at the expense of relations with France. They hoped rather to bring Germany back into the Concert of Europe, where she could be more easily controlled. The conversations are also significant for the fact that Hitler for the first time introduced new tactics in his relations with Britain. Instead of merely offering concessions, he now also applied pressure—over colonies and over armaments. He was not seriously interested in colonies at this stage; he merely used the issue as a means of convincing Britain of the need to come to terms with Germany and concede her wishes in the Continental field in return for German cooperation outside Europe. Similarly,

Germany had by no means reached air parity with Britain, but by lying Hitler was able to apply pressure from another quarter.

Although Britain refused to be drawn into a comprehensive agreement with Germany, Hitler's tactics were partially successful, for, on 18 June 1935, Britain completely undermined the Stresa Front by finally signing a naval agreement with Germany without having previously discussed the matter with her partners. The agreement allowed Germany to rebuild her navy up to 35 per cent of the strength of the British navy and 100 per cent of the British submarine force. Hitler's directives to the German negotiators led by Ribbentrop had laid down: 'An understanding must be reached between the two great Germanic peoples through the permanent elimination of naval rivalry. One will control the sea, the other will be the strongest power on land. A defensive and offensive alliance between the two will inaugurate a new era.'[9] On hearing the news of the successful completion of the agreement, Hitler described it as 'the happiest day of his life'[10] He said 'he was convinced that the British regarded the agreement with us in this sphere as only a preliminary to much wider cooperation. An Anglo-German combination would be stronger than all the other powers'.[11]

(iii) The creation of the Rome-Berlin axis and the growing disillusionment with Britain: 1935–37

Soon after the Anglo-German Naval Agreement, the Stresa front was further undermined by a change in Italian policy towards Germany, a development which was to transform the European scene. Under the influence of a pro-German group led by his son-in-law, Galeazzo Ciano, Mussolini was becoming convinced that association with Germany offered the best opportunities for Italian expansion. On 30 May 1935, less than two months after the Stresa conference, the German ambassador in Rome noted that relations between Germany and Italy had improved so much recently 'that one might almost speak of a reversal of Italy's attitude towards Germany'.[12] This trend received added impetus from developments in Abyssinia. Mussolini had assumed that, in return for his cooperation over the German threat to Austria, Britain and France would be prepared to give him *carte blanche* in Abyssinia. His assumption proved erroneous. When the Italians began their invasion in October 1935, the

[9] E. Kordt, *Nicht aus den Akten* (Berlin 1950), p. 100; quoted in A. Kuhn, *Hitlers aussenpolitisches Programm* (Stuttgart 1970), p. 168.

[10] *The Ribbentrop Memoirs* (London 1954) p. 41.

[11] Kordt, *op. cit.*, p. 109.

[12] *Documents on German Foreign Policy*, series C. vol. iv. p. 230.

Emperor of Abyssinia appealed to the League of Nations for support. After an attempt to reach a compromise at the expense of Abyssinia had been rejected by British public opinion, the new British Foreign Secretary, Anthony Eden, took the initiative in the League of Nations to impose economic sanctions on Italy. Germany remained officially neutral on the issue but refused to join the blockade and continued to supply Italy with raw materials.

In January 1936, it appeared as if Italy was becoming bogged down in Abyssinia, thereby weakening her position in Austria. In this event, Austria was likely to turn for support to the Western powers. In this situation, on 6 January, the Ciano group persuaded Mussolini to approach Germany with a proposal for an agreement by which Austria would in effect become a satellite of Germany. The German Foreign Ministry wished to reject the idea for fear that Mussolini was using the Austrian issue to play Germany and the Western powers off against each other. Hitler, however, responded more positively. On 17 January, he received von Hassell, the German ambassador in Rome, who reported on his interview as follows:

496

After a short discussion of the resultant situation, the Führer and Chancellor sent for the Foreign Minister and in the presence of us both drew a picture of the political position as it appeared to him at present. He said he had no illusions at all about the fact that Germany was at present as good as completely isolated. We possessed no really reliable friends. No real trust could be placed in Poland's policy and Italy was herself in a very difficult position. It would be highly undesirable if this isolation should, as the result of a collapse of Fascism in Italy, become a moral isolation as well. We must do everything to prevent the various opponents throughout the world of the authoritarian system of government from concentrating upon us as their sole object. But apart from this it was also in our interests that Italy as a piece upon the European chessboard should not be weakened too much. There was a time, especially after Mussolini's well-known demonstrations at the Brenner Pass, when perhaps we might not have wished to see Italy emerge from the conflict too great or too victorious, but nowadays this danger surely no longer existed to any considerable degree. On the contrary, it was much more to be feared that Fascism, and indeed Italy herself, might be destroyed or at least emerge seriously impaired by the ordeal. We Germans, for our part, could not but wish to make every effort to prevent such a collapse, in so far as we were in a position to do so. He had therefore resolved to continue our benevolent neutrality towards Italy. Indeed, he had even at times considered going further and undertaking some form of action towards peace and thus of mediation in the Italo–Abyssinian conflict. The idea had then again been dropped, but the benevolent neutrality so far observed would continue to be our guiding principle. Similarly he could only welcome it if relations of mutual trust between Italy and Germany were restored. It was a mistake to pursue a policy of emotion in such questions; regardless of what one's own personal feelings might be, it was politically correct to treat the events of 1934 as a closed chapter.

On 27 January, Hassell replied to Mussolini in general but positive terms and the Duce assured him in turn that 'Stresa was dead'.[13]

On 7 March 1936, Hitler exploited the differences between the Western powers and their preoccupation with the Abyssinian question to spring his next surprise—the reoccupation of the Rhineland which had been demilitarized by the Versailles Treaty. Apart from his more general motives, this action was regarded by the Army leadership as essential for the realization of the strategic and rearmament planning which it had initiated in December 1933. Hitler made this decision in mid-February and took the ratification of the Franco–Soviet Pact by the French Chamber of Deputies on 4 March as a pretext to terminate the Locarno Treaty of 1925 which guaranteed the Franco–German frontier. Relations between Germany and Italy being still somewhat ambiguous, Mussolini had not been informed beforehand. Britain discouraged France from taking action because she did not want to risk war to prevent Germany from walking into her own 'back garden', as one observer put it. Had any action been taken, the German forces would have been vastly outnumbered; but the addition of several police divisions helped to give the impression that the German troops were more numerous than they really were. The occupation of the Rhineland represented not only a great diplomatic *coup*, but also a strategic victory by which Germany had closed a gap in her western flank which had hitherto made her extremely vulnerable to French pressure. Characteristically, Hitler accompanied his aggressive move with a conciliatory gesture. Thus, the announcement justifying the reoccupation contained an offer to sign new agreements:

497

The German Government has continually emphasized during the negotiations of the last years its readiness to observe and fulfil all the obligations arising from the Rhine Pact so long as the other contracting parties were ready on their side to maintain the pact. This obvious and essential condition can no longer be regarded as being fulfilled by France. France has replied to Germany's repeated friendly offers and assurances of peace by infringing the Rhine Pact through a military alliance with the Soviet Union directed exclusively against Germany. In this manner, however, the Locarno Rhine Pact has lost its inner meaning and ceased

[13] Ibid, Doc. No. 525.

in practice to exist. Consequently, Germany regards herself for her part as no longer bound by this dissolved Treaty. The German Government is now constrained to face the new situation created by this alliance, a situation which is rendered more acute by the fact that the Franco–Soviet Treaty has been supplemented by a Treaty of Alliance between Czechoslovakia and the Soviet Union exactly parallel in form. In accordance with the fundamental right of a nation to secure its frontiers and ensure its possibilities of defence, the German Government has today restored the full and unrestricted sovereignty of Germany in the demilitarized zone of the Rhineland.

In order, however, to avoid any misinterpretation of its intentions and to establish beyond doubt the purely defensive character of these measures, as well as to express its unalterable longing for a real pacification of Europe between states equal in rights and equally respected, the German Government declares itself ready to conclude new agreements for the creation of a system of peaceful security for Europe.

Specifically, Germany offered a non-aggression pact with France and Belgium, to be guaranteed by Britain and Italy, an air agreement with Britain and even the return of Germany to the League of Nations which it was hoped would prove particularly tempting to Britain.

The final victory of Italy in the Abyssinian war in May 1936 boosted Mussolini's self-confidence, while the feeble performance of the Western democracies during the affair confirmed his view of their decadence, a view towards which he had already been tending on eugenic grounds. He contrasted the declining birth rates in France and Britain with the apparent success of the Third Reich in not only halting but even reversing the decline in the German birth rate. At the beginning of 1935, he declared that 'the German nation had answered the call' and that 'Germany is unwilling to connive at its own extinction unlike the miserly and aging nations of the West.'[14] Finally, he was persuaded by the theories of the influential Italian military strategist, General Douhet, that the air force was the key to future warfare and that it would transform the balance of power in the Mediterranean to the disadvantage of Britain, traditionally dominant there through its naval power. Italy, therefore, could now afford to dispense with close links with Britain and seek her advantage in association with the dynamic revisionist power to the north.

On 9 June, Mussolini replaced the Foreign Minister, Suvich, who favoured close links with France and Britain, with Ciano. At the same time, he gave his blessing to the agreement between Germany and Austria, which was finally signed on 11 July, by which Germany acknowledged Austrian independence and in return Austria agreed to pursue a foreign

[14] Cf. J. Petersen, *Hitler–Mussolini Die Entstehung der Achse Berlin–Rome 1933–1936* (Tübingen 1973) p. 485.

policy in line with German interests. This was, in fact, the realization of his January proposal.

A week later, a development began which was further to cement relations between Germany and Italy. On 17 July 1936, civil war broke out in Spain. A group of right-wing army officers led by General Franco rebelled against the Government of the Republic, which consisted of a coalition of the Left. Right from the start Germany was involved on the rebel Nationalist side. Her intervention was initiated by the *Auslandsorganisation*, a Nazi organization which controlled relations with Germans living abroad. Its agents in Spain by-passed the Foreign Office and through Party contacts managed to gain direct access to Hitler and win his support for Franco. He agreed to provide the vital transport necessary to bring the elite Moroccan division to the mainland. Italy also soon sent troops and arms to the Nationalists, while Russia supplied the Republicans with arms and Comintern-organized international brigades of foreign Communists and other pro-Republicans.

Intervention in the civil war gave Germany a number of advantages: she had her eye on the valuable raw materials to be found in Spain, iron ore and tungsten, and the war also offered a valuable testing ground for the new German weapons and particularly the air force. But most important were the political factors. In the first place, a pro-German Government in Spain would, it was thought, threaten France and if necessary Britain as well. Secondly, the war would ensure that Italy and France remained in conflict and would therefore bind Italy more firmly to Germany and tie her down in the Mediterranean, leaving Germany a freer hand in the east. Finally, German intervention on the side of the Nationalists could be portrayed by Germany as an anti-Bolshevist move which, it was hoped, would find sympathy with conservative circles in Britain. Moreover, the anti-Bolshevist aspect was not just a propaganda weapon. Hitler feared and was determined to prevent a victory of the Left in Spain, which he believed would strengthen Bolshevism and therefore the Jews, as well as complicating his own strategic objectives.

The Spanish Civil War polarized opinion in Europe, heating the ideological temperature and welding Germany and Italy together. In September 1936, Hitler sent the Nazi legal expert, Hans Frank, on an exploratory visit to Rome which resulted in the visit of Ciano, the Italian Foreign Minister, to Germany in the following month. Hitler made special efforts to please the Italians and took a personal interest in the details of Ciano's reception in Munich, which included a gala performance of *Don Giovanni*. After a trip to Berlin, Ciano met Hitler at Berchtesgaden, where the two men signed the secret 'October Protocols' which covered cooperation on a number of points—opposition to Communist propaganda, recognition of Franco as the rightful head of the Spanish Government, and an understanding that Germany recognized the Italian empire and had no wish to interfere in the Mediterranean. Hitler referred in grandiose terms to Mussolini as 'the first statesman of the world with whom no one else had the right even remotely to compare himself' and succeeded in overcoming Mussolini's reserve shown during Frank's visit in September. On 1 November, Mussolini made a speech at Milan in which he revealed his satisfaction at Ciano's visit and referred for the first time to a 'Rome/Berlin axis'.

498

The meeting at Berlin resulted in an agreement between the two countries on certain questions, some of which are particularly interesting in these days. But these agreements, which have been included in special statements and duly signed—this vertical line between Rome and Berlin is not a partition, but rather an axis around which all the European States animated by the will to collaboration and peace can also collaborate. Germany, although surrounded and solicited, did not adhere to sanctions. With the agreement of 11 July there disappeared any element of dissension between Berlin and Rome, and I may remind you that even before the Berlin meeting Germany had practically recognized the Empire of Rome.

Yet, although Hitler had now clearly shifted his main attention to Italy, he did not give up his attempts to win over Britain, the other ally envisaged in his pre-1933 programme, despite a growing sense of disillusionment. The Naval Agreement of 1935 had not, after all, turned out to be the great turning-point in Anglo-German relations for which he had hoped. Moreover, his experience of the weakness and indecisiveness of British policy during the Abyssinian crisis had seriously undermined his belief in British strength and purpose, an impression that was to be confirmed by British policy towards the Spanish Civil War.

In March 1936, the German ambassador to Britain, Leopold von Hoesch, died. Hitler seized the opportunity to replace him with the man who in the meantime had become his chief, though unofficial, advisor on British affairs, Joachim von Ribbentrop. Ribbentrop, a former champagne salesman who had married into a wealthy German champagne firm, had only joined the Nazi Party in 1932, but his social contacts had won him a position close to Hitler. In particular, Ribbentrop managed to impress Hitler with his experience of foreign countries, experience which the Führer himself so singularly lacked. After the Nazi take-over, Hitler, who wished to reduce his dependence on the conservative officials in the Foreign Ministry, relied more and more on Ribbentrop for unofficial diplomatic missions to Britain and France. In the spring of 1934, he appointed Ribbentrop his representative for disarmament questions so as to give him official status, and Ribbentrop established his own office, the Ribbentrop Bureau, which became in effect a rival diplomatic service to the Foreign Ministry.

Like Hitler, Ribbentrop had begun by regarding an alliance with Britain as essential to Germany's re-establishment as a great power. However, his negotiations with British statesmen during 1933–35, and in particular his experience during the naval negotiations in 1935, had disillusioned him about the prospects of such an alliance. He became aware that the British government was not prepared to do a deal on the basis of a free hand for Germany in Eastern Europe in return for German support for the British Empire. Moreover, unlike Hitler he was more committed to a German overseas empire than to the conquest of living space in Russia, a goal which was liable to involve a confrontation with Britain.

Since Britain was proving uncooperative, Ribbentrop began to seek alternative partners for Germany. After trying to cultivate closer relations with France with only limited success, he came to focus his attentions on Italy and Japan. During the Abyssinian war, Ribbentrop encouraged the German rapprochement with Italy, without however having a major influence on developments there. His most important contribution at this stage was his role in the establishment of closer relations with Japan. Initially, Ribbentrop had not envisaged a partnership with Japan as intrinsically anti-British, but primarily directed against the Soviet Union. The agreement, which was finally signed between the two countries on 25 November 1936, was specifically aimed against the Communist International or Comintern and was colloquially termed the 'Anti-Comintern Pact'.

At Ribbentrop's final interview with Hitler before his departure for London, the Führer gave him the following instructions:

499

Ribbentrop . . . get Britain to join the Anti-Comintern pact, that is what I want most of all. I have sent you as the best man I've got. Do what you can . . . But if in future all our efforts are still in vain, fair enough, then I'm ready for war as well. I would regret it very much, but if it has to be, there it is. But I think it would be a short war and the moment it is over, I will then be ready at any time to offer the British an honourable peace acceptable to both sides. However, I would then demand that Britain join the Anti-Comintern pact or perhaps some other pact. But get on with it Ribbentrop, you have the trumps in your hand, play them well. I'm ready at any time for an air pact as well. Do your best. I will follow your efforts with interest.

During his period in London, Ribbentrop played the anti-Bolshevik card as well as he could, trying to frighten Britain with the dangers of Bolshevism, as exemplified in Russian intervention in the Spanish Civil

War, and to portray Nazi Germany as a bastion of anti-Bolshevism. His aim was to persuade Britain that her traditional 'balance of power' principle was no longer relevant in the light of this new threat and that the opponents of Bolshevism must now stand together. This was the main tenor of Ribbentrop's activities in Britain and the propaganda found a receptive climate, particularly among the upper classes. Harold Nicholson, a writer and Member of Parliament associated with the Conservatives, noted in his diary on 16 July 1936 that 'the majority of the National [Conservative and National Labour] Party are at heart anti-league [of Nations] and anti-Russian and what they would really like would be a firm agreement with Germany and possibly Italy by which we could purchase peace at the expense of the smaller states.'[15] However, the British government remained unwilling to commit itself to Germany on the basis of an anti-Bolshevik crusade and Ribbentrop's initial scepticism was confirmed.

Meanwhile, Hitler had begun to conclude that he could after all dispense with the British alliance since Britain apparently lacked both the strength and the will to oppose him. Indeed, he now considered that, for the time being at any rate, a partnership with Italy was likely to be more productive since it would allow Italy to concentrate on Mediterranean affairs, freeing Germany's hands for action in the South-East. A partnership with Britain, on the other hand, would force Italy back into the hands of France. On 2 December, Dertinger of the Propaganda Ministry gave the German press the following confidential briefing on Hitler's views:[16]

500

Apart from the untruthfulness of English policy . . . even an honest German–English rapprochement could offer Germany no concrete, positive advantages in the present situation. The process of German–English understanding would at best bring Germany this or that colonial strip, which it would not be able to defend in an emergency, and where based on direct German–English agreement would not be large enough to bring Germany significant economic advantages, but would be large enough to drive Belgium, Portugal and France properly into a united anti-German front. Above all in the event of German–English understanding, Italy would lose its entire basis for its Mediterranean policy and having been denuded of its German support would have to capitulate to England. The consequence

[15] H. Nicholson, *Diaries and Letters,* ed. N. Nicholsen (London 1966) p. 263.

[16] We owe this document and much of the argument in this section to an important article in the Hossbach Memorandum shortly to appear in *Militärgeschichtliche Mitteilungen*. We are very grateful to its authors Dr Jonathan Wright and Dr Paul Stafford for permission to use the article prior to publication.

would be a natural Italian attempt to achieve compensation in Central Europe. Rome will then be automatically driven to France's side. France and Italy together would then at any time be in a position to obstruct Germany even in the most modest attempt at a new order in South East Europe. In this event England would not be in a position or would not want to help Germany carry out its Central European plans against Italian–French opposition. The policy of an understanding with England would therefore only bring an effective colonial success but in practice with the consequence of the impossibility of South-East European expansion. From these considerations the Führer concludes that Germany must stay unaltered at Italy's side and has no interest in coming to an understanding with England. Only so long as relations between Berlin and London are on ice is Italy in a position to conduct Mediterranean policy and therefore to submit to Germany in central Europe.

It seems likely that Hitler would in reality still have preferred to have secured the British alliance. However, anything short of a total commitment by Britain, i.e. a global arrangement, was of less value to him than the relationship with Italy, indeed would undermine that relationship. In fact, he became increasingly convinced that that was the intention behind British approaches to Germany.

Hitler later referred to 1937 as the 'year of awareness' in the sense of his final recognition that he would have to dispense with the British alliance—at any rate for the time being—and seek alternative arrangements. Of these the most important remained the Rome-Berlin axis which was strengthened by a state visit to Germany by Mussolini in September, during which Hitler impressed him with a display of German power. Two months later Italy joined the Anti-Comintern pact.

1937 was also a 'year of awareness' in the sense that by the autumn Hitler appears to have concluded that time was not on Germany's side and that she must go onto the offensive sooner rather than later. For the problem was that, by embarking on a massive rearmament programme, Germany had started an arms race. Moreover, because of her limited resources by comparison with her rivals it was a race she was bound to lose if it went on for any length of time. She thus came under growing pressure to act quickly, using her temporary superiority to expand her resources by plundering her neighbours.

(iv) The Rearmament Issue and the 'Hossbach Memorandum'

Germany's rearmament programme was already coming up against the limits of Germany's productive capacity, given the numerous other demands made on her resources of labour and raw materials: the vast industrial investment required to fulfil the targets of the Four Year Plan launched in 1936, the continuing Autobahn programme, extensive urban development, prestige building projects such as the Nuremberg Party rally complex and numerous Gau Party buildings, and last but not least, the requirements of production for export in order to provide the foreign exchange for raw material imports essential to the rearmament drive. All these demands competed with the requirements of the armed services, which in turn competed against one another. The problem was that the rearmament programme had rapidly acquired its own momentum, sustained by a mutually reinforcing combination of Hitler's political goals on the one hand, and the professional concerns, ambitions, and rivalry of the three armed services on the other. Neither Hitler nor the service chiefs took sufficient account of the strategic and the economic implications of their various programmes.

The Army's armament goals had expanded dramatically since December 1933. The December programme had envisaged a peacetime army of 21 divisions (300,000 men) by 1938 and a field army of 63 divisions. In May 1934, however, Hitler had demanded that the target of 300,000 men should be achieved by October of that year. The Army High Command succeeded in postponing the date to 1935 and by the end of February 1935 the Army had already reached a total of 280,000 men. Then, on 6 March 1935, a general staff (*Truppenamt*) memorandum, approved by the Commander-in-Chief, Fritsch, advocated a peacetime army of 30–36 divisions, a figure adopted by Hitler in his declaration of conscription on 16 March. By the autumn of 1936, the Army had in fact expanded to 36 infantry and 3 armoured divisions.

Not only did the Army rapidly expand in size during 1934–6, but it also underwent a fundamental reorientation of emphasis both in its composition and its direction. The rearmament programme of December 1933 had been geared to provide the basis for fighting a 'defensive war on several fronts with some prospect of success', as General Beck put it in a memorandum of 14 December 1933.[17] However, in October 1935, the first three armoured divisions were established, representing the culmination of a campaign fought by a number of officers over the years to convince the Army leadership of the need to overcome the restrictions of Versailles by increasing the mobility of the German Army. The successful trials of armoured formations on manoeuvres in the summer of 1935 had convinced both Hitler and the Army leadership of the value of this new weapon. Concentration on the use of armoured formations tended, however, to shift the emphasis away from defence towards offensive operations. Initially, this was envisaged in terms of 'offensively conducted defence', but the transition from this to envisaging operations which were plainly offensive in intent had

[17] Cf. K.-J. Müller, *General Ludwig Beck* (Boppard 1980). p. 339.

already occurred in a highly influential memorandum in which General Beck summed up the implications of armoured warfare for the future composition and direction of the Army. The memorandum to the Commander-in-Chief had the title 'Considerations on increasing the Offensive Capacity of the Army' and was dated 30 December 1935:

501

1. The present plan for building up the Army and its present organization were determined by the requirement to provide the Army initially with the necessary defensive capability for a war on several fronts.

The considerations concerning an increase in the offensive capacity of the Army raise the question, therefore, whether such an increase would not contradict this initial requirement.

Stategic defence can only be successful if it can also be carried out in the form of an attack. For this reason an increase in offensive capacity represents a simultaneous strengthening of defensive capacity. Thus, the response to such a question must be unequivocally negative.

2. An examination of the present plan for building up the Army in terms of its offensive capacity suggests the following possible improvements:

(a) An increase in the number of tank units envisaged (hitherto 3 brigades = 12 units, in addition to the 3 tank brigades contained in the armoured divisions), in order to secure the most vital offensive capability of the field army.

(b) The reorganization of infantry divisions into (mot) divisions in order to increase operational and tactical mobility.

3. In addition, consideration should be given to:

(a) increasing the prospects for success of pure tank units through the feasibility of a temporary transfer of highly mobile infantry units (e.g. mot. infantry regiments).

(b) via a restructuring of the infantry.

4. Re: Paragraph 2a (tanks):

. . . (b) A realistic goal which must be achieved and can be achieved is the formation of a sufficient number of tank units so that every army corps in peacetime can include 1 tank brigade with two regiments each containing 2 units i.e. 48 units in 12 army corps. Or in the future field army with 24 army corps one tank unit each would be dropped and there would be the same number of units (24), organized in regiments and brigades, as there were troops available (12 regiments with 2 units each and 6 brigades with two regiments). That also makes 48 units.

Such an increase in the number of tank units may, however, in certain circumstances, have to be paid for by dispensing with the 12 corps anti-tank units. However, since the tank is to some extent capable of replacing the anti-tank gun, provided it is equipped with a tank-busting weapon, this could be risked, provided we ensure that a number of anti-tank units are kept prepared in the event of war.

A separate matter for consideration is whether the three major tasks of the armoured troops: infantry support (Inf. tank), anti-tank operations, independent operational deployment in association with other motorized weapons (at the moment armoured divisions), permit the use of the same types of tank and in the same combinations for all the current tank units (regiments and brigades) and for those still planned, or whether different types will have to be used . . .

7. Re: paragraph 3a (Increasing operational and tactical mobility in the deployment of tank formations.

(a) In requesting an increase in the number of tank units we have operated on the assumption that a frontal assault on an opponent more or less equal in strength and numbers and who is encountered in a state of readiness and on terrain favourable to him can hardly expect to succeed without the participation of tanks.

In addition, at those places where one starts out by envisaging ambitious targets these can only have a prospect of success through the commitment of strong armoured formations. In such cases *armoured divisions* appear to be the most suitable, or at least units whose composition ensures that their infantry can rapidly follow the armoured formations and hold on to their gains or fully exploit them.

One can only confirm the efficacy of the current composition of an armoured division on the basis of practical experience. As long as the restriction of the Army to 36 divisions prevents a further expansion of armoured divisions—except at the expense of infantry divisions—it will be necessary to form additional such units.

For the time being, the only conceivable supplement to the pure tank units are motorized infantry units . . .

The implication of this memorandum was that the German Army should be reorganized to ensure a significant increase in armoured and motorized units, which would be available either for 'offensively conducted defence' or for 'ambitious [or extended] targets' and this is indeed what happened.

During the summer and autumn of 1936, the Army leadership worked out a new armaments programme which envisaged that by October 1939 Germany would have a peacetime army of 36 infantry divisions, of which four would be motorized, 3 armoured divisions, 3 light divisions, 1 mountain division, and 1 cavalry brigade—a total of 830,000 men, and a field army of 4,626,000 men.

This new programme involved a vast increase in the financial and economic resources required. The Army leadership hoped to acquire these from the Four Year plan which Hitler had launched almost certainly to coincide with this programme.

Nor was the armaments problem confined to the Army. As Britain had increasingly emerged as a potential opponent so the Navy had begun to play a growing part in Hitler's calculations, though not in the sense of having to deal with an immediate threat. After the Anglo-German Naval Agreement of 1935, the Navy had operated on the basis of a programme to achieve 35 per cent of the British fleet by the end of 1942. However, during early 1937, Hitler had given instructions for the inclusion of a further six large battleships, in addition to the four already envisaged, for completion by 1944. This was not because he expected war with Britain in the immediate future. He gave no orders for preparations for such a war and in any case the time-span for completion of the battleships made them inappropriate for such a task. It was rather the fact that, with Britain now a potential enemy instead of an ally, he felt under growing pressure to telescope the various stages of his programme. To achieve world hegemony against the United States, possibly in alliance with Britain, he would need a powerful battle fleet. Although a fleet including only ten battleships by 1944 would be insufficient for such a task, it would provide a powerful deterrent against attacks on the new continental empire which he hoped to have achieved by that date. This would provide a breathing space during which Germany could build up her navy and air force for the coming challenge for world power. The problem was, however, that by telescoping the stages of his programme, Hitler had to devote Germany's limited resources to providing the means to achieve a multiplicity of tasks more or less simultaneously. He needed to build up the Army for territorial conquest in Europe, the Navy initially for deterrence and eventually for the achievement of world hegemony, and the air force both as a tactical weapon for close support of the Army and as a strategic weapon for long-range attacks on Britain and the United States.

By the summer of 1937, it was already clear that even the previous naval programme involving only four battleships was subject to growing delays. The Navy faced competition for resources not only from the Army but also from Göring who was not only head of a rival service, the Luftwaffe, but also responsible for both the vast investment programme of the Four Year Plan and the export drive.

On 25 October, the C-in-C Navy, Admiral Raeder, wrote in desperation to Blomberg about the effects of these delays and of the cuts in the programme which would have to be introduced because of the shortages, particularly of steel:

502

. . . Thus, by the scheduled completion date for naval rearmament we would have at our disposal a battle fleet with only two ships of 35,000 tons, which would be neither capable of taking on any of our conceivable opponents nor would possess adequate alliance potential. The postponements and cuts would thus not only produce a considerable reduction in the Navy's readiness for war, they would also have decisive diplomatic effects in the event of a peaceful development. Since the measures in question [i.e. cuts] will have consequences going beyond my sphere of responsibilities, I consider myself unable to take on the responsibilities for proposing the overturning of the naval rearmament programme. I consider it necessary to secure an immediate decision by the Führer.

Hitler responded to this request, and to the general conflict over priorities in the allocation of raw materials and labour, by summoning a meeting in the Reich Chancellery for 5 November 1937. It was attended by the Reich War Minister (Blomberg), the Commanders-in-Chief of the Army (Fritsch), Navy (Raeder), and Air Force (Göring), and by the Foreign Minister (Neurath). Hitler decided to use the occasion for a major speech outlining his views on the current diplomatic situation and on Germany's future course of action. A report of this meeting, based partly on memory and partly on notes taken at the time, was made five days later by Hitler's military adjutant, Colonel Friedrich Hossbach, who also attended. The surviving version printed here is not the original but a copy of a copy. However, it is regarded by the overwhelming majority of historians as authentic.

The Hossbach memorandum has been the subject of considerable controversy. It was taken by the Nuremberg Tribunal as evidence of a 'plot' to wage war which had been carefully 'planned', as a blueprint for Hitler's intentions. In fact, it was not Hitler's practice to commit himself in this way. Moreover, it has been pointed out that his timetable proved wrong and the moves against Austria and Czechoslovakia did not occur in the way he envisaged. Finally, the speech omits the most important of Hitler's aims, namely living space in the East. (This was probably in order not to alarm his audience and because he was only dealing with the second stage in his programme—Austria and Czechoslovakia.) All this has persuaded some historians to play down the significance of the document. A. J. P. Taylor, for example, has argued that Hitler's speech was primarily a move in domestic politics, and that Hitler simply launched into a *tour d'horizon* on foreign policy in order to avoid committing himself on the armaments' issue. Nevertheless, in view of the other evidence that has recently come to light on Hitler's thinking during this period, it seems more likely to have been a genuine attempt by Hitler to persuade his audience, most of whom were sceptical, about his views on the dispensability of an agreement with Britain, and to convey to them his own sense of urgency, his awareness of the pressures building up both at home and abroad as a result of rearmament, and his determination to pursue a more aggressive policy abroad before the favourable diplomatic and military situation changed to Germany's disadvantage.

503

The Führer began by stating that the subject of the present conference was of such importance that its discussion would, in other countries, be a matter for a full Cabinet meeting, but he, the Führer, had rejected the idea of making it a subject of discussion before the wider circle of the Reich Cabinet just because of the importance of the matter. His exposition to follow was the fruit of thorough deliberation and the experiences of his four-and-a-half years of power. He wished to explain to the gentlemen present his basic ideas concerning the opportunities for the development of our position in the field of foreign affairs and its requirements, and he asked, in the interest of a long-term German policy, that his exposition be regarded, in the event of his death, as his last will and testament.

The Führer then continued:

The aim of German policy was to make secure and to preserve the racial community [*Volksmasse*] amd to enlarge it. It was therefore a question of space.

The German racial community comprised over 85 million people and, by reason of their number and the narrow limits of habitable space in Europe, it constituted a tightly packed racial core such as was not to be found in any other country and such as implied the right to a greater living space than in the case of other peoples. If there existed no political result, territorially speaking, corresponding to this German racial core, that was a consequence of centuries of historical development, and in the continuance of these political conditions lay the greatest danger to the preservation of the German race at its present peak. To arrest the decline of Germanism [*Deutschtum*] in Austria and Czechoslovakia was as little possible as to maintain the present level in Germany itself. Instead of increase, sterility was setting in, and in its train disorders of a social character must arise in course of time, since political and ideological ideas remain effective only so long as they furnish the basis for the realization of the essential vital demands of a people. Germany's future was therefore wholly conditional upon the solving of the need for space, and such a solution could be sought, of course, only for a foreseeable period of about one to three generations.

Before turning to the question of solving the need for space, it had to be considered whether a solution holding promise for the future was to be reached by means of autarky or by means of an increased participation in world economy.

Autarky

Achievement possible only under strict National Socialist leadership of the State, which is assumed; accepting its achievement as possible, the following could be stated as results:

A. In the field of raw materials only limited, not total, autarky:

1. In regard to coal, so far as it could be considered as a source of raw materials, autarky was possible.

2. But even as regards ores, the position was much more difficult. Iron requirements can be met from home resources and similarly with light metals, but with other raw materials—copper, tin—this was not so.

3. Synthetic textile requirements can be met from home resources to the limit of timber supplies. A permanent solution impossible.

4. Edible fats, possible.

B. In the field of food the question of autarky was to be answered by a flat 'No'.

Hand in hand with the general rise in the standard of living compared with that of thirty to forty years ago, there has gone an increased demand and an increased home consumption even on the part of the producers, the farmers. The fruits of the increased agricultural production had all gone to meet the increased demand, and so did not represent an absolute increase in production. A further uncrease in production by making greater demands on the soil, which already, in consequence of the use of artificial fertilizers, was showing signs of exhaustion, was hardly possible, and it was therefore certain that, even with the maximum increase in production, participation in world trade was unavoidable. The not inconsiderable expenditure of foreign exchange to ensure food supplies by imports, even when harvests were good, grew to catastrophic proportions with bad harvests. The possibility of disaster grew in proportion to the increase in population, in which, moreover, the excess of births of 560,000 annually produced, as a consequence, an even further increase in bread consumption, since a child consumed more bread than an adult.

It was not possible over the long run, in a continent enjoying a practically common standard of living, to meet the difficulties of food supply by lowering that standard and by rationalization. Since, with the solving of the unemployment problem, the maximum consumption level had been reached, some minor modifications in our home agricultural production might still, no doubt, be possible, but no fundamental alteration was possible in our basic food position. Thus autarky, in regard both to food and to the economy as a whole, could not be maintained.

Participation in world economy

To this there were limitations which we were unable to remove. The establishment of Germany's position on a secure and sound foundation was obstructed by market fluctuations, and commercial treaties afforded no guarantee for their actual observance. In particular it had to be remembered that since the world war those very countries which had formerly been food exporters had become industrialized. We were living in an age of economic empires in which the primitive urge to colonization was again manifesting itself: in the cases of Japan and Italy, economic motives underlay the urge for expansion; with Germany also, economic need would supply the stimulus, For countries outside the great economic empires, opportunities for economic expansion were severely obstructed.

The boom in world economy caused by the economic effects of rearmament could never form the basis of a sound economy over a long period, and the latter was impeded above all by the economic disturbances resulting from Bolshevism. There was a pronounced military weakness in those States which depended for their existence on foreign trade. As our foreign trade was carried on over the sea routes dominated by Britain, it was a question rather of security of transport than of foreign exchange, which revealed in time of war the full weakness of our food situation. The only remedy, and one which might seem to us visionary, lay in the acquisition of greater living space—a quest that has in every age been the origin of the formation of States and of the migration of peoples. That this quest met with no interest at Geneva or among the satiated nations was understandable. If, then, we accept the security of our food situation as the principal point at issue, the space needed to ensure it can be sought only in Europe, not, as in the liberal-capitalist view, in the exploitation of colonies. It is not a matter ot acquiring population but of gaining space for agricultural use. Moreover, areas producing raw materials can be more usefully sought in Europe, in immediate proximity to the Reich, than overseas; the solution thus obtained must suffice for one or two generations. Whatever else might later prove necessary must be left to succeeding generations to deal with. The development of the great galaxies of world politics progressed, after all, only slowly, and the German people with its strong racial core would find the most favourable prerequisites for such achievement in the heart of the continent of Europe. The history of all ages—the Roman Empire and the British Empire—had proved that expansion could be carried out only by breaking down resistance and taking risks; setbacks were inevitable. There had never in former times been spaces without a master, and there were none today; the attacker always comes up against someone in possession.

The question for Germany was: Where could she achieve the greatest gain at the lowest cost?

German policy had to reckon with two hate-inspired antagonists, Britain and France, to whom a German colossus in the centre of Europe was a thorn in the flesh, and both countries were opposed to any further strengthening of Germany's position either in Europe or overseas; in support of this opposition they were able to count on the consensus of all their political parties. Both countries saw in the establishment of German military bases overseas a threat to their own communications, a safeguarding of German commerce, and as a consequence, a strengthening of Germany's position in Europe.

Because of opposition from her Dominions, Britain could not cede any of her colonial possessions to us. After England's loss of prestige through the passing of Abyssinia into Italian possession, the return of East Africa was not to be expected. British concessions could at best be expressed in an offer to satisfy our colonial demands by the appropriation of colonies which were not British possessions. e.g. Angola; French concessions would probably take a similar line.

Serious discussion of the question of the return of colonies to us could not be entered upon except at a moment when Britain was in difficulties and the German Reich armed and strong. The Führer did not share the view that the Empire was unshakeable. Opposition to the Empire was to be found less in the countries conquered than among her competitors. The British Empire and the Roman Empire could not be compared in respect of permanence; the latter was not confronted by any powerful political rival of a serious order after the Punic Wars. It was only the disintegrating effect of Christianity, and the symptoms of age which appear in every country, which caused ancient Rome to succumb to the onslaught of the Germans.

Beside the British Empire there existed today a number of States stronger than she. The British motherland was able to protect her colonial possessions, not by her own power, but only in alliance with other States. How, for instance, could Britain alone defend Canada against attack by America, or her Far Eastern interests against attack by Japan?

The emphasis on the British Crown as the symbol of the unity of the Empire was already an admission that, in the long run, the Empire could not maintain its position by power politics. Significant indications of this were:

(a) the struggle of Ireland for independence;

(b) the constitutional struggles in India, where Britain's half-measures had given the Indians the opportunity of using later on, as a weapon against Britain, the non-fulfilment of her promises of a constitution;

(c) the weakening by Japan of Britain's position in the Far East;

(d) the rivalry in the Mediterranean with Italy who, under the spell of her history, driven by necessity and led by a genius, was expanding her power position, which was inevitably coming more and more into conflict with British interests. The outcome of the Abyssinian War was a loss of prestige for Britain which Italy was striving to exploit by stirring up trouble in the Mohammedan world.

To sum up, it could be stated that, with 45 million Britons, the position of the Empire, despite its theoretical soundness, could not in the long run be maintained by power politics, The ratio of the population of the Empire to that of the motherland of 9:1 was a warning to us, in our territorial expansion, not to allow the foundation constituted by the numerical strength of our own people to become too weak.

France's position was more favourable than that of Britain.The French Empire was territorially better placed; the inhabitants of her colonial possessions represented a supplement to her military strength. But France was going to be confronted with internal political difficulties. In a nation's life, about 10 per cent of its span is taken up by parliamentary forms of government and about 90 per cent by authoritarian forms. Today, none the less, Britain, France, Russia, and the smaller States adjoining them, must be included as factors [*Machtfaktoren*] in our political calculations.

Germany's problem could be solved only by the use of force, and this was never without attendant risk. The Silesian campaigns of Frederick the Great, Bismarck's wars against Austria and France, had involved unheard-of risk, and the swiftness of Prussian action in 1870 had kept Austria from entering the war. If the resort to force with its attendant risks is accepted as the basis of the following exposition, then there remain still to be answered the questions 'When?' and 'How?' In this matter there were three contingencies [*Fälle*] to be dealt with:

Contingency 1: Period 1943–45

After this date only a change for the worse, from our point of view, could be expected.

The equipment of the Army, Navy and Luftwaffe, as well as the formation of the officer corps, was nearly completed. Equipment and armament were modern; in further delay there lay the danger of their obsolescence. In particular, the secrecy of 'special weapons' could not be preserved for ever. The recruiting of reserves was limited to current age groups; further drafts from older untrained age groups were no longer available.

Our relative strength would decrease in relation to the rearmament which would by then have been carried out by the rest of the world. If we did not act by 1943–45, any year could, owing to a lack of reserves, produce the food crisis, to cope with which the necessary foreign exchange was not available, and this must be regarded as a 'waning point of the regime'. Besides, the world was expecting our attack and was increasing its counter-measures from year to year. It was while the rest of the world was still fencing itself off [*sich abriegele*] that we were obliged to take the offensive.

Nobody knew today what the situation would be in the years 1943–45. One thing was certain, that we could wait no longer.

On the one hand there was the great Wehrmacht, and the necessity of maintaining it at its present level, the ageing of the movement and its leaders; and on the other, the prospect of a lowering of the standard of living and of a limitation of the birth-rate, which left no choice but to act. If the Führer was still living, it was his unalterable determination to solve Germany's problem of space by 1943–45 at the latest. The necessity for action before 1943–45 would arise in contingencies 2 and 3.

Contingency 2:
If internal strife in France should develop into such a domestic crisis as to absorb the French army completely and render it incapable of use for war against Germany, then the time for action against the Czechs would have come.

Contingency 3:
If France should be so embroiled in war with another State that she could not 'proceed' against Germany.

For the improvement of our politico-military position our first objective, in the event of our being embroiled in war, must be to overthrow Czechoslovakia and Austria simultaneously in order to remove the threat to our flank in any possible operation against the West. In a conflict with France it was hardly to be regarded as likely that the Czechs would declare war on us on the very same day as France. The desire to join in the war would, however, increase among the Czechs in proportion to any weakening on our part, and then her participation could clearly take the form of an attack in the direction of Silesia, toward the north or toward the west.

If the Czechs were overthrown and a common German–Hungarian frontier achieved, a neutral attitude on the part of Poland could be all the more surely counted upon, in the event of a Franco-German conflict. Our agreements with Poland only retained their force so long as Germany's strength remained unshaken. In the event of German setbacks, Polish action against East Prussia, and possibly against Pomerania and Silesia as well, had to be reckoned with.

Assuming a development of the situation, leading to action on our part as planned, in the years 1943–45, the attitude of France, Britain, Italy, Poland, and Russia could be conjectured as follows:

Actually, the Führer believed that almost certainly Britain, and probably France as well, had already tacitly written off the Czechs and were reconciled to the fact that this question would be cleared up in due course by Germany. Difficulties connected with the Empire, and the prospect of being once more entangled in a protracted European war, were for Britain decisive reasons against taking part in a war against Germany. France's attitude would certainly not be uninfluenced by that of Britain. An attack by France without British support, and with the prospect of the offensive being brought to a standstill on our western fortifications, was hardly probable. Nor was a French march through Belgium and Holland without British support to be expected: nor would this course be contemplated by us in the event of a conflict with France, because it would certainly entail the hostility of Britain. It would of course be necessary to maintain a strong defence [*eine*

Abriegelung] on our western frontier during the prosecution of our attack on the Czechs and Austria. And in this connexion it had to be remembered that the defence measures of the Czechs were growing year by year in strength, and that the actual quality of the Austrian army was also steadily increasing. Even though the populations concerned, especially that of Czechoslovakia, were not sparse, the annexation of Czechoslovakia and Austria would mean an acquisition of foodstuffs for 5–6 million people, on the assumption that the compulsory emigration of 2 million people from Czechoslovakia and a million people from Austria was practicable. The incorporation of these two States with Germany meant a substantial advantage from the political-military point of view, because it would mean shorter and better frontiers, the freeing of forces for other purposes, and the possibility of creating new units up to a level of about twelve divisions, that is, one new division per million inhabitants.

Italy was not expected to object to the elimination of the Czechs, but it was not possible at the moment to estimate what her attitude on the Austrian question would be; that depended essentially upon whether the Duce were still alive.

The degree of surprise and the swiftness of our action were decisive factors for Poland's attitude. Poland, with Russia at her rear, will have little inclination to engage in war against a victorious Germany.

Military intervention by Russia must be countered by the swiftness of our operations; but whether such intervention was a practical contingency at all was more than doubtful, in the attitude of Japan.

Should contingency 2, the crippling of France by civil war, occur, the situation thus created by the elimination of our most dangerous opponent must be seized upon, whenever it occurs, for the blow against the Czechs.

The Führer saw contingency 3 coming definitely nearer; it might emerge from the present tensions in the Mediterranean, and he was resolved to take advantage of it whenever it happened, even as early as 1938.

In the light of past experience, the Führer saw no early end to the hostilities in Spain. If one considered the length of time which Franco's offensives had taken up till now, it was entirely possible that the war would continue another three years. Neither, on the other hand, from the German point of view was a 100 per cent victory for Franco desirable; our interest lay rather in a continuance of the war and in the keeping up of the tension in the Mediterranean. Franco in undisputed possession of the Spanish Peninsula precluded the possibility of any further intervention on the part of the Italians or of their continued occupation of the Balearic Islands. As our interest lay rather on the prolongation of the war in Spain, it must be the immediate aim of our policy to strengthen Italy's rear with a view to her remaining in the Balearics. But the permanent establishment of the Italians on the Balearics would be intolerable both to France and Britain, and might lead to a war of France and England against Italy—a war in which Spain, should she be entirely in the hands of the Whites, might come out on the side of Italy's enemies. The probability of Italy's defeat in such a war was slight, for the road from Germany was open for the supplementing of her raw materials. The Führer pictured the military strategy for Italy thus: on her western frontier with France she would remain on the defensive, and carry on the war with France from Libya against the French North African colonial possessions.

As a landing by Franco–British troops on the coast of Italy could be ruled out, and a French offensive over the Alps against northern Italy would be very difficult and would probably come to a halt before the strong Italian fortifications, the crucial point [*Schwerpunkt*] of the operations lay in North Africa. The threat to French lines of communication by the Italian Fleet would largely cripple the transportation of forces from North Africa to France, so that France would have only home forces at her disposal on her Italian and German frontiers.

If Germany made use of this war to settle the Czech and Austrian questions, it was to be assumed that Britain, herself at war with Italy, would decide not to act against Germany. Without British support, no warlike action by France against Germany was to be expected.

The time for our attack on the Czechs and Austria must be made dependent on the course of the Anglo–French–Italian war and would not necessarily coincide with the commencement of military operations by these three States. Nor had the Führer in mind military agreements with Italy; he wanted, while retaining his own independence of action, to exploit this favourable situation, which would not occur again, to begin and carry through the campaign against the Czechs. This descent upon the Czechs would have to be carried out with 'lightning speed'.

In this address Hitler had for the first time expressed a concrete commitment to war in terms of specific goals—*Anschluss* with Austria and the destruction of Czechoslovakia—and within a specific time limit—1943–5. The main reasons for this were economic and diplomatic, Germany could not sustain her massive rearmament indefinitely with the limited resources available to her; at the same time, Hitler was not prepared to reduce rearmament because that would be a confession of the bankruptcy of his whole programme. Furthermore, he recognized that Germany was engaged in an armaments race in which she was liable to lose her head start once the superior resources of her potential opponents were mobilized. Thus, she must exploit or endeavour to create a favourable diplomatic situation for the deployment of her armed forces in an offensive war.

Secondly, Hitler had in effect openly revised his programme. Britain had—for the time being at least—joined France as a 'hate-inspired antagonist' in his eyes. However, since he considered that she lacked both the power and the will to oppose him, he would pursue his goals in the East counting on her neutrality. If he could not achieve living space with Britain as an ally, he would do so without her and if necessary against her, although he still hoped that eventually she would see sense. In the meantime, he agreed to the Navy's demand for an increased allocation of steel and then ordered an expansion of the U-Boat programme up to 100 per cent parity with Britain as envisaged in the Anglo-German Naval Agreement of 1935.

It is clear from the following account in Hossbach's *Memoirs* that Hitler had not succeeded in convincing his audience:

504

At times the discussion became quite heated, above all between Blomberg and Fritsch on the one hand and Göring on the other, while Hitler for the most part remained a spectator. I do not recall the substance of the dispute. However, I remember very clearly that the sharp divergence of opinion both in form and substance did not fail to make an impression on Hitler as I could see from the expression on his face. In view of his attitude, the behaviour of Blomberg and Fritsch must have made it clear to the Führer that his political ideas had simply produced sober and objective counter-arguments instead of applause and approval. And he knew very well that the two generals rejected any involvement in a war provoked by us.

In fact, Fritsch visited Hitler on 9 November to express his concern about the danger of French and British intervention in any German military action such as he had envisaged in his speech. Hitler reassured him that he did not contemplate any such action in the immediate future. Neurath shared the concern of the military and expressed it to Hitler in mid-January 1938, pointing out that 'his policy could lead to a world war . . . Many of his goals could be achieved peacefully—though somewhat more slowly'. Significantly, Hitler replied that 'he had no more time'.[18]

Concern about Hitler's willingness to ride roughshod over British opinion and interests was shared by Göring, who had already arranged an invitation for Lord Halifax, a senior British statesman, to visit Germany in an informal capacity in the hope of improving relations.

Meanwhile, the British government had decided that the best way to proceed was to try and achieve a 'general settlement' with Germany by which, in return for satisfying what were seen as legitimate German grievances through limited concessions in Eastern Europe (Austria and Czechoslovakia) and over colonies, Germany would give guarantees of good behaviour in the future and return to the Concert of Europe and the League of Nations. Hitler, however, having changed his views about the desirability of the English alliance had little time for such negotiations with Britain, which would fail to provide Germany with living space, and he only reluctantly agreed to meet Halifax on 19 November. Their conversation and, in particular, Halifax's statements concerning Britain's willingness to accept a limited revision of the frontiers in Eastern Europe merely confirmed his view of British weakness.

[18] Cf. H. Gackenholz, 'Reichskanzlei 5 November 1937' in *Forschungen zu Staat und Verfassung. Festgabe für Fritz Hartung* ed. R. Dietrich. (Berlin 1958) pp. 471 ff.

505

HALIFAX: . . . The Prime Minister held the view that it should be possible to find a solution (of our differences) by an open exchange of views. The solution of even difficult problems could be facilitated by mutual confidence. If Germany and England were to succeed in reaching an understanding or even in approaching nearer to such an understanding, it would be necessary, in the English view, that those countries which stood politically close to Germany and England should be at the appropriate time brought into our discussions. One should mention in this context Italy and France, to whom it must be made clear from the beginning that an Anglo-German *rapprochement* would not mean an attempt to divide France and England. The impression should not be given that the Berlin–Rome axis or the good relations between London and Paris would be prejudiced by an agreement between England and Germany. After the ground had been prepared by agreement between England and Germany, the four Great Powers of Western Europe must together create the basis upon which a lasting European peace would be built. In no case should one of the four Powers be left outside this collaboration for in that case the situation of insecurity which would arise would never find an end.

HITLER: There were two possibilities in the shaping of relations between the peoples:

The interplay of free forces, which was often synonymous with great and grave encroachments upon the life of the peoples and which could bring in its train a serious convulsion which would shake the civilisation we had built up with so much trouble. The second possibility lay in setting up in the place of the play of free forces the rule of a "higher reason"; in this case, however, one must clearly realise that this higher reason must lead to approximately similar results to those which had followed from the working of free forces. He (the Chancellor) had often asked himself during recent years whether humanity today was intelligent enough to replace the play of free forces by the method of higher reason.

In the year 1919 a great chance to apply this new method had been missed. At that time a solution of unreasonableness had been preferred: as a consequence Germany had been forced back on the path of the free play of forces, because this was the only possible way to make sure of the simplest rights of mankind. It would be decisive for the future whether the one method were chosen, or the other. When considering the sacrifices which would certainly be demanded here and there by the method of reason one should realise what sacrifices would have to be made, were one to return to the old method of the free play of forces. One would then realise that the former alternative cost less.

HALIFAX: On the English side it was not necessarily thought that the *status quo* must be maintained under all circumstances. It was recognised that one might have to contemplate an adjustment to new conditions, a correction of former mistakes and the recognition of changed circumstances when such need arose. In doing so England made her influence felt only in one way—to secure that these alterations should not take place in a manner corresponding to the unreasonable solution mentioned by the Chancellor, the play of free forces, which in the end meant war. He must emphasise once more in the name of H.M. Government that possibility of change of the existing situation was not excluded, but that changes should only take place upon the basis of reasonable agreements reasonably reached. If on both sides there was agreement that the world was not static, one should try to put the recognition of this fact into practice so that the energies at the disposal of mankind should be directed in mutual confidence to a common objective . . .

LORD HALIFAX asked the Chancellor, if, subject to a satisfactory solution of pending questions, he saw any possibility of leading Germany back to a close cooperation with other nations in the League of Nations or in what respect the Covenant of the League in his opinion must be altered before Germany could once more become a member of the League. There was no doubt that the virtues of the League might have been exaggerated by its too enthusiastic supporters. Nevertheless, one must admit that the League used its influence for a peaceful method of solving international difficulties. If it was possible to put these methods into force, one would have practically realised the second alternative which the Chancellor had previously described as the "reasonable method," in contra-distinction to the free play of forces. If one were to use the League, which was an international method, the details of which one might perhaps alter, in this manner, it would have considerable effect upon the re-establishment of confidence between the nations. He therefore inquired of the Chancellor his attitude toward the League and to disarmament. All other questions fell into the category of possible alterations in the European order which might be destined to come about with the passage of time. Amongst these questions were Danzig, Austria, and Czechoslovakia. England was interested to see that any alterations should come through the course of peaceful evolution and that methods should be avoided which might cause far-reaching disturbances, which neither the Chancellor nor other countries desired.

The colonial question was doubtless difficult. The English Prime Minister adopted the attitude that it could only be solved as a part of a new start and of a general settlement.

During the course of the discussions which followed Hitler's address on 5 November 1937 and in the subsequent conversation with Fritsch on 9 November, he had reassured the generals that he would implement his plans only when the requisite conditions had been created and, in particular, he would strive to avoid a two-front war. On this basis, the military leadership went ahead and incorporated Hitler's aims in their planning. Hitherto German strategic planning had concentrated on dealing with the threat of a French invasion. Late in 1935, the first major deployment plan, 'Operation Red', was drawn up to meet this eventuality. But the military planners were also obliged to deal with the possibility of intervention by France's ally Czechoslovakia. By 1937 the General Staff had worked out a plan for a pre-emptive strike against Czechoslovakia to forestall precisely such intervention in the case of a war with France—'Operation Green'. On 24 June 1937 a general plan was drawn up which incorporated both 'Operation Red' and 'Operation Green'. In this plan 'Operation Red' took precedence. The extent to which the plan reflected aggressive intentions is in dispute. On the one hand, the preamble to the plan stated that 'the general political situation permits the assumption that Germany need not expect an attack from any quarter', while on the other hand it added that 'a permanent state of readiness of the German Wehrmacht' was necessary 'to take military advantage of any politically favourable opportunities which might arise', Nevertheless, the emphasis of the plan was in general more defensive than aggressive.

On 7 December 1937, however, following on the Hossbach meeting, the Chief of Operations Staff at OKW, General Jodl, amended the plan in such a way as to give it a definite aggressive slant. From now onwards 'Operation Green' was to take precedence over 'Operation Red' and the invasion of Czechoslovakia was no longer conceived as a pre-emptive strike for essentially defensive purposes but as an 'offensive war' for the purpose of solving 'the German problem of living space':

506

. . .

(1) The further development of the diplomatic situation makes 'Operation Red' increasingly less likely than 'Operation Green'. . . .

(3) The political preconditions for the activation of 'Operation Green' have changed following the directives of the Führer and Reich Chancellor, and the objectives of such a war have been expanded.

The previous Section II of Part 2 of the directive of the High Command of the Armed Forces of 24 June 1937 is therefore to be deleted and replaced by the enclosed new version. . . .

The main emphasis of all mobilization is now to be placed on 'Operation Green'. . . .

II. *War on two fronts with main effort in south-east ('Operation Green')*

1. *Prerequisites*

When Germany has achieved complete preparedness for war in all spheres, then the military conditions will have been created for carrying out an offensive war against Czechoslovakia, so that the solution of the German problem of living space can be carried to a victorious conclusion even if one or another of the Great Powers intervene against us.

Apart from many other considerations, there is in the first place the defensive capacity of our western fortifications, which will permit the western frontier of the German Reich to be held with weak forces for a long time against greatly superior strength.

But even so the Government [*Staatsführung*] will do what is politically feasible to avoid the risk for Germany of a war on two fronts and will try to avoid any situation with which, as far as can be judged, Germany could not cope militarily or economically.

Should the political situation not develop, or develop only slowly, in our favour, then the execution of 'Operation Green' from our side will have to be postponed for years. If, however, a situation arises which, owing to Britain's aversion to a general European War, through her lack of interest in the Central European problem and because of a conflict breaking out between Italy and France in the Mediterranean, creates the probability that Germany will face no other opponent than Russia on Czechoslovakia's side, then 'Operation Green' will start *before* the completion of Germany's full preparedness for war.

2. The military objective of 'Operation Green' is still the speedy occupation of Bohemia and Moravia with the simultaneous solution of the Austrian question in the sense of incorporating Austria into the German Reich. In order to achieve the latter aim, military force will be required only if other means do not lead or have not led to success.

In accordance with this military objective it is the task of the German Wehrmacht to make preparations so that:

(a) the bulk of all forces can invade Czechoslovakia with speed, surprise and the maximum impetus;

(b) reserves, mainly the armed units of the SS, are kept ready in order, if necessary, to march into Austria;

(c) in the west, security can be maintained with only a minimum of forces for rearguard protection of the eastern operations. . . .

(v) Ribbentrop's conclusions on the Anglo-German Relationship and his Policy of the 'World Triangle'—Germany–Italy–Japan

It is probable that a significant part in Hitler's reassessment of the future role of Britain in his plans was played by the reports of his ambassador in London, Ribbentrop, for whom he had developed a considerable admiration. On 28 December 1937, Ribbentrop summed up his views on 'The Anglo-German Relationship and the Way to deal with the Chamberlain Initiative' in a major report with that title, and then, on 2 January 1938, prepared a brief 'Note for the Führer' in which he stressed the importance of regarding Britain as a future enemy and the need to cultivate good relations with Italy and Japan in particular:

507

. . . I. For centuries England has always fought for three principles:

1. For English supremacy at sea.
2. For the inviolability of the so-called 'low countries' (Holland and Belgium) and
3. For the balance of power in Europe.

Re: 1. World naval supremacy no longer exists. Since the Naval Agreement [of 1935] the question of naval rivalry between Germany and Britain is no longer so acute as before the War. However the following point should be borne in mind: The British Admiralty calculates that, in the event of war, the ratio of 100:35 laid down in the Naval Agreement would in fact be at the most 60 per cent in the North Sea because normally 40 per cent of the English fleet has to remain elsewhere. If the English Admiralty had to reckon with the hostility of Italy and possibly of Japan, the figure would move still further to England's disadvantage, despite the inclusion of the allied French fleet.

Re: 2. Following the emergence of air power, France has now joined the 'Low Countries', in line with the Baldwin thesis that England's frontier is on the Rhine. Thus, strategically, England regards the countries, Holland, Belgium, and France, as a kind of glacis for English defence. In my view, it is a fact that English foreign policy is totally linked to that of the French, which in the last few years has become increasingly dependent on the [British] Foreign Office out of fear of Germany's renewed strength. For this reason, England has done its utmost, on the one hand to discourage a Franco-Geman rapprochement, and, on the other hand, to prevent the weakening of France, for example through Bolshevism.

Re: 3. Since the seizure of power by National Socialism and the rearmament of Germany, England sees the possibility of a disturbance of the previous balance of power in Europe which would remove its role as the arbiter of Europe and thereby its freedom of manoeuvre, and furthermore could even threaten England directly. The enduring memory of the achievements of the German Army in the war against the Allies plays an important part in these English fears. Thus, Germany is regarded . . . as the most dangerous of possible opponents. For, while other possible opponents e.g. Japan threaten important English interests, these lie in the first instance on the periphery of its empire, Italy threatens the quickest but not the only route to its most important possession, India, but Germany alone can threaten the heart of the British Empire, namely the British Isles . . .

II. Since the formation of the Rome–Berlin axis and Mussolini's visit to Germany, since the concern about the outcome of the Spanish Civil War and its incalculable repercussions on the English position in the Mediterranean, since Italy has joined the Anti-Comintern movement, and since Japan's advance into China, Britain's fears concerning a disturbance of the balance of power in Europe and in the world have generally increased. England now sees its East Asian possessions threatened by Japan, its sea route through the Mediterranean to India by Italy, and the mother country, the British Isles, by Germany.

III. England has initially dealt with this development through its tremendous rearmament programme and also through strengthening its friendly alliance with France. Since the beginning of the year, England has also been attempting to secure America as a source of raw materials . . . However, England's final goal is undoubtedly to win over America once more as an ally in the event of a European conflict.

IV. However, the main question for England, which naturally sees the maintenance of peace as the best guarantee for the maintenance of the Empire, remains as before whether it will *still be possible to come to an arrangement with Germany*, which secures world peace and maintains the European balance of power. It is conceivable that there are men in the English government (on the basis of my own experience and observations I doubt whether they include Chamberlain and

Halifax) who still believe in the possibility of a friendly arrangement with Germany on the following basis:

The return of some German colonies and the leaving open of a solution to the Austrian question which could prepare a peaceful *Anschluss*, as well as an improvement in the situation of the Sudeten Germans, possibly to the extent of granting them cultural autonomy, in return for a repetition of Germany's guarantee not to attack her neighbours and the guarantee to solve all problems with her neighbours only on the basis of peaceful negotiations; furthermore, a clear agreement at least on a qualitative limitation of air force rearmament on the model of the Anglo–German Naval Agreement, for example through a ban on bombing, a limitation of bombers, and possibly a quantitative limitation through the publication and eventually limitation of the [arms] budget.

In my view this would be more or less the maximum which those people who believe in principle in an accommodation with Germany (i.e. those who do not regard the existence of a Germany governed by the so-called expansionist National Socialist ideology as an insuperable obstacle to an Anglo–German understanding) envisage as involved in an arrangement with Germany.

The English ruling class will today just as in the past fight to the limit, i.e. to the point of war, to defend both its important material interests and its position of power in the world so long as there is a chance of winning. England will never risk such a commitment lightly. It will always carefully weigh up the situation and if necessary postpone decisions. If at some point it has the advantage it will fight. The non-intervention by England in the Abyssinian War is in my view not the result of a lack of heroism but a result of the fact that England had criminally neglected its armaments and of the false assessment of the situation by the English Government, which believed that Italy would get bogged down there and would give up the adventure of its own accord . . .

England has for some time considered it possible that sooner or later Germany might be compelled by the internal conditions in Czechoslovakia to intervene there and also in Austria by force. It is hoped that such a solution, particularly as regards Czechoslovakia can be prevented if at all possible. If it cannot be done, then England, which could be drawn into such a conflict at any time by a possible French intervention, wishes to make absolutely sure that it does not begin at a time when its rearmament has not reached at least a certain stage. One often hears and reads of 1939 as the year in which England can make its weight felt more. In my view, it is likely to be later, particularly in the light of the English naval programme. If such a conflict broke out earlier, it would be just as inconvenient as the Abyssinian campaign last year. For this reason, the Foreign Office has been pressing Prague for a long time to improve matters in the Sudeten questions. Halifax's remark at Berchtesgaden to the effect that the status quo in Austria and Czechoslovakia cannot be maintained and in the longer term could, in view of the English concern about military conflict, be intended to prevent us from carrying out solutions by force at an inappropriate time for England, which we are allegedly intending, by offering us the prospect of English understanding and even support for a peaceful solution of these and, other (colonial) questions. The tactic of concealing one's true intentions is a long-practised tradition in English politics. An example of this is England's attitude before the World War, when it concealed its intentions so well that 'German foreign policy collapsed with the unexpected entry of England into the war', and the fact that there are politicians today who believe that at the time England was not consciously working for the encirclement of Germany . . .

To sum up: we should have no great illusions about the further development of Anglo–German relations. Nevertheless, it seems to me correct for our future policy vis-à-vis England to be aimed at conciliation (*Ausgleich*). This must not, however, cause any damage to our relations with other friendly countries.

For this reason, and with your agreement, the embassy has in the past year always treated the Rome–Berlin axis and the Anti-Comintern relationship with Japan as permanent factors of our foreign policy in our work concerning England.

508

Note for the Führer 2.1.1938

. . . The hopes of those English politicians who are friendly to Germany—insofar as they are not already simply playing a prearranged role—that there can be an understanding will gradually disappear with the recognition that Germany does not want to bind herself to the status quo in Central Europe. This then raises the vital question: will Germany and England in the final analysis inevitably move into opposite camps and, one day march against each other again? In order to answer this question, one has to bear in mind the following points:

An alteration of the status quo in the East in the interests of Germany can only be carried out by force. So long as France knows that England, which has so to speak taken over as the guarantor of France against Germany, will support her, then France is likely to march in defence of its Eastern allies, or at least it is always possible that she will do so and that will mean an Anglo–German war . . .

Italy and Japan have just as strong an interest in a strong Germany as we have in a strong Italy and Japan. The existence of the new Germany has been of great benefit to the expansionist efforts of both of them in recent years. In view of this, and of common goals which must be achieved later, it ought to be possible to get these powers to declare their solidarity with us at the appropriate time. In such a situation, it might be possible that England would prevent France from intervening in the event of an Eastern conflict between Germany and one of her [France's] allies so that the conflict remains localised and England is not compelled to fight possibly in three different places—in East Asia, in the Mediterranean, and in Europe—under the most unfavourable conditions for its world empire. I do not think it would risk a fight for the existence of its world empire for the sake of a local Central European problem even if, in consequence, Germany was significantly strengthened. In such an event, France would presumably hardly dare to attack Germany's Western fortifications alone and without Britain . . .

5. We must draw the following conclusions:
   1) Outwardly our declared policy should be an understanding with England, while protecting the interests of our friends.

2) Construction secretly, but with absolute determination, of a network of alliances against England, i.e. in practice a strengthening of our friendship with Italy and Japan—further, the inclusion of all states whose interests coincide with our own—close and friendly cooperation of the three great powers to this end.
This is the only way to deal with Britain, whether or not one day we come to an agreement or into conflict. England will be a strong and tough opponent in this diplomatic game.

6. The particular question of whether, in the event of Germany becoming involved in a conflict in Central Europe, France and thus England will intervene depends on the circumstances and the timing of the outbreak of such a conflict and on military considerations which cannot be assessed here. I have some points to make orally to the Führer on this.

This is my view of the situation after having considered all the circumstances. I have worked for years for friendship with England and nothing would make me happier than if it could be achieved. When I asked the Führer to send me to London, I was sceptical whether it would work. However, in view of Edward VIII a final attempt seemed appropriate. Today, I no longer believe in an understanding. England does not want a powerful Germany nearby which would pose a permanent threat to its islands. It will fight to prevent it. People believe National Socialism is capable of formidable things. Baldwin recognized this and Edward VIII had to abdicate because they were not certain whether he would cooperate with a policy hostile towards Germany. Chamberlain has now appointed Vansittart, our most important and toughest opponent, to a position from which he can intervene decisively in the diplomatic game against Germany.[19] No matter what temporary and tactically motivated attempts are made to reach an understanding with us, in future every day on which our political considerations are not based on the view of England as our most dangerous opponent will be a gain for our enemies.

[19] On 1 January 1938 Sir Robert Vansittart had been appointed permanent diplomatic adviser to the Foreign Secretary, a position which, despite its impressive-sounding title, in fact largely removed him from the decision-making process (eds).

CHAPTER 28

German Foreign Policy 1938–1939: The Road to War

(i) The Purge of Conservatives—Winter 1937–8

The winter of 1937–38 marked the beginning of a new phase not only in foreign policy and strategy but in the development of the regime itself. Hitler now took steps to evict a number of conservatives from influential positions. One factor prompting this move may have been the doubts expressed during the 'Hossbach Conference' of the advisability of Hitler's intentions by Admiral Raeder, Field-Marshal von Blomberg, and von Neurath, the Foreign Minister. Moreover, on 9 November, the Commander-in-Chief of the Army, General von Fritsch, had expressed to Hitler the concern of the military leaders lest Germany should become involved in a war before her military preparations were complete.

The critical attitude of the Army leadership towards his policy probably made Hitler decide to take the first opportunity of replacing these generals with more pliable men. This was achieved by manufacturing or exploiting personal scandals involving Blomberg and Fritsch and using these as an excuse to ease them out of their posts. Fritsch was replaced as Commander-in-Chief of the Army by General von Brauchitsch, while Hitler abolished the position of War Minister held by Blomberg and took over from him as Commander-in-Chief of the Armed Forces in addition to the post of Supreme Commander of the Armed Forces which he already held as Head of State. To replace the old Wehrmacht Office he established a new High

Command of the Wehrmacht (OKW) of which he appointed General Keitel, the former head of the Wehrmacht Office, as the chief. In addition, fourteen senior generals were retired and forty-six others were required to change their commands. The reorganization of the High Command was based on the following decree issued on 4 February 1938.

509

From now onwards I will exercise direct command over the whole Wehrmacht personally. The present Wehrmacht Office in the War Ministry will come directly under my command as the 'Supreme Command of the Wehrmacht' [Oberkommando der Wehrmacht = OKW] retaining its responsibilities and acting as my personal staff.

At the head of the Staff of the Supreme Command of the Wehrmacht will be the present Chief of the Wehrmacht Office as Chief of the High Command of the Wehrmacht. His rank is equivalent to that of a Reich Minister.

The High Command of the Wehrmacht will also fulfil the duties of the Reich War Ministry, the Chief of the High Command of the Wehrmacht will carry out the responsibilities hitherto pertaining to the Reich War Minister in my name.

The High Command of the Wehrmacht is responsible under my direction for the unified preparation of the defence of the Reich in time of peace.

But the purge was not confined to the military. Schacht had resigned as Minister of Economics in November 1937 after differences with Hitler over the pace of rearmament and the policy of autarky. These differences found institutional expression in the undermining of his authority by the growth of Göring's Four-Year Plan Office. Schacht's departure and the rise of the Four-Year Plan Office reflected the extent to which the economy had become subordinate to the political and strategic goals of the regime in the form of the priority given to accelerating rearmament. Lastly, on 4 February 1938, the same day as Hitler made the changes in the military leadership, he appointed Ribbentrop as Foreign Minister in place of Neurath so that the conservative Foreign Office also was now finally 'coordinated'.

This purge of the conservatives marked a new departure for the regime. If June–August 1934 saw the close of the first phase in the 'seizure of power', November 1937–February 1938 marked the beginning of the end of the period of compromise with the conservative elites. This development partly reflected Hitler's growing self-confidence in matters of foreign and military policy. The fact that he had consistently been proved right and his expert advisers wrong over such matters as the introduction of conscription and the occupation of the Rhineland gave him the confidence to take the reins more firmly into his own hands. But the purge also reflected Hitler's decision to increase the pressure in a way which he knew would alienate the conservatives, who were now increasingly concerned that he was embarking on what they regarded as an extreme and hazardous action which, successful or not, would inevitably shatter that delicate balance between old and new forces which had existed since 1934.

(ii) The Anschluss with Austria, March 1938

Hitler's first initiative after the 'Hossbach Conference' concerned Austria. In the period after the abortive Austrian Nazi putsch of 1934 Hitler had refrained from any overt pressure on Austria in order not to jeopardize the growing *entente* with Italy. In the Austro-German agreement of 11 July 1936 Germany had recognized the sovereignty of Austria, both countries agreed on non-interference in each other's domestic affairs, and Austria promised to follow a foreign policy based on the principle that 'Austria acknowledges herself to be a German State'. The Austrian Government also agreed to give a share of political responsibility to the 'national opposition'. The two Governments, however, had different interpretations of the significance of the agreement. Schuschnigg, the Austrian Chancellor, viewed it as a settlement of differences which relieved him of German pressure. Hitler, on the other hand, saw it as a means of increasing German influence in Austria.

During 1937, it was in fact Göring who increasingly took the initiative over Austria. He favoured an evolutionary policy in which the *Anschluss* would inexorably follow a peaceful German penetration of Austria through a combination of attraction and pressure, both political and economic. In the course of the year, he stepped up the pressure, particularly when it became clear that Austria was resisting closer economic integration with the Reich.

Hitler adopted a more cautious attitude since he was very concerned not to alienate Mussolini. Because he was loath to raise the matter of Austria with the Duce during his visit to Germany in September, he left it to Göring, while at the same time making it clear that he had 'not approved Göring's approach hitherto which is too tough'. He declared that 'the Austrian problem should by no means be brought to a head in the foreseeable future . . . One must simply ensure that in the event of the Austrian question being brought to a head by someone else it will be possible for Germany to intervene.'[1]

---

[1] A. Kube *Pour le mérite und Hakenkreuz: Hermann Göring im Dritten Reich* (Munich 1986) p. 236.

Göring, however, continued to believe that a tough line was right with Mussolini and on the Duce's visit to his estate, Carinhall, he showed him a map of Europe in which Austria had been included in Germany. Mussolini remarked drily 'that the Reich was fulfilling its programme punctually', which Göring interpreted as a green light.[2] Hitler, although convinced after his conversation with Halifax in November that Britain would not intervene to prevent an *Anschluss,* was still anxious not to provoke Mussolini. He needed to increase the momentum without taking undue risks.

The opportunity Hitler was seeking was provided by the Austrian Chancellor. Schuschnigg had been having increasing difficulty with the Austrian Nazis and in January 1938 the police exposed a plot by Tavs, the Nazi leader in Vienna to stage a *coup*. Schuschnigg took his problem to von Papen, now ambassador in Vienna but in process of being recalled. Papen, who also resented the interference of the Austrian Nazis, persuaded him to seek an interview with Hitler in order to sort the matter out. When Papen informed Hitler of Schuschnigg's desire to meet him, Hitler jumped at the opportunity of putting new pressure on the Austrians. The interview took place in Berchtesgaden on 12 February. Hitler already knew through a security leak of the concessions Schuschnigg was willing to make and proceeded to browbeat him into meeting Germany's demands. The following agreement was reached:

510

. . . II

(1) The Austrian Government shall from time to time enter into a diplomatic exchange of views on questions of foreign policy of common concern to both countries. Austria shall on request give moral, diplomatic, and press support to the desires and actions of the German Reich, to the extent that circumstances permit. The Reich government assumes the same obligation toward the Austrian Government.

(2) Federal Chancellor Schuschnigg declares that he is willing to take State Counsellor Dr Seyss-Inquart[3] into his Government and entrust him with Security.

(3) The Federal Chancellor states that the Austrian National Socialists shall in principle have opportunity for legal activity within the framework of the Fatherland Front and all other Austrian organizations. This activity shall take place on an

---

[2] Ibid. p. 237.

[3] Arthur Seyss-Inquart, who became Minister of the Interior and Security in Schuschnigg's Government, was a Vienna lawyer with pan-German ambitions. Although not formally committed to the Austrian Nazis, he became the chief spokesman for their interests.

equal footing with all other groups, and in accordance with the constitution. Dr Seyss-Inquart has the right and the duty to see to it that the activity of the National Socialists can develop along the lines indicated above, and to take appropriate measures for this purpose.
(4) The Austrian Government shall immediately proclaim a general amnesty for all persons in Austria punished by the courts or the police because of their National Socialist activities. Such persons whose further stay in Austria appears detrimental to relations between the two countries shall, after an examination of each individual case and by agreement between the two Governments, be made to transfer their residence to the Reich.
(5) Disciplinary measures in the fields of pensions, annuities, and public welfare, especially the withholding or reduction of benefits, and in education as well, because of National Socialist activities, shall be revoked and restitution promised.
(6) All economic discrimination against National Socialists shall be eliminated.
(7) The unhindered observance of the press truce agreed upon between the Governments shall be assured by the appointment of Dr Wolf to an important post in the Austrian Press Service.
(8) Military relations between the German and Austrian armed forces shall be assured by the following measures:
(a) the replacement of General Jansa by General Böhme;
(b) a systematic exchange of officers (up to the number of 100);
(c) regular conferences between the General Staffs;
(d) a systematic cultivation of comradely and professional military relations.
(9) All discrimination against National Socialists, especially that affecting enrolment in and completion of military service, shall be stopped. All past discriminatory actions shall be cancelled.
(10) Preparations shall be made for the intensification of commerce between Austrian and German economies. For this purpose, Dr Fischböck shall be appointed to a leading post.

The Federal Chancellor declares that he is prepared to carry out all measures agreed upon under II (2), (4), (5), (7), by 18 February 1938, subject to the definitive reply agreed upon under II.

Hitler was satisfied that compliance with these demands would make Austria a satellite of Germany. On 26 February, therefore, when he met five leading Austrian Nazis, he ordered them to remain in Germany for the time being. Wilhelm Keppler, now Hitler's agent in Austria, recorded Hitler's statement of policy at the meeting:

511

The Führer stated that in the Austrian problem he had to indicate a different course for the Party, *as the Austrian question could never be solved by a revolution*. There remained only two possibilities: force or evolutionary means. He wanted the evolutionary course to be taken, whether or not the possibility of success could today be foreseen. The Protocol signed by Schuschnigg was so far-reaching that, if completely carried out, the Austrian problem would be automatically solved. He did not now desire a solution by violent means, if it could be at all avoided, since the danger for us in the field of foreign policy became less each year and our military power greater.

Under pressure from German military manoeuvres near the frontier, Austria complied with the German demands and declared an amnesty for political prisoners, mainly Austrian Nazis. Seyss-Inquart, now Minister of the Interior, travelled to Berlin on 17 February to receive instructions from Hitler, and he increasingly dominated the Austrian Government. Schuschnigg, however, then attempted to retrieve the situation by a desperate move. On 9 March, against the advice of Mussolini, he announced a plebiscite on the question of the independence of Austria in three day's time.

Hitler was completely stunned by this bold move on the part of the man who had been so submissive at Berchtesgaden and was uncertain of what to do next. On the one hand, the whole question had become a matter of prestige. Furthermore, in view of the voting conditions, he had reason to doubt whether the vote would go in Germany's favour. Voting was restricted to those over 24 (thus excluding many members of the Nazi Party, who tended to be young), there was no up-to-date electoral register, and the wording of the plebiscite question was tendentious. On the other hand, Hitler was still concerned about the attitude of Mussolini. At noon on 10 March, therefore, Hitler dispatched Prince Philip of Hesse to Rome with a letter justifying German intervention and giving the following assurances:

512

I now wish solemnly to assure Your Excellency, as the Duce of Fascist Italy:
1. Consider this step only as one of national self-defence. . . . You too, Excellency, could not act differently if the fate of Italians were at stake. . . .
2. In a critical hour for Italy I proved to you the steadfastness of my sympathy. Do not doubt that in the future there will be no change in this respect.
3. Whatever the consequences of the coming events may be, I have drawn a definite boundary between Germany and France and now I draw one just as definite between ourselves and Italy. It is the Brenner. This decision will never be questioned or changed.

Göring appears to have seized the initiative from a hesitant Hitler and successfully argued for the toughest measures. Military plans were hurriedly drawn up since no preparations had been made for such an eventuality—the only existing plans dealing with Austria were to forestall a restoration of the Habsburg Monarchy, the so-called 'Operation Otto'. At two o'clock in the morning of the 11th, Hitler issued Directive No. 1 for 'Operation Otto' which, as the first sentence indicates, still did not commit Germany to an invasion of Austria:

513

1. If other measures prove unsuccessful, I intend to invade Austria with armed forces to establish constitutional conditions and to prevent further outrages against the pro-German population.
2. The whole operation will be directed by myself. . . .
5. The behaviour of the troops must give the impression that we do not want to wage war against our Austrian brothers. It is in our interest that the whole operation shall be carried out without violence but in the form of a peaceful entry welcomed by the population. Therefore any provocation is to be avoided. If, however, resistance is offered it must be broken ruthlessly by force of arms.

Austrian units who come over to us come immediately under German command.
6. On the remaining German frontiers no security measures are to be taken for the time being.

Meanwhile, Göring had effectively taken charge of events and, having despatched Seyss-Inquart to Vienna with a draft telegram to be sent requesting the sending of German troops, set about raising the stakes from hour to hour. He began by demanding the postponement of the plebiscite and the substitution of an alternative question. Then, when this was conceded, he insisted on the resignation of Schuschnigg. When this too had been accepted, he demanded the appointment of Seyss-Inquart as Chancellor. Here, however, he came up against the Austrian President, Wilhelm Miklas, who refused the request and stuck to his refusal despite the threat of invasion. The following transcripts of the telephone conversations between Göring and Seyss-Inquart on the afternoon and evening of 11 March, monitored by Göring's personal phone-tapping service, the *Forschungsamt*, illustrate the development of the crisis and Göring's role:

514

Telephone call from S at 15.55:

S reported to the Field Marshall [Göring] that the Chancellor Schuschnigg has gone to Federal President Miklas to hand in his and his government's resignation. In reply to the F's question whether S was certain to be asked to form a cabinet, S stated that he would inform F about that by 17.30 at the latest. F declared categorically that this was an irrevocable demand in addition to the resignation of Chancellor Schuschnigg.

Field Marshall Göring to Seyss-Inquart 11.3.38 Vienna–Berlin 17.26–17.31

. . . G. Please note the following: You must go at once together with Lieut.-Gen. Muff(?) to the Federal President and tell him that if the demands made so far, you know what they are, are not accepted, then an invasion by the troops already mobilized on the border will follow tonight and that will be the end of Austria . . . The invasion will only be stopped and the troops remain at the border if we hear by 7.30 [p.m.] that Miklas has handed over the Chancellorship to you . . . and you must let the National Socialists loose throughout the whole country. They are now to be allowed to go on the streets everywhere. So I want to hear by 7.30 . . . If Miklas hasn't got that in 4 hours then he will have to get it in 4 minutes.

Seyss-Inquart, Vienna reports to Field-Marshal Göring 11.3.38 Vienna–Berlin 19.57–20.03

S. Dr Schuschnigg will announce on the radio that the Reich Government is presenting an ultimatum.

G. I have heard that.

S. And the government has left office. General Schiwaski has command of the military and will withdraw the military. The gentlemen are adopting the position that they will wait for the invasion.

G. So you haven't been appointed. And you haven't been given office—it's been refused?

S. They are still refusing. They are taking the line that they will just let the invasion happen and, on the basis of the invasion, authority will be transferred to other people.

G. O.K. I will give the order to invade and you see to it that you take over power. Make clear to the leading people there what I am telling you now: anyone who opposes or organizes opposition will be immediately subject to our courts martial, the courts martial of the invading troops. Is that clear?

Göring insisted on Seyss-Inquart sending the telegram which was received in Berlin at 9.40 p.m. on the 11th. Göring had in fact already given the order for the invasion 'in the name of the Führer' at 8.45 p.m. The Nazi leadership were reassured by news of a broadcast by Schuschnigg ordering the Austrian army not to oppose an invasion. This freed Hitler from the odium of spilling the blood of fellow Germans and reduced the prospect of foreign intervention. This prospect was made even less likely by the news which he received in a telephone call from Prince Philip of Hesse at 10.25 p.m. Hitler's replies indicate the degree of his relief at the news of Mussolini's acquiescence in the invasion:

515

Hesse: I have just come back from the Palazzo Venezia. The Duce accepted the whole thing in a very friendly manner. He sends you his regards.
Hitler: Then please tell Mussolini I will never forget him for this.
Hesse: Yes
Hitler: Never, never, never, whatever happens. As soon as the Austrian affair is settled, I shall be ready to go with him, through thick and thin, no matter what happens.
Hesse: Yes, my Führer.
Hitler: Listen, I shall make any agreement—I am no longer in fear of the terrible position which would have existed militarily in case we had got into a conflict. You may tell him that I thank him ever so much—never, never shall I forget.
Hesse: Yes, my Führer.
Hitler: I will never forget, whatever may happen. If he should ever need any help or be in any danger, he can be convinced that I shall stick to him, whatever may happen, even if the whole world were against him.
Hesse: Yes, my Führer,

No actual plans had been made for the implementation of the *Anschluss*. Indeed, the decision to integrate Austria completely into the Reich was taken by Hitler on the spur of the moment during a triumphal visit to his former home town of Linz.

In the meantime, Hitler received an approach from Britain. The British Government had now decided to try to buy peace in Europe by making concessions outside Europe—in Africa. The offer was prompted by a statement which Hitler had made in the course of his conversation with Halifax the previous November to the effect that 'between Germany and England there was only one difference, namely the colonial question'. The British offer was communicated to Hitler by Sir Nevile Henderson, the British ambassador in Berlin, who was received on 4 March 1938. After stressing the confidential nature of the discussions—'no information would be given the French, much less the Belgians, Portuguese or Italians'—Henderson emphasised that

516

the offer did not mean a commercial transaction, but an attempt to establish the basis for a genuine and cordial friendship with Germany beginning with an improvement of the atmosphere and ending with the creation of a new spirit of friendly understanding. . . . He stressed the importance of German collaboration in the pacification of Europe, to which he had already referred in previous conversations with Herr von Neurath and Herr von Ribbentrop. This pacification could be furthered by limitation of armaments and by appeasement in Czechoslovakia and Austria. . . .

Concerning the colonies, the British ambassador expressed the sincere willingness of the British Government not only to examine the colonial question, but to make progress towards its solution. Prime Minister Chamberlain had given his full personal attention to this problem. . . .

Henderson then read out a proposal for 'a scheme based on the idea of a new regime of colonial administration in a given area of Africa, roughly corresponding to the conventional zone of the Congo Basin Treaties, acceptable and applicable to all the powers concerned on exactly equal terms'.

Hitler, who according to Henderson was in a bad temper when he arrived, was not impressed. He had raised the colonial issue not for its own sake but in order to persuade Britain to give him *carte blanche* in Europe in return for his dropping it. Now the British were taking him at his word and offering him the precise opposite of what he wanted. He was not prepared to limit himself in Europe for the sake of minor gains overseas. After complaining about the British press, Hitler continued:

. . . that he personally was known as one of the warmest friends of England, but he had been ill-rewarded for this friendship. Perhaps nobody had been oftener and more grievously offended by England than he. It was, therefore, understandable that he had now withdrawn into a certain isolation, which still seemed to him more respectable than to make advances toward someone who did not want him and persistently snubbed him. . . .

Concerning central Europe, it should be noted that Germany would not tolerate any interference by third powers in the settlement of her relations with kindred countries or with countries having large German elements in their population, just as Germany would never think of interfering in the settlement of relations between England and Ireland. It was a question of preventing the continuance or the renewal of an injustice to millions of Germans. In this attempt at a settlement Germany would have to declare most seriously that she was not willing to be influenced in any way by other parties in this settlement. . . .

. . . England need not fear any interference from the Germans. Germany did not meddle in Empire affairs. She was, however, obliged to accept a negative reaction by England when Germany tried to solve her own difficulties. Any attempted settlement toward the east was met by 'No' from Britain and so was the colonial problem, and the British press in particular opposed Germany everywhere and conducted a campaign of slander against this country. . . .

On the issue of the colonies:

The Führer replied that Germany was of course primarily interested in the question of the disposition of her former colonies. Instead of establishing a new and complicated system, why not solve the colonial question in the simplest and most natural way, namely by returning the former German colonies? He, the Führer, must openly admit, however, that he did not consider the colonial problem ripe for settlement as yet, since Paris and London had declared themselves much too firmly opposed to their return. Therefore, neither did he wish to press the issue. One could wait quietly for four, six, eight or ten years. Perhaps by that time a change of mind would have taken place in Paris and London, and they would understand that the best solution was to return to Germany her rightful property acquired by purchase and Treaty. . . .

So far as Hitler was concerned, the British offer was merely a sign that his new policy of intimidating Britain into remaining neutral was proving effective. He now felt all the more prepared to move on to his next objective.

(iii) The Czech crisis, 1938–39

While driving into Austria at the time of the Anschluss, Hitler had remarked to his companion, General Halder: 'This will be very inconvenient to the Czechs.' The Anschluss had indeed seriously undermined the strategic position of Austria's neighbour. Yet Czechoslovakia still had a powerful army, well-equipped by the Skoda arms works, and formidable fortifications. Even before 1933, Hitler had regarded the Czechs as a serious threat to Germany both because of their alliance with France and because of their proximity to important German industrial centres, including Berlin, which would be vulnerable to air attack. Moreover, Hitler's own background as a pre-1918 Austrian probably contributed to his attitude a degree of personal animosity, rooted in the Czech–German rivalry of the prewar era. This was accentuated by ideologically based resentment at the fact that Czechoslovakia was a successful democracy. But it was the strategic factor which was decisive. Germany could not dare to launch ambitious plans either in the west or in the east until Czechoslovakia had been dealt with.

The means for dealing with Czechoslovakia lay ready to hand in the country's complicated ethnic structure. The new State, created by the Versailles settlement, contained apart from Czechs and Slovaks a number of minority groups of whom the most important were the three-and-a-quarter million Germans. Most of these lived in the Sudetenland, an area on the northern border with Germany. Hitler now proceeded to use the ethnic diversity of the country as a lever with which to break it up into its ethnic components. The most obvious group with which to start were the Sudeten Germans. For years they had been clamouring for greater recognition of their rights by the Czech Government and there was some justice in their case. But the rise of Nazi Germany had given an added impetus to their demands and in 1935 the German Foreign Office had begun secretly financing the Sudeten German Party, which by 1938 had succeeded in establishing itself as the leading representative of the Sudeten Germans.

After the Anschluss, Hitler summoned the leaders of the Sudeten German Party, Konrad Henlein and Karl Frank, to Berlin and at an interview on 28 March gave them instructions for their future activity:

517

. . . The Führer stated that he intended to settle the Sudeten German problem in the not-too-distant future. He could no longer tolerate Germans being oppressed or fired upon. He told Henlein that he knew how popular he, Henlein, was and that he was the rightful leader of the Sudeten German element, and as a result of his popularity and attractiveness he would triumph over circumstances. To Henlein's objection that he, Henlein, could only be a substitute, Hitler replied: I will stand by you; from tomorrow you will be my Viceroy (*Statthalter*]. I will not tolerate difficulties being made for you by any department whatsoever within the Reich.

The purport of the instructions which the Führer has given to Henlein is that demands should be made by the Sudeten German Party which are unacceptable to the Czech Government. Despite the favourable situation created by the events in Austria, Henlein does not intend to drive things to the limit, but merely to put forward the old demands for self-administration and reparation of the Party Rally (23–24 April 1938). He wishes to reserve for later on a suggestion of the Führer's that he should demand German regiments with German officers, and military commands to be given in German. The Reich will not intervene of its own accord. Henlein himself will be responsible for events for the time being. However, there must be close cooperation. Henlein summarized his view to the Führer as follows: We must always demand so much that we can never be satisfied. The Führer approved this view. . . .

The demands mentioned by Henlein were made at his Party's Congress at Carlsbad on 24 April and consisted of full autonomy for the Sudeten Germans. These demands were intended to be unacceptable to the Czechs but to appear eminently reasonable to foreign opinion which would then gain the impression of Czech obstinacy and injustice:

518

1. Restoration of complete equality of the German national group with the Czech people;
2. Recognition of the Sudeten German national group as a legal entity for the safeguarding of this position of equality within the State;
3. Confirmation and recognition of the Sudeten German settlement area;

4. Building up of Sudeten German self-government in the Sudeten German settlement area in all branches of public life in so far as questions are involved affecting the interests and affairs of the German national group;
5. Introduction of legal provisions for the protection of those Sudeten German citizens living outside the defined settlement area of their national group;
6. Removal of wrong done to the Sudeten German element since the year 1918, and compensation for damage suffered through this wrong;
7. Recognition and enforcement of the principle: German public servants in the German area;
8. Complete freedom to profess adherence to the German element and German ideology.

At this stage Hitler was in no hurry to solve the Czech question and on 20 May he presented to his generals an interim draft for an attack on Czechoslovakia ('Operation Green').

519

1. *Political assumptions*: It is not my intention to smash Czechoslovakia by military action in the immediate future without provocation, unless an unavoidable development of the political conditions *within* Czechoslovakia forces the issue, or political events in Europe create a particularly favourable opportunity which may perhaps never recur.
2. *Political possibilities for commencing the operation*: A sudden attack without convenient outward excuse and without adequate political justification cannot be considered in the present circumstances, in view of the possible results of such action.

Operations will preferably be launched,
either: (*a*) after a period of increasing diplomatic controversies and tension linked with military preparations, which will be exploited so as to shift the war guilt on the enemy.

But even such a period of tension preceding the war will be terminated by sudden military action on our part with as much of the surprise element as possible, alike in regard to time and extent;

or: (*b*) by lightning action as the result of a serious incident which will subject Germany to unbearable provocation and which, in the eyes of at least a part of world opinion, affords the moral justification for military measures.

Case (b) is more favourable, both from a military and a political point of view.

3. *Conclusions for the preparation of 'Operation Green'* based on the possible cases mentioned in 2(a) and (b):
(a) For the military operation it is essential to create in the first four days a strategic situation which demonstrates to enemy States which may wish to intervene the hopelessness of the Czech military position, and also provides an incentive to those

States which have territorial claims upon Czechoslovakia to join in immediately against her.

In this case the intervention of Hungary and Poland against Czechoslovakia can be expected, particularly if France, as a result of Italy's unequivocal attitude on our side, fears, or at least hesitates, to unleash a European war by intervening against Germany. In all probability attempts by Russia to give Czechoslovakia military support are to be expected.

If concrete successes are not achieved in the first few days by land operations a European crisis will certainly arise. . . .

However, a few days earlier, he had expressed a preference for 'a solution of the Sudeten question by the end of the year, since the [diplomatic] constellation could deteriorate'.[4] Then, an event occurred which prompted him to act sooner rather than later. On 20 May, rumours spread of German military preparations near the Czech border. In response, the Czech Government ordered a partial mobilization, and Britain and France warned Germany of the consequences if Hitler took any action. Hitler was forced to deny the rumours which were in fact untrue and the foreign press interpreted the affair as a climb-down by Hitler.

After a week's brooding in Berlin, Hitler returned to Berlin for a meeting with his service chiefs on 28 May. In the meantime, his naval adjutant, Puttkamer, had informed the naval chiefs of Hitler's new priorities in the light of the threat from Britain revealed by the May crisis: an acceleration of U-Boat construction, the bringing forward of the construction of the first two battleships (F = Bismarck and G = Tirpitz) by six months to spring 1940, and an acceleration in the increase in the firepower of the two pocket battleships (D = Scharnhorst and E = Gneisenau). This was clearly still insufficient for a full-scale naval war with Britain, but in Hitler's view would provide a useful deterrent against her, in any case, unlikely intervention in the coming continental war. It was, however, the most specific indication to the naval chiefs hitherto of Hitler's anticipation of a future war with Britain. Furthermore, he ordered the construction of six slipways for 'very large ships' whose building schedule clearly anticipated a future confrontation with Britain and/or the United States around 1944–5.

On 28 May Hitler outlined his views on the new situation to his service chiefs as his adjutant, Fritz Wiedemann, recalled after the war:

520

I remember that, on 28 May 1938, Hitler summoned a meeting of all the responsible people from the Foreign Ministry, the Army, and other leading figures in the

---

[4] *Die Weizsäcker-Papiere 1933–1950* ed. L. E. Hill (Frankfurt 1974) p. 128.

Winter Garden of the Reich Chancellery. Those present included, as I recall, Göring, Ribbentrop, von Neurath, General Beck, Admiral Raeder, General Keitel, and General von Brauchitsch. Hitler used the occasion to make the following statement: 'I am utterly determined that Czechoslovakia should disappear from the map'. Then Hitler revealed the outlines of his plan of attack on Czechoslovakia. Hitler turned to the generals and said: 'Right, we will deal with the situation in the East First [i.e. Czechoslovakia]. Then I shall give you three or four years and then we will sort things out in the West.' With 'things in the West' he meant war with France and England. I was very shocked by this statement and, on leaving the Chancellery, said to Neurath: 'Well, what do you think of these revelations?' Neurath thought that 'the situation was not as serious as it looked and that nothing would happen before Spring 1939'.

General Beck had taken down Hitler's address in note form, of which the following is an extract:

521

. . . Germany needs space: (a) In Europe
(b) in colonies.
It is up to our generation to solve the problem.
Opponents of Germany:
1. France: Every step will hurt France, it will always be our enemy. Is not stronger than 1914 but probably weaker.
2. England: was near to collapse in the Great War, the organization of the Empire has become other than envisaged; also opposed to an expansion of German power.
3. Czechoslovakia: in every coalition our enemy. Has 3 enemies: Poland, Hungary, Germans—Czechoslovakia has 7 million Czechs.
Czechoslovakia always our most dangerous enemy in the event of war in the West. She stands in the way of certain success in the West.
The aim of a war in the West (France and England) is now an extension of coastal basis (Belgium, Holland).
Danger of Belgian and Czech neutrality . . .
After rejecting the idea of an immediate attack on Czechoslovakia, Hitler nevertheless put forward:
Reasons for quick action:
(a) [Czech] fortifications are still improvised, moment of weakness will have been missed in 2–3 years.
(b) Lightning action (English rearmament will not come into effect before 1941/42. French rearmament will also still last many years) because of the international situation: tension between England, France–Italy is very great. Italy's ambitions are not satisfied. Directed against Tunisia. (Warning against underestimation of Italians). France's situation has changed: Italy will exploit every French weakness. It is necessary to create absolutely unambiguous relations.

Russia: will not take part, not geared up for a war of aggression.
Poland and Romania: Fear of Russian aid, will not act against Germany.
East Asia: Reason for England's caution. Lightning action is necessary.
Conclusions: Unambiguous attitude towards the powers that are with us.

Italy: no interest in the Mediterranean, prepared for any military agreement with Italy; any support for Japan.
No thought that we can avoid the crisis [Ernstfall]
Favourable moment must be seized (Politicians are only partly in control of it).
Military preparations:
(a) Strongest possible build up [in fortifications] in the West and their manning.
(b) Lightning march into Czechoslovakia . . .

General Jodl noted in his diary:

522

The intention of the Führer not to touch the Czech problem as yet is changed because of the Czech strategic troop concentrations of 21 May, which occurs without any German threat and without the slightest cause for it.

Because of Germany's self-restraint, its consequences lead to a loss of prestige of the Führer, which he is no longer willing to take. Therefore the new order is issued for 'Green' on 30 May.

523

II. *War on two fronts, with main effort in South-East*
(*Strategic concentration 'Green'*)
1. *Political assumptions*: It is my unalterable decision to smash Czechoslovakia by military action in the near future. It is the business of the political leadership to await or bring about the suitable moment from a political and military point of view.

An unavoidable development of events within Czechoslovakia, or other political events in Europe providing a suddenly favourable opportunity which may never recur, may cause me to take warlike action. . . .

A covering letter from Keitel stated that the execution of the plan 'must be assured by 1 October 1938 at the latest'.

Hitler envisaged a *Blitzkrieg* or 'lightning war' against Czechoslovakia which, by defeating her in a matter of days, would present the Western powers with a *fait accompli*. This strategy simultaneously exploited Germany's advantage in rearmament, while at the same time minimizing the risk of getting involved in a major war for which her resources would be inferior to those of the Allies, a risk which he was nevertheless prepared to take. However, to deter intervention by the Western powers he ordered a crash programme to build the so-called 'West Wall' fortifications along the French frontier, delaying the date for the attack on Czechoslovakia until 1 October, the last feasible moment before the onset of autumn reduced the impact of German armour and air superiority, both crucial to the *Blitzkrieg* concept. In the meantime, he concentrated on psychological warfare against the Czechs through a propaganda campaign. During August and September the German press was full of alleged Czech atrocities against Sudeten Germans.[5] The tactics behind this campaign were to frighten the Western Powers into putting pressure on the Czechs to make concessions. It was hoped that the Czechs would refuse and that the Western Powers would then feel morally justified in washing their hands of Czechoslovakia.

This campaign did not fail to have its effect on the Western Powers. Both Britain and France urged the Czech government to make concessions to the Sudeten Germans. But when, on 4 September, the Czech Government finally conceded Henlein's demand for autonomy, the Sudeten Germans, following Hitler's instructions to avoid a compromise, evaded the issue by claiming that Czech atrocities precluded further negotiations. The attitude of the British Government at this time may be gauged by an interview on 23 August between the German *chargé d'affaires* in Britain, Kordt, and Sir Horace Wilson, the Prime Minister's closest adviser. Kordt states that he left Wilson in no doubt 'that we would agree to no solution which left the State intact in its present extent'. He also insisted that Czechoslovakia must end its ties with France and Russia. Yet, he says, Wilson replied that

524

. . . a policy of this nature could quite well be discussed with Great Britain. It was only necessary that this policy should not be rendered impossible by the sudden use of force by us. He completely agreed with my remarks on the present unnatural and absurd position of Czechoslovakia. If there was a possibility here of settling the question by peaceful political means, the British Government was prepared to enter into serious negotiations. He asked me if the Führer were prepared to regard such a solution of the Czechoslovak problem as the beginning of further negotiations on a larger scale. The Führer had used the simile to an Englishman (he thought it was Lord Halifax) that European culture rested on two pillars which must be linked

[5] For details on the orchestration of this campaign by the Propaganda Ministry see Vol. 2 p. 395.

by a powerful arch: Great Britain and Germany. Great Britain and Germany were in fact the two countries in which the greatest order reigned and which were the best governed. Both were built up on the national principle, which had been designed by nature itself as the only working principle of human relationship. The reverse of this, Bolshevism, meant anarchy and barbarism. It would be the height of folly if these two leading white races were to exterminate each other in war. Bolshevism would be the gainer thereby.

Wilson then turned to Germany's south-eastern policy. A constructive solution of the Czech question by peaceful means would leave the way clear for Germany to exert large-scale policy in the south-east. He himself was not one of those who held the view that Germany wanted to organize south-eastern Europe and then to use its resources for the annihilation of the British Empire. In these areas he could see possibilities of action for Germany better than any that could be imagined. The Balkan countries were the natural buyers of German manufactured goods, and on the other hand were the natural sources of raw materials essential to Germany. There was no sense in sending a turkey from Budapest to London instead of to Berlin. Neither had Great Britain any intention of opposing development by Germany in a south-easterly direction. Her only wish was that she should not be debarred from trade there. . . .

The implication of this conversation was clear. Britain was quite prepared for Germany to annex the Sudetenland, provided she did it by negotiation. Britain was also willing for Germany to turn the whole of south-east Europe into a German sphere of influence. This, it was hoped, would appease Germany and enable Europe to settle down into a situation where no single power would claim dominance. If, however, Germany insisted on military action, this would have to be resisted, however, unwillingly, because such action would imply a German claim to hegemony which would threaten the other major powers. This was to be the basic line followed by Britain throughout the rest of the crisis.

Hitler's campaign culminated in a violent speech to the Nuremberg Party rally on 12 September in which he demanded self-determination for the Sudeten Germans and threatened war. This in turn brought to a head the increasing anxiety of the British and French Governments about becoming involved in a war with Germany over Czechoslovakia. Chamberlain decided that a final approach should be made to Hitler to try to reach a peaceful solution. On 15 September, therefore, the British Prime Minister flew to Hitler's residence at Berchtesgaden in Bavaria.

Hitler was delighted. Chamberlain's visit offered him the opportunity of persuading Britain to demand from Czechoslovakia the cession of the Sudetenland. When the Czechs refused, as he assumed they would, Britain would, he believed, wash its hands of Czechoslovakia, and France would be obliged to follow suit. Hitler began the interview by saying that since his youth he had had the idea of Anglo–German cooperation and that although in recent years 'this idealistic belief in Anglo–German racial affinity had suffered very severe blows' he still hoped that 'at the eleventh hour' it would be possible to achieve the agreement he had been seeking.[6] He then came to the crux of the matter. There was, he said, only one problem outstanding, Czechoslovakia, which he would solve by one means or another. He was already forty-nine and if there had to be a world war he would prefer it now rather than later. The question was 'Would Britain agree to the secession of these areas [the Sudetenland] or would she not?' If Britain publicly announced its agreement, 'then no doubt it would be possible by this means to bring about a degree of pacification in the regions in question'. Chamberlain replied that he 'recognized the principle of the detachment of the Sudeten areas' and thought that, provided this were done peacefully, it might offer a solution.

Chamberlain then returned to London and under British and French pressure the Czechs agreed to the secession of the Sudetenland. This was of course not at all what Hitler had expected or desired. However, he had taken precautions against just such an eventuality. During the conversation at Berchtesgaden, Chamberlain had asked Hitler whether the Sudeten Germans were all that Germany was interested in or whether 'she was not aiming over and above this at the dismemberment of the Czechoslovak State'. Hitler replied that 'apart from the demands of the Sudeten Germans similar demands would of course be made by the Poles, Hungarians and Ukrainians living in Czechoslovakia which it would be impossible to ignore in the long run, but that he was not of course their spokesman'. Now, however, he proceeded to provoke these demands. Thus, at an interview with the Hungarian Prime Minister and Foreign Minister on 21 September, recorded by an official of the Foreign Ministry, Hitler

525

. . . reproached the Hungarian gentlemen for the undecided attitude of Hungary in the present time of crisis. He, the Führer, was determined to settle the Czech question even at the risk of a world war. Germany demanded the entire German area. He was convinced that neither England nor France would intervene. It was Hungary's last opportunity to join in, for, if she did not, he would not be in a position to put in a word for Hungarian interests. In his opinion the best thing would be to destroy Czechoslovakia. In the long run it was quite impossible to tolerate the existence of this aircraft carrier in the heart of Europe. He presented two demands to the Hungarians: (1) that Hungary should make an immediate

[6] For the following see *Documents on German Foreign Policy,* series D Vol. 2 Dor No. 487 and *Documents diplomatigues français* 2d. Series Vol 11, Doc. No. 188.

demand for a plebiscite in the territories which she claimed, and (2) that she should not guarantee any proposed new frontiers for Czechoslovakia. In certain circumstances Hungary might threaten to resign from the League of Nations and to establish a Freikorps. The Czechoslovak problem would be settled by the Führer in three weeks' time at the latest. . . .

The Führer declared further that he would present the German demands to Chamberlain with brutal frankness. In his opinion, action by the Army would provide the only satisfactory solution. There was, however, the danger of the Czechs submitting to every demand. . . .

Prime Minister Imrédy promised to send the Führer today a document, to be treated as confidential, in which Hungarian demands would be set down in detail. The Führer intends to make good use of this document at Godesberg in talks with the British.

Counsellor of Legation Brücklmeier gave me the further information that Ambassador Lipski had been requested to obtain a similar document from the Polish Government. . . .

Chamberlain returned to Germany on 22 September with the Czech agreement to secession in his pocket. At the meeting with Hitler at Bad Godesberg, according to the postwar account of Ivone Kirkpatrick, Head of Chancery at the British Embassy in Berlin, who was present, Chamberlain began by proudly announcing that he had secured the Czech Government's consent:

526

. . . Mr Chamberlain recalled that at Berchtesgaden Hitler had declared that he would be satisfied with nothing but self-determination, that was to say Anschluss, for the Sudeten Germans. He himself had been unable to give an immediate reply, but he had undertaken to consult his Cabinet and the French Government. He had done so and was happy to say that the British and French Governments agreed in principle. Moreover they had been able just in time to secure the assent of the Czechoslovak Government. The question of principle having been settled, it only remained to discuss the ways and means of transferring the territory in an orderly manner. On this point he had proposals to make which would doubtless be the subject of discussion at the present meeting. The statement was then translated into German. As Schmidt[7] finished speaking, Mr Chamberlain looked inquiringly at Hitler. But Hitler merely gazed down the table and said in a dry rasping voice: 'Es tut mir leid, aber das geht nicht mehr.'And with these words he pushed his chair back from the table, crossed his legs, folded his arms and turned to scowl at Mr Chamberlain. Schmidt translated: 'I am very sorry, but all that is no longer any use.' There was a long pause of pained silence.

---

[7] Paul Schmidt, Hitler's official interpreter (eds).

That was the atmosphere in which the Godesberg peace negotiations began. Mr Chamberlain, when he had recoverd from his amazement, acidly inquired why an arrangement which had been declared satisfactory to Germany a few days before had now become unacceptable. Hitler rather lamely replied that Mr Chamberlain's proposals were no longer sufficient because in the meantime Hungary and Poland had tabled new claims on Czechoslovakia. Hungary and Poland, he added, were good friends and Germany would insist that their claims must be met.

We seemed to have reached a deadlock, but for internal reasons Hitler did not want an early breakdown. So after a considerable period of ill-tempered floundering on both sides he suggested that it might be well to have a look at Mr Chamberlain's proposals in regard to the ways and means of meeting the German demands. Hitler listened to these proposals with increasing impatience and replied that he must decline to accept them on the ground that they involved an intolerable delay. Whilst we were arguing, he said, Germans were being killed by the Czechs, and that was a state of affairs for which he could not be responsible. At intervals little scraps of paper were sent in to Hitler reporting fresh outrages against the Sudeten Germans. No, he shouted, the territory within the so-called language boundary must be ceded at once, without any delay, and occupied by German troops. Mr Chamberlain said that he could not accept an immediate German military irruption. Let Hitler send in police if public order were threatened, but British opinion would be outraged by a military occupation. Hitler must remember that Britain was not ruled by a dictator and that he should take into account the Prime Minister's situation before Parliament and the public. Hitler characteristically retorted that his role depended on the suffrage of the German people and Mr Chamberlain must take into account the rising anger of the German nation at the Czech maltreatment of Germans. The argument waxed hotly and Schmidt had a trying time.

During his conversation with Chamberlain, Hitler had insisted that the Czechs should evacuate the Sudetenland between 26 and 28 September. On the following day, he postponed the date to 1 October. He claimed this to be a great concession but in fact it made no difference since his military plans for an invasion had all along been fixed for 1 October. Chamberlain agreed to put Hitler's terms to the British and Czech Governments. On 25 September, the British Cabinet decided they could not recommend the terms to Czechoslovakia and, on the following day, Britain promised France support in the event of her becoming involved in a war with Germany in defence of Czechoslovakia. On the same day, Germany was informed of the rejection of Hitler's demands by the Czechs. Yet far from deflecting Hitler from his proposed course of action, this news made him even more belligerent. In a speech in the Berlin Sports Palace that evening he outdid himself in violent abuse of the Czechs. He warned that he had made the Czech Prime Minister 'an offer which is nothing but the carrying out of what he himself had promised. The decision now lies in his hands:

Peace or War'.[8] He ended, however, by publicly thanking Chamberlain 'for all his efforts' and assuring him once more 'that at the moment when Czechoslovakia solves her problems, that is to say, when the Czechs have come to terms with their other minorities, and that peaceably and not through oppression, then I shall have no further interest in the Czech State. And I can guarantee him we want no Czechs.'

In the days following the Sports Palace speech, however, a number of developments caused Hitler to draw back from the brink. In the first place news came of the beginning of French mobilization and of the mobilization of the British fleet, suggesting that the Western Powers were not bluffing. Moreover, the Army and Navy leaders made clear their doubts of Germany's ability to face a war with Britain and France while simultaneously engaged against Czechoslovakia. Secondly, Göring advised against war and Mussolini, while assuring Hitler of his support, made clear his concern. Finally, Hitler observed with his own eyes the unenthusiastic response of the German people to the military preparations. Thus, when the British Government appealed to Mussolini to mediate and when Mussolini gave his support to the idea of an international conference to discuss the issue, Hitler grudgingly agreed. It was arranged that a conference between Germany, Italy, Britain and France should be held immediately in Munich. The conference took place on 29 September and the basis for discussion was provided by a memorandum which had been drafted by Neurath, Göring and Weizsäcker in order to circumvent Ribbentrop who was opposed to the idea of a conference. The memorandum was then shown to Hitler and, after its approval, was passed to the Italians who then produced it at the conference as if it was their own. Agreement was finally reached on the early morning of the 30th:

527

Germany, the United Kingdom, France and Italy, taking into consideration the agreement which has already been reached in principle for the cession to Germany of the Sudeten German territory, have agreed on the following terms and conditions governing the said cession and the measures consequent thereon, and by this agreement they each hold themselves responsible for the steps necessary to secure fulfilment:

1. The evacuation shall begin on 1 October.
2. The United Kingdom, France and Italy agree that the evacuation of the territory shall be completed by 10 October, without any existing installations having been

[8] Cf. M. Domarus, ed. *Hitler: Reden und Proklamationen 1932–1945* (Neustadt 1962) Vol. 1 pp. 923–33.

destroyed, and that the Czechoslovak Government shall be held responsible for carrying out the evacuation without damage to the said installations.
3. The conditions governing the evacuation shall be laid down in detail by an international commission composed of representatives of Germany, the United Kingdom, France, Italy and Czechoslovakia.
4. The occupation by stages of the predominantly German territory by German troops shall begin on 1 October. The four territories marked on the attached map will be occupied by German troops in the following order: The territory marked No. I on 1 and 2 October, the territory marked No. II on 2 and 3 October, the territory marked No. III on 3, 4 and 5 October, the territory marked No. IV on 6 and 7 October. The remaining territory of preponderantly German character shall be ascertained by the aforesaid international commission forthwith and shall be occupied by German troops by 10 October.
5. The international commission referred to in Paragraph 3 shall determine the territories in which a plebiscite is to be held. These territories shall be occupied by international bodies until the plebiscite has been completed. The same commission shall fix the conditions on which the plebiscite is to be held, taking as a basis the conditions of the Saar plebiscite. The commission shall also fix a date, not later than the end of November, on which the plebiscite shall be held.
6. The final determination of the frontiers shall be carried out by the international commission. This commission shall also be entitled to recommend to the four Powers, Germany, the United Kingdom, France and Italy, in certain exceptional cases, minor modifications in the strictly ethnographical determination of the zones which are to be transferred without plebiscite.
7. There shall be a right of option into and out of the transferred territories, the option to be exercised within six months from the date of this agreement. A German–Czechoslovak commission shall determine the details of the option, consider ways of facilitating the transfer of population and settle questions of principle arising out of the said transfer.
8. The Czechoslovak Government shall within a period of four weeks from the date of this agreement release from their military and police forces any Sudeten Germans who may wish to be released, and the Czechoslovak Government shall within the same period release Sudeten German prisoners who are serving terms of imprisonment for political offences.

Annex to the Agreement

His Majesty's Government in the United Kingdom and the French Government have entered into the above agreement on the basis that they stand by the offer, contained in Paragraph 6 of the Anglo–French proposals of 19 September, relating to an international guarantee of the new boundaries of the Czechoslovak State against unprovoked aggression.

When the question of the Polish and Hungarian minorities in Czechoslovakia has been settled, Germany and Italy for their part shall give a guarantee to Czechoslovakia.

The Munich Agreement, then, enabled Hitler to march his troops into the Sudetenland on 1 October after all. The fact that this was to be done in stages after international agreement made no difference in practice. The plebiscite envisaged in paragraph 5 was never held and the cession of the Sudetenland, which was followed on 10 October by the cession of Teschen to Poland, meant that Czechoslovakia was now totally exposed to any future attack since the area ceded included the fortifications and the mountains which formed a natural barrier.

It has been disputed among historians whether or not Hitler was bluffing all along during the Munich crisis. In fact, there is evidence from several sources to suggest that, far from feeling elated about the agreement as one would expect had he been bluffing, he resented being, as he thought, cheated of a military victory, Thus, according to Ivone Kirkpatrick, during the conference 'he was obviously in a black mood, furious with the whole business', and on his return to Berlin Schacht overheard him remarking to SS officers: 'That fellow Chamberlain has spoiled my entry into Prague.' The State Secretary in the Foreign Ministry, von Weizsäcker, summed up his view of the background to the Agreement in an entry in his diary on 9 October 1938:

528

. . .We appeared to have won the game when Chamberlain announced his visit to the Obersalzberg [Berchtesgaden] in order to preserve peace. This represented a rejection of Czechoslovakia's crisis politics. One could have reached an agreement without difficulty, on the basis of English mediation, about how the Sudetenland was to be split off and transferred to us in a peaceful manner.

However, we were dominated by the determination to have a war of revenge and destruction against Czechoslovakia. Thus, we conducted the second phase of discussions with Chamberlain in Bad Godesberg in such a way that, despite our basic agreement, what had been decided was bound to fail. The group who wanted war, namely Ribbentrop and the SS had nearly succeeded in prompting the Führer to attack. Among numerous similar statements made by the Führer in my presence during the night of 27–28 September was one to the effect that he would now annihilate Czechoslovakia. Ribbentrop and I were the sole witnesses of these words; they were not designed to have an effect on a third party.

Thus, the assumption that the Führer was intending a huge bluff is incorrect. His resentment stemming from 22 May, when the English accused him of pulling back, led him on to the path of war. I have not quite managed to establish what influences then finally decided him to issue invitations to the four power meeting in Munich on 28 October and thereby to leave the path of war. Naturally one can find 100 different reasons for this change of course. Herr von Neurath is quite wrong to describe himself as one of them because, in a dereliction of duty, he failed to make his voice heard in the months of June–September, including the 27–29 September.

Two factors were probably decisive: (a) His observation that our people regarded the approach of war with a silent obstructiveness and were far from enthusiastic. (Dr Goebbels said that loudly to the Führer at table in the Reich Chancellery over the heads of all those present), and (b) Mussolini's appeal at the last moment, i.e. on the morning of the 28th, when the mobilization was planned for 2 p.m. The idea of a four power conference was first mentioned in my presence by the Führer and received general and warm approval with the exception of those referred to above. Herr von Ribbentrop was still working against the agreement on the evening of the 28th and on the 29th since he obviously considered war to the best solution.

The fact that the 29th could be an important date for the future orientation of Europe was clear to everyone. However, such a shift did not accord with the aims of Germany i.e. its decision-makers. This was already apparent in the negotiations in the International Commission where, for reasons which are not clear, we pushed through the boundary settlement in a rapacious fashion instead of letting the plebiscite on the Sudetenland border go ahead. To ensure the permanence of the boundary over the long term the latter procedure would undoubtedly have been better.

Hitler had evidently been shocked by the pacific attitude displayed by the Geman people during the crisis. On 10 November he outlined his views on the impotant role of propaganda during the Czech crisis and in preparing the nation for war in a secret speech made to a gathering of 400 representatives of the German press in Munich.

529

We have set ourselves several tasks this year which we want to achieve through our propaganda—and I consider the press present here among the main instruments of propaganda.

First, the gradual preparation of the German people themselves. For years circumstances have compelled me to talk about almost nothing but peace. Only by continually stressing Germany's desire for peace and her peaceful intentions could I achieve freedom for the German people bit by bit and provide the armaments which were always necessary before the next step could be taken. It is obvious that such peace propaganda also has its doubtful aspects, for it can only too easily give people the idea that the present regime really identifies itself with the determination to preserve peace at all costs. That would not only lead to a wrong assessment of the aims of this system, but above all it might lead to the German nation, instead of being prepared for every eventuality, being filled with a spirit of defeatism which in the long run would inevitably undermine the success of the present regime. It was only out of necessity that for years I talked of peace. But it was now necessary gradually to re-educate the German people psychologically and to make it clear that there are things which *must* be achieved by force if peaceful means fail. To do this, it was necessary not to advocate force as such, but to depict to the German people certain diplomatic events in such a light that the inner voice of the nation itself gradually began to call for the use of force. That meant, to portray certain events in such a way that the conviction automatically grew in the minds of the broad mass of the people: If things cannot be settled amicably, force will have to be used, but in any case things cannot go on like this. This work took months; it was begun according to plan, carried out according to plan, and intensified. Many people did not understand this, gentlemen; many thought all this was rather exaggerated. Those were the over-cultured intellectuals who have no idea, even when the thunder and lightning start, how one gets a nation to stand together.

. . . Furthermore, it was necessary to use the press and other propaganda methods to influence the enemy which confronted us, namely Czechoslovakia. There may have been some people who did not understand many of the measures taken during the past few years. Gentlemen! After 21 May it was quite clear that this problem had to be solved one way or another [*so oder so*]! Each further postponement could only make it more difficult and make its solution more bloody. Now we know also that it was, I would say, the last moment at which this problem could be solved in the way it was solved. One thing is certain, gentlemen: a delay of only one or two years would have put us into an extraordinarily difficult situation from the military point of view. Our enemies in the rest of the world would have remained. The aircraft carrier in the heart of Germany [i.e. Czechoslovakia] would have strengthened and fortified itself more and more, and gradually all the additional weapons produced by our rearmament programme would have been swallowed up by the task of having to solve this problem first before tackling any other. . . .

It was vital for this problem to be solved now. It could no longer be postponed. The preparations which had to be carried out for the first time for the ultimate event were so tremendous that concealment no longer seemed feasible. Above all, one could no longer assume that in the circumstances our neighbours would have believed in it any longer. Somehow, I think that this disc, the pacifist disc, is now worn out as far as we are concerned. People would probably no longer have listened to this melody or believed in its content. I was convinced that the only way left was the other one, that is to tell the truth quite brutally and ruthlessly, no more and no less. In my view that must in the long run have a paralysing effect on the state which was most affected [i.e. Czechoslovakia] . . . I was convinced that through this activity going on for months I would slowly but surely destroy the nerves of these gentlemen in Prague. And the press had to help in this. It had to cooperate in slowly grinding down the nerves of these people, and in fact they did not stand up to it.

I would like to state now that this propaganda has worked superbly this year, quite superbly and that the press has got completely used to this work and that I personally looked through the numerous German papers each day with great pleasure. . . . The greatness of this success became clearest to me at that moment when, for the first time, I stood in the middle of the Czech fortifications. Then it became clear to me what it means to capture nearly 2000 km. of fortifications without having fired a shot. Gentlemen, this time we really have gained 10 million people with over 100,000 square km. through propaganda in the service of an idea. That is tremendous! . . .

The press, gentlemen, can achieve tremendous things and have a tremendous effect if it is a means to an end.

We have tried to mould the press into an effective weapon like that here in Germany. And, as this year comes to an end, I can assure all of you that I am more than content with this attempt. It has proved itself to be brilliantly effective. We still have major tasks in front of us. There is one task, gentlemen, which is the most important of all. We must now step by step strengthen the self-confidence of the German people. I realize that that is not a task that can be achieved in one or two years. What we need is a firm and strong public opinion, if possible extending into our intellectual circles (movement and laughter). You must realize that it is only in this way that a successful policy can be pursued in the long term . . .

Gentleman, it used to be my greatest pride to have built up a Party that stood behind me steadfastly and fanatically even in bad times—especially in bad times. That was my greatest pride and a tremendous comfort. We must get the whole German people to do this. They must learn to believe in final victory so *fanatically* that even if we were occasionally defeated, the nation would regard it from an overall point of view and say: This is a temporary phase; victory will be ours in the end! It was a Prussian general who best illustrated this character trait—Blücher, the man who was perhaps more defeated than anyone else, but who had a fanatical belief in final victory, and that was what mattered. We must educate our whole nation to that end. They must be educated to the absolute, steadfast, optimistic belief that in the end we will achieve all that is necessary. We can only succeed in this by a continuous appeal to the strength of the nation, by stressing the qualities of the nation and by disregarding the so-called negative sides as much as possible.

To achieve this, it is also necessary for the press in particular to hold blindly to the principle: The leadership is always right! Gentlemen, we must all be allowed to make mistakes. Newspapermen are not exempt from that danger either. But all of us can only survive if we do not let the world see our mistakes but only the positive things. In other words, it is necessary, by removing any possibility of admitting mistakes or of argument, always to stress the correctness of the leadership. That is the decisive point. . . .

Above all, that is necessary for the sake of the people, for I often hear people ask the question—it is a regression to liberal notions: Shouldn't one put that to the nation sometime? Well, gentlemen, you know I have the feeling that I have achieved a fair amount, at any rate more than some shoemaker or some milkmaid or other. Nevertheless, it may well happen of course that I do not quite agree in the assessment of a problem with other gentlemen who have also achieved quite a lot. What is certain, however, is that a decision has to be taken. It would be quite impossible for me to put this decision in the hands of dairymaids, herdsmen, and shoemakers. That is impossible. So, it does not matter at all whether in the final analysis such a decision is absolutely right. That is completely irrelevant. What is decisive is that the whole nation closes ranks behind that decision. There must be a united front and then whatever is not quite right about the decision will be compensated for by the determination with which the nation stands behind it . . .

In front of the people there can only be one opinion. Gentlemen, that is an absolutely clear principle. If we insist on that absolutely then the German people will become great and powerful through this leadership. Then in 1938 we shall not be at the end of an historical epoch but we will be only at the beginning of a great historic epoch of our nation . . .

Despite his bloodless victory in the Sudetenland, Hitler was by no means satisfied with the Munich Agreement. He now believed that he had been wrongly advised and that Britain and France would not after all have gone to war over Czechoslovakia. He saw the Agreement as an attempt by the Western powers to lock Germany into international arrangements designed to limit her freedom of manoeuvre in general and his ambitions in Eastern Europe in particular. He had no intention of giving the guarantee of the boundaries of Czechoslovakia contained in the annex to the agreement. He still found the existence of an independent Czechoslovakia intolerable and it was really only a question of time before he took steps to eliminate it. This intention became clear in the military directive which he signed on 21 October 1938:

530

The future tasks of the Wehrmacht and the preparations for the conduct of war resulting from these tasks will be laid down by me in a later directive.

Until this directive comes into force, the Wehrmacht must at all times be prepared for the following eventualities:

1. securing the frontiers of the German Reich and protection against surprise air attacks;
2. liquidation of the remainder of the Czech State;
3. the occupation of Memelland. . . .

2. LIQUIDATION OF THE REMAINDER OF THE CZECH STATE

It must be possible to smash at any time the remainder of the Czech State should it pursue an anti-German policy. . . .

In fact, the new Czech Government went out of its way to be accommodating towards Germany. But this was not enough for Hitler. As far as he was concerned. the fact that Czechoslovakia retained some independence and the fact that it still retained a significant army and military resources meant that it represented a troublesome wedge in Germany's south-eastern flank which would still pose a threat to Germany in the event of her being involved in war on her other frontiers. In addition, there was his personal resentment against the Czechs which made him sensitive to the least provocation. In short, after Munich the question was only how and when the remnants of Czechoslovak independence could be destroyed.

In a secret speech to a large number of senior officers on 10 February 1939, Hitler reviewed the developments in foreign policy since the Nazi take-over of power. Although his emphasis on the extent to which events had gone according to plan must be taken, in part at any rate, as an *ex post facto* assessment, the speech is illuminating both on the extent to which Hitler believed he was following a programme and in showing his increased self-confidence since 1933:

531

All our actions during 1938 represent only the logical extension of the decisions which began to be realized in 1933. It is not the case that during this year of 1938—let us say—a particular action occurred which was not previously envisaged. On the contrary, all the individual decisions which have been realized since 1933 are not the result of momentary considerations but represent the implementation of a previously existing plan, though perhaps not exactly according to the schedule which was envisaged. For example, in 1933 I was not exactly certain when the withdrawal from the League of Nations would occur. However, it was clear that this withdrawal had to be the first step towards Germany's revival. And it was further clear that we would have to choose the first appropriate moment. We could see from the start that the next step would have to be rearmament without the permission of foreign countries, but naturally we could not gauge the exact speed and extent of this rearmament right from the start. It was also further obvious that, after certain period of rearmament, Germany would have to take the daring step of proclaiming to the world its freedom from restrictions on rearmament. At the beginning, naturally one could not foresee the right moment for this step. Finally, it was further clear that every further step must first involve the remilitarization of the Rhineland. The date for this was in fact envisaged as being one year later: I did not think I would carry it out until 1937. The circumstances at the time made it seem appropriate to carry it out as early as 1936. It was also quite obvious that the Austrian and the Czech problems would have to be solved in order further to strengthen Germany's political and, in particular, her strategic position. To start with, I was not quite sure whether both problems ought to be or could be solved simultaneously or whether one should deal first with the question of Czechoslovakia or with the Austrian questions. There was no doubt that these questions would have to be solved and so all these decisions were not ideas which were realized at the moment of their conception, but were long-made plans which I was determined to realise the moment I thought the circumstances at the time would be favourable.

After Munich Hitler was merely waiting for a favourable moment to deal with Czechoslovakia. As far as the methods were concerned, the same weapon lay ready to hand that he had used so successfully before—ethnic disaffection. Whereas previously he had used the Sudeten Germans as a lever against the Czech Government, now he proposed to use the Slovaks in a similar role. After Munich, the Czech Government had been forced to give a considerable degree of autonomy to the Slovaks, and Hitler now proceeded to encourage the Slovaks to claim complete independence. Eventually, the Czechs responded to the growing Slovak separatism by dismissing the Slovak Government on 9 March 1939 and by declaring martial law. The new Slovak Government opposed secession and in this it appears to have had the support of the majority of the Slovak people. Hitler, however, had no intention of allowing this opportunity to pass. On 13 March, he presented the former Slovak Prime Minister, Tisò, with an ultimatum: he was either to declare that the Slovaks desired independence, or to stand by and let Hungary, which had designs on Slovakia, take over the country:

532

. . . He wanted a final confirmation as to what Slovakia really wanted. He did not want Hungary to reproach him for preserving something which did not want to be preserved. . . . It was a question not of days but of hours. He had previously said that if Slovakia wished to become independent he would support and even guarantee her efforts in that direction. He would keep his promise so long as Slovakia clearly expressed the desire for independence. If she hesitated or refused to be separated from Prague he would leave the fate of Slovakia to events for which he was no longer responsible. Then he would look after German interests only, and they did not extend east of the Carpathians. Germany had nothing to do with Slovakia. She had never belonged to Germany.

. . . The Reich Foreign Minister also emphasized that a decision was a matter of hours, not days, He handed to the Führer a report just received announcing Hungarian troop movements on the Slovak frontier. The Führer read this report, told Tiso of its contents and expressed the hope that Slovakia would reach a decision soon. . . .

Tiso then returned to Slovakia and pushed the declaration of independence through Parliament under the threat of German occupation if it were not accepted.

Hitler was genuine in his assurance that Germany had no interest in Slovakia. It was a predominantly agricultural area and its situation posed no strategic threat to Germany. He was therefore content for it to remain a satellite of Germany. It was the Czech areas of Bohemia and Moravia, industrialised and strategically important, whose independence Hitler was determined to eliminate. The significance for Hitler of Slovakia's demand for independence was that it enabled the British and French Governments to evade their Munich guarantee of the boundaries of Czechoslovakia on the ground that the State had already disintegrated from within.

On 14 March, the Czech Government made a desperate attempt to avert the German invasion, President Hácha and the Foreign Minister, Chvalkovsky, travelled to Berlin to make a direct appeal to Hitler. Hitler, however, had already given orders for the invasion to begin. His justification of his action to Hácha significantly laid stress on the size of the Czech army:

533

. . . In the autumn he had not wished to draw the final conclusions because he had thought a coexistence possible, but already at that time, and later during his conversations with Chvalkovsky, he had left no doubt that if the Beneš[9] tendencies did not disappear completely he would destroy this State ruthlessly. Chvalkovsky had understood that at the time and had begged the Führer to have patience. The Führer had recognized this, but months had passed without any change taking place. The new regime had not succeeded in making the old one disappear psychologically; he saw this in the press, in propaganda by word of mouth, in the dismissal of Germans, and in many acts which were to him symbolic of the whole situation. He had not understood this at first, but when it had become clear to him he definitely drew his conclusions, for, had things continued to develop along these lines, the relationship with Czechoslovakia would, in a few years, again be exactly where it had been six months ago. Why had Czechoslovakia not at once reduced her Army to reasonable proportions? Such an Army was a tremendous burden for such a State; it made sense only if it supported the State in its role in foreign affairs. As, however, the Czechoslovak State no longer had a role in foreign affairs, such an Army had no justification. He quoted several examples which had proved to him that the spirit in the Army had not changed. This symptom had convinced him that the Army also was a heavy political liability for the future. Add to this the relentless development of a situation of economic stringency, and furthermore the protests from the minorities who could no longer put up with a life of this kind. . . .

President Hácha was then threatened with the bombing of Prague if he did not order the Czech troops to lay down their arms. After suffering a heart attack, from which he was revived by an injection from Hitler's doctor, he agreed to sign a communiqué which in its unctuous mendacity was remarkable even for the Nazis:

534

. . . The conviction was unanimously expressed on both sides that the aim of all efforts must be the safeguarding of calm, order and peace in this part of central

[9] The former Czech President (eds).

Europe. The Czechoslovak President declared that, in order to serve this object and to achieve ultimate pacification, he confidently placed the fate of the Czech people and country in the hands of the Führer of the German Reich. The Führer accepted this declaration and expressed his intention of taking the Czech people under the protection of the German Reich and of guaranteeing them an autonomous development of their ethnic life as suited to their character.

In the meantime German troops had already crossed the Czech border on their way to Prague.

(iv) The 'Z Plan' and problems of German rearmament

Meanwhile, the events of 1938 had exacerbated the problems of German rearmament. Although the Navy had managed to secure a measure of priority at the 'Hossbach meeting' on 5 November 1937, Hitler had increased his demands on it after the 'May Crisis' of 1938, while simultaneously launching the crash programme for the construction of the West Wall which absorbed vast quantities of labour and building materials. Moreover, in view of the impending war with Czechoslovakia, the Army and the Air Force had managed to assert claims for priority with some success. Finally, after Munich Hitler had ordered a fivefold increase in the Air Force to meet the threat from Britain. Since Germany did not have the resources to meet all these demands simultaneously, which ultimately flowed from Hitler's own promptings and decisions, by the winter of 1938 the Führer was obliged to confront the difficult question of priorities.

There were not only problems over the competition for scarce resources but also differences over strategy. A number of naval chiefs were unhappy about Hitler's emphasis on the construction of large battleships preferring to concentrate on cruisers, destroyers, and U-Boats which, it was thought, would prove more effective in a war with Britain who, since May 1938, had emerged as Germany's main potential naval opponent. They failed to appreciate that Hitler was primarily concerned not with meeting an immediate threat from Britain, which he thought unlikely, but rather with the construction of a large battle fleet with which Germany could take on both United States and if necessary Britain after having secured a continental empire. He did not envisage this war for world hegemony before 1944 at the earliest by which time the first ten battleships would have been built. In the meantime, a limited expansion of U-Boat construction and an acceleration of the first battleships would serve as a deterrent to a Britain which in his view lacked the will to fight.

In November 1938, confronted by Raeder with the prospect of a delay in the completion of the naval programme until 1947/8, and urged to postpone the battleships in favour of U-Boat construction, Hitler refused to budge. Threatening to hand over naval tasks to the Air Force if the Navy could not do the job, he insisted on priority being given to his original plan of an additional six large battleships to be completed by 1944, telling Raeder: 'If I could build the Third Reich in six years then surely the Navy can build these six ships in six years.'[10] On 17 January 1939, a new 'Z Plan' was agreed which envisaged four pocket battleships (*Panzerschiffe*) being completed by 1943 and six larger battleships (H Class) by 1944. These would have priority over U-Boat and other naval construction going on simultaneously. To enable Raeder to achieve this, Hitler agreed to his request for priority for naval requirements over all other claims on German resources. On 27 January, he signed the following edict:

535

It is my express wish that the naval construction which I have ordered should be given priority over all other tasks including the rearmament of the other two services and including exports. The construction covers the implementation of the new programme as well as the maintenance of the preparedness of the naval forces for war.

The Commander-in-Chief of the Navy shall put direct and indirect requests for personnel, materials, and finance to the Delegate of the Four Year Plan, Field-Marshal Göring, who is responsible for ensuring their urgent fulfilment on schedule by conveying corresponding instructions to the Reich agencies involved.

On the same day, Hitler agreed to Göring's request to transfer operational control over the fleet air arm from the Navy to the Luftwaffe, presumably envisaging that Göring's Air Force would in the short term compensate for the lack of a fleet specially designed for attacking Britain.

With Hitler's edict in his pocket Raeder had some success in increasing the allocation of resources to the Navy. Thus, the Navy increased its quota of iron and steel from 12 per cent of total *Wehrmacht* consumption in the second half of 1938 to 26 per cent in the first half of 1939 and 31 per cent in the second half, of nickel from 33–46.6–63.3 per cent, and other raw materials correspondingly.

This reallocation of resources within the *Wehrmacht* did not, however, resolve the crucial problem of German rearmament, namely the failure of Germany's resources to match the demands made upon them.[11] For example, by February 1939, there was already a shortage of one million workers and the Army Ordinance Office estimated that for all the various pro-

[10] Cf. J. Dülffer, *Hitler und die Marine* op. cit., p. 502 to which this section is much indebted.

[11] For further material on German economic constraints see vol. 2 pp. 292 ff.

grammes to be carried out an 870 per cent increase in the number of workers would be necessary. Moreover, there were limits on the extent to which the German labour force could be mobilized—at any rate in peacetime—because of shortages in housing in industrial areas and the unpopularity of labour conscription. In this situation the regime turned increasingly to the recruitment of foreign labour initially through voluntary means in countries such as Poland and Italy. Significantly, by 1 June 1939, 40,000 skilled workers had been acquired from defeated Czechoslovakia, not to mention large quantities of military equipment, raw materials, and productive capacity. Three German armoured divisions were equipped with Czech combat vehicles for the French campaign. Plunder was emerging as the way out of Germany's constraints most appropriate to the Nazi regime.

This question of the relationship between demands and the resources to meet them raised major political and strategic issues. The *Wehrmacht* Economic Office under General Thomas was in theory responsible for the coordination of the demands of the three services on the economy. Thomas wished to implement systematic arrangements for the allocation of scarce resources on the basis of a comprehensive armaments programme involving a clear set of priorities. Hitler, however, refused to permit his freedom of action to be restricted in any way. Thus, significantly, Raeder had secured priority for the naval programme by bypassing the *Wehrmacht* High Command and securing an edict from Hitler. Under pressure from the rapidly developing international situation between 1933–39, to which his own actions had largely contributed, Hitler was continually shifting his priorities. He tended simply to encourage each of the service chiefs to press ahead with achieving their own particular goals, sometimes, as in the case of the Navy, with the threat of transferring tasks to a rival if they proved insufficiently committed. Moreover, the fact that the various stages in his programme, which had originally been intended to be achieved consecutively, had now been telescoped and were being carried out almost simultaneously meant that he required a massive expansion of the Navy, which was originally envisaged for the final stage, before the Army had secured the continental empire.

Hitler's sense of being under time pressure encouraged him to concentrate on the production of the immediate requirements of the three services: weapons, ammunition, equipment, and limited reserves (armament in breadth) rather than a proper coordination of the economy and the preparation of productive capacity and raw material supplies for a long war (armament in depth). It is true that the Four Year Plan represented an attempt to achieve a measure of 'armament in depth'. However, fulfilment of the plan was undermined by the pressures for the diversion of resources to more immediate tasks. In Hitler's eyes the Four Year Plan was essentially a stop-gap measure to avoid the worst bottlenecks until Germany could conquer the supplies of raw materials she needed. The combination of a head start over other powers in the supply of actual war *matériel* with the lack of means to expand production over the longer term led logically to a strategy of Blitzkrieg, by which Germany would expand her resources through a series of lightning predatory wars. By concentrating her limited but well-equipped forces, Germany would knock out her opponents one by one, seizing their resources in preparation for the next stage. Germany had in effect to make war in order to continue her rearmament in a vicious circle of destruction.

The emphasis on armament in breadth at the expense of armament in depth was criticized by General Thomas in a lecture given at the Foreign Ministry on 24 May 1939:

536

. . . In conclusion we can state that the total German rearmament, in the field of personnel as well as of war *matériel*, represents an achievement of the German people probably unique in the world, and a testimony to resolute leadership and to the energy and creativeness innate in the German people. The great efforts of German industry and of the German people in both finance and hard work have undoubtedly yielded the desired result and we can perceive today that German armament in its breadth and its state of preparedness has a considerable start over the armament of all other countries.

But if one compares the armament situation not in terms of its breadth and preparedness, but in terms of the depth of armament or, to put it another way, the possibility of endurance in the event of a new world war, the picture looks different. . . .

II

Gentlemen! All the time I have been in charge of my department, I have always pointed out the difference between armament in breadth and armament in depth.

By armament in breadth I mean the number and strength of the armed forces in peacetime and the preparations made to increase them in the event of war.

Armament in depth, on the other hand, embraces all those measures, particularly those affecting materials and of an economic nature, which serve to provide supplies during war and therefore strengthen our powers of endurance.

We are all clear about our present superiority in breadth and in the initial striking power of our armament; now we must analyse whether we can retain this superiority in an armaments race and thereby achieve superiority in depth of armament.

Allow me first to say a few words about the dangers which can develop if too much attention is paid to armament in breadth at the expense of armament in depth.

We all know that in every war, soon after the beginning of operations, a request comes for new formations and that then all available resources are recklessly released to provide these new formations. At the same time, there is a request for increased amounts of munitions and all the other necessities, and woe betide the leadership of economic warfare if it is not in a position to fulfil these demands owing to a lack of reserves of finished goods or raw materials and semi-finished products. Here again the old proverb still holds good: 'Save in time of plenty and you will have something in time of need.' You will understand if, particularly at the present time in which the sections of the armed forces are considerably enlarged every year, I emphasize in all seriousness the need of improving our armament in depth. . . .

The information which we have so far received does not indicate that the western Great Powers are as yet pursuing rearmament with the same energy as we are. But should the political situation lead to a long-drawn-out armaments race we must of course realize that the Western Powers, considering the capacity of their economies for producing armaments, will be in a position to catch up with the German lead in 1–1½ years. The combined economic strength of Britain, America, and France is in the long run greater than that of the Axis Powers and in an armaments race the Western Powers will not have the same difficulties which Germany and Italy will always have on account of their lack of raw materials and manpower. If it comes to such an armaments race and then to a war the result of that war will, in my opinion, depend on whether the Axis States succeed in bringing about a decision by a quick decisive blow. If they do not succeed in this, if it comes to a struggle like that of the World War, then the depth of military economic power, that is, the powers of endurance, will decide the issue.

It is not my task to speculate on the possible success or failure of such a lightning war [*Blitzkrieg*]. I myself do not believe that a conflict between the Axis Powers and the Western Powers will be a question of a lightning war, that is, a matter of days and weeks. As far as I am concerned, as Chief of Defence Economic Staff, it is essential for the armaments industry to be prepared for a long war. Our preparations must concentrate on strengthening our armament in depth as much as possible.

There are three particularly important points which must chiefly concern us in this connexion:

1. The securing of the German food situation;[12]
2. The securing of iron ore supplies;
3. The oil and rubber question. . . .

. . . Another problem is that considerable financial resources are called for and are employed on projects which do not serve German armament and could be postponed for a few years. At the moment our German economy is not 100 per cent employed but 125 per cent. And these superfluous 25 per cent are the contracts which bring disorder into the economy and lay upon us a considerable financial burden. In our present military and economic situaton, we must in my opinion follow one path only, that of bringing back the old order into the economy and concentrating all our economic resources on the strengthening of our economic armament.

---

[12] Thomas emphasizes in particular the shortage of fats (eds).

Concentration of our resources must be our watchword in all spheres, in personnel as in materials, in the regulation of manpower as in the distribution of raw materials and machinery. . . .

(v) The attack on Poland

One of the factors prompting Hitler to destroy the remnants of Czechoslovakia had been the desire to put pressure on Poland. The attitude of Poland would clearly be crucial for future German action either in the east or in the west. Hitler could attack neither France nor Russia without first being sure of Poland. During the winter of 1938–39, he appears to have been moving in the direction of an attack on Russia. Thus he cultivated good relations with France which, on 6 December, culminated in a joint declaration guaranteeing the existing frontier, that is, the abandonment by Germany of Alsace and Lorraine. In return, he clearly hoped that France would cease to interest herself in Eastern Europe despite her alliances with Poland and the U.S.S.R. German relations with Poland had been good since the Non-Aggression Pact of 1934 and, after the Munich Agreement, Poland had acquired Teschen from Czechoslovakia with Germany's connivance. But Hitler now wanted guarantees of Poland's good behaviour; he wanted to turn Poland into a satellite of Germany. Once Poland had accepted this position, he could undertake an attack on Russia with Poland as an ally, or if necessary turn against France.

As far as Hitler was concerned, the test of Polish willingness to become a satellite was whether or not she would agree to the return of Danzig, a German-speaking city placed by the Treaty of Versailles under the control of the League of Nations, and to a road and rail link through the 'Polish Corridor' which separated East Prussia from the rest of Germany. These demands were first put in a friendly way by Ribbentrop at a meeting with the Polish ambassador, Josef Lipski, on 24 October 1938. Lipski gave an evasive reply. But the Germans were not to be put off and when the Polish Foreign Minister, Beck, visited Berlin in January 1939, Hitler repeated these demands, at the same time hinting at their common hostility to Russia and that Germany would have no objection to Polish acquisitions in the Ukraine:

537

. . . On the part of Germany he could state emphatically that there had not been the slightest change in Germany's relations with Poland as based on the non-agression declaration of 1934. Germany would under all circumstances be interested in maintaining a strong nationalist Poland, quite irrespective of developments in

Russia. Regardless of whether Russia was Bolshevist or Tsarist or anything else, Germany's attitude towards that country would always be one of the greatest caution and for that reason she was decidedly interested in seeing Poland's position preserved. Purely from the military point of view the existence of a strong Polish Army meant a considerable easing of Germany's position; the divisions stationed by Poland at the Russian frontier saved Germany just so much additional military expenditure. . . .

From the German point of view the remaining problem in direct German–Polish relations, apart from the question of Memel, which would be settled in the German sense (it appeared that the Lithuanians intended to cooperate towards a sensible solution), was that of the Corridor and Danzig, on which Germany was psychologically very sensitive. . . .

Danzig is German, will always remain German, and will sooner or later become part of Germany. He could give the assurance, however, that no *fait accompli* would be engineered in Danzig.

With regard to the Corridor . . . the necessity for Poland to have access to the sea had definitely to be recognized. In the same way, however, to have a connexion with East Prussia was a necessity for Germany; here too, by using entirely new methods of solution one could perhaps do justice to the interests of both.

If it should be possible on this rational basis to bring about a definite settlement of the individual problems, which would of course have to do justice to both sides, the time would have come to supplement in a positive sense, in the manner of the agreements with France, the somewhat negative declaration of 1934 by a German guarantee of Poland's frontiers clearly laid down in a Treaty. Poland would then obtain the great advantage of having her frontier with Germany, including the Corridor, secured by Treaty. . . .

Beck's reply, however, was evasive. The Poles were determined to resist their inclusion in Germany's sphere of influence and recognized equally with the Germans that to yield on Danzig would be a tacit acceptance of satellite status. Their attitude has sometimes been interpreted as arrogance; it was certainly based on a gross overestimation of their own strength, clearly demonstrated by their continuing refusal to contemplate an agreement with Russia. But in view of Hitler's actions during 1938, their suspicions were understandable, while an agreement with Russia was also problematic. Poland's position was unenviable.

Three months after Beck's interview with Hitler came the German invasion of Czechoslovakia in which Hitler's motive was probably partly the desire to exert pressure on Poland to come to terms. If so, the impact of the invasion was the reverse of that intended. For Britain, now totally disillusioned by Hitler's annexation for the first time of non-German-speaking territory, decided to try to retrieve the situation by issuing a warning to Germany against further aggression. This warning took the form of a British guarantee of those countries which were regarded as most threatened by Germany—Poland, Romania and Greece. With a guarantee from Britain (31 March) in their pocket, the Poles were even less willing to accede to the German demands.

Hitler was furious at the British guarantee and on 3 April, seeing that now there was much less likelihood of Polish acquiescence, he ordered military preparations for an attack on Poland to begin at any time after 1 September. The directive for 'Operation White' (the attack on Poland), was issued on 11 April:

538

OPERATION WHITE

The present attitude of Poland requires, over and above the plan 'Frontier Security East' the initiation of military preparations, to remove if necessary any threat from this direction for ever.

1.) *Political Requirements and Aims*

German relations with Poland continue to be based on the principles of avoiding any disturbances. Should Poland, however, change her policy towards Germany, which so far has been based on the same principles as our own, and adopt a threatening attitude towards Germany, a final settlement might become necessary in spite of the Treaty in force with Poland.

The aim then will be to destroy Polish military strength, and create in the East a situation which satisfies the requirements of national defence. The Free State of Danzig will be proclaimed a part of the Reich territory at the outbreak of hostilities, at the latest.

The political leaders consider it their task in this case to isolate Poland if possible, that is to say, to limit the war to Poland only.

The development of increasing internal crises in France and resulting British restraint might produce such a situation in the not too distant future.

Intervention by Russia, if she were in a position to intervene, cannot be expected to be of any use to Poland, because this would mean Poland's destruction by Bolshevism.

The attitude of the Baltic States will be determined wholly by German military superiority.[13] (In the course of further developments it may become necessary to occupy the Baltic states up to the border of the former Courland and to incorporate them in the Reich.)

Germany cannot count on Hungary as a certain ally. Italy's attitude is determined by the Rome-Berlin Axis.

2.) *Military Conclusions*

The great objectives in the reconstruction of the German Wehrmacht will continue to be determined by the antagonism of the Western Democracies.

[13] The word 'superiority' is crossed out by hand in the original and 'demands' inserted (eds).

'Operation White' constitutes only a precautionary complement to these preparations. It is not to be looked upon in any way, however, as the necessary prerequisite for a military conflict with the Western opponents.

The isolation of Poland will be all the more easily maintained, even after the outbreak of hostilities, if we succeed in starting the war with sudden, heavy blows and in gaining rapid successes.

The overall situation will require, however, that in all cases precautions be taken to safeguard the western frontier and the German North Sea coast, as well as the air above them.

Against the Baltic States—Lithuania in particular—security measures are to be carried out in case of a Polish march through this country.

3.) *Tasks of the Wehrmacht*

The task of the Wehrmacht is to destroy the Polish Armed Forces.To this end a surprise attack is to be aimed at and prepared. Camouflaged or open general mobilization will not be ordered earlier than the day before the attack and at the latest possible moment. The forces provided for "Frontier Security West (section I, "Frontier Security") must not be employed for the time being for any other purpose.

All other frontiers are to be kept under observation only; the Lithuanian frontier is to be covered.

Hitler's first diplomatic success in his preparation for war with Poland was in securing at long last an alliance with Italy. During May, Mussolini had overcome his earlier qualms about tying himself in this way (Berlin had proposed the alliance in October 1938). His annexation of Albania in April, which had been opposed by the Western Powers, had driven him into greater dependence on Germany and so he now agreed to turn the Rome-Berlin axis into a 'Pact of Steel', a ten year 'pact of friendship and alliance' with Germany, which was signed on 22 May 1939. Hitler was delighted since he hoped it would increase pressure on Britain and France to remain neutral.

On the following day, 23 May, Hitler outlined his current views to a meeting of twelve senior Army commanders, together with Admiral Raeder and Göring.

539

. . . Germany was outside the circle of the Great Powers. A balance of power had been established without Germany's participation.

This balance is being disturbed by Germany's claiming her vital rights and her reappearance in the circle of the Great Powers. All claims are regarded as "breaking in".

The English are more afraid of economic dangers than of ordinary threats of force.

The ideological problems have been solved by the mass of 80,000,000 people. The economic problems must also be solved. To create the economic conditions necessary for this is a task no German can disregard. The solution of the problems demands courage. The principle must not prevail that one can accommodate oneself to the circumstances and thus shirk the solution of the problems. The circumstances must rather be adapted to suit the demands. This is not possible without 'breaking in' to other countries or attacking other people's possessions.

Living space proportionate to the greatness of the State is fundamental to every Power. One can do without it for a time but sooner or later the problems will have to be solved by hook or by crook. The alternatives are rise or decline. In fifteen or twenty years' time the solution will be forced upon us. No German statesman can shirk the problem for longer.

At present we are in a state of national ebullience as are two other states: Italy and Japan . . .

It is not Danzig that is at stake. For us it is a matter of expanding our living space in the East and making food supplies secure and also solving the problem of the Baltic States. Food supplies can only be obtained from thinly populated areas. Over and above fertility, the thorough German cultivation will tremendously increase the produce.

No other openings can be seen in Europe.

Colonies: A warning against gifts of colonial possessions. This is no solution to the food problem. Blockade!

If fate forces us into a showdown with the West it is good to possess a largish area in the East. In war time we shall be even less able to rely on harvests than in peace time.

The populations of non-German territories do not render military service and are available for labour service.

The problem 'Poland' cannot be dissociated from the showdown with the West. Poland's internal solidarity against Bolshevism is doubtful. Therefore Poland is also a doubtful barrier against Russia.

Success in war in the West with a rapid decision is questionable and so is Poland's attitude.

The Polish regime will not stand up to Russian pressure. Poland sees danger in a German victory over the West and will try to deprive us of victory.

There is therefore no question of sparing Poland and we are left with the *decision*:

To attack Poland at the first suitable opportunity.

We cannot expect a repetition of Czechia. There will be war. Our task is to isolate Poland. Success in isolating her will be decisive.

Therefore the Führer must reserve to himself the final order to strike. It must not come to a simultaneous showdown with the West (France and England).

If it is not definitely certain that a German-Polish conflict will not lead to war with the West then the fight must be primarily against England and France.

Thesis: Conflict with Poland—beginning with an attack on Poland—will only be successful if the West keeps out of the ring.

If that is not possible it is better to fall upon the West and finish off Poland at the same time . . .

The Führer doubts whether a peaceful settlement with England is possible. It is necessary to be prepared for a showdown. England sees in our development the establishment of a hegemony which would weaken England. Therefore England is our enemy and the showdown with England is a matter of life and death . . .

The idea of getting out cheaply is dangerous; there is no such possibility. We must then burn our boats and it will no longer be a question of right or wrong but of to be or not to be for 80,000,000 people.

Question: *Short or long war*?

Everybody's Armed Forces and/or Government must strive for a short war. But the Government must, however, also prepare for a war of from ten to fifteen years' duration.

History shows that wars were always expected to be short. In 1914 it was still believed that long wars could not be financed. Even today this idea buzzes in a lot of heads. However, every State will hold out as long as it can unless it is immediately seriously weakened (for instance the Ruhr). England is similarly vulnerable. England knows that to lose the war means the end of her world power . . .

In reply to Field Marshal Göring the Führer lays down that:

(a) the branches of the Armed Forces determine what is to be constructed;
(b) nothing will be changed in the shipbuilding programme;
(c) the armaments programme will be completed by 1943 or 1944.

The threat of a German attack on Poland, to which the Western powers had given a guarantee, enhanced the importance of the Soviet Union to both sides. As far as Britain and France were concerned, without Russian cooperation they would find it difficult to come to Poland's assistance. Britain and Russia were already engaged in negotiations, but neither side took them very seriously. Chamberlain was extremely hostile to the Soviet Union on ideological grounds and also shared the contemptuous view of Soviet military power held by the British General Staff. For Stalin had recently purged several thousand officers from the Red Army and as a result it was widely assumed outside Russia that the Red Army would be ineffective. In any case, the Poles were extremely suspicious of the Soviet Union. Russia too was very wary of committing herself. The abandonment of Czechoslovakia by the Western Powers at Munich and the exclusion of the Soviet Union from the conference had given her good grounds for suspicion. Russia was afraid that Britain and France wished to involve her in a war with Germany while they came to terms with Hitler. In a speech to the Communist Party Congress on 10 March, Stalin had warned that he would 'not let our country be drawn into conflict by warmongers, whose custom is to let others pull their chestnuts out of the fire'. And in May he replaced Litvinov, who had favoured a pact with the Western Powers, with Molotov as Foreign Minister.

Ribbentrop and Hitler rightly interpreted these moves as signs that the Russians might be prepared to alter their policy towards Germany. The idea of an arrangement with the Soviet Union had long been supported by a group within the German Foreign Ministry and the Wehrmacht. Their arguments were reinforced by the need for Germany to gain access to Russian raw materials in the increasingly probable event of an economic blockade of Germany by the Western Powers. Hitler had hitherto resisted this pressure for improved relations with Russia, preferring the idea of the conquest of living space in association with Poland as a junior partner. But with Poland's acceptance of the guarantee by Britain and France he was forced to reconsider his position. For, if Russia intervened on the side of Poland, Germany would once more be faced with a two front war, whereas if Russia could be won over then Poland would be isolated and encircled. Hitler expressed his view of the new situation in the following two statements. The first was made to Carl Burckhardt, the League of Nations Commissioner in Danzig, on 11 August 1939.

540

Everything I undertake is directed against the Rusians; if the West is too stupid and blind to grasp this, then I shall be compelled to come to an agreement with the Russians, beat the West, and then after their defeat turn against the Soviet Union with all my forces. I need the Ukraine so they can't starve us out like in the last war.

The second statement was addressed to his military commanders at a meeting held on 22 August at his mountain retreat near Berchtesgaden. No official minutes were taken. The following version is based on notes taken by Admiral Canaris:

541

It was clear to me that a conflict with Poland had to come sooner or later. I had already made this decision in the spring, but I thought that I would first turn against the West in a few years, and only after that against the East. But the sequence of these things cannot be fixed. Nor should one close one's eyes to threatening situations. I wanted first of all to establish a tolerable relationship with Poland in order to fight first against the West. But this plan, which appealed to me, could not be executed, as fundamental points had changed. It became clear to me that, in the event of a conflict with the West, Poland would attack us. Poland is striving for access to the sea. The further development appeared after the occupation of the Memel Territory[14] and it became clear to me that in certain circumstances a conflict with Poland might come at an inopportune moment. I give as reasons for this conclusion:

[14] Germany had annexed Memel on 23 March 1939 (eds).

1. First of all two personal factors:

My own personality and that of Mussolini.

Essentially all depends on me, on my existence, because of my political talents. Furthermore, the fact that probably no one will ever again have the confidence of the whole German people as I have. There will probably never again in the future be a man with more authority than I have. My existence is therefore a factor of great value. But I can be eliminated at any time by a criminal or a lunatic.

The second personal factor is the Duce. His existence is also decisive. If anything happens to him, Italy's loyalty to the alliance will no longer be certain. The Italian Court is fundamentally opposed to the Duce. Above all, the Court regards the expansion of the empire as an encumbrance. The Duce is the man with the strongest nerves in Italy.

The third personal factor in our favour is Franco. We can ask only for benevolent neutrality from Spain. But this depends on Franco's personality. He guarantees a certain uniformity and stability in the present system in Spain. We must accept the fact that Spain does not as yet have a Fascist party with our internal unity.

The other side presents a negative picture as far as authoritative persons are concerned. There is no outstanding personality in England and France.

It is easy for us to make decisions. We have nothing to lose; we have everything to gain. Because of our restrictions [*Einschränkungen*] our economic situation is such that we can only hold out for a few more years. Göring can confirm this. We have no other choice, we must act. Our opponents will be risking a great deal and can gain only a little. Britain's stake in a war is inconceivably great. Our enemies have leaders who are below the average. No personalities. No masters, no men of action.

Besides the personal factors, the political situation is favourable for us: In the Mediterranean, rivalry between Italy, France and England; in the Far East, tension between Japan and England; in the Middle East, tension which causes alarm in the Mohammedan world.

The English Empire did not emerge stronger from the last war. Nothing was achieved from the maritime point of view. Strife between England and Ireland. The Union of South Africa has become more independent. Concessions have had to be made to India. England is in the utmost peril. Unhealthy industrialization. A British statesman can only view the future with concern.

France's position has also deteriorated, above all in the Mediterranean.

Further factors in our favour are these:

Since Albania, there has been a balance of power in the Balkans. Yugoslavia is infected with the fatal germ of decay because of her internal situation.

Rumania has not grown stronger. She is open to attack and vulnerable. She is threatened by Hungary and Bulgaria. Since Kemal's death, Turkey has been ruled by petty minds, unsteady, weak men.

All these favourable circumstances will no longer prevail in two or three year's time. No one knows how much longer I shall live. Therefore, better a conflict now.

The creation of Greater Germany was a great achievement politically, but militarily it was doubtful, since it was achieved by bluff on the part of the political leaders. It is necessary to test the military [machine]. If at all possible, not in a general reckoning, but by the accomplishment of individual tasks.

The relationship with Poland has become unbearable. My Polish policy hitherto was contrary to the views of the people. My proposals to Poland (Danzig and the Corridor) were frustrated by England's intervention. Poland changed her tone towards us. A permanent state of tension is intolerable. The power of initiative cannot be allowed to pass to others. The present moment is more favourable than in two or three years' time. An attempt on my life or Mussolini's could change the situation to our disadvantage. One cannot for ever face one another with rifles cocked. One compromise solution suggested to us was that we should change our convictions and make gestures. They talked to us again in the language of Versailles. There was a danger of losing prestige. Now the probability is still great that the West will not intervene. We must take the risk with ruthless determination. The politician must take a risk just as much as the general. We are faced with the harsh alternatives of striking or of certain annihilation sooner or later.

Reference to previous hazardous undertakings.

I should have been stoned if I had not been proved right. The most dangerous step was the entry into the neutral zone. Only a week before, I got a warning through France. I have always taken a great risk in the conviction that it would succeed.

Now it is also a great risk. Iron nerves, iron resolution.

The following special reasons fortify me in my view. England and France have undertaken obligations which neither is in a position to fulfil. There is no real rearmament in England, but only propaganda. A great deal of harm was done by many Germans, who were not in agreement with me, saying and writing to English people after the solution of the Czech question: The Führer succeeded because you lost your nerve, because you capitulated too soon. This explains the present propaganda war. The English speak of a war of nerves. One factor in this war of nerves is to boost the increase of armaments. But what are the real facts about British rearmament? The naval construction programme for 1938 has not yet been completed. Only the reserve fleet has been mobilized. Purchase of trawlers. No substantial strengthening of the Navy before 1941 or 1942.

Little has been done on land. England will be able to send at most three divisions to the Continent. A little has been done for the Air Force, but it is only a beginning. Anti-aircraft defence is in its initial stages. At the moment England has only 150 anti-aircraft guns. The new anti-aircraft gun has been produced. There is a shortage of predictors. England is still vulnerable from the air. This can change in two or three years. At the moment the English Air Force has only 130,000 men, France 72,000, Poland 15,000. England does not want the conflict to break out for two or three years.

The following is typical of England. Poland wanted a loan from England for her rearmament. England, however, only granted credits in order to make sure that Poland buys in England, although England cannot make deliveries. This suggests that England does not really want to support Poland. She is not risking eight million pounds in Poland, although she poured five hundred millions into China. England's position in the world is very precarious. She will not take any risks.

France is short of men (decline in the birth rate). Little has been done for rearmament. The artillery is obsolete. France did not want to embark on this adventure. The West has only two possibilities for fighting against us:

1. Blockade: It will not be effective because of our autarky and because we have sources of supply in Eastern Europe.

2. Attack in the West from the Maginot line: I consider this impossible.

Another possibility would be the violation of Dutch, Belgian and Swiss neutrality. I have no doubt that all these States, as well as Scandinavia, will defend their neutrality with all available means. England and France will not violate the neutrality of these countries. Thus in actual fact England cannot help Poland. There still remains an attack on Italy. Military intervention is out the question. No one is counting on a long war. If Herr von Brauchitsch had told me that I would have replied: 'Then it cannot be done.' It is nonsense to say that England wants to wage a long war.

We will hold our position in the West until we have conquered Poland. We must bear in mind our great production capacity. It is much greater than in 1914–1918.

The enemy had another hope, that Russia would become our enemy after the conquest of Poland. The enemy did not reckon with my great strength of purpose. Our enemies are small fry. I saw them in Munich.

I was convinced that Stalin would never accept the English offer. Russia has no interest in preserving Poland, and Stalin knows that it would mean the end of his régime, no matter whether his soldiers emerged from a war victorious or vanquished. Litvinov's replacement was decisive. I brought about the change towards Russia gradually. In connection with the commercial treaty we got into political conversations. Proposal for a non-aggression pact. Then came a comprehensive proposal from Russia. Four days ago I took a special step, which led to Russia replying yesterday that she is prepared to sign. Personal contact with Stalin is established. The day after tomorrow von Ribbentrop will conclude the treaty. Now Poland is in the position in which I wanted her.

We need not be afraid of a blockade. The East will supply us with grain, cattle, coal, lead and zinc. It is a mighty aim, which demands great efforts. I am only afraid that at the last moment some swine or other will yet submit to me a plan for mediation.

The political objective goes further. A start has been made on the destruction of England's hegemony. The way will be open for the soldiers after I have made the political preparations.

Today's announcement of the non-aggression pact with Russia came as a bombshell. The consequences cannot be foreseen. Stalin also said that this course will benefit both countries. The effect on Poland will be tremendous.

In reply, Göring thanked the Führer and assured him that the Wehrmacht would do their duty.

After an adjournment, Hitler continued with some further remarks:

542

Things can also work out differently regarding England and France. It is impossible to prophesy with any certainty. I am expecting an embargo on trade, not a blockade, and furthermore that relations will be broken off. The most iron determination on our part. No shrinking back from anything. Everyone must hold the view that we have been determined to fight the Westen Powers right from the start. A life and death struggle. Germany has won every war when she was united. An inflexible, unflinching bearing, above all on the part of superiors, firm confidence, belief in victory, overcoming the past by becoming accustomed to the heaviest burdens. A long period of peace would not do us any good. It is therefore necessary to be prepared for anything. A manly bearing. It is not machines that fight each other, but men. We have better men as regards quality. Spiritual factors are decisive. On the opposite side they are weaker men. The nation collapsed in 1918 because the spiritual prerequisites were insufficient. Frederick the Great only achieved final success by his fortitude.

The destruction of Poland has priority. The aim is to eliminate active forces, not to reach a definite line. Even if war breaks out in the West, the destruction of Poland remains the priority. A quick decision in view of the season.

I shall give a propagandist reason for starting the war, no matter whether it is plausible or not. The victor will not be asked afterwards whether he told the truth or not. When starting and waging a war it is not right that matters, but victory.

Close your hearts to pity. Act brutally. Eighty million people must obtain what is their right. Their existence must be made secure. The stronger man is right. The greatest harshness.

Swiftness in making decisions is necessary. Firm faith in the German soldier. Crises are due solely to leaders having lost their nerve.

On the same day as this speech to the military commanders, Ribbentrop had flown to Moscow with Hitler's authority to agree to a non-aggression pact which also included a division of Poland and other parts of Eastern Europe with the Soviet Union. The agreement signed on 23 August 1939 included a secret annex which contained the details of this division of the spoils:

543

The Government of the German Reich
and
The Government of the Union of Soviet Socialist Republics,

directed by the wish to strengthen the cause of peace between Germany and the U.S.S.R. and proceeding upon the basic provisions of the Treaty of Neutrality concluded between Germany and the U.S.S.R. in April 1926, have reached the following agreement:

Article 1. The two contracting parties undertake to refrain from any act of violence, any aggressive action, or any attack against one another, whether individually or jointly with other powers.

Article 2. In case any of the contracting parties should become the object of warlike acts on the part of a third power, the other contracting party will not support that third power in any form.

Article 3. The Governments of the two contracting parties will in future remain in contact with each other through continuous consultation in order to inform each other concerning questions affecting their mutual interests.

Article 4. Neither of the two contracting parties will participate in any grouping of powers which is indirectly or directly aimed against the other party.

Article 5. Should disputes or conflicts arise between the contracting parties regarding questions of any kind whatsoever, the two parties would clear away these disputes or conflicts solely by means of friendly exchanges of views or if necessary by arbitration commissions.

Article 6. The present Treaty is concluded for a period of ten years with the provision that unless one of the contracting parties denounces it one year before the end of this period the duration of the validity of this treaty is to be regarded as automatically prolonged for another five years.

Article 7. The present Treaty is to be ratified within the shortest possible time. The documents of ratification are to be exchanged in Berlin. The Treaty becomes effective upon signature.

SECRET ADDITIONAL PROTOCOL

On the occasion of the signature of the Non-Aggression Treaty between the German Reich and the Union of Soviet Socialist Republics, the undersigned plenipotentiaries of the two parties discussed in strictly confidential conversations the question of the delimitation of their respective spheres of interest in Eastern Europe. These conversations led to the following result:

1. In the event of a territorial and political transformation in the territories belonging to the Baltic States (Finland, Estonia, Latvia, Lithuania), the northern frontier of Lithuania shall represent the frontier of the spheres of interest both of Germany and the U.S.S.R.. In this connexion the interest of Lithuania in the Vilna territory is recognized by both parties.

2. In the event of a territorial and political transformation of the territories belonging to the Polish State, the spheres of interest of both Germany and the U.S.S.R. shall be bounded approximately by the line of the rivers Narev, Vistula and San.

The question of whether the interests of both parties make the maintenance of an independent Polish State appear desirable and how the frontiers of this State should be drawn can be definitely determined only in the course of further political developments.

In any case both Governments will resolve this question by means of a friendly understanding.

3. With regard to south-eastern Europe, the Soviet side emphasizes its interests in Bessarabia. The German side declares complete political *désintéressement* in these territories.

4. This Protocol will be treated by both parties as strictly secret.

Hitler was convinced that the Non-Aggression Pact with the Soviet Union would ensure that Britain and France would not fulfil their guarantee to Poland. Reports from German visitors to Britain and from the German ambassador had already given evidence of Britain's anxiety to reach an agreement with Germany.

On 23 August, after hearing that the negotiations with Russia had gone well, Hitler provisionally fixed the date for the attack on Poland for the 26th. Meanwhile, Chamberlain had responded to the news of the German–Soviet Pact by warning Hitler publicly in a speech and in the following letter that Britain was no less determined to support Poland if she were attacked. Hitler received this letter later on the 23rd:

544

Your Excellency will have already heard of certain measures taken by His Majesty's Government and announced in the press and on the wireless this evening. These steps have, in the opinion of His Majesty's Government, been rendered necessary by military movements which have been reported from Germany and by the fact that apparently the announcement of a German–Soviet Agreement is taken in some quarters in Berlin to indicate that intervention by Great Britain on behalf of Poland is no longer a contingency that need be reckoned with. No greater mistake could be made. Whatever may prove to be the nature of the German–Soviet Agreement, it cannot alter Great Britain's obligation to Poland, which His Majesty's Government have stated in public repeatedly and plainly and which they are determined to fulfil.

It is alleged that if His Majesty's Government had made their position more clear in 1914, the great catastrophe would have been avoided. Whether or not there is any force in that allegation, His Majesty's Government are resolved that on this occasion there shall be no such tragic misunderstanding.

If the case should arise, they are resolved and prepared to employ without delay all the forces at their command, and it is impossible to foresee the end of hostilities once engaged. It would be a dangerous illusion to think that if war once starts it will come to an early end, even if a success on any one of the several fronts on which it will be engaged should have been secured. Having thus made our position perfectly clear, I wish to repeat to you my conviction that war between our two peoples would be the greatest calamity that could occur. I am certain that it is desired neither by our people nor by yours, and I cannot see that there is anything in the questions arising between Germany and Poland which could not and should not be resolved without use of force, it [*sic*] only a situation of confidence could be restored to enable discussions to be carried out in an atmosphere different from that which prevails today.

We have been, and at all times will be, ready to assist in creating conditions in which such negotiations could take place and in which it might be possible concurrently to discuss the wider problems affecting future international relations, including matters of interest to us and to you . . .

But I am bound to say that there would be slender hope of bringing such negotiations to a successful issue, unless it were understood beforehand that any settlement reached would, when concluded, be guaranteed by other Powers. His Majesty's Government would be ready, if desired, to make such contribution as they could to the effective operation of such guarantees.

At this moment I confess I can see no other way to avoid a catastrophe that will involve Europe in war.

After an initial frosty response to Chamberlain in a letter of 24 August, the following day Hitler decided to exploit Britain's unwillingness to go to war if it could possibly be avoided. Receiving the British ambassador at 1.30 p.m. on the 25th, he outlined to him the following 'large and comprehensive offer':

545

. . . 3. The problem of Danzig and the Corridor must be solved. The British Prime Minister had made a speech which was not in the least calculated to induce any change in the German attitude. At the most, the result of this speech could be a bloody and incalculable war between Germany and England. Such a war would be bloodier than that of 1914 to 1918. In contrast to the last war, Germany would no longer have to fight on two fronts. The agreement with Russia was unconditional and signified a change in the foreign policy of the Reich which would last a very long time. Russia and Germany would never in any circumstances again take up arms against each other. Apart from this, the agreements reached with Russia would also render Germany secure economically for the longest possible period of war.

The Führer had always wanted German–British understanding. War between England and Germany could at the best bring some profit to Germany but none at all to England.

The Führer declared that the German–Polish problem must be solved and would be solved. He is, however, prepared and determined, after the solution of this problem, to approach England once more with a large comprehensive offer. He is a man of great decisions, and in this case also he will be capable of a great action. He accepts the British Empire and is ready to pledge himself personally for its continued existence and to commit the power of the German Reich for this, if:

(1) His colonial demands, which are limited and can be negotiated by peaceful methods, are fulfilled and in this case he is prepared to fix the longest time limit;

(2) His obligations towards Italy are not touched—in other words, he does not demand that England give up her obligations towards France and similarly for his own part he cannot withdraw from his obligations towards Italy.

(3) He also desires to stress the irrevocable determination of Germany never again to enter into conflict with Russia. The Führer is ready to conclude agreements with England which, as has already been emphasized, would not only guarantee the existence of the British Empire in all circumstances as far as Germany is concerned, but would also if necessary assure the British Empire of German assistance regardless of where such assistance should be necessary. The Führer would then also be ready to accept a reasonable limitation of armaments which would correspond to the new political situation and be economically tolerable. Finally, the Führer renewed his assurances that he is not interested in Western problems and that a frontier modification in the West does not enter into consideration. The Western fortifications [*Westwall*], which have been constructed at a cost of thousands of millions, were the final Reich frontier on the West.

If the British Government would consider these ideas, a blessing for Germany and also for the British Empire might result. If they reject these ideas, there will be war. In no case would Great Britain emerge stronger from this war; the last war had already proved this.

The Führer repeats that he is a man of great decisions by which he himself is bound, and that this is his last offer. Immediately after the solution of the German–Polish question he would approach the British Government with an offer.

Then, at 3.00 p.m., following Henderson's departure, Hitler confirmed 26 August as the date for the attack on Poland, clearly hoping that his offer would divert the British from intervening. An hour later, he received news that the Anglo–Polish treaty, agreed in April, had at last been signed. No sooner had he received this ominous news than he heard from the Italian ambassador that Italy was not yet ready to go to war. In view of these two developments, Hitler decided to postpone the attack on Poland, scheduled for the following day, to 1 September, in order to give himself more time to manoeuvre.

The following days until the outbreak of war were dominated by Hitler's attempt to drive a wedge between Britain and Poland and to gain a propaganda advantage in the coming conflict with Poland. Britain, however, was by now thoroughly disillusioned with German guarantees which had been consistently broken. Moreover, with the British guarantee the Poles had a trump card which the unfortunate Czechs had lacked. Britain continued to insist on a peaceful settlement of the Polish question *before* she would consider broader Anglo–German issues.

In their reply to Hitler's offer the British government mentioned that they had secured Polish agreement to direct discussions between Poland and Germany. Hitler now seized on this to try and gain a propaganda advantage. On 29 August, he issued what was effectively an ultimatum demanding that the Poles send a plenipotentiary the following day. The Poles, however, refused to yield to this pressure and Britain declined to compel them to do so. At midnight on the 30th, Henderson delivered the

British reply to Ribbentrop. He reported to the Foreign Office on the interview that followed:

546

I told von Ribbentrop this evening that His Majesty's Government found it difficult to advise Polish Government to accept procedure adumbrated in German reply and suggested that he should adopt normal contact i.e. that when German proposals were ready to invite Polish Ambassador to call and to hand him proposals for transmission to his Government with a view to immediate opening of negotiations. I added that if basis afforded prospect of settlement His Majesty's Government could be counted upon to do their best in Warsaw to temporize negotiations.

2. Herr von Ribbentrop's reply was to produce a lengthy document which he read out in German aloud at top speed. Imagining that he would eventually hand it to me I did not attempt to follow too closely the sixteen or more articles which it contained. Though I cannot therefore guarantee accuracy the main points were: restoration of Danzig to Germany; southern boundary of Corridor to be line Marienberg [*sic*], Graudenz, Bromberg, Schölanke; plebiscite to be held in the Corridor on basis of population on Janary 1, 1919, absolute majority to decide; international commission of British, French, Italian and Russian members to police the Corridor and guarantee reciprocal communications with Danzig and Gdynia pending result of the plebiscite; Gdynia to be reserved to Poland; Danzig to be purely commercial city and demilitarized.

3. When I asked von Ribbentrop for text of these proposals in accordance with undertaking in the German reply of yesterday he asserted that it was now too late as Polish representative had not arrived in Berlin by midnight.

4. I observed that to treat matter in this way meant that request for Polish representative to arrive in Berlin on August 30 constituted in fact an ultimatum in spite of what he and Herr Hitler had assured me yesterday. This he denied saying that idea of an ultimatum was figment of my imagination. Why then I asked could he not adopt normal procedure and give me copy of proposals and ask Polish Ambassador to call on him just as Herr Hitler had summoned me a few days ago and hand them to him for communication to Polish Government. In the most violent terms Herr von Ribbentrop said that he would never ask the Ambassador to visit him. He hinted that if Polish Ambassador asked him for interview it might be different. I said that I would naturally inform my government so at once. Whereupon he said while those were his personal views he would bring all that I had said to Herr Hitler's notice. It was for Chancellor to decide.

5. We parted on that note but I must tell you that von Ribbentrop's whole demeanour during an unpleasant interview was aping Herr Hitler at his worst. He inveighed incidentally against Polish mobilization but I retorted that it was hardly surprising since Germany had also mobilized as Herr Hitler himself had admitted to me yesterday.

Having, as he thought, gained a propaganda advantage through Poland's rejection of a 'generous offer', which was in fact never seriously intended, Hitler went ahead and, at 12.30 p.m. on 31 August, signed the Directive No. 1 for the Conduct of the War. The war had already been postponed once, a week had been lost, and with the autumn rains not far off, he was under pressure to act even at the risk of Britain and France becoming involved, a risk which he still did not rate very highly:

547

1. Now that every political possibility has been exhausted for ending by peaceful means the intolerable situation on Germany's eastern frontier I have determined on a solution by force.
2. The attack on Poland is to be carried out in accordance with the preparations made for 'Operation White [*Fall Weiss*]', with the alterations, in respect of the Army, resulting from the fact that strategic deployment has by now been almost completed.

Assignment of tasks and the operational objective remain unchanged.

Day of attack . . .	1 September 1939
Time of attack . . .	4.45 a.m.

This timing also applies for the Gdynia/Gulf of Danzig, and Dirschau Bridge operations.
3. In the west, it is important that the responsibility for the opening of hostilities should be made to rest squarely on Britain and France. Insignificant frontier violations should, for the time being, be opposed by purely local action.

The neutrality on which we have given assurances to Holland, Belgium, Luxemburg and Switzerland must be scrupulously respected.

On land, the German west frontier is not to be crossed at any point without my express permission.

At sea, the same applies for all warlike actions which could be regarded as such.

The defensive measures of the Luftwaffe are, for the time being, to be restricted to those necessary to counter enemy air attacks at the Reich frontier, whereby the frontiers of neutral States are to be respected as long as possible in countering single aircraft and smaller units. Only if large French and British formations are employed over the neutral States in attacks against German territory and the air defence in the west is no longer assured, are counter-measures to be allowed even over these neutral territories.

The speediest reporting to OKW of any violation of the neutrality of third-party States by our western opponents is particularly important.
4. If Britain and France open hostilities against Germany, it is the task of the Wehrmacht formations operating in the west to contain their forces as much as possible and thus maintain the conditions for a victorious conclusion of the operations against Poland. Within these limits enemy forces and their military economic resources are to be injured as much as possible. Orders to go over to the attack are reserved to me in every case.

The Army will hold the West Wall and make preparations to prevent its being outflanked in the north through violation of Belgian or Netherlands territory by the Western Powers. If French forces enter Luxemburg, the demolition of frontier bridges is authorized.

The Navy will carry on warfare against merchant shipping, directed mainly at Britain. To intensify the effects a declaration of danger zones may be expected. OKM[15] will report in which sea areas, and to what extent, danger zones are considered expedient. The wording of a public announcement is to be prepared in consultation with the Foreign Ministry and submitted to me through OKW for approval.

The Baltic Sea is to be protected from enemy raids. The Commander-in-Chief of the Navy will decide whether the approaches to the Baltic Sea should be blocked by mines for this purpose.

The Luftwaffe is, in the first place, to prevent the French and British air forces from attacking the German army and German living space.

In conducting the war against Britain, preparations are to be made for the use of the Luftwaffe in disrupting British supplies by sea, the armaments industry, and the transport of troops to France. A favourable opportunity is to be taken for an effective attack on massed British naval units, especially against battleships and aircraft carriers. Attacks against London are reserved for my decision.

Preparations are to be made for attacks against the British mainland, bearing in mind that partial success with insufficient forces is in all circumstances to be avoided.

(vi) Hitler's 'programme' and German foreign policy 1933–39

There is disagreement among historians about the significance of Hitler's 'programme' for his conduct of foreign policy. One historian has described the ideas outlined in *Mein Kampf* and elsewhere as 'day dreams'[16] and it has rightly been pointed out that *Mein Kampf* provides no specific guide to the foreign policy which Hitler carried out between 1933 and 1939, a policy which in fact culminated in a pact with the Soviet Union, the very power which he had claimed to wish to destroy, and in a war with Britain, whom he had originally envisaged as an ally.

Some historians have argued that Hitler's expansionist drive was not so much the product of a coherent programme as basically the incoherent expression of dynamic forces which derived from the nature of the regime itself. A regime based on a charismatic form of authority which thrived on crisis, a regime whose ideology declared struggle to be the essence of life and which systematically militarized society and launched a masssive rearmaments programme, a regime whose ideology not only glorified conflict but embraced conflicting values and which, instead of providing a framework within which social conflict could be resolved peacefully, simul-

[15] Oberkommando der Marine—the Naval High Command (eds).

[16] A. J. P. Taylor, *The Origins of the Second World War* (London 1963), p. 69.

taneously suppressed it by terror and denied it through propaganda—such a regime, it is argued, created a dynamic which was bound to explode into war. According to Martin Broszat, for example, Hitler's programmatic goals merely provided 'symbolic metaphors' for this dynamic rather than coherent and systematically pursued objectives which determined policy. In other words, in this view, the Third Reich was a regime inherently geared to war, towards the unleashing of a drive for plunder and exploitation which was essentially without direction, whose logic lay within itself and was therefore essentially irrational and therefore nihilistic.

However, and without denying the dynamic and nihilistic aspects of the regime, it is doubtful whether Hitler's programmatic goals can be dismissed merely as 'symbolic metaphors' without decisive significance for policy. It seems more likely on the basis of the evidence that, while Hitler adhered all along to his major objective of acquiring *Lebensraum* in the East, he was not committed to any specific policies for achieving it. In July 1924, he had emphasized the difference between a 'programme maker' or theoretician and a politician. 'The theoretician must always preach the pure idea and have it always before his eyes: the politician, however, must not only think of the great objective but also the way that leads to it.'[17] Flexibility was characteristic of his whole approach, at any rate until the war. Thus, in the period between 1919 and 1933 he had invariably adapted his tactics in domestic politics to the conditions imposed by a developing situation, first changing from a putsch to a parliamentary tactic and then switching from a demand for a Nazi-dominated Government to the acceptance of a coalition with a strong Conservative contingent. His attitude in foreign policy was similar. For a long time he hoped that he would secure a far-reaching arrangement with Britain, and the Anglo–German Naval Agreement of 1935 seemed to confirm the correctness of his analysis. When an arrangement eventually eluded him and he found himself faced with a threat from the west which represented a permanent obstacle to the achievement of his eastern objective, he postponed his eastern campaign and even allied himself with his intended victim in order to remove the more immediate obstacle, although significantly, even after the outbreak of war, he still hoped that Britain would agree to an alliance. Similarly, although Hitler probably began by merely wishing to detach the smaller powers of Central and Eastern Europe from France and turn them into German satellites, the failure of the Austrian, Czech and Polish Governments to accept the satellite status envisaged for them, their attempt to retain a measure of independence forced him to go further than perhaps

[17] Cf. W. Jochmann (ed), *Nationalsozialismus und Revolution* (Frankfurt 1963), p. 133; see also A. Hitler, *Mein Kampf,* trs. (London 1969), pp. 191–2, where this distinction was reaffirmed.

he originally intended at particular stages. He was not, for example, intending an immediate annexation of Austria—he would have been content, for the time being at any rate, with its 'coordination'—but the situation developed in such a way that annexation proved possible. It would be a mistake, however, to assume from these tactical shifts that he was not guided by any long-term objectives.

Hitler began with several distinct advantages over his predecessors. The reparations issue which had restricted German foreign policy so much in the past had been solved; France had been forced to modify her intransigent line in the light of her experience with the Ruhr invasion and the attitude of her main ally, Britain; above all, the impact of the economic depression had dissolved the ties of international solidarity and had induced everywhere an attitude of *sauve-qui-peut*. It was a situation which provided the necessary freedom of manoeuvre for a power which was bent on exploiting the differences between the other States and on playing them off, one against the other, by means of bilateral rather than the traditional multilateral agreements. Nevertheless, although the diplomatic situation was now distinctly more favourable than that faced by his predecessors, there is no doubt that Hitler exploited his opportunities with exceptional skill. One of his great gifts as a politician was his ability to sense the points of weakness in his opponents' armoury. He sensed the deep unwillingness of the peoples of Western Europe to go to war again. He was aware of the fear of Bolshevism which dominated the European upper and middle classes. He knew that the treatment of Germany under the Treaty of Versailles had left many, particularly in Britain, with a bad conscience. He appreciated that the refusal of the right of self-determination to the Austrian Germans, the creation of German minorities in countries such as Poland and Czechoslovakia, and finally, the imposition on Germany of permanent restrictions while the other powers showed no signs of disarming—that all these aspects of the Treaty appeared to a greater or lesser extent unjust and thus helped to undermine the will of the Allies to defend its principles, particularly if defence of the settlement would involve another major war. Hitler ruthlessly exploited these weaknesses. He combined every move against the Versailles settlement with an assertion of his desire for peace and often with a claim that the particular issue involved represented Germany's final grievance and that in future she would be satisfied; he projected an image of the Third Reich as an anti-Bolshevik bastion against the threat from Soviet Russia; and finally he justified every move against the Versailles settlement in terms of the principles of the settlement itself. Thus, the invasion of the Rhineland and of Austria, and the annexation of the Sudetenland in Czechoslovakia, were all justified on the grounds of national self-determination.

Up until 1939 this tactic proved extremely successful. Yet, from 1938 onwards, he appears to have been governed by a mounting impatience. This may have reflected increasing tensions within the regime itself such as the growing economic crisis produced by a rearmament programme which was not balanced by restraint in other sectors of the economy. For these economic problems were bound in the long run to have political repercussions. Hitler was acutely sensitive to public opinion and having built his regime on an identification of his leadership with expectations of national glory and material well-being he now had to fulfil them. He was aware that the population would not remain content indefinitely with a diet of nationalist rhetoric and ersatz products for which it was having to work long hours.

His impatience may also have reflected a growing fear on Hitler's part that he would not survive long enough to carry out his objectives. An operation for a benign polyp in his throat in 1935 had no doubt reminded him of his mortality. It may equally have reflected his growing self-confidence in his mastery of diplomacy and strategy, as each of his coups was crowned with success despite the doubts of the experts, coupled with a growing contempt for his opponents—a combination which, when reinforced by the ceaseless flattery of his subordinates, was calculated to produce a growing hubris and detachment from reality.

However, perhaps decisive was Hitler's awareness that the other major powers had begun crash rearmament programmes. For, just as it is a mistake to assume that Hitler had no long term goals, it would be equally wrong to imagine that Hitler was in control of events, adjusting his tactics to suit the prevailing situation with a sovereign freedom. Apart from the fact that there were others involved in the formation of foreign policy, notably Ribbentrop and Göring, who were on occasion (e.g. the Anschluss) capable of influencing events decisively, Hitler's options were circumscribed. In particular, he was subject to the repercussions of his own previous actions both at home and abroad (e.g. the crash rearmament programm)—which created pressures and constraints which in turn helped determine his future foreign and strategic policies. Britain's refusal to fulfil the role envisaged in his programme and the arms race which he himself had initiated, forced him to accelerate the fulfilment of his plans, telescoping the various stages of his programme with the final result that within three days his continental war had become a world war, a war for which Germany was not properly prepared.

Certainly, whatever the reasons, from 1938 onwards Hitler increased the stakes almost from month to month. His risks were still calculated. It was, for example, a reasonable assumption that the Nazi–Soviet pact of August 1939 would rule out the possibility of Allied intervention in support of Poland, particularly in view of their behaviour on previous occasions.

However, Hitler seemed increasingly willing to face the prospect of a general war. Since war with the West was inevitable and since Germany had a head start in rearmament—an advantage which would soon be eroded—it would be better to have a war there and then, rather than later. Furthermore, the policy of appeasement had undermined his respect for the capacity of Britain and France to resist him. As a result, when it became clear that, contrary to his expectations, Britain and France would fight over the Polish issue, he did not draw back. On 29 August, Göring implored him not to play *va banque*. Hitler replied: 'Throughout my life I have always played *va banque*'.[18]

[18] Cf. A. Kube, *Hermann Göring* op. cit., p. 319.

CHAPTER 29

The Successful Blitzkriege 1939–1940

(i) The attack on Poland

The German attack on Poland began in the early morning of 1 September with offensives carried out by an Army Group North operating from Pomerania and East Prussia and an Army Group South based in Silesia and Czechoslovakia. It had been preceded by a incident organized by the SD. One hundred and fifty concentration camp inmates clothed in Polish uniforms were obliged to stage a mock attack on a German transmitter at Gleiwitz near the Polish border; their corpses were to provide proof of Polish provocation.

Later in the day, Hitler addressed the Reichstag:

If I called up the Wehrmacht and if I now demand sacrifices from the German people, and if necessary the supreme sacrifice, I have a right to do so. For I myself am just as prepared as I was before to make any personal sacrifice. I am not demanding of any German man anything more than what I myself was ready to do voluntarily for four years. There will be no privation in Germany which I myself will not share from the start. From now onwards, even more than before, my whole life belongs to my people. I do not want to be anything other than the first soldier of the German Reich.

I have once more put on the uniform which was once the most holy and precious to me. I shall only take it off after victory or I shall not live to see the end.

If anything happens to me in this struggle my first successor will be party comrade Göring. If anything happens to party comrade Göring then the next successor will be party comrade Hess. You would then be bound to them as Führer in blind loyalty and obedience as much as to me. If anything happens to party comrade Hess then I shall summon the Senate by law which will choose the most worthy i.e. the bravest from their midst.[1]

As a National Socialist and as a German soldier, I am going into this struggle strong in heart. My whole life has been nothing but a struggle for my people, for their revival, for Germany. This struggle has been fought continually under the banner of my faith in this nation. There is one word which I have never learnt: capitulation. But if anyone thinks we may be heading for difficult times then I would ask him to remember that in the past a Prussian king[2] with a ridiculously small state opposed one of the greatest of coalitions and, after fighting three campaigns, finally achieved victory because he possessed that stout heart and faith which we too need at this time. And so I would now like to assure the whole world: German history will never see a repetition of November 1918.

Just as I myself am ready to risk my life at any time—anyone could take it—for my people and for Germany, so I demand the same of everyone else. But anyone who thinks that he can oppose this national commandment, whether directly or indirectly, will die! Traitors can expect nothing but death.

Thus, we all confess our faith in our traditional principle: It is totally unimportant whether or not we live, but it is vital that our people live, that Germany lives . . .

In fact, Hitler still hoped that Britain was bluffing, and that once the war had started and she was forced to face the fact that Britain could not effectively assist Poland, she would accept the inevitable as she had accepted so much already. But Britain was not bluffing and, on 3 September, Chamberlain issued an ultimatum: unless Germany withdrew her troops from Poland by 11 a.m. British Summer Time a state of war would exist between the two countries. The French government issued a similar ultimatum. The German government interpreter, Paul Schmidt recalled after the war the reception of the British ultimatum by the Nazi leaders:

549

. . . I then took the ultimatum to the Chancellery, where everyone was anxiously awaiting me. Most of the members of the Cabinet and the leading men of the Party were collected in the room next to Hitler's office. There was something of a crush and I had difficulty in getting through to Hitler.

[1] Hitler intended at one point to create a Senate but in fact never did so (eds).

[2] Frederick the Great (eds).

'What's the news?' anxious voices asked. I could only answer: 'Class dismissed.'

When I entered the next room Hitler was sitting at his desk and Ribbentrop stood by the window. Both looked up expectantly as I came in. I stopped at some distance from Hitler's desk, and then slowly translated the British Government's ultimatum. When I finished, there was complete silence.

Hitler sat motionless, gazing before him. He was not at a loss, as was afterwards stated, nor did he rage, as others allege. He sat completely silent and unmoving.

After an interval which seemed an age, he turned to Ribbentrop, who had remained standing by the window. 'What now?' asked Hitler with a savage look, as though implying that his Foreign Minister had misled him about England's probable reaction.

Ribbentrop answered quietly: 'I assume that the French will hand in a similar ultimatum within the hour.'

As my duty was now performed, I withdrew. To those in the anteroom pressing round me I said: 'The English have just handed us an ultimatum. In two hours a state of war will exist between England and Germany.' In the anteroom also this news was followed by complete silence.

Göring turned to me and said: 'If we lose this war, then God have mercy on us!'

Goebbels stood in a corner, downcast and self-absorbed. Everywhere in the room I saw looks of grave concern, even amongst the minor Party people.

The German advance was rapid and, on 6 October, the last Polish units capitulated. The Germans benefited from a strategic situation which rendered an effective Polish defence extraordinarily difficult. For they could attack Poland from the north (East Prussia), the north-west (Pomerania), the west (Silesia), and the south (Czechoslovakia), while the Soviet Union launched an invasion from the East on 17 September to secure the territory promised to it under the Nazi-Soviet pact. The Germans also had the advantage of surprise and of an Army which was better equipped and better led. The balance of forces was as follows:

550

German-Polish Balance of Forces 1 September 1939

Total Number of troops		Incl border defence units	Panzer and mot. Division	Inf. Div.	Mountain Div.	Cavalry Brig.	Total no. of units	Armoured vehicles	Aircraft	Ships
Wehrmacht										
Eastern Front	1.5 Mill.	90,000	15	37	1	1	54	3600	1929	40
Poland	1.3 Mill.	60,000	1 Brig.	37	—	11	49	750	900	50

Apart from their overwhelming superiority in modern equipment, the Germans used new 'Blitzkrieg' tactics—highly mobile operations involving the deployment of armour, motorized infantry and air power in coordinated attacks, thereby achieving rapid penetration followed by the encirclement of an enemy which was bound by static and inflexible defensive tactics. Last but not least, the Germans benefited from the fact that Britain and France failed to come to Poland's assistance. Had the Allies launched an offensive in the West, particularly during the first half of September, the Germans would have been highly vulnerable. However, the two western powers were adopting a defensive strategy on the assumption that time was on their side in view of the superiority of their potential resources and the anticipated effects of their blockade of Germany. Losses in the Polish campaign were as follows:

551

	Poland against Germany	Poland against the Soviet Union	Germany	Soviet Union
Dead	70,000	50,000	11,000	700
Wounded	133,000	?	30,000	1,900
Missing	?	?	3,400	?
Prisoners	700,000	300,000	—	—
Fled abroad	220,000	—	—	
Armoured vehicles	?	?	300	?
Other vehicles	?	?	5,000	?
Aircraft	330		560	?

Hitler expressed his view of the situation after the defeat of Poland to Alfred Rosenberg, the leading Nazi ideologue, on 1 November 1939, who recorded it in his diary:

552

The Führer mentioned several times that he still considered a German–English understanding to be desirable, particularly in the longer term. But since the Thirty Years War England had got used to looking down on Germany and playing it off against others. We had done everything possible, but a crazy Jewish-led minority was dominant. Chamberlain was a spineless old man. It looked as if they wouldn't see the light until they had been given a fearful bash. He couldn't grasp what they were really after. Even if England secured a victory, the real winners would be the United States, Japan and Russia. England would come out of a war shattered in any case, let alone if it suffered a military *defeat*. He even thought that, despite their sympathy, many Americans had certainly rubbed their hands at the British losses so far.

ROSENBERG: Yes, the USA wants to inherit control over South America. Apart from that, I think one should avoid a psychological danger when making public speeches, namely of first explaining what one had offered in return for friendship with England and then going on to portray England as a murderer, liar, hypocrite, and international rapist. One should explain that there are two Englands, a strong England which is an important security factor and of cultural value, and a second unscrupulous one led by Jews. We had hoped to work with the *first*, but it wasn't our fault if the second had won.

THE FÜHRER: You are quite right there . . . The only one would be L[loyd] G[eorge]. Before 1914 he too was against the war, although when it could no longer be avoided, he fought it energetically. Mosley has shown himself to be brave. Something like a sense of blood has come to life in *this* Briton. . . .

(ii) Operation 'Weser Exercise' and Operation 'Yellow'—April–May 1940

The ease and speed of the conquest of Poland gave Hitler renewed self-confidence. He had already informed the commanders-in-chief of the three services of his desire to exploit Germany's military advantage to 'smash' France and then, having secured naval and air bases in Belgium, Holland, and northern France, to 'bring England to its knees'.[3] At the same time, he probably retained a slender hope that Britain would now appreciate its foolishness in having entered a war in support of a guarantee which it could do nothing effective to fulfil. To encourage this reappraisal, he made a speech to the Reichstag on 6 October in which, while attacking 'Messrs Churchill & Co', he insisted that he was anxious for peace. Significantly, however, he made no concrete proposals. He clearly hoped to exploit the division within the British Cabinet between the former appeasers and Churchill, who had just joined the Government as First Lord of the Admiralty, but, as he later told the Italian Foreign Minister he did not believe that this would make a deep impression on the enemy. He was doing it only in order to place the enemy in the wrong.[4]

On 9 October, Hitler presented his views on the need for a rapid offensive in the West to the Commander-in-Chief of the Army, von Brauchitsch, and the Chief of the General Staff, Franz Halder, in the form of a lengthy memorandum:

[3] Franz Halder, *Kriegstagebuch* I pp. 89 ff. 27 and 28, September 1939.

[4] *Documents on German Foreign Policy,* Series D. Vol. VIII p. 189.

553

. . . The British and French war aim is to break up or rather to smash once again the state of 80 millions [Germany] in order to restore the European balance of power, i.e. the situation of a balance of forces which is in their own interest. Thus, the German people will have to face this struggle at some point one way or the other. Nevertheless, the great successes of the first month of war could, in the event of an immediate peace, serve to strengthen the Reich both psychologically and materially to such an extent that, from a German point of view, there could be no objection to concluding the war, provided the success won by our arms was not jeopardized by the peace treaty . . .

After rejecting this proposal, Hitler continued:

. . . The German war aim, on the other hand, must consist of the final military defeat of the West, i.e. the destruction of the strength of the Western powers and of their ability once more to oppose the political consolidation and further development of the German people within Europe.

This fundamental aim must clearly be adjusted from time to time for propaganda purposes and to suit the psychological requirements of individual cases vis-à-vis the outside world. This does not alter the war aim itself. It is and remains the destruction of our Western opponents. . . .

Time

In this war as in all historical events time is not a factor which is valuable in itself but must be assessed in the light of the situation. In this case it is more probable that time is an ally of the Western powers than of ours.

Reasons: The success of the Polish campaign has made possible the war on one front which was the impossible dream of decades, that is Germany can take on the West with all its forces, apart from a few troops left to cover the East.

The other European states are neutral either through concern about their own fate or from a lack of interest in the conflict, or from an interest in a particular outcome of the struggle which, however, forbids them to intervene either at all or prematurely.

The following should be borne in mind:

Russia: There is no treaty and no agreement which can ensure that Russia remains neutral over the long term. At the moment all the signs are against her breaking her neutrality. In eight months, in a year's time, let alone in several years, this may change. The last few years have abundantly demonstrated the limited importance of treaties. The greatest security against any Russian intervention lies in the clear demonstration of German superiority or in other words in the rapid demonstration of German strength.

Italy: As long as the Italian political leadership sees the future of Italy in the recreation of a great imperial Roman empire, it will tend to lean towards Germany. For this imperial idea can only be realized at the expense of France and England. Its realization is only conceivable with the help of Germany or on the basis of

German successes. This imperial vision is carried by Fascism and in the first instance by its creator, Benito Mussolini. A weakening of Fascist influence in Italy, let alone the death of the Duce, would lead to a strengthening of the influence of the Court and ultimately to the renunciation of these aims which are rooted in the nation but unattractive to dynasties because they are dangerous. In this case, therefore, time can in no circumstances be regarded as an ally of Germany. It can only represent a threat.

. . . *America*: The attempt on the part of certain circles in the USA to lead the continent in an anti-German direction is certainly at the moment without effect but in the future it may be successful. Here too time can be regarded as working against Germany.

East Asia: Japan will decide its own position purely on the basis of its own interests: its aim will be to exploit any weakening of the European states in East Asia with the smallest possible expenditure of its own forces. Here too time cannot count as an ally of Germany but only success.

Threats to the German position:

The first threat to Germany lies in the fact that if the war lasts a long time, in certain circumstances other states may be drawn into the opposing front either on grounds of economic necessity or through the development of particular interests.

The second danger lies in the fact that through a long drawn out war states which might be basically favourable to joining Germany, in view of the experience of the last war, may take the very length of the war as a warning and therefore avoid intervening on our behalf.

The third danger involved in a lengthy war lies in the difficulty of feeding our population and securing the means for fighting the war in view of the limited basis for food supplies and raw materials. The morale of the population will at the very least be adversely affected.

The biggest and most serious threat lies in the following:

The precondition for the successful conduct of the war is to maintain the production of the Ruhr area intact. Any serious loss of production in this area cannot be compensated for elsewhere. It must lead sooner or later to the collapse of the German war economy and thereby of our powers of defence. . . .

Since this weakness is as well known to England and France as it is to us, in their conduct of the war, which is intended to ensure the destruction of Germany, they will endeavour to secure this aim under all circumstances. Indeed, the less England and France can hope to destroy the German army in the field through a series of battles, the more the two states will try to secure the conditions for the effective waging of a long drawn out war of attrition and destruction. However, the precondition for this is to push the Anglo-French forces up to the German border, thereby violating Dutch neutrality. . . .

The probability, indeed the certainty of such an Anglo-French decision is strengthened by the undeniable fact that, *vice versa*, the possession of this territory in German hands would be one of the few factors which would benefit Germany in the event of a long drawn out war.

The German War Aim

In the event of the final conflict with France and England the German war aim can only be the complete annihilation of the French and British forces. Territorial gains are significant only in so far as they facilitate the destruction of our opponents or, alternatively, are important for the future conduct of the war in the long run. We must, therefore, seek primarily the destruction of the enemy forces and only secondarily the occupation of enemy soil. Naturally, there is an inevitable connexion between the two goals. . . .

If it must be the aim of German military operations to destroy the effective offensive and defensive forces of our enemies then the most favourable moment for this is before the build-up of the British forces has given France a valuable psychological and material advantage. Above all, we must avoid our opponents overcoming the flaws in their own armaments, particularly in the sphere of anti-tank and anti-aircraft defence, and thereby once more achieving parity.

With regard to this, every further month which is lost has a negative impact on Germany's offensive capability. Psychologically, swift action is not to be underestimated because its impetus both galvanizes the one side and deters the other. At the moment, the German soldier is once more considered the best in the world. His self-esteem is as great as the respect in which he is held by others. Six months of hesitancy in the conduct of war and effective enemy propaganda will once again weaken this important imponderable of morale. . . .

For this reason attack is invariably preferable to defence as a decisive method of war. It cannot begin soon enough. The coming months will not lead to a significant increase in our own offensive capability but almost certainly to a crucial increase in the defensive strength of our enemies. . . .

On the same day, 9 October, Hitler issued OKW Directive No. 6 for the Conduct of the War, in which he declared: 'If it becomes clear that Britain, and under its leadership France also, are not prepared to end the war, I am determined to go on the offensive without delay.' On 12 October, Chamberlain rejected the idea of a peace which confirmed Germany's conquests, finally convincing Hitler that further victories would be necessary to force Britain to come to heel.

The Army leadership was extremely sceptical about the feasibility of an early attack in the West. They were concerned both about Germany's lack of military preparedness—the Polish campaign had used up substantial quantities of the available war matériel—and about the strength of the opposition: memories of the First World War were still potent. On 5 November, Brauchitsch presented Hitler with a memorandum setting out the military arguments against an early offensive. Hitler responded angrily and scheduled the attack for 12 November. Bad weather, however, forced its cancellation.

A week later, on 23 November, Hitler addressed some 200 senior members of the armed forces in an attempt to convince them of the need for an early offensive in the West:

554

The purpose of this conference is to give you an idea of the thoughts which govern my view of future events, and to tell you my decisions. The building up of our armed forces was only possible in connexion with the ideological [*weltanschaulich*] education of the German people by the Party. When I started my political work in 1919, my strong belief in final success was based on thorough observation of the events of the day and on a study of the reasons for their occurrence. I never, therefore, lost my faith in the midst of setbacks which were not spared me during my period of struggle. Providence has had the last word and has brought me success. In addition, I had a clear understanding of the probable course of historical events, and the firm will to take brutal decisions. The first decision was in 1919 when after long inner struggles I became a politician and took up the struggle against my enemies. That was the hardest of all decisions. I had, however, the firm belief that I would achieve my goal. Above all, I desired a new system of selection. I wanted to educate a minority which would take over the leadership. After fifteen years, I arrived at my goal, after hard struggles and many setbacks. When I came to power in 1933, a period of the most difficult struggle lay behind me. Everything existing before that had collapsed. I had to reorganize everything, beginning with the mass of the people and extending it to the armed forces. First internal reorganization, the removal of symptoms of decay and defeatist ideas, education for heroism. In the course of the internal reorganization, I undertood the second task: to release Germany from its international ties. I would like to mention two points in particular: secession from the League of Nations and denunciation of the disarmament conference. It was a hard decision. The number of prophets who predicted that it would lead to the occupation of the Rhineland was large, the number of believers was very small. I was supported by the nation, which stood firmly behind me when I carried out my intentions. After that came the order for rearmament. Here again there were numerous prophets who predicted misfortunes, and only a few believers. In 1935, the introduction of compulsory military service. After that the militarization of the Rhineland, again a development considered impossible at that time. The number of people who put their trust in me was very small. Then the beginning of the fortification of the whole country especially in the west.

One year later came Austria. This step too was considered doubtful. It brought about a considerable reinforcement of the Reich. The next step was Bohemia, Moravia and Poland. But this could not be accomplished in one campaign. First of all, the western fortification had to be finished. It was not possible to reach the goal in one go. It was clear to me from the first moment that I could not be satisfied with the Sudeten German territory. That was only a partial solution. The decision to march into Bohemia was made. Then followed the establishment of the Protectorate and with that the basis for the action against Poland was laid, but I was not quite clear at that time whether I should start first against the east and then in the west or vice versa. Moltke often made the same calculations in his time. The pressure of events imposed the decision to fight with Poland first. One might accuse me of wanting to fight and fight again. In struggle I see the fate of all beings. Nobody can avoid struggle if he does not want to lose out. The increasing number of people requires a larger living space [*Lebensraum*]. My goal was to create a logical relationship between the number of people and the space for them to live in. The struggle must start here. No people can get away from the solution of this task, or it must yield and gradually die out. That is the lesson of history. . . . If the Polish war was won so quickly, it was owing to the superiority of our armed forces. The most glorious event in our history. Unexpectedly small losses of men and matériel. Now the eastern front is held by only a few divisions. It is a situation which we regarded previously as unattainable. Now the situation is as follows: Our opponent in the west lies behind his fortifications. There is no possibility of coming to grips with him. The decisive question is: how long can we endure this situation? Russia is at present not dangerous. It is now weakened by many developments. Moreover, we have a Treaty with Russia. Treaties, however, are only kept as long as they serve their purpose. Russia will hold herself to it only so long as Russia herself considers it to be to her benefit. Bismarck thought so too. Think of the Reinsurance Treaty. Now Russia has far-reaching goals, above all the strengthening of her position in the Baltic. We can oppose Russia only when we are free in the west. Further, Russia is seeking to increase her influence in the Balkans and is pressing toward the Persian Gulf. That is also the goal of our foreign policy. Russia will do what she considers best for her. At the present moment, she has withdrawn from internationalism. If she renounces it, she will go over to pan-Slavism. It is difficult to see into the future. It is a fact that at the present time the Russian army is of little account. For the next year or two the present situation will remain. . . .

Everything is determined by the fact that the moment is favourable now; in six months it may not be so any more.

As the last factor I must in all modesty name my own person: irreplaceable. Neither a military nor a civil person could replace me. Assassination attempts may be repeated. I am convinced of the powers of my intellect and of decision. Wars are always ended only by the destruction of the opponent. Everyone who believes differently is irresponsible. Time is working for our adversaries. Now there is a relationship of forces which can never be more propitious, but can only deteriorate. The enemy will not make peace when the relationship of forces is unfavourable for us. No compromise. Sternness towards ourselves. I shall strike and not capitulate. The fate of the Reich depends on me alone. I shall deal accordingly. Today we have a superiority such as we have never had before. After 1918 our opponents disarmed themselves of their own accord. England neglected the expansion of her fleet. . . .

We have an Achilles' Heel: the Ruhr. The progress of the war depends on the possession of the Ruhr. If England and France push through Belgium and Holland to the Ruhr, we shall be in the greatest danger. That could lead to the paralysing of the German power of resistance. Every hope of compromise is childish: Victory or defeat! The question is not the fate of National Socialist Germany, but who is to dominate Europe in the future. The question is worthy of the greatest efforts. Certainly England and France will assume the offensive against Germany when they have rearmed. England and France have means of pressure to bring Belgium and Holland to request their help. In Belgium and Holland the sympathies are all for France and England. . . . If the French army marches into Belgium in order to attack us, it will be too late for us. We must anticipate them. One more thing.

U-boats, mines, and Luftwaffe (also for mines) can strike England effectively, if we have a better starting-off point. Now a flight to England demands so much fuel that sufficient bomb loads cannot be carried. The invention of a new type of mine is of the greatest importance for the Navy. Aircraft will be the chief minelayers now. We shall sow the English coast with mines which cannot be cleared. This mine warfare with the Luftwaffe demands a different starting-off point. England cannot live without its imports. We can feed ourselves. The permanent sowing of mines on the English coast will bring England to her knees. However, this can only occur if we have occupied Belgium and Holland. It is a difficult decision for me. No one has ever achieved what I have achieved. My life is of no importance in all this. I have led the German people to a great height, even if the world does hate us now. I am staking my life's work on a gamble. I have to choose between victory or destruction. I choose victory. Greatest historical choice, to be compared with the decision of Frederick the Great before the first Silesian war. Prussia owes its rise to the heroism of one man. Even there the closest advisers were disposed to capitulation. Everything depended on Frederick the Great. Even the decisions of Bismarck in 1866 and 1870 were no less crucial. My decision is unalterable. I shall attack France and England at the most favourable opportunity. Breach of the neutrality of Belgium and Holland is irrelevant. No one will question that when we have won. We shall not bring about the breach of neutrality as idiotically as it was done in 1914. If we do not break the neutrality, then England and France will. Without an attack the war cannot be ended victoriously. I consider it only possible to end the war by means of an attack. The question whether or not the attack will be successful no one can answer. Everything depends upon the favourable moment. The military conditions are favourable. A prerequisite, however, is that the leadership must give an example of fanatical unity from above. There would be no failures if leaders always had the courage a rifleman must have.

The enemy must be beaten only by attack. Our chances are different today than they were during the offensive of 1918. So far as numbers go, we can deploy more than a hundred divisions. There are reserves of men. The supply situation is good. Moreover that which is not ready today must be ready tomorrow. It is not merely the outcome of a single action that is involved by that of the war itself. What is at stake is not just a single issue but the very existence of the nation.

I ask you to pass on the spirit of determination to all the lower echelons.

1. The decision is irrevocable.
2. The only prospect for success lies in the determination of all the armed forces.

The spirit of the great men of our history must hearten us all. Fate demands from us no more than from the great men of German history. As long as I live I shall think only of the victory of my people. I shall shrink from nothing and shall destroy everyone who is opposed to me. I have decided to live my life so that when I have to die I can stand unashamed. I want to destroy the enemy. Behind me stands the German people, whose morale can only grow worse. Only he who struggles with destiny can have a good intuition. In the last years I have experienced many examples of intuition. Even in the present development I see the work of Providence.

If we come through this struggle victoriously—and we shall—our age will enter into the history of our people. I shall stand or fall in this struggle. I shall never survive the defeat of my people. No capitulation to the enemy, no revolution from within.

The offensive in the West suffered repeated postponments during the winter of 1939–40 prompted by Hitler's concern about the weather and the transport situation. In January, he finally decided to postpone the attack until the spring. In the meantime, his attention was diverted to another area, Scandinavia. There were two spheres in which Scandinavia was of vital importance to the German war effort. In the first place, nearly half of Germany's iron ore supplies came from Sweden, much of which were transported down the Norwegian coast from the port of Narvik. Secondly, the Navy regarded Norway as of key significance because Germany's main submarine route passed between Norway and the Shetland Islands.

The outbreak of war with Britain and France already in 1939, instead of in 1944 or later as envisaged in the Z-Plan, had filled the Naval Commander-in-Chief, Admiral Raeder, with deep pessimism. On 3 September, he noted down the following 'Thoughts of the Commander-in-Chief of the Navy on the outbreak of war on 3 September 1939':

555

Today the war against England-France has broken out which, according to the Führer's previous statements, we did not need to anticipate before about 1944, and which the Führer thought he could avoid until the last moment (Address to the Commanders-in-Chief of the Armed Forces on the Obersalzberg on 22.8),[5] even if a comprehensive settlement of the Polish question was postponed as a result. At the turn of the year 1944/5, which was the date envisaged for the implementation of the naval Z Plan according to the Führer's instructions, Germany could have embarked on a war with England with the following naval forces distributed across the oceans for the purpose of attacks on trade:

3 fast battleships
3 modified pocket battleships
5 heavy cruisers
some M and reconnaisance cruisers
2 aircraft carriers
roughly 190 U-boats . . .

With the English fleet in pursuit of these German forces, which would be scattered across the oceans attacking trade, two groups of 3 each of the heaviest battleships with 40 cm guns would have had the task of attacking and destroying the major English units which would be more or less dispersed in their pursuit [of the German forces]. In this way, and particularly with the cooperation of Japan and Italy, who

[5] See above, pp. 739–43.

would have neutralized part of the English fleet, there would have been a good prospect of destroying the English fleet and of cutting off English supply lines, i.e. of finding the final solution to the English question.

On 3.9.1939, Germany entered the war with England because the latter—contrary to the Führer's assumption that England did not *need* to fight on account of the Polish question—*believed* it *ought to fight* at this moment, using the Polish question as an excuse, because in its view sooner or later it would have to fight Germany and then possibly under less favourable military circumstances (the completion of the construction of the German fleet).

As far as the Navy is concerned, it is of course not at all adequately armed for the great struggle with England. It has, it is true, created in the short time since 1935 (Naval Agreement)[6] a well-trained and effectively built-up U-boat arm, of which at the moment 26 boats are operational for the Atlantic, but which is nevertheless too weak to achieve a *decisive effect on the war*. The surface fleet, however, is so much weaker in numbers and fighting capacity compared to the English fleet that—assuming that it is fully committed in action—it can only demonstrate that it knows how to go down with dignity and is determined thereby to create the basis for a later reconstruction. The pocket battleships (at the outbreak of war only *Deutschland*[7] and *Graf Spee* are operational for the Atlantic), will be able to carry out a cruiser war on the high seas for a time if they are well captained; *Scharnhorst* and *Gneisenau*, which in addition, are far behind in their readiness for action and reliability, will have to endeavour to restrict enemy battle cruisers to their home waters and keep them from the pocket battleships. But even the pocket battleships cannot have a *decisive effect on the war*.

556

The Fleets of the great Naval Powers on 1 September 1939

	Britain	USA	Japan	France	Italy	Germany
Battleships	15	15	9	7	4	2
Pocket battleships	—	—	—	—	—	3
A/C carriers	7	6	6	1	—	—
Heavy cruisers	15	18	12	7	7	1
Light cruisers	49	19	25	11	14	6
Destroyers	192	236	112	61	61	21
Torpedo boats	—	—	12	12	70	12
U-boats	62	96	60	79	106	57

Raeder was convinced that if the Navy were to mount a campaign against British shipping it would need bases providing direct access to the Atlantic. On 10 October, he pointed out to Hitler the value of bases on the Norwegian coast for German U-boat warfare without, however, apparently

[6] See above, p. 667.
[7] Later renamed the *Lützow* (eds).

convincing him. Then, with the outbreak of the Russo-Finnish war on 30 November, Scandinavia became a major focus of interest for the great powers. The Navy feared that Britain might use the excuse of sending assistance to Finland to carry out a 'cold occupation' of Norway. On 12 December, Raeder persuaded Hitler to receive the Norwegian fascist leader, Quisling. Quisling evidently convinced Hitler of the danger of British intervention in Norway and, two days later, he ordered OKW to set up a staff to look into the possibility of the invasion of Norway. Then, on 16 February 1940, a British destroyer attacked a German ship, the *Altmark*, which was sailing in Norwegian waters, and freed British prisoners held on board. This incident prompted Hitler to accelerate the preparations. On 1 March, he issued the directive for Operation 'Weser Exercise':

557

1. The development of the situation in Scandinavia requires the making of all preparations for the occupation of Denmark and Norway by a part of the Wehrmacht (*Fall Weserübung*). This operation should prevent British encroachment on Scandinavia and the Baltic. Further it should guarantee our ore base in Sweden and give our Navy and Luftwaffe a wider start-line against Britain.

The part which the Navy and the Luftwaffe will have to play, within the limits of their capabilities, is to protect the operation against the interference of British naval and air striking forces.

In view of our military and political power in comparison with that of the Scandinavian States, the force to be employed in the *Fall Weserübung* will be kept as small as possible. The numerical weakness will be balanced by daring actions and surprise execution.

On principle, we will do our utmost to make the operation appear as a *peaceful* occupation, the object of which is the military protection of the neutrality of the Scandinavian States. Corresponding demands will be transmitted to the Governments at the beginning of the occupation. If necessary, naval and air demonstrations will provide the necessary emphasis. If, in spite of this, resistance should be met with, all military means will be used to crush it. . . .

3. The crossing of the Danish border and the landings in Norway must take place *simultaneously*. I emphasize that the operations must be prepared as quickly as possible. In case the enemy seizes the initiative against Norway, we must be able to apply immediately our own countermeasures. It is most important that the Scandinavian States as well as the Western opponents should be taken *by surprise* by our measures . . .

Although the conclusion of peace between Russia and Finland on 13 March removed the immediate threat of British intervention, Raeder still pressed for action on the grounds that 'sooner or later Germany will be faced with the issue of carrying out the Weser Exercise'.[8] Hitler agreed and, on 2 April, ordered the attack to go ahead on 9 April. In the meantime, however, Britain was preparing plans to mine the approaches to Narvik with the intention of provoking a German response which would then justify British intervention.

The attack on Denmark achieved success within a few hours. In Norway, however, the Germans not only came up against stiffer resistance from the Norwegian defences, but clashed with British naval forces which had begun laying mines the day before. Moreover, since a British expeditionary force was already prepared, it could be rapidly deployed against the German invasion. Although the Germans succeeded in capturing Oslo and a number of ports, they had limited numbers of troops, were scattered, and their reinforcement proved difficult. During the first week of the operation, the nerve of the German leadership almost cracked. A staff officer in OKW reported that 'people had lost their heads' and that Hitler 'sat ignored on a chair in the corner staring gloomily in front of him'.[9] At one point, Hitler wanted to evacuate Narvik and agreed to a section of the German forces if necessary crossing the border into Sweden to be interned. However, the Allied forces, lacking air support and artillery, and poorly led by comparison with the Germans, proved incapable of exploiting the situation. In any case, by June the campaign had been overtaken by events in France and the Allies finally withdrew on 8 June.

Meanwhile, Hitler's attention had reverted once more to the west. Preparations had been continuing all through the winter and, in the meantime, the plans had undergone an important modification. (See the map on page 1209 below.) The plans envisaged an attack by three Army Groups—A in the centre, B in the north and C in the south. Under the version of Deployment Directive 'Yellow', of 19 October, it was planned that the main thrust should come from Army Group B, which formed the right wing under General von Bock. Its main task would be to occupy Holland and thrust into Belgium north and south of Liège. The main task of Army Group A in the centre under General von Rundstedt would be to cover the southern flank of Army Group B by crossing the Meuse between Fumay and Mouzon and advancing into north-eastern France. Army Group C, under General von Leeb, would cover the Maginot Line further south.

This was a rather conventional plan which bore some similarity to that followed in the initial stages of the First World War. It would have come

---

[8] Cf. *Lagevorträge des Oberbefehlshabers der Marine vor Hitler 1939–1945*, ed., G. Wagner (Munich 1972) p. 86 (26.3.1940).

[9] W. Warlimont, *Im Hauptquartier der deutschen Wehrmacht 1933–1945* (Frankfurt a. M. 1964) p. 95 f.

as no surprise to the Allies. Moreover, its objectives were extremely limited. Hitler was not alone in being unsatisfied with the plan and during the next few days he suggested that the emphasis of the attack should be south of Liège. However, he finally settled for a dual-pronged attack by Army Group B north and south of Liège with each prong tipped with Panzer divisions. Holland would be excluded from the invasion. This plan was incorporated in a revised version of 'Yellow' dated 29 October:

558

(a) *Deployment Directive 'Yellow'*

1. *General intention*. The attitude of the Western Powers may require the German army in the west to go over to the offensive. All available forces will be committed with the intention of bringing to battle on north French and Belgian soil as many sections of the French army and its allies as possible. This will create favourable conditions for the further conduct of the war against England and France on land and in the air.

2. *Deployment and tasks*. (*a*) The attack will be made under my command by Army Groups B and A with the aim of destroying the Allied forces in the area north of the Somme and of breaking through to the Channel coast. Army Groups B and A will assemble east of the Reich frontier between Geldern and Mettlach (south of Trier) under camouflage so that they can take up the necessary positions for crossing the frontier within the space of six night marches and attack on the morning of the 7th. The time by which they must be ready will be given separately. Army Group C will have to hold the fortifications in its sector with a minimum of forces. A separate order will deal with the question of simulated attacks. . . .

3. *Tasks of the attacking front*. (*a*) After breaking through the Belgian frontier fortifications, Army Group B will initially advance in a westerly direction. One attacking force will be sent north of Liège to the area round Brussels, the other south of Liège to the area south and south-west of Namur, so that without loss of time the attack of the Army Group can be continued either in a westerly or in a north-westerly or south-westerly direction depending on the situation. After the breach of the fortified frontier zone, motorized forces must be committed as quickly and in as great a strength as possible. In the area of the northern attacking force they must be pushed forward in the direction of Ghent, in the area of the southern attacking force in the direction of Thuin with the aim, by means of ruthless attack, of preventing the formation of an enemy battle front and so that in mutual cooperation, and following the directives of the Army Group, they may create favourable conditions for the supporting forces to sustain the attack. If necessary, Army Group B will concentrate the motorized units of both attacking forces wherever favourable opportunities exist for a rapid advance. The motorized units of one attacking force must not be allowed to lie idle when they could be effectively employed by the other. With the release of the motorized forces for the advance, their leadership must be separated from that of the infantry divisions which are following. Army Group B will organize the employment of the Army High Commands for the

various tasks. The fortresses of Liège and Antwerp are to be surrounded in accordance with the orders of Army Group B. The enemy must be prevented from escaping from the areas of the fortresses. . . .

(*b*) Army Group A will cover the attack of Army Group B against an enemy advance from the south and south-west. For this purpose it will push its right wing as quickly as possible over the Meuse near and south of Fumay and through the fortified French frontier zone in the general direction of Laon. . . .

However, Hitler was still unhappy about this plan and, when it was captured after a staff officer had landed in Belgium, he became convinced that the only way to surprise the enemy was to concentrate the attack further South on the southern Meuse in the direction of Sedan. Initially, however OKH regarded this plan as too risky because the wooded Ardennes hills, through which the attack would have to pass, were considered impassable for tanks. At this stage, Hitler lacked the military self-confidence to press his point. Meanwhile, however, the Chief of Staff of Army Group A, General von Manstein, probably the most brilliant strategic brain on the General Staff, had also expressed his disquiet about the plan for 'Yellow'. He too wished more emphasis to be given to the thrust in the Centre in order to cut off the Allied forces in Belgium on the Somme, and he ascertained from the tank warfare expert General Heinz Guderian, that the Ardennes were not an insuperable obstacle provided sufficient tank forces were employed. After securing the backing of his commander, von Rundstedt, Manstein pressed his views in several memoranda to OKH. The Army High Command resented this interference which they may well have assumed sprang merely from a desire to increase the role of Manstein's own Army Group. They decided, therefore, to transfer him to a command in eastern Germany, well out of the way. Before leaving, however, Manstein succeeded in putting his point of view to Hitler's Wehrmacht adjutant and, when Hitler learnt that one of the acknowledged military experts appeared to be thinking along the same lines as himself, he called him for interview on 17 February 1940. Then, confirmed in his own opinion, Hitler ordered the redrafting of 'Yellow' in accordance with Manstein's plan, thereby transferring the 'centre of gravity' of the attack from Army Group B in the north to Army Group A in the centre. In fact, meanwhile, a series of war games had already persuaded OKH that Manstein had been correct after all.

This new draft of 24 February embodied the famous *Sichelschnitt* ('Sickle Cut') strategy which was to prove so devastatingly successful in May. The key to the plan was that, since the wooded hills of the Ardennes facing Army Group A were considered impassable for tanks, this section of the front would be more lightly defended. Allied forces would concentrate further north to meet the expected German thrust through Belgium. Once through the Ardennes, the German armour would be in the plains of northern France and could make straight for the Channel coast, thereby cutting the Allied forces in half and squeezing the main allied force in Belgium between Army Group A advancing from the south and Army Group B in the north. The following were General von Manstein's suggestions to Hitler made on 17 February 1940 for the alteration of 'Yellow':

559

1. *The aim of the Western offensive* must be *to bring about the decision on land.* The political and military stakes are too high for partial objectives such as are contained in the existing plan of attack, namely, the destruction of as large a part of the enemy forces as possible in Belgium and the occupation of parts of the Channel coast.

From the outset, therefore, those directing the operations must aim at the destruction of the French powers of resistance.

2. For this it is necessary that, contrary to the deployment directive, right from the start the centre of gravity of the attack should be in the southern wing [the centre], i.e. should be transferred to Army Group A instead of remaining with B or being left undecided. Under the existing plan at best one can only smash the advancing Franco-British forces in Belgium in a frontal attack and throw them back on the Somme, where the operation could come to a standstill.

The southern wing, i.e. Army Group A, must push through southern Belgium over the Meuse and in the direction of the lower Somme. By definitely transferring the centre of gravity in this way, the strong enemy forces which may be expected in north Belgium and which will have been thrown back by Army Group B through frontal attack, will be cut off and destroyed. This will only be possible if Army Group A pushes through quickly to the lower Somme. This must be the first part of the campaign. The second part, the encirclement of the French army by means of a strong right-wing movement, will follow on from it.

3. For such a task it will be necessary to divide Army Group A into three armies. Thus another Army will have to be inserted in its right wing.

The northernmost Army of the Army Group (2nd) has the task of crossing the Meuse and breaking through to the lower Somme in order to cut off the enemy forces withdrawing from Army Group B.

South of that, a second Army (12th) must advance over the Meuse on either side of Sedan and then turn south-westward and, by taking the offensive, defeat all French attempts to mass troops for a counter-attack.

The third Army (16th) has the initially defensive role of covering the southern flank of the operation between the Meuse and the Moselle.

It is essential that the Air Force destroys the French concentration early on, because if the French attempt anything it will be a large-scale counter-attack to the west or on both sides of the Meuse, possibly reaching up to the Moselle.

The idea of committing only the XIX (motorized) Corps to the Meuse near Sedan is a half-measure. If the enemy attack us with strong motorized forces in south Belgium, the Corps will be too weak to destroy these quickly while crossing the Meuse with the remainder of its forces. If the enemy limit themselves to holding the line of the Meuse with forces of some strength, relatively to the present balance of forces, the Corps will not be able to cross the Meuse on its own.

If one is going to commit motorized forces, there must be at least two Corps in the present sector of the Army Group which can cross the Meuse simultaneously near Charleville and Sedan, independently of the commitment of tank forces on the Meuse near Givet by the 4th Army. Thus the XIV Armoured Corps must be placed beside Guderian's Corps from the beginning. It must not be earmarked for the use of Army Group A or B [but definitely for A].

The Führer expressed his agreement with these statements. A short time afterwards, the new and final deployment directive was issued.

The following was the new draft of Directive 'Yellow' dated 24 February, incorporating Manstein's suggestions:

560

1. The offensive 'Yellow' is intended to remove the threat of a British occupation of Dutch territory by means of the rapid occupation of Holland, to defeat as many sections as possible of the Anglo-French army by an attack through Belgium and Luxemburg, and thereby to pave the way for the destruction of the military power of the enemy.

The centre of gravity of the attack through Belgium and Luxemburg will lie south of the line Liège–Charleroi.

The forces in action north of this line will break through the Belgian frontier defences. By a further offensive in a westerly direction they will eliminate any direct threat to the Ruhr area from north-east Belgium and draw as large a section as possible of the Anglo-French army toward them.

The forces in action south of the line Liège–Charleroi will force a crossing of the Meuse between Dinant and Sedan (both inclusive) and open up a way through the French frontier defences in the north in the direction of the lower reaches of the Somme.

2. The attack north of the line Liège–Charleroi will be led by the Supreme Command of Army Group B with the 18th and 6th Armies, the attack south of this line by the Supreme Command of Army Group A led by the 4th, 12th and 16th Armies.

Army Group C will tie down the enemy opposite its position and remain prepared to ward off diversionary attacks by the enemy. . . .

5. *Tasks of the Army Groups and initial tasks of the armies.* The task of Army Group B is to occupy Holland by means of motorized forces and to prevent the linking up of the Dutch army with Anglo-Belgian forces. It will destroy the Belgian frontier defences by a rapid and powerful attack and will throw the enemy back over the line Antwerp–Namur.

The fortress of Antwerp will be surrounded from the north and east, the fortress of Liège from the north-east and north of the Meuse. . . . The task of Army Group A will be to force a crossing of the Meuse between Dinant and Sedan (both inclusive) as quickly as possible, while covering the left flank of the whole offensive against enemy attack from the protected region round Metz and Verdun. Then, while continuing to cover the flanks, it will break through in the rear of the French frontier fortifications in the north in the direction of the mouth of the Somme as rapidly and in as great strength as possible. For this purpose Army Supreme command 2 will be available as an additional Army Supreme Command.

Strong motorized forces in deep formation must be sent ahead of the front of the Army Group towards the Dinant–Sedan sector of the Meuse. Their task is to smash the enemy forces which have advanced into south Belgium and Luxemburg, to gain the west bank of the Meuse in a surprise assault and thereby to secure favourable conditions for the continuation of the offensive toward the west. . . .

The German offensive in the west was finally launched on 10 May. The balance of forces on both sides was as follows:

561

I. Army

	Divisons	Artillery pieces	Tanks
France	104[a]	10,700	3,063[a]
Great Britain[b]	10	1,280	310
Belgium	22	1,338	10
Netherlands	8	656	
Total	144	13,974	3,383
Germany	141	7,378[c]	2,445[d]

II. Air Force

	Aircraft total	Fighters	Bombers	Reconnaissance
France	1,368[e]	637	242	489
Great Britain[b]	456	261	135	60
Belgium	250	90	12	120
Netherlands	175	62	9	50
Great Britain (Home strength)	850	540	310	
Total	3,099	1,590	708	719
Germany	5,446	1,736	2,224	700
Operational (on 4.5.1940)	4,020	1,220	1,559	535

a) Only northeast front including reserves and a Polish Division; b) Expeditionary force; c) Excluding Norway and the East; d) total available: 3,505; e) operational aircraft in home bases.

Although the Allies had a slight advantage in terms of both numbers and matériel (with the significant exception of aircraft—particularly dive-bombers), this was heavily outweighed by the single German command structure and by the superiority of German *blitzkrieg* tactics operating according to Manstein's plan. The Germans deployed twenty-nine divisions under Army Group B in the north and forty-four divisions, including the bulk of the armour, under Army Group A in the Centre. Army Group C with seventeen divisions covered the southern flank and posed a threat to the French eastern flank. Everything went according to plan. By 23 May, the major portion of the British Expeditionary Force, the Belgians and several French divisions were trapped between Army Group B in the north and Army Group A in the south. Moreover, the spearheads of the German panzer units of Army Group A were only a few miles from Dunkirk, the only available port of evacuation for the British troops. (See the map on page 1210 below.) Yet on that day these tanks received the order to halt, an order which gave the British the necessary breathing space to organize defences so that the evacuation could go ahead. The following documents show who was responsible and the reasons for this decision:

562

(*a*) *War Diary of Army Group A*
24.v.40. . . . At 11.30 the Führer arrives and receives a summary of the situation from the C.-in-C. of the Army Group. He comlpletely agrees with the opinion that the infantry should attack east of Arras while the motorized units should be held on the line Lens–Béthune–Aire–St Omer–Gravelines in order to 'catch' the enemy who are being pushed back by Army Group B. He gives it added emphasis by stating that it is necessary to conserve the tank units for the coming operations and that a further narrowing of the pocket would result in an extremely undesirable restriction of Luftwaffe operations. . . .

(*b*) *OKW Jodl Diary*
25.v.40. In the morning the C.-inC. of the Army arrives and asks permission for the tanks and motorized divisions to come down from the heights of Vimy–St Omer–Gravelines into the plains towards the east. The Führer is against, leaves the decision to Army Group A. They turn it down for the time being since the tanks must have time to recover in order to be ready for the tasks in the south. . . .

From these documents it is clear that the initial decision to halt was that of von Rundstedt, Commander of Army Group A. When he arrived on the scene Hitler confirmed this decision and made it a Führer command, thereby overriding the Army High Command (OKH). Hitler had been urged by Göring to let the Air Force finish off the retreating British and his own experience of the First World War persuaded him to concentrate on the primary task of defeating France and capturing Paris for fear of the offensive becoming bogged down. He was particularly concerned about the German armour which had suffered a high rate of attrition. Nevertheless, it is clear from the second document that on the following day he left the decision to Army Group A.

The decision to halt caused consternation in the headquarters of OKH, and the Chief of Staff, General Halder, who had become an enthusiastic convert to the 'Sickle Cut', commented bitterly on it in his diary:

563

25.v.40. The day begins once again with unpleasant arguments between von Br[auchitsch] and the Führer concerning the future course of the battle of encirclement. I had envisaged the battle going as follows: Army Group B would mount a heavy frontal assault on the enemy, which would be making a planned withdrawal, with the aim merely of tying them down. Army Group A, meeting a beaten enemy, would tackle it from the rear and bring about the decision. This was to be achieved by means of the motorized troops. Now the political leadership gets the idea of transferring the final decisive battle from Flanders to northern France. In order to disguise this political aim it is explained that the Flanders terrain with its numerous waterways is unsuitable for tanks. The tanks of the other motorized troops, therefore, had to be halted after reaching the line St Omer–Béthune.

In other words the position is reversed. I wanted the Army Group A to be the hammer and B to be the anvil. Now B is made the hammer and A the anvil. Since B is faced with an organized front this will cost a lot of blood and take a long time. For the Air Force on which hopes were pinned is dependent on the weather. . . .

At 1.30 p.m. on the 26th, Hitler ordered the German armour to continue the advance, but the forty-eight hours delay was sufficient for the construction of defences to allow the evacuation of the bulk of the BEF as well as a sizeable French contingent during the following week.

564

Evacuation of Allied troops from the area round Dunkirk

Date	From the beach	From Dunkirk harbour	Altogether	Total
27.5.		7,669	7,669	7,669
28.5.	5,930	11,874	17,804	25,473
29.5.	13,752	33,558	47,310	72,783
30.5.	29,512	24,311	53,823	126,606
31.5.	22,942	45,072	68,014	194,620
1.6.	17,348	47,081	64,429	259,049
2.6.	6,695	19,561	26,256	285,305
3.6.	1,870	24,876	26,746	312,051
4.6.	622	25,553	26,175	338,226
	98,671	239,555	338,226	

Including the roughly 28,000 who were evacuated before 27 May, nearly 370,000 allied soldiers including 139,000 French, escaped capture.

Following the capture of Dunkirk, the Germans launched the second phase of their invasion, Operation 'Red', on 5 June. It soon achieved rapid success with the capture of Paris nine days later. On 18–19 June, Hitler met Mussolini in Munich. Ciano recorded the event in his dairy:

565

JUNE 18 and 19, 1940. During the rail journey the German welcome is very warm. At Munich a meeting with Hitler and von Ribbentrop. The Duce and the Führer are locked in conference. Von Ribbentrop exceptionally moderate and calm, and in favour of peace. He says at once that we must offer lenient armistice terms to France, especially concerning the fleet; this is to avoid the French fleet joining with the English fleet. From von Ribbentrop's words I feel that the mood has changed also as regards England. If London wants war it will be a total war, complete, pitiless. But Hitler makes many reservations on the desirability of demolishing the British Empire, which he considers, even to-day, to be an important factor in world equilibrium. I ask von Ribbentrop a clear-cut question: 'Do you prefer the continuation of the war, or peace?' He does not hesitate a moment. 'Peace.' He also alludes to vague contacts between London and Berlin by means of Sweden. I speak of our desiderata with respect to France. In general I find him understanding, but von Ribbentrop does not want to push the conversation further because he does not know as yet Hitler's precise ideas. He says only that there is a German project to round up and send the Jews to Madagascar.

The conference then continued with Hitler, Mussolini, and the military authorities. In principle the terms of the armistice with France are fixed. Mussolini shows himself to be quite intransigent on the matter of the fleet.

Hitler, on the other hand, wants to avoid an uprising of the French Navy in favour of the British. From all that he says it is clear that he wants to act quickly to end it. Hitler is now the gambler who has made a big scoop and would like to get up from the table risking nothing more. To-day he speaks with a reserve and a perspicacity which, after such a victory, are really astonishing. I cannot be accused of excessive tenderness towards him, but to-day I truly admire him.

Mussolini is very much embarrassed. He feels that his role is secondary.

The armistice signed between Germany and France on 22 June contained a set of relatively modest demands, since Hitler was anxious not to provoke the French Government into continuing resistance from the French colonies and handing over their fleet to the British. The Germans restricted their occupation to three-fifths of the country, comprising the north and a coastal strip in the west, while the remainder was granted partial independence under the government of Marshal Pétain based at Vichy. The losses on both sides during the campaign were as follows:

566

Countries	Dead	Wounded
Germany	27,000	111,000
France	92,000	200,000
Great Britain	69,637	
Belgium	7,500	15,850
Netherlands	2,890	6,900
Italy	1,247	4,782

CHAPTER 30

Strategic Vacillation, June–December 1940

(i) Policy towards Russia and Britain, June–September 1940

Hitler was aware that the decisions which he reached over the next few months would probably decide the outcome of the war. With the defeat of France, the questions of Britain and Russia became the main preoccupation of the German leadership. Hitler hoped that the defeat of France would make Britain come to terms. On the basis of his reading of history, he believed that Britain intervened on the Continent only when she could use an ally as her 'Continental sword'. Now, with the defeat of France, this sword had been struck from her hands, and, although he began making preparations for an invasion of Britain, this was intended to force her to make peace rather than destroy her. According to Hanno von Etzdorf, the Foreign Ministry liaison official with OKH, Germany sought 'contact with England on the basis of partitioning the world',[1] while his superior, State Secretary von Weizsäcker, reckoned that 'it will probably turn out that we will suggest to the English that, having received a black eye, they should remove themselves from the Continent and leave it to us'.[2]

On 15 July 1940, a journalist, Dr Hans-Joachim Kausch, recorded the following 'strictly confidential' briefing provided by the Propaganda Ministry for the editorial departments of Germany's leading newspapers:

1. F. Halder, *Kriegstagebuch* I, p. 308. (21.5.1940.)
2. *Weizsäcker-Papiere*, p. 204. (23.5.1940.)

567

New authentic information has clarified the recent political soundings which have taken place between Germany and Britain during the pause in hostilities. It is now certain that Germany's views have been passed on to Churchill directly via leading Swedish circles i.e. via Stockholm and that contact has been further sought with Halifax via the British ambassador in Madrid, Sir Samuel Hoare. About twelve or thirteen days ago, these soundings were broken off as a result of the hostile attitude of the British ruling class.

Germany's views about the possibilities of a political peace, already mentioned, involved Britain withdrawing from Europe, i.e. from the continent and the Mediterranean and agreeing to a complete revision of the colonial sphere in Africa. Until the soundings were broken off, the Führer was of the opinion that sooner or later Germany would have to work together with the healthy section of the British people and therefore that it was not appropriate to destroy the whole [British] empire, since this would simply mean that the Russians, the Japanese, and the Americans could secure an easy inheritance which is not in our interest. In the Führer's view sooner or later the racially valuable germanic element in Britain would have to be brought in to join with Germany in the future secular struggles of the white race against the yellow race or the germanic race against Bolshevism.

Now, we cannot expect to avoid a very hard and costly military blow against Britain. Here in Berlin people are dubious about there being an early landing. Probably the air bombardment will be stepped up so much that there will still be the possibility of the British people being softened up before a major confrontation, involving an invasion etc., occurs.

The Führer wants an early end to the war. In the first place, as I explained, the economic problems in Europe require to be solved centrally which can only be properly and carefully achieved in peace time. Furthermore, the Führer wants to consolidate the Reich in all spheres of life during the period in which he is in full possession of his energies. All attempts to create new particularisms must be nipped in the bud. Socialism will crown the Führer's work and these efforts too can only flourish in peace time. Furthermore, there are big building plans ahead and the Führer is also keen to take on the great and revolutionary problems involved in adjusting Europe to German hegemony . . .

As far as Russia was concerned, Hitler was aware of the advantage of cooperation with the Soviet Union at least in the short term. On 8 March 1940, he had expressed his view on German–Russian relations with Russia in a letter to Mussolini, who was hostile to the Nazi–Soviet Pact:

568

. . . Germany's relationship to Russia is the outcome of:

1. An over-all appraisal of the general European development and
2. Consideration of the special situation in which the Reich finds itself today.

The appraisal of the general situation gives the following result:
Since Stalin's final victory, Russia has without doubt experienced a modification of the Bolshevist principle in the direction of a nationalist Russian way of life, which is out of the question for us, but which could not be replaced by anything else in Russia herself at the present time. That which made National Socialism the mortal enemy of Communism was the latter's Jewish-international leadership with its avowed goal of destroying the non-Jewish nations or their leading forces. How far-reaching this, to our minds, epochal change in Russia has been is somethig which the Reich Foreign Minister will be able to describe to you, Duce, from his personal impressions and experience. For my part I merely wish to say that since Litvinov's departure there has unquestionably been a change in Russia's attitude toward Germany. There can be no doubt that the conditions for establishing a reasonable relationship between the two countries exist today. We no longer have any reason for believing that any Russian agency is trying to exert influence on German domestic affairs. I do not have to emphasize, moreover, that National-Socialist Germany is completely immune to any ideological attacks by Bolshevism. Accordingly, nobody here thinks of making concessions. But if Bolshevism in Russia is developing into a Russian naftional state ideology and economy, it constitutes a reality which we have neither interest nor reason to combat. On the contrary! In our struggle against the blockade of the world by the plutocratic democracies, Duce we can only welcome every factor and every assistance. Germany and Russia have often lived in peace and friendship for very long periods of time. Our economies complement each other to an extraordingary degree. There is almost no raw material which we need that Russia does not possess or could not make available to us within a reasonable time. And, conversely, there is not a product of German industry which Russia does not either already need or will not in the foreseeable future. The trade agreement which we have concluded with Russia, Duce, means a great deal in our situation!
Specifically, however, what Germany has done was simply a clear-cut delimitation of zones of interest with respect to Russia, in which nothing will ever change again. I took here only the same step that I took with you earlier, Duce, when I accepted the Brenner as the final line of demarcation between the lives and destinies of our two peoples. The emigration of more than 200,000 Germans from Italy will ratify this decision for all time and thus give it final sanction.

However, the rapid victory over France and the refusal of Britain to come to terms created a new situation for both Russia and Germany requiring them to reappraise their relationship.

Russia had anticipated a long war between Germany and France exhausting both powers and leaving her as the 'laughing third'. Stalin now responded to the unexpected development by acting fast to acquire new territory both as a means of improving Russian defences vis-à-vis Germany and in pursuit of Russian imperialist goals. Thus, he now claimed his side of the bargain, contained in the Russo-German pacts of August and September 1939, by annexing the Baltic states of Lithuania, Estonia, and

Latvia in June–July 1940. In addition, he demanded territory from Romania: the province of Bessarabia, taken from Russia in 1918, through which the Danube flowed into the Black Sea, and the province of Bukovina.

These Russian actions caused concern in Germany, particularly the pressure on Romania which was an important source of German oil. While accepting Russian annexation of Bessarabia, Germany insisted that Russia limit herself to the northern part of Bukovina. The development of German policy towards Russia in the crucial months of June–December 1940 can be best traced in the War Diaries of General Halder, Chief of the General Staff. One clue to this policy lies in German military dispositions for which Hitler was ultimately responsible but in which Halder played an independent role.

Once the defeat of France had become clear Hitler ordered a reduction of the Army by 35 divisions to 120 divisions. As Halder pointed out, the assumption was that with 'the now imminent final collapse of the enemy [France], the Army's task has been fulfilled . . . the Navy and Air Force will then have the task of continuing the war against England on their own'.[3] At the same time, however, Halder planned the transfer of the headquarters of 18th Army and fifteen infantry divisions to secure the Eastern frontier, and his instructions for their deployment indicate that he intended any enemy attack to be countered with *offensive* tactics.[4] Initially, there were no plans to deploy armoured units on the Eastern frontier. By 25 June, however, Halder was thinking in terms of creating a 'force with striking power' in the East and for this purpose an armoured group under General Guderian was to be deployed to reinforce the infantry divisions of the 18th Army.

Halder's move reflected his growing concern, first, about recent Russian activities in the Balkans—the annexation of Bessarabia and the demand for Bukovina from Romania, and secondly, about Russia's future behaviour in the event that Britain refused to make peace, a situation which would increase German dependence on Russian goodwill. Halder's growing concern was evidently shared by Hitler, whose view of events Weizsäcker reported to Halder on 30 June: 'Eyes concentrated on the East . . . England will probably need another demonstration of our military force before it yields and leaves our rear free for the East.'[5]

3. F. Halder, *Kriegstagebuch* I, p. 357. (15.6.1940.)

4. Cf. E. Klink, 'Die Militärische Konception des Krieges gegen die Sowjetunion' in: *Das Deutsche Reich und der Zweite Weltkrieg*. Bd. 4 *Der Angriff auf die Sowjetunion* eds H. Boog *et. al.*

5. F. Halder, *op. cit.* p. 375.

Halder became particularly concerned about two concentrations of troops in Western Russia. Although he did not fear an attack on Germany itself, he was worried about the possibility of Soviet action against Romania which would threaten German oil supplies. By 3 July, he had become convinced that the question of the East 'must be treated mainly from the point of view of how a military blow against Russia can be carried out to force it to recognize Germany's dominant role in Europe'.[6]

The questions of Britain and Russia came up at Halder's interview with Hitler on 13 July as he recorded in his diary:

569

. . . 12.00 Interview with Hitler about attack on England . . .
Military review of the political situation:
(*a*) It seems advisable not to disband about 20 of the 35 divisions intended for demobilization, but only to send them back home on leave as a source of labour so that these divisions can be reactivated at once [Proposal of C. in C. Army].
(*b*) Political observations [of Hitler].
1. Führer wants to bring Spain into play in order to build up the enemy front against England from the North Cape to Morocco. Ribbentrop will go to Spain.
2. Russia's interest in not letting us get too big is recognised. Russia's aspirations towards the Bosphorus are inconvenient for Italy.

The Führer is most concerned about the question of why Britain will not yet make peace. He sees the answer, as we do, in the fact that Britain still has hopes of Russia. He reckons therefore that England will have to be compelled to make peace by force. But he does not like doing this. The reason is that if we crush England's military power the British Empire will collapse. That is of no use to Germany. German blood would be shed to accomplish something that would benefit only Japan, America, and others.

On 16 July 1940, however, the logic of the situation created by Britain's refusal to come to terms compelled Hitler to issue a directive for the invasion of Britain, Directive No. 16:

570

On the preparation of a landing operation against England
Since England, despite her hopeless situation in the military sense, still shows no sign of willingness to come to terms, I have decided to prepare a landing operation against England, and if necessary to carry it out.

6. Ibid II. p. 6.

The aim of this operation is to eliminate the English homeland as a base for the carrying on of the war against Germany, and, if it should become necessary, to occupy it completely.

To this end I order the following:

1. The *Landing* must be carried out in the form of a surprise crossing on a broad front approximately from Ramsgate to the area west of the Isle of Wight, in which Luftwaffe units will take the role of the artillery, and units of the Navy the role of the engineers. Whether it is practical before the general landing to undertake *subordinate actions*, such as the occupation of the Isle of Wight or of the County of Cornwall, is to be determined from the standpoint of each branch of the Wehrmacht and the result is to be reported to me. I reserve the decision for myself. The preparations for the entire operation must be completed by *mid-August*

2. To these preparations also belong the creation of those conditions which make a landing in England possible:

(*a*) The English air force must be so beaten down in morale and in fact, that it can no longer display any appreciable aggressive force in opposition to the German crossing.

(*b*) Mine-free channels must be created.

(*c*) By means of a closely concentrated mine-barrier the Straits of Dover must be sealed off on both *flanks* as well as the western entrance to the Channel at the approximate line Alderney–Portland.

(*d*) The area off the coast must be dominated and given artillery protection by strong coastal artillery.

(*e*) It would be desirable shortly before the crossing to tie down the English naval forces in the North Sea as well as in the Mediterranean (by the Italians), in which connexion the attempt should be made now to damage the English naval forces which are in the homeland by air and torpedo attacks in strength.

3. *Organization of the command and of the preparations*. Under my command and in accordance with my general directives the Commanders-in-Chief will command the forces to be used from their branches of the Wehrmacht. The operations staffs of the Commander-in-Chief of the Army, the Commander-in-Chief of the Navy and the Commander-in-Chief of the Luftwaffe must from 1 August onwards be placed within a radius of at most 50 km. from my headquarters (Ziegenberg). Quartering of the restricted operations staffs of the Commanders-in-Chief of the Army and Navy together at Giessen seems to me advisable.

Hence, for the command of the landing armies the Commander-in-Chief of the Army will have to employ an Army Group headquarters.

The project will bear the code name *Seelöwe* [Sea Lion].

In the preparation and carrying out of the undertaking the following duties will fall to the various branches of the Wehrmacht:

(*a*) *Army*: Will draw up first of all the operational plan and the transport plan for all formations to be shipped across as the first wave. The anti-aircraft artillery to be transported with the first wave will at the same time be attached to the Army (to the individual crossing groups) until such time as a division of tasks in support and protection of ground troops, in protection of the ports of debarkation and in protection of the air bases to be occupied, can be carried out. The Army furthermore will distribute the means of transport to the individual crossing groups and establish the embarkation and landing points in agreement with the Navy.

(*b*) *Navy*: Will secure the means of transport and will bring them, corresponding to the desires of the Army and according to the requirements of seamanship, into the individual embarkation areas. In so far as possible, ships of the defeated enemy States are to be procured. For every ferrying point it will provide the necessary naval staff for advice on matters of seamanship, with escort vessels and security forces. It will protect, along with the air forces employed to guard the movement, the entire crossing of the channel on both flanks. An order will follow on the regulation of the command relationship during the crossing. It is further the task of the Navy to regulate, in a uniform manner, the building up of the coastal artillery, that is, all batteries of the Army as well as of the Navy, which can be used for firing against sea targets, and to organize the fire control of the whole. As large an amount as possible of *very heavy artillery* is to be employed as quickly as possible to secure the crossing and to protect the flanks from enemy operations from the sea. For this purpose, railway artillery (supplemented by all available captured pieces), less the batteries (K5 and K12) provided for firing on targets on the English mainland, is to be brought up and emplaced by using railway turn-tables.

Independently of this, the heaviest available platform batteries are to be opposite the Straits of Dover, so emplaced under concrete that they can withstand even the heaviest aerial attacks and can thereby dominate permanently within their effective range the Straits of Dover in any circumstances.

The technical work is the responsibility of the Todt Organization.

(*c*) *The mission of the Luftwaffe is*: To hinder interference from the enemy air force. To overcome coastal defences which could do damage to the landing places, to break the first resistance of enemy ground troops and to smash reserves which may be coming up. For this mission the closest cooperation of individual units of the Luftwaffe with the crossing units of the Army is necessary. Furthermore, to destroy important transport routes for the bringing up of enemy reserves, and to attack enemy naval forces coming up, while they are still far away from the crossing points, I request proposals on the use of parachute and glider troops. In this regard it is to be determined in conjunction with the Army whether it is worthwhile to hold parachute and glider troops here in readiness as a *reserve* to be quickly committed in case of emergency.

4. The Wehrmacht Chief of Communications will carry out the necessary preparations for communication connexions from France to the English mainland. The installation of the remaining 80-km. East Prussian cable is to be provided for in conjunction with the Navy.

5. I request the Commanders-in-Chief to submit to me as soon as possible:

(*a*) the intentions of the Navy and Luftwaffe for achieving the necessary conditions for the crossing of the Channel;

(*b*) the construction of the coastal batteries in detail (Navy).

(*c*) a survey of the tonnage to be employed and the methods of getting it ready and fitting it out. Participation of civilian agencies? (Navy);

(*d*) the organization of aerial protection in the assembly areas for troops about to cross and the means of crossing (Luftwaffe);

(*e*) the crossing and operations plan of the Army, composition and equipment of the first crossing wave;

(*f*) the organization and measures of the Navy and the Luftwaffe for the carrying out of the crossing itself, security of the crosing, and support of the landing;

(*g*) proposals for the commitment of parachute and glider troops, as well as for the detailing and command of anti-aircraft artillery, after an extensive occupation of territory on English soil has been made (Luftwaffe);

(*h*) proposals for the setting up of the operations staffs of the Commanders-in-Chief of the Army and of the Navy;

(*i*) the attitude of Army, Navy and Luftwaffe on the question whether and what subsidiary actions *before* the general landing are considered practical;

(*k*) proposals of Army and Navy on the overall command *during* the crossing.

But three days later, on 19 July, in a speech to the Reichstag Hitler made a final attempt to persuade Britain to negotiate a peace settlement. Again there were no concrete proposals, and it was primarily a propaganda gesture rather than a serious peace offer:

571

. . . Mr Churchill has just declared again that he wants the war. About six weeks ago he began to fight in the sphere in which he seems to think he is particularly strong, namely the air war against the civilian population, though under the pretence that the targets are important for the war effort. Since Freiburg[7] these targets have been open cities, market towns and villages, houses, hospitals, schools, nursery schools and whatever else is being hit.

So far I have hardly bothered to respond to this. But that need not mean that this is or will remain my only answer.

I am quite aware of the fact that people will suffer incredible misery and misfortune from our impending response. Naturally this will not affect Mr Churchill, for he will certainly be in Canada where the property and the children of the most important people who have an interest in the war have already been taken. But for millions of other people there will be great misery. And perhaps Mr Churchill should believe me for once when I prophesy the following:

A great empire will be destroyed. A world empire that I never intended to destroy or even damage. But it is clear to me that the continuation of this struggle will end with the complete destruction of one of the two opponents. Mr Churchill may believe that this will be Germany. I know that it will be England.

At this hour I feel compelled by conscience once more to appeal to reason in England. I believe I am in a position to do this because I am not the vanquished begging favours. As victor, I am speaking in the name of reason. I can see no reason why this war should go on.

7. German aircraft bombed Freiburg by mistake on 10 May 1940, killing 57 inhabitants including 22 children. The raid was blamed on the Allies by German propaganda which used it to excuse their own terror raids such as that on Rotterdam on 13 May (eds).

I regret the sacrifices it will demand. I would like to spare my own people them also. I know that millions of German men and youths are aglow with the thought of at last being able to face the enemy who has declared war on us for the second time and for no reason.

But I also know that there are many wives and mothers at home who, despite their readiness to make the utmost sacrifices, are clinging to this last hope with all their hearts.

Mr Churchill may reject this declaration of mine by shouting that it is only the product of my fear and my doubts of final victory. But at least I have relieved my conscience before the events that threaten. . . .

Meanwhile, Halder had responded to what he saw as a growing Russian threat by revising the instructions for the 18th Army. He now envisaged a preventive attack to be carried out in the event of Russian preparations for aggression, i.e. Germany would no longer merely respond offensively to a Russian attack but would strike first. The aim of such a German attack would be to seize Russian territory in order to ensure the security of Germany's eastern frontier, to compel Russia to accept German hegemony in Europe, and to remove from Britain the hope of Russian intervention in the war. This plan for a preventive attack was contained in the deployment directive given to the 18th Army on 22 July.[8]

On the previous day, the C. in C. Army, von Brauchitsch, had had an interview with Hitler the results of which Halder recorded in his Diary on the 22 July:

572

22.7. C. in C. Army reports on his *Conference with the Führer* on 21.7 in Berlin . . .

(*b*) Führer: not clear what is going on in England. The preparations for a decision through force of arms must be completed as quickly as possible. The Führer does not want to let the military-political initiative be taken out of his hands. As soon as things become clear he will once more take the political and diplomatic initiative.

(*c*) Reasons for the continuation of the war by England:

1. Hope of a change in America. (Roosevelt is uncertain. Industry won't invest. England runs the risk of losing its position as the number one naval power to America.)

2. Places hope on Russia.

England's position is hopeless. We have won the war. A reversal in the prospects of success impossible . . .

(*e*) The Führer regards the crossing of the Channel as a great risk. So a crossing only if there is no other way of dealing with Britain.

(*f*) England may see the following possibilities: Create trouble in the Balkans through Russia in order to cut off our fuel supply and so paralyse our Air Force.

8. Cf. E. Klink, *op. cit.*

To achieve the same end by inciting Russia against us. To bomb our hydrogenation plants . . .

(*h*) If England wants to carry on the war, then attempt will be made to confront her with a solid political front including Spain, Italy, Russia.

(*i*) England must be finished off by mid-September if we attack. Will be carried out by Air Force and U-boats . . .

(*k*) Appraisal of the effect of the peace feelers. Press initially very hostile, then milder. Lloyd George: letter to King and Parliament. Duke of Windsor: letter to King. Thomsen[9]: News from England. Situation considered hopeless. English ambassador in Washington (Lothian): England has lost the war. It should pay up. But not do anything contrary to its honour. Possibility of a cabinet consisting of Lloyd George, Chamberlain, Halifax . . .

7. Stalin is flirting with England to keep her in the fight and to tie us down in order to have time to take what he wants and what he won't be able to take when peace comes. He will have an interest in not letting Germany get too strong. But there are no indications of Russian activity against us.

8. Deal with Russian problem. Prepare ideas for it. The Führer has been informed:

(*a*) Build-up of German forces will take 4–6 weeks.

(*b*) Aim to defeat Russian army or at least seize as much Russian territory as is necessary to prevent air attacks on Berlin and Silesian industrial area.

Desirable to penetrate far enough so that we can destroy Russia's strategic areas with our Air Force.

(*c*) Political goal: Ukrainian empire.
Baltic confederation.
White Russia–Finland.
Baltic states as a 'thorn in the flesh' [of Russia]. . . .

It seems doubtful whether these comments represented a commitment by Hitler to a total war for living space in Russia. The goals referred to accord more with the plans developed by Halder in OKH, which Brauchitsch presumably put to Hitler at the interview. Indeed, the references to a 'Ukrainian empire' and a 'Baltic Confederation' appear more similar to the conditions contained in the Brest-Litovsk peace imposed on Russia by the German High Command in March 1918 than to Hitler's ideas of the conquest of living space.

This discussion of an attack on Russia clearly concentrated the minds of the Army leadership, who came to the conclusion that it would after all be preferable to maintain good relations with Russia if possible. At the same time, it had become clear that neither the Navy nor the Air Force had much enthusiasm for an invasion of Britain as is apparent from the following entry in Halder's Diary:

9. Hans Thomsen, the German ambassador in Washington (eds).

573

30.7 . . . Greiffenberg arrives back from Conference with OKM.

(*a*) Naval Operations Staff under no circumstances ready before 15.9. Earliest jump-off date 20/26.9. (Moon phases). If not then, next May. Air Force is not doing anything about invasion matters at present.

(*b*) Speedier construction of landing craft impossible . . .

(*c*) The operation cannot be protected against English forces. *Scharnhorst*, *Gneisenau*, *Scheer* are in dry dock. *Hipper* is available. *Prince Eugen* will be commissioned in late autumn. In addition, only 4 destroyers, 3 torpedo boats, (48 U-boats).

(*d*) Insufficient tide mines available.

(*e*) Protection against mines cannot be provided for the invasion fleet . . .

C. in C. Army (20.00–22.00) comes over to discuss overall situation in the light of the statement by the Navy. We agree on the following points:

(*a*) As far as can be seen, the Navy will not provide us with the preconditions for a successful invasion of England this autumn. If the Navy reckons it can only provide us with the available ships by mid-September, we have two options:

To postpone the attack to the bad weather period. That may have certain localised advantages for the invasion, but in general will be disadvantageous, or to wait until spring 1941 (May). Our position vis-à-vis England will not be thereby improved. The English can improve their defences, augment their armaments, increase their number of aircraft. America can make itself felt.

However, it is possible that the Air Force and the Navy will reduce Britain's resources.

(*b*) The greatest risk involved in postponement lies in the fact that we shall not retain the initiative sufficiently.

(*c*) If we decide we cannot achieve success against the British Isles this autumn the following options remain:

1. An attack in Gibraltar (by land through Spain).
2. Support for Italy in North Africa by sending armoured divisions (Egypt).
3. An attack on the English in Haifa.
4. An attack on the Suez Canal.
5. To incite Russia to move on the Persian Gulf.

(*d*) In the event of our being unable to force a decision against England and of the danger of England allying herself with Russia, the answer to the question of whether one should then launch a two front war against Russia is that it is better to keep on friendly terms with Russia. A visit to Stalin would be desirable. Russia's aspirations towards the Straits and in the direction of the Persian Gulf need not worry us. In the Balkans, which are in our economic sphere of interest, we can keep out of each other's way. Italy and Russia will not harm each other in the Mediterranean.

Subject to this prerequisite, we could deliver the English a decisive blow in the Mediterranean, assist the Italians in building up their Mediterranean sphere, and consolidate the empire which we have created in north and west Europe and even have Russian assistance in doing so. We need then have no fears about facing a lengthy war with England.

Hitherto, Halder's preparations for military action in the East had been carried out largely on his own initiative. Hints had been dropped by Weizsäcker and others that the Führer was concerned about the East, and, at the interview with Brauchitsch on 21 July, discussion about the need to deal with Russia had evidently been more specific. As yet, however, there had been no definite instructions from Hitler to the Army to prepare for Germany to launch a full-scale war of aggression against the Soviet Union. These came on 31 July, when Hitler summoned a meeting of military and naval chiefs to Berchtesgaden. Halder recorded the results in his Diary:

574

Führer:

(a) Stresses his scepticism regarding technical feasibility[10]; however, satisfied with results produced by Navy.

(*b*) Emphasizes weather factor.

(*c*) Discusses enemy resources for counteraction. Our small Navy is only 15 per cent of enemy's, 8 per cent of enemy's destroyers, 10–12 per cent of his motor torpedo boats. So we have nothing to bring into action against enemy surface attacks. That leaves mines (not 100 per cent reliable), coastal Artillery (good!), and Air Force.
In any decision we must bear in mind that even if we take risks, the prize too is big.

(*d*) In the event that invasion does not take place, our aim must be to eliminate all factors that let England hope for a change in the situation. To all intents and purposes the war is won. France no longer available for protecting British convoys. Italy is pinning down British forces.
Submarine and air warfare may bring about a final decision, but this will take one or two years.
Britain's hope lies in Russia and the United States. If the hopes pinned on Russia are disappointed then America too will fall by the wayside, because elimination of Russia would tremendously increase *Japan's power* in the Far East.
Russia is the Far Eastern sword of Britain and the United States pointed at Japan. Here an ill wind is blowing for Britain. Japan has her programme which she wants to carry through before the end of the war . . .
Russia is the factor on which Britain is relying the most. Something must have happened in London!
The British were completely down; now they have perked up again. Intercepted telephone conversations. Russia is painfully shaken by the swift development of the Western European situation.

10. Of Sealion (eds).

All that Russia has to do is to hint that she does not care to have a strong Germany, and the British will take hope, like one about to go under, that the situation will undergo a radical change within six or eight months.
With Russia smashed, Britain's last hope would be shattered. Germany will then be master of Europe and the Balkans.
Decision: Russia's destruction must therefore be made a part of this struggle. Spring '41. The sooner Russia is crushed the better. Attack achieves its purpose only if Russian State can be shattered to its roots with one blow. Holding only part of the country will not do. Standing still during the winter would be perilous. So it is better to wait a little longer, but with the resolute determination to eliminate Russia. This is necessary also because of the situation in the Baltic. We can do without having another major power [Russia] there. If we start in May '41, we would have five months to finish the job in. Tackling it this year would still have been the best, but unified action would be impossible at this time.
Aim: destruction of Russia's vital strength. Divided into:
1. Thrust towards Kiev along the Dnieper. Air Force to destroy the Odessa river crossings.
2. Thrust: Border states and drive to Moscow.
Finally, a link up of northern and southern prongs. Later limited drive on Baku oil fields. How far we can interest Finland and Turkey remains to be seen.
Later: Ukraine, White Russia, Baltic States to us. Finland extended to the White Sea. . . .
Spread rumours: Spain, North Africa, England. [i.e. preparations for Russian offensive to be disguised as other operations]

(ii) The 'Peripheral' or Mediterranean Strategy and the 'World Coalition'

Britain's refusal to come to terms coupled with the political drawbacks and technical difficulties involved in an invasion of Britain had placed Hitler in a dilemma. He could not sit tight and adopt a 'hedgehog position' for the simple reason that in the long run Germany's control of central and western Europe was threatened not so much by Britain, but rather by the intervention of the other world powers—Russia and the United States. If Germany did nothing, her political and economic dependence on the Soviet Union would increase. Russian supplies of oil, grain and other raw materials under the economic agreement between the two countries had now become essential to the German war machine. And Stalin made it abundantly clear that he would claim a reward for his neutrality. He had been disconcerted by the speed of Germany's victory over France and during June, without consultation, Russia had occupied the Baltic States, which had been assigned to her under the 1939 pact, and begun to apply pressure on Romania, Germany's main source of oil imports. This was primarily a defensive move on the part of the Russians who wanted as large a buffer area as possible between themselves and Germany, but it was unwelcome to Hitler in view of his long term objectives in the east. And it was not only Russia that Hitler had to consider. The United States also posed a threat. In a speech on 19 July President Roosevelt had declared America's support for Britain stopping short only of war. Although at this time her Army was far too small to intervene, the lesson of 1917 was not lost on Hitler and he realized that, with America's enormous resources now being devoted to rearmament, she would eventully be able to intervene decisively on the side of Britain.

In this situation, there were three possible strategies. In the first place, he could try to defeat Britain directly—by an invasion. Secondly, he could try to approach the same goal indirectly by attacking the British position in the Mediterranean and the Middle East with the help of Italy, Spain and Vichy France, and threaten the British position in the Far East by encouraging the Japanese to take the offensive in the Pacific. Russia might even be persuaded to switch her emphasis from the west to the south toward the Persian Gulf and India. Finally as part of this indirect strategy he could intensify the U-boat campaign against British shipping. These strategies would either destroy Britain as a power or force her to come to terms. In either case this would remove, for the time being at any rate, the basis for American intervention and would secure Germany's rear for an attack on Russia. The third alternative strategy would be to try to defeat Russia in a *Blitzkrieg*. This would then give Germany the security and the basis of raw materials necessary to defeat Britain and, if necessary, the United States. This had essentially been the strategy contained in his original programme which had been upset by the entry of Britain into the war.

During the following months, Hitler vacillated between these three strategies, sometimes pursuing them simultaneously. His decisions were shaped, as always, by a combination of his assessment of the situation and ideological factors. As far as he was concerned, both pointed in the direction of an attack on Russia. For, apart from the fact that the securing of *Lebensraum* in Russia had formed the core of his programme, there were also strategic considerations involved. He had become convinced that Britain's refusal to come to terms derived from her hopes of Russia as a substitute 'Continental sword' for France and of future American intervention. In this situation, and in the light of the political and technical problems associated with an invasion of Britain, he decided that the best plan would be a *Blitzkrieg* against Russia whose military capabilities he grossly underestimated. The defeat of Russia would, he thought, not only remove the threat from that quarter and destroy British hopes, it would also free Japan to expand in the Pacific. This in turn would threaten the United States, which, in order to concentrate on this threat, would have to remain neutral in the war between Britain and Germany. However, it was too late in the year for a Russian campaign and so, while initial planning for a war with

Russia got under way, in the meantime Hitler concentrated on the other two strategic alternatives.

Although the Army pressed ahead with the preparations for Sea Lion, the Navy and Air Force were much less enthusiastic and, in any case, by the middle of September it had become clear that the Luftwaffe had been defeated in the Battle of Britain. On 14 September, Hitler ordered the postponement of the invasion and, on 12 October, it was finally put off until the spring.

Hitler was now obliged to fall back on the remaining alternative strategy—that of trying to create a coalition of powers which would be able to attack Britain indirectly, in the Mediterranean and North Africa, and which would put sufficient pressure on the United States to ensure that they remained neutral.

The entry of Italy into the war on 10 June 1940 had given the Axis powers the opportunity to strike telling blows in the Mediterranean through which ran Britain's vital links with her oil reserves in the Middle East and with India and the Far East. The problem was that relations between Germany and Italy were from the beginning plagued by a total lack of coordination which sprang from Mussolini's determination to fight 'not with Germany, not for Germany, but only for Italy alongside Germany',[11] an attitude which was paralleled by Hitler's conception of 'a policy of separate spheres' in which Germany would concentrate on northern Europe, while Italy would be left free to establish a new version of the Roman Empire in the South. The stalemate in northern Europe which set in with the frustration of the invasion of Britain, however, obliged Germany to direct her attention towards the Mediterranean as the only sphere, apart from the bombing offensive, in which the war could be effectively continued against Britain. The question was: Should Germany henceforward concentrate on the Mediterranean as the main area of attack and regard the defeat of Britain as the primary objective, or should this be considered a temporary measure, a stop-gap operation undertaken during the period before the attack on Russia could get under way?

This strategy, however, had its problems. In the first place, Hitler regarded the Mediterranean as Mussolini's sphere of influence and he was anxious not to offend the Duce by too great an interference in that area. In particular, the problem of reconciling French, Italian and Spanish interests in the area was acute. Indeed according to Hitler it would only be possible through a 'grandiose fraud'.[12] Secondly, Hitler was unwilling

11. Quoted in Lothar Gruchmann, 'Die "verpassten strategishen Chancen" der Achsenmächte im Mittelmeerraum 1940–41', *Vierteljahrshefte für Zeitgeschichte,* Bd. 18 (1970), pp. 456 ff.

12. F. Halder, *Kriegstagebuch* II. p. 124. (3.10.1940.)

to tie down large German forces in the south, for his main objective remained an attack in the east in the following spring though he was not yet totally committed to it.

The Mediterranean strategy was pressed strongly by the armed forces and in particular by the Naval High Command under Admiral Raeder. Already, during a conference on 6 September, Raeder had pressed Hitler to concentrate on capturing Gibraltar and the Suez Canal as an alternative to the risky venture of an invasion of England. Three weeks later, after the postponement of the invasion and having learnt of the plans for an invasion of Russia, Raeder requested an interview with Hitler *tête à tête*. Afterwards he explained in a minute that 'it was my fear that the war might go off on the wrong track and turn away from the main danger, which was Britain, which prompted me to seek the interview *tête à tête* with the Führer'.[13]

575

Report of the Commander-in-Chief, Navy, to the Führer on 26 September 1940 at 1700 hours. (Without witnesses.)

The Commander-in-Chief, Navy, requests permission to give the Führer his views on the progress of the war, including also matters outside his sphere of operations.

The British have always considered the Mediterranean the pivot of their world empire. Even now eight of the thirteen battleships are there; strong positions are held in the Eastern Mediterranean; troop transports from Australia and New Zealand have been sent to Egypt and East Africa. While the air and submarine war is being fought out between Germany and Britain, Italy, surrounded by British power, is fast becoming the main target of attack. Britain always attempts to strangle the weaker enemy. Germany, however, must wage war against Great Britain with all the means at her disposal and without delay, before the United States is able to intervene effectively. For this reason the Mediterranean question must be cleared up *during the [coming] winter months*.

(*a*) *Gibraltar* must be seized. The Canary Islands must be secured beforehand by the Air Force.

The *Suez Canal* must be captured. It is doubtful whether the Italians can accomplish this alone; support by German troops will be needed. An advance from Suez through Palestine and Syria as far as Turkey is necessary. If we reach that point, Turkey will be in our power. The Russian problem will then appear in a different light. Basically, Russia is afraid of Germany. It is doubtful whether an advance against Russia from the north will then be necessary. There is also the question of the Dardanelles. It will be easier to supply Italy and Spain if we control the Mediterranean.

13. Quoted in M. Salewski, *Die deutsche Seekriegsleitung 1935–1941* (Frankfurt am Main 1970), vol. 1, p. 284.

Protection of East Africa is assured. The Italians can wage naval warfare in the Indian Ocean.

An operation against India could be feigned.

(*b*) The question of *North-West Africa* is also of decisive importance.

All the indications are that Britain, with the help of De Gaulle France, and possibly *also of the U.S.A.*, wants to make this region a centre of resistance and to establish air bases for attacks on Italy. Britain will try to prevent us from gaining a foothold in the African colonies.

In this way Italy would be defeated.

Thus action must be taken against *Dakar*. The U.S.A already has a consul there, the Italians two repesentatives, and we are not represented *at all*. The economic situation will quickly deteriorate, but the attitude towards the British is *still* hostile. In spite of demobilization there are still about 25,000 troops left in this area; in the neighbouring British territory, on the other hand, there are only about six to eight battalions. The possibility of action on the part of France against the British is therefore very promising. It is very desirable that support be given to the French, possibly by permitting the use of the STRASBOURG.

It would be advisable to station air forces in Casablanca in the near future. In general, it appears important to cooperate with France in order to protect North-West Africa—after certain concessions have been made to Germany and Italy. The occupation of France makes it possible to compel her to maintain and defend the frontiers advantageous to us.

The Führer agrees with the general trend of thought. When the alliance with Japan has been finalized he will immediately confer with the Duce, and possibly also with France. He will have to decide whether cooperation with France or with Spain is more profitable; probably with France, since Spain demands a great deal (French Morocco) but offers little. France must guarantee beforehand to fulfil certain German and Italian demands; an agreement could then be reached regarding the African colonies. Britain and the U.S.A. must be excluded from North-West Africa. If Spain were to cooperate, the Canary Islands, and possibly also the Azores and the Cape Verde Islands would have to be seized beforehand by the Air Force.

An advance through Syria would also depend on the attitude taken by France; it would be quite possible, however. Italy will be *against* the cession of the Dardanelles to Russia. Russia should be encouraged to advance towards the south, or against Persia and India, in order to gain an outlet to the Indian Ocean which would be more important to Russia than the positions in the Baltic Sea.

The Führer is also of the opinion that Russia is afraid of Germany's strength; he believes, for instance, that Russia will not attack Finland this year.

The Führer is obviously hesitant about releasing additional French forces at Toulon; he feels himself bound by previous decisions.

With the invasion of Britain frustrated, and faced with a delay of eight months before the attack on Russia could go ahead, Hitler now went some way towards adopting this strategy of an indirect offensive against Britain. The Foreign Minister, von Ribbentrop, had for some time been urging the creation of a 'world triangle' between Germany, Italy and Japan aimed at

Britain. This had been his aim for the Anti-Comintern Pact of 1937.[14] However, Japan had wished the pact to be directed against its nominal target, the Soviet Union, and had reacted negatively to the Nazi–Soviet Pact of August 1939. Now, after the German victory in the West, the Japanese saw the opportunity of exploiting the defeat of France and Holland to take-over their colonies in the Far East and so were anxious for an accommodation with Germany over the division of spheres of interest. Thus, on 27 September 1940, Ribbentrop's conception of the 'world triangle' came to fruition with the conclusion of the Tripartite Pact with Italy and Japan:

576

The Governments of Japan, Germany, and Italy, considering it as the condition precedent of any lasting peace that all nations of the world be given each its own proper place, have decided to stand by and cooperate with one another in regard to their efforts in Greater East Asia and the regions of Europe respectively wherein it is their prime purpose to establish and maintain a new order of things calculated to promote the mutual prosperity and welfare of the peoples concerned. Furthermore it is the desire of the three Governments to extend cooperation to nations in other spheres of the world as may be inclined to put forth endeavours along lines similar to their own, in order that the ultimate aspirations for a world peace may thus be realized. Accordingly the Governments of Japan, Germany and Italy have agreed as follows:

I Japan recognizes and respects the leadership of Germany and Italy in the establishment of a new order in Europe.

II Germany and Italy recognize and respect the leadership of Japan in the establishment of a new order in Greater East Asia.

III Japan, Germany and Italy agree to cooperate in their efforts on the aforesaid lines. They further undertake to assist one another with all political, economic and military means when one of the three contracting parties is attacked by a power at present not involved in the European war or in the Sino-Japanese conflict.

IV With a view to implementing the present pact joint technical commissions, the members of which are to be appointed by the respective Governments of Japan, Germany and Italy, will meet without delay.

V Japan, Germany and Italy affirm that the aforesaid terms do not in any way affect the political status which exists at present as between each of the three contracting parties and Soviet Russia.

VI The present pact shall come into effect immediately upon signature and shall remain in force for 10 years from the date of its coming into force.

---

14. See above p. 673 ff.

At proper time before the expiration of the said term the high contracting parties shall, at the request of any one of them, enter into negotiations for its renewal. . .

Hitler hoped that the Tripartite Pact would bind Japan to the Axis, encourage her to attack British possessions in the Far East, and intimidate the United States into remaining neutral through the threat of a war on two fronts. He outlined his current thoughts to Mussolini at a meeting on 4 October 1940:

577

Now the question arose as to why the English continued to hold out despite everything in a situation which was hopeless for them from a military point of view. In his opinion this fact was due to two hopes. Great Britain placed her hopes in America and in Russia.

But America would only be able to deliver materiel. The figures published on her delivery capacity were lies pure and simple. It was possible to construct a rather good picture of the production capacity of the American airplane industry by considering the number of workers employed, the amount of aluminum produced, and the possibilities for manufacturing engines; one came to the conclusion that the American possibilities in this field stayed within moderate bounds. In this connection the Führer stressed the difficulties in Britain's supply of aluminum.

And now America had also been warned by the Tripartite Pact. The Führer termed the official reaction very cowardly, and expressed his conviction that seeing the possibility of a two-front war would have quite a dampening effect on America.

England's second hope was based on Russia. In this connection the Führer remarked that a year ago Stalin had certainly believed there would be a long European war accompanied by a general attrition of Europe. He had certainly expected this to result in a relief for Russia and new perspectives in a Europe which had been bled white, and now he was doubtless disappointed at the quick conclusion of the war. The Kremlin had calculated wrong this time. Germany was not afraid of Russia and had prepared everything for defense. To be sure, 17 divisions of older age groups had been demobilized, but 40 new divisions had been organized, so that after March a total of 100 first-class divisions, 24 of them armoured, would be available. He (the Führer) considered it out of the question that Russia would undertake anything.

The Reich Foreign Minister underscored these statements and pointed out that in his opinion the Russians were afraid of Germany and Stalin would certainly not undertake anything on his own initiative: the Duce readily granted this.

The Führer then said he approved directing the Russians toward India or at least the Indian Ocean, but added that he doubted it would be possible really to set the Russians in motion actively in this direction. In any case the Russians would not represent any problem for Germany even if worst came to worst. However, as the well-known Pravda article on the Tripartite Pact proved, they seemed to regard matters very reasonably.

Thus both hopes of the English were illusory and would bring only disappointments sooner or later. Independent of the question of the direct attack on England, however, it was a matter of attacking the British Empire at other places too, and of inflicting injury on it at every possible point . . .

. . .At the moment, however, the ideal solution consisted in creating a European coalition against England including France and Spain. The question was whether one could find a compromise between the French hopes and the Spanish wishes, and possibly feelers would have to be put out to the French to ascertain whether they were willing to relinquish at least part of Morocco for British Nigeria. The German colonial claims were moderate, as he had already mentioned. They consisted merely in rounding off the former German colonial possessions in Central Africa to consolidate the [word illegible] German colonies as compactly as possible. Germany was not out to win the greatest possible number of square kilometres of colonial territory, but simply needed raw materials, in particular timber, whose lack made itself unpleasantly felt in the production of the new Vista fibre. Then she also wanted to obtain oils and fats from the colonies. In connection with this there arose the necessity of securing the sea route to the new German colonies by means of bases along the French coast, and access to the open sea through the development of the Norwegian positions. Germany would never get out of Norway. She intended to develop Trondheim as a large naval harbour.

If a compromise between the French and the Spanish interests should not be possible, however, one should consider very carefully which of the then available possibilities to prefer. An attack on Gibraltar was technically quite feasible. Germany possessed certain specialized troops that had successfully accomplished similar tasks in the west, and they could doubtless also achieve the conquest of the Rock. At any rate the war was won for the Axis Powers unless they should do something very inept. For this reason, too, there must in no circumstances be a reversal.

Next, therefore, Hitler tried to gain the cooperation of France and Spain for his Mediterranean strategy against Britain. In particular, he sought Spanish cooperation for an attack on Gibraltar (Operation Felix). However, despite a personal visit from the Führer in October, both Marshal Pétain and Generalissimo Franco proved evasive. They were suspicious of German promises, of Italian designs in the Mediterranean and North Africa, and of each other. Above all, neither was willing to commit his country irrevocably to support the Axis until Britain's defeat was final. Spain, in particular, was still vulnerable to British naval pressure.

Meanwhile, relations with Russia had entered a difficult phase as a result of the clash of interests in Finland and Romania. Finland had been assigned to the Russian sphere of influence under the Nazi–Soviet Pact of August 1939 and Germany had been careful not to intervene in the Russo–Finnish war of November 1939–March 1940. However, Finland supplied Germany with nickel, crucial for the special steel alloys needed for armaments and, having taken the decision to attack the Soviet Union, Hitler was now less sensitive to Russian interests and more concerned about guaranteeing

German supplies of nickel. At the end of July, therefore, Germany resumed arms supplies to Finland and in September she signed an agreement with Finland granting her the right to send troops to Norway via Finland and also to station troops there to protect the route. This move was regarded by the Russians as a breach of the Nazi–Soviet pact and raised suspicions about future German intentions.

Romania was of even greater importance to Germany than Finland because of her oilfields. On 30 August, Germany and Italy had responded to Russian pressure on Romania by guaranteeing its territorial integrity, including south Bukovina, as part of a deal (the Second Vienna Award), by which Romania ceded half of Transylvania to Hungary and southern Dobruja to Bulgaria. Moreover, during the autumn of 1940, Hitler took steps to turn Romania into a virtual satellite of Germany. This too was resented by the Russians.

The deterioration in Russo–German relations was of particular concern to Ribbentrop. Even before his success with the Nazi–Soviet Pact, Ribbentrop had been urging closer relations with Russia as a vital element in the achievement of what he saw as the major goal—the defeat of Britain. As a means to this, he now sought Russian membership of the Tripartite Pact with the aim of drawing Russia into a world-wide coalition against Britain thereby turning the 'triangle' into a quadrilateral. Ribbentrop persuaded Hitler to agree to invite the Russian Foreign Minister, Molotov, to Berlin for discussions on 12 November. The aim was to redirect Russian interests away from the Balkans, where they conflicted with those of Germany and Italy, and towards the Persian Gulf, which was a British sphere.

The question of Hitler's policy towards Russia in the autumn of 1940 is one of the most obscure and controversial aspects of his whole career. Many historians argue that his negotiations with the Russians were designed merely to gauge their immediate objectives and to mislead them about his own plans for an invasion. The fact that he specifically ordered those plans to be continued during the negotiations appears to lend weight to the view. On the other hand, it is equally plausible to argue that Hitler was undecided in his strategy at this point. While remaining committed to an eventual confrontation with Russia, in order to settle the question of European hegemony and to secure *Lebensraum*, he may well have been tempted by the possibility of at least a short-term arrangement with the Russians. This would either finally persuade the British that they could not count on Russian intervention, and thus force them to come to terms, or enable him to concentrate all his forces against Britain in the spring of 1941. It would ensure that he would not have to fight a two-front war against both Russia and Britain.

The Army leadership was certainly unclear about what he intended. In his interview with Hitler on 2 November the first point which General

Halder wished to raise was: 'To request a decision on the *major goals* which the Army's preparations are intended to serve'.[15] Hitler's response was Directive No. 18 of 12 November 1940 which, however, did not really clarify matters:

578

The measures of the High Commands which are being prepared for the conduct of the war in the near future are to be in accordance with the following guiding principles:

1. *Relations with France*

The aim of my policy toward France is to cooperate with this country in the most effective way for the future prosecution of the war against England. For the time being France will have the role of a 'nonbelligerent power' which will have to tolerate German military measures on her territory, in the African colonies especially, and to give support, as far as possible, even by using her own means of defence. The most pressing task of the French is the defensive and offensive protection of their African possessions (West and Equatorial Africa) against England and the de Gaulle movement. From this task the participation of France in the war against England can develop in full force . . .

2. *Spain and Portugal*

Political measures to induce the prompt entry of Spain into the war have been initiated. The aim of *German* intervention in the Iberian Peninsula (code name *Felix*) will be to drive the English out of the Western Mediterranean.

For this purpose:

(*a*) Gibraltar should be taken and the Straits closed;

(*b*) The English should be prevented from gaining a foothold at another point of the Iberian Peninsula or of the Atlantic islands . . .

3. *Italian Offensive against Egypt*

If at all, the commitment of German forces comes into consideration only when the Italians have reached Mersa Matrûh. Even then the commitment initially of German air forces is envisaged only if the Italians make available the requisite air bases.

The preparations of the branches of the armed forces for commitment in this or in any other North African theatre of war are to be continued within the following framework:

Army:

Holding in readiness of an armoured division (composition as previously provided for) for commitment in North Africa . . .

4. *Balkans*

The Commander in Chief of the Army will make preparations in order, in case of necessity, to occupy the *Greek mainland* north of the Aegean Sea, entering from

15. F. Halder, *Kriegstagebuch* II. p. 159.

Bulgaria, and thereby make possible the commitment of German air forces units against targets in the Eastern Mediterranean, especially against those English air bases which threaten the Rumanian oil area . . .

5. *Russia*

Political discussions have been initiated with the aim of clarifying Russia's attitude for the coming period. Regardless of what results those discussions will have, all preparations for the East which already have been orally ordered, are to be continued.

Directives on this will follow as soon as the outline of the Army's plan of operations is submitted to, and approved by me.

6. *Landing in England*

Because, with changes in the over-all situation, the possibility or necessity may arise to return in the spring of 1941 to Operation Sealion, the three branches of the armed forces must earnestly try in every way to improve the groundwork for such an operation.

7. *Reports of the Commanders in Chief*

Will be expected by me regarding the measures envisaged in this directive. I shall then issue orders regarding the methods of execution and the synchronization of the individual actions . . .

Hitler decided to use Molotov's visit to Berlin to sound him out about the prospects of an arrangement. At their first meeting on 12 November Hitler sketched out his view of future Russo–German relations:

579

He (the Führer) now had pondered the question how, beyond all petty momentary considerations, further to clarify in bold outline the collaboration between Germany and Russia and what direction future German–Russian developments should take. In this matter the following viewpoints were of importance for Germany:

1. Need for space. During the war Germany had acquired such large areas that she would require one hundred years to utilize them fully.
2. Some colonial expansion in Central Africa was necessary.
3. Germany needed certain raw materials, the supply of which he would have to safeguard in all circumstances.
4. she could not permit the establishment by hostile powers of air or naval bases in certain areas.

In no event, however, would the interests of Russia be affected. The Russian empire could develop without in the least prejudicing German interests. (Molotov said this was quite correct.) If both countries came to realize this fact, they could collaborate to their mutual advantage and could spare themselves difficulties, friction, and nervous tension. It was perfectly obvious that Germany and Russia would never become one world. Both countries would always exist separate from each other as two powerful elements of the world. Each of them could shape its future as it liked, if in so doing it considered the interests of the other. Germany herself had no interests in Asia other than general economic and commercial interests. In particular she had no colonial interests there.

In addition, there was the problem of America. The United States was now pursuing an imperialistic policy. It was not fighting for England, but only trying to get the British Empire into its grasp. They were helping England, at best, in order to further their own rearmament and to reinforce their military power by acquiring bases. In the distant future it would be a question of establishing a great solidarity among those countries which might be involved in an extension of the sphere of influence of this Anglo-Saxon power which had a more solid foundation, by far, than England. In this case, it was not a question of the immediate future; not in 1945 but in 1970 or 1980, at the earliest, would the freedom of other nations be seriously endangered by this Anglo-Saxon power. At any rate the Continent of Europe had to adjust itself now to this development and had to act jointly against the Anglo-Saxons and against any of their attempts to acquire dangerous bases. Therefore, he had undertaken an exchange of ideas with France, Italy, and Spain in order with these countries to set up in the whole of Europe and Africa some kind of Monroe Doctrine and to adopt a new joint colonial policy by which each of the powers concerned would claim for itself only as much colonial territory as it could really utilize. In other regions, where Russia was the power in the foremost position the interests of the latter would, of course, have to come first. This would result in a great coalition of powers which, guided by sober appraisal of realities, would have to establish their respective spheres of interest and would assert themselves against the rest of the world correspondingly. It was surely a difficult task to organize such a coalition of countries; and yet, to conceive it was not as difficult as to carry it out.

However, while agreeing on the possibility of future collaboration between Germany and Russia, Molotov insisted on raising detailed questions about Finland, about Russia's Balkan and Black Sea interests, and about the significance of the Tripartite Pact: 'What was the meaning of the new order in Europe and in Asia and what role would the USSR be given in it?'

The Führer replied that the Tripartite Pact was intended to regulate relationships in Europe in the sphere of the natural interests of the European countries and, consequently, Germany was now approaching the Soviet Union in order that she might express herself regarding the areas of interest to her. In no case was a settlement to be made without Soviet Russian cooperation. This applied not only to Europe, but also to Asia, where Russia herself was to cooperate in the definition of the Greater East Asian sphere and where she was to designate her claims. Germany's task in this case was that of a mediator. Russia by no means was to be confronted with a fait accompli.

When the Führer undertook to try to establish the above-mentioned coalition of powers, it was not the German–Russian relationship which appeared to him to be the most difficult point, but the question of whether a collaboration between

Germany, France, and Italy was possible. Only now that he believed this problem could be solved and after a settlement in broad outlines had in effect been accepted by the three countries, had he thought it possible to contact Soviet Russia for the purpose of settling the questions of the Black Sea, the Balkans, and Turkey.

In conclusion, the Führer summed up by stating that the discussion to a certain extent, represented the first concrete step toward comprehensive collaboration, with due consideration for the problems of Western Europe, which were to be settled between Germany, Italy and France, as well as for the issues of the East, which were essentially the concern of Russia and Japan, but in which Germany offered her good offices as mediator. It was a matter of opposing any attempt on the part of America to "make money on Europe." The United States had no business either in Europe, in Africa, or in Asia.

Molotov expressed his agreement with the statements of the Führer regarding the role of America and England. The participation of Russia in the Tripartite Pact appeared to him entirely acceptable in principle, provided that Russia was to cooperate as a partner and not be merely an object. In that case he saw no difficulties in the matter of participation of the Soviet Union in the common effort. But the aim and the significance of the Pact must first be more closely defined, particularly because of the delimitation of the Greater East Asian sphere . . .

At this point the conversation was broken off because of a possible air raid. When they resumed the following day the two sides quickly became bogged down in a somewhat acrimonious discussion of the working of the existing Russo–German agreements and the recent actions of the two countries. Hitler kept urging the Russians to look beyond these temporary problems, caused by the necessities of war, towards the broader prospects raised by future collaboration:

580

The Führer replied that if German-Russian collaboration was to show positive results in the future, the Soviet Government would have to understand that Germany was engaged in a life and death struggle, which, at all events, she wanted to conclude successfully. For that, a number of prerequisites depending upon economic and military factors were required, which Germany wanted to secure for herself by all means. If the Soviet Union were in a similar position, Germany on her part would, and would have to, demonstrate a similar understanding for Russian needs. The conditions which Germany wanted to assure did not conflict with the agreements with Russia. The German wish to avoid a war with unforeseeable consequences in the Baltic Sea did not mean any violation of the German-Russian agreements according to which Finland belonged in the Russian sphere of influence. The guarantee given upon the wish and request of the Romanian Government was no violation of the agreements concerning Bessarabia. The Soviet Union had to realize that in the framework of any broader collaboration of the two countries advantages of quite different scope were to be reached than the insignificant revisions which were now being discussed. Much greater successes could then be achieved, provided that Russia did not now seek successes in territories in which Germany was interested for the duration of the war. The future successes would be the greater, the more Germany and Russia succeeded in fighting back to back against the outside world and would become the smaller, the more the two countries faced each other breast to breast. In the first case there was no power on earth which could oppose the two countries.

In his reply Molotov voiced his agreement with the last conclusions of the Führer. In this connection he stressed the viewpoint of the Soviet leaders, and of Stalin in particular, that it would be possible and expedient to strengthen and activate the relations between the two countries. However, in order to give those relations a permanent basis, issues would also have to be clarified which were of secondary importance, but which spoiled the atmosphere of German-Russian relations. Finland belonged among these issues. If Russia and Germany had a good understanding, this issue could be solved without war, but there must be neither German troops in Finland nor political demonstrations in that country against the Soviet Russian Government . . .

In conclusion the Führer stated on this point that Germany did not desire any war in the Baltic Sea and that she urgently needed Finland as a supplier of nickel and lumber. Politically, she was not interested and in contrast to Russia, had occupied no Finnish territory. Incidentally, the transit of German troops would be finished within the next few days. No further troop trains would then be sent. The decisive question for Germany was whether Russia had the intention of going to war against Finland . . .

In reply to the statements of Molotov regarding the absence of military danger to the Finnish question, the Führer stressed that he too had some understanding of military matters, and he considered it entirely possible that the United States would get a foothold in those regions in case of participation by Sweden in a possible war. He (the Führer) wanted to end the European war, and he could only repeat that in view of the uncertain attitude of Sweden a new war in the Baltic would mean a strain on German-Russian relations with unforeseeable consequences. Would Russian declare war on the United States in case the latter should intervene in connection with the Finnish conflict?

When Molotov replied that this question was not of present interest, the Führer replied that it would be too late for a decision when it became so. When Molotov then declared that he did not see any indication of the outbreak of war in the Baltic, the Führer replied that in that case everything would be in order anyway and the whole discussion was really of a purely theoretical nature.

Summarizing, the Reich Foreign Minister pointed out that:

(1) The Führer had declared that Finland remained in the sphere of influence of Russia and that Germany would not maintain any troops there;

(2) Germany had nothing to do with demonstrations of Finland against Russia, but was exerting her influence in the opposite direction;

(3) The collaboration of the two countries was the decisive problem of long-range importance, which in the past had already resulted in great advantages for Russia, but which in the future would show advantages compared with which the matters

that had just been discussed would appear entirely insignificant. There was actually no reason at all for making an issue of the Finnish question. Perhaps it was a misunderstanding only. Strategically, all of Russia's wishes had been satisfied by her peace treaty with Finland. Demonstrations in a conquered country were not at all unnatural, and if perhaps the transit of German troops had caused certain reactions in the Finnish population they would disappear with the end of those troop transits. Hence, if one considered matters realistically, there were no differences between Germany and Russia.

The Führer pointed out that both sides agreed in principle that Finland belonged to the Russian sphere of influence. Instead, therefore, of continuing a purely theoretical discussion, they should rather turn to more important problems.

After the conquest of England the British Empire would be apportioned as a gigantic world-wide estate in bankruptcy of 40 million square kilometres. In this bankrupt estate there would be for Russia access to the ice-free and really open ocean. Thus far, a minority of 45 million Englishmen had ruled 600 million inhabitants of the British Empire. He was about to crush this minority. Even the United States was actually doing nothing but picking out of this bankrupt estate a few items particularly suitable to the United States. Germany, of course, would like to avoid any conflict which would divert her from her struggle against the heart of the Empire, the British Isles. For that reason, he (the Führer) did not like Italy's war against Greece, as it diverted forces to the periphery instead of concentrating them against England at one point. The same would occur during a Baltic war. The conflict with England would be fought to the last ditch, and he had no doubt that the defeat of the British Isles would lead to the dissolution of the Empire. It was a chimera to believe that the Empire could possibly be ruled and held together from Canada. In those circumstances there arose worldwide perspectives. During the next few weeks they would have to be settled in joint diplomatic negotiations with Russia, and Russia's participation in the solution of these problems would have to be arranged. All the countries which could possibly be interested in the bankrupt estate would have to stop all controversies among themselves and concern themselves exclusively with apportioning the British Empire. This applied to Germany, France, Italy, Russia, and Japan.

Molotov replied that he had followed the argument of the Führer with interest and that he was in agreement with everything that he had understood. However, he could comment thereon less than the Führer, since the latter had surely thought more about these problems and formed more concrete opinions regarding them. The decisive thing was first to be clear regarding German-Russian collaboration, in which Italy and Japan could be included later on. In this connection nothing should be changed that had been started; rather, there should be in prospect only a continuation of what had been begun.

The Führer mentioned here that the further efforts in the sense of the opening up of great prospects would not be easy and emphasized in this connection that Germany did not want to annex France, as the Russians appeared to assume. He wanted to create a world coalition of interested powers which would consist of Spain, France, Italy, Germany, Soviet Russia, and Japan and would to a certain degree represent a coalition—extending from North Africa to Eastern Asia—of all those who wanted to be satisfied out of the British bankrupt estate. To this end all internal controversies between the members of this coalition must be removed or at least neutralized. For this purpose the settlement of a whole series of questions was necessary. In the West, i.e. between Spain, France, Italy, and Germany, he believed he had now found a formula which satisfied everybody alike. It had not been easy to reconcile the views of Spain and France for instance, in regard to North Africa; however, recognizing the greater future possibilities, both countries finally had given in. After the West was thus settled, an agreement in the East must now be reached. In this case it was not a matter of relations between Soviet Russia and Turkey only, but also of the Greater Asian sphere. The latter consisted not only of the Greater East Asian sphere, but also of a purey Asiatic area oriented toward the south, that Germany even now recognized as Russia's sphere of influence. It was a matter of determining in bold outlines the boundaries for the future activity of peoples and of assigning to nations large areas where they could find an ample field of activity for fifty to a hundred years.

Molotov replied that the Führer had raised a number of questions which concerned not only Europe but, beyond that, other territories too. He wanted to discuss first a problem closer to Europe, that of Turkey . . .

There followed a long discussion of Russia's interests in the Balkans and the Black Sea, including a query from Molotov about Germany's response to a Russian 'guarantee' of Bulgaria corresponding to Germany's guarantee of Romania. Hitler ducked the question by asking whether Bulgaria had requested such a guarantee and by claiming the need to consult Mussolini.

At this point in the conversation the Führer called attention to the late hour and stated that in view of the possibility of English air attacks it would be better to break off the talk now, since the main issues had probably been sufficiently discussed.

Summarising, he stated that subsequently the possibilities of safeguarding Russia's interests as a Black Sea power have to be examined further and that in general Russia's further wishes with regard to her future position in the world would have to be considered.

In a closing remark Molotov stated that a number of important and new questions had been raised for Soviet Russia. the Soviet Union, as a powerful country, could not keep aloof from the great issues in Europe and Asia . . .

It must have been clear to Hitler from these conversations that Molotov was unimpressed by his grand visions. He was primarily concerned with issues involving Russia's concrete interests in Europe not with vague promises of future gains in Asia at the expense of a country which had still to be defeated. When, at their last meeting on the same day, Ribbentrop presented him with a proposal for a new pact, Molotov replied:

581

. . . For the Soviet Union, as the most important Black Sea Power, it was a matter of obtaining effective guarantees of her security. In the course of her history, Russia had often been attacked by way of the Straits. Consequently paper agreements would not suffice for the Soviet Union; rather would she have to insist on effective guarantees of her security. Therefore this question had to be examined and discussed more concretely. The questions which interested the Soviet Union in the Near East concerned not only Turkey but Bulgaria, for instance, about which he, Molotov, had spoken in detail in his previous conversation with the Führer. But the fate of Romania and Hungary was also of interest to the Soviet Union and could not be immaterial to her in any circumstances. It would further interest the Soviet Government to learn what the Axis contemplated with regard to Yugoslavia and Greece, and likewise what Germany intended with regard to Poland. He recalled the fact that, regarding the future form of Poland, a protocol existed between the Soviet Union and Germany, for compliance with which an exchange of opinion was necessary. He asked whether from the German viewpoint this protocol was still in force. The Soviet Government was also interested in the question of Swedish neutrality, and he wanted to know whether the German Government still took the stand that the preservation of Swedish neutrality was in the interests of the Soviet Union and Germany. Besides, there existed the question of the passages out of the Baltic Sea (Store Bælt, Lille Bælt, Öresund, Kattegat, Skagerrak). The Soviet Government believed that discussions must be held on this question similar to those now being conducted about the Danube Commissions. As to the Finnish question, it was sufficiently clarified during his previous conversations with the Führer.

Somewhat in desperation Ribbentrop replied that German action in the Balkans

. . . was motivated exclusively by the circumstances of our war against England. As soon as England conceded her defeat and asked for peace, German interests in the Balkans would be confined exclusively to the economic field, and German troops would be withdrawn from Romania. Germany had—as the Führer had repeatedly declared—no territorial interests in the Balkans. He could only repeat again and again that the decisive question was whether the Soviet Union was prepared and in a position to cooperate with us in the great liquidation of the British Empire. On all other questions we would easily reach an understanding if we could succeed in extending our relations and in defining the spheres of influence. Where the spheres of influence lay had been stated repeatedly. It was therefore—as the Führer had so clearly put it—a matter of the interests of the Soviet Union and Germany requiring that the partners stand not breast to breast but back to back, in order to support each other in the achievement of their aspirations. He would appreciate it if M. Molotov would comment on this matter. Compared to the great basic issues, all others were completely insignificant and would be settled automatically as soon as an over-all understanding was reached. In conclusion, he wished to remind M. Molotov that the latter owed him an answer to the question of whether the Soviet Union was in principle sympathetic to the idea of obtaining an outlet to the Indian Ocean.

In his reply Molotov stated that the Germans were assuming that the war against England had already actually been won. If, therefore, as had been said in another connection, Germany was waging a life and death struggle against England, he could only construe this as meaning that Germany was fighting 'for life' and England 'for death'. As to the question of collaboration, he quite approved of it, but he added that they had to come to a thorough understanding. This idea had also been expressed in Stalin's letter. A delimitation of the spheres of influence must also be sought. On this point, however, he (Molotov) could not take a definitive stand at this time, since he did not know the opinion of Stalin and of his other friends in Moscow in the matter. However, he had to state that all these great issues of tomorrow could not be separated from the issues of today and the fulfilment of existing agreements. The things that were started must first be completed before they proceeded to new tasks. The conversations which he—Molotov—had had in Berlin had undoubtedly been very useful, and he considered it appropriate that the questions raised should now be further dealt with through diplomatic channels by way of the Ambassadors on either side.

The following confidential Propaganda Ministry briefing, recorded by Dr Kausch and dated 19 November, suggests that the outcome of Molotov's visit did not produce immediate disillusionment in Berlin. Indeed, the initial reaction appears quite positive:

582

. . . According to all our reliable information, the Soviet Union, as hitherto, has not the slightest intention of entering the war. So there is no question of any kind of military pact. Russia is disinterested in the new Europe. The organization of this area, together with the colonial territory in Africa, is solely a matter for Germany and its European allies. Russia is only interested in Finland and, in particular, in the port of Petsamo and its sources of raw materials. It was not difficult to achieve an agreement over this.

. . . We pointed out to the Russians that the Straits would cease to be of interest to Russia the moment the way had been cleared for Russia's expansionist drive towards the Persian Gulf. This is the old German line in negotiations with Russia. Germany has nothing against Russia establishing a strong influence over Afghanistan, Iran, Beludschistan, and even India. Such a large state as the Soviet Union must secure far more by gaining access to the Indian Ocean than by posession of the Straits, which does not promise any further opportunities for expansion, since

Italian hegemony will be established in the Mediterranean itself and will not be restricted.

Apparently, the Russians i.e. Molotov, accepted this advice. Molotov declared that Russia had no interest in the Straits or in Turkey—with one small qualification: in the event of a war between Turkey and Germany and Italy certain border areas between Iran and Turkey, i.e. in Eastern Turkey, are to be given to Russia in order to expand access to Persia.

In addition, Russia has promised to use its influence with Turkey to stay out of the war and it is very likely that Mr Sarcoglu will be instructed accordingly next week in Moscow. Saracoglu's trip to Moscow has already been announced.

It all depends on whether Stalin confirmed Molotov's agreements. Naturally Molotov will have to give Stalin a detailed account and secure Stalin's final agreement. However, it is anticipated in Berlin that Stalin will honour the broad lines of the agreements . . .

However, it is probable that Hitler was less positive but wanted to await Stalin's response before reaching a final decision on his future actions.

Russia eventually presented her conditions for joining the Tripartite Pact, which included the demand that Germany remove her troops from Finland and agree to a treaty between Russia and Bulgaria which would secure Russian control of the Dardanelles. Hitler ignored the Russian response, which merely confirmed the impression he had formed in his talks with Molotov, namely that Russia was not prepared to agree to German domination of Europe. On 5 December, he ordered the C.-in-C. Army and the Chief of the General Staff to accelerate the preparations for the attack on Russia in spring 1941 commenting: 'the decision over European hegemony will be made in the struggle against Russia'.[16] On 7 December, Franco's final refusal to participate forced Hitler to cancel the planned attack on Gibraltar (Operation Felix). Thus both the 'world coalition strategy' and the Mediterranean strategy had reached a cul de sac. On 18 December, Hitler issued a military directive for the invasion of Russia which was to be code-named 'Operation Barbarossa':

583

. . . The German Wehrmacht must be prepared *to crush Soviet Russia in a quick campaign* (Operation Barbarossa) even before the conclusion of the war against England.

For this purpose the *Army* will have to employ all available units, with the reservation that the occupied territories must be secured against surprises.

For the *Luftwaffe* it will be a matter of releasing such strong forces for the Eastern campaign in support of the Army that a quick completion of the ground

16. *Ibid*. p. 186.

operations can be counted on and that damage to eastern German territory by enemy air attacks will be as slight as possible. This concentration of the main effort in the east is limited by the requirement that the entire combat and armament area dominated by us must remain adequately protected against enemy air attacks and that the offensive operations against England, particularly against her supply lines, must not be permitted to break down.

The main effort of the *Navy* will remain unequivocally directed against England, even during an Eastern campaign.

I shall order the *concentration* against Soviet Russia possibly eight weeks before the intended beginning of operations.

Preparations requiring more time to get under way are to be started now, if this has not yet been done, and are to be completed by 15 May 1941.

It is of decisive importance, however, that the intention to attack does not become apparent.

The preparations of the High Commands are to be made on the following basis:

I. *General Purpose*

The mass of the Russian *Army* in western Russia is to be destroyed in daring operations, by driving forward deep armoured wedges; and the retreat of units capable of combat into the vastness of Russian territory is to be prevented.

In quick pursuit a line is then to be reached from which the Russian air force will no longer be able to attack the territory of the German Reich. The ultimate objective of the operation is to establish a cover against Asiatic Russia from the general line Volga-Archangel. Then, in case of necessity, the last industrial area left to Russia in the Urals can be eliminated by the Luftwaffe.

In the course of these operations the Russian *Baltic Sea Fleet* will quickly lose its bases and thus will no longer be able to fight.

Effective intervention by the Russian *Air force* is to be prevented by powerful blows at the very beginning of the operation.

II. *Probable allies and their tasks*

1. On the wings of our operation the active participation of *Romania* and *Finland* in the war against Soviet Russia is to be expected.

The High Command will in due time arrange and determine in what form the armed forces of the two counties will be placed under German command at the time of their intervention.

2. It will be the task of *Romania* to support with selected forces the attack of the German southern wing, at least in its beginnings; to pin the enemy down where German forces are not committed; and otherwise to render auxiliary service in the rear area.

3. *Finland* will cover the concentration of the German *North Group* (parts of the XXI Group) withdrawn from Norway and will operate jointly with it. Besides, Finland will be assigned the task of eliminating Hango.

4. It may be expected that *Swedish* railroads and highways will be available for the concentration of the German North Group, from the start of operations at the latest. . . .

Hitler had probably not held out much hope for an agreement with Russia, though it was an option he was prepared to test. The decision to attack Russia was much easier for him springing as it did from that combination of ideological and strategic motives which invariably determined his decisions and all of which now pointed in that direction: racism—the superiority of the Aryan Germans over the Slavs and their right to secure vital *Lebensraum* at the Slavs' expense; the necessity of destroying the plague of 'Jewish Bolshevism' which threatened civilization; strategic necessity—the need to force Britain to make peace by removing her remaining 'continental sword'; and economic considerations—the need to acquire large sources of food and raw materials to enable Germany to continue the war for world hegemony against the Anglo-Saxon powers with their vast resources. Finally, he was convinced of the impossibility of any kind of peaceful coexistence with the Soviet Union in the long run and believed that the cultural and racial inferiority of the Russians would ensure a German victory.

CHAPTER 31

From Blitzkrieg To World War: January–December 1941

(i) The Preparations for 'Barbarossa'—the Invasion of the Balkans

On 9 January 1941, Hitler summed up his view of the strategic situation in a conference with military commanders:

A landing in England was only feasible if complete air superiority had been achieved and if England had been partially paralysed. Otherwise it would be a criminal act. The English war aim was ultimately to beat Germany on the continent. However, it lacked the means to do so. The British Navy was weaker than ever because it was deployed on two military theatres which were far apart; it could not be decisively reinforced. The British air force was faced with bottlenecks in the supply of raw materials, particularly aluminium, because of the decline in imports, and the effects of the German air and naval warfare were having a very deleterious effect on British industry. The aircraft industry had been so badly damaged that there had been a decrease rather than an increase in production. This damage inflicted by the German air force must be continued more systematically than hitherto. As far as the British army was concerned, it was incapable of mounting an invasion. What kept England going were the hopes it vested in the United States of America and in Soviet Russia, for the destruction of the English homeland was in time inevitable. But England hoped to hold on until it had brought together a great continental block against Germany. The diplomatic preparations for this were clearly apparent.

Stalin, the master of Russia, was a clever man; he would not act openly against Germany, but one must expect that he will increasingly make difficulties in situations which are difficult for Germany. He wants to gain the inheritance of an impoverished Europe, needs successes and is animated by the urge to expand to the West. He is also absolutely clear about the fact that after a total victory by Germany the situation of the Soviet Union would be very difficult.

The possibility of a Russian intervention in the war is keeping the English going. They would only give up the race if the last continental hope was destroyed. For, if they lost the war they would no longer have the strength to keep the empire together. However, if they could keep going and raise 40–50 divisions, and the USA and Russia helped them, then a very serious situation would develop for Germany. That must not happen.

Until now he had operated on the basis of always destroying the most important enemy position in order to move a step forward. For this reason Russia must be beaten. Then, either the English would give in or Germany would be able to continue the fight against Britain under more favourable circumstances. The destruction of Russia would also enable Japan to move against the USA with all its forces. That would keep the latter from entering the war . . .

Before the attack on Russia could go ahead, however, an awkward situation which had developed in the Balkans had to be cleared up. It was a result of Italy's abortive attempt to capture Greece with an attack launched from Albania on 28 October 1940. This attempt by Mussolini to realize Italian ambitions in the Mediterranean had not been coordinated with Germany and went directly counter to the German interest in keeping the Balkans quiet preparatory to the attack on Russia. But Mussolini had resented Hitler's failure to give him adequate warning of German actions. As he told Ciano on 12 October; 'Hitler always faces me with *faits accomplis*. This time I am going to pay him back in his own coin. He will find out from the papers that I have occupied Greece'.[1]

The whole affair illustrated the dangers of the lack of coordination between the Axis powers. Not only did the Italian attack fail to make headway, but it opened the way for Britain to establish bases in Greece, as an ally, thereby exposing the Romanian oilfields and the southern flank of the German offensive in Russia to Allied air attacks. On 5 December 1940, therefore, Hitler approved 'Operation Marita', an attack on Greece via Bulgaria, for the spring. Then, on 27 March 1941, a coup replaced the pro-German government in Yugoslavia with a pro-British one. Hitler responded by including an invasion of Yugoslavia in the campaign against Greece launched on 9 April.

1. *Ciano's Diary 1939–1945*, ed. M. Muggeridge (London, 1947) p. 297.

Although the German offensive was quickly successful, it did mean a postponement of the Russian campaign by four weeks and the southern prong of the German advance was slightly weakened by the diversion of troops. In his last days, Hitler blamed Mussolini for the loss of the war owing to this postponement, which meant, he maintained, that the German armies had not had time to defeat Russia before the onset of winter. This, however, was undoubtedly an exaggeration. Apart from anything else, the muddy conditions in western Russia in spring 1941 would not have allowed an effective attack before June.

So confident were the German leadership of victory over Russia that, on 11 June, even before Operation Barbarossa had begun, General Walter Warlimont of OKW was drafting a directive for the conduct of the war after the successful conclusion of the Russian campaign:

585

A. After the destruction of the Soviet armed forces, Germany and Italy will dominate the European mainland militarily—with the exception, for the time being, of the Iberian peninsula . . .

At that point a serious threat to the European sphere on land will no longer exist. Both in order to secure it and for the purpose of further offensives which are envisaged the Army will require much smaller forces than have had to be maintained hitherto. The main emphasis of armament production can be shifted to the Navy and the Air Force.

The expansion of Franco-German cooperation must and will contain further English forces.

Spain will be faced in the foreseeable future with the question of whether or not it is prepared to participate in the expulsion of the English from Gibraltar.

The possibility of exercising strong pressure on Turkey and Iran enhances the prospects of using these countries as well—either directly or indirectly—for the struggle against England.

B. On the basis of this situation, which will emerge after the victorious completion of the Eastern campaign, the following strategic tasks may emerge for the Wehrmacht in the late autumn of 1941 and the winter of 1941/42.

1. The newly won eastern territory must be organized, secured and, with the full cooperation of the Wehrmacht, economically exploited.

2. A continuation of the struggle against the British position in the Mediterranean and in the Near East through concentric attacks which are envisaged from Libya through Egypt, from Bulgaria through Turkey, and in certain circumstances from Transcaucusus through Iran.

(*a*) In North Africa the main thing is to finish off Tobruk and thereby provide the basis for continuing the German-Italian attack on the Suez Canal. It must be prepared for around November with the proviso that the German Africa Corps must be brought up to the highest possible level in terms both of personnel and *matériel* and be provided with sufficient reserves of all kinds.

(*b*) In view of the anticipated reinforcement of the English position in the Near and Middle East for the defence of the Suez Canal, we shall have to contemplate a German operation from Bulgaria through Turkey with the goal of attacking the English position on the Suez Canal from the East as well.

For this purpose we must ensure that strong forces are assembled in Bulgaria as soon as possible sufficient to make Turkey politically submissive or to break its resistance by force.

(*c*) When the collapse of the Soviet Union has created the preconditions for it, we must prepare to launch a motorized expeditionary force from Transcaucusus against Irak in association with the operations under (*b*).

(*d*) Exploitation of the Arab freedom movement. In the event of major German operations, the position of the English in the Middle East will become that much more difficult the more forces can be tied down at the appropriate moment by disaffection or uprisings. All military, political, and propaganda measures must be carefully coordinated during the period of preparation.

3. The closing of the Western entrance to the Mediterranean through the elimination of Gibraltar.

The preparations for 'Operation Felix',[2] plans for which already exist, must once more be set in motion even during the operations in the East . . . The exploitation of West African bases by the Navy and Air Force, possibly through the occupation of Atlantic islands, will be facilitated by the possession of the Straits.

4. In addition to these possible operations against the British position in the Mediterranean, after the conclusion of the Eastern campaign, the 'siege of England' must be taken up again by the Navy and Air Force with full force.

On 21 June 1941, the day before Operation 'Barbarossa', Hitler wrote to Mussolini to explain the reasons for his decision to attack:

586

DUCE: I am writing this letter to you at a moment when months of anxious deliberation and continuous nerve-racking waiting are ending in the hardest decision of my life. I believe—after seeing the latest Russian situation map and after appraisal of numerous other reports—that I cannot take the responsibility for waiting longer, and above all, I believe that there is no other way of obviating this danger—unless it be further waiting, which, however, would necessarily lead to disaster in this or the next year at the latest.

The situation: England has lost this war. With the right of the drowning person, she grasps at every straw which, in her imagination might serve as a sheet anchor.

2. The attack on Gibraltar (eds).

Nevertheless, some of her hopes are naturally not without a certain logic. England has thus far always conducted her wars with help from the Continent. The destruction of France—in fact, the elimination of all west European positons—is directing the glances of the British warmongers continually to the place from which they tried to start the war: to Soviet Russia.

Both countries, Soviet Russia and England, are equally interested in a Europe fallen into ruin, rendered prostrate by a long war. Behind these two countries stands the North American Union goading them on and watchfully waiting. Since the liquidation of Poland, there is evident in Soviet Russia a consistent trend, which, even if cleverly and cautiously, is nevertheless reverting firmly to the old Bolshevist tendency to expand the Soviet State. The prolongation of the war necessary for this purpose is to be achieved by tying up German forces in the east, so that—particularly in the air—the German Command can no longer vouch for a large-scale attack in the west. I declared to you only recently, Duce, that it was precisely the success of the experiment in Crete that demonstrated how necessary it is to make use of every single airplane in the much greater project against England. It may well happen that in this decisive battle we would win with a superiority of only a few squadrons. I shall not hesitate a moment to undertake such a responsibility if, aside from all other conditions, I at least possess the one certainty that I will not then suddenly be attacked or even threatened from the east. The concentration of Russian forces—I had General Jodl submit the most recent map to your Attaché here, General Marras—is tremendous. Really, all available Russian forces are at our border. Moreover, since the approach of warm weather work has been proceeding on numerous defences. If circumstances should give me cause to employ the Luftwaffe against England, there is danger that Russia will then begin her strategy of extortion in the south and north, to which I would have to yield in silence, simply from a feeling of air inferiority. It would, above all, not then be possible for me, without adequate support from an air force, to attack the Russian fortifications with the divisions stationed in the east. If I do not wish to expose myself to this danger, then perhaps the whole year of 1941 will go by without any change in the general situation. On the contrary, England will be all the less ready for peace for she will be able to pin her hopes on the Russian partner. Indeed, this hope must naturally even grow with the progress in preparedness of the Russian armed forces. And behind this is the mass delivery of war material from America which they hope to get in 1942 . . .

(6) Whether or not *America* enters the war is a matter of indifference, inasmuch as she supports our opponent with all the power she is able to mobilize.

(7) The situation in England itself is bad; the provision of food and raw materials is growing steadily more difficult. The martial spirit to make war, after all, lives only on hopes. These hopes are based solely on two assumptions: Russia and America. We have no chance of eliminating America. But it does lie in our power to exclude Russia. The elimination of Russia means, at the same time a tremendous relief for Japan in East Asia, and thereby the possibility of a much stronger threat to American activities through Japanese intervention . . .

As far as the war in the east is concerned, Duce, it will surely be difficult, but I do not entertain a second's doubt as to its great success. I hope, above all, that it will then be possible for us to secure a common food supply base in the Ukraine for some time to come, which will furnish us such additional supplies as we may need in the future . . .

Whatever may now come, Duce, our situation cannot become worse as a result of this step; it can only improve. Even if I should be obliged at the end of this year to leave 60 or 70 divisions in Russia, that is only a fraction of the forces that I am now continually using on the eastern front. Should England nevertheless not draw any conclusions from the hard facts that present themselves, then we can, with our rear secured, apply ourselves with increased strength to the dispatching of our opponent. I can promise you, Duce, that what lies in our German power, will be done . . .

In conclusion, let me say one more thing, Duce. Since I struggled through to this decision, I again feel spiritually free. The partnership with the Soviet Union, in spite of the complete sincerity of the efforts to bring about a final conciliation, was nevertheless often very irksome to me, for in some way or other it seemed to me to be a break with my whole origin, my concepts, and my former obligations. I am happy now to be relieved of these mental agonies. With hearty and comradely greetings,

Yours

Adolf Hitler.

(ii) Operation 'Barbarossa': the first phase, 22 June–August 1941

Operation 'Barbarossa' began at dawn on 22 June 1941. (See the map on page 1211 below.) The Germans committed all their available units which were ready and equipped for action—153 divisions, a total of 3,050,000 men. They included seventeen of the twenty-one panzer divisions—two were in Libya and two being re-equipped—with 3,350 tanks, all thirteen of the motorized divisions, and virtually all the artillery units, with 7,146 guns. There were only 385,000 available troops in reserve until November, when those born in 1922 were due for call-up. As General Fromm of the Reserve Army pointed out, this was sufficient only for a summer campaign. The air force could only deploy around 68 per cent of its strength—2,510 aircraft, of which 1,945 were ready for action—fewer than for the Western campaign of 1940. The remaining 1,766 (1,162 ready for action) had to be deployed at home or on the other fronts, an example of the extent to which German resources were already being overstretched. Deployed against them were 2.8 million Russians in the western districts—150 divisions with 1,800 tanks and 1,540 modern aircraft and 5,000 older types.

The German forces were divided into three Army Groups. Army Group North under Field-Marshal von Leeb consisted of two armies (18 v.Busch and 16 v.Küchler) and one panzer group (4 Hoepner), with a total of 26 divisions, of which three were panzer and three motorized. Von Leeb was to advance from East Prussia through the Baltic States towards Leningrad. The most powerful thrust came from Army Group Centre under Field Marshal von Bock, which contained two armies (9 Strauss and 4 v.Kluge) and two panzer groups (3 Hoth and 2 Guderian) comprising fifty divisions, of which nine were panzer and six motorized. Von Bock was to advance north of the Pripet marshes due east towards Smolensk. Army Group South under Field Marshal von Rundstedt contained three armies (6 v.Reichenau, 17 v.Stülpnagel, and 11 v.Schobert) and one panzer group (1 v.Kleist), comprising 41 German divisions, of which five were panzer and three motorized, and the equivalent of 14 Romanian divisions. Rundstedt was to advance in two separate wings, one from Poland and one from Romania. The remaining divisions were in OKH reserve.

Initially the German armies made rapid progress. Stalin had ignored warnings of the attack from the Allies and from his Intelligence, because he could not believe that the Germans would dare to initiate a war on two fronts and assumed the Allies were trying to provoke him into the war. He assumed the German preparations were bluff designed to force him to be more conciliatory. And, indeed, in the months preceding the attack he had made serious attempts to be conciliatory. As a result, the Germans were able to take full advantage of the element of surprise and in the first two days half the Russian air force was wiped out on the ground. Within the first three weeks the German forces had managed to advance 450–500 kilometres on the northern front, up to 600 on the central front, and 300–350 on the southern front. In his diary entry of 3 July Halder was already thinking in terms of the next phase of the war against Britain on the assumption that Russia had already been defeated:

587

On the whole, then, it may already be said that the aim of shattering the bulk of the Russian army this side of the Dvina and the Dnieper has been accomplished. I do not doubt the statement of the captured Russian Corps CG that, east of the Dvina and the Dnieper, we would encounter nothing more than partial forces, not strong enough to hinder the realization of German operational plans. It is thus probably no overstatement to say that the Russian campaign has been won in the space of two weeks. Of course, this does not yet mean that it is closed. The sheer geographical vastness of the country and the stubbornness of the resistance, which is carried on with every means, will claim our efforts for many more weeks to come.

Future plans:

(*a*) For the continuance of the Russian operations it will be of primary importance to gain a new jump-off line between Smolensk and Moscow and another base around Leningrad. From here we could proceed to the capture of northern Russia and the industrial region round Moscow, and subsequently, in conjunction with AGr. South, of the Donetz industrial region.

Once we are across the Dvina and Dnieper, it will be less a question of smashing enemy armies than of denying the enemy possession of his production centres and so prevent his raising a new Army with the aid of his gigantic industrial potential and his inexhaustible manpower resources.

(*b*) As soon as the battle in the East changes from an effort to annihilate the enemy armed forces to one of paralyzing the enemy economy, our next tasks in the war against England will come to the foreground and require preparation.

Preparations must be made for the offensive against the land route between Nile and Euphrates, both from Cyrenaica and through Anatolia, and perhaps also for an offensive from the Caucasus against Iran . . .

However, although the Russian armies were driven back, they cleverly exploited the difficult terrain and the vulnerability of the German lines of communication, for example using the Pripet marshes as a base for the Russian 5th Army to launch damaging attacks on the German 6th Army on the northern flank of Army Group South. These difficulties in turn prevented the fully effective coordination of panzer and infantry units essential for Blitzkrieg tactics. The infantry tended to lag behind the panzer units enabling significant numbers of Russian troops to escape encirclement. Moreover, although large numbers of Russian troops were surrounded in pockets by the pace of the German advance, notably at Minsk (300,000) and, Smolensk (300,000) on the central front, they continued to put up a stubborn resistance, thereby delaying the advance and increasing German losses in men and matériel. By the end of July, the German forces had suffered 213,301 casualties, including 46,470 dead and 11,758 missing, nearly 30 per cent more than in the West European campaign and 100 per cent more officers. By the middle of July, the motorized forces had lost approximately 50 per cent of their combat strength and the infantry divisions around 80 per cent. German reserves had to be drawn upon earlier and to a greater extent than had been envisaged.

Before the campaign both Hitler and the German military leadership had totally underestimated the strength of the Red Army, arguing partly from the purge of officers in 1937 and partly from its poor performance in the Russo-Finnish war of 1939–40. They estimated that the Russians would be defeated in a matter of two months, and this opinion was shared by most military experts in the Allied countries. This helps to explain what in hindsight appears to be the incredible folly of the German attack. During August, however, they began to become aware of the size of the task they had taken on. This changing appreciation of the situation is evident in the entry for 11 August in General Halder's diary:

588

The whole situation makes it increasingly plain that we have underestimated the Russian colossus, who consistently prepared for war with that utterly ruthless determination so characteristic of totalitarian States. This applies to organizational and economic resources, as well as to the communications system and, most of all, to the strictly military potential. At the outset of the war we reckoned with about 200 enemy divisions. Now we have already counted 360. These divisions indeed are not armed and equipped according to our standards, and their tactical leadership is often poor. But there they are, and if we smash a dozen of them, the Russians simply put up another dozen. The time factor favours them, as they are near their own resources, whereas we are moving farther and farther away from ours. And so our troops, sprawled over an immense front line, without any depth, are subjected to the enemy's incessant attacks. Sometimes these are successful, because in these enormous spaces too many gaps have to be left open.

(iii) Disagreements on strategy between the OKH and Hitler, July–August 1941*

At this point, when it became clear that German resources were inadequate for continuing the attack on three fronts with equal momentum, the issue of priorities arose. The question was: on which of the three fronts—North, Centre, or South—should the main emphasis of the German advance lie? Right from the start of the planning for Barbarossa, there had been a latent clash between Hitler and OKH over this question. General Halder advocated that the main thrust should come from Army Group Centre towards Moscow on the grounds that the Russians would commit the bulk of their forces for the defence of the capital. The Germans would thus have the opportunity of destroying those forces and thereby creating a large gap in the Red Army front, and also of capturing the seat of government and a key communications centre, as well as the valuable industrial centres north and south of the city.

Hitler, however, was more concerned with political and economic aspects. His priorities were first, to establish secure communications with Sweden and Finland, ensuring continued access to supplies of iron ore and nickel. This would require the capture of Leningrad, removing the threat from the Russian fleet in the Baltic. Secondly, he was anxious to capture the rich agricultural area of the Ukraine and the industrialized Donetz basin (Donbas) in the south, and to secure the oilfields in the Caucasus. He also believed that a German advance on the Caucasus would apply pressure on Turkey to enter the war on the Axis side. He regarded the

*See the map on pages 1212–3 below.

attack on Moscow as of lesser significance than these objectives in north and south. Moreover, following an OKW (v.Lossberg) draft for Barbarossa, he had assumed that the continuation of the offensive on Moscow would depend on the progress made on the flanks. However, while Army Group Centre had achieved its initial objective, Smolensk, by mid-July, Army Group North had not yet captured Leningrad and Army Group South was lagging behind.

This controversy, which had rumbled on during July and early August, came to a head when, on 15 August, Hitler ordered Panzer Group 3, on the northern flank of Army Group Centre, to move to assist Army Group North which was facing a dangerous Soviet counter-attack on its southern flank. In a memorandum, dated 18 August 1941, prepared by OKH and put before Hitler by Brauchitsch, Halder tried to persuade Hitler to concentrate the main thrust on Army Group Centre and head for Moscow:*

589

1. *The enemy situation*
The distribution of the enemy forces indicates that at the present time, after the annihilation of the enemy forces facing Army Group South and with the impending successes of Army Group North, the bulk of the intact military forces of the enemy is in front of Army Group Centre. The enemy therefore appear to regard an attack by Army Group Centre in the direction of Moscow as the main threat. They are employing every means (troop concentrations, fortifications) in order to block this attack. It is unlikely that the enemy will significantly weaken their forces in front of Army Group Centre in order to reinforce those in front of Army Groups South and North. It is more likely that, in view of their increasingly evident shortage of forces, they will attempt to achieve a tight defensive position by pulling back advanced outposts, thereby shortening the front as much as possible.

2. *The objective of the operation*
The further objectives of Army Groups South and North are, apart from the defeat of the enemy forces confronting them, in the first instance to capture essential industrial areas and to eliminate the Russian fleet. The immediate objective of Army Group Centre, on the other hand, is, above all, the destruction of the strong enemy forces confronting it, thereby breaking down the enemy's defences. If we succeed in smashing these enemy forces, the Russians will no longer be capable of establishing a defensive position. This will create the necessary conditions for the occupation of the industrial area of Moscow. Only the elimination of this industrial area, together with the successes of Army Groups South and North, will remove the possibility of the enemy's rebuilding their defeated armed forces and re-establishing them on an operationally effective basis.

The decision about the operational objective for Army Group Centre must take into account the following basic points:

*See the map on pages 1212–3 below.

(*a*) The time factor. The offensive by Army Group Centre cannot continue after October on account of weather conditions. The suggested offensive in the direction of Moscow can be carried out as far as can be judged within this time limit. On the other hand, this whole period will be required in view of the distances involved and the resistance of the enemy. As a result, we will not be able to push forward with the motorized units on their own without support from the infantry.

(*b*) Even after refuelling, the motorized units can only be effective over short distances and with diminishing combat strength. As a result, they must be only used for the essential tasks involved in the decisive operation.

(*c*) The suggested operation can only be successful if the forces of Army Group Centre are systematically concentrated on this single goal to the exclusion of other tactical actions which are not essential for the success of the operation. Otherwise, time and energy will not suffice to deal a decisive blow against the enemy forces confronting Army Group Centre and their sources of supply during the course of this year. This, however, must remain the objective of the military leadership. Army Group South and Army Group North will be able to fulfil the tasks assigned to them with their own resources. . . .

Hitler remained unconvinced. In addition to the priority he gave to his strategic goals in the Baltic and the Ukraine, he was now tempted by the opportunity of encircling a huge concentration of Russian forces around Kiev. He therefore rejected the OKH memorandum and ordered Guderian's Panzer Group 2 from Army Group Centre to be switched to Army Group South and insisted that the advance on Moscow should be delayed until the objectives in north and south had been achieved. His reply was dated 22 August 1941:

590

The proposal drawn up by the Commander-in-Chief of the Army on 18 August 1941 for the future operations of Army Group Centre in conjunction with Army Groups South and North prompts me to go over once again the salient points in this campaign.

1. The objective of this campaign is finally to eliminate Russia as a Continental ally of Great Britain and thereby to remove from Britain all hope of changing the course of events with the help of the last remaining Great Power.

2. This objective can only be achieved:

(*a*) through the annihilation of the Russian combat forces;

(*b*) through the occupation, or at least destruction, of the economic bases which are essential for a reorganization of the Russian armed forces.

One must point out in this connexion that the destruction or removal of essential sources of raw materials is more decisive than the occupation or destruction of industrial manufacturing plant. . . .

In accordance with the initial decision on the relative importance of the individual combat zones in the east, the following are and remain the most essential points:
1. The destruction of the Russian position in the Baltic, and
2. The occupation of the Ukrainian areas and those round the Black Sea which are essential in terms of raw materials for the planned reconstruction of the Russian armed forces.

3. As already mentioned, in addition, there is the concern for our own oil in Romania and the necessity of pressing on as fast as possible to a position which offers Iran at least the prospect of assistance in the foreseeable future.

As a result of the circumstances which have developed, partly because an order of mine or rather of the OKW was ignored, Army Group North is clearly not in a position, within a short space of time and with the forces at its disposal, to advance on Leningrad with a right flanking movement and thereby to be certain of surrounding and destroying this base and the Russian forces defending it. The situation now demands that Army Group North should be rapidly supplied with the forces which were intended for it at the beginning of the campaign since it is numerically weaker. I hope that the three divisions which are being sent will suffice to enable Army Group North to achieve its objective and to deal with any crises. The cleaning up and securing of its south-eastern flank can, however, only be carried out by forces of Army Group Centre.

The faster Army Group North is enabled to clear up its position, i.e. to surround or destroy the Russian opponent through the support of the forces transferred to it by the Army and through the concentration of the Air Force by the Reich Marshal, the more quickly will the forces of this Army Group, particularly the motorized units, become available. Then they can use the motorized units put at their disposal by Army Group Centre to concentrate on their sole remaining objective, namely to help the advance of Army Group Centre on Moscow.

Just as important, however, in fact even more important, is the clearing up of the situation between Army Group Centre and Army Group South.

The objection that time would be lost and that the attack on Moscow might occur too late or that the tank units would then be unable to fulfil this task for technical reasons is not valid; since after the destruction of the Russian forces, which are still threatening the flank of Army Group Centre, the task of advancing on Moscow will not be more difficult, but considerably easier. For either the Russians will withdraw part of their forces from the central front to cover the gap opening up in the south, or they will immediately bring up the forces which are being created in the rear. In either event, the situation will be better than if the Centre Group tried to advance with the undefeated Russian 5th Army as well as the Russian forces east and west of Kiev acting as a continual threat to its flanks and with the Russians able, in addition, to bring up new formations from the rear as reinforcements. . . .

For these reasons, I am unable to give my general approval to the draft submitted to me by the Army on the further conduct of the operations.

This is a strategic opportunity such as fate only very rarely provides in war. The enemy is in a salient nearly 300 kilometres long, triangular in shape and surrounded by two Army Groups. It can only be destroyed if at this time Army Group considerations are not allowed to predominate but are subordinated to the interests of the overall conduct of the campaign. The objection that time would then be lost and that the units would no longer be technically equipped for their advance on Moscow is not decisive in view of this opportunity. The suggestion that Army Group South should also contribute to this task can be disregarded. For the decisive point is whether it can contribute. If it can, all the better; if not, then its task must under no circumstances be therefore neglected and in consequence remain uncompleted. . . .

A key reason for Hitler's rejection of the OKH memorandum was his growing realization that it might not be possible to defeat Russia before the winter. While he continued to hope that it would be possible to reach Moscow and the Caucasus before the winter, he was not prepared to sacrifice his major priorities of Leningrad and Ukraine for the sake of a bid to capture Moscow: This revised view of the strategic situation was reflected in an OKW memorandum of 13 September approved by Hitler:

591

. . . For our own prosecution of the war, therefore, the following is necessary:
1. The next and decisive war aim is the collapse of Russia, which must be achieved through the commitment of all the forces which can be spared from the other fronts. If it proves impossible to realize this objective completely during 1941, the continuation of the eastern campaign has top priority for 1942. The acquisition of territory on the southern flank will have great political and economic implications.

Our main aim must be to achieve an alteration in our favour in the political attitude of Turkey. This would significantly improve the military situation in the south-east.
2. Only after the exclusion of Russia as a power factor will it be feasible to concentrate on the battle in the Atlantic and in the Mediterranean against Britain, if possible with the help of French and Spanish bases. Even if Russia was largely crushed by the end of the year, the army and air forces necessary for decisive operations in the Mediterranean, the Atlantic and on the Spanish mainland will not be available until the spring of 1942.
3. It is important that political and military contacts with France and Spain should not be broken off before next spring. On the contrary, they should be strengthened in order to keep France in tow and to continue to persuade her to strengthen West Africa from a military point of view to resist any Anglo-American attack. The difficulty for us, as far as France is concerned, is the need to take into account the rightful interests of our Italian ally. But from a military point of view she is absolutely essential if we are to defeat Britain in the foreseeable future, and therefore she must be approached.
4. On this expanded basis, then, the increasing U-boat offensive can only receive more support from the Air Force from next spring to enable it to continue the blockade of England with greater success.

5. Operations in the eastern Mediterranean are only feasible when the Transcaucasus has been reached.
6. The invasion of Britain can only be seriously considered if, despite the collapse of Russia, all means fail to get Spain or France to take part in the war on the side of the Axis, and if, on account of this, the battle of the Atlantic is not sufficiently successful to ensure the defeat of Britain by this method.

Hitler's decision to switch Guderian's Panzer Group south to Kiev contributed to the destruction of the whole of the Soviet South West Front (Army Group) by 24 September, leading to the capture of 665,000 prisoners and a vast quantity of booty. However, in the meantime, German losses in men and equipment had increased. By 26 September, German casualties had reached 534,000, the bulk of them infantry and the reserves were inadequate to replace them. When the advance of Army Group Centre began again on 2 October, many of the motorized units were at only 30–40 per cent of their full strength.

Although the offensive started well with the destruction of 45 Soviet divisions near Vyazma and the capture of 650,000 prisoners, by the second week of October the autumn rains slowed down the advance, since only tracked vehicles could move effectively through the mud. And then the Russian winter set in early and with full force. The warnings of the Army High Command in their August memorandum on the time factor and the technical problems now proved correct. It was a premiss of the *Blitzkrieg* strategy that Russia would be defeated before the onset of winter. As a result, the German army was not equipped with winter clothing, nor was the German military equipment and transport designed for the extreme conditions of the Russian winter. With supply lines over-extended, the breakdown in transport, made worse by the existing shortage of locomotives and rolling stock, was potentially disastrous. Last but not least, the Russians mounted a brave and stubborn defence.

Hitler's mood during November and the inadequacy of his style of leadership can be gauged from the following comments by his OKH adjutant, Major Engel. They were written down after the war on the basis of jottings made at the time and should, therefore, be treated with caution:

592

12.11.1941. Above all there is the devastating realization that F does not express or justify clearly enough what he wants. The result is that C.in.C. and Ch.of.St. give up and do what they think is right on the basis of the F's unclear statements . . .
22.11.1941. This evening Hitler speaks to a small group about the things which have been on his mind for the past months. From everything he says it is clear that

he is still not quite sure what he wants. The whole situation leads him to make decisions which unfortunately are dependent on the pressures to which he is subject: Party, old party comrades, State, and lastly Wehrmacht . . . From all he says the aims of the campaign have not been achieved, on the other hand, German successes would not be without effect in prestige terms on Germany's world position. All wars, he said, were to start with not racial *(völkisch)* but economic in structure, without merchants no war has ever been decided. The small tradesman determines the production of guns, tanks, and munitions. He [Hitler] must deploy sufficient resources for German armaments production so as to leave the others standing. This was how the war in the East must be fought. To undermine the opportunities of the other side and monopolize them oneself—that was the precondition for final victory.
24.11.1941. Once more an unsatisfactory and unclear situation. The Führer does not give orders but only holds long discussions and at the end the C.in.C and Ch. of St. go home with the sense that they can do what they want—the F suddenly has another train of thought and then what was once true no longer is and OKH is to blame. This is not so, but Field Marshal [Brauchitsch] is not the man to put up a fight.
25.11.1941. In the evening once more long discourses about the continuation of operations. F expatiates. Great concern about Russian winter and weather, claims we started a month too late. Ideal solution would be the fall of Leningrad, the capture of the Southern region and then possibly a pincer movement from S and N on Moscow, combined with a frontal attack. Then one could construct an Eastern Wall with military bases similar to that of the Habsburg Monarchy in the Balkans; but time was his greatest nightmare.

(iv) The Reverse in front of Moscow in December 1941—The Failure of the Blitzkrieg Strategy

During November, despite the appalling conditions, Hitler and OKH urged on the troops in the hope that the Russians were on the point of collapse and that a final push would secure Moscow. However, by the end of November, the armies were exhausted and, with German spearheads in the northern suburbs of Moscow, the advance ground to a halt. Then, on 5 December, the Russians launched a massive counter-offensive both north and south of Moscow with fifty-seven fresh infantry, and seventeen armoured, divisions drawn largely from Siberia and well equipped for winter fighting. Writing two days after the counter-attack began, the Commander-in-Chief of Army Group Centre, von Bock, reviewed the factors which had led to that situation:

593

. . . Three things have led to the present crisis:

1. The setting in of the autumn mud season. Troop movements and supplies were almost completely paralysed by the mud-covered roads. It is no longer possible to exploit the victory of Vyazma.
2. The failure of the railways.
   Weaknesses in the organization, a shortage of wagons, of locomotives and of trained personnel—the inability of the locomotives and the equipment to withstand the Russian winter.
3. The underestimation of the enemy's resistance and of his reserves of men and material.

The Russians have understood how to increase our transport difficulties by destroying almost all the bridges on the main lines and roads to such an extent that the front lacks the basic necessities of life and of fighting equipment. Ammunition, fuel, food, and winter clothing do not reach the front line. . . .

The Russians have managed in a surprisingly short time to reconstitute divisions which had been smashed, to bring new ones from Siberia, Iran, and the Caucasus up to the threatened front, and to replace the artillery which has been lost by numerous rocket launchers. There are now twenty-four more divisions in the sector of this Army Group than there were on 15 November. By contrast, the strength of the German divisions has sunk to less than half as a result of the unbroken fighting and of the winter, which has arrived with full force; the fighting strength of the tanks is even less. The losses of officers and N.C.O.s are terribly high and at the moment replacements for them are even more difficult to get than new troops. . . .

During the next days panic spread among the German forces and the Army Commanders advised a withdrawal. Hitler, however, was aware that no defences had yet been prepared in the rear and was afraid that a retreat might become a rout. On 16 December, therefore, he ordered all the German armies to stand firm and fight to the last, an order which he reaffirmed in a directive to Army Group Centre on 20 December:

594

. . . 1. The fanatical will to defend the ground on which the troops are standing must be injected into them with every possible means, even the toughest. If every unit is equally imbued with it then the enemy's attacks—even if they lead to breaches or breakthroughs at particular points—will ultimately be doomed to fail. However, where this will is not fully present the front will begin to crumble without any prospect of stabilizing it once more in a prepared position. For, every officer and soldier must understand that a withdrawal will expose them to the dangers of the Russian winter far more than staying put in a position, however inadequately equipped it may be—quite apart from the very considerable and unavoidable losses of *matériel* involved in a withdrawal. The Russians will immediately pursue a unit which is withdrawing, they will not let it come to rest, they will keep attacking it without the unit being able to find a refuge because prepared positions in the rear are lacking. Talk of Napoleon's retreat is threatening to become reality. Thus, there must only be withdrawals where there is a prepared position in the rear. The soldier will only understand the withdrawal when he sees that, after withdrawing from the enemy, he will move into a position which has been prepared, however makeshift it is. Only a retreat carried out in this way can avoid undermining the trust between the unit and its leadership. If, however, a unit is forced to leave a position without being offered a satisfactory alternative, then every withdrawal threatens to produce a crisis of confidence in the leadership.

. . . 3. Every piece of territory which has to be abandoned to the enemy must be rendered unusable as far as possible. Every settlement must be burnt down and destroyed without consideration for the population to deprive our opponents of all shelter. That must be prepared. If the destruction is unsuccessful, then those settlements which have not been destroyed must be subsequently annihilated by the Luftwaffe. For, in view of the cold, the enemy will be just as dependent on shelter as our own troops. His position as the attacker will be even more difficult than that of our own troops when they acquire a reasonably equipped position.

4. The enemy will gradually bleed themselves to death with their attacks. They are hurling the last available forces into the battle. Their equipment and armament may in individual cases be very good, but in most places they are fighting with badly-led and poorly-armed masses. There is thus no reason for the troops to lose the sense of superiority over this opponent which they have demonstrated hitherto. On the contrary, it is essential to strengthen everywhere this justified self-confidence and to have the will to deal with this opponent and the difficulties caused by the weather until sufficient reinforcements arrive and the front is thereby finally secured.

Generals who withdrew were dismissed, including the panzer hero, Heinz Guderian. One, Hans von Sponeck, the Commander of the XXXXII Army Corps, was even courtmartialled and sentenced to death. His sentence was commuted to imprisonment in a fortress, but he was then executed after the July 1944 plot against Hitler. By the spring of 1942, 35 generals had been replaced for various reasons, an indication of the effect of months of heavy fighting and the impact of the Soviet offensive. On 19 December, Hitler accepted the resignation of the C.in C. Army, Field Marshal von Brauchitsch, and took over himself. A few days earlier, Halder had noted in his diary: 'The C.in C. is little more than a postman', and from then onwards Hitler's interference at all levels of Army operations increased still further.

Hitler's order did have the effect of stabilizing the situation somewhat and, on 15 January, OKH gave the order for a phased withdrawal. In practice, however, the Soviet offensive continued and the front could not be properly stabilized until March/April when it ran some 150–300 kilometres further back from the line reached by the German armies at the beginning of December 1941. The cost in casualties was high.

Later, after the crisis was over, Hitler reflected on the experience of the reverse in front of Moscow. At a meeting with Speer on 24 May 1942 to discuss the transport problem, which had played such a vital role in the crisis, Hitler explained how he had coped with the problem. The experience had confirmed for him the key importance of will power, a view which had long dominated his whole political approach:

595

THE FÜHRER: The transport problem is crucial; it must be solved. Throughout my life I have confronted decisive issues which had to be resolved–above all last winter. I was repeatedly told by so-called experts and people who were supposed to have leadership qualities: 'that's impossible, that won't work'. I can't accept that. There are problems which absolutely must be solved. Where the right leaders are available they have always been solved and will always be solved. One can't always achieve it by amiable means; but for me the question of amiability does not arise, just as I am completely indifferent to what posterity may say about the methods I had to use. As far as I am concerned, there is only one issue which has to be resolved, namely, we must win the war or Germany will be destroyed. As a result, I am not concerned about how we win the war but only that we do it. Unfortunately, I frequently came across cases of inadequate leadership. I responded by intervening ruthlessly. I even sent home people who were very close to me, like for example, two colonel-generals; their strength was exhausted, they couldn't go on. One of these gentlemen came to me in the winter and said: 'My Führer, we can't hold on, we must retreat'. I asked him: 'Sir, where in God's name do you intend to go back to, how far do you want to go back?' 'Well, he told me, I don't know how far.' 'Do you want to go back 50 km; do you think it is less cold there; do you think that the transport problem for the supplies can be solved better there? And if you go back—do you intend to take your heavy weapons with you, can you take them with you?' The gentleman replied: 'No, I can't' 'So you want to leave them to the enemy and how do you intend to fight your way back without heavy weapons?' He replied: 'My Führer, at least rescue the army without their weapons'. I asked him: 'Do you want to go back to the Reich frontier or where are you going to stop?' 'Yes, my Führer', he replied, 'we probably have no other alternative, I must confess that to you quite frankly'.

I could only say to the gentlemen: 'Gentlemen, you go back to Germany, as fast as possible yourselves, but leave the Army here under my leadership; it will stay up front.'

There were nerve-wracking days. Almost everybody failed, apart from a few men who fought alongside me; day and night I had to think things through without sleep: what can I do? What must be done? How can I fill this gap or that? For, I knew that a retreat would mean suffering the fate of Napoleon. And I managed it! The fact that we have survived this winter and are now in a position to go on the offensive again victoriously, viz; Kertsch, viz: the great battle of the Kharkov pocket, in which I think 250–400,000 Russians are trapped, all this is only due to the bravery of the soldiers at the front and my determined will to hold on come what may . . .

THE FÜHRER: On the basis of a briefing by the Reich Marshal [Göring] about the transport situation, I have decided to intervene in this matter, since victory depends on it. I too once began with nothing as a unknown soldier of the World War and I only did so when all the others, who appeared much more qualified for leadership than I was, had failed. I only had my will power and yet I succeeded. The whole course of my life proves that I never capitulate. The war problems must be mastered!

Let me remind you of the recent briefing on the shipping situation during which the experts repeatedly used the word 'impossible'. And afterwards the problem was easily solved and it will produce results.

In the front line I see tremendous heroism. Only the simple soldier in the most forward position has any right to find something difficult and to regard it as impossible, if anybody is to have that right. And yet there every task is completed!

I repeat: for me the word 'impossible' does not exist, it does not exist for me! Coal and iron and transport must be ruthlessly put in order . . . Younger people must be brought in to fulfill my demands, the old no longer have the requisite energy. Our whole leadership is about the same age. It consists of the old soldiers of the World War ranging from the mid-forties to the late fifties. Later, we will all go at the same time, and so we must ensure that the succession is secure. For that reason, I have nominated my best man [Göring], who is a little younger than I am, to be my successor. Unfortunately, the second deputy whom I named [Hess] has failed me. I have, therefore, decided to dismiss State Secretary Kleinmann [Transport Ministry] since he has proved not up to the job and to appoint Ganzenmüller, who has come from the front where he proved effective, to carry out the vital tasks for the railways . . . The war must not be lost because of the transport problem; it will therefore be solved.

The reverse in front of Moscow had been a disastrous setback for Germany; it confirmed the bankruptcy of their whole *Blitzkrieg* strategy. They were now faced with a long war on two fronts, the very situation which Hitler had planned to avoid.

(v) Germany's declaration of war on the United States, 11 December 1941

Less than a week after the beginning of the Russian counter offensive, Germany's strategic situation suffered another devastating blow from a different area, a blow that was partly self-inflicted. On 7 December 1941, Japan attacked the United States' fleet at Pearl Harbor. Hitler had envisaged the alliance with Japan as a means of attacking Britain's Far Eastern position and of intimidating the Americans into maintaining their neutrality. He had not envisaged a Japanese attack on the United States. Even so, under the Tripartite Pact of September 1940, Germany was not bound to come to Japan's assistance unless Japan was attacked by another power. Germany, therefore, was not bound to join Japan in the war against America. Now, however, overestimating Japanese strength, Hitler convinced himself not only that the Japanese attack was to Germany's advantage, in terms of distracting America from the Battle of the Atlantic against Britain and of tying it down in the Pacific, but also that Germany should itself declare war on the United States. He had long resented American assistance to Britain and now believed that if Germany declared war it would simply replace a virtual state of war with an actual one.[3] He considered that it would take America at least a year to mobilize her forces sufficiently to intervene effectively in the European war and by then he hoped to have defeated Russia. Then, with Russia's vast resources underpinning the German war machine, he could take on the Anglo-Saxon powers. How far of course Hitler was actually convinced by his own arguments or whether he had sensed that his gamble had failed and was now engaged on a desperate *Flucht nach vorn* (a policy of 'when in a tight spot attack') so characteristic of his style of politics is a moot point. In any event, on the afternoon of 11 December 1941, Hitler made a devastating attack on President Roosevelt in the Reichstag:

596

. . . And now by contrast let me comment on that other world which is represented by that man who, while nations and their soldiers fought in snow and ice, tactfully made a habit of chatting from his fireside, in other words above all the man who bears the main guilt for this war . . .

The forces which supported Herr Roosevelt were the forces which I fought for the sake of my people and from my deepest conviction. The 'brains trust' which the new American president had to make use of consisted of members of the same nation whom we fought in Germany as a parasitic human phenomenon and began to exclude from public life. And yet we both had something in common: Franklin Roosevelt took over a state with an economy in decline as a result of democratic influences and I too became head of an empire which also, thanks to democracy, was facing ruin. The United States had 13 million unemployed, Germany 7 million and 7 million more short time workers. In both states public finances were ruined . . . Whereas in the German Reich under national socialist leadership within a few years there was a tremendous revival, a revival of the economy, of culture, of art etc., President Roosevelt did not succeed in producing the slightest improvement in his own country . . .

3. See, for example, Hitler's letter to Mussolini of 21 June 1941 on p. 816 above.

And so the influence of the American president began to make itself felt in terms of creating conflicts or in deepening existing conflicts, at any event in preventing conflicts from being peacefully resolved. For years the one desire of this man has been to see conflict break out somewhere in the world, most of all in Europe, to give him the opportunity of linking the American economy with that of one of the two opponents and thereby establishing a political nexus which might gradually draw America into such a conflict and thereby divert attention away from an economic policy which had failed at home.

From November 1938 onwards, he began systematically to sabotage any chance of a policy leading to European peace . . .

From July 1940 onwards Roosevelt's measures, whether through the entry of American citizens into the British Air Force or through the training of English air force personnel in the United States, moved further and further in the direction of war. And, already in August 1940, agreement was reached on a common military programme for the United States and Canada.

In September 1940, he came even closer to war. He handed over 50 destroyers from the US fleet, accepting in return military bases in the British possessions in north and central America. . . . After England was no longer in a position to pay cash for American deliveries he imposed on the American people the Lend-Lease Act . . . In March (1941) occurred the expropriation of all German ships by the American authorities. . . . And, on 9 April, came the first English report that, on the basis of an order of President Roosevelt, an American warship had dropped depth charges on a German U-Boat near Greenland.

On 14 June, contrary to international law, German accounts in the United States were blocked. On 17 June, President Roosevelt demanded, on the basis of mendacious excuses, the withdrawal of German consuls and the closing of German consulates. . . . At the same time, he sent a promise of aid to the Soviet Union. On 10 July, the Navy Minister, Knox, suddenly announced that the USA had issued an order to fire on German warships. On 4 September, the US cruiser *Greer*, following orders, operated in conjunction with English aircraft against German U-Boats in the Atlantic . . . Finally, on 11 September, Roosevelt made a speech in which he himself reiterated the order to fire on all Axis ships.

The fact that, after years of negotiations with this con man, the Japanese government finally had had enough of allowing itself to be mocked in such an undignified fashion fills us all, the German people, and I believe the other decent people throughout the world with deep satisfaction. I have, therefore, handed the American Chargé d'Affaires his passports and informed him of the following:

In pursuit of a policy aimed at unlimited world dictatorship, the United States under President Roosevelt, in conjunction with England, have shrunk from no means of threatening the basis of existence of the German, Italian, and Japanese peoples. The governments of England and the United States have for this reason not only for the present but also for the future opposed any justifiable revision with the aim of a new and better world order.

Since the beginning of the war, the American President Roosevelt has increasingly been guilty of a series of the most serious crimes against international law. Illegal attacks on ships and other property of German and Italian citizens were combined with threats against and even with the deprivation of the personal liberty of those affected through internment.

The increasingly sharp attacks of the President of the United States finally culminated in his order to the American Navy, contrary to all the rules of international law, to attack ships flying the German and Italian flag on sight, to fire upon them and sink them. American ministers proudly boasted of having sunk German U-boats in this criminal fashion. German and Italian merchant ships were attacked by American cruisers, commandeered, and their innocent crews led off to prison. Moreover, President Roosevelt's plan to launch an attack on Germany and Italy in Europe itself, by 1943 at the latest, has now been published in America without any attempt at an official denial by the American government. This has destroyed the honest efforts of Germany and Italy to prevent an extension of the war and to maintain relations with the US, efforts which have demonstrated an exemplary patience in the face of intolerable provocations by President Roosevelt which have been going on for years. Germany and Italy have now found themselves finally compelled to undertake a struggle for their defence and thereby for the maintenance of the freedom and independence of their nations and empires against the United States of America and England, side by side with Japan, in fulfilment of the provisions of the Tripartite Pact of 27 September 1940.

While Hitler was making this speech, Ribbentrop was addressing the American Chargé d'Affaires in the following terms:

597

. . . Mr Chargé d'Affaires: The Government of the United States of America, having violated in the most flagrant manner and in ever increasing measure all rules of neutrality in favour of the adversaries of Germany and having continually been guilty of the most severe provocations toward Germany ever since the outbreak of the European War, provoked by the British declaration of war against Germany on 3 September 1939, has finally resorted to open military acts of aggression.

On 11 September 1941, the President of the United States of America publicly declared that he had ordered the American Navy and Air Force to shoot on sight at any German war vessel. In his speech of 27 October 1941, he once more expressly affirmed that this order was in force.

Acting under this order, vessels of the American Navy, since early September 1941, have systematically attacked German naval forces. Thus, American destroyers, as for instance the *Greer*, the *Kearney* and the *Reuben James*, have opened fire on German submarines according to plan. The Secretary of the American Navy, Mr Knox, himself confirmed that American destroyers attacked German submarines.

Furthermore, the naval forces of the United States of America under order of their Government and contrary to international law have treated and seized German merchant vessels on the high seas as enemy ships.

The German Government therefore establishes the following facts:

Although Germany on her part has strictly adhered to the rules of international law in her relations with the United States of America during every period of the present war, the Government of the United States of America from initial violations of neutrality has finally proceeded to open acts of war against Germany. It has thereby virtually created a state of war.

The Government of the Reich consequently discontinues diplomatic relations with the United States of America and declares that in these circumstances brought about by President Roosevelt Germany also, as from today, considers herself as being in a state of war with the United States of America.

Accept, Mr Chargé d'Affaires, the expression of my high consideration.

RIBBENTROP

CHAPTER 32

The Turning-Point 1942–1943

(i) The 'Co-ordination' of Axis Strategy 1942

Until December 1941, the war had been primarily a European engagement with a small global dimension in the form of a peripheral North African theatre and the participation of colonial and Commonwealth troops on the Allied side. With the entry of Japan and the United States it came to embrace much of the world. This created problems for both sides of coordinating their activities to ensure that maximum pressure was brought to bear on the various fronts. On the evening of 11 December 1941, the three Axis powers signed an agreement on the joint conduct of the war:

. . . In the unshakeable determination not to lay down their arms until the common war against the United States of America and England has been brought to a victorious conclusion, the German Government, the Italian Government, and the Japanese Government have agreed on the following provisions:

I. Germany, Italy, and Japan will conduct the war forced upon them by the United States of America and England with all the means at their disposal until a victorious conclusion.

II. Germany, Italy, and Japan mutually guarantee that they will not seek an armistice or make peace with either the United States of America or England without full agreement with each other.

III. After the victorious conclusion of the war, Germany will cooperate in the closest fashion for the purpose of achieving a just new order on the basis of the Tripartite Pact signed by them on 27 September 1940.

IV. This agreement comes into effect immediately upon its signature and stays in effect as long as the Tripartite Pact of 27 September 1940 remains valid . . .

On 3 January 1942, Hitler met the Japanese ambassador, Oshima, to discuss his future plans and cooperation between the two powers:

599

. . . For the time being he did not intend to carry out any more attacks in the centre of the front. His goal was an offensive on the southern front. Picking up the thread of his argument again, the Führer declared that he was determined to take up once again the offensive in the direction of the Caucasus as soon as the weather was favourable. The thrust in this direction was the most important one: we must get to the oil and to Iran and Iraq. Once we were there, he hoped that we could help to unleash the freedom movement of the Arab world. Naturally, in addition, he would do everything possible to destroy Moscow and Leningrad.

. . . All of us and Japan as well were engaged in a joint life and death struggle and so it was vital that we share our military experience.

. . . With the aid of a map the Führer explained to the Japanese ambassador the situation in the naval war in the Atlantic and emphasized that he regarded it as his most important task to get the U-boat war into top gear. The U-boats were being redeployed. He had first of all recalled all the U-boats operating in the Atlantic. As already mentioned, they would now be posted in front of the US ports and later in front of Freetown and the big ones down as far as Cape Town. He hoped that by February he would be able to deploy 20–24 boats on the coast of the United States alone. These boats were in a position to lie there for four weeks before they had to return. After making a number of other points with reference to the map, the Führer pointed out that however many ships the USA built, one of their main problems was a shortage of personnel. For this reason merchant ships would also be sunk without warning with the aim of drowning as large a proportion of their crew as possible. If word got around that, in the event of being torpedoed, most sailors were lost, the Americans would soon have difficulty in recruiting new people. The training of seamen took a long time. We were fighting for our existence and therefore could not allow a humanitarian viewpoint to dictate our actions. For this reason he must give the order that if foreign seamen could not be taken prisoner, which was not usually possible on the high seas, then the U-boats must surface after torpedoing and fire upon the lifeboats.

Ambassador Oshima warmly agreed with these statements by the Führer and said that the Japanese were also compelled to use these methods. When Singapore had fallen the Allies would be in a completely different position: the English fleet could then only go to Ceylon or perhaps Bombay. Calcutta was already very dangerous for them. He did not think that the United States and England would be able to agree on how to conduct the war . . .

[Hitler then] emphasized that it was probably the first time in history that two such powerful military powers, which were so far apart from one another, stood together in battle. Provided their military operations were coordinated, this offered the possibility of creating leverage in the conduct of the war which must have enormous effects on the enemy, since they would be thereby compelled continually to shift their centres of gravity and in this way would hopelessly fritter away their forces. He did not believe the United States would have the courage to conduct offensive operations in the East Asian sphere . . . the Fuhrer continued 'If England loses in India a world will collapse. India is the cornerstone of the English empire. England acquired all its wealth from India . . .'.

The Führer is of the opinion that England can be destroyed. He is not yet sure how the USA can be defeated. The South American States would, in his opinion gradually move away from the United States. In reply to a comment by the Foreign Minister [Ribbentrop] that Japan might be in a position to attack Russia in May, the Führer said that the most important thing from Germany's point of view was that Japan was not defeated by the Anglo-Saxon powers. It must on no account prematurely dissipate its forces. For us too England was the main enemy. We would certainly not be defeated by Russia. He pointed out to Oshima the long-term danger of the United States and England establishing themselves in a big way on the Australian continent. Oshima is of the same opinion and convinced that Japan would soon secure bases in Australia. In addition, it was obvious that Japan must one day beat Russia, for otherwise the new order in East Asia would be impossible. At the moment, she was still heavily committed with her troops in China. However, he was convinced that the Chungking government would get progressively weaker in the coming months and then Japan would be in a position to withdraw troops from China.

Roosevelt's greatest mistake was to impose sanctions on Japan without at the same time being sufficiently well-armed. This was a really crazy policy. The Führer was of the same opinion and said that if one did not want to wait until one's throat was cut one simply must strike first and Japan had correctly recognized that and done it. The Führer is of the opinion that it is extremely important for Japan and Germany to exchange their military inventions. Germany has no interest in East Asia and Japan none in Europe and Africa . . .

On 18 January 1942, the diplomatic agreement between the Axis powers of 11 December 1941 was supplemented by a military one. According to this, the world was divided into two zones of military operations along the line of 70° longitude, with Japan being responsible for the area east of the line and Germany and Italy for that west of it. In practice however, it was the Allies who proved more effective in coordinating their efforts. For, while the United States, Britain and Russia cooperated, albeit with some friction, in all the various theatres, Germany and Italy on the one hand and Japan on the other fought entirely separate wars in Europe and the Far East. In particular, Japan declined to enter the war with Russia, initially with Hitler's blessing, later despite requests from Germany to do so. Finally, even the relationship between Germany and Italy was marked by barely concealed resentment, suspicion, and contempt on both sides, while Italy's actions in North Africa and Greece had proved more of a hindrance than a help to their German allies.

On 29 April 1942, Hitler met Mussolini in Salzburg to inform him about future operations. The Italian Foreign Minister commented cynically on the meeting in his Diary:

600

There is much cordiality, which puts me on my guard. The courtesy of the Germans is always in inverse ratio to their good fortune. Hitler looks tired. He is strong, determined, and talkative; but he is tired. The winter months in Russia have weighed heavily upon him. I see for the first time that he has many grey hairs. Hitler talks with the Duce, I talk with Ribbentrop, but in two separate rooms, and the same record is played in both. Ribbentrop, particularly, plays his usual record. I have reported the conversation elsewhere. Napoleon, the Beresina, the drama of 1812, all this is brought to life in what he says. But the ice of Russia has been conquered by the genius of Hitler. This is the strong dish that is served up to me. But what of to-morrow? What does the future hold? On this matter Ribbentrop is less explicit. An offensive against the Russians in the south with the oil wells as a politico-military objective? When Russia's sources of oil are exhausted she will be brought to her knees. Then the British Conservatives, and even Churchill himself, who, after all, is a sensible man, will bow in order to save what remains of their mauled Empire. Thus spoke Ribbentrop. But what if all this doesn't happen? What if the British, who are stubborn, decide to continue? What course must be followed to change their minds? Aeroplanes and submarines, says Ribbentrop. We turn back to the 1940 formula. But this formula failed then and was put up in the attic. Now they pull it out again, and, after having dusted it thoroughly, they want to offer it to us again. I am little convinced by it, and say so to Ribbentrop, much to Alfieri's dismay.[1] Alfieri understands very little of what he hears but always says yes.

America is a big bluff. This slogan is repeated by everyone, big and little, in the conference rooms and in the antechambers. In my opinion, the thought of what the Americans can and will do disturbs them all, and the Germans shut their eyes to it. But this does not keep the more intelligent and the more honest from thinking about what America can do, and they feel shivers running down their spines.

Hitler talks, talks, talks, talks. Mussolini suffers—he, who is in the habit of talking himself, and who, instead, has to remain practically silent. On the second

1. Dino Alfieri, the Italian Ambassador in Berlin (eds).

day, after lunch, when everything has been said, Hitler talked uninterruptedly for an hour and forty minutes. He omitted absolutely no argument: war and peace, religion and philosophy, art and history. Mussolini automatically looked at his wrist-watch, I had my mind on my own business, and only Cavallero[2], who is a phenomenon of servility, pretended he was listening in ecstasy, continually nodding his head in approval. The Germans, however, dreaded the ordeal less than we did. Poor people. They have to endure it every day, and I am certain there isn't a gesture, a word, or a pause which they don't know by heart. General Jodl, after an epic struggle, finally went to sleep on the divan. Keitel was yawning, but he succeeded in keeping his head up. He was too close to Hitler to let himself go as he would have liked to do.

(ii) The German Campaign in Russia 1942–43

While the Navy continued to urge the need to concentrate on attacking Britain by focusing on the Mediterranean theatre and by establishing close cooperation with Japan, Hitler—while accepting the importance of the Battle of the Atlantic against Britain—continued to regard victory in Russia as the key to the defeat of Britain. After the disastrous set-back in front of Moscow, the Germans had eventually managed to stabilize their front and remained on the defensive until May 1942. Hitler had learnt his lesson from the over-ambitious attempt to attack on three separate fronts simultaneously and, in any case, Germany clearly now lacked the resources to do so. He therefore decided to concentrate on what had always been his main goal—the capture of the industrial Donbas and above all the oilfields of the Caucasus. At the same time, however, he hoped that one final push would suffice to capture Leningrad, which had been under siege all winter, and thereby enable the German forces to link up with the Finns and control the Baltic.

OKW Directive No. 41 of 5 April 1942 ordered a major offensive on the southern front 'to destroy the remaining military forces of the Soviets once and for all' and 'as far as possible to remove from them the most important economic resources necessary for the war effort'. The offensive was to be conducted in four phases: 1) a thrust due east with the aim of encircling large Soviet forces near Voronezh; 2) a thrust further south to destroy the Russian armies on the central part of the river Don; 3) an encircling movement involving two thrusts up and down the Don aiming to trap Russian forces in the Don bend north-west of Stalingrad; 4) a thrust south to conquer the Caucasus up to the line Batumi-Baku. This would then provide the basis for a move down into Iran and Iraq to link up with the German Afrika Korps moving eastwards into Egypt.*

2. Marshal Count Ugo Cavallero was the Italian Commander-in-Chief (eds).

*See the map on p. 1214 below.

An OKW study of 6 June 1942 on 'The Strength of the Wehrmacht in Spring 1942' concluded that 'on account of the impossibility of a complete replenishment of matériel and personnel, it was viewed overall as less strong than in spring 1941'.[3] However, by concentrating on a single major offensive the Germans were able to assemble a powerful force of 68 divisions (including 8 panzer and 7 motorized infantry), together with 10 Italian divisions and 3 brigades, and 27 Romanian and 13 Bulgarian divisions, although the fighting capacity of these allied units was rated as only 50 per cent of that of the German ones.

During May 1942, the Soviet forces launched a series of attacks which were repulsed with heavy Russian losses and led to German territorial gains. However, these actions, together with weather problems, delayed the start of the main German offensive by two weeks until 28 June. Moreover, although the Germans secured a rapid breakthrough, they failed to achieve the objective of the first two phases of the offensive: the destruction of the bulk of the Russian forces in front of the Don. Hitler responded to this situation with OKW Directive No. 45, dated 23 July 1942, which determined the future conduct of the campaign:

601

I. In a campaign lasting little more than three weeks the major goals which I set for the southern flank of the eastern front have been essentially achieved. Only weak enemy forces of Timoschenko's armies have succeeded in avoiding encirclement and in reaching the southern bank of the Don. We must anticipate their reinforcement from the Caucasus.

The concentration of further enemy forces in the Stalingrad area, which our opponents will presumably defend tenaciously, is in progress.

II. Goals of future operations.

A. Army

1. The next task of Army Group A is to encircle the enemy forces, which have escaped over the Don, in the area south and south-east of Rostov and destroy them . . .

2. *After the destruction of the enemy forces* south of the Don, the most important task of Army Group A is to occupy the whole of the eastern coast of the Black Sea and thereby to eliminate the Black Sea ports and the enemy Black Sea fleet . . .

A further force composed of all remaining mountain and light infantry divisions will force a passage of the Kuban, and occupy the high ground around Maykop and Armavir . . .

3. Cf. *Deutschland im Zweiten Weltkrieg Bd. 2 Vom Überfall auf die Soviet-union bis zur sowjetischen Gegenoffensive bei Stalingrad*, K. Drechsler *et al.* (Berlin-East 1983) p. 329.

3. *At the same time*, a force composed mainly of mobile units will give flank cover in the east and capture the Groznyy area. Detachments will block the military road between Osetia and Groznyy, if possible at the top of the passes.

Following that the Baku area will be occupied by a thrust along the Caspian coast . . .

4. The task of Army Group B is, as previously laid down, to envelop the Don defences and, by a thrust forward to Stalingrad, to smash the enemy forces concentrated there, to occupy the town, and to block the land communications between the Don and the Volga, as well as the Don itself.

Closely connected with this, highly mobile forces will advance along the Volga with the task of thrusting through to Astrakhan and blocking the main course of the Volga in the same way . . .

With this directive Hitler in effect decided to operate on the assumption that the goals of the first two phases of the offensive had been achieved by giving orders for the implementation of the next two phases. Moreover, whereas Directive No. 41 had envisaged the thrust towards Stalingrad and the move down into the Caucasus as successive operations (phases 3 and 4), Directive No. 45 ordered them to be carried out simultaneously on the fatally mistaken assumption that Russian resistance in front of Stalingrad was crumbling. Indeed, the 4th Panzer Army was diverted from the Stalingrad offensive south to attack Rostov, while the 6th Army was left to advance on Stalingrad alone minus much of its fuel and armour in what was assumed to be merely a mopping-up operation. In fact, however, within a week after the issuing of Directive No. 45 Soviet resistance in front of Stalingrad had stiffened to such an extent that OKH was obliged to transfer the 4th Panzer Army from the Caucasus back to the Stalingrad front, thereby crucially weakening the Caucasus offensive.

The battle for Stalingrad began on 19 August and on the 23rd the 6th Army received the order to take the city. The fighting became extraordinarily fierce with every street and every block bitterly contested. Losses were heavy. Between 21 August and 16 October, the 6th Army took 40,000 casualties. In a desperate attempt to capture the city German units were withdrawn from the flanks to the north and south and thrown into the attack. Defence of the flanks was left in the hands of the 3rd and 4th Romanian armies which were inadequately trained and equipped and hence vulnerable to a counter attack. However, OKH assumed the Russians were too weak to mount such an attack and largely ignored appeals from General Paulus, Commander of the 6th Army, for his flanks to be reinforced.

Meanwhile, the offensive into the Caucasus was also bogged down as a result of stubborn Russian resistance and problems of supply. Although advance German units managed to capture a key pass in the high Caucasus, they lacked the strength to exploit it. By the autumn, it was clear that

Army Group A had failed to achieve the objectives laid down in Directive No. 45 of capturing the Black Sea coast and the main oilfields of the Caucasus. Only part of the oil field had been secured.

At this point, Hitler's generals began to advise him to withdraw to less exposed positions. However, he was determined to hold on to the Russian territory which had been won at such cost, in particular to Stalingrad. Apart from its importance as the hub of Russian transport and communications in the south-eastern part of European Russia, the name of the city had symbolic significance. In a speech to his old Party comrades on 8 November at the annual reunion in commemoration of the Munich putsch, Hitler committed himself to its capture:

602

. . . I have always been ridiculed as a prophet. Innumerable people who laughed then do not laugh now, and those who laugh now will perhaps after a time stop laughing. Realization of this will spread from Europe throughout the whole world. International Jewry will be recognized in all its devilish power, we National Socialists will see to that. In Europe this danger has been recognized and State after State is imitating our legislation. So in this gigantic struggle there is only one possible outcome: complete success. . . . What our soldiers have achieved in terms of speed is tremendous. And what has been achieved this year is enormous and historically unprecedented. The fact that I don't do things the way other people want—well, I consider what the others are likely to think and then I do things differently on principle. So if Mr Stalin expected us to attack in the centre—I had no intention of attacking in the centre. Not only because Mr Stalin may have believed that I wanted to, but because I was not interested. I wanted to get to the Volga at a certain point near a certain town. As it happens, its name is that of Stalin himself. But please do not think I marched there for that reason—it could be called something quite different—I did so because it is a very important place. Thirty million tons of transport can be cut off there, including nearly nine million tons of oil. All the wheat from the vast Ukraine and the Kuban area converges there in order to be transported north. Manganese ore is mined there; it is a huge reloading point. I wanted to take it and, you know, we are being modest, for we have got it! There are only a few very small places left not captured. Now others are saying: 'Why don't you fight more quickly then?' Because I do not want a second Verdun there but I prefer to do it with quite small detachments of assault troops. Time is no object here. Not a single ship is now getting up the Volga. And that is the decisive thing! . . .

The decisive factor in this war is, Who deals the final blow? And you may be sure that it will be us!

Meanwhile, the Russians had secretly prepared a massive counter-offensive on the Stalingrad front, involving roughly sixty per cent of their available armoured and motorized units and more than twice the artillery fire power of the December 1941 counter-offensive in front of Moscow. They launched their attack at the weak points on the German flanks north and south of Stalingrad, defended by the 3rd and 4th Romanian armies respectively. (See the maps on page 1215 below.) On 19 November, they struck from Kletskaya to the north of the city and on the 20th from the 'Beketovka bell' to the south. By 22 November, the two Russian pincers had joined together twelve miles south east of Kalach trapping some 240,000 troops of the German 6th Army and elements of two Romanian armies in a pocket stretching some thirty-five miles from the east at Stalingrad to the west and some twenty miles from north to south.

The commander of the 6th Army, General von Paulus and his superior, the Commander of Army Group B, General von Weichs, both requested that the German forces should be permitted to break out towards the south-west, a request supported by the new Chief of the General Staff, General von Zeitzler. However, a commitment by Göring to supply the besieged army with some 500 tons of supplies per day by air, a promise which flew in the face of the advice of his Luftwaffe commander on the spot, von Richthofen, reinforced Hitler's inclination to insist that the Army should stay put until it could be relieved. On 24 November, therefore, Hitler ordered the 6th Army to hold its position, encouraged by the optimistic assessment of General von Manstein about the feasibility of a relief operation.

In fact, it soon became clear that the Luftwaffe could not adequately supply Stalingrad in the harsh winter conditions. On average less than 120 tons of supplies per day arrived. On 12 January, the bread ration was reduced to forty grams per day—a large slice. An attempt to relieve Stalingrad, launched on 12 December from Kotelnikovo, sixty miles south-west of Stalingrad, by an Army Group under General Hoth with 232 tanks, failed. Although the attack reached the Myshkova river, the last Russian defensive position before the city, it was held on the 20th and the German forces were then forced back by a major Russian offensive, launched on 16 December north-west of Stalingrad, which burst through the Italian 8th Army holding that sector and threatened to outflank the relief force. The 6th Army had to be left to its fate. When the siege finally ended on 2 February 1943, the Axis forces had lost twenty-two divisions and 160 other units, and had taken more than 150,000 casualties. Nearly 90,000 prisoners were taken by the Russians including twenty-four generals.

The course of events during the battle was recorded in the War Diary of the OKW:

603

7 November 1942. The Chief of General Staff of the Army reports at the briefing that, according to agents' reports, a Supreme Council Meeting [*Kronrat*] took place on 4 November in Moscow at which all the Commanders-in-Chief were present. At this meeting it was decided to carry out a major offensive either on the Don front or in the Centre by the end of the year. . . .

19 November 1942. During the day, alarming reports arrive from the Chief of the General Staff of the Army concerning the Russian offensive which has long been awaited by the Führer and which began this morning in the sector held by the 3rd Romanian Army.[4]

20 November 1942. The Chief of the General Staff of the Army reports that the Russians have driven a deep wedge into the 3rd Romanian Army sector. The situation is not yet clear. In the afternoon, the Führer orders the evacuation of the Army High Command II from Vitebsk to the Army Group B in order that it may take over the High Command for the Don region with the 3rd and 4th Romanian Armies, the 4th Panzer Army and the 6th Army subordinate to it.

21 November 1942. The Russian breakthrough in the front of the 3rd Romanian Army between Kletskaya and Scrafimovich has deepened considerably. By midday on 20 November Russian tank spearheads had reached the Guryev region in the upper Liska valley and the area to the south. South of Stalingrad too and in the Kalmyk steppes the Russians have launched an attack with strong forces and large numbers of tanks against the eastern flank of the 4th Panzer Army and the 4th Romanian Army.

In the evening, the Führer orders the 6th Army, whose headquarters is apparently in Kalach, to hold the western and southern corners of their position under all circumstances.

22 November 1942. The two wedges of the major Russian offensive in the Don-Volga region have joined together near Kalach. In consequence, the 6th Army is surrounded between the Volga and the Don. . . .

25 November 1942. The 6th Army which is now surrounded has held its fronts, though its supply situation is critical and, in view of the unfavourable winter weather and the enemy superiority in fighters, it is very doubtful whether the 700 tons of food, ammunition, fuel, etc. per day, which the Army has requested, can be transported to the pocket by air. Air Fleet 4 has only 298 transport planes, whereas 500 are required. The General in command of the VIII Flying Corps in action near Stalingrad, Colonel-General Freiherr von Richthofen, has therefore suggested to the Führer that the 6th Army should for the time being retire to the west in order to be able to go over to the offensive later. But the Führer rejected the idea from the outset. . . .

4. North-west of Stalingrad (eds).

23 January 1943. . . . The Führer has replied in the negative to the question put by Zeitzler[5] yesterday evening as to whether the 6th Army could now be permitted to capitulate. The Army must fight on to the last man in order to gain time. General Paulus replied to a radio message in this vein from the Führer which was sent to the 6th Army: 'Your commands will be carried out. Long live Germany!'
28 January 1943. The main subject of discussion at the briefing today was the re-establishment of the 6th Army, which the Führer wishes to be carried out as quickly as possible.
31 January 1943. In the morning the last radio message from the Southern Group of the 6th Army arrived from Stalingrad.
2 February 1943. In the morning the last radio message from the Northern Group of the 6th Army arrived. The Foreign Armies East section of the General Staff of the Army [German Intelligence] assesses the number of Russian units which will have become available for deployment through the annihilation of the 6th Army at 107 divisions and 13 tank regiments.

Meanwhile, the Russian offensive launched on 16 December towards the south-west in the direction of Rostov was moving so rapidly that there was a serious danger of the whole of Army Group A being cut off in the Caucasus. OKW decided, therefore, to withdraw most of it to a bridgehead on the Taman peninsula, obliging the 17th Army and the 1st Panzer Army to pull back 450 kilometres in three weeks. In the Ukraine too the German armies were in headlong retreat and, during February, the Russians liberated the cities of Kursk, Kharkov, and Belgorod. Meanwhile, in January, the Russians had managed to break the blockade of Leningrad and improvise a railway link to the city along the southern shore of Lake Ladoga.

However, by mid-February, the Russian supply lines were overextended and their offensive was beginning to flag. By withdrawing from exposed positions and drawing on reserves, the Germans had managed to concentrate forces in the South for a counter-attack which began on 19 February and, within less than a month, had succeeded in recapturing Kharkov and Belgorod. At this point, however, their advance was halted by stiffening Russian resistance and the onset of the spring rains.

In their winter offensive the Russians had failed to achieve their objectives of cutting off Army Groups A and South and of capturing the bridges over the river Dnieper, and the Germans had finally succeeded in stabilising their front and in recapturing the initiative. Nevertheless, during the winter campaign of 1942–43, the Germans had lost virtually all the territory gained in the summer offensive of 1942 as well as large amounts of men and equipment. It was a major defeat. Moreover the winter and spring of 1942–43 also represented a turning point in two theatres where the Germans were fighting the Western Allies.

5. General Kurt Zeitzler was the new Chief of the Army General Staff. Halder had been dismissed in the autumn because of disagreement over Stalingrad (eds).

(iii) The North Africa Campaign June 1942–May 1943

On 26 May 1942, the Axis launched a highly successful campaign in North Africa under the overall command of General Rommel, which culminated in the capture of the fortress of Tobruk on 21 June. However, during the first three weeks of July, the Axis advance was halted eighty kilometres west of Alexandria in the first battle of El Alamein. Moreover their attempt to break through the Alamein line at the end of August was blocked in the battle of Alam Halfa. Finally, on 23 October, the British and Commonwealth Eighth Army launched an attack on the well-prepared Axis positions at El Alamein in Egypt:

604

The Balance of Forces at the Start of the Battle of El Alamein 24 October 1942.

	Axis	*Allies*
Troops	96,000	150,000
Tanks	500	1,114
Field guns	*c.* 600	880
Aircraft	372	*c.* 850

Within two weeks they had achieved a major victory, inflicting 25,000 casualties and taking 30,000 prisoners, of whom just over 10,000 were Germans, and the German Afrika Korps was in full retreat. Then, on the night of 7–8 November 1942, 106,000 American and British troops landed on the coasts of Algeria and Morocco in Operation 'Torch'. After brief French resistance, the Allies reached an agreement with Admiral Darlan for a French capitulation, which had already been secretly approved by Marshal Pétain.

Hitler responded at once to these events. On 10 November, he ordered the despatch of German forces to Tunisia and the following day the occupation of Vichy France. By 9 December, the Germans had established a 5th Panzer Army in Tunisia consisting of two German Panzer divisions, a Panzergrenadier division, and two infantry divisions as well as three Italian infantry divisions—a total of 78,000 German and 27,000 Italian troops—to which further units were later added. However, although these forces succeeded in delaying the Allied advance, since the Allies largely dominated the Mediterranean, they could not be effectively supplied. On 3 March 1943, Field-Marshal Kesselring, Hitler's senior military representative in the Mediterranean area, wrote to OKW as follows:

605

. . . Supplies are not meeting current needs. The stocks required to repulse a major attack can only be built up if we start getting over 140,000 tons per month. However, since it is impossible to achieve such provisioning on account of the existing difficulties, the reinforcement of the German troops is proceeding very slowly. Italian equipment is inadequate. The units which have been formed after the retreat have little cohesion. In view of this situation, the C. in C. of the Army Group Africa has requested a decision on how we are planning to continue the war in Tunisia in the long term.

In fact, on 7 March, General Rommel, the C.in C. of the new Army Group Africa, which combined the Afrika Corps and the Fifth Panzer Army, flew to Hitler's headquarters to request the evacuation of what was now in effect merely a bridgehead in Tunisia. Hitler, however, refused since he was not prepared to face the loss of prestige involved so soon after Stalingrad, and he was supported in this by the Italian High Command. Yet, despite desperate efforts by the German Navy, which gave priority to the supplying of Army Group Africa, the supply situation failed to improve significantly as can be seen from the following figures for April 1943:

606

Transports by Sea for the Army Group Africa in April 1943.

Landed	*Lost*
18,690 t. of supplies	15,516 t. of supplies
2,500 soldiers	2 destroyers
26 field guns	14 freighters
46 tanks	1 tanker
268 trucks	12 small ships
13 motor cycles	17 field guns
	3 tanks
	170 trucks
	41 motor cycles

Crucial was petrol of which the German forces were in chronically short supply.

On 12 May 1943, Tunis—the last remaining Axis outpost in North Africa—fell to the Allies. 238,243 soldiers were taken prisoner, of whom approximately half were German.

Even more serious than the failure of the Axis navies to prevent Operation 'Torch' and to supply the Army Group Africa was the development of the Battle of the Atlantic during the Spring of 1943.

(iv) The Battle of the Atlantic, September 1940–December 1943

After the cancellation of Operation 'Sealion' in September 1940, the German Navy had taken on the main burden of the fight against Britain, concentrating on trying to cut her supply lines across the Atlantic. Initially, the Navy had tried to fight both a 'cruiser war', using surface ships against British merchant shipping, and a U-boat war. However, although the few German large ships, which outclassed their British counterparts, had some success—for example, the two battleships, *Scharnhorst* and *Gneisenau*, sank thirty ships with a total tonnage of 149,680 during February–March 1941—the sinking of the largest and most modern German battleship, *Bismarck*, on 27 May 1941, convinced the Naval High Command (OKM) that a cruiser war in the Atlantic against the vastly superior British surface fleet posed too many problems. Instead, they decided to keep the remaining large ships in port and restrict them to limited excursions, maintaining them as a 'fleet in being' and thereby posing a permanent latent threat to British convoy operations. As a result of this decision, the main burden of the Battle of the Atlantic fell on the U-boats.

Between June–December 1940, operating from new bases in north-west France and Norway, German U-boats had succeeded in sinking 343 British ships with a total tonnage of 1,754,501. The British and American yards were then producing some 200,000 tons of shipping per month, so that at that stage the British merchant fleet was facing gradual attrition rather than imminent collapse. U-boat operations were hampered throughout the war by a shortage of submarines. In a memorandum dated 1 September 1939, Admiral Dönitz, the chief of U-boat operations had mentioned the figure of 300 U-boats as the minimum necessary for a decisive victory over Britain in the Atlantic. At the outbreak of war, Germany had only twenty-five U-boats suitable for Atlantic operations. By 1 June 1940, this figure had increased to fifty and by 1 March 1941 to 109. However, of these the vast majority were either under test or being used for training purposes, with the result that in February 1941 only twenty-two were fully operational. Attempts to increase the number of U-boats had been consistently thwarted by the priority given to armaments for the various land operations in 1940–41. Hitler promised to devote more resources to U-boat construction after the successful completion of 'Barbarossa'. The result of this shortage of U-boats, when combined with improved British defences, was a decline in the number of sinkings during 1941.

In part, this decline had been attributable to growing American cooperation. However, with the United States' entry into the war, the German Navy no longer had to restrain its activities for fear of provoking the Americans. On 9 December 1941, two days before the German declaration of war on America, the Navy ordered its U-boats to attack American warships on sight, and from then on they took full advantage of the weak defences off the East coast of the United States and, in particular, of America's failure to introduce a convoy system during the first six months of 1942. During 1942, the numbers of sinkings increased substantially, partly also because of the increasing numbers of U-boats coming into service and because of a break-down in Allied signals intelligence. However, during the second half of 1942, the numbers of U-boats destroyed also increased sharply as the Allies began to improve their tactics and equipment.

Admiral Dönitz, the chief of U-boat operations, was aware that, despite German successes, the U-boat war was still not having a decisive effect on the Western Allies. Angered by the diversion of U-boats to the Mediterranean, to attack the North African supply lines, where they had suffered heavy losses (two thirds in the 'Torch' operation), Dönitz now insisted that priority be given to their deployment in the Atlantic, where they were less vulnerable and more effective. However, in his view, even more emphasis should be given to the U-boat war, if necessary at the expense of the surface fleet.

In January 1943, Dönitz acquired a powerful ally. Already under stress because of Stalingrad, Hitler's anger and disillusionment over the failure of the German surface fleet to intervene decisively in the war had finally boiled over. For, at the turn of the year, Operation 'Rainbow', an attack by German surface ships on a Russian convoy, on which Hitler had pinned great hopes, had proved a fiasco: not one transport was sunk. On 6 January 1943, Hitler ordered the scrapping of the large surface ships. This prompted the resignation of the Commander-in-Chief, Admiral Raeder, who had always been a leading advocate of the surface fleet strategy, to which indeed Hitler himself had hitherto been a strong adherent. On 2 February, Raeder was replaced by Dönitz, a move symbolizing the absolute priority now being given to U-boat warfare in the Atlantic and which Dönitz spelled out to the assembled department heads of OKM on that day:

607

. . . Naval warfare means the U-boat war. All other requirements must be ruthlessly subordinated to its demands. We must secure dock yard capacity and labour supplies for the construction and repair of U-boats and provide the U-boats with improved weapons and the best crews. Only with the U-boat weapon will the Navy be able to make a decisive contribution to victory. Every sacrifice must be made to achieve this goal.

Although Dönitz concentrated all his efforts on the U-boat war, he managed to persuade Hitler of the advisability of continuing to maintain the big surface ships as a 'fleet in being' in Norwegian waters in order to force Britain to provide large escort ships for the Russian convoys. However, all the major ships being built as part of the 1939 'Z' plan had already been scrapped. Dönitz proposed a new naval construction programme, concentrating on U-boats and small surface vessels such as torpedo boats. This was approved by Hitler, who issued an order on 31 May 1943 for the construction of at least forty U-boats per month, compared with the 19–20 which had been built hitherto. The final five year programme envisaged 480 U-boats per year, eight destroyers, twelve torpedo boats, and a whole range of other small surface ships.

Meanwhile, however, the Battle of the Atlantic had already been lost. On the one hand, the Navy's assumption that they could sink more ships than the Allies could build was undermined by improved British construction rates in the first quarter of 1943 (643,000 tons), as a result of a reduction in the German bombing of dockyards, and, above all, by the massive construction programme of the United States (1.7 million tons during the same period). On the other hand, the rate of U-boat successes declined sharply in May and was never to recover, while the rate of U-boat losses increased sharply. The last major U-boat success against an Allied Atlantic convoy was the attack on Convoys H 229 and SC 122 in March 1943, the biggest convoy battle of the war. The Allies lost 21 ships with a total tonnage of 140,842 in the actual battle, while eleven other ships were torpedoed, most of which sank later. Only one U-boat was lost.

The following figures tell the story of the shifts in the U-boat war:

608

1939	*Allied ships sunk*	*Tonnage*	*U-boats sunk*
September	41	153,879	2
October	27	134,807	5
November	21	51,589	1
December	25	80,881	1
Total	114	421,156	9

1940			
January	40	111,263	2
February	45	169,566	4
March	23	62,781	3
April	7	32,467	5
May	13	55,580	1
June	58	284,113	—
July	38	195,825	2
August	56	267,618	3
September	59	295,335	—
October	63	352,407	1
November	32	146,613	2
December	37	212,590	—
Total	471	2,186,158	23

1941			
January	21	126,782	—
February	39	196,783	—
March	41	243,020	5
April	43	249,375	2
May	58	325,492	1
June	61	310,143	4
July	22	94,209	1
August	23	80,310	3
September	53	202,820	2
October	32	156,554	2
November	13	62,196	5
December	26	124,070	10
Total	432	2,171,754	35

1942	*Allied ships sunk*	*Tonnage*	*U-boats sunk*
January	62	327,357	3
February	85	476,451	2
March	95	537,980	6
April	74	431,664	3
May	125	607,247	4
June	144	700,235	3
July	96	476,065	11
August	108	544,410	10
September	98	485,413	11
October	94	619,417	16
November	119	729,160	13
December	60	330,816	5
Total	1,160	6,266,215	87
1943			
January	37	203,128	6
February	63	359,328	19
March	108	627,377	15
April	56	327,943	15
May	50	264,852	41
June	20	95,000	17
July	46	252,145	37
August	16	86,579	25
September	20	118,841	9
October	20	97,407	27
November	14	66,585	18
December	13	86,967	8
Total	463	2,321,300	237
1944			
January	13	92,728	15
February	18	92,923	20
March	23	142,944	25
April	9	62,149	20
May	4	24,424	22
June	11	57,875	25
July	12	63,351	22
August	18	98,729	33
September	7	43,368	21
October	1	7,176	13
November	7	29,592	7
December	9	58,518	14
Total	132	773,767	237

German U-boat Strength 1939–44.

Date	Operational	Training and trials	Total	New boats commissioned in previous quarter
September 1939	49	8	57	7
January 1940	32	24	56	4
April 1940	46	6	52	9
July 1940	28	23	51	15
October 1940	27	37	64	22
January 1941	22	67	89	30
April 1941	32	81	113	47
July 1941	65	93	158	53
October 1941	80	118	198	69
January 1942	91	158	249	49
April 1942	121	164	285	49
July 1942	140	191	331	59
October 1942	196	169	365	61
January 1943	212	181	393	69
April 1943	240	185	425	69
July 1943	207	208	415	71
October 1943	175	237	412	61
January 1944	168	268	436	78
April 1944	166	278	444	62

The turning-point in the Battle of the Atlantic came in May 1943 when forty-one U-boats were lost, containing 1,336 personnel of whom 95 were officers. This rate of loss could not be sustained and on 24 May Dönitz ordered all U-boats away from the North Atlantic and from the convoy routes and deployed them south-west of the Azores. On 31 May, he explained to Hitler what he saw as the reasons for the failure:

609

The reason for the present crisis in the U-boat war is the considerable increase in enemy air strength. In the Iceland-Faeroe Islands gap our listening service has picked up in one day the same number of planes which a few weeks ago would only have appeared in one week. In addition, there is the deployment of aircraft carriers with North Atlantic convoys so that all sea lanes are now under surveillance by the enemy airforce. However, the U-boat crisis would not have been caused solely by the increase in aircraft. The decisive point is that through a new direction-finding device, which also appears to be being used by surface ships, the aircraft are in a position to locate the U-boats and then to launch surprise attacks in low cloud, poor visibility, or at night. If the aircraft did not have this direction-finding equipment they would not be able to locate the U-boats in rough seas or at night. The losses are distributed accordingly. The vast majority have been caused by aircraft. Only a small proportion involve surface ships, although as a result of a particularly unfortunate weather situation (the sudden onset of mist) during the convoy operation on 8 May, this month a fairly large number of U-boats (5) were surprised by destroyers. This ability to surprise us in mist is also only possible through direction-finding devices.

Corresponding to this situation, 65 per cent of the losses happened en route or in a waiting position and only 35 per cent during attacks on convoys. That is natural since, during the largest part of the six to eight weeks mission, the U-boat is either in a waiting position or en route. Here, in the event of poor visibility or darkness, the danger of being suddenly attacked from the air by an opponent who has not been previously spotted is particularly great. In the past month the losses have increased from roughly 14 U-boats = thirteen per cent of those at sea to thirty-six if not thirty-seven = around thirty per cent of those U-boats at sea. These losses are too high. We must now husband our forces, otherwise it would only benefit the enemy.

Dönitz was correct in emphasizing the key role played by the Allied airforces in anti-submarine operations. For, at this point, RAF Coastal Command squadrons based in Iceland and Northern Ireland and a Canadian squadron based in Newfoundland acquired long-range Liberators enabling them to close the gap in air cover for the convoys. However, a vital element in their success was the fact that they were deployed precisely in support of those convoys which were in particular danger from U-boat attack. The key to this lay in the other essential ingredient in the victory in the Battle of the Atlantic: 'Ultra'—the British operation for decoding the German 'Enigma' cyphers used in the transmission of signals between the Commander of U-Boats in Berlin and the submarines at sea. From the beginning of June 1941, the British could read the German naval signals and thereby locate the submarines and determine their course. As a result, convoys could be diverted away from them. Ultra made a vital contributon during these difficult months. However, on 1 February 1942, the Germans introduced a modified machine which produced a black-out for the decryption of U-boat wireless traffic until the cypher could be cracked on 13 December. By January–February 1943, it was once more possible to read the German signals and, with the exception of some breaks in March and between June and September 1943, from then onwards the German U-boat signals could be read with only a few hours delay.

Dönitz had assumed that the set-back in May 1943 would only be temporary and, in the Autumn, he launched another U-boat offensive in the Atlantic, using a new and more effective acoustic homing torpedo. However, the continuous air escort of convoys by land and carrier-based-planes, using new high-frequency location devices and more effective anti-submarine weapons, and working in coordination with surface escorts on the basis of Ultra intelligence was to prove an unbeatable combination.

(v) Germany and its allies, 1943–4

(a) The Scheme for a 'European Confederation':

The German defeats in Russia and North Africa during the winter of 1942–43 had a distinctly unsettling effect on Germany's allies who began to contemplate ways and means of extricating themselves from the war. They were already becoming disillusioned by the heavy losses incurred by their forces on the Eastern front. Italy, for example, had suffered 150,000 casualties and prisoners out of the 230,000 members of their expeditionary corps and the Hungarians and Romanians had suffered comparable losses. There was growing resentment at the extent to which their economies were being in effect plundered in the interests of the German war machine. And there was uncertainty and increasing concern about what the future held in store, irrespective of whether or not the Axis eventually won the war. What would be their place in the German 'new order'? Would they be reduced to mere vassal states in a German-dominated Europe? On 23 March 1943, for example, the Finnish ambassador told State Secretary von Weizsäcker about 'the uncertain mood among our allies and the general desire prevalent among them to hear from us how in broad terms we envisage the future organization of Europe'. And he complained about 'the lack of an overall concept which would be suitable as a motto for our friends and the neutrals in Europe'.[6]

Two days earlier, on 21 March, Ribbentrop had approached Hitler with a scheme for a European confederation which he had already put to the Führer during the Stalingrad battle without success. The following notes formed the basis of his proposal:

610

Re: *European Confederation*
As I proposed in my previous notes for the Führer, in my view we should proclaim the European Confederation in a quite concrete form as soon as possible, in fact as soon as we have achieved a significant military success.

6. Cf. *Deutschland im Zweiten Weltkrieg. Bd 3. Der grundlegende Umschwung im Kriegsverlauf* (November 1942 bis September 1943), W. Schumann *et al.* (East Berlin, 1982) p. 427.

For the inaugural ceremony I envisage inviting all the heads of state of the European states in question and their governments to a safe place, e.g. Salzburg or Vienna, who would then ceremonially sign the inaugural documents of this federation.

Initially, the following states would come into consideration: Germany, Italy, France, Denmark, Norway, Finland, Slovakia, Hungary, Romania, Bulgaria, Croatia, Serbia, Greece, and Spain (?). To those would be added any states in the occupied territories to which the Führer might wish to grant independence.

In my view, only a definite act like that can secure for us the success which we seek.

The question of the territorial demarcation of the various states must not be dealt with at the inaugural ceremony. It must of course be left open until the definitive peace treaties.

I want to recommend the setting up of this confederation in the warmest possible terms. If we always appoint the right people as our representatives in these states, people who take a hard line and, despite conciliatory appearances, uncompromisingly follow the concrete political goal, we will not prejudice anything by forming such a confederation. In fact, the formation of the Greater German Reich at the end of the war will then be a matter of course . . .

The creation of a European Confederation would have the following advantages for us:

1. It would remove from our friends and allies the fear that straight after the peace had been signed, they would all have a German *Gauleiter* imposed on them.

2. It would remove from the neutral states the fear that at the end of the war they would be incorporated into Germany.

3. It would remove from Italy the fear that a powerful Germany would push them to the wall.

4. If the Führer were prepared to create out of certain occupied territories a number of more or less independent states, which would then still be completely in our sphere of influence, this would ensure a significant calming down and relaxation of the situation in those countries.

5. It would produce in the Russians the feeling that the whole of Europe was opposed to them and thus Russia's fighting strength would be weakened.

6. It would have a paralysing effect on the English and Americans if they were not liberating the European states but attacking a unified and united Europe.

7. It would have a paralysing effect on the domestic situation in both England and America.

8. It would ensure that both France and the other occupied territories would undoubtedly contribute to the war effort both in terms of personnel and *matériel* in a totally different way than hitherto . . .

9. We would thereby prevent some neutral states such as, for example, Sweden, Turkey, Portugal etc. from establishing close links with England and America . . .

A new 'Europe Committee' was set up in the Foreign Ministry to work out the details of the 'New Order' and in his directive for its activities Ribbentrop indicated the main ideological cement which was intended to hold it together: 'A very effective method of preparing the European nations for the future New Order lies in exploiting the fears provoked in all countries by the thought of the expansion of Bolshevism into Europe'.[7]

The Foreign Ministry continued to work on plans for a European Confederation during 1943, prompted also by the need to counter Allied propaganda about their plans for the post-war world. German propaganda emphasized the claim that Britain had always opposed European unity, encouraging conflicts among the European states to secure a free hand for building up its empire overseas.

However, the prerequisite for the launching of the Confederation project was a German military success. Otherwise, it would appear too obviously as a concession from weakness and would in any case have little attraction for the other states if it appeared that Germany would eventually lose the war. Since this prerequisite never materialized the project was still-born, although German propaganda continued to use the theme of European unity against Eastern Bolshevism and Western plutocracy.

Hitler showed little interest in such schemes. He expressed his views on Europe and Germany's future role in it in a speech to Gauleiters on 8 May 1943:

611

. . . From all this the Führer deduced that all the rubbish of small nations [Kleinstaaten-Gerümpel] still existing in Europe must be liquidated as fast as possible. The aim of our struggle must be to create a unified Europe. The Germans alone can really organize Europe. There is practically no other leading power left. In this connexion the Führer re-emphasized how happy we can be that there are no Japanese on the European continent. Even though the Italians today give us many a headache and create difficulties, we must nevertheless consider ourselves lucky that they cannot be serious competitors in the future organization of Europe. If the Japanese were settled on the European continent the situation would be quite different. Today we are practically the only power in the European mainland with a capacity for leadership.

. . . The Führer gave expression to his unshakeable conviction that the Reich will be the master of all Europe. We shall yet have to engage in many fights, but these will undoubtedly lead to magnificent victories. Thereafter the way to world domination is practically certain. To dominate Europe will be to assume the leadership of the world.

7. Ibid., p. 411.

In this connection we naturally cannot accept questions of right and wrong even as a basis of discussion. The loss of this war would constitute the greatest wrong to the German people, victory would give us the greatest right. After all, it will only be the victor who can prove to the world the moral justification for this struggle. . . . We still have so many chances to hand that we can await further developments with a clear conscience. The Führer rightly recalled that his prophecies in 1919, 1920, and 1921 seemed insolent and impudent. Today they are proved to have been the results of his realistic thinking and of his comprehensive view of the general situation. We must never have the slightest doubt of victory. The Führer is firmly determined to fight this fight through to the end.

There will never be any rebellion within the Reich against our leadership. The people would never think of such a thing. There is no Jewish leadership here for it. The criminals in such a serious crisis would be stood up against a wall.

(b) The Defection of Italy—September 1943:

In an increasingly difficult situation Germany found she could not rely on her two major allies. During 1942–43, Japan ignored repeated and urgent requests from Germany for military action against Russia. She was far too preoccupied with meeting the growing Allied threat in the Far East to do more than maintain a token presence on the Russian frontier with Manchuria. In the case of Italy the situation was even worse.

The loss of North Africa had completed Italy's disillusionment with the Axis, which had begun with the defeat of Stalingrad if not before. Germany's continual demands on the Italian economy and her failure to maintain essential supplies of vital necessities such as coal produced serious inflation and growing discontent, while the arrogance and barely concealed contempt displayed towards Italian government officials and the armed forces by their German comrades-in-arms wounded Italian pride. Mussolini himself remained committed to the Axis largely because he rightly felt that he had burned his boats, and he could rely on the support of hard-line Fascists such as Roberto Farinacci. However, many Conservatives close to the Court, the new Commander-in-Chief, General Ambrosio, and his deputy General Castellano, leading industrialists such as Pirelli, and even some leading Fascists, such as the former ambassador in London, Dino Grandi, and the former Foreign Minister and Mussolini's son-in-law, Galeazzo Ciano, were determined to take Italy out of the war even if it meant overthrowing Mussolini.

The Allied invasion of Sicily on 9 July 1943 brought the crisis to a head. On 24 July, at a meeting of the Grand Fascist Council, a motion to transfer the Supreme Command of the Armed Forces from Mussolini to the King was agreed by nineteen votes to seven. On the following day, at an audience with the King, Mussolini was dismissed as head of the government and arrested on his departure. The Fascist regime was replaced by a military dictatorship under Marshal Badoglio. Under cover of public declarations that the new regime would continue the war, Badoglio then negotiated an armistice with the Western powers on 3 September, which came into effect on the 8th to coincide with the Allied landing at Salerno.

The Germans had long suspected that the loss of North Africa, let alone Allied landings on Italian soil, might prompt Italy to seek a separate peace and had meanwhile devised plans—Operation 'Axis'—to occupy Italy and disarm all the Italian forces throughout Europe. For this purpose they had increased the number of their divisions in Italy from eight on 1 August to twenty on 8 September. By the latter date, there were, for example, 60,000 German soldiers in Rome, who also controlled the airports, facing 65,000 less well-equipped Italian soldiers. At 8.00 pm on 9 September, the order was given for Operation 'Axis' which, despite some opposition from Italian forces, quickly achieved success—apart from the escape of the bulk of the naval and air forces. By December 1943, 725,000 Italian soldiers had been interned, 615,000 of whom were sent as forced labour to Germany. On 12 September, Mussolini was freed from his hotel prison on the Gran Sasso, the highest mountain of the Abruzzi, by a special German paratroop unit, and, on the 18th he established a new regime which was named the 'Republic of Salò' after the town on Lake Garda nearest the villa where Mussolini was staying. It was a puppet state of the Germans, whose writ ran only in northern Italy and could only be enforced with German approval and cooperation, since it lacked an effective administrative substructure.

Thanks to their prompt intervention, the attempted defection of Italy did not prove the disaster for the Germans which it otherwise might have been. They were able to establish a firm front south of Rome, forcing the Allies to engage in a hard and punishing slog up the peninsula. However, the Italian campaign was a drain on both sides and the Germans could afford the cost in men and *matériel* less than the Allies. Above all, it diverted troops from the Russian front where the outcome of the war was being decided.

CHAPTER 33

The Road to Defeat 1943–1945

(i) Operation 'Citadel' and the Russian offensives of 1943–45

Germany's strategic situation in the spring of 1943 after the defeat of Stalingrad and the loss of North Africa was serious. Apart from the waning commitment of her allies, her resources, particularly in manpower, were being increasingly stretched. Thus, although the Germans were managing to maintain or even increase the numbers of troops on the Eastern front, nothing could disguise the gradual deterioration in their quality as Germany was forced to mobilize her reserves. Moreover, many of them had to be transferred from other fronts, a situation which could only last so long as those fronts remained inactive.

In this situation the Wehrmacht High Command (OKW) determined to adopt a defensive strategy by turning occupied Europe into a fortress. The aim was to establish a strong defensive line along the frontiers and a large central reserve, which could then be deployed to meet attacks on any sector of the front. The enemy would then gradually bleed to death through their unavailing attempts to storm this 'fortress Europe'. It was hoped that this defensive strategy would give Germany a breathing space in which to mobilize and exploit all the resources of occupied Europe in preparation for a later offensive strategy. It was also hoped that the ideological and political divisions among the Allies would eventually lead to a break-up of the Grand Alliance.

The problem with this approach was, first, the fact that while the Red Army remained a powerful threat in the East, Germany would be forced to commit all her reserves to meeting the danger in that sphere, thereby weakening the other parts of the 'fortress'. There was thus a danger of Germany herself bleeding to death as she dealt with repeated Soviet attacks on different sectors of the Eastern front. Secondly, it was vital for political reasons—both at home and abroad—for Germany to give the impression that she was still on the offensive, otherwise both her allies and the German people would begin to doubt a German victory, with consequent devastating effects on morale and hence on the war effort.

The Army leadership (OKH), responsible for the Russian front, was more acutely aware of the need to deal with the Soviet threat than was OKW, which was responsible for the other fronts and for German strategy as a whole. However, both OKH and OKW were directly subordinate to Hitler and for him the political and economic aspects were decisive. Thus, Hitler supported the OKH in its desire for an offensive on the Russian front against the OKW's inclination to rely on defensive operations to facilitate the creation of a strong strategic reserve.

In the Spring of 1943 OKH developed a plan for a quick, powerful, and concentrated attack aimed at destroying the offensive capacity of the Red Army and allowing Germany to regain the strategic initiative on the Eastern front. This operation, codenamed 'Citadel', took into account Germany's limited resources. Whereas Barbarossa had involved three separate offensives on a front of 2,000 kilometres, and the campaign of Summer 1942 had involved two offensives on a front of 600 kilometres, 'Citadel' envisaged an attack on a front of only 150 kilometres. The aim was to pinch out a large Russian salient—approximately 150 kilometres long and 200 kilometres deep—which projected westwards into the centre of the German front between what were in effect two German salients, the Orel salient in the north and the Kharkov-Belgorod salient in the south. (See the maps on page 1217 below.) On 15 April 1943, Hitler approved OKH Order No. 6 for the preparation of Operation 'Citadel', confirming an earlier order No. 5 of 13 March:

612

I have decided to launch the 'Citadel' attack as the first of this year's offensive blows as soon as weather conditions permit.

This attack is of decisive importance. It must be a quick and conclusive success. It must give us the initiative for this spring and summer. For this reason, all the preparations must be carried out with great care and energy. The best units, the best weapons, the best officers, large quantities of munitions must be deployed at the centres of gravity of the attack. Every officer, every soldier must be convinced of the decisive importance of this attack. The victory of Kursk must shine like a beacon to the world.

To achieve this, I hereby issue the following orders:
1. The aim of the attack is to surround and destroy the enemy forces in the Kursk area through a concentric attack by one army from the Belgorod district and one army from the South of Orel advancing in concentrated, ruthless, and rapid thrusts.

In the course of this attack the front must be shortened along the line: Neshega-Korotscha sector-Skorodnoye-Tim-east of Schtschigry-Ssossna-Sector, in order to conserve our forces.
2. We must be sure:

(*a*) That the advantage of surprise is maintained and, above all, that the enemy is left uncertain about the timing of the attack.

(*b*) to concentrate the attacking forces as tightly as possible on a narrow front in order to ensure that by achieving a massive local superiority in all offensive means (tanks, assault guns, artillery, multiple rocket launchers, etc.) we can drive through in one thrust until the two attacking armies come together and thereby secure the pocket.

(*c*) to transfer forces from the rear as quickly as possible to cover the flanks of the spearheads so that the spearheads themselves can simply push forwards.

(*d*) to keep the enemy off balance and accelerate his destruction by early thrusts from all sides into the pocket.

(*e*) to carry out the attack so swiftly that the enemy can neither evade encirclement nor bring up strong reserves from other fronts.

(*f*) to free units and particularly the mobile formations as early as possible for further tasks through a rapid construction of the new front . . .
11. It is of crucial importance for the success of the offensive to ensure that the enemy does not succeed in securing a postponement of 'Citadel' or the premature transfer of formations earmarked for the offensive by mounting attacks on other sectors of Army Groups South and Centre.

Thus, by the end of the month, both Army Groups must prepare the defensive battle on the other sectors of the front with all means in addition to the "Citadel" offensive.

The plan envisaged an attack from the northern sector of the salient southwards towards Kursk by General Model's 9th Army, and an attack from the southern sector northwards by General Hoth's 4th Panzer Army and by a Panzer Group under General Kempf from von Manstein's Army Group South. The two German thrusts would then meet trapping the Russian forces in a double envelopment. Two key aspects of the plan were speed and surprise. However, in the event neither could be realized. Originally, the Germans had timetabled the operation for the first half of May. However, it was repeatedly postponed because General Model demanded more formations to reinforce his thrust and Hitler wished to deploy more heavy Tiger tanks, which were just beginning to come off the production lines in large numbers. As a result, the operation did not finally begin until 4 July. Meanwhile, the Russians had exploited the two month delay to reinforce the salient with an elaborate defensive system and large numbers of troops, tanks, and weapons including the new KV85 heavy tanks and SU self-propelled guns. Furthermore, there could be no question of the Germans achieving surprise. As early as 12 April, Stalin and his sector generals had decided at a war council that the Kursk salient would be the most likely focus of a German summer offensive, and field intelligence had then reported the massive German build-up to the north and south of it. Moreover, a Russian spy in OKW, codenamed 'Lucy', reported that Hitler had given the final go-ahead for the operation at a conference on 1 July and that it would start on 4–6 July.

The aim of the Germans was to punch holes in the Russian defences by concentrating a mass of armour and infantry on a few very narrow fronts and then exploit the breakthroughs by pouring more forces through the gaps. The two thrusts by Army Group South were carried out by a total of eleven panzer and *Panzergrenadier* divisions, of which four were elite Waffen-SS divisions with over two hundred tanks and assault guns each, and one was the elite *Panzergrenadier* division 'Grossdeutschland', and by ten infantry divisions. General Model's northern thrust deployed eight panzer and *Panzergrenadier* divisions and seven infantry divisions. The Germans committed nearly seventy per cent of the tanks and assault guns on the Eastern front to the battle and the offensive was supported by two air fleets (*Luftflotten* 4 and 6).

The Russians planned to absorb the German offensive in their defence system and then, having ground down the German forces, go on to the offensive themselves, striking towards Orel in the north and south-west towards Kharkov.

The Battle of Kursk began on the afternoon of 4 July with a preliminary attack on the southern front by German forces aiming to capture the high ground which lay between the German and Soviet positions. The Russians responded that evening with massive artillery barrages on both fronts designed to disrupt the preparations for the main German attack which was now expected the following morning. Despite the disruption caused, the German attacks went in on time and soon a fierce battle was raging on both northern and southern sectors of the salient. On the northern front, the Germans made comparatively little progress, advancing only some ten miles before their thrust was blocked. Moreover, they were soon obliged to move forces north to deal with a Soviet offensive against the Orel bulge, which began on 12 July and threatened to outflank them. However, the southern thrust, which was the more powereful one, was more successful, penetrating some twenty miles. Indeed, after a week of fighting, it looked as if the German forces might drive through the last Soviet defensive line before Kursk.

The decisive engagement came on 11–12 July in the tank battle of Prokhorovka, when 4th Panzer Army tried to capture the high ground north-west of the small town of Prokhorovka in order to outflank the Soviet defences from the East and open the way to Kursk. On 11 July, the Germans launched two armoured thrusts towards the town from the South and West and a diversionary thrust towards the town of Oboyan. At dawn, the 6th, 7th, and 19th *Panzer* divisions, together with three infantry divisions, moved towards Prokhorovka from the south, at 9.00 am the 3rd and 11th Panzer divisions attacked towards Oboyan; and half an hour later the SS *Panzer* divisions, *Totenkopf*, *Adolf Hitler*, and *Das Reich* launched the main assault on Prokhorovka from the south-west.

Meanwhile, the Russians had planned to launch a major offensive in the southern sector, aimed at encircling the German forces, which was scheduled for 12 July. The result was that on that day the two sides clashed near Prokhorovka in the biggest tank battle of the Second World War. Each side fielded approximately 900 tanks together with air support. At the end of the day, more than 300 German tanks had been destroyed, including 70 of the 100 Tigers. The Russians had suffered comparable losses and the battle of Kursk continued for another ten days. However, the essential point was that the German attack had been held and, with their elite armoured divisions severely mauled, the whole offensive had lost its impetus. Operation 'Citadel' had failed. General Guderian, recently appointed 'Inspector of the Panzer Troops' recognized it as a 'decisive defeat'.

On 3 August, the Russians exploited their successes at Kursk by launching an offensive against Belgorod (liberated on the 5th) and Kharkov (liberated on the 23rd). Stalin's aim was to throw the German armies back to the river Dnieper and recover the industrially important Donbas and the breadlands of the eastern Ukraine. Meanwhile, on 11 August, Hitler had decided to make a stand on the so-called *Ostwall* or Panther line, running from Kerch in the south northwards along the Dnieper, aiming to hold on to the Western Ukraine and Byelorussia. However, the Russians had crossed the Dnieper in places by the end of September and recaptured Kiev on 6 November. A German counter-offensive in mid-November was checked after achieving only limited success.

On Christmas Eve, the Russians resumed their offensive. Stalin placed the main emphasis on the northern and southern fronts. The northern offensive recaptured Leningrad on 26 January 1944, when the Moscow-Leningrad railway was cleared. However, the main thrust occurred in the south, where almost half the German troops on the Eastern front and just under three quarters of the German armour were concentrated. Here all six Soviet tank armies were deployed with the object of recapturing the western Ukraine and the Crimea and destroying Army Group South between the Dneiper and Dneister rivers.

By 12 May 1944, which saw the capture of Sebastapol and the final liberation of the Crimea, five German armies had been destroyed during the winter offensives—6th, 8th, 16th, 17th, and 18th. Three Panzer armies had been badly mauled, leaving only 3rd Panzer Army with Army Group Centre relatively intact. The Germans had been virtually driven out of the Ukraine, with its valuable economic resources, and of the Crimea, and Russian forces had penetrated Romania threatening the oilfields crucial to the German war economy. The winter campaign of 1943–44 had resulted in almost one million Axis casualties, most of them German. In the capture of Sebastopol alone, 110,000 members of 17th Army had been killed, wounded, or captured. Only on the Central front did the Germans still hold a substantial chunk of Russian territory in Byelorussia—apart from the Baltic States, which Russia had annexed in 1940 and which were still in German hands.

With the defeat of Kursk and the subsequent Russian offensives, Germany had lost the strategic initiative. From now onwards, instead of dictating events to his opponents, Hitler was forced to react to moves made by others. By the winter of 1943–44, at the latest, the outcome of the war had already been decided on the Eastern front where, in December 1943, Germany had deployed more than 60 per cent of her total strength (4,906,000 men) and over 50 per cent of her armour (5,400 tanks). Germany was now bound to lose the war; the only question was how long it would take and what the post-war map of Europe would look like. In determining the answers to these vital quesions the role of the Western allies proved crucial.

(ii) The Second Front: Operation 'Overlord', 6 June 1944

On 6 June 1944—'D-Day'—the Western Allies finally opened the second front which the Russians had been demanding and the Germans had been expecting for so long. Hitler had already responded to the threat of an invasion as early as 3 November 1943 in his OKW directive No. 51:

613

The hard and costly struggle against Bolshevism over the last two and a half years has placed a severe strain on our military strength and efforts. That is understandable in view of the enormity of the threat and of the overall situation. In the meantime, things have changed. The threat in the East has remained, but an even greater one is emerging in the West: the Anglo-Saxon invasion. In the East the size of the area involved ensures that even in the most extreme case there will only be a considerable loss of territory without Germany being lethally crippled.

In the West the situation is very different. If the enemy succeeds in breaking through our defences on a broad front, within a short time the consequences will be incalculable. All the signs suggest that the enemy will attack the western front at the latest in the spring and perhaps even earlier.

I can, therefore, no longer justify the West being weakened any further in favour of other war theatres. I have thus decided to strengthen its defences in particular at the place from which we are going to begin the long-range struggle against England.[1] For the enemy must and will attack there and that is where—if we are not deceiving ourselves—the decisive battle will be fought.

We can expect attacks on other fronts intended to divert and tie us down. Even a major attack on Denmark cannot be excluded. It would be more difficult for the Navy and cannot be supported so successfully from the air. However, in the event of its succeeding, it will have the greatest political and operational effects.

At the start of the battle, the whole offensive power of the enemy will inevitably be concentrated against the coastal defences. In the short time still available to us our defences on the coast can only be strengthened by the strongest consolidation, which must be increased to the greatest possible extent by the mobilization of all the available forces of the home front and the occupied territories both in terms of personnel and matériel.

The static weapons which will shortly be delivered to Denmark and the occupied territories in the West (anti-tank guns, immobile tanks for digging into the ground) coastal artillery, static artillery, mines etc.) are to be concentrated at the most threatened sections of the coast. The fact that the defensive strength of the less threatened sections will thereby suffer in the immediate future must be accepted.

If, as a result of concentrating his forces, the enemy nevertheless succeeds in achieving a landing, he must be dealt with by a counter-attack carried out with the greatest force. We must ensure through the adequate and rapid movement of forces and matériel and through intensive training that the existing large units are turned into crack, offensive and fully-mobile reserves which, through a counter-attack, can prevent the expansion of an invasion and can hurl the enemy back into the sea.

In addition, once the enemy has landed we must throw at him everything which is at all fit for action from those sections of the coast which have not been attacked and from the home front, on the basis of temporary measures which have been carefully prepared beforehand.

The Air Force and Navy must ruthlessly counter the strong attacks which can be expected from the air and sea with all the forces that can be mobilised . . .

Continuing to underestimate the power of the Soviet Union and the significance of the German defeats there in 1943–4, Hitler was convinced that the decisive battle would be fought in the West. This was not simply because an invasion in the West would enable the Allies to strike quickly at the Ruhr, the heart of German industry, but also because he believed that by defeating the invasion, Germany could then concentrate its forces on the Russian front and achieve a decisive victory there as well. Moreover,

1. The V1 and V2 rocket attacks (eds).

such was Hitler's contempt for the quality of the British and American forces, confirmed for him by their relatively ineffective operations in Italy, and his exaggeration of the strength of the German fortifications on the French coast, that he positively welcomed the prospect of the invasion as he explained to Marshal Antonescu of Romania on 27 February 1944:

614

. . . On the basis of this situation, he could only hope that the English and Americans who, by the way, were becoming increasingly aware of the difficulties of their undertaking, would actually attack. He was confident that on the basis of these preparations he could ensure the collapse of their aggressive intentions. Once a major landing operation had failed, one could assume that the English and Americans would not go on to the attack a second time this year both for reasons of morale and of matériel. The shock effect on public opinion in England and America of such a failure, and the enormous losses which it would inevitably incur, could not be overemphasized and would in all probability represent a turning-point in the war. With one blow large forces would become available which could be deployed in the East not only for a stabilization of the front but for an offensive against the Russians . . .

In part, no doubt, Hitler's optimism was intended to reassure his ally and was also a form of whistling in the dark. However, Hitler had the ability to convince himself—and others—by such arguments. Two months later, on 22 April 1944, he explained his view of the prospects of the war, particularly in relation to the Western powers, to Mussolini. In its mixture of shrewdness and naivety, ignorance of British and American life and values its self-dramatization and fanaticism, his monologue is a typical expression of Hitler's mind and rhetoric:

615

. . . The Führer did not know whether or when an invasion would occur, but the English had adopted measures which could only be maintained for 6–8 weeks and a serious crisis would break out in England if the invasion did not occur. He would then deploy new technical weapons which were effective within a radius of 250–300 kilometres and would transform London into a heap of ruins . . . The decision in this war would occur in the West and it was clear that a successful enemy offensive which succeeded in pushing through to Germany's industrial areas would bring about the decision. The Führer would never under any circumstances capitulate, he would fight to the last gun. But this was not only his attitude but that of the German people as a whole. We knew that this was a matter of life and death not only for Germany but also for its allies; for, if Europe did not destroy its enemies, in ten or fifteen years the English and Russians would once again attack. Besides, all measures had been taken in the West to ensure the best possible defence. The huge defensive position of the West Wall now represented only sixty-five per cent of the Atlantic wall. In addition, there were the huge U-boat bunkers and the single regiment which had gone into action at Dieppe had shown what we were capable of in the West . . .[2]

However, one must also consider the political sector. The Führer had spent a lot of time reading history recently and had noted that most coalitions hardly lasted for five years. The fact that our allies had remained loyal to us, despite the long period of war, was only because Fascism ruled in Italy and because the Hungarians, Romanians and Finns were bound to us by the Russian threat. Our enemies' coalition was unnatural. It involved two different worlds. One could rather imagine a German-Russian coalition than one between the egoistical capitalism of England and America and egoistical Bolshevism or anti-capitalism. Both sides were still dominated by imperialism but one in which the imperialist tendencies were opposed to and clashed with each other. In the Near East the desire for oil was the reason for conflict. The English and Americans could not be indifferent to a Russian push towards the North Sea through Finland and northern Norway, or to a Russian move towards India, or to them trying to get their hands on the Persian Gulf.

The Duce interjected that Russian activities in the Mediterranean would have provoked a war between England and Russia.

In addition, there was the conflict between England and America. America was quietly and without making a fuss about it plundering England on the basis of a system of pledges. The things that America delivered were being eaten in so far as they were foodstuffs and being fired off in so far as they were weapons. By contrast, America was acquiring pledges in the form of bases, islands, the granting of air routes, oil, mines etc. While England was giving away its substance, America was only giving part of its production. If we remained firm and held on unshakeably, the break between England and America would inevitably come because one day the substance would involve England's world position and then an Englishman would emerge to make a stand against it.

If one read the English and American press, one could see that tension was growing. One could now read things which would have been inconceivable five months ago. One could hear speeches from statesmen which would not have been made two months ago. Articles were adopting a tone such as exists between dog and cat. The Americans had already announced that they wanted to keep the bases for ever.

If the Americans came into contact with our new weapons during an invasion they would lose enthusiasm for the struggle in Europe and the debate about the point of American participation in the war would begin. With us there was a strong sense of duty. In America, even at the beginning of the war, there was no enthusiasm and now the war was only accepted with disquiet. Strikes, the shortage of petrol and tyres, the plundering of the community because of the lack of any sense of national discipline, the greed of the gangsters and the development of the 'black

2. A reference to the abortive raid on Dieppe by Canadian troops on 19 August 1942 (eds).

market' characterized the situation in America and in the long term would not fail to have its effect on the Americans. For, the Americans were not willing to accept restrictions in the long term. With us, workers were still used to going by tram or on the Underground, whereas in America they went to work by car. The restrictions on travel by car were felt particularly acutely by the Americans.

Although the Führer was absolutely convinced that we would finally overcome our enemies militarily, the other side would also be unable to wage the political struggle in the long run. However, it was essential that the enemy did not spot any split on our side and clearly understood that a capitulation was out of the question for us . . .

The most important thing was to hold on stubbornly at all events, since the front of our opponents must break down one day. . . One could not see when, but the example of Frederick the Great in the Silesian War showed that the coalition between Russia, Austria, and France collapsed one day and out of this very tough struggle emerged the foundations of the Prussian state. The future belonged to the authoritarian states, the time of the Jewish democracies was past . . .

The Führer emphasized that he did not simply wait but did everything one could do, but politically time was on our side . . . We had had a run of bad luck. The winter of 1941–2 was twice as hard as that 1812, then came Stalingrad, then the muddy winter, and finally Badoglio's treason. But one day our luck would turn. The year 1923 had brought the Führer bad luck as well.[3] For six hours he had been in control of events and then had gone to prison where he wrote *Mein Kampf*. Then came the trial. He had had difficulty in getting parole, the Party had disintegrated, he had been banned from speaking, he had been expelled from various states, the Party was prevented from wearing a uniform, and then one day our luck turned. He felt like a garden spider. He was lying in wait for a run of good luck and one must only be ready and prepare everything for this moment. States were never without blame for their own downfall. There was truth in the principle of the single righteous man of Sodom and Gomorrha because of whom the city was to be saved, and so he too would carry the flag alone as he had done in 1918. In 1939 Germany had begun with a small number of new divisions without battle experience and had achieved tremendous things and now the Führer was unshakeable in his belief in success. The English and Americans were fighting for capitalist interests, whereas the Führer was fighting for the existence of his people and was totally convinced that one day the historic reward would come and, if the German people showed no understanding, he would fight on alone; however, the German people supported his leadership . . .

The Führer thought the English would have the shock of their lives if they landed in the West. We were feverishly awaiting the moment when our defences could start operating like clockwork. The decision to launch an invasion was very difficult because it demanded the deployment of one's best troops. The Führer had also been faced with this decision in 1940. The precondition was always the elimination of the enemy's air force. In addition, there was the fact that in the West the ports, in particular, would be defended. They could only be captured after a very large

3. The abortive Munich Beer Hall putsch of 8–9 November. See Vol. I pp. 26 ff (eds).

sacrifice of blood and yet they were essential for supplying the invasion. The English, whose invasion methods we had been able to study at Nettuno,[4] were well-known to be rigid followers of the rules, whereas the Americans were dilettantes. When the invasion came there would only be one surprise and that would be the one the English would receive when they landed.

The D-Day operation achieved complete surprise both in its timing and in its location. The Germans had not anticipated a landing that night and the majority of the generals believed that it would come in the Pas de Calais district, the most geographically obvious point, an opinion to which Hitler was committed. This view had been encouraged by a brilliant deception exercise (Operation 'Fortitude') by British Intelligence. The result was that the Germans felt obliged to retain considerable forces in the Pas de Calais for at least a month after the Normandy landings, on the assumption that another landing would occur there. Moreover, on the morning of 6 June, they committed their reserves towards Calais at the crucial stage when the bridgeheads were still narrow and when there was still a chance of driving the Allies back into the sea. Of the three panzer divisions available for deployment, only one—the 21st—was sent into action and, as a result of its being initially deployed towards Calais, even this division was not ready for action until after 4 p.m. on 6 June, though it proved effective in blocking Montgomery's advance towards Caen. The result was that under cover of an enormous naval bombardment, overwhelming air superiority, and effective sabotage of German communications by the French Resistance, the Allies managed to consolidate their beachheads. Although they did not manage to make a decisive break-out from their enlarged bridgehead until the offensive towards Avranches (Operation 'Cobra') on 25 July, it had long been clear to the German military leadership on the spot that the Allies would soon overrun northern France. On 15 July, Rommel had sent the following message to Hitler requesting a withdrawal:

616

The situation on the Normandy Front is becoming more difficult every day.

As a result of the fierceness of the fighting, the extremely large amounts of matériel used by the enemy, particularly in terms of artillery and tanks, and the impact of the enemy air force which is in absolute control of the combat area, our own losses are so high that they seriously reduce the operational effectiveness of

4. Near Anzio in Italy where the Allies had landed on 22 January 1944 (eds).

our divisions. Replacements from the homeland are few and, owing to the difficult transport situation, only reach the front after several weeks. Compared with the loss of approximately 97,000 men, including 2160 officers and among them 28 generals and 354 commanding officers, i.e. on average 2500–3000 men per day, we have so far received only 6000 men. The losses of matériel by the troops in action are also extremely high and only a small amount can be replaced, e.g. out of 225 tanks only 17.

The new divisions which have been sent are inexperienced in combat and, in view of the small amount of artillery and anti-tank weapons at their disposal, are in the long run incapable of successfully repulsing major offensives which are preceded by several hours of artillery bombardment and heavy air attacks. As has been demonstrated by the battles so far, even the bravest troops are destroyed piecemeal by the amount of matériel employed by the enemy.

The supply situation is so difficult, because of the destruction of the railway network and the vulnerability of the roads to air attack up to 150 kilometres behind the front, that only the most necessary supplies can be brought up and we have to economize carefully, especially on artillery and mortar ammunition. We can no longer send significant numbers of new troops to the Normandy front. The enemy front line units, on the other hand, receive new forces and supplies of war material every day. Our Air Force has no effect on the enemy supply lines. The pressure of the enemy is becoming greater and greater.

In these circumstances, we must assume that the enemy will succeed in the foreseeable future—a fortnight to three weeks—in breaking through our own front line, above all, that held by the 7th Army, and will go forward deep into France. The consequences will be incalculable.

The troops are fighting everywhere with heroism, yet the unequal struggle is coming to an end. I must request that you draw the necessary conclusions from this situation. I feel myself duty bound as Commander-in-Chief of the Army Group to make myself clear.

However, instead of agreeing to a withdrawal, Hitler and the OKW ordered a counter-attack against the exposed flank of the American forces now ranging deep into Brittany. Soon after midnight on 7 August, five Panzer divisions with roughly 190 tanks attacked towards Mortain. Despite initial progress, the counter-attack had been tracked by Ultra and, by the end of the afternoon, smashed by rocket-firing Typhoon fighter bombers. At this point, British and Canadian forces in Caen began moving south to link up with the American, Polish, and French forces moving north-east, thereby creating a pocket near Falaise in which the 5th Panzer Army and the 7th Army were trapped. Although 20–40,000 German troops, including most of the generals, escaped before the trap closed, the Allies still captured some 50,000 and killed 10,000 within the pocket as well as capturing or destroying vast quantities of matériel. The way was now open to Paris, which fell on 25 August, and Brussels on 3 September. Meanwhile, on 15 August, the Americans had landed in the South of France (Operation 'Anvil'/'Dragon'). Between D-Day and the end of September, the Germans lost some twenty-nine divisions in the West, a total of 32,000 dead, 97,000 wounded, and 284,000 missing. This compared with Allied figures of 40,000 dead, 164,000 wounded, and 20,000 missing up to 11 September 1944.

(iii) The Ardennes offensive of December 1944—Hitler's last gamble

By October 1944, the impetus of the Allied offensive in the West was beginning to wane, partly because of supply difficulties as their advance moved further and further from the ports and supply bases of northern France, and partly because of stiffening German resistance on the borders of the Reich behind the fortifications of the West Wall. Noting this development and exaggerating its significance, Hitler determined to seize the initiative once more with a bold stroke which he hoped would transform the situation in the West. He aimed to exploit the fact that the Allies lacked sufficient troops to cover their 800 mile front with equal strength and the fact that the deteriorating weather in late autumn would weaken the impact of Allied air superiority. He decided to launch a major offensive by concentrating the bulk of his remaining reserves against a weak point in the Allied front and one from where the Germans would be strategically placed to achieve a decisive blow.

The point he chose was a seventy mile sector between Monschau and Echternach in the wooded Ardennes hills near the Belgian/German border. (See the map on page 1219 below.) His aim was to strike north-west over the river Meuse between Namur and Liège, passing east of Brussels and on towards Antwerp. This would first slice into the rear of the US 1st Army, trapping the American forces massing for the attack on the Ruhr, and then cut off the British 21st Army Group in the Netherlands. Some twenty-five to thirty allied divisions would be smashed, vast quantities of *matériel* would be captured and the Allies would be prevented from exploiting Antwerp as a forward supply base for an invasion of the Reich. Above all, Hitler envisaged that such a damaging blow would not only secure the postponement of the invasion of Germany for several months, thereby enabling her to prepare more effective defences against the imminent Russian offensive, but would also have serious political repercussions on the Allies, whose 'unnatural' coalition he continued to consider extremely fragile.

The German military leadership were extremely sceptical about the success of such an ambitious operation and advocated much more modest goals aimed at cutting off the Allied salient protruding into the West Wall around Aachen and, at the most, driving the Allies back to the Meuse and capturing Liège. Then they could decide on whether to continue the offensive to Antwerp. However, although Hitler was aware that Antwerp was a highly ambitious goal given the limited forces available, nevertheless he was determined to stake everything on this gamble because he was convinced that a primarily defensive strategy would only postpone the evil day. It could never achieve a decisive strategic impact and bring the Allies to the negotiating table.

The offensive was launched on 16 December with the main thrust being carried out by the 6th Panzer Army in the north, comprising nine divisions, four of which were panzer, supported by the 5th Panzer Army in the centre with seven divisions, of which four were panzer, and with the 7th Army with seven divisions, including one mobile formation, responsible for protecting the southern flank of the offensive. Between six and seven divisions, mainly panzer or motorized divisions were held in reserve to exploit the breakthrough. Although the offensive achieved complete surprise and a rapid breakthrough in a sector held by the US 1st Army with only four or five divisions covering a one hundred mile front, the Allies recovered quickly and, through the stubborn defence of key points (Bastogne, St Vith), delayed the German advance, enabling reinforcements to be rushed from the north and south and deployed against the flanks of the bulge created by the German thrust. The result was that, although the 5th Panzer Army made progress, penetrating forty miles into the Allied front in the centre, the failure of the 6th Panzer Army in the north and the 7th Army in the south to sustain the offensive left its flanks increasingly vulnerable. Moreover, Hitler refused to exploit the success in the centre by switching the main thrust from the 6th SS Panzer Army in the north to the 5th Panzer Army in the centre, probably partly because of his anxiety that the SS should win the battle honours. The German advance had been hampered by bottlenecks caused by the stubborn Allied resistance at key points and by the adverse terrain and weather conditions which largely restricted the advance to the roads. The result was that many of the German forces could not be deployed against the enemy. Then, when the weather finally cleared on 23 December, the Allies could exploit their air superiority to full effect, hammering the German bases and exposed supply columns and starving the enemy advance of fuel and ammunition. On 3 January 1945, the Allies began a counter-offensive which forced Hitler to order a withdrawal on the 8th.

(iv) The End

Although the Germans had taken some 25,000 prisoners in the 'Battle of the Bulge' and given the western Allies a nasty shock, delaying the Allied advance into Germany by some six weeks, Hitler's gamble had failed and most of the remaining reserves had been lost: there had been 100,000 casualties and 800 tanks destroyed. The result was that when the Russians launched a major offensive between the 12 and 15 January on a front stretching from the Carpathians to East Prussia, the Germans had no more reserves to throw against them or against the Western allies when they resumed their offensive on 8 February. Although the German forces fought bravely, particularly in the East, it was a very unequal struggle which ended at Rheims on 7 May 1945, when General Jodl and Admiral von Friedeburg signed an unconditional surrender of all the German armed forces which was presented to them jointly by the representatives of the Soviet Union, the United States, Great Britain, and France.

617

Estimated losses during the Second World War.

	Dead	% of Pre-war Population	Military	Civilian
USSR	20,600,000	10.4	13,600,000	7,000,000
China	10,000,000	2.0		
Poland	6,123,000	17.2	123,000	6,000,000
Germany*	6,850,000	9.5	3,250,000	3,600,000
Japan	2,000,000	2.7		
Yugoslavia	1,706,000	10.9		
France	810,000	1.9	340,000	470,000
Greece	520,000	7.2		
USA	500,000	0.4	500,000	—
Austria	480,000	7.2		
Romania	460,000	3.4		
Hungary	420,000	3.0		
Italy	410,000	0.9	330,000	80,000
Czechoslovakia	400,000	2.7		
Great Britain	388,000	0.8	326,000	62,000
Netherlands	210,000	2.4	198,000	12,000
Belgium	88,000	1.1	76,000	12,000
Finland	84,000	2.2		
Canada	34,000	0.3		
Albania	28,000	2.5		
India	24,000	0.01		
Australia	12,000	0.2		
Norway	10,262	0.3		
New Zealand	10,000	0.6		
Luxemburg	5,000	1.7		
Total	*c.* 52,172,262			

* Approximately 10,000,000 of the 13,600,000 Germans killed, wounded, or missing and made prisoner met their fate on the Eastern front.

CHAPTER 34

*The Nazi Empire**

Nazi imperialism involved a great variety of policies in the countries under its sway. They were determined by a whole range of considerations—strategic, political, economic, and ideological—whose particular combination and relative weight varied from case to case and developed in different ways during the course of the war. Because of this great variety it is impossible to document the Nazi empire in any systematic way within the limited space available. This chapter will thus simply provide an overview with a selection of some of the most significant documents, particularly in the economic field, while the following chapter will document in more detail one of the most important examples of Nazi occupation—Poland. Here the racial imperialism at the core of Nazism found perhaps its most ruthless expression.

(i) The structures of German rule

Broadly speaking, four major categories of Nazi treatment of the occupied territories emerged in the course of the war:[1]

(1) *The Incorporated Territories* which were immediately integrated more or less completely into the Reich itself: the western parts of Poland[2] and the Cantons of Eupen, Malmédy, and St Vith in eastern Belgium.

---

* See the map on p. 1321 below.

[1] These categories are taken from *Survey of Internatonal Affairs. Hitler's Europe I* eds. A. Toynbee and V. M. Toynbee (London 1954), pp. 91 ff. The author (C. J. Child) uses an additional category 'Zones of Operation' to refer to those territories formerly administered by Italy which were occupied by Germany in September 1943 after the fall of Mussolini. See also the map on p. 1321 below.

[2] See below p. 924.

(2) *The Territories under a Chief of Civil Administration* which were intended for rapid integration into the Reich: Alsace and Lorraine in north-east France, Luxembourg, part of Yugoslavia bordering on the *Ostmark* (Austria), and the district of Białystok in eastern Poland. These territories were attached to their nearest German Gau with the Gauleiters appointed as Chiefs of Administration, for example Erich Koch Gauleiter of East Prussia became Chief of Administration in Białystok, and Robert Wagner, Gauleiter of Baden became Chief of Administration in Alsace. Alsace and Baden were in fact combined to form the new Gau Westmark, but this was only a Party not an administrative arrangement. This category differed from the first one in that these territories were never formally annexed to the Reich by law. However, both categories (1) and (2) saw far-reaching measures of germanization, including the changing of place names and surnames and the compulsory use of German, and in both the customs, post, telegraph services and railways were integrated into those of the Reich.

(3) *The Appended Territories* were intended for eventual integration into the Reich and, largely for this reason, they had a rather vaguely defined status as neither part of the Reich as such nor independent of it: the General Government in Poland,[3] the *Reichskommissariate* in the Ukraine and Ostland (the Baltic States and White Russia),[4] and the Reich Protectorate of Bohemia and Moravia. The Reich Protectorate differed from the others in retaining a nominally 'autonomous' administration with a head who was entitled 'to the full honours of the head of a sovereign government' and the right of diplomatic representation in Berlin. Also whereas the others had an overwhelmingly German administration, the Reich Protectorate had a large Czech bureaucracy operating under German supervision. In practice, however, the Reich Protector (von Neurath 1939–41, Frick 1942–5) was a straw man, apart from a brief interlude under Heydrich (September 1941–May 1942), and the Protectorate was in fact ruled by his 'general deputy', the State Secretary and Higher SS and Police Leader, Karl Hermann Frank, a Sudeten German and protégé of Himmler. Hitler had established the basic guidelines for the treatment of the Reich Protectorate in the autumn of 1939 as is clear from the following report by the German Army commander there, General Frederici, dated 15 October 1940:

[3] See below pp. 925 ff. and 957 ff.

[4] See below pp. 914.

618

The Reich Protector's office held an official conference on 9 October last year at which State Secretary SS *Gruppenführer* K. H. Frank made the following statement:

The solution of the Czech problem has been considered by official party circles and industrial groups, as well as the central authorities in Berlin ever since the creation of the protectorate of Bohemia and Moravia.

After much discussion, the Reich Protector gave his views about the various plans in a memorandum which contained three possible solutions:

(a) German penetration of Moravia and the restriction of the Czech nation to a rump Bohemia.

This solution is regarded as unsatisfactory since the Czech problem will continue to exist albeit in a reduced form.

(b) Many arguments can be made against the most radical solution, the deportation of all the Czechs. Thus, the memorandum concluded that it cannot be implemented within a reasonable length of time.

(c) Assimilation of the Czechs, i.e. absorption of about half the Czech nation by the Germans, in so far as this is of significance in view of its value from a racial or other standpoint. This will also be the consequence among other things of increasing the employment of Czechs in Reich territory (apart from the Sudeten German border district), in other words by dispersing the concentrated Czech population group.

The remaining half of the Czech nation must be deprived of its power, removed and deported from the country by all sorts of methods. This is particularly true of the section which is racially Mongolian and of the majority of the intellectual class. The latter can hardly be converted ideologically and would cause difficulties by constantly making claims for leadership over the other Czech classes and thus interfering with rapid assimilation.

Elements which oppose the plan for germanization must be treated roughly and should be eliminated.

The above development naturally presupposes an increased influx of Germans from the Reich into the protectorate.

After a discussion, the Führer chose solution (*c*) (assimilation) as a directive for the solution of the Czech problem and decided that, while maintaining the autonomy of the Protectorate on the surface, germanization must be carried out in a centralized way by the office of the Reich Protectorate for years to come . . . This is the line which has always been taken from here . . .

(4) *The Occupied Territories* comprised the remaining countries occupied by the German *Wehrmacht*. Their forms of administration varied greatly depending on strategic and political considerations. In areas which were of particular strategic importance, such as Belgium and northern France or Greece, there was a military administration under a military commander. However, Hitler preferred to avoid giving too much power to the military on the grounds that they lacked ideological commitment

and political skill. In the case of Holland and Norway, therefore, which were regarded as 'germanic' and contained pro-Nazi movements which could be exploited, political considerations assumed primary importance and civilian Reich Commissioners were appointed: Josef Terboven, the Gauleiter of Essen, to Norway, and Arthur Seyss-Inquart, an Austrian lawyer who had played a major part in the Anschluß,[5] to Holland. Terboven ruled Norway through the leader of the Norwegian 'Nazi' Party (the Nasjonal Samling), the notorious Quisling, who became Prime Minister on 1 February 1942. Seyss-Inquart ruled Holland through the so-called 'headless government', composed of the permanent Secretaries General of the former Dutch Ministries whose powers were considerably increased. However, the increasing German demands on Holland prompted these civil servants to resign one by one and, in order to replace them with ideologically reliable officials, Seyss-Inquart was forced to fall back on members of the Dutch 'Nazi' Party (the NSB). This was in fact more Dutch nationalist than Nazi and opposed Nazi plans for the annexation of Holland by Germany. It was also unpopular with the Dutch: its membership was never more than 110,000 out of a population of nine million and many of these were opportunists. Nevertheless, it became the sole political party when all the others were dissolved on 4 July 1941 and its leader, Anton Mussert, was recognized as 'Führer of the Dutch people' by Hitler in December 1942. However, Hitler refused Mussert's request to be made Prime Minister and power in Holland as in Norway remained essentially with the Reich Commissioner and his German officials.

Denmark was an anomaly among its neighbours. Unlike his Norwegian and Dutch counterparts, the King of Denmark had not fled the country and on 9 April 1940 he and the Prime Minister issued a proclamation announcing that the Danish Government had 'decided under protest to handle the affairs of the country with dispatch' and that it was 'the duty of the people to refrain from any resistance to German troops' and to 'maintain a calm and thoughtful attitude' and an 'attitude of loyalty to the authorities.'[6] In response, Hitler agreed to allow the government and even the Parliament in Denmark to continue to operate and the Army to remain in existence. German relations with Denmark were initially conducted via a German plenipotentiary who used diplomatic channels and was responsible to the Foreign Ministry. In a press interview on 12 April 1940, General Kaupisch, the German commander in Denmark, declared that Denmark would remain a sovereign state under German military protection.

---

[5] See above pp. 700 ff.

[6] Cf. *Documents on International Affairs 1939–46* Vol. II *Hitler's Europe* ed. M. Carlyle (Oxford 1954) pp. 212–3.

Denmark is a good example of the problematic nature of satellite status. As the war continued so German pressure increased, raising economic demands, for example, or demands for the deportation of the Danish Jews. The Danish authorities were forced to make more and more concessions, thereby provoking growing resentment among the Danish population who were gaining confidence from the lack of German military success after the summer of 1942. The result was increasing resistance which, in October 1942, prompted Hitler to change the whole basis of the occupation. He appointed a new Military Commander—General von Hanneken, a keen Nazi, and replaced the German Plenipotentiary, von Renthe-Fink, a diplomat, with Werner Best, a former Gestapo department chief and deputy of Heydrich. A memorandum on Denmark by Werner von Grundherr of the Foreign Ministry reported Hitler's views as follows:

619

The Führer proceeded on the principle that the declarations of 9 April 1940, on which the relationship of Germany and Denmark hitherto rested, had, through the developments of the past years and the conduct of the Danes themselves, become obsolete. He had for some time regarded these commitments as troublesome and unsuitable. These declarations had had their justification at a time when a long duration of the war was not expected and when the developments which had occurred in the meantime had not been foreseen. Now they must be eliminated. For the future it was impossible that in the New Europe established under German leadership there should exist a form of state with a democratic government and under a royal house which up to now had displayed nothing but ill-will. For the future it was entirely impossible that he, the Führer, should restore Denmark in its previously existing form (meaning that German troops should leave Denmark). On the contrary, he needed Denmark, as he needed Norway, to hold England in check and for this the possession of Denmark was essential. Denmark must become a German province.

For the fact that things had gone as far as they had, the Danes themselves, with their King and Government, were to blame. The King and the Royal House had never concealed their unfavourable attitude and their preference for Sweden and England. A Danish Minister had been allowed to leave the country[7] and the volunteers of the Freikorps Dänemark[8] had been ridiculed and mistreated. The Danish Government and the King had let the opportunity escape and had never made us an offer of North Schleswig. The royal house and the present form of government were disturbing factors in developments as a whole and therefore he had finally come to the conclusion that both should be put aside.

[7] Christmas Moeller, a Conservative leader, had escaped to London in May 1942 (eds).

[8] A unit of Danish Nazis which had fought on the Eastern front (eds).

For the way things had gone, so the Führer had expressly declared, no blame could be cast on either the Plenipotentiary von Renthe-Fink or on General Lüdke. They had within the limits of their respective spheres acted correctly according to their instructions then in force. From now on, however, there would be new basic principles.

As Plenipotentiary would come a hard-fisted National Socialist and the Military Commanding Officer as well as the armed forces would regard themselves not in a friendly but in a hostile country . . . The members of the armed forces must break off ali relationships with Danes.

As regards the government, the aim must be to establish as soon as possible a regime under the leadership of the Danish National Socialists. Whether the party leader of the Danish National Socialists, Dr Frits Clausen, was the right person or whether he had a large or small proportion of the Danish people behind him was completely unimportant. The Führer needs in Denmark a puppet government which will do everything he requires of it. Even the English have set up puppet governments in Iran and Iraq. The head of this government must always be conscious that in case of a possible withdrawal of German troops he would be hanged on the nearest lamp post. The Führer in this connection would see that the new Plenipotentiary to be appointed would receive the necessary instructions.

Any resistance, even the slightest, must be suppressed by force. Should it appear that the Danish police force does not suffice or does not act in accordance with our desires, additional military forces, possible also SS troops will be made available.

In fact in addition to Best, a tough Higher SS and Police Leader, Günther Pancke, was brought in with SS reinforcements to control police operations.

Denmark had been permitted to retain a large measure of autonomy for so long, partly because of the special political circumstances which had arisen in April 1940, partly because it was much more convenient for the Germans to secure their goals through a cooperative native government than through direct rule, partly because of Denmark's relatively modest strategic importance, and partly for ideological reasons—the Danes were seen as a closely related Germanic people.

Denmark thus bore a closer resemblance to the puppet states of Slovakia, Croatia, and Vichy France that it did to its immediate neighbours, Norway and Holland. These states, which were products of German action, possessed varying degrees of independence at different periods. Slovakia, for example, had been permitted to retain a considerable amount of independence during the first year or so of its existence because Germany was anxious 'to create with Slovakia a classic example of our conception of a protective relationship with a Southeastern Slav state' as Ernst von Drüffel, the head of the German diplomatic mission in Bratislava, put it in a message to Berlin on 25 March 1939.[9] Germany hoped to persuade other states in

[9] Cf. N. Rich, *Hitler's War Aims. The Establishment of the New Order* (London 1974) p. 60.

the area of the advantages of such a relationship. However, the independent line taken by the Slovak government, for example on the Jewish question and in its commitment to political Catholicism, soon proved irksome to the Germans. Thus, in the summer of 1940, with Germany's international position consolidated by the victories in the West, the new German diplomatic representative, Hans Bernard, decided that 'the time has come to make perfectly plain once again, particularly with reference to the countries of Southeastern Europe that Slovakia is in our *Lebensraum*, that is our wishes alone count'.[10] Prime Minister Tisa and his cabinet were summoned to Berlin at the end of July and forced to reconstruct the government with ministers more acceptable to Germany. Hitler reaffirmed the German guarantees of Slovakia's political independence and territorial integrity but 'in return Germany demanded that Slovakia adhere loyally and unequivocally to the German cause in her domestic politics'.[11] From then until the Slovakian uprising of August–October 1944 Slovakia remained a docile member of the Nazi empire, for example joining the war against the Soviet Union on 24 July 1941.

Croatia proved a more difficult state to control. Created after the defeat of Yugoslavia on 15 April 1941 as a counterweight to the Serbs, it was ruled by Ante Pavelić, the Poglavnik or Führer of the Ustaša movement. This was a fanatical Croatian nationalist and Roman Catholic organisation which had long been in opposition to the new Serb-dominated Yugoslav state created in 1919. The Pavelić government took full control of the civil administration and police, while the Germans retained an army of occupation in the east of the country and gained certain economic privileges. Hitler regarded Croatia as part of the Italian sphere of influence with the result that the Croatians faced more pressure from Italy than from Germany. The German military representative in Agram (Zagreb), General Edmund von Glaise-Horstenau, had no authority to intervene in Croatia's domestic affairs, while the German political representative, Siegfried Kasche, was a SA leader who was out of his depth in the political sphere and allied himself with the Pavelić regime against the Italians and the German military. Pavelić ingratiated himself with the Germans by cooperating with their Jewish policy and acceding to their economic demands, but his policy of virtual genocide against the ethnic and religious minorities in Croatia, in particular the Serbs, turned the area into a hotbed of partisan activity providing major problems for the Germans, which Glaise-Horstenau lacked the resources or authority to deal with.

---

[10] *Ibid.* p. 62.

[11] *Ibid.* p. 63.

German ideas on the future of France had fluctuated sharply in the course of the summer of 1940. Initially, they had contemplated large-scale annexation, as is clear from the following official and confidential briefing to the German press by the Propaganda Ministry, dated 12 July 1940:

620

The new order for Europe is to be quite consciously placed under Germany's sole auspices. It was already clear from the directives of the Propaganda Ministry that in future France would only play a role as a small Atlantic state. One must envisage this quite concretely: apart from Italy's territorial demands on France, our demands too will be very large. The Führer has not yet said the final word and one is dependent on guessing as to the size of the German demands which will be contained in the peace treaty with France. It seems certain, however, that, apart from Alsace-Lorraine, we will also add the main parts of Burgandy, with the Plateau of Langres and Dijon as the capital, to the territory of the Reich. People are already beginning to talk of a '*Reichsgau* Burgundy'. Also the Channel ports such as Dunkirk, Bologne [*sic!*] etc. will at least become German naval bases if not Reich territory as such . . .

As far as France is concerned, the maxim will be: the destruction of the Peace of Westphalia. Some people are even talking of a revocation of the partition agreed in the Treaty of Verdun of 843. For this reason, everything which serves to encourage an economic, political, or economic revival of France will be destroyed. We have no faith in any attempts at renewal in an authoritarian direction in France. We consider that all these attempts are simply camouflage and that the ideas of 1789 will soon show through again together with a revived chauvinism. For this reason, we shall have to draw certain sober conclusions which will indeed be drawn. The peace treaty will eliminate France not only as a great power but as a state with any political influence in Europe. As far as the colonial issue is concerned, things are not yet clear. . .

However, given Britain's refusal to make peace, Hitler had soon come to the conclusion that, for the time being at any rate, it would be better to grant France relatively generous terms in the hope of winning her cooperation in the war against Britain.[12] These included permission for the continued existence of a semi-independent rump French state under Marshal Pétain as head of state with its capital in the town of Vichy.

The Vichy Government was responsible for administering the French population in both Occupied and Unoccupied France, with the exception of Alsace and Lorraine, the departments Nord and Pas de Calais, and the

[12] See above pp. 777–8.

so-called Closed Zone in the north-east between the departments of the Jura and the Somme. However, in the Occupied Zone French officials were under the direct supervision of the German military commander and his subordinate officers. Vichy also exercised full authority over most of France's overseas empire and controlled the large French navy and merchant fleet. Although the collaboration of the Vichy government with the Germans greatly facilitated Nazi control over France and, in particular, its economic exploitation, this collaboration stopped short of providing Germany with support which might have proved of crucial strategic importance. Pétain was a right-wing French nationalist who defended French national interests as he saw them. He therefore declined to join in the war against Britain, scuttled the French fleet after the German occupation of the Unoccupied Zone on 8 September 1943 rather than let it fall into German hands, and refused to allow Germany to use Vichy French ports or the North African colonies as bases for attacks on the British position in the Mediterranean. Finally, while cooperating with German anti-semitic policies out of ideological prejudice, the Vichy authorities retained a vestigial sense of loyalty to the concept of French citizenship and its dignity. Thus, while happy to sacrifice foreign refugee Jews to the Nazis, they resisted attempts to deport Jews who were French citizens, with some measure of success.

The outer ring, so to speak, of the Nazi empire consisted of a group of allies and satellites over which Germany could exercise influence to a greater or lesser extent. Finland, Hungary, Romania, and Bulgaria had all gained territory as a result of German actions and were to a varying degree obliged to gear their foreign policy and economies to German needs. However, they retained considerable independence. Finland, for example, maintained diplomatic relations with the United States contrary to German wishes and Bulgaria declined to join in the invasion of the Soviet Union. While agreeing to introduce anti-semitic measures (except Finland), which were in line with their ideological stance, all four resisted German pressure to deport their own Jews to the death camps in Poland.[13] On 19 March 1944, the Germans occupied Hungary and SS *Sturmbannführer* Adolf Eichmann arrived with his staff to organize the deportation of the Hungarian Jews. In Finland, Bulgaria, and Romania, however, the Red Army arrived before the Germans could intervene successfully to shore up their dwindling influence.

---

[13] See below p. 1191.

Finally, among the states associated with the Nazi empire, Italy had a unique status as Germany's junior partner. Initially, Hitler envisaged recognising the Mediterranean and North Africa as Italy's sphere of influence. However, talk of a Rome-Berlin Axis and Hitler's respect for Mussolini could only obscure for a time the real disparity of power which existed between the two countries. As the war continued and Italy's failures mounted, so her treatment by Germany became increasingly condescending. Less and less attention was paid to Italy's needs and interests in a process which, after Mussolini's fall in September 1943, culminated in the German occupation of the country and the creation of Mussolini's puppet state of Salò (the R.S.I) in northern Italy.

(ii) The 'New Order' and the concept of a Grossraumwirtschaft

The most obvious area in which Germany could benefit from her empire was in the economic sphere. German economic goals covered both the long and the short term. Initially, during the phase when it appeared as if the war would soon be won, policy-makers and those who tried to influence policy devoted a considerable amount of time and energy formulating longer term goals for German economic imperialism. Even before Dunkirk, a meeting had been held on 24 May 1940 in the Foreign Ministry under the chairmanship of its leading expert on economic matters, Karl Ritter, to discuss 'European *Grossraumwirtschaft*' (a large economic sphere of interest). The meeting, which was attended by, among others, representatives of the Economics Ministry, the Reichsbank, the Four Year Plan, and the *Wehrmacht*, was intended to coordinate plans for the 'New Order' in Europe 'in view of the new development in Germany's economic-political situation'.

This meeting was followed by a flood of memoranda from various ministries, semi-official and Party agencies, business organizations, and particular industries outlining plans for the 'New Order' in Europe which it now seemed that Germany had the power to create. These provide a fascinating insight into the imperialist goals of various sections of the German administration and economy. An early example was by Werner Daitz, an associate of Rosenberg and member of his 'Foreign Policy Office of the NSDAP'. Daitz was a prolific author and long-time advocate of *Grossraumwirtschaft*—the concept of a world divided into large economic spheres of interest. On 21 October 1939, Daitz had established the 'Society of European Economic Planning and *Grossraumwirtschaft*' of which he was president, and the following document contains excerpts from his memorandum advocating the 'Creation of a Reich Commission for Grossraumwirtschaft' dated 31 May 1940:

621

For more than two decades I have been pointing out in numerous articles, speeches and books that the liberal world economic system, which operated under the auspices of the English pound and the English fleet will inevitably dissolve into several autonomous or autarkic economic blocks or large economic spheres [*Grossraumwirtschaften*]: into a dollar block, a yen block, a rupee block, and a continental European mark block.

This development has been accelerated as a result of the English blockade of Germany in the years 1914–1918 and now again during 1939–1940. The present blockade, in particular, has rendered unavoidable the construction of a continental European *Grossraumwirtschaft* under German leadership as a measure of economic self-defence on the part of the European mainland. The reorganization of the European continent, this eternal core area of the white race, will thereby secure the economic recovery and independence which are essential. This economic cooperation of the continental European nations must follow the motto: Europe for the Europeans. European economic requirements must be met in the first place by goods produced in Europe itself and exchanged there, and only then by those of other economic blocks or *Grossraumwirtschaften* in exactly the same way as other *Grossraumwirtschaften* which are in the process of formation declare: America for the Americans, East Asia for the Asians, India for the Indians etc. As a final goal to ensure peace, a continental European *Grossraumwirtschaft* under German leadership must embrace all the peoples of the mainland from Gibraltar to the Urals and from the Noth Cape to the island of Cyprus with their natural colonial extensions radiating out into Siberia and beyond the Mediterranean into Africa. . .

It is essential, however, to note that for foreign policy reasons this continental European *Grossraumwirtschaft* under German leadership must not be termed a *German Grossraumwirtschaft*; for, the moment that happens then, presumably for reasons of prestige, the Italians will want to set an Italian *Grossraumwirtschaft*, Soviet Russia as Soviet Russian *Grossraumwirtschaft* etc. This would seriously complicate the construction of a genuine *continental European Grossraumwirtschaft* under German leadership or indeed make it impossible. A *Grossraumwirtschaft* embracing the whole of the European mainland is, however, necessary in order to take on successfully the huge economic blocks of North and South America, the Yen block, and the possible surviving remnants of the Pound block. Thus, it appears politically inappropriate to seek to create merely a *German Grossraumwirtschaft*, although of course the firm economic integration of those countries of western, northern, and south-eastern Europe which are directly dependent on Germany must be our first war and peace aim. If we wish to secure the economic leadership of the European continent which is absolutely necessary in order to strengthen the economy of the European continent as the core area of the white race, and which will in fact do so, then for understandable reasons we must not publicly proclaim it as a *German Grossraumwirtschaft*. As a matter of principle, we must always only speak of Europe, for German leadership of it will emerge naturally from the political, economic, cultural, and technological weight of Germany and from its geographical position. Similarly, with the help of our German economic system, as it has been created by the National Socialist revolution and through a skilful trade policy, the Mark will establish itself as the standard currency on its own, just as the pound, the dollar, and the yen have established themselves as the standard currencies in their economic spheres. . .

Daitz did not himself hold a powerful position, but the long campaign which he and others had waged for the concept of *Grossraumwirtschaft* was now bearing fruit as it was adopted by more influential figures. Among them was Karl Ritter who presented a memorandum on 1 June from which the following extracts are taken.

622

I. THE GREATER ECONOMIC SPHERE

The possibility of a future greater economic sphere under German leadership is now taking shape. This sphere comprises:

1. Greater Germany (including Bohemia, Moravia, and Poland) as its economic and political center.

2. Holland, Belgium, Luxembourg, Denmark, and Norway are to be incorporated in it in economic-political forms yet to be determined. The possible forms are a system of preferential tariffs, a customs union, a customs and monetary union, or an economic union. It would appear reasonable to put off the final decision regarding the economic-political form until clarification of the future status of these countries with respect to constitutional and international law, and even then to progress gradually from the easier to the more difficult phases of economic integration in order to mitigate the inevitable economic readjustments and difficulties in these countries. Nevertheless I believe that as soon as the military and political situation permits we should promptly advance to the definitive and final form of economic integration, i.e., the economic union. War, debasement of currency, and reconstruction will automatically lead to extensive economic and social changes in these countries. If we carry the proposed transformation in economic policy immediately to its ultimate phase at that time, this process will be accomplished in one clean-up or, rather, one reconstructive effort. The reverse procedure, a progression by stages from preferential tariffs through customs union and customs and monetary union and finally to economic union would lead these nations year after year from one readjustment to another. It would be best if they were given from the outset a definitive foundation on which to base their effort of reconstruction and readjustment.

3. Already incorporated into the greater economic sphere in fact, though not in any specific economic-political form, are the countries of the Danube area. Greater Germany already has a position of economic preponderance with respect to the imports and exports of these countries, accounting on the average for 50 per cent thereof. In one instance this preponderance has already attained nearly 70 per

cent. With Holland, Belgium, Luxembourg, Denmark, and Norway incorporated into the greater economic sphere, this preponderance will automatically be increased by additional percentages. Moreover, this position will be further enhanced over the course of the years, as the potentialities for trade between the Nordic area and the Danube area neglected in the past are systematically developed.

No new economic-political forms are therefore needed with respect to the countries of the Danube area. Cultivation and further expansion of existing relations will suffice.

4. The remaining countries of the Nordic area, Sweden, Finland, Lithuania, Latvia, and Estonia, must be more firmly integrated in a practical manner similar to that of the Danube area. This has already been accomplished with regard to the three Baltic nations through the recent treaties.[14] These treaties assure Greater Germany a decisive economic preponderance even now. It will suffice for us to defend and maintain this preponderance in the face of the recently observed intensified activity of the Soviet Union. Just now we are at the beginning of economic negotiations with Sweden and Finland. The principal object of these negotiations is to lay the foundation now for a reorientation of these two countries away from the world market and overseas countries, and toward the greater European economic sphere and the Baltic. To accomplish this, advantage is being taken of the presently strong pressures, but on the other hand it will be necessary, by accommodation and perhaps even sacrifices in certain areas, to offer them a positive inducement for such a reorientation.

Such a greater economic sphere comprises approximately 200 million people. These people have for the most part a consumption and production capacity above the average.

This greater economic sphere will by and large be able to feed itself given average crops and provided that readjustment of agriculture in several countries, a step necessary in any event, is carried out and a constructive price policy is pursued. In the matter of bread cereals, potatoes, meat, and dairy products the greater economic sphere is self-sufficient. Grain for fodder will have to be imported from abroad to make up for a relatively small deficit. A large deficit exists in edible fats, and a lesser in sugar.

Generally lacking are tropical and subtropical vegetable raw materials and certain metals (cf. part II, "Future Exports," and III, "Colonial Empire".)

Two stipulations must be borne in mind for the peace treaties in this connection. One is to demand, in lieu of financial reparations in money, the free delivery of the required amounts of foodstuffs and raw materials over 3, 4, or 5 years (at a rate of about 3 to 4 billion reichsmarks a year). The second is transfer of rights and interests (ownership shares, securities) in industrial and transport establishments situated in the greater economic sphere, which belong to enemy powers or their nationals, e.g., the French copper mines in Yugoslavia, the Anglo-Canadian nickel mines in Finland, and the Anglo-French petroleum interests in Rumania. This would at the same time act as a potent means of economic cohesion within the greater economic sphere. . . .

[14] This refers to economic agreements between Germany and Latvia, Lithuania and Estonia signed between December 1939 and May 1940 (eds).

III. THE COLONIAL EMPIRE

A colonial empire comprising the German colonies in Africa, Belgian Congo, French Equatorial Africa (and possibly British Nigeria), after a prolonged period of intensive development, could in a large measure supply the requirements of Greater Germany and of the greater economic sphere in tropical and subtropical vegetable raw materials and articles of luxury consumption, and in addition a large part of the copper requirements. Possibly some other mineral raw materials will also be found. In 10 to 15 years the colonies will be able to supply our entire needs for edible vegetable fats, which is very important because edible fats account for the largest shortage in the greater economic sphere. They will also supply all or part of the requirements in cocoa, coffee, tea, tobacco, cotton, rubber, fancy woods, tanning extracts, etc.

The prerequisite is a considerate policy toward natives and labour. The question of labour is the most difficult problem in this respect.

Reichsmark as currency.

In principle there are to be no customs between Greater Germany and the colonial empire. An exception, for revenue reasons, would probably be made in the case of articles of luxury consumption such as coffee, tea, and tobacco.

Temporary acceptance of Belgian and French colonial officials for a period of transition, until a staff of German officials has been trained.

Invitation to settlers of German origin in South America and other countries to move to the colonial empire.

A colonial empire of this kind is not adapted to large-scale settlement. Neither would this be necessary. . .

On 20 June 1940, Hitler told his chief engineer and Minister of Munitions, Fritz Todt:

623

The course of the war shows that we have gone too far in our efforts to achieve autarky. It is impossible to try and produce everything we lack through synthetic processes or other measures . . . We must follow another path and must conquer the things we need but lack. The one-off commitment of man-power which that will require will not be as large as the manpower which will be continuously needed for the synthetic plants. Thus, our aim must be to secure all those territories which are of special interest to our defence economy through conquest.

Two days later, on 22 June, the Reich Economics Minister, Walther Funk, was assigned by Göring the responsibility for the 'preparations and the establishment of appropriate planning procedures for the reorganization of Europe' which were to involve:

624

1. The integration of the occupied territories and those incorporated into the Reich into the Greater German economy.
2. The economic conflict with the enemy states.
3. The reconstruction of the continental economy led by Germany and its relations with the world economy.

Six weeks later, on 6 August 1940, Funk presented Göring with his proposals for the 'New Order':

625

. . . The question of what form the European economy will finally take cannot of course be answered definitively at the present time.

I am working on the assumption that the integration of the occupied territories in the economy of Greater Germany and the reconstruction of a continental European economy under German leadership will not occur through a single political act such as the conclusion of a customs or currency union, but that this goal will be achieved through a series of individual measures which will begin at once and to some extent have already begun. The decisive factor must be to link the European economies as completely and as closely as possible with the economy of Greater Germay. In the process, all measures which are designed to improve the satisfaction of German needs and to strengthen German economic influence in the various countries concerned must be given priority, while vice versa all measures which, from the standpoint of our greater German interests, are unimportant must be prevented or be postponed until later. From this point of view, at the moment the following measures are important and have priority:
1. The securing of as large a proportion as possible of European production for German requirements.
2. The extension of European production with a view to a further improvement in the possibilities of satisfying German needs from within Europe, i.e. the application of the principles of the Four Year Plan and the German Battle of Production[15] to the European economy.
3. The creation of a European payments system (Central Clearing) on the basis of the *Reichsmark*, which in the first instance will provide the technical means for paying for the influx of European goods onto the German market and, secondly, will deal with the gold and credit aspects of the exchange of goods within Europe.
4. The control of international trade within Europe as well as European trade with overseas countries through inter-state agreements involving the exercise of German

[15] The 'Battle of Production' was launched in 1934 to increase German agricultural production (eds).

power and influence. The control of the economic and financial policy of the European states with the aim of aligning the economic-political methods and forms of economic activity practised by them as far as possible with the German norms.

These questions are being dealt with at this moment in the territories occupied by the German Wehrmacht; it must be our next task gradually to create a similar state of affairs in the other countries which are dependent on us.

5 The linking of the European economies with the greater German economy under German leadership in the following spheres:

(*a*) The organisation of the economy: the creation of organisational forms such as those represented in Germany by the Organisation of Business [*Organisation der gewerblichen Wirtschaft*] and the Reich Food Estate and the fusion of these organisations into a combined European organisation under German leadership.

(*b*) The inclusion of the relevant branches of European business in the German market-regulating associations (Cartells) at the same time ensuring that German leadership is firmly secured (iron, coal, metals, chemicals, electricity etc.)

(*c*) Securing control of the capital of the most important European industrial undertakings (armaments industry, iron and metal industries etc.).

(*d*) The infiltration of the decisive posts in European business with suitable German experts.

6. Simplification of the practice of granting permits for international trade within Europe, the removal of restrictive regulations, the adaptation of the customs arrangements to the need for an intensification of trade and cooperation in the industrial, raw material, and agrarian spheres.

As far as point 2 of your commission, ' Economic conflict with the enemy states', is concerned, I consider it premature to make you any suggestions at present. Preparations are, however, underway in house. In this connection, I would like to reiterate my view that in order to construct a unified European *Grossraumwirtschaft* under German leadership it is vital to take over the leading business posts in Europe which at the moment are all in the possession of Englishmen and Frenchmen. Similarly, we need a reserve of foreign exchange and raw materials for the transitional period in order to be able to remove the restrictions on German consumption as soon as possible. I am thinking in terms of a sum of circa ten billion gold marks, which represents the equivalent of the value of the German private property stolen by the Allies.

I would be grateful if you could inform me of your approval of the proposed work programme and of any further wishes you may have in connection with it. The relevant Ministries, in particular the Reich Ministry of Food and Agriculture and the Foreign Ministry, have expressed their approval of the programme.

On 17 August 1940, Göring replied to Funk as follows:

626

I quite agree with you that during the war the production of foodstuffs and goods vital to the war effort in the area controlled by Germany must be increased as much as possible for the benefit of the German war economy in accordance with the goals of the Four Year Plan. All measures required for this purpose which promise to produce results during the war must be taken as quickly as possible. I also share your view that in the post-war period it is vital to extend Germany's economic sphere of influence in Europe and the rest of the world as far as possible and to provide the German people with the highest possible standard of living while securing the needs of the defence economy. Germany's economic leadership will have to achieve this goal after the war (with the simplest possible administrative apparatus) by laying down the main economic-political guidelines and supervising their implementation. After the removal of the raw material and foreign exchange bottlenecks, the rapid dismantling of the economic controls in every sphere, which were an emergency measure, will receive priority. However, decisions cannot yet be reached on the matter, since the point at which and the forms through which these goals will be realisable in the post-war period depend so much on political developments.

Göring went on to emphasise the need for measures to bring about as quickly as possible 'a mutual integration and linkage of interests between the Germany economy and those of Holland, Belgium, Norway and Denmark'.

Meanwhile, individual firms had been submitting their views and requests to the Government. On 3 August 1940, two directors of the huge chemical combine, IG Farben, Georg von Schnitzler and Kurt Krüger, wrote to Gustav Schlotterer, head of the special department 'Preparation and Order' in the Economics Ministry enclosing a 'New Plan'. The following document contains excerpts first from the letter and then from the plan itself:

627

1. Our assumption is that in the process of creating a European *Grossraumwirtschaft* it will be necessary to develop a plan for the chemical industry. The aim of such a plan is:
(*a*) to secure the economic independence of this area in the sense of ensuring the supply of the bulk of what it requires.
(*b*) to organize the productive capacity of this area in a planned way through the rational exploitation of the available plant to adapt it to present needs and those of the foreseeable future in such a way that wastage of labour and capital is avoided.
2. After the war this continental *Grossraum* will receive the task of organising the exchange of goods with other *Grossräume* and to compete with the productive forces of other *Grossräume* in competitive markets—a task which includes, in particular, the regaining and securing of the world position of the German chemical industry. The ideas and plans in this connection must above all take into account the trends and shifts in the balance of international economic forces which were triggered off by the last war, such as have become increasingly apparent in the

increased influence of the USA in Latin America, of Japan in the Far East and of Italy in South-East Europe and in the Near East.

3. A *Grossraumwirtschaft* organized in terms of self-sufficiency and planned in relation to the other economic spheres of the world must at the same time take account of all the factors which arise from the needs of the defence economy of the Greater German Reich. These requirements must not only be seen in relation to the supply of imports which are of importance to the defence economy, but also from the point of view that links between those European countries in the German sphere of influence and countries outside Europe, which may once have existed or may exist in the future, and which may affect their military potential in the chemical sphere, should be organized in such a way that Greater German interests are taken fully into account: I am thinking in this connection of cartels, capital stakes, and exchange of information . . .

The New Plan

General Section . . .

One will undoubtedly be unable to return to the conditions which existed at the outbreak of the [First] World War and to reverse the economic development which has occurred in particular countries or spheres over the past twenty years at Germany's expense. To some extent, the deterioration in Germany's position compared with 1914 will have to be accepted as irreversible. In the planning of a European *Grossraumwirtschaft* it may appear all the more justifiable to envisage the German chemical industry once more acquiring a leading position, a position which corresponds to its technical, economic, and scientific rank. It will be vital for all planning for a European sphere to ensure a decisive and tough leadership for the inevitable confrontation with the *Grossraumwirtschaften* which are already emerging outside Europe.

To ensure that the Greater German or continental European chemical industry can successfully maintain its position in this confrontation, it is vital to recognise those forces which will play a decisive role in the world market after the war. Their importance is briefly sketched as follows:

1. The main emphasis in the confrontation over a reorganisation of the world market will depend on our situation vis à vis the North American concerns. Pushed out of the European market for reasons which were already operative before the war and which will be even stronger after the war, the Americans will use all their efforts to try and maintain and develop the build-up of their chemical exports to non-European countries (which they managed to achieve during the war). In the forefront of their efforts is the Latin American market . . .

The extent to which and the speed with which Europe, and in particular, Germany, will be able as a pure 'trading partner' to restore, maintain, and build up its position in the Latin American continent will depend, on the degree of order or disorder in the European economic area and on the creation of a purposeful trading policy. Moreover, what has been said about Latin America will also be true to some extent of Canada. The second main area of confrontation with the USA will be the countries of the Far East . . .

The above comments show the extent and importance of the shifts which have taken place at the expense of the German chemical industry as a result of the effects of the World War. Apart from a review of the past, a description has been provided of those forces with which not only the German but in the final analysis the continental European chemical industry will be confronted in a serious conflict. The review and the forecast demonstrate the need to gear all plans towards securing success in this confrontation and for this purpose to subordinate interests which diverge from this goal in all those European industrial countries whose economic policies can be influenced by Germany . . .

France . . .

To achieve the desired reorganisation and to compensate for the damage which has been done in and by France the most appropriate solution appears to be for the German dyestuffs industry to acquire a stake in the French diestuffs industry and thereby ensure that in the future French production and marketing are controlled in such a way that German exports can no longer be harmed. Concrete proposals could be made for this such as our suggestion that the IG is permitted to acquire fifty per cent of the French dyestuffs industry from the Reich . . .

Finally, influential businessmen put forward proposals such as those for the future of the British economy put forward by Karl E. Markau, President of the German Chamber of Commerce in London until the outbreak of war, which he sent to the Foreign Ministry and OKW on 27 September 1940:

628

. . . The take-over of this inheritance, our inclusion in English trade channels and the opportunity simultaneously to train our junior members of staff not only provide the quickest way for the desired development of German exports but also at the same time prepare the path towards the final goal of the transfer of this commercial expertise and experience to Germany.

Through these measures Germany would be in a position to acquire the following:

1. Direct access to Great Britain's raw material possessions, such as zinc mines, copper works, rubber plantations, tea plantations, rice fields, cocoa plantations etc.[16]

2. The utilization of the trade channels and agencies of these firms for our own purposes.

3. To train our junior businessmen in these commercial firms which have been placed under German control, to send them to the overseas agencies as necessary and thereby to acquire trained personnel in the shortest possible time.

The same is true of those industries which are of interest to us.

The final goal of these measures is the transfer of expertise, trade channels, and all the influence which was previously in English hands to Germany and to do so in the quickest and most effective way . . .

[16] Here followed a list of the most important British commercial firms which were to be brought under German control through the acquisition of fifty per cent of the shares (eds).

One must remember that, having been defeated, England can only be a shadow of her former self: the English pound has lost its influence; no government can pay the huge debts with which the war has burdened the English people. A degree of impoverishment will occur such as the English in particular are incapabe of conceiving. On the other hand, the English people, who owe their living to a large extent to trade and industry, must go on existing. The only possibility of doing so is through commerce. Moreover, since Europe was the largest export market for all their raw materials, basic and semi-luxury foodstuffs and will continue to be so and since exports to the continental countries will be controlled by Germany, the English will have no alternative but to accept such German measures which will also be equivalent to measures of support for them.

In view of the indefinite postponement of the invasion of Britain and the prospect of the war continuing into 1941, the Economics Ministry felt obliged to lay down some guidelines and, in particular, to put a stop to the indiscriminate plunder characteristic of some sections of German industry. On 3 October 1940, Gustav Schlotterer of the Reich Economics Ministry explained the broad outlines of his Minister's policy on the question of the 'European *Grossraumwirtschaft*' to a meeting of the Grand Council of the Reich Group Industry. The following document contains excerpts from his speech and the reply by Wilhelm Zangen:[17]

629

. . . That raises the whole question of how we view our relations with other European states. One can take the view that we can simply dictate what is to happen in the economic field in Europe, i.e. that we simply regard matters from a one-sided standpoint of German interests. This is the criterion which is sometimes adopted by private business circles when they are dealing with the questions of the future structure of the European economy from the point of view of their own particular sphere of operations. However, such a view would be wrong because in the final analysis we are not alone in Europe and we cannot run an economy with subjugated nations.

It is quite obvious that we must avoid falling into either of two extremes: on the one hand, that we should swallow up everything and take everything away from the others and, on the other, that we say: we are not like that, we don't want anything. Of course we want something, of course we must want something, for, if in the final analysis, we are in control in Europe, then we must have influence, and the precondition for that is that we acquire those positions in Europe that we need in order to play our leading role. . . . We are not in a position to fulfil every

[17] Wilhem Zangen, head of the large Mannesmann steel and heavy engineering firm had been chairman of the Reich Group Industry since November 1938 (eds).

wish of this or that businessman with regard to acquiring stakes in enterprises. One wants to buy a brewery, another a textile factory, a third a villa, a fourth to buy into a mining business and often they look to the military commander for assistance. We can't do things that way and we have no need to. It is obvious that the German authorities will back you if you are working for German interests abroad. We urgently want to acquire stakes in businesses. But if the firm X turns up in Belgium and wants a fifty per cent stake in the Belgian firm Y, we can't simply order the Belgian firm to obey.

If everything is not as we would wish after one month then we shall simply have to take time. We believe that our economic position in Europe in general and the economic position of particular German economic groups are so strong that during the next months and years when the European *Grossraumwirtschaft* has crystallised further you will find ways and means of enforcing your will, in skilful cooperation with the German authorities . . .

It is obvious that, in addition, we will endeavour to secure the major and important things that we need in the coming peace treaties. But I would like to emphasize once again: we want German firms themselves to use the right methods of applying pressure and the appropriate opportunities. What matters is that we secure a healthy mixture between German interests and those of other nations and countries in Europe. These countries are dependent on cooperation with us and that will push them in our direction and that will compel them to work with us . . .

Thus, we must not regard our task in the sphere of industrial policy as being to suppress the other industries let alone to destroy them. We must rather attempt to secure a sensible cooperation and division of labour in Europe. The right thing to do is not to destroy European industry outside Germany but to reorganise it. . . . For, in the final analysis, why are we constructing a European *Grossraum*? Because we want to produce a sensible division of labour between the agrarian and industrial areas of Europe, because we want to produce as cheaply as possible in the European *Grossraum*, i.e. we shall close centres of production which are useless which have only shot up under the protection of foreign exchange, customs, or quota arrangements . . .

All of you who are actively engaged in the business world, who run industrial concerns may not find it very pleasant having to put up with the fact that industries with which you were engaged in tough competition, are allowed to keep going and even to boom to a certain extent because they are no longer being treated as foreign industries but as European industrial concerns which belong to us. You will have to get used to thinking European in economic matters as well. We are moving towards a situation in which sharp distinctions between German and European will gradually have to disappear. If we are already adopting the position that the various national economies of Europe represent a community, a *Grossraum* under German leadership, then we must draw the consequences from that and be prepared to treat these national economies correctly within the framework of our interests and on the basis of leadership by us and no longer adopt a narrow German yardstick but rather a broad European one.

However, it is not the case that we want to unleash our own competitors. We cannot be indifferent to what is going on outside. We cannot permit people to attack our markets in an undisciplined fashion. For this reason the problem of economic cooperation in Europe, in particular in the industrial field, must be resolved by business itself and through economic means.

First, the mutual integration of capital holdings, in particular the acquisition of stakes in European businesses. If one is facing unpleasant competition abroad then one wonders whether one could not acquire influence over this competition by securing a stake, by going in with one's own people and thereby creating the possibility of controlling the management of the firm or at least of influencing it.

The wish has been expressed in the highest quarters that the method of taking capital stakes should be given particular emphasis by German industry. I am well aware of the fact that that is not always easy and that one cannot achieve it overnight. But our goal for the next few years must be to aim to penetrate as deeply as possible into European businesses in every sphere, in particular into industrial firms, by acquiring capital holdings so that we can direct things from there. Then, instead of competition, wild unregulated competition, at least a regulated form of competition or even cooperation will emerge.

You will be aware, gentlemen, that we are providing the necessary foreign exchange for the acquisition of capital stakes in Holland, Belgium, France, and also Norway, in the northern coutries and in the south-east. You can have any amount (General Director Zangen: Hear Hear!). Yes, I give you my word. You can rely on it. It is important to us that you succeed in penetrating these countries and that we can thereby make our influence felt there.

The second method, gentlemen, is to include the industries of these countries in our system of market regulations. In other words, the people out there must not be allowed to run around out of control. I would like to emphasize the point that in future there will be no question of allowing our economic development and our economic goals in Europe or overseas to be disturbed by, for example, a Dutch or a Swiss concern. Naturally, the people can work and live with us; naturally Belgian railway carriage factories can go on producing carriages and exporting them. But, in the future it will be impossible for them to force down our prices by cheap offers. They will have to come to an arrangement with us about the sale of carriages. That is obvious. And, in this connection the question arises as to whether the creation of cartells, associations and syndicates can play a European role as well.

Our view in the Reich Economics Ministry—and we know that we are in agreement with the Reich Group Industry on this—is that where the cartel or syndicate or any other association represents a useful institution for regulating the market, one should not hesitate to turn it into a European institution. . . . And the things which aren't suitable for cartels or associations should be left outside and one should put up with a certain amount of competition there.

The third method: Where cartels or associations cannot be created—things will vary in the different spheres—the question arises as to whether one cannot work with general market agreements, arrangements for protecting particular spheres etc. within the framework of the [German] Organisation of Business [*Organisation der gewerblichen Wirtschaft*]. The precondition for that is that similar business organisations are created outside Germany on the German model. There has been a very great response to this idea abroad, sometimes perhaps too great and too enthusiastic. At any rate, they are setting about creating such an organisation in Holland at the moment. Similar efforts are going on in Belgium and things are moving in the south-east. Thus, this will prove a major task for the Organisation of Business and in the sphere of Industry for the Reich Group Industry.

Gentlemen! From the comments which I have made on this question you can see that we envisage the European *Grossraumwirtschaft* essentially as a product of the initiative of business itself. We as the State can of course reach economic agreements [with other states]. We can set up a customs or currency union here and there or implement a transfer agreement. But that can only lead to a general form of regulation and will remain suspended in mid-air unless it is underpinned by business itself. It is obvious that we will support you and that we must give the lead. But I must emphasize very strongly that this European *Grossraumwirtschaft* ought be to a matter for business itself and be something administered by business [*Selbstverwaltung der Wirtschaft*].

These problems raised by the *Grossraumwirtschaft* must be resolved:

1. at the level of the private firms which must be interlinked and integrated as closely as possible in terms of personnel and capital holdings.
2. at the level of cartels, associations etc. where such collaboration is appropriate.
3. at the level of the self regulation of business, the organisation of business as such.

Zangen: What you have just told us about industrial policy was new to most of those present. Various negotiations have already been conducted with prospects of success. We can only welcome the fact that you view matters in the way you have outlined, for compulsory agreements do not last for ever. When the drawing up of the political boundaries has been dealt with then a true peace on both sides must consist of cooperation and your proposals are in our view most welcome. Gentlemen, we of the Reich Group Industry have received a commission from the Reich Economics Ministry to travel to Paris to deal with these matters with the French and Belgian industrialists. Holland will follow. Here too the question of creating an organisation is of immediate importance, for it is obvious that it is impossible for us to work over there if we cannot deal with a united organization such as exists here. I may remind you that we were close to concluding a coal agreement with the English in March 1938 and that that had of course taken ten years because the English could not get their mine owners to agree. So there are important issues to be prepared. I had a discussion with Herr Schneider of Schneider-Creusot[18] a few weeks ago and tried to introduce him to the idea of creating an organization. At the moment the idea is totally unfamiliar to the French.

We altogether welcome the far-sighted policy which you have elucidated here in connection with all the issues relating to European reconstruction and which you have established as your guiding principle, a policy which if I have understood you correctly is geared to the natural economic facts of life and natural economic principles.

You may be convinced that, as I said at the beginning, we have no doubt that, in view of Germany's situation of dearth and in view of the European cooperation which is now to take place, the direction of the economy not only in Germany but

[18] A big French coal and steel combine (eds).

in Europe is absolutely essential and that we are glad to go along with everything which must be done in this respect. And if you interpret the direction of policy in terms of avoiding interference in particular questions, as you have just said, then you will have our full cooperation in the future just as in the past.

The summer of 1940 was the high point of plans for a 'New Order' and a German dominated *Grossraumwirtschaft*. From autumn 1940 onwards, the Nazi regime felt increasingly compelled to concentrate on policies which would produce the most immediate benefits in terms of the German war effort, in other words on extracting the maximum resources from the occupied territories. Hitler himself had little interest in high flown ideas of a 'New Order' and a *Grossraumwirtschaft*. In contrast to these more sophisticated versions of imperialism advocated by German diplomats and economic officials, which echoed Wilhelmine plans for a German-dominated *Mitteleuropa*, Hitler was primarily interested in territorial conquest and direct economic exploitation. His comments at a conference held on 16 July 1941 to discuss plans for the occupation of Russia provide a good insight into his notion of imperialism. Bormann took the minutes:

630

A conference attended by Rechsleiter Rosenberg, Reich Minister Lammers, Field-Marshal Keitel, the Reich Marshal [Göring], and myself was held today by order of the Führer at 3.00 p.m. in his quarters. The conference began at 3.00 p.m. and, including a break for coffee, lasted until about 8.00 p.m.

By way of introduction the Führer emphasized that he wished first of all to make some basic statements. Various measures were now necessary; this was confirmed, among other events, by an assertion made in an impudent Vichy newspaper that the war against the Soviet Union was Europe's war and that therefore it had to be conducted for Europe as a whole. Apparently by these hints the Vichy paper meant to say that it ought not to be the Germans alone who benefited from this war, but that all European States ought to benefit from it.

It was essential that we should not proclaim our aims before the whole world; moreover, this was not necessary, but the chief thing was that we ourselves should know what we wanted. In no case should our own way be made more difficult by superfluous declarations. Such declarations were superfluous because we could do everything wherever we had the power, and what was beyond our power we would not be able to do anyway.

What we told the world about the motives for our measures ought therefore to be conditioned by tactical reasons. We ought to proceed here in exactly the same way as we did in the cases of Norway, Denmark, Holland and Belgium. In these cases too we said nothing about our aims, and if we were clever we would continue in the same way.

We shall then emphasize again that we were forced to occupy, administer and secure a certain area; it was in the interest of the inhabitants that we should provide order, food, traffic, etc.; hence our measures. It should not be made obvious that a final settlement is thereby being initiated! We can nevertheless take all necessary measures—shooting, resettling, etc.—and we shall take them.

But we do not want to make enemies of any people prematurely and unnecessarily. Therefore we shall act as though we wanted to exercise a mandate only. It must be clear to *us*, however, that we shall never withdraw from these areas.

Accordingly we should take care:

1. to do nothing which may obstruct the final settlement, but to prepare for it only in secret;
2. to emphasize that we are liberators.

In particular:

The Crimea must be evacuated by all foreigners and be settled by Germans only.

In the same way the former Austrian part of Galicia will become Reich territory.

Our relations with Romania are at present good, but one does not know what our relations will be at any future time. This we have to take account of, and draw our frontiers accordingly. One ought not to be dependent on the good will of other people; we have to arrange our relations with Romania in accordance with this principle.

In principle we have now to face the task of cutting up the giant cake according to our needs, in order to be able, first, to dominate it, second, to administer it, and third, to exploit it.

The Russians have now given an order for partisan warfare behind our front. This partisan war again has some advantage for us; it enables us to exterminate everyone who opposes us.

Principles:

Never again must it be possible to create a military power west of the Urals, even if we have to wage war for a hundred years in order to attain this goal. All successors of the Führer must know: that security for the Reich exists only if there are no foreign military forces west of the Urals; that it is Germany who undertakes the protection of this area against all possible dangers. Our iron principle must be and must remain:

We must never permit anybody but the Germans to carry arms!

This is especialy important; even when it seems easier at first to enlist the armed support of foreign, subjugated nations, it is wrong to do so. This will prove some day to be absolutely and unavoidably to our disadvantage. Only the German may carry arms, not the Slav, nor the Czech, nor the Cossack, nor the Ukrainian!

On no account should we apply a wavering policy such as was done in Alsace before 1918. What distinguishes the Englishman is his constant and consistent following of *one* line and *one* aim. In this respect we must learn absolutely from him . . .

This notion of imperialism was shared by much of the Nazi leadership. Goebbels, for example, expressed it in two confidential statements he made during 1940. The first was on 5 April to the German press:

631

We are carrying out the same revolution in Europe as we carried out on a smaller scale in Germany. If anyone asks how do you conceive the new Europe, we have to reply that we don't know. Of course we have some ideas about it. But if we were to put them into words it would immediately create more enemies for us. Once we have the power then they'll know, and we too will know what to do with it. . . . In 1914 it was thought one could tell the nation that the coalfields of northern France were a worthwhile war aim. The man in the street isn't interested in these coalfields. Today, we talk about living space. Anybody can interpret it as they wish. When the time comes we will know very well what we want . . .

The second was on 26 October 1940 to leaders of the NSDAP in Vienna:

632

One can replace everything else in political life but not the substance of a nation, the blood of a nation, and that has to be committed in war. And so our first principle in the conduct of this war was: long preparations, short wars and not short preparations and long wars. . . Of course we are involved in a life and death struggle, naturally we have risked a high bid, but we risked it in a situation in which it appeared most likely to bring a reward. One cannot criticize German and Austrian policy before the World War for going to war in 1914, but one can criticize it for not going to war six years earlier when the situation was far more favourable . . .

I have the impression that at the moment the world is being carved up again and in a different way from that which it was done previously. And since we came off badly in the previous distributions, our motto can only be: join the queue and push to the front. If anyone asks me what do you really want, I cannot give him a precise answer. That depends on the circumstances. It depends on how much we want and how much we can get. We want living space. Yes, but what does that mean? We will provide a definition after the war . . . When this war is over we want to be masters of Europe . . . Then at last we will belong to the 'have' nations, we will possess raw materials and resources and then we will have a large colonial empire. . . .

We National Socialists have always taken the view that the war was not over in 1918. That was only the end of the first act and then came the long interval. The final act is being played at the moment. This drama will end with a German victory and won't be a tragedy.

(iii) Economic exploitation

First and foremost Nazi occupation policy was geared to the economic exploitation of the empire. This was most ruthlessly and brutally practised in Poland and the Soviet Union. The attitude of the German authorities in the early phase of the Russian campaign is illuminated by the following excerpt from the minutes of a meeting of State Secretaries to discuss plans to exploit the Soviet Union held on 2 May 1941:

633

1. The war can only be continued if the whole of the *Wehrmacht* is fed from Russia during the third year of war.
2. Tens of millions of people will undoubtedly die of starvation if we take what we need from the country.
3. The most important thing is to get hold of and take away oil seeds and oil cake whereas wheat is subordinate to that.
4. Industry should only be restarted in spheres where there are shortages.

However, economic exploitation was by no means confined to the east. The mentality governing the conduct of German occupation policy is also illuminated by the minutes of a conference at which Göring addressed the Reich Commissioners and Military Commanders of the occupied territories, which took place on 6 August 1942 in the Hermann-Göring-Hall of the Air Ministry and from which the following extracts are taken:

634

Göring . . . In all the occupied territories I see the people living there stuffed full of food, while our own people are starving. For God's sake, you haven't been sent there to work for the well-being of the peoples entrusted to you, but to get hold of as much as you can so that the German people can live. I expect you to devote your energies to that. This continual concern for the aliens must come to an end once and for all.

I have the reports of what you are planning to deliver in front of me. When I contemplate your countries it seems like nothing at all. I could not care less if you tell me that your people are collapsing from hunger. They can do that by all means so long as no German collapses from hunger.

Heavy attacks have been made on German cities in the Ruhr area. The population have suffered appallingly. Next door to the Ruhr area lies rich Holland. It could send far more vegetables to this hard hit area that it has done. I could not care less what the Dutch gentlemen think about that. It would not be a bad thing if the resistance of the Dutch population was greatly weakened, for they are nothing but a nation of traitors to our cause. I don't really blame them for that. In their place I might well do the same. But we do not have the job of feeding a nation which inwardly rejects us. If this nation is so weak that it can no longer lift a hand except where we can employ it, all the better. If it is that weak then it won't revolt just when our rear is being threatened. I am only interested in the people in the occupied territories who work producing armaments and food. They must get just sufficient so that they can do their work. I could not care less whether the Dutch gentlemen are Teutons or not. Because if they are then they will be all the more stubborn, and great personalities in the past have already shown how one deals with stubborn Teutons. Even if various complaints are made, you have done the right thing because the fate of the Reich is the only thing that matters . . .

Now, as to the deliveries to the Reich. Last year France delivered 550,000 tons of bread corn and now I demand 1.2 m. tons. I want suggestions on how it is to be done within a fortnight. No more discussion. It does not matter what happens to the French: 1.2 m. tons will be delivered. 550,000 of fodder grain, now 1 million! 135,000 of meat, now 350,000: 23,000 of fats last year, now 60,000! Cheese—last year they didn't deliver any, so this year they will deliver 25,000. Last year 125,000 of potatoes, this year 300,000. No wine last year, this year six million hectolitres. 15,000 of vegetables last year, this year 150,000. 200,000 of fruit last year, this year 300,000. Those are the deliveries from France.

The Netherlands: 40,000 of bread grains, 45,000 of fodder grains, 35,000 of meat, 20,000 of fats, 85,000 of potatoes, 45,000 of root crops, 30,000 of sugar, 16,000 of cheese, 1 million of vegetables, 10,000 of vegetable seeds. (Interjection from Seyss-Inquart)

They ought to find it easy to make 1 million. Then take the whole harvest. You can swop around: a bit less vegetables, a bit more fats. I don't care.

Belgium is a poor country. But not as poor as all that or as you try to make out. They won't need to deliver bread grains, but they won't get any. But don't forget to send me 50,000 tons of fodder corn. They won't get fats, I don't want any either. I want 20,000 tons of sugar, 50,000 tons of potatoes, 95,000 tons of fruit.

Norway: They've got fish: 400,000.

(Terboven 'We delivered more last year')

500,000!

(Terboven: Then I must ask you to get the Navy to return the trawlers).

I know, we must discuss that with the Navy. You must give some meat, How much?

(Interjection: Nothing)

Haven't you got any fodder corn either?

(No!)

(Terboven: The *Wehrmacht* is largely fed by me) . . .

Gentlemen. I would like to add something. I have an incredible amount to do and an incredible amount of responsibility. I haven't time to read letters and memos in which you tell me that you can't do what I ask of you. I only have time to find out from time to time through a short report from Backe[19] whether the demands are being met. If not, then we shall have to meet again in rather different circumstances.

---

[19] Herbert Backe who was in charge of the Reich Ministry of Agriculture (eds).

The economic exploitation of their empire by the Germans took a variety of forms. First, occupied territories were obliged to pay for the costs of German occupation which were fixed far in excess of the actual costs:

635

Payments of occupation costs in billions of RM

Country	*1940 (2.half)*	*1941*	*1942*	*1943*	*1944 till Sept.*	*Total*
France	1.75	5.55	8.55	11.10	8.30	35.25
Holland	0.80	1.90	2.20	2.20	1.65	8.75
Belgium	0.35	1.30	1.50	1.60	0.95	5.70
Denmark	0.20	0.20	0.25	0.55	0.80	2.00
Italy				2.00	8.00	10.00
Others	0.90	1.05	4.50	7.55	8.30	22.30
Total	4.00	10.00	17.00	25.00	28.00	84.00

Secondly, the Reichsmark was set at an artificially high rate in relation to other currencies:

636

Overvaluation of the Reichsmark in Comparison to its Pre-war Purchasing Power

Occupied country	*Currency*	*Purchasing power of the RM*	*Fixed rate*	*Overvaluation in %*
Netherlands	hfl	0.53	0.75	42
Belgium	bfr	1.67	2.50	50
France	ffr	12.30	20.00	63
Denmark	dkr	1.45	2.00	38
Norway	nkr	1.24	1.67	34

Thirdly, a large percentage of the foodstuffs, industrial raw materials, and manufactured goods produced by the occupied territories were earmarked by Germany. The percentage of levies varied from country to country. According to official figures, the percentage of German levies of raw materials in relation to French production was as follows:

637

Coal, 29 per cent; electric power, 22 per cent; petroleum and motor fuel, 80 per cent; iron ore, 74 per cent; steel products, crude and half-finished, 51 per cent; copper, 75 per cent; lead, 43 per cent; zinc, 38 per cent; tin, 67 per cent; nickel 64 per cent; mercury, 50 per cent; platinum, 76 per cent; bauxite, 40 per cent; aluminium, 75 per cent; magnesium, 100 per cent; sulphur carbonate, 80 per cent; industrial soap, 67 per cent; vegetable oil, 40 per cent; carbosol, 100 per cent; rubber, 38 per cent; paper and cardboard, 16 per cent; wool, 59 per cent; cotton, 53 per cent; flax, 65 per cent; leather 67 per cent; cement 55 per cent; lime, 20 per cent; acetone, 21 per cent.

Levies of manufactured goods and the products of the mining industry:
Automobile construction, 70 per cent; electrical and radio construction, 45 per cent; industrial precision parts, 100 per cent; heavy castings, 100 per cent; foundries, 46 per cent; chemical industries, 34 per cent; rubber industry, 60 per cent; paint and varnish, 60 per cent; perfume, 33 per cent; wool industry, 28 per cent; cotton weaving, 15 per cent; flax and cotton weaving, 12 per cent; industrial hides, 20 per cent; buildings and public works, 75 per cent; wood work and furniture, 50 per cent; lime and cement, 68 per cent; naval construction, 79 per cent; aeronautic construction, 90 per cent.

Moreover, like the other parts of the Nazi empire, France was penalised by the 'clearing' system which Germany had instituted to handle the financial side of her trade with the various members of the empire. Under so-called clearing agreements each member was obliged to allow Germany to purchase vast quantities of goods and services on credit since they were unable to purchase equivalent amounts from her. Under the agreements these inbalances would only be settled after the war. It has been estimated that by September 1944 these German debts had reached a total of some 42 billion RM. The debt to France by the end of July 1944 was 8.2 billion RM. According to Alan Milward, the payments to Germany were 49 per cent of total French public expenditure over the years 1940–44 and in 1943 were as high as sixty per cent. This was 8.2 per cent of German GNP in 1943.[20]

By taking control of the banking system in the occupied territories, the Germans were not only able to acquire the gold and foreign currency reserves of these countries (though in some cases they had already been removed to a safe place), but also to remove restrictions on note issue and the granting of credit. This enabled the banks to pay for the occupation costs by in effect printing money. However, the combination of the

[20] A. S. Milward, *War, Economy and Society* 1939–1945 (London 1977) pp. 139, 141.

increased circulation of notes plus the shortage of goods as a result of German levies produced serious inflation. This trend was also encouraged by issuing a form of occupation money in the shape of so-called *Reichskreditkassen* notes for the use of the German occupying forces, at least during the first phase of the occupation.

German domination over industry in the occupied territories was secured by a variety of techniques. First, the distribution of raw materials and fuel was controlled through a system of licences issued by a network of commodity control offices which worked under close German supervision. In addition, there was the sanction that idle plant could be closed down or confiscated. Secondly, through their control of international trade within German-occupied Europe they were able to exert a decisive influence not only on industry within the occupied territories but also on that of their allies.

Thirdly, the Germans secured direct control over a substantial number of major firms throughout continental Europe by using a variety of techniques. The simplest was confiscation, or sequestration for the duration of the war under a form of trusteeship. This technique was widely practised in the incorporated territories, and in the General Government, in the Protectorate and the Soviet Union where the Germans acted with fewer scruples than elsewhere. Alternatively, direct control could be acquired by 'Aryanization' of Jewish property or the purchase of majority shareholdings with the help of the over-valued Reichsmark and the reserves which had accumulated from the occupation payments, reinforced by various forms of intimidation. This technique was widely practised in the occupied territories of western Europe and in the satellite and allied countries of South East Europe. Finally, commissioners could be appointed to oversee firms which were of particular strategic importance or where the management was considered inadequate.

Nazi imperialism benefited enormously from the fact that it could harness the skills and ambitions of the German business community. In addition to firms operating on their own initiative to take over or acquire large stakes in companies in the occupied territories, they also provided much of the personnel for the official economic agencies which controlled the subject economies. These individuals could and to some extent did exploit their official positions to benefit the companies to which they belonged.

However, it would be a mistake to assume that the major firms were invariably able to secure their objectives, let alone that Nazi imperialism was determined by the goals of big business. Many of the officials in the government agencies came from smaller firms which were traditional rivals of the major combines and, in any case, Nazi party officials tended to be suspicious of 'trusts' such as IG Farben. Moreover the regime developed its own combines, notably the huge Hermann Goering Werke AG, which was far more actively engaged in economic plunder than any other firm and provided serious and increasing competition for the old-established companies. The cooperation between big business and the regime was one between unequal partners and firms felt obliged to come to terms with Nazi imperialism out of the need to defend their respective positions against rivals as much as out of greed for new acquisitions which in some cases were of dubious value. Thus, the Nazis succeeded in utilising the dynamics of capitalism but geared them to fulfilling their own priorities which were essentially political.

Nazi Germany failed to create a New Order in Europe in the sense in which the economic planners of 1940 had envisaged, i.e. a rationally ordered economic system based on a optimum international division of labour which, while primarily geared to German interests, would be based on a degree of mutual cooperation rather than perpetual and overt subjugation by force. The arrogant contempt for the conquered peoples characteristic of Nazi occupation policy combined with the increasingly pressing needs of the German war machine to ensure that the German economic order in Europe between 1940 and 1945 was in fact one of naked and ruthless exploitation.

In theory, the Germans could undoubtedly have improved their yield from the occupied territories—for example, through a more rational organization of their administration there, whose competing agencies (Göring, Speer, Sauckel, Himmler, *Wehrmacht* etc.) operated with the massive degree of friction so typical of the Nazi bureaucratic machine, and which, in addition, was riddled with corruption. Equally, a more conciliatory policy towards their subject populations might well have earned dividends. But the leopard could not change its spots. And, in any case, despite the grave inadequacies in their occupation policy the Germans drew very considerable benefits from it. In 1943–4, when deliveries from the occupied territories were at their peak, almost thirty per cent of 'Greater German' production of coal (98.5 million tons) came from there, above all from Polish Upper Silesia, and (including Austria) around forty per cent of its raw steel production (34.6 million tons)[21]. On 11 July 1944, Speer reported that 'up to the present twenty-five per cent to thirty per cent of the German war production had been furnished by the occupied western territories and Italy, by Italy alone twelve and a half per cent'.[22] The value of manufactured goods, agricultural produce, raw materials and services derived from France alone was equivalent to roughly one quarter of Germany's GNP in

[21] See *Deutschland im Zweiten Weltkrieg, op. cit.*, vol. 4, p. 164.

[22] *Survey of International Affairs 1939–1946. Hitler's Europe* eds. A. and V. M. Toynbee (Oxford 1954) p. 280.

[23] A. S. Milward, *op. cit.* p. 144.

1938.[23] Furthermore, one of the most crucial benefits which the Nazis gained from their empire, was the exploitation of foreign labour within the German economy, thereby easing a shortage of labour which was already critical before the outbreak of war and, with the call-up of German workers into the armed forces, would otherwise have become catastrophic. The following statistics show the significance of foreign labour for the German war machine:

638

Foreign workers in the German War economy

	1939	*1940*	*1941*	*1942*	*1943*	*1944*
Agriculture						
Germans	10,732,000	9,684,000	8,939,000	8,969,000	8,743,000	8,460,000
Foreign civilians	118,000	412,000	769,000	1,170,000	1,561,000	1,767,000
P.O.W's	—	249,000	642,000	759,000	609,000	635,000
Total foreigners	118,000	661,000	1,411,000	1,929,000	2,230,000	2,402,000
Foreigners as % of all employees	1.1	6.4	13.6	17.7	20.3	22.1
All non-agricultural pursuits						
Germans	28,382,000	25,697,000	24,947,000	23,298,000	22,278,000	21,340,000
Foreign civilians	183,000	391,000	984,000	1,475,000	3,276,000	3,528,000
P.O.W's	—	99,000	674,000	730,000	954,000	1,196,000
Total foreigners	183,000	490,000	1,658,000	2,205,000	4,230,000	4,724,000
Foreigners as % of all employees	0.6	1.9	6.4	8.9	16.5	19.0
Economy as a whole						
Germans	39,114,000	35,239,000	34,528,000	33,026,000	31,690,000	30,435,000
Foreign civilians	301,000	803,000	1,753,000	2,645,000	4,837,000	5,295,000
P.O.W's	—	348,000	1,316,000	1,489,000	1,623,000	1,831,000
Total foreigners	301,000	1,151,000	3,069,000	4,134,000	6,460,000	7,126,000
Foreigners as % of all employees	0.8	3.2	8.5	11.6	17.7	19.9

Foreign Workers (including Prisoners of War) as a Percentage of Total Employment, by Major Economic Division within the Reich as of May 31, 1939–1944

Economic division	*1939*	*1940*	*1941*	*1942*	*1943*	*1944*
Agriculture	1	6	13	18	20	22
Industry	1	3	9	14	26	29
Handwork	1	3	8	9	13	16
Transport	1	2	4	8	13	17
Distribution	—	—	2	3	5	7
Administration and Services	—	1	3	3	5	6
Domestic service	—	1	2	5	5	5
All Occupations	1	3	9	12	17	20

Distribution of Foreign Workers in the Reich According to Sex and Origin in Autumn 1943 (in thousands)

	Civilian Men	*POW's*	*Total Men*	*% of Total Men*	*Total Women*	*% of Total Women*
France	605	739	1344	26.3	44	2.6
Soviet Union	817	496	1313	25.8	899	52.4
Poland	1094	29	1123	22.0	527	30.7
Belgium	195	53	248	4.9	33	1.9
Bohemia-Moravia	244	—	244	4.8	42	2.5
Holland	236	—	236	4.6	20	1.2
Serbia	34	94	128	2.5	11	0.7
Italy	103	—	103	2.0	14	0.8
Others	303	54	357	7.1	124	7.2
Total	3631	1465	5096	100.0	1714	100.0

Last but not least, the exploitation of their empire ensured that the German people were able to maintain a standard of nourishment which was not only superior to that of the population of the occupied territories but was higher than that which they had enjoyed during the First World War, a fact which clearly played a significant part in sustaining German morale. Ironically, France provided as much food as the eastern occupied territories—Hitler's *Lebensraum*—combined. The following figures make this clear:

639

(a) Net imports of foodstuffs into Germany, 1936–44, and the part of major suppliers by value (in millions of Reichsmarks).

Year	U.S.S.R.‖	South-eastern Europe*	Belgium-Luxemb'g†	Czecho-slovakia‡	Denmark	France	Italy	Nether-lands	Norway	Poland§	Spain	Sweden	Total Imports: current prices	Total Imports: constant 1925 prices
1936	4·0	285·9	11·6	4·6	134·2	0·5	114·8	83·1	43·7	21·8	54·7	21·7	1411·8	3034
1937	1·2	437·3	14·7	19·2	137·0	9·0	119·5	112·6	43·1	28·9	43·4	25·7	1956·3	3978
1938¶	1·9	451·1	15·4	14·9	143·4	19·6	135·2	97·6	39·3	43·9	33·6	31·8	2050·2	4367
	6·2	621·8	15·1	21·1	144·7	20·7	155·6	100·8	40·5	56·6	31·9	32·1	2326·6	4897
1939	6·3	598·1	11·3	19·0	157·4	6·2	158·0	86·6	26·3	32·5	61·7	26·6	1917·2	3966
1940	197·9	728·3	18·4	29·6	466·0	29·2	268·9	247·1	43·4	−30·4	9·0	16·6	2243·5	3679
1941	139·5	640·9	−60·2	25·5	376·1	141·6	467·1	297·0	49·2	−10·4	89·1	7·2	2407·5	3063
1942	281·2	866·7	4·1	16·9	232·4	321·6	455·4	228·1	50·4	86·0	81·5	2·1	2713·1	2662
1943	132·4	1034·3	−14·3	29·3	350·0	483·4	301·9	237·3	−74·8	103·0	119·1	−4·6	2720·5	2010
1944	0	n.a.	−33·2	44·9	458·0	328·5	215·6	109·6	39·7	15·2	n.a.	−3·0	2131·0	n.a.

Foodstuffs are defined according to the classification Ernährungswirtschaft in the new German trade classification of 1936. This includes all kinds of food and drink for human consumption, animal fodder, livestock and tobacco.

* Bulgaria, Greece, Hungary, Romania, Turkey, Yugoslavia.

† After 15 August 1940 Belgium only.

‡ After March 1939 Slovakia only.

§ From 1940 the 'General-Government of Poland'.

‖ In 1940 includes Estonia, Latvia, Lithuania. From 1942 to June 1943 is the Reichskommissariat Ostland plus Reichskommissariat Ukraine plus other occupied eastern territories.

¶ The top line includes the Sudetenland in Germany after October but excludes Austria. The bottom line includes Austria after April. The Protectorate of Bohemia and Moravia is counted as Germany from the start of October 1940.

(b) The Provisioning of the German Reich and the Occupied Territories in the Second World War (Calories contained in the rations of a normal consumer, i.e. one not eligible for additional rations).

	1941	*1942*	*1943*	*1944*
Germany	2445	1928	2078	1981
Occupied Territories (without Poland and the S.U.)	1617	1495	1503	1494
Poland	845	1070	855	1200
Line 2 in % of Line 1	66	78	72	75
Line 3 in % of Line 1	35	56	41	61

(c) The Normal German Rations of Flour, Meat and Fats in the First and Second World Wars (Grams per week on a yearly average).

		Flour	
1914	. . . . . .	1800 g = 114	1939
1915	1575 g = 100	1688 g = 107	1940
1916	1400 g = 89	1688 g = 107	1941
1917	1540 g = 98	1688 g = 107	1942
1918	1400 g = 89	1818 g = 115	1943
		Meat	
1914	. . . . . .	500 g = 200	1939
1915	. . . . . .	500 g = 200	1940
1916	250 g = 100	400 g = 160	1941
1917	250 g = 100	350 g = 140	1942
1918	250 g = 100	250 g = 100	1943
		250 g = 100	1944
		Fats	
1914	. . . . . .	270 g = 270	1939
1915	. . . . . .	270 g = 270	1940
1916	100 g = 100	270 g = 270	1941
1917	100 g = 100	206 g = 206	1942
1918	70 g = 70	216 g = 216	1943
		219 g = 219	1944

(iv) Internal criticism of Nazi occupation policy and attempts at a change of course

The trend towards a more ruthless exploitation of the occupied territories and in particular the mass recruitment of forced labour provoked growing resistance. This in turn produced increasingly vicious reprisals on the part of the German authorities, including the taking and shooting of large numbers of hostages in retaliation for the assassination of German military and civilian personnel and, particularly in eastern Europe and the Soviet Union, the burning down of thousands of villages believed to harbour resistance fighters and the execution of many or all of their inhabitants.

The policy of ruthless exploitation and repression aroused the opposition of some of those who held responsible positions within the Nazi empire. For example, Dr Otto Bräutigam, the head of the Main Political Department in the Reich Ministry of the Eastern Territories (Soviet Union), produced a memorandum dated 25 October 1942 which contained a damning indictment of German occupation policy in Russia:

640

In the east, Germany is carrying on a threefold war: a war for the destruction of Bolshevism, a war for the destruction of the Greater Russian empire, and finally a war for the acquisition of territory for colonial settlement and for economic exploitation . . .

. . . It was soon apparent that, because of the vast areas involved and the enemy's inexhaustible reserves of manpower and matériel, the war could not be decided in a short time by arms alone, but that as in all great wars of recent times a disintegration of morale would also have to take place, and that in the final analysis the war would have to be transformed into a civil war, especially since the German armed forces do not intend to occupy the whole territory of the Soviet Union. . . .

As we all know, the peoples of the Soviet Union have been through very difficult times. Their wishes are therefore incredibly modest, even in the political sphere. A form of administration which was not intent simply on plunder and exploitation and which abolished Bolshevist methods would have kindled the greatest enthusiasm and would have put at our disposal a mass consisting of millions. And the enthusiasm in the occupied territories in the east would have had its impact on the powers of resistance of the Red Army. It would have been easy to persuade the Red Army man to say to himself: 'I am fighting for a system which is far worse than that which I can expect in the event of a defeat. Under the Germans things will be much better than they have been up to now.' If this view had become general among the members of the Red Army, the war would soon have been over.

Appreciating this, the Main Political Department believed it to be its primary duty to devote its energies towards assisting the combat troops with a propaganda campaign aimed at crippling the powers of resistance of the Red Army and in this way at shortening the war. Among the measures proposed for the attainment of this goal there are two of particular importance which differ essentially from Bolshevist policies: the Agrarian Decree and religious freedom.

In view of the exceptional significance of the agrarian question in the Soviet Union, the Main Political Department had demanded even before the beginning of the eastern campaign that the kolkhoz[24] be dissolved and an individual agrarian economy be reintroduced. This proposal was turned down by the Four-Year Plan with the remark that organizational changes were not to be considered during the war. So not before August of last year was it possible to put through an increase in farmland.

But before this plan could be realized, the Four-Year Plan had recognized that the fierce pressure of the whole peasant population for the dissolution of the collective farms would have to be met in some way in the interests of production. The demand of the Main Political Department for the dissolution of the collective farms found expression in the new Agrarian Decree.[25] A few months had been sufficient to make clear, not only to all the *Wehrmacht* units down to the youngest lieutenant in the most forward position, but also to the military posts at home and to the civil administration in the occupied Eastern territories, the need for reform in the constitution of the kolkhoz. The only exceptions to this general recognition of the situation were the two Reich Commissioners, whose disagreement unfortunately caused a delay of several weeks. The new Agrarian Decree was published shortly before the spring planting and was made the basis of a big propaganda campaign in the territories by the press and propaganda departments of the Main Department.

1. Its immediately sucessful result was a hitherto inconceivable productivity on the part of the population in the spring planting, which could be undertaken despite unfavourable conditions. In spite of this, there has been no lasting effect on the enemy so far. Naturally enemy propaganda has countered our Agrarian Decree with every means available. Their main argument was that it was only a promise which aimed at temporary tactical successes, and that Germany intended later to make use of the land exclusively for her own purposes. This argument found support in the very slow enforcement of the decree, which is to be partly attributed to practical reasons (lack of surveyors, land registration, survey instruments etc.).

It was intended that, during 1942, 20 per cent of the collective farms would be transformed into agricultural cooperatives. The enlarging of the farmland, which forms the main criterion of a communal economy and which should have been carried through everywhere immediately, particularly since it was decreed in August 1941 as mentioned above, has still not been achieved with even 10 per cent of the collective farms. The transformation into agricultural cooperatives was only begun a short time ago and, according to the directives of the Farmers' Leader, Körner,[26] at the end of August, it is not to reach more than 10 per cent this year. Considering this state of affairs, it is understandable that large sections of the Ukrainian

[24] Collective farms (eds).

[25] Published on 26 February 1942 (eds).

[26] Hellmut Korner, chief of the agricultural section in the Ukraine (eds).

peasantry are under the influence of enemy propaganda and have lost faith in the seriousness of our intentions.

Freedom of religion was also intended to produce a propaganda shock effect. But after months of negotiations, it was eventually decided to make no formal announcement of religious freedom, but to let it come into force as quietly as possible. As a result the propaganda effect amounted to nil.

When the Main Political Department noticed the hesitation over the decision in the church question, it looked for a substitute in another means of propaganda, in the question of returning property rights to the individual. In this the whole world could be clearly shown that National Socialism decisively repudiates Bolshevist measures of expropriation in the Baltic States, which Bolshevism had ruled for less than a year and where consequently one could have reverted to the previous property arrangements without further ado. But, to the absolute astonishment of the population, the German administration preferred to play the role of receiver of the goods stolen by the Bolshevists. The necessity of the restoration of private ownership for the correct psychological handling of the population was referred to by all the General Commissioners in the Baltic States. It is intended, as is well known, to win this population for German nationality *[Deutschtum]*. Yet even after the Four-Year Plan gave up its original objections in recognition of the fact that further delay in the restoration of private ownership would also damage German economic interests, a basic commitment to the restoration of the pre-Bolshevik property situation did not follow, although the refusal was contrary to all political sense and was based merely on the unfounded objection of the Reich Commissioner.

Again a vital weapon for the disintegration of the enemy front had been wrested from our hands, a weapon whose effects should not be underestimated. For the expropriation of private property by the Bolshevists without compensation had at the time aroused the horror not only of bourgeois circles in Russia, including the better-off peasants, but of the whole civilized world. The world, including the labourers and peasants of the Soviet Union who were disillusioned with Bolshevism, now awaited a clear policy on this question from Germany. This silence on the part of Germany was obviously of use to the enemy propaganda which could argue persuasively to the Soviet masses that Germany did not plan to restore individual ownership.

The Main Political Department has, moreover, always emphasized that the eastern peoples must be told something concrete about their future. It referred to the fact that if we do not counteract the Stalinist propaganda, the peoples would be bound to succumb to this propaganda, i.e. they would believe that Germany intended to enslave them. The Main Department has therefore, in accordance with numerous suggestions from *Wehrmacht* departments, repeatedly referred to the advisability of assurances from an authoritative German source being given the Slav peoples of the east as regards their future. The best method, it was suggested, would be the establishment of a sort of counter-government to Stalin with a captured Red General or, if one wished to avoid the term 'government', then just a defector General somewhat after the model of de Gaulle, who could become the focal point for all Red soldiers dissatisfied with Stalin. The correctness of this conception has been subsequently confirmed by countless statements of prisoners of war who have all stated independently of one another that the total silence of Germany with regard to the future of Russia leaves it open to people to fear the worst. Many would like to desert, but they do not know to whom they are going. Under the banner of a recognized counter-revolutionary leader they would fight gladly and bravely against the Bolshevist regime.

All the suggestions concerning this were in essence rejected. Permission for front-line duty was secured only for units of the Turkish and Caucasian peoples and finally, after several refusals, for the Estonians as well. Because of the difficulty of recruiting troops, the units in general turned to the enlistment of prisoners of war and civilians, primarily for service in the rear areas. But they were employed even in the front line and fought excellently. Not until the last few weeks, under the pressure of danger from the partisans, was the formation of native units allowed, and then only for action against the bandits. But even this measure will remain ineffective so far as propaganda is concerned, if their commitment at the front is not permitted and if a personality with a big name is not put at the head of the units.

In order to achieve its goal outlined above, the Main Political Department was compelled to rescind or at least to alter substantially measures introduced on the German side which strengthened the enemy's powers of resistance.

Here one should mention the treatment of prisoners as a factor of primary importance. It is no longer a secret from friend or foe that hundreds of thousands of them have literally died of starvation and cold in our camps.[27] It is alleged that there were not enough supplies of food on hand for them. But it is strange that food supplies are lacking only for prisoners of war from the Soviet Union, while complaints about the treatment of other prisoners—Poles, Serbs, French and English—have not been voiced. It is obvious that nothing was more calculated to strengthen the resistance of the Red Army than the knowledge that in German captivity they were faced with a slow and painful death. It is true that the Main Political Department has by unceasing efforts succeeded in achieving a substantial improvement in the lot of the prisoners of war. But this improvement is not to be ascribed to political acumen, but to the sudden realization that our labour market urgently needs replacements. We now experience the grotesque spectacle that after the tremendous starvation of prisoners of war, millions of labourers must hurriedly be recruited from the occupied Eastern territories in order to fill the gaps which have appeared in Germany. Now the question of food was no longer important. With the usual unlimited abuse of Slav people, 'recruiting' methods were used which can only be compared with the blackest periods of the slave trade. A veritable man-hunt was launched. Without regard for health or age people were shipped to Germany, where it soon turned out that well over 100,000 had to be sent back because of serious illness and other disabilities. It needs no elaboration to appreciate that these methods, which of course are being applied in this form not to nationals of enemy countries like Holland or Norway, but only to the Soviet Union, have

---

[27] Approximately 3.3 million of the 5.7 million Russian POWs died or were killed in German captivity (57.8 per cent). Of these around two million died between 22 June 1941 and the end of February 1942. By comparison, only 5.4 per cent of the 1.4 million Russian POWs died in German captivity during World War I. See Christian Streit, *Keine Kameraden. Die Wehrmacht und die Sowjetischen Kriegsgefangenen 1941–1945* (Stuttgart 1979) p. 10 (eds).

their repercussions on the resistance of the Red Army. In fact we have made it very easy for Soviet propaganda to increase hatred of Germany and of the National Socialist system. The Soviet soldier fights more and more bravely despite the efforts of our politicians to find another name for this bravery. More and more valuable German blood must flow in order to break the resistance of the Red Army. Of course the Main Political Department has struggled ceaselessly to put the methods of roping in workers and the treatment of the workers in Germany on a rational foundation. Originally it was intended in all seriousness to get maximum performance out of the workers sent to Germany with minimum nourishment. Here also it was not political insight that led to an improvement, but the most elementary knowledge of biology. Now 400,000 female household workers are to go to Germany from the Ukraine and already the German press is announcing publicly that they are to have no right to free time, that they will not visit the theatre, cinemas or restaurants, and that they can only leave the house for three hours a week at the most, apart from exceptions in the line of duty.

In addition there is the question of the treatment of the Ukrainians in the Reich Commissariat itself. With unequalled presumption we ignore all political experience and, to the joyful astonishment of the whole coloured world, treat the peoples of the occupied Eastern territories as second-class whites, to whom providence is alleged to have given the task of slaving for Germany and Europe. They are allowed only the most limited education, and can be given no welfare services. We are interested in feeding them only in so far as they are still capable and they are given to understand that in every respect we regard them as inferior.

In view of this situation, one can state the following:

1. As the population has become aware of our true attitude towards it, so to the same degree has the resistance of the Red Army and the strength of the partisan movement increased. The feats of arms of our magnificent Army have therefore been neutralized, just as in 1918, by an inadequate political policy. Our political policy has forced both Bolshevists and Russian nationals into a common front against us. The Russian is today fighting with exceptional bravery and self-sacrifice for nothing more or less than the recognition of his human dignity.

2. Our political policy of using the Ukraine as a counterweight against mighty Russia, against Poland and the Balkans and as a bridge to the Caucasus, has proved a complete fiasco. The 40 million Ukrainians who greeted us joyfully as liberators are today indifferent to us and are already beginning to swing into the enemy camp. If we do not succeed in checking this situation at the last movement, we risk the overnight emergence in the Ukraine of a partisan movement which would not only eliminate the Ukraine as a source of food supply, but would also tie up the reinforcements of the German army, threaten its existence and thereby involve the danger of a German defeat. . . .

As the tide of war turned against Germany, such pressure for a change of policy even begun to find echoes at the top of the Nazi hierarchy. In the diplomatic sphere, for example, attempts were made by Ribbentrop to maintain the support of Germany's allies by a new stress on the war as a European crusade against Bolshevism and Anglo-Saxon plutocracy.[28] Another example, was the following directive issued by Goebbels to the Reichsleiters, Gauleiters, and Gau Propaganda leaders of the NSDAP concerning the attitude to be taken towards the population in the occupied territories of Eastern Europe dated 15 February 1943:

641

In his proclamation on the occasion of the 30 January 1943, the Führer referred directly to the National Socialist struggle and its importance in the past, the present and the future not only for Germany but beyond that for Europe as a whole . . .

From this arise the following clear requirements for the treatment of those European nations living outside Germany, including the eastern nations, as well as for the treatment of Reich plans for the east in speeches, articles, and other publications.

1. To secure victory we must mobilise not only all the available energies of the German people but also those nations which inhabit the territories which have been occupied and conquered by us in the course of the war. All the forces of the European continent, including above all the eastern nations, must be deployed in the struggle against Jewish Bolshevism.
2. The entire propaganda activity of the NSDAP and the National Socialist state must, therefore, be geared towards convincing not only the German people but also the other European nations including the nations in the eastern territories that the victory of Adolf Hitler and of German arms is in their very own interest.
3. It is incompatible with this goal to disparage these nations and, in particular, the members of the eastern nations, either directly or indirectly in public speeches or articles and to offend their sense of self-esteem.

One cannot call these people of the eastern nations, who are hoping to be liberated by us, beasts, barbarians etc. and then expect them to be interested in a German victory . . .

4. Portrayals of the future new order in Europe from which members of foreign nations can derive the impression that the German leadership intends to maintain them in a permanent state of subordination are equally inappropriate.

Observations to the effect that Germany will establish colonies in the east and follow a colonial policy in which the land and its inhabitants will be regarded as an object of exploitation are completely inappropriate. They would provide Soviet propaganda with a welcome opportunity to maintain that Germany was placing the nations of the east on the same level as negroes. This would only strengthen the resistance of the population and the Soviet troops to the German *Wehrmacht* and the German Reich.

---

[28] See above pp. 855 ff.

5. It is equally wrong to talk of new German settlements or even major settlements and of the expropriation of land or to write articles theorizing about the question of whether the peoples or the land should be Germanized. The National Socialist principle that only the land can be Germanized is already being used by the enemy to proclaim that the Reich has a plan for the massive deportation of these peoples. Enemy and particularly Soviet propaganda must not be given a pretext for this since this would result in a strengthening of the eastern peoples' will to resist. Above all, there must be no discussion about the deportation of the long-established inhabitants.

However, a softer line in the Occupied Territories clearly went against the grain as far as Hitler was concerned and he merely paid lip service to it rather than giving it his active support. His sympathies lay far more with the SS, whose position in the Nazi empire was enhanced by the growing resistance movement, since it was responsible for security.

(v) The role of the SS in the Nazi Empire

The SS drew its strength primarily from the significance for the Nazi empire of its two main functions: the maintenance of security and the implementation of Nazi racial policies. It also benefited from effective leadership by Himmler and Heydrich and from having the resources of a large organization and an apparatus which could be imposed more or less uniformly throughout the occupied territories. By contrast, its rivals tended to be fragmented and isolated, individual office holders in the various territories with no one to turn to apart from Hitler. His support was often difficult to activate, sustain, or apply effectively in the bureaucratic warfare, particularly against Himmler who could normally count on the Führer to back him. The only comparable organizations which could remotely compete with the SS were first, the *Wehrmacht*, which was preoccupied with its military functions and anxious to avoid political involvement as far as possible, a sentiment which was encouraged by Hitler; and secondly, the Nazi party whose influence was largely confined to the Incorporated Territories in which there was a sizeable ethnic German presence for it to organize. The fact that Gauleiters and other senior Party officials (for example Hans Frank) acquired major posts in the occupied territories by no means guaranteed that the Party organization as such (Bormann's Party Chancellery) could exercise much influence on or through them.

In the occupied territories the SS operated through two main institutions. First, there were the territorial leaders—the Higher SS and Police Leaders and SS and Police Leaders. At the end of 1937 a Higher SS and Police Leader had been appointed to each military district within the Reich with the responsibility of coordinating the various branches of the SS within the area—General SS, Waffen SS, Order Police, and Security Police and SD.

However, they were only activated on 25 August 1939. Outside the *Altreich* Higher SS and Police Leaders were eventually appointed to each of the occupied countries with the same function of coordinating the various branches of the SS, while SS and Police Leaders performed the same function at district level in some of the occupied territories. The Higher SS and Police Leaders were answerable directly to Himmler.

The second important SS institution in the Nazi empire was the Security Police and SD, which had been reorganised shortly after the outbreak of war. On 27 September 1939, Himmler ordered the amalgamation of the Central Office of the Security Police (*Gestapa* and Reich Criminal Police Office) with the Central Office of the SD to form a new Reich Security Main Office (*Reichssicherheitshauptamt*—RSHA) under Reinhard Heydrich. The RSHA was not a properly official body of the state and its title was only used for internal purposes. It was a hybrid organization in which the Security Police and SD both in effect continued to exist under the umbrella of the RSHA. Thus, the SD office for ideological investigation became *Amt* II (later VII) of the RSHA; its office for research into popular opinion became *Amt* III (SD-Inland), and its office for foreign intelligence became *Amt* VII of the RSHA. These offices all remained under the auspices of the Party. At the same time, the Security Police continued in the form of *Amt* I and later II (Administration), *Amt* IV (Gestapo), and *Amt* V (Crime), all of which were state bodies. The only real element of amalgamation was in *Amt* IV which included not only the *Gestapa* but also absorbed *Zentralabteilung* III 2 of the SD Main Office. The functions of *Amt* IV of the RSHA—security and the organization of the deportation of the Jews—were carried out in the field by Inspectors (in the east Commanders) of the Security Police and SD. They received their orders directly from the RSHA in Berlin, but were also subordinate to the Higher SS and Police Leader in their territory.

Himmler summed up the role which he envisaged the SS playing in the occupied territories in a notorious speech to SS leaders in Posen on 4 October 1943:

642

. . .

One basic principle must be the absolute rule for the SS man: we must be honest, decent, loyal, and comradely to members of our own blood and to nobody else. What happens to a Russian or to a Czech does not interest me in the slightest. What the nations can offer in the way of good blood of our type we will take, if necessary by kidnapping their children and raising them here with us. Whether nations live in prosperity or kick the bucket[29] interests me only in so far as we need them as slaves for our *Kultur*; otherwise, it is of no interest to me. Whether 10,000 Russian females fall down from exhaustion while digging an anti-tank ditch interest me only in so far as the anti-tank ditch for Germany is finished. We shall never be rough and heartless when it is not necessary, that is clear. We Germans, who are the only people in the world who have a decent attitude towards animals, will also assume a decent attitude towards these human animals. But it is a crime against our own blood to worry about them and give them ideals, thus causing our sons and grandsons to have a more difficult time with them. When somebody comes to me and says, 'I cannot use women and children to dig the anti-tank ditch; it is inhuman, it would kill them', then I have to say, 'You are a murderer of your own blood because if the anti-tank ditch is not dug, German soldiers will die, and they are sons of German mothers. They are our own blood.' That is what I want to instil into the SS and what I believe I have instilled into them as one of the most sacred laws of the future. Our concern, our duty is our people and our blood. It is for them that we must provide and plan, work and fight, nothing else. We can be indifferent to everything else. I wish the SS to adopt this attitude to the problem of all foreign, non-Germanic peoples, especially Russians. All else is vain, false to our own nation, and an obstacle to the early winning of the war. . . .[30]

If the peace is a final one, we shall be able to tackle our great work of the future. We shall colonize. We shall indoctrinate our boys with the laws of the SS. I consider it to be absolutely necessary to the life of our peoples that we should not only impart the meaning of ancestry, grand-children and future, but feel these to be part of our being. Without there being any talk about it, without our needing to make use of rewards and similar material things, it must be a matter of course that we have children. It must be a matter of course that the most copious breeding should be from this racial elite of the German people. In twenty to thirty years we must really be able to provide the whole of Europe with its ruling class. If the SS together with the farmers, and we together with our friend Backe[31], then run the colony in the east on a grand scale, without any restraint, without any question of tradition, but with nerve and revolutionary impetus, we shall in twenty years push the national boundary *[Volkstumsgrenze]* 500 kilometres eastwards.

Today I have asked the Führer that the SS, if we have fulfilled our task and our duty by the end of the war, should have the privilege of holding Germany's most easterly frontier as a defence frontier. I believe this is the only privilege for which we have no competitors. I believe that not a single person will dispute our claim to this privilege. We shall be in a position there to train every young age-group in the use of arms. We shall impose our laws on the east. We shall charge ahead and push our way forward little by little to the Urals. I hope that our generation will successfully bring it about that every age-group has fought in the east, and that every one of our divisions spends a winter in the east every second or third year. Then we shall never grow soft, then we shall never have SS members who come

[29] *Verrecken*, a slang term, used of cattle. (eds).

[30] For the part of this speech dealing with the Jews, see below pp. 1199–1200

[31] Herbert Backe had replaced Darré as acting Minister of Agriculture on 23 May 1942 (eds).

to us only because it is distinguished or because the black coat will naturally be very attractive in peacetime. Everyone will know: 'If I join the SS, there is the possibility that I may be killed.' He has contracted in writing that every other year he will not dance in Berlin or attend the carnival in Munich, but that he will be posted to the eastern frontier in an ice-cold winter. Then we will have a healthy elite for all time. Thus we will create the necessary conditions for the whole Germanic people and the whole of Europe, controlled, ordered and led by us, for the Germanic people, to be able, in generations to come, to stand the test in her battles of destiny against Asia, which will certainly break out again. We do not know when that will be. Then, when the mass of humanity of 1–1½ milliards lines up against us, the Germanic people, numbering, I hope, 250–300 millions, and the other European peoples, making a toal of 600–700 millions (and with an outpost area stretching as far as the Urals, or in a hundred years beyond the Urals), must stand the test in its vital struggle against Asia. It would be an evil day if the Germanic people did not survive it. It would be the end of beauty and of *Kultur*, of the creative power of this earth. That is the distant future. It is for that we are fighting, pledged to hand down the heritage of our ancestors.

We see into the distant future, because we know what it will be. That is why we are doing our duty more fanatically than ever, more devoutly than ever, more bravely, more obediently and more thoroughly than ever. We want to be worthy of being permitted to be the first SS-men of the Führer, Adolf Hitler, in the long history of the Germanic people stretching before us.

Now let us remember the Führer, Adolf Hitler, who will create the Germanic Reich and will lead us into the Germanic future.

Our Führer Adolf Hitler
Sieg Heil!
Sieg Heil!
Sieg Heil!

Of all the occupied territories it was above all in Poland that the SS succeeded in establishing its power. Here it did indeed form virtually a state within the state, particularly in the General Government, the part of Poland not directly annexed to Germany.

CHAPTER 35

The German Occupation of Poland

Of all the countries occupied by Germany, Poland suffered the worst. Six million people, around eighteen per cent of the population of Poland, died as a result of Nazi policies, of whom half were Jews. Poland became the main killing ground of the Jews, both from within and outside the country, and a kind of laboratory for Nazi racial ideology. Indeed, as a doctrine of racial imperialism, in many ways Nazism achieved its purest expression in Poland.

Yet, until 1939, Hitler's policies towards Poland had been reasonably moderate—by comparison, for example, with Czechoslovakia. His Non-Aggression Pact with Poland of 25 January 1934 represented a reversal of the anti-Polish policy consistently pursued by the German Foreign Ministry since the loss of Prussia's Polish territories in 1919; and his requests for Danzig and for guaranteed access through the Polish corridor were on the surface modest.[1] At that stage, Hitler appears to have merely wanted to turn Poland into a satellite of Germany. However, her refusal to make any concessions and, above all, the fact that she was able to mobilise Britain and France in her defence to the extent of going to war transformed Hitler's behaviour towards Poland.

With the outbreak of war in September 1939, Hitler was clearly bent on large-scale annexation and the only question was whether he would be prepared to permit the existence of semi-independent rump Polish state. Initially, he seems to have leant in this direction, mainly in the hope of

---

[1] See above pp. 661,773.

securing diplomatic advantages from it, in particular peace with Britain and France. At an interview with Ciano on 1 October, Hitler gave the impression that he was prepared to allow a Polish rump state to exist as a satellite of Germany. In his Reichstag speech on 6 October he referred to the 'ridiculous Polish state' which was simply 'a spoilt child of the western democracies and deserved 'to be swept from the face of the earth'. But he also talked about 'the formation of a Polish state so constituted and governed as to prevent its becoming again either a hot-bed of anti-German activity or a centre of intrigue against Germany and Russia'.[2]

However, little was done to prepare for the creation of such a Polish state and the few feelers put out by Poles sympathetic to Germany, notably by the leading Germanophile, Władysław Studnicki, were ignored or rejected. Moreover, Russia's opposition to the idea of a rump Polish state and, in particular, her decision to annex permanently a large slice of eastern Poland, to a large extent pre-empted the decision, since no Polish Government would be prepared to tolerate such a loss of territory or retain credibility if it did so. In fact, Hitler appears not to have been very enthusiastic about the idea from the start and, once it became clear that Britain and France were not prepared to make peace, so he moved towards a policy of large-scale annexation and exploitation. For a time, until the late spring of 1940, he envisaged a rump Polish state under direct German control as a 'homeland for the Polish people'. But then, in his euphoria over the victory in the West, and with his plans for 'living space' in the Ukraine and the Baltic blocked—for the time being at any rate—by the pact with Moscow, he moved towards the goal of germanizing the whole of Poland through racial selection and mass resettlement. Such ambitions echoed but went beyond those which Pan-Germans such as General Ludendorff had attempted to realize during the First World War and which had been kept alive by academics and right-wing pressure groups during the 1920s and 1930s.

(i) The Political Reorganization of Poland in October 1939[3]

Under the Nazi-Soviet Pact of 24 August 1939, which was revised on 28 September, Germany had acquired 188,000 square kilometres (km.) of Polish territory containing a population of 20.2 million, of whom 17.3 million were Poles and 675,000 Germans. The Soviet Union had acquired 201,000 square km. with a population of 11.9 million, of whom 4.7 million were Poles and the remainder Ukrainians, Ruthenes and Jews. Under the revision of the Nazi-Soviet Pact of 28 September 1939, Russia handed over

[2] See M. Domarus, *Hitler. Reden 1932 bis 1945*: Vol. 2 (Wiesbaden 1973) p. 1391.

[3] See the map p. 1320 below.

to Germany the district of Lublin and the eastern part of the district of Warsaw, agreeing to move the demarcation line back to the river Bug in the centre, in return for Germany's willingness to grant her control over Lithuania.

The question remained of how much Polish territory Germany should incorporate directly into the Reich and what should be done with the rest. Whereas the Foreign Ministry and the Interior Ministry wanted to restrict the amount of Polish territory incorporated into Germany more or less to the Prussian areas transferred to Poland under the Versailles Treaty of 1919, Hitler and Göring both insisted on Germany acquiring a much larger slice of territory. The result was that the so-called 'incorporated territories' finally covered 90,000 square km. with ten million inhabitants, of whom some eighty per cent were Poles—an area almost double the size of the previous Prussian territory.

Under the new arrangement the Prussian province of East Prussia was extended eastwards to include the Suwalki salient, and southwards to include both the small district of Soldau, which had been ceded to Poland by Germany in 1919, and some 12,000 square km. of the Polish district of Warsaw, bounded on the south by the Vistula and on the east by the Narew. Suwalki was added to the *Regierungsbezirk* Gumbinnen and Soldau to *Regierungsbezirk* Allenstein. The remaining area, which was renamed *Regierungsbezirk* Zichenau, extended to within twenty miles of the city of Warsaw and contained around 800,000 Poles, 80,000 Jews, and 15,000 Germans.

The new *Reichsgau* Danzig-West Prussia incorporated *Regierungsbezirk* Marienwerder which had been detached from the western side of East Prussia. It also included the Free City of Danzig and the Polish province of Pomorze. It consisted of 25,000 square km. and had a population of 2.15 million. Of the three *Regierungsbezirke* into which the *Gau* was divided, Danzig had 55 per cent German population, Marienwerder 35 per cent, and Bromberg 14 per cent.

South of Danzig-West Prussia, the new *Reichsgau* Posen (from 29 January 1940 renamed Warthegau) included the pre-1918 German province of Posen (Polish province of Poznán) but extended another 150-200 km further east to take in the bulk of the Polish province of Łódź and part of the province of Warsaw. The population of 4.2 million contained 3.96 million Poles (85 per cent), 327,000 Germans (7 per cent), and 366,000 Jews (8 per cent).

The Prussian province of Silesia was extended beyond its pre-1918 boundaries to include the whole coal and iron basin of south-west Poland, the coal mining districts of Teschen and parts of the Polish provinces of Cracow and Kielce. It gained 10,000 square km. from Galicia (pre-1918 Austrian Poland) and from Congress Poland (pre-1918 Russian Poland) and around

2.5 million population, of whom the vast majority were Poles. Upper Silesia was divided at the end of January 1941 into Lower Silesia (Breslau) and Upper Silesia (Kattowitz).

The remaining German-occupied Polish territory, which was not incorporated into the Reich, consisted of some 98,000 squre km. and had a population of some eleven million. It comprised the Polish province of Lublin and parts of the provinces of Warsaw and Cracow. It was intially termed the 'General Government of the Occupied Polish Areas', but on 31 July 1940 was renamed the 'General Government' (*Generalgouvernement*). This change reflected the decision to give it the status of an 'adjunct territory (*Nebenland*) of the Reich' and to adopt a policy of germanization.

Under the 'guidelines for the establishment of a military administration in the occupied eastern territory', issued on 8 September 1939, civil administrative staffs were assigned to each of the three military districts into which German-occupied Poland was divided. Significantly, Hitler appointed hard-line Nazis to head these staffs: Albert Forster, the *Gauleiter* of Danzig (West Prussia), Arthur Greiser, the President of the Danzig Senate (Posen), and Dr Hans Frank, a *Reichsleiter* of the Nazi Party and a Reich Minister without portfolio (Łódź and the remaining occupied territory). This military government began to operate on 25 September and before long tension developed between the military and civilian staffs over the latter's ruthless ideologically inspired policies. The Army soon became anxious to escape the burden of responsibility for such unpleasant measures and Hitler was delighted to oblige by removing Polish territory from military administration as fast as possible. On 6 October, he announced in his Reichstag speech that he wanted 'all the territory which was to be united with Germany to be integrated into the Reich at the same time'. Two days later, on 8 October 1939, he signed the following Decree on the Organisation and Administration of the Incorporated Eastern Territories, which came into effect on 26 October 1939, five days earlier than originally envisaged:

643

§ 1. (1) In the process of reorganizing the Eastern territories the *Reichsgaue* of West Prussia and Posen (Poznań) will be incorporated in the German Reich.

(2) At the head of each *Gau* there will be a Reich Governor [*Reichsstatthalter*].

(3) The Reich Governor of West Prussia will have his offical residence in Posen.

§ 2. [4] The *Gau* of West Prussia shall be divided into the administrative districts of Danzig, Marienwerder, and Bromberg (Bydgoszcz).

(2) The *Gau* of Posen shall be divided into the administrative districts of

Hohensalza (Inowrocław), Posen, and Kalisch (Kalisz).[4]
§ 3. (1) The provisions of the law regarding the setting up of the administration in the *Reichsgau* Sudetenland (Sudetengau Law) of 14 April 1939 shall apply to the setting up of the administration of these *Gaus* except where modified by this decree.

(2) All branches of the administration shall be subject to the jurisdiction of the Reich Governor. The Reich Minister of the Interior shall decide, in agreement with the responsible Reich Minister, upon the transfer of particular branches of the administration to the existing special agencies of the Reich. Special offices for regional districts shall be subject to the jurisdiction of the *Landräte* until further notice.
§ 4. With regard to those parts of the territories which lie on the frontiers, the administrative district of Kattowitz (Katowice) will be included in the province of Silesia and the administrative district of Zichenau (Ciechanów) in the province of East Prussia . . .
§ 6 . Residents of the incorporated territories who are of German or kindred blood shall become German nationals in accordance with provisions to be issued later.

(2) Ethnic Germans [*Volksdeutsche*] in these territories shall become Reich citizens in accordance with the Reich Citizenship Law.[5]
§ 7. The laws hitherto in force shall remain operative in so far as they do not conflict with the process of incorporation into the German Reich.
§ 8. The Reich Minister of the Interior may, in consultation with the responsible minister concerned, introduce Reich law and Prussian law by decree . . .
§ 12. (1) The Reich Minister of the Interior shall be the central authority with responsibility for the reorganization of the Eastern territories . . .

(2) He shall issue such judicial and legislative regulations as are necessary for the implementation and amplification of this decree.
§ 13. (1) This decree shall take effect from 1 November 1939.

Then, on 12 October 1939, Hitler approved the following Decree on the Administration of the Occupied Polish Territories. This decree focused on the Polish territory occupied by Germany which was not intended to be incorporated into the Reich:

644

In order to restore and maintain public order and public life in the occupied Polish territories, I decree
§ 1. The territories occupied by German troops shall be subject to the authority of the Governor General of the occupied Polish territories, except in so far as they are incorporated in the German Reich.
§ 2. (1) I appoint Reich Minister Dr Frank as Governor General of the occupied Polish territories.

---

[4] From 1940 Litzmannstadt (Łódź) (eds).

[5] See Vol. 2, pp. 534 ff. (eds).

(2) I appoint Reich Minister Dr Seyss-Inquart as Deputy Governor General.
§ 3. (1) The Governor General shall be directly responsible to me.
(2) All branches of the administration shall be directed by the Governor General.
§ 4. The laws at present in force shall remain in force, except in so far as they conflict with the taking over of the administration by the German Reich.
§ 5. (1) The Council of Ministers for the Defence of the Reich, the Commissioner for the Four Year Plan, and the Governor General may make laws by means of decrees . . .
§ 7. (1) The cost of administration shall be borne by the occupied territory . . .
§ 8. (1) The central authority for the occupied Polish territories shall be the Reich Minister of the Interior.
2. The administrative decrees required to implement and supplement the present decree shall be issued by the Reich Minister of the Interior.
§ 9. (1) The present decree shall come into force as soon as and to the extent to which I withdraw the order given to the Commander-in-Chief of the Army for the exercise of military administration.

Hitler ordered German military administration in the 'Polish occupied territories' to cease on 26 October 1939 and the decree came into effect on that date.

(ii) The ideological programme for Poland

Hitler made clear at an early stage his views on the future treatment of Poland in an interview with Rosenberg on 27 September 1939, as the latter noted in his diary:

645

. . . The Poles: a thin germanic layer, underneath frightful material. The Jews, the most appalling people one can imagine. The towns thick with dirt. He's learnt a lot in these past weeks. Above all, if Poland had gone on ruling the old German parts for a few more decades everything would have become lice-ridden and decayed. What was needed now was a determined and masterful hand to rule. He wanted to split the territory into three strips: 1. Between the Vistula and the Bug: this would be for the whole of Jewry (from the Reich as well) as well as all other unreliable elements. Build an insuperable wall on the Vistula—even stronger than the one in the west. 2. Create a broad cordon of territory along the previous frontier to be germanized and colonized. This would be a major task for the whole nation: to create a German granary, a strong peasantry, to resettle good Germans from all over the world. 3. In between, a form of Polish state [*Staatlichkeit*]. The future would show whether after a few decades the cordon of settlement would have to be pushed further forward.

On 17 October 1939, Hitler informed Keitel of his views on the future government of Poland:

646

1. The armed forces should welcome the opportunity of avoiding having to deal with administrative questions in Poland. On principle there cannot be two administrations.
2. Poland is to be made autonomous. It will be neither a separate part of the German Reich nor an administrative district of the Reich.
3. It is not the task of the administration to turn Poland into a model province or a model state in accordance with the principles of German order; nor is it its task to put the country on a sound basis economically and financially. The Polish intelligentsia must be prevented from forming itself into a ruling class. The standard of living in the country is to remain low; it is of use to us only as a reservoir of labour. Poles too are to be used for the administration of the country. But the formation of national political groups will not be permitted.
4. The administration must work on its own responsibility and must not be dependent on Berlin. We do not want to do anything there which we do in the Reich. Responsibility does not rest with the Berlin ministries, since no German administrative unit is involved. The accomplishment of this task will involve a hard ethnic struggle [*Volkstumskampf*] which will not permit any legal restrictions. The methods will be incompatible with the principles which we otherwise adhere to. . . .
5. *Our interests are as follows:* The territory is important to us from a military point of view as an advanced jumping-off point and can be used for the strategic concentration of troops. To that end, the railways, roads and lines of communications are to be kept in order and utilized for our purposes. Any tendencies toward stabilizing the situation in Poland are to be suppressed. 'Polish muddle' must be allowed to flourish. The fact that we are governing the territory should enable us to purify the Reich territory also of Jews and Polacks. Collaboration with the new *Reichsgaue* (Posen and West Prussia) only for resettlement purposes (compare Himmler mission). Purpose: Shrewdness and severity must be the maxims in this ethnic struggle in order to spare us from having to go into battle again on account of this country.

The key role in the racial and settlement policies in Poland was played by the SS. On 25 August 1939, a special section 'Operation Tannenberg' had been set up in the Security Police Main Office to organize five special task forces (*Einsatzgruppen*). One was allocated to each army and each was subdivided into four *Einsatzkommandos* of 100–150 men allocated to the Army corps. Their role was defined as follows: 'The task of the *Einsatzkommandos* of the Security Police is to combat all anti-Reich and anti-German elements in enemy territory behind the front line troops.' They were specifically instructed to arrest all persons 'who opposed the measures of official German agencies or are obviously intending to provoke unrest and, on the basis of their position and prestige are in a position to do so.'[6] The following two documents contain excerpts from Heydrich's instructions to the Security Police and SD on its task in Poland issued at meetings in the Reich Security Main office (RSHA). The first is dated 7 September 1939:

647

. . . A Protectorate-type government is not envisaged for Poland but rather a purely German administration. This will correspondingly require a major commitment of the Gestapo and criminal police . . .

The leadership class in Poland is to be rendered harmless as far as possible. The remaining inferior population will not be given any particular schools but will be suppressed in some way or other.

5. The expulsion of the Polish Jews from Germany must be carried out, including those Jews who came from Poland and have meanwhile acquired German citizenship.

The transfer of prisoners is causing problems. It has been decided that the leadership class, which must on no account remain in Poland, will be put in German concentration camps, while temporary concentration camps will be established on the frontier behind the *Einsatzgruppen* for the lower classes who can then be deported to the remaining part of Poland immediately.

Two days later, Heydrich summed up his policy to Lieut-General Carl-Heinrich von Stülpnagel by telling him that 'the nobility, the clerics (*Popen*) and the Jews must be killed'.[7] The following document is dated 27 September 1939:

648

. . . It is initially envisaged that developments in what was previously Poland will take the form of the creation of German Gaus in the former German provinces and, in addition, the creation of a Gau with a foreign population with its capital in Cracow. Seyss-Inquart[8] is envisaged as the possible leader of this Gau. This foreign Gau will lie outside the new East Wall which is to be created. The East Wall will contain all the German provinces and the foreigh Gau will be a virtual no-man's-land in front of it. The RFSS will be appointed as settlement commissioner

---

[6] See *Deutschland im Zweiten Weltkrieg* Bd. 1. (Berlin (East) 1975), p. 187.

[7] See *Deutschland im Zweiten Weltkrieg* Bd. 1. *op. cit.*, p. 186.

[8] Dr Arthur Seyss-Inquart had played a leading role in the Anschluß, see above pp. 700 ff. He was to become Reich Commissioner of the Netherlands 1940–1945 (eds).

for the east. The deportation of the Jews into the foreign Gau, expulsion over the demarcation line, has been approved by the Führer. However, the whole process is to be phased over the period of a year. The solution of the Polish problem—as has frequently been explained—will vary between the leadership section (Polish intelligentsia) and the lower working class Poles. Three per cent of the political leadership at the most is still in the occupied territories. This three per cent must also be rendered harmless and be put in concentration camps. The *Einsatzgruppen* must draw up lists in which the notable leaders are included, and then lists of the middle class: teachers, priests, nobility, legionnaires, returning officers etc. These too must be arrested and deported to the remaining area [i.e. the General Government-to-be] . . . [9]

The leaders of the *Einsatzgruppen*, in particular Schäfer for the industrial area [Upper Silesia] and Damzog for the north east [Danzig and West Prussia], must consider how, on the one hand one can integrate the primitive Poles into the work force while at the same time expelling them. The aim is for the Poles to remain permanently seasonal and migrant workers; their main place of residence must be the district of Cracow.

Himmler's appointment as 'settlement commissioner', forecast by Heydrich, was formally announced in the Decree of the Führer and Reich Chancellor for the Strengthening of German Nationality of 7 October 1939:

649

The consequences of the Versailles Treaty have been removed in Europe. As a result, the Greater German Reich now has the opportunity of admitting into its territory and resettling those Germans who were hitherto obliged to live abroad, and to arrange the settlement of the population groups within its sphere of interest so as to improve the lines of demarcation between them. I entrust the *Reichsführer SS* with execution of this task according to the following regulations:

§1. In accordance with my directives the Reichsführer has the duty:

(1) of repatriating persons of Germanic race or nationality resident abroad who are considered suitable for permanent return to the Reich;

(2) of eliminating the harmful influence of those alien sections of the population which constitute a danger to the Reich and German national community;

(3) of forming new German settlements by the transfer of population and, in particular, by settling persons of German race or nationality returning from abroad.

The *Reichsführer SS* is authorized to issue such general regulations and to take such administrative measures as may be necessary to carry out these duties.

In order to carry out the tasks assigned to him in §1 (2) above the *Reichsführer SS* can assign specific areas of settlement to the sections of the population concerned . . .

---

[9] For this section of the document which refers to the Jews, see below p. 1053 (eds).

§3. The tasks assigned to the *Reichsführer* with regard to the reorganization of the German peasantry will be carried out by the Reich Minister of Food and Agriculture following the general directives of the *Reichsführer SS*.

For other matters connected with his duties, the *Reichsführer SS* will make use within the territory of the German Reich of the existing authorities and institutions of the Reich, the states and the municipalities as well as other public bodies and the existing settlement associations. . . .

Himmler's appointment as Reich Commissioner for the Strengthening of German Nationality (RKFDV) reflected the fact that he had already been given the responsibility for resettling the Germans of South Tyrol, which had been agreed with Italy in June 1939, and had already established a staff to carry it out under SS *Brigadeführer* Ulrich Greifelt. Moreover, the task would also involve extensive use of his police apparatus.

Himmler saw his role as RKFDV as involving two main tasks. On the one hand, he maintained that 'the removal of all persons of alien race from the annexed eastern territories is one of the most important aims to be achieved in the German east'. However, on the other hand, he believed it was equally vital to regain German 'blood' which had been 'lost' through intermarriage with inferior races: 'It is therefore an absolute national-political necessity to "screen" the incorporated eastern territories and later also the General Government for such persons of Teutonic blood in order to make this lost German blood available again to our own people'.[10] The guidelines which governed the general settlement policy of the Staff Main Office of the RKFDV were defined in the introduction to a book published in 1940 with the title 'Basic Principles, Guidelines, and Directives for Manpower Deployment (*Menscheneinsatz*)' from which the following excerpt is taken:

650

. . . The sections of German nation living beyond the borders of the Reich will be relieved of their role of acting as a cultural fertiliser for foreign states . . . The Führer's call to various ethnic groups to return to the Reich represents a complete revolution in German policy regarding the national issue. The previous and often romantic enthusiasm for the fact that Germans were scattered throughout the world has given place to the demand for the return of valuable German blood in order to strengthen the Reich. However, those Germans who return will be required to adapt themselves organically [!] to the discipline and order of the Greater German Reich. We cannot and will not allow a situation to continue in the German east

[10] See N. Rich, *Hitler's War Aims, op. cit.* Vol. 2. p. 80.

where, for example, a Baltic German group exists side by side with Volhynian and Bessarabian German groups. The concept of Baltic, Volhynian and Bessarabian Germans must, on the contrary, be eliminated as soon as possible . . .

As far as SS policy in Poland was concerned, on 15 May 1940, Himmler produced a memorandum entitled 'Some Thoughts on the Treatment of the Alien Population in the East' which was endorsed by Hitler:

651

In our treatment of the foreign ethnic groups in the east we must endeavour to recognize and foster as many such individual groups as possible, i.e. apart from the Poles and the Jews, the Ukrainians, White Russians, Gorales, Lemkes, and Kaschubians. If there are any more ethnic splinter groups to be found then these too.

I mean to say that we not only have a major interest in not uniting the population in the east but, on the contrary, we need to divide them up into as many parts and splinter groups as possible.

Also, within the ethnic groups themselves we have no interest in leading them to unity and greatness or in gradually giving them a sense of national consciousness and national culture, but rather in dissolving them into countless little splinter groups and particles.

We will of course use the members of all these ethnic groups and, in particular, the small ones, as policemen and mayors.

The senior positions in such ethnic groups must be restricted to mayors and local police authorities; in the case of the Gorales, the individual chieftains and tribal elders, who are in any case always feuding. There must not be a concentration of these groups at a higher level because only the dissolution of this ethnic mishmash of fifteen million in the General Government and eight million in the eastern provinces will enable us to carry through the racial screening process which must form the basis of our concern to fish out the racially valuable people from this mishmash, take them to Germany and assimilate them there.

For example, within a few years—I imagine four or five—the term 'Kaschubian' must have been forgotten because there will no longer be a Kaschubian people (that also applies, in particular, to the West Prussians). I hope to see the term 'Jew' completely eliminated through the possibility of a large-scale emigration of all Jews to Africa or to some colony. Over a slightly longer period it must also be possible to ensure the disappearence of the ethnic categories of Ukranians, Gorales, and Lemkes from our territory. Making allowances for the larger area involved, what has been said about these splinter groups should also apply in the case of the Poles.

A basic issue as far as the solution of all these questions is concerned is the question of schools, and therefore that of sifting and assessing the young people. The non-German population of the eastern territories must not receive any education higher than that of an elementary school with four forms. The objective of this elementary school must simply be to teach: simple arithmetic up to 500 at the most, how to write one's name, and to teach that it is God's commandment to be obedient to the Germans and to be honest, hard working, and well-behaved. I consider it unnecessary to teach reading.

There must be no schools at all in the east apart from this type of school. Parents who wish to provide their children with a better education both in the elementary school and later in a secondary school, must make an application to the Higher SS and Police Leader. The decision on the application will be primarily determined by whether or not the child is racially first class and comes up to our requirements. If we recognise such a child as being of our blood then the parents will be informed that the child will be placed in a school in Germany and will remain in Germany indefinitely.

However cruel and tragic each individual case may be, if one rejects the Bolshevik method of physically exterminating a people as fundamentally un-German and impossible, then this method is the mildest and best one.

The parents of these children of good blood will be given the choice of either giving up their child—they will then probably not produce any more children and so remove the danger that this sub-human people of the east might acquire a leader class from such people of good blood, which would be dangerous for us because they would be our equals—or they would have to agree to go to Germany and become loyal citizens there. One has a strong weapon against them in their love of their child whose future and education would depend on the loyalty of the parents.

Apart from the examination of the petitions which parents put forward for a better education, all 6–10 year-olds will be sifted each year to sort out those with valuable blood and those with worthless blood. Those who are selected as valuable will be treated in the same way as the children who are admitted on the basis of the approval of the parents' petition.

I consider it obvious both from an emotional and from a rational point of view that the moment the children and parents arrive in Germany they should not be treated in school and life as outcasts but—after changing their names and despite being treated with vigilance—should be integrated into German life on the basis of trust. The children must not be made to feel rejected; for, after all, we believe in our own blood, which through the mistakes of German history has flowed into a foreign nation, and are convinced that our ideology and ideals will find an echo in the souls of these children which are racially identical to our own. In this respect, above all, teachers and HJ leaders must change their tune and we must never again make the same mistake as was made in the past with the people of Alsace and Lorraine of, on the one hand, wanting to win them over to become Germans and, on the other hand, of using every opportunity to hurt their pride, offend their sense of honour, and undermine their human dignity through mistrust and abuse. Abusive expressions such as 'Polack' or 'Ukrainian' and such like must be out of the question.

Education must be carried out in a pre-school and after four forms one can then decide whether to let the children continue in a German elementary school or whether they should be transferred to a National Political Educational Institution [Napola].[11]

After these measures have been systematically implemented during the next ten years, the population of the General Government will inevitably consist of an inferior remnant, which will include all the people who have been deported to the eastern provinces as well as from those parts of the German Reich which contain the same racial and human type (for example parts containing the Sorbs and Wends).

This population will be available as a leaderless labouring class and provide Germany with migrant and seasonal workers for special work projects (road building, quarries, construction); even then they will get more to eat and have more from life than under Polish rule and, while lacking in culture themselves, under the strict, consistent and fair leadership of the German people will be called upon to participate in their eternal cultural deeds and monuments and, in view of the amount of heavy labour required to produce them, may even make them feasible at all.

Although the officials of the SS-Police and the Nazi Party were to be the main instruments of Nazi racial imperialism, the regime was anxious to develop the correct *Herrenmensch* attitudes towards their new colonial subjects among the German people as a whole. In this they benefited from a long tradition of German ethnic arrogance towards the Poles reflected, for example, in the term *Polnische Wirtschaft* ('Polish muddle' or shambles), and somewhat reminiscent of traditional British attitudes towards the Irish. In January 1940 the Press Information Service of the Reich Propaganda Ministry issued the following directive to German newspapers:

652

. . . The attention of the Press is drawn to the fact that articles dealing with Poland must express the instinctive revulsion of the German people against everything which is Polish. Articles and news items must be composed in such a way as to transform this instinctive revulsion into a lasting revulsion. This should be done, not by special articles, but by scattering phrases here and there in the text.

Similarly, it must be suggested to the reader that Gypsies, Jews, and Poles ought to be treated on the same level. This is particularly important since there is no doubt that for a long time we shall be obliged to employ Poles as agricultural labourers in Germany. It is, therefore, desirable to build up a defensive front in the heart of the German nation.

---

[11] See Vol. 2, p. 435.

Further, in composing news items, the principle must be adopted that everything representing civilization and economic activity in Polish territory is of German origin.

It will be as well also to avoid speaking in sympathetic terms of Polish prisoners of war. It is preferable to say nothing at all about them in the Press.

(iii) The 'Incorporated Territories'

The decision to incorporate large areas of Poland into the Reich posed the major problem of what to do about the Poles living in those areas who, after all, formed the vast majority of the population. In both *Mein Kampf* and his so-called 'Second Book' of 1928 Hitler had contemptuously rejected traditional policies of assimilation through education and discrimination, which had been practised by both Germans and Poles in these areas since the late nineteenth century. Both he and Himmler wished to clear the Poles and Jews out of the area and replace them with German settlers (germanization of the land rather than the people). This objective determined the first phase of Nazi policy and, even when it came up against insuperable obstacles during wartime, remained their long-term goal. Agreements were reached with Estonia on 15 October 1939 and with Latvia on 30 October for the repatriation of the Baltic Germans to the Reich, and with Russia, on 3 November, to repatriate the Germans in the Russian-occupied part of Poland. The pressing need to resettle the 55,000 ethnic Germans from Latvia, the 15,000 from Estonia, and the 135,000 from eastern Poland provided an added impetus to the policy of expelling Poles and Jews from the incorporated territory upon which the Nazis were already determined.

The autumn and winter of 1939–40 saw a period of more or less unrestrained terror in Poland, particularly in the 'incorporated territories'. It was facilitated by the decision to end military government before a proper civilian administration was in place. The legal and administrative vacuum thereby created was filled by Nazi Party activists and by the *Einsatzgruppen* of the Security Police and SD which, though disbanded on 20 November 1939, were replaced by permanent Security Police headquarters in the major towns. Both the Party and the SD had already established close links with ethnic German groups in the area and now encouraged them to form so-called 'self defence' organizations. These vigilante groups operating under SS leadership were particularly active in West Prussia where nationalist rivalries between Germans and Poles were of long standing. Moreover, these tensions had been intensified by incidents which occurred after the outbreak of war in which some 5,400 ethnic Germans had been killed for allegedly assisting the invaders. These incidents were fully exploited by Nazi propaganda and Hitler had personally ordered that, in place of the official figure of 5,400 casualties, the figure of 58,000 ethnic Germans killed or missing should be published. The 'self defence organizations' exploited the opportunity to drive out their Polish rivals seizing their property, farms, businesses, and professional practices. These expulsions through informal terror coincided with official deportation programmes organized by the SS,

Responsibility for the detailed organization of the deportations in the field lay with the Higher SS and Police Leaders (HSSPF) and Commanders of the Security Police and SD in the Reich Gaus, while the overall planning was handled by the RSHA in Berlin. In December 1939, Heydrich officially appointed Adolf Eichmann who, as the head of the Jewish desk (B 4) in Amt IV (Gestapo) of the RSHA, was already responsible for the expulsion of the Jews from Austria and the Reich Protectorate of Bohemia and Moravia, to organize the deportation of the Jews and Poles from the incorporated territories. In May 1940, the RSHA established a 'Central Resettlement Office' (*Umwandererstelle*-UWZ) in Łódź, which organized the deportation programme from the Warthegau which was by far the largest. The following document contains excerpts from the directives of the HSSPF in *Reichsgau* Posen [Warthegau] for the 'deportation of Jews and Poles' dated 12 November 1939:

653

1. In his capacity as Reich Commissioner for the Strengthening of German Nationality the *Reichsführer* SS and Chief of the German Police has ordered that the following people should be deported from the former Polish territories which now belong to the Reich:
(*a*) all Jews and
(*b*) all those Poles who either belong to the intelligentsia or because of their Polish nationalist attitudes might constitute a threat to the strengthening of German nationhood. Criminal elements are to be treated in the same way.
The deportation is intended (*a*) to purge and secure the new German territories. (*b*) to create accommodation and employment opportunities for the immigrant ethnic Germans. These goals must definitely be achieved by the evacuation action without any regard for other considerations.
2. It was decided at a meeting with the Governor General in Cracow that the deportations from the Warthegau will initially include 200,000 Poles and 100,000 Jews during the period 15 November 1939–28 February 1940.
3. The reception area for those being deported from here will be the territory south of Warsaw and Lublin.
4. In this first action all Jews from the country districts are to be deported and, in addition, at least 2,000 Poles from the smallest districts and a correspondingly larger number from the larger ones . . .

The area will only have been effectively purged and secured when the intellectual leadership, the whole of the intelligentsia, as well as all political and criminal elements have been removed. All those who are politically aware are also to be deported. In the case of the intellegentsia, deportation is not restricted to those involved in actual political or anti-German activity.

In addition, full consideration must be given to the need to create accommodation and jobs for the immigrant Reich and ethnic Germans. All aspects must be taken into account in determining which persons and circles are politically dangerous: among other things, membership of national political organisations, of political parties of every persuasion, of Catholic clerical and lay circles etc.

7. The deportations will as far as possible proceed in such a way that comprehensive expulsions are carried out district by district. Transport will be solely by the Reich railways. The available trains can carry 900–1,000 persons . . . Each train must be provided with an escort unit composed of six police officials and thirty self-defence people . . .

9. The Poles and Jews to be deported may take with them:

(*a*) Provisions for the period of their stay in the deportation camp and their rail journey.

(*b*) A suitcase with essential clothing and equipment.

(*c*) Cash solely in Polish currency up to a limit of 200 Zl. per head. It is forbidden to take bonds, foreign exchange, precious metals, jewelry, art objects. In the case of Jews, the amount of everything which they are permitted to take with them must be considerably reduced. The amount of cash must not exceed 50 Zl. per head.

The *Oberbürgermeister* and *Landräte* must secure the cash, arrears, and bank accounts, which exceed the amount permitted to be taken, by transferring them to the Reich Governor's deposit account at the *Bank für Handel and Gewerbe* in Posen.

12. The *Oberbürgermeister* and *Landräte* are responsible for the evacuation measures in their areas. All agencies of the Party and the State are required to provide all necessary assistance and cooperation in the execution of this historic task which has been set by the Führer.

The following is an account of her deportation to the General Government by a Mrs J. K. of Gdynia in West Prussia:

654

On 17 October 1939, at 8 a.m. I heard someone knocking at the door of my flat. As my maid was afraid to open it, I went to the door myself. I found there two German gendarmes, who roughly told me that in a few hours I had to be ready to travel with my children and everybody in the house. When I said that I had small children, that my husband was a prisoner of war, and that I could not get ready to travel in so short a time, the gendarmes answered that not only must I be ready, but that the flat must be swept, the plates and dishes washed and the keys left in the cupboards, so that the Germans who were to live in my house should have no trouble. In so many words, they further declared that I was entitled to take with me only one suit-case of not more than fifty kilograms in weight and a small handbag with food for a few days.

At 12 noon they came again and ordered us to go out in front of the house. Similar groups of people were standing in front of all the houses. After some hours' waiting, military lorries drove up and they packed us in one after the other, shouting at us rudely and also striking us. Then they took us to the railway station, but only in the evening did they pack us into filthy goods trucks, the doors of which were then bolted and sealed. In these trucks, most of which were packed with forty people, we spent three days, without any possibility of getting out. I hereby affirm that in my truck there were six children of under ten years of age and two old men, and that we were not given any straw, or any drinking utensils, that we had to satisfy our natural needs in the tightly packed truck, and that if there were no deaths in our transport it was only because it was still comparatively warm and we spent only three days on the journey. We were unloaded, half dead at Czestochowa,[12] where the local population gave us immediate help, but the German soldiers who opened the truck exclaimed 'What! Are these Polish swine still alive?'

Later transports of Poles and Jews in the dead of winter suffered even worse with many deaths.[13] Moreover, many, particularly members of the upper classes and the intelligentsia, were simply shot out of hand.

The Army leadership in Poland became increasingly concerned about this terror. The attitude of sections of the Army is apparent in the following excerpts from a memorandum, dated 6 February 1940, prepared by Colonel-General Blaskowitz, commander of the Ober-Ost military region for a visit by the Army C in C. It was the second such memorandum by Blaskowitz, a man who was not one of the leading opponents of Hitler among the generals, being a typical professional soldier of limited horizons. His protest cost him a Field-Marshal's baton and eventually his command.

655

. . .

It is misguided to slaughter tens of thousands of Jews and Poles as is happening at present; because, in view of the huge population neither the concept of a Polish State nor the Jews will be eliminated by doing so. On the contrary, the way in which this slaughter is being carried out is causing great damage; it is complicating the problems and making them much more dangerous than they would have been with a considered and systematic approach. The consequences are:

(a) Enemy propaganda is provided with material which could nowhere have been more effectively devised. It is true that what the foreign radio stations have broad-

[12] In the General Government. (eds).

[13] See below pp. 1057–8.

cast so far is only a tiny fraction of what has happened in reality. But we must reckon that the clamour of the outside world will continually increase and cause great political damage, particularly since the atrocities have actually occurred and cannot be disproved.

(b) The acts of violence against the Jews which occur in full view of the public inspire among the religious Poles not only deep disgust but also great pity for the Jewish population, to which up to now the Poles were more or less hostile. In a very short time we shall reach the point at which our arch-enemies in the eastern sphere—the Pole and the Jew, who in addition will receive the particular support of the Catholic Church—will, in their hatred against their tormentors, combine against Germany right along the line.

(c) The role of the armed forces, who are compelled impotently to watch this crime and whose reputation, particularly with the Polish population, suffers irreparable harm, need not be referred to again.

(d) But the worst damage which will accrue to the German nation from the present situation is the brutalization and moral debasement which, in a very short time, will spread like a plague among valuable German manpower.

If high officials of the SS and police demand acts of violence and brutality and praise them publicly, then in a very short time we shall be faced with the rule of the thug. Like-minded people and those with warped characters will very soon come together so that, as is now the case in Poland, they can give full expression to their animal and pathological instincts. It is hardly possible to keep them any longer in check, since they can well believe themselves officially authorized and justified in committing any act of cruelty.

The only way of resisting this epidemic is to subordinate those who are guilty and their followers to the military leadership and courts as quickly as possible.

The C.-in-C. of the southern section of the front, General of the Infantry Ulex, expressed himself on 2 February 1940 as follows:

To the C.-in-C. East
Spala

The acts of violence by the police forces, which have increased recently, demonstrate a quite incredible lack of human and moral feeling, so that it can be called sheer brutalization. And even so I believe that my headquarters only hears of a small number of the acts of violence occurring.

It seems as if the superiors privately approve of this activity and do not wish to intervene.

I see the only way out of this ignoble situation, which besmirches the honour of the whole German nation, in the recall and disbanding at a stroke of all the police units, including all their superior officers and all those leaders in the departments of the 'General Government' who have witnessed these acts of violence for months, and their replacement by sound honourable units.

[signed] ULEX

. . .

The attitude of the troops to the SS and police alternates between abhorrence and hatred. Every soldier feels repelled and revolted by these crimes which are being perpetrated in Poland by nationals of the Reich and representatives of the State authority. He does not understand how such things can happen with impunity, particularly since they occur, so to speak, under his protection.

Every police search and confiscation is accompanied by a tendency for those of the police involved to rob and plunder. It is clearly the normal custom for confiscated articles to be distributed among the police and SS units.

In a conference with the Governor-General on 23 January 1940, Major-General Ruhrmann reported to the representative of the Four-Year Plan that his skilful director of external departments, a certain Captain Schuh in the cavalry, had succeeded in getting the SS to give up large quantities of watches and gold objects.

Considering such a state of affairs it is naturally not surprising that the individual uses every opportunity to enrich himself. He can do this with no danger to himself, since if everybody steals the individual thief need fear no punishment. There is no doubt that the defenceless Polish population, who have to look on at these crimes and are driven to despair by them, will give fanatical support to any revolt or movement of vengeance. Many people who have never thought of revolt before will use every opportunity of organizing one and will flock to support it, determined to fight. The large peasant population particularly, which, if treated reasonably and objectively by the German administration, would have worked calmly and peacefully for us, is being driven by force, so to speak, into the enemy camp.

The resettlement programme is causing especial and growing discontent throughout the country. It is obvious that the starving population, which is fighting for its existence, can only observe with the greatest concern how the masses of those being resettled are left to find refuge with them completely penniless and, so to speak, naked and hungry.

It is only too understandable that these feelings reach a pitch of uncontrolled hatred at the numbers of children dying of starvation on every transport and the wagons of people frozen to death.

The idea that one can intimidate the Polish population by terrorism and rub their noses in the dirt will certainly prove to be false. This people's capacity for enduring suffering is too great for that . . .

Hitler was unimpressed by these arguments. On 18 November 1939, his adjutant, Major Engel, had recorded in his diary Hitler's reaction to Blaskowitz's first memorandum as follows:

656

Siewert asks me to come and see him and hands over to me a memorandum from General Blaskowitz concerning conditions in Poland: very great concern about illegal shootings, arrests, and confiscations, worries about the discipline of the troops who witness these things with their own eyes, local discussions with SD and Gestapo without success—they refer to instructions from the SS leadership. Request to reestablish conditions of legality, above all that executions should only be carried out after due process of law. Place the memorandum, which is very moderately phrased, before the Führer that very afternoon. At first, he reads it calmly, but then once again starts making serious criticisms of the 'childish attitudes' among the Army leadership; one can't fight a war with Salvation Army methods. This also confirms his long-held aversion to General Bl. whom he had never trusted. He had also been opposed to his appointment to command an army and thinks that Bl. should be relieved of his command since he is unsuitable. I inform C-in-C. Army and Sievert, also Oqu.IV . . .

Himmler was later obliged to defend the SS policies to the Army leadership in a lecture. He referred to his commission from the Führer and asserted the need to pursue harsh policies in order to deal with the threat of subversion by Polish nationalists and Jewish Bolshevism. The Army washed its hands of the matter and turned with relief to preparing the operations in the west. Moreover, the tremendous success of those operations helped to overcome any residual doubts. Thus, on 22 July, 1940, General von Küchler, the Commander of the XVIII Army, which had just been transferred to the east, issued the following order:

657

. . . 2. I wish to emphasize the necessity of ensuring that all soldiers of the Army and, in particular, the officers refrain from any criticism of the struggle being waged with the population in the General Government, for example the treatment of the Polish minorities, the Jews, and Church matters. The achievement of a final solution of this ethnic struggle, which has been raging for centuries along our eastern frontier, requires particularly tough measures.

The carrying out of this ethnic struggle has been delegated to certain units of the Party and the State.

Soldiers must keep away from these matters in which other units are involved. That means that they must also not criticize these activities.

It appears extremely important to issue instructions concerning this problem immediately to those soldiers who have only recently been transferred from the west to the east, since otherwise they may hear rumours and receive false information concerning the aim and significance of this struggle.

Quartermaster

I request senior officers to inform all officers and officials of their units of the contents of the Commander's order immediately after their arrival in the east.

However, the deportation of Poles and Jews to the General Government met with increasing opposition. It came both from the Governor General, Hans Frank, who complained about the problems caused by having to absorb thousands of homeless and penniless people in an area which, contrary to Nazi myth, was in fact already well populated, and from the *Wehrmacht* Armaments Office, which objected to the economic disruption being caused. These complaints met with a sympathetic response from Göring. He intervened in February 1940 to insist that deportations to the General Government should be restricted to those necessary for the resettlement of the immigrant ethnic Germans and to those Poles who were not required for work in the Reich. These objections and growing transport problems slowed down the operation. However, the SS were determined to continue the resettlement programme and Himmler increased the pressure by agreeing in May 1940 to repatriate 30,000 ethnic Germans from the General Government (Cholm) and 50,000 from Lithuania after its annexation by the Soviet Union in June. Then, in the autumn of 1940, he accepted 135,000 more ethnic Germans from Soviet-occupied Bessarabia and North Bukhovina and another 80,000 from Old Romania.

According to RKFDV statistics, by May 1943 almost 800,000 ethnic Germans had arrived from the East, of whom 408,000 had been successfully re-settled in the incorporated territories and 74,000 in the *Altreich*. However, well over 300,000 had not been resettled or were not regarded worthy of resettlement and were languishing in camps. For, eventually, these ethnic Germans were subjected to racial selection procedures by special 'assessors' (*Eignungsprüfer*) from the SS Race and Settlement Main Office, (Ru.SHA), who were attached to the Central Office for Immigration (EWZ) of the Security Police in Łódź. These assessors were mainly SS officers who were ineligible for front-line duties and had undergone a four-week crash course in biology, anthropology, and eugenics. The Ru.SHA issued guidelines for its racial selection procedures which involved filling out R (race) cards according to physical, racial, and sociological criteria. A medical examination looked for signs of hereditary illness or deformity. The medical examination involved 21 different physical characteristics, of which 15 referred to the head, mainly the face. The following criteria were involved in the final assessment:

658

Assessment of Physique

9. Ideal figure. 8. Excellently developed physique. 7. Very well-developed physique. 6. Well-developed physique. 5. Satisfactory physique. 4. Barely satisfactory physique. 3. Unsatisfactory physique. 2. Inadequate physique. 1. Malformed physique.

Racial Assessment

The racial assessment involves five levels which have also been drawn up on the basis of the nordic race being the most important for the German people. They are as follows:

(*a*) Purely nordic, purely phalian or nordic-phalian. (*b*) Predominantly nordic or predominantly phalian, with a slight strain of one of the other European races. (*c*) A balanced cross of the nordic, phalian or dinarian race with elements of the other European races. (*d*) *Ostisch*, purely *ostisch*, purely east Baltic, further unbalanced crosses of these races, also unbalanced crosses of these races with a small nordic phalian and dinarian element. (*e*) Non-European blood strain.

Overall Assessment

The overall assessment is divided into six grades:
AI Very suitable
AII Suitable
AIII In general suitable
BI No longer suitable (barely suitable)
BII Unsuitable
C Ethnically or biologically unsuitable
The overall assessment is by no means the sum of the physical and racial judgments but is the expression of the evaluation of the whole personality of the individual being assessed. A person whose physical and racial assessment is very good can receive a negative overall assessment if defects of intellect, character or of a hereditary nature are present.

General Assessment of the Family (Sippe)

Since the racial assessment is concerned with an overall assessment of a person's hereditary characteristics, a final judgement can only be made after a consideration of the whole family: parents, children, and brothers and sisters. The family assessment has proved particularly necessary for the work involved in strengthening the German nationality in terms both of the bringing in of ethnic Germans and of the integration of hitherto ethnically alien persons into the German nation.

Family Assessment

Group I Very suitable, i.e. desirable as additional population. (These are the pure or predominantly nordic and phalian types, who are first class in terms of their genetic health and social efficiency. They are equivalent to aAI-bAII).

Group II Suitable, i.e. acceptable as additional population. (These are the balanced crosses with a significant proportion of nordic, phalian or dinaric race, with a small addition of other European races, who are satisfactory in terms of their genetic health and social efficiency. They are equivalent to bAIII-cAIII).

Group III+ Barely suitable, i.e. just acceptable as additional population. (These are the crosses in which *westisch, ostisch*, or east Baltic racial strains are predominant, but in whom elements of the nordic, phalian, or dinarian race are still clearly visible and who are therefore considered to be just adequate as a balanced cross. It is a precondition for inclusion in this category that the respective persons and families are genetically very healthy and socially very efficient. They fall between cAIII and c/dBI).

Group III Unsuitable, i.e. undesirable as additional population. (These are the crosses in which *westisch*, *ostisch*, or east Baltic racial strains are predominant, in which however nordic, phalian, or dinarian racial elements are still faintly discernible. Additional confirmation for this judgement is provided when the genetic health of the persons concerned is poor or when they are of below average social efficiency. They are equivalent to c/dBI).

Group IV Completely unsuitable, i.e. unacceptable as additional population. (These include racially pure *ostisch* and east Baltic types, unbalanced crosses of the European races, as well as those with serious hereditary defects and people or families who are socially weak or incompetent). They are equivalent to dBII.

Group IVF Totally unacceptable as additional population. (These are racial crosses with non-European races and alien races.)

After the war, the man responsible for training the assessors, SS *Hauptsturmführer* Heinrich Ruebel recalled:

659

Initially, the assessors made their assessment purely on the basis of a person's physical, i.e. external features. When Schwalm took over the training of the assessors he insisted on including in the evaluation not only a person's purely physical features, but also his character, his intelligence, his achievements both personal and social and whatever psychological characteristics could be determined . . . He tried to make a psychological assessment of the person being examined through conversations, through questions about his or her family, job, particular interests politics etc. When he had formed a certain impression of the person concerned, he went on to look at the actual physical characteristics—the anthropological characteristics such as shape of head, shape of face, colour of eyes, colour of hair, the proportions of the body, physical size. The assessor included in his final assessment these various impressions, together with the psychological impressions, the racial assessment and what he had gathered from the documentation about the personal achievements of the person concerned, his performance in his career, his diligence etc.

In order to make room for the ethnic Germans who were being resettled in the incorporated territories, by the end of 1940, 261,517 Poles had been deported to the General Government from Warthegau, 17,413 from Upper Silesia, 31,000 from Danzig-West Prussia, and 15,000 from Zichenau—an overall total of nearly 325,000. The SS planned another massive deportation operation for 1941. However, the build-up for Operation Barbarossa imposed such heavy demands on the transport system and on accommodation in the General Government that the chief of *Amt* IV in the RSHA

(Gestapo), Heinrich Müller, was obliged to impose a ban on further deportations to the General Government from 16 March 1941, which remained in effect until the end of the war. The result was that the final overall total of Poles deported to the General Government had only increased slightly to 365,000. However, between March 1941 and the end of the war, another 400,000 or so Poles in the incorporated territories were driven from their homes and farms to make way for ethnic Germans without actually being deported. Around one in ten of the Poles in the incorporated territories had been expelled from their homes during the war.

The increasing difficulties involved in deporting Poles from the incorporated territories focused attention on an alternative approach to the problem—the selection of Poles for germanization.[14] Originally, the intention had been to deport nationalist-minded Poles and Jews and then grant the remainder of the Polish population German nationality while reserving Reich citizenship to the ethnic Germans. This was a policy favoured in particular by the Reich Interior Ministry. However, since the issue was closely bound up with Nazi racial ideology, the Nazi Party and the SS soon took the matter into their own hands. In Posen, the local SD specialist for ethnic questions, SS *Obersturmführer* Dr Strickner, persuaded Reich Governor Greiser to establish a new body, on 28 October 1939, to prepare a 'German Ethnic Register' (*Deutsche Volksliste*—DVL) under Dr Karl Coulon, who was simultaneously the head of the NSDAP Gau Office for Ethnic Questions and the Reich Governor's desk officer for ethnic questions. Initially, the DVL contained two categories—A for those ethnic Germans who had shown their commitment to the German nation by participation in ethnic German organizations before the German invasion, and B for those who were clearly of German origin but who had shown no such commitment. In May 1940, however, when it became clear that Hitler himself favoured the incorporation into the German nation of around one million people with Polish connexions, particularly from the ethnically mixed groups of Cashubians, Masurians, and Upper Silesians ('Water Poles') and Poles closely related to Germans, a new C category was introduced for persons of German origin who had come under Polish influence, as well as persons of foreign blood who, having married Germans, had come to adopt German ways and customs. Finally, in January 1941, a fourth D category was introduced for 'renegades' of German blood who 'politically had become completely Polish'. By a decree of 4 March 1941, the DVL system developed in the Warthegau was introduced throughout the incorporated territories with the categories A–D merely changed to

[14] For the following see M. Broszat, *Nationalsozialistische Polenpolitik 1939–1945* (Stuttgart 1961), pp. 118 ff. This chapter is much indebted to this book.

1–4. Different types of citizenship were introduced to correspond with the DVL categories. Those in categories 1–2 were entitled to Reich citizenship with effect from 26 October 1939, though only those in category 1 were to be admitted to the Party. Those in category 3 were only entitled to be German 'state members' while those in category 4 were only entitled to state membership 'on probation'. The members of categories 3 and 4 were removed to the *Altreich* where they underwent a germanization programme after being subjected to assessment by the Ru.SHA assessors. The Ru.SHA leader in Breslau issued the following directives for the germanization of Polish families in 1942:

660

Experience has shown that the Polish leadership, in particular that of the insurgent or resistance movement, have a significant proportion of nordic blood which, in contrast to the otherwise fatalistic slavic strains, has enabled them to take the initiative.

It is for this reason, in particular, that the racially valuable Polish families ought to be creamed off so that at least the next generation of these former carriers of germanic blood can be restored to the German nation through a programme of education in the *Altreich*. However, this requires a careful selection of those families who are to be re-germanized. In proposing people for germanization . . .

1. If possible only propose whole families, since good looking individuals are no proof of the hereditary value of the person with those characteristics.
2. The family must stand out from the rest of the Polish and ethnic German population through its bearing, diligence, cleanliness, and health even when living in deprived circumstances.
3. The family must make a harmonious impression in a racial and psychological sense.
4. Since families which are eligible for germanization must be above the average of the social group to which they belong, the nordic-dinarian blood strain must predominate, i.e. from a layman's point of view these families must in general stand out from the mass through their height.
5. A lack of knowledge of the German language or past political activity are not grounds for objecting to a proposal for germanizaton, since the persons will be placed under police supervision in the *Altreich* and will only receive German nationality on probation.

Those who were approved as 'eligible for re-germanization' were sent to particular locations, allocated jobs and received special identity cards denoting their status. The process was applied to other groups such as

Luxemburgers, Lorrainers etc. A total of 30–50,000 people were 'regermanized' in this way. Those Poles in the incorporated territories who did not come under any of the categories of the DVL were 'placed under German protection'.

An elaborate network of racial selection boards was established to process the applications for membership in the DVL and sort them out into the various categories. Application was compulsory and, as the war turned against Germany, penalties for failure to register were increased, particularly since membership of categories 1–2 involved being drafted into the *Wehrmacht*. Decisions were taken by committees composed of representatives of the Party, the Security Police, the civil administration, and the ethnic German community. Guidelines issued by Himmler on 12 September 1940 suggested the following considerations to be taken into account: racial characteristics, language, religious denomination, school attendance, surnames and Christian names, ethnic German sponsors, and documents such as birth and marriage certificates, military papers etc. On the question of racial characteristics, the guidelines pointed out:

661

Distinctive racial characteristics frequently prove that there were Germans among the applicant's ancestors. But in view of the situation in the Reich Gau, racial characteristics cannot be put forward as reliable bases for judging German nationality. On the contrary, it may be frequently remarked, particularly in the neighbourhood of the town of Posen, that the nordic element among Poles who were politically active is particularly strong. These politically active persons very rarely fail to take a definite stand vis-à-vis the national struggle. One cannot hope to win over these distinctly nordic Poles by any kind of compromise.

In practice, the implementation of the DVL procedures was far less systematic than the legislation and official guidelines suggest. In West Prussia and Upper Silesia, the proportion of ethnic Germans and those with German connections was in general much higher than in the Warthegau. In the case of Upper Silesia, economic considerations too favoured a more relaxed attitude towards ethnic questions, because of its industrial importance. Here, therefore, the policy adopted was far less rigid than in the Warthegau. In West Prussia, in particular, Reich Governor Forster was determined to retain control over ethnic questions in the hands of his Party organization. Moreover, his more pragmatic policy reflected his desire to impress Hitler with the speed with which his Gau had been 'germanized' and also to avoid a long-drawn-out period of uncertainty and tension.

On 14 December 1940, Forster presented a programme which he had drawn up with his specialist for ethnic questions, Wilhelm Löbsack, which gave his district Party leaders a wide discretion within certain broad guidelines and of which the following extracts provide a flavour:

662

. . . In general the germanization action will initially have to be confined to agricultural and factory workers, artisans, and small peasants. However, there will be *individual cases* where one will not be able to keep to this restriction, e.g. in the case of businessmen and tradesmen of German origin who have been partly Polonified [*angepolt*!] . . . The examination of professional competence and efficiency is a valuable tool in assessing a family . . . One will be able to assume the presence of German blood in a family on the basis of typically German abilities and gifts (e.g. technical skills, a sense of how to look after household and farm appliances properly). In this connexion, one should also point out the need to assess personal and domestic hygiene . . .

A post-war report by a member of the *Volksdeutsche Mittelstelle* (VOMI) resettlement organization described his experiences in West Prussia as follows:

663

. . . During the process of germanizing Poles on the basis of the Ethnic Register, there were many cases where whole villages or towns were compulsorily entered in the register according to fixed quotas laid down by Forster. For example, a [Nazi] local branch leader or mayor was instructed to enter eighty per cent of his village in the register although it was at least eighty per cent Polish. When the local branch leader refused, he was reported by the district leader to the Gauleiter, Then the Gauleiter himself came to the village and gave the branch leader such a dressing down in an inn in front of all the Germans and Poles that the branch leader promptly sat down, lined up all the Poles and simply entered them in the Ethnic Register. The following night, the Poles who had been compulsorily registered flung their rejections into the branch leader's or mayor's letter box, declaring themselves to be Poles. I reported this incident to Heinz Bruckner [VOMI]. Bruckner simply said that he had passed on my information to Himmler but that Forster allowed no one to interfere with his ethnic policy but based his position on Hitler's support . . .

Greiser too complained to Himmler about Forster's activities in a letter dated 16 March 1943:

664

. . . Right from the start I avoided trying to win cheap successes by germanizing people who could not provide clear proof of their German origin . . . I fixed a minimum of fifty per cent German ancestry for entry in the German Ethnic Registry . . . This prevented the categories 3 and 4 of the Registry becoming larger in relation to the total number of Germans than the political work of a Gau can cope with without running into serious difficulties. There are around 400,000 Category 1 and 2 cases, which can be regarded as wholly reliable compared with 56,000 Category 3 and 20,000 Category 4 cases . . . As I have frequently pointed out in my discussions with you, my ethnic policy is threatened by that pursued in the Reich Gau Danzig–West Prussia in so far as the policy followed there initially appears to many superficial observers to be more successful . . .

In his reply, Himmler reassured him: 'I am particularly pleased by the healthy ratio between the 3–4 cases and the 1–2 cases in your Gau. I still consider the policy you have followed so far in this connection to be the only feasible one.'[15] Himmler informed Forster in a letter of 26 November 1941 of Hitler's views as follows:

665

I do not wish the Gauleiters of the eastern Gaus to enter into a competition to see who will be the first to report after two or three years: 'My Führer, the Gau has been Germanized'. Instead, I wish to have a population which is racially impeccable and am content if a Gauleiter can report it in ten years time . . . You yourself are such an old National Socialist that you know that one drop of false blood which comes into an individual's veins can never be removed.

In January 1944, out of a population of 9,500,000 in the incorporated territories, around 2.75 million were registered in the DVL; 370,000 were Reich Germans, 353,000 ethnic German immigrants and the remaining six million were Poles. Of those who had been registered in the DVL, some 1.7 million were placed in Categories 1–2, becoming Reich citizens or German nationals automatically. Around the same number, of whom 1.6 million were in West Prussia and Upper Silesia, were placed in Category 3 and could acquire German nationality through individual naturalization. They were subject to various forms of discrimination—exclusion from the civil service and restricted property and civil rights, such as the need to get permission to marry. Thirdly, there were those in Category 4, a small

[15] M. Broszat *Nationalsozialistische Polenpolitik 1939–1945, op. cit*, p. 130, fn. 1.

number, who could acquire German nationality by individual naturalization on probation. However, they were subject to strict supervision by the Party and the Gestapo and their property was subject to confiscation like that of the Poles; and those who were considered 'asocial' 'hereditarily inferior', or politically unreliable were sent to concentration camps. A number of children of parents who were considered ethnically German but for some reason unsuitable for naturalisation were taken from their parents and transferred to the Reich to be brought up as Germans.

Finally, there were the Poles who fell into none of the DVL categories and yet, even after the mass deportations, made up two thirds of the population of the incorporated territories. As merely 'protected members of the German Reich' they were subject to massive discrimination in every sphere of life.

On 10 September 1941 Greiser issued the following directive which confirmed previous oral instructions:

666

Male Poles may not marry until the end of their 28th year, female Poles until the end of their 25th year.

While this unpublished regulation initially applied only to the Warthegau, on 27 May 1943 a new Reich Law concerning Protected Membership of the German Reich confirmed it's general introduction. Poles were also forbidden to marry those in Categories 1–4 of the DVL under a decree of 25 April 1943 confirming earlier regulations. Poles who had sexual relations with German women were condemned to death, for the Poles were no longer regarded as Aryans.

The policy towards Polish schools in the incorporated territories varied somewhat between the various *Reischsgaue* and even within them. In general, however, Polish schools were few and far between and were restricted to the elementary level. Teachers were German as was the language of instruction—at least in theory. In practice many teachers had to use Polish much of the time. Poles were of course not admitted to German schools. The following instructions were issued in the Warthegau on 20 September 1939:

667

1. The aim of putting Polish children through school is in the first instance to educate them to be clean and orderly, to behave decently, and to be obedient to Germans.

2. The language of teaching in the Polish schools is German.
3. The schools will instruct the children in a precisely defined body of knowledge which is geared to the later use of their labour.
Period of instruction limited to two hours per day.

Poles in the incorporated territories were also subjected to humiliating regulations such as the following one issued by the German police chief in the town of Thorn (Toruń) in West Prussia on 27 October 1939:

668

In order to curb the insolent behaviour of a section of the Polish population, I decree as follows:
1. Polish inhabitants of both sexes must stand aside for the representatives of German authority in so far as the latter can be recognized through their uniforms or armbands. The streets belong to the victors and not to the vanquished.
2. Male Polish inhabitants must show their respect to all leading personalities of the State, the Party, and the military forces by uncovering their heads.
3. Poles are forbidden to use the German form of greeting by raising the right hand and crying 'Heil Hitler'.
4. In shops and at market stalls all representatives of German authority, members of their families and all German nationals must be served first before the vanquished.
5. The wearing of Polish school uniforms, of caps with Polish badges etc., as well as the wearing of uniforms or badges by Polish railway and postal officials is prohibited.
6. It is forbidden particularly for young people to gather in the streets and at street corners.
7. Anyone molesting or accosting a German woman or girl will receive exemplary punishment.
8. Polish women who accost or molest Germans will be confined in brothels . . .

On 8 November 1940, the following police order was issued in Posen:

669

§ (1) In those groceries which are marked with the sign 'German Shop' only German customers may be served in the mornings.
(2) Between 6.00 and 9.15 during the period 1 April–30 September and between 7.00 and 9.15 during the period 1 October–31 March market stalls may sell goods only to Germans.
(3) The shopping hours in butchers which are reserved for Germans will be individually fixed by the Food Office of the Gau capital, Posen.

§ 2. (1) It is forbidden to hold back goods from sale during the shopping hours reserved for Germans.
(2) Goods in short supply which arrive in the afternoon may only be sold on the morning of the following day.

§ 3. Poles are forbidden to enter groceries, butchers shops, and market places during the shopping hours reserved to Germans.

§ 4. Germans may shop in groceries, butchers, and in markets throughout the period when they are open for business. They must always be served before Poles.

The Poles in the incorporated territories were also liable to have their property confiscated. Following the ad hoc seizures during the winter months of 1939–40, the practice was formalised in the Decree concerning the Treatment of the Property of Citizens of the Former Polish State of 17 September 1940 from which the following are extracts:

670

§ 1. (1) The property of citizens of the former Polish state within the territory of the Greater German Reich, including the incorporated Eastern Territories is subject to sequestration, trustee administration, and confiscation in accordance with the following provisions.
(2) § 1 (1) does not apply to the property of persons who, in accordance with § 6 of the decree of the Führer and Reich Chancellor relating to the organization and administration of the Eastern Territories dated 8 October 1939[16] . . . have acquired German nationality. The agency having jurisdiction under § 12 may allow further exemptions.
(3) Citizens of Polish nationality of the former Free City of Danzig shall have the status of citizens of the former Polish state.

2. (1) Sequestration shall be ordered in connection with the property of:
(*a*) Jews,
(*b*) Persons who have fled or who are not merely temporarily absent.

(2) Sequestration may be ordered
(*a*) if the property is required for the public welfare particularly in the interests of Reich defence or the strengthening of German nationhood,
(*b*) if the owners or other title holders immigrated into the then territory of the German Reich after 1 October 1918.

(3) Sequestration may be confined to individual items of property.

(4) The following shall as a general rule be exempted from sequestration:
(*a*) movable objects serving exclusively personal needs.
(*b*) cash, bank current and deposit accounts and securities up to a total value of one thousand Reich Marks.

[16] See above pp. 925–6.

§ 3. Property is defined as: immovable and movable objects (together with all accessories), claims, shares, rights and interests of all kinds.

§ 4. (1) In the case of sequestration, those previously entitled to the sequestrated property shall lose the right of disposal over it . . .

(2) Owners or trustees of sequestrated property shall hold and administer it until further notice. Changes in or dispositions relating to the property or the proceeds thereof shall be admissable only within the limits of orderly administration. All other transactions and particularly the disposal of land, shall require the permission of the agency having jurisdiction under § 12.

§ 5. (1) Administration through trustees may be ordered in respect of property subject to sequestration if the orderly administration requires it.

(2) The imposition of trustee administration is equivalent to sequestration . . .

§ 12. (1) The Commissioner for the Four Year Plan—*Haupttreuhandstelle Ost*—shall be competent for measures and decisions based on the present decree . . .

§ 20. (1) A fine and imprisonment or either of these penalties shall be imposed on anyone who, in order to gain a material advantage for himself or another, undertakes to withold a sequestrated item of property from the authorities designated in § 12 or from agents appointed by them, or to prevent, circumvent or impede the effects of the sequestration in any other manner.

(2) In serious cases the penalty is imprisonment. If the culprit acts from opposition to the new political order, or if the case is particularly serious for some other reason, then the death penalty shall be imposed . . .

No compensation was paid for property seized from Poles, transferred to the *Haupttreuhandstelle Ost* and then sold to Germans at knock down prices. Official figures for February 1941 show that the *Hauptreuhandstelle Ost* was administering the following Polish enterprises in February 1941:

671

264 large industrial enterprises;
9,000 medium-sized industrial enterprises;
76,000 small industrial enterprises;
9,120 large commercial firms;
112,000 small commercial firms.

These figures do not include those businesses which had already been transferred to German ownership by February 1941.

Of the four incorporated territories, the Reichsgau Wartheland saw the most ruthless and systematic practice of Nazi policy. Its Reich Governor, Artur Greiser, aimed for it to become a 'model Gau' in which Nazi ideology would be fully realised. 'The National Socialist state is being constructed in the Warthegau' he proudly stated in a reply to a critic of his church policies, and he could count on the full support of Hitler, Himmler, and

Bormann in the pursuit of his goal.[17] Greiser was determined to achieve the segregation and degradation of the Polish population in his Gau. On 22 September 1940, he issued the following directive to the Higher SS and Police Leader in Posen of which copies were sent to all German authorities in the Warthegau:

672

From the very beginning the *Reichsgau* has followed the political line of adopting the principle of the segregation of Germans and Poles. This clear line of segregation is, however, violated in numerous individual cases owing to the close coexistence of the German population in the *Reichsgau* Wartheland with the Polish population, which still considerably exceeds the German population in numbers. It will require a long period of education to achieve a state of affairs in which every German citizen adopts an attitude to Poles which corresponds to our national dignity and the aims of German policy. Until all those belonging to the German community comprehend such an attitude to things Polish as something entirely natural, it is necessary for relations with Poles to be ruthlessly restricted to those which are essential in connection with services performed by the Poles and with regard to economic considerations. Since we are still obliged to use Polish labour, it is impossible to avoid everyday contact between Germans and Poles working in the same sphere. Similarly, owing to the shortage of accommodation and domestic staff, it is not yet possible to avoid having Poles as neighbours or even living in the same house. Thus, it is vital to alert the German population, with the aid of appropriate measures, to the necessity of observing a strict segragation in their personal relations with individuals belonging to the Polish national community.

I consider it highly desirable that you and the departments subordinate to you should place great emphasis on such educative efforts. With reference to the discussions between the Inspector of the Security Police and SD and the head of the State Police and the experts on ethnic questions, I urge you to instruct other departments of equal status in future to observe in general the following guide lines which are in accordance with the policy applied hitherto:

1. Any individuals belonging to the German community who maintain relations with Poles which go beyond those deriving from the performance of services or economic considerations will be placed in protective custody. In serious cases, especially when an individual belonging to the German community has seriously injured the ethnic interests of the Reich through relations with Poles, *he will be transferred to a concentration camp*.

2. *In all cases the maintenance of repeated friendly contacts with Poles must be regarded as failure to observe the prescribed distance*. The only exception is contact with the relatives of a husband of wife belonging to an alien national community. Any one belonging to the German community whom police patrols find associating

[17] M. Broszat, *op. cit.*, p. 168.

in public with members of the alien nationality is obliged, on demand, to prove that his contact with Poles is based on economic requirements.
3. Members of the German community who are caught publicly associating on *friendly terms with Poles without a proper reason for doing so based on a relationship of service may be liable to protective custody*.
4. Members of the German community who enter into physical relations with Poles will be placed in protective custody. Poles of the female sex who permit physical relations with members of the German community may be sent to a brothel. Whether in any particular case, and especially in cases of lesser importance, the objective, i.e. the enlightenment and education of members of the German community can be achieved by instruction and admonition, is left to the discretion of the Inspector of the Security Police and SD or the person authorized by him.
5. In so far as the above remarks apply to youths under the age of sixteen, the prescribed penalties for relations with Poles are to be applied in accordance with their particular level of education. The youth welfare department should be informed of any case in which protective custody is imposed.
6. In addition to the repressive measures indicated in points 1 and 5, officials who permit the violation of these guidelines must be reported for disciplinary action by the appropriate department. In addition, my department must be informed of every such case.

The most notorious examples of Greiser's imposition of Nazi ideology on his Gau were his policies towards the Jews[18] and the Churches. Large numbers of clergy had been arrested and some killed by the *Einsatzgruppen* during the purge of the Polish intelligentsia in the autumn of 1939. Greiser, however, pursued a systematic policy of destroying not just the Polish churches but the German ones as well, using as his henchman August Jäger, who had played a major role in the Nazi attempt to 'coordinate' the German churches in 1933–4. It began with a decree of 14 March 1940 ending the German state's traditional role of providing arrangements to assist the Churches financially. Greiser responded to a complaint from the Superintendent of the Protestant Church in Posen about restrictions on the church with the following illuminating rebuff:

673

. . . As far as the remnants of the Church organization are concerned, according to National Socialist legal concepts the Church has ceased to be a pillar of the German community in terms of public law. The fact that superficially it continues to possess this legal form in the *Altreich* does not represent a new recognition of this legal form on the part of National Socialism but rather the fact that these things

[18] See below p. 1083.

have not yet been reorganised. However, in an area in which as a result of the historic reorganization the old legal form of the Church has disappeared, we will not be giving the remnants of the Church a form which, according to our legal concepts, has already been superceded. Instead, we will only permit its continued existence in the forms which the National Socialist community and state consider acceptable for such organizations.

On 19 September 1941, Greiser moved to give the Church in the Warthegau the form appropriate to 'National Socialist legal conceptions'. With the support of Bormann, who was a hardliner on the religious issue, Greiser bypassed the official legislative procedures in the Reich, ignoring the responsibility of the Reich Church Minister, and issued a decree which restricted the German Protestant and Catholic Churches in the Warthegau to the role of 'private associations', limited membership to adults, and required that future members should only be admitted after a personal declaration, of which the local Registry Office had to be informed. In addition, the decree imposed a strict supervision of the Churches by the Reich Governor's Office. Then, just over a fortnight later, on 5–6 October 1941, the majority of the remaining Polish clergy were arrested and transferred to Dachau. A Church report on the situation in the Diocese of Posen-Gnesen, which covered only part of the Warthegau, for the month of October recorded:

674

Of 681 priests (1939) 22 are not permitted to perform their functions, 120 are in the General Government, 74 have been shot or died in concentration camp, 24 are in exile beyond the Reich borders, 12 are missing, 451 are in prison or concentration camp. Of 431 former churches and 74 chapels, only 30 churches and 1 chapel are still open.

By the end of 1941, Dachau had become the main place of confinement for Polish clergy; of 1,700 clergy imprisoned there almost half did not survive the war.

Many of the ideologically inspired measures were implemented in the Warthegau by the police, which operated largely independently of the local government administration. However, in order to ensure a smooth operation, Greiser endeavoured to appoint hard-line Nazis to local government posts of *Landrat* and *Bürgermeister*. Initially, a number of qualified and moderate civil servants had been appointed to posts in the Warthegau, often as a form of punishment for their failure to get on with Party officials in their previous posts in the *Altreich*. However, these were soon purged on the grounds that they lacked 'the ability to serve in the East'

(*Ostdienstfähigkeit*). One such local government civil servant was Alexander Hohenstein, mayor of the town of Poniatowec near Łódź, January 1941–June 1942. A German nationalist rather than a Nazi, although he was a Party member, Hohenstein followed a well-meaning paternalist policy in his town which soon brought him into conflict with the Party. He relates in his diary how he discussed the situation with the acting *Landrat* on 11 October 1941:

675

Landrat Thieler shares my tentatively expressed view that the Poles are not being correctly treated. He too is of the opinion that the Kaiser's government adopted a much more successful policy towards the Polish population in Posen . . .

'How are your relations with the Party, with your local branch leader?' (he finally asked me). I stalled. Smiling, he understood what I was anxious not to say outright and skirted round with circumlocations.

'Is there any possibility of you being given the district on a permanent basis?' (I asked the Landrat).

'Unfortunately, not. I am a lawyer but not a Party official. Only Party people get given posts as *Landrat* here, in other words district leaders who have been specially trained in the *Ordensburgen*. Purely legal knowledge is no longer sufficient for leading posts. We experts will always be simply the henchmen of political power-holders.'

'That's a pity.'

'A great pity. We merely carry out policy. Our knowledge, our work is considered of secondary importance. The Party is creating a special type of political leader. I lack certain basic character traits for that. You presumably too, mayor.'

I could not deny it but remained guarded. 'I have difficulty in proving my ability to serve in the East. I have the impression that I am only tolerated here.'

'I doubt that, although I am not unaware of your extraordinary tolerance—towards the ethnic aliens.' [*Fremdvölkische* = the official term used for eastern ethnic groups].

Hohenstein was dismissed at the end of May 1942 for maintaining too close contacts with Poles.

(iv) The General Government 1939–1944

(*a*) *The development of German Policy 1939–1944*

Under the Decree on the Administration of the Occupied Polish Territories of 12 October 1939,[19] which came into effect on 26 October, the Governor

[19] See above pp. 926–7.

General, Hans Frank, was given virtual sovereign power within the General Government as Hitler's direct representative. His authority was limited only by the right of the Reich Finance Minister to approve the budget, the power of the Ministerial Council of Reich Defence to issue laws for all territories subordinate to the Reich, the Delegate of the Four Year Plan's authority to issue directives in the economic sphere, and by certain residual military powers of the *Wehrmacht*, including supervision of armaments' industries. Frank clearly demonstrated his own perception of his role by setting up his headquarters in the royal castle of the Wawel in Cracow. He established an 'Office of the General Governor' under a long-time associate, Dr Josef Bühler, as State Secretary, which was divided into twelve 'central departments' corresponding to the Reich Ministries and forming a kind of cabinet. Indeed, on 31 July 1940 Frank issued a decree renaming the 'Office' 'Government'. By a decree of 26 October 1939, he divided the General Government into four administrative districts, (Cracow, Warsaw, Lublin and Radom), headed by District Governors, each of which was subdivided into ten *Kreishauptmannschaften* (urban or rural counties). In 1941, after the invasion of the Soviet Union, an additional district (Galicia) was added.

The problem with this structure was that the establishment of departments in Cracow, corresponding to the Reich Ministries in Berlin, encouraged the latter to treat the departments as their field offices in the General Government, thereby undermining Frank's control over his 'government', though he had some success in resisting this development. It also tended to produce an overblown and top-heavy bureaucratic structure. Secondly, since the administration in the districts operated according to the *Führerprinzip*, and since the districts and counties were very large and the total number of German officials was very small (4,000–5,000 in January 1944, apart from the railways and Post Office) and of very varied and generally inferior quality, supervision by the central government over its field administration proved very difficult. Each district governor and *Kreishauptmann* tended to regard his district or county as a private fief and give priority to local needs at the expense of the criteria laid down by the central government in Cracow.

However, the most serious problem was that Nazi policy towards the General Government was fundamentally flawed by inconsistency and the pursuit of irreconcilable objectives. Initially, Nazi policy towards the General Government took the line that it must be ruthlessly stripped of raw materials and equipment and treated as a dumping ground for racial undesirables (Jews and Poles), in particular from the incorporated territories, and as a reserve of labour. This policy emerged in Göring's Directive on the Economic Treatment of the Different Areas of Occupied Poland of 19 October 1939:

676

At the meeting of 13 October I gave detailed instructions for the economic administration of the occupied territories, I summarize them again here:

1. The objectives of the economic treatment of the various administrative areas differ according to whether the region in question is one which is to be in-corporated politically in the German Reich or whether it is the General Government which will probably not be incorporated.

In the first-mentioned areas the reconstruction and expansion of their economy and the safeguarding of their production and supplies must be pushed forward with a view to complete absorption in the German economic system as soon as possible. In the General Government, on the other hand, all raw materials, scrap, machinery, and so forth which can be used in the German war economy must be removed from the territory. Enterprises which are not absolutely essential for the maintenance at a low level of the bare existence of the inhabitants must be transferred to Germany, unless such transfer would take a disproprortionately long time and therefore it would be more practical to carry out German orders in the factories where they now stand . . .

By the beginning of 1940, however, Nazi policy had undergone a change of direction. On 19 January, at a meeting with his department heads, Frank reviewed developments since the beginning of the General Government as follows:

677

On 15 September 1939, I received the commission to take on the administration of the conquered eastern territories with particular orders ruthlessly to exploit this area as a war zone and a land ripe for plunder, to turn its economic, social, cultural, and political structure into a heap of ruins so to speak. The work of enlightenment undertaken during the past months has produced a complete change of attitude. Nowadays, the area of the General Government is regarded as a valuable part of the German living space. The principle of total destruction has changed into one of developing this area to the extent that it can produce benefits for the Reich in its present situation. An important effect of this new principle has been the introduction of the Four Year Plan in this area which has thereby been geared to the overall German objectives. This has provided new opportunities for the working population of this country . . .

The decisive point now is the need to rebuild production in the General Government. Until now the dominant view was to regard this country as fit for plunder. But this stage is now over. Now we must rebuild production out of the original elements and place this production at the service of the Reich. . . . Thus the factories must slave away and work. The Poles who are employed in these plants must be made to work so hard—in a disciplined fashion—that they don't know whether they are coming or going, that they don't have time to carry out acts of sabotage . . .

If this programme is to be carried out then the plants must be given favoured treatment . . . For the 10–12 Złoty which they earn each day, these workers must be able to purchase all their most pressing needs. I must ask all departments to assist me in completely fulfilling the wish and command of the Führer and that of the Field-Marshal [Göring]. This command is to extract for the German defence economy whatever can be extracted. In this connection, my relationship with the Poles is the same as that between an ant and a greenfly. If I treat the Poles well and tickle them in a friendly way, so to speak, then I do it in the expectation that their work will be to my advantage. This is not a political issue but a purely tactical and technical one. . . . In cases where, in spite of all these measures, their performance does not improve or where the slightest act prompts me to intervene, I would not hesitate to take the most draconian action.

This change of course was also reflected in the important directive on the economy of the General Government which Göring issued on 25 January 1940:

678

To fulfil the task of placing the economic power of the General Government in the service of the German defence economy within the framework of the Four Year Plan, I hereby issue the following

Directives

1. In view of the present requirements of the defence economy of the Reich, the economic policy of the General Government *cannot for the time being be geared to the longer term.* On the contrary, the economy of the General Government must be directed in such a way that within the shortest possible time it can produce the maximum contribution which can be secured from the resources of the General Government for the immediate reinforcement of the military power of the Reich.
2. The economy of the General Government is expected to make the following specific contributions:
(*a*) the *intensification of agricultural production* . . .
(*b*) the utmost *exploitation of the forests* which will involve the temporary abandonment of long-term forest management . . .
(*c*) *An increase in the production of raw materials in the industrial sector* . . .
(*d*) The exploitation and if necessary the partial extension of the existing industrial capacity of the General Government for the purpose of the most *rapid execution of orders to be placed by the Reich in the General Government*, while maintaining the production of plants which are considered vital for the continuing operation of the economic structure of the General Government using the most strict criteria.
(*e*) The maintenance of the productive capacity of plants which, though not yet in receipt of any armament orders, have been selected as *reserve plants* for the use of undertakings which are important to the war effort and which have been or are to be evacuated from the Reich.

(*f*) The razing of plants which are neither to be turned into armaments works nor reserve plants and the utilisation of the scrap, including the demolished buildings.
(*g*) *The provision and transportion to the Reich of a least 1 million male and female agricultural and industrial workers*—including approximately 750,000 agricultural workers, of whom at least fifty per cent must be women—in order to safeguard agricultural production and supply the deficiency in industrial labour in the Reich.
3. To achieve the anticipated contributions, provision should be made:
(*a*) to complement the organisational measures designed to increase agricultural production and restore the stocks of cattle which have considerably diminished owing to the war by ensuring the supply of seeds and fertiliser, if necessary by importing them from the Reich . . .
(*f*) To guarantee the supply of Polish labour required for the Reich by ensuring that the Labour Offices coordinate the recruitment of labour for the Reich with the labour requirements of the General Government and that its despatch occurs sufficiently early for the transport to be completed during April.
4. To ensure that the economy of the General Government is wholly geared to the fulfilment of the present tasks, the following measures must be taken:
(*a*) In connection with the supply of foodstuffs to the population, measures must be taken to guarantee at all costs that people employed in plants of vital or military importance maintain their efficiency, while the rest of the population are reduced to a minimum supply of food while the food shortage continues.
(*b*) All production which is based on the use of raw materials of military importance, which are not absolutely vital within the framework of the present plan, must be ruthlessly prohibited if it proves impossible to switch to raw materials available in sufficient quantities (e.g. production of wooden clogs while the production of leather shoes and boots for the indigeneous population is prohibited). Furthermore the regulations regarding the economical use of raw materials and the prohibitions and rules relating to their production and use which are in operation in the Reich, must be enforced in the General Government at least to the same extent.
(*c*) The despatch of raw materials to the Reich is to be restricted to the amounts which are not absolutely necessary to maintain production in the General Government which is important to the war economy . . .

Between October 1939 and May 1940, Hitler appears to have envisaged the General Government as becoming a Polish 'homeland' under German control and serving German needs. At a meeting of the officials of the district of Radom on 25 February 1940 Frank made the following points:

679

Whether and in what form this territory will become part of the German Reich is still completely uncertain . . . We must, therefore, treat the General Government as a Polish territory which has been entrusted to us as a result of the war. This territory has been initially designated by the Führer as the homeland of the Polish people. In Berlin the Führer and Field-Marshal Göring impressed on me repeatedly that the territory will not be subjected to germanization. It must be secured as the homeland of the Polish nation. It is to be a reservation put at the disposal of the Polish nation in the name of the German people . . . according to the Führer's decree.

In accordance with our directives, the Polish laws are still in force here. We must never dream of giving the Poles the benefit of our laws. It is not right for you to oppose or prevent the Poles living in their own way and continuing to do so. We have no reason to build a model state here and thereby ensure that one day they are left with a structure which is more efficient and rational than ever before in Poland. I make a particular point of this because the border between the territories which have been incorporated in the German Reich and which are not Reich Gaus and the General Government must be very sharply drawn . . .

At a meeting of the Reich Defence committee on 2 March 1940, Frank laid down policy guidelines:

680

The day before yesterday, I spent two and half hours discussing the problems of the east once more with the Führer in the Reich Chancellery. The Führer is absolutely sticking to this goal. The General Government is initially to be designated as the homeland of the Poles—Poles who will be under German sovereignty but not German citizens and will receive a kind of reservation here. Thus, initially there will be no comprehensive trend towards germanizing the Poles in the area of the General Government. I must stress very strongly, gentlemen, that it would be a major violation of the bases of the Führer's policy if any attempt were made to introduce such measures by force. The Führer has for the time being declared that this country will be a reservation for the Poles. What this country's position will be after victory has been achieved remains to be seen. That task will undoubtedly be solved in the same masterly fashion as all the others . . .

. . . So if we rule and administer here and carry out our overall task without this obsession that we must follow a policy of germanization and spread a German gloss over everything, then we have the tremendous responsibility of ensuring that this area remains firmly under German control, that the Poles' backbone is permanently broken and that there is never again the slightest resistance to German Reich policy from this area.

This task cannot be fulfilled through a gigantic extermination programme in which people are, so to speak, mowed down. We cannot after all kill 14,000,000 Poles. This struggle can also not be fought through systematic terror, for we do not have enough personnel to build up the apparatus required. It can only be carried out with a compact administrative apparatus which must rapidly prove its effectiveness . . .

From an economic point of view the General Government is now an empty shell. The Four Year Plan has as far as possible removed whatever raw materials there were. That was a good thing because the Reich has a tremendous need for raw materials. We did whatever we could to help in this sphere. There cannot be any economic prosperity in the General Government so long as there is a war economy in the Reich. The living standards of the Polish section of the population here cannot be in the least bit better than those of the German people. We will if necessary take all the steps which are necessary to ensure that the living standards of the Polish people are regulated in such a way that they are just sufficient to sustain life but are in a state of decline by comparison with the situation in the German Reich. If one looks at the life of the Polish people one can confirm that is indeed the position. In general the food situation in many large areas of this country is catastrophic. If the German Reich did not provide continual help, very grave difficulties would occur . . .

On 30 May, at a meeting of police chiefs in Cracow, Frank reported a complete change of policy towards the General Government which he alleged had been under discusson for months but which in fact almost certainly reflected the prospects of imminent victory on the western front:

681

. . . There then occurred a remarkable change of course. As late as the beginning of October [1939], the Führer told me that he wanted this territory to be a rump territory for the Polish nation, a sort of rump state which we would eventually return to the Polish nation. However, not least under the influence of reports which started coming in about the agrarian and industrial potential, about the opportunity for great German colonial activity, and also impressed by the fact that the mass of ordinary common Poles, namely the workers and peasants, were in general perfectly prepared to work under strict control, under the influence of all these reports, the Führer told me—and I can remember clearly that it was at the beginning of November: We will keep the General Government, we will not give it up. In view of this change in the situation, we had to arrange a completely new programme. The matter which the Führer had repeatedly talked over with me now increasingly became the subject of discussion, namely that the territory of the General Government would remain in the German sphere, not in the form of a Protectorate or something like that, but rather in the form of a political structure of the German Reich under German rule in which the absolute leadership of the German nation vis-à-vis the Polish lower class of workers would be secured and in which, after the conclusion of the germanization and resettlement of the Germans in the Warthegau, West Prussia, southern East Prussia, and Upper Silesia, germanization will be carried out on a large scale. I speak quite openly of germanization, for the problem was no different for our ancestors of a thousand years ago when the same alien Slav people was crowded together here. Frequently, we are surprised to find a blond and blue-eyed child speaking Polish and I say to myself: If we were to educate this child as a German then it would be a pretty German girl. Thus, we consider that this nation has a completely German racial core and by developing, fostering and encouraging this racial core we will make it possible to claim this area of the General Government for the German nation.

I have discussed all this with the Führer and we are in agreement about the fact that this territory must gradually be won for the German nation in this way. At the moment we are not interested in how long it will take, whether it will occur in 50 of 100 years. The decisive point—and that is the vital thing and the reason why we are gathered here today—is that we must use every opportunity which is provided for us in order to achieve this goal and work productively towards it . . .

Frank then continued by describing the difficulties caused by the resettlement of Poles, Jews, and Gypsies in the General Government who allegedly included 'an active leadership which is embittered' and would have to be dealt with:

682

There is only one thing I can say about all that: I can only carry out this policy with your help. Excuse me for being so blunt. But if I did not have the old National Socialist fighters, the Police and the SS here to help me, who else could I possibly use to carry out this policy? I couldn't do it with the *Wehrmacht* or with anybody else. These are matters of such gravity and we, as National Socialists, are faced with such an incredibly difficult and responsible task that we can only talk about these things in the most intimate circles.

If, in view of all these difficulties we wish to achieve the goal of the total domination of the Polish nation in this area then we must seize our opportunity. On 10 May, the offensive in the West began, i.e. on that very same day the outside world ceased to be particularly interested in the goings-on here. You can't imagine the trouble which the atrocity propaganda and the lying reports about the activities of the National Socialist rulers in this area have caused for us vis-à-vis the outside world. Well, I would not have cared a bit if the Americans or the French or the Jews or even the Pope had got worked up about it, but it has been terrible for me during the past few months and for all of you as well to keep hearing comments from the Propaganda Ministry, from the Foreign Ministry, from the Interior Ministry, even from the *Wehrmacht* to the effect that we have a murderous regime here, that we must stop these atrocities etc. And so it was obvious that we had to declare that we would stop them. And it was equally clear that during a period when the searchlights of the world were on this territory we could not carry out such things on a large scale. However, since the 10th May this atrocity propaganda no longer bothers us. Now we must seize the available opportunity. If every minute and every second thousands of people of the best German blood must be sacrificed, then as National Socialists we have a duty to bear in mind that the Polish nation must not be allowed to rise again at the expense of this sacrifice of German blood. Thus, it was at this point that I discussed this remarkable pacification programme with comrade Streckenbach[20] in the presence of SS *Obergruppenführer* Krüger,[21] a pacification programme which is intended to finish off at an accelerated pace the mass of the rebellious resistance politicians and other politically suspect individuals who are in our hands and, at the same time, to clear up the remnants of the earlier Polish criminal element. I must quite openly admit that that will cost the lives of a few thousand Poles, above all from the intellectual leadership of Poland. But all of us as National Socialists have a duty at this time to ensure that no further resistance emerges from the Polish people. I know what a responsibility we are taking on here. But it is clear that we can do it, particularly since we are required to take over the protection of the eastern flanks of the Reich. Moreover, SS *Obergruppenführer* Krüger and I have decided to speed up the pacification action. I must ask you gentlemen to give us all the help you can in carrying out this task. I appeal to you as National Socialist fighters and I don't think I need to say any more. We will carry out this measure and I can tell you in confidence that we shall be implementing an order which I received from the Führer. The Führer told me that the implementation of German policy in Poland is a matter for the men who are in charge in the General Government to deal with themselves. He put it this way: We must liquidate those people whom we have discovered form the leadership in Poland; all those who follow in their footsteps must be arrested and then got rid of after an appropriate period. We do not need to burden the Reich organisation of the German police with that. We don't need to bother to cart these people off to concentration camps in the Reich because then we would only have trouble and an unnecessary correspondence with their relatives. Instead, we will finish the thing off here. We will do it in the simplest way. Gentlemen, we are not murderers. It is a fearful task for the policemen and SS man who is obliged to carry out the execution. We can easily sign hundreds of death sentences here; but it is a terrible burden to have to assign their execution to German men, to decent German soldiers and comrades . . .

In his discussion of a 'pacification programme' Frank was referring to the notorious AB action, in which during the summer of 1940 thousands of Poles, particularly from the intelligentsia[22], were arrested and then either taken to the Palmiry forest outside Warsaw and shot, or transferred to the new concentration camp at Auschwitz in Silesia.[23]

By the winter of 1941, Frank was dreaming of the great future role which his General Government would play in the Greater German Reich, dreams

---

[20] SS *Brigadeführer* Bruno Streckenbach, Commander of the Security Police and SD in Cracow (eds).

[21] The Higher SS and Police Leader in the General Government (eds).

[22] The 'intelligentsia' was defined by Frank as 'teachers, clergy, doctors, dentists, vets, officers, ranking bureaucrats, big merchants, big landowners, writers, journalists, as well as persons who had university or high school diplomas. See J. T. Gross, *Polish Society under German Occupation* (Princeton 1979), p .47, fn. 2.

[23] On Auschwitz see below pp. 1173–1189.

which almost certainly derived from conversations with Hitler. On 16 December 1941, he told a meeting of the government of the General Government:

683

Above all, we must bear the following in mind: after the regermanization of the eastern territories of the Reich, this territory of the General Government will be the next to be totally germanized. We will build the great Reich autobahns which will go straight across our country. Great settlements will grow up alongside these autobahns. Major military centres will be established at carefully selected strategic points around which German life will gradually develop over a broad zone. Since we will then have the opportunity to transfer any unwanted ethnic aliens to the east, it will not be an insuperable task to ensure that the German ethnic element puts down roots while the ethnically alien element is progressively squeezed out.

For this reason, you must adopt the five points which I have put forward which, beginning with the germanic settlement of this territory, and going up to the war of 1941, provide the Germans with a series of legal claims to this territory. For the Führer has given me authority to initiate preparations along these lines. The Goths' Gau will be set up further east and the General Government will then be able to become the Vandals' Gau. It is well-known that the Vandals are the Germanic tribe who have been slandered the most. Their homes were here: here they began the first germanic culture. This Vandals' Gau will thus help to eliminate before the whole world this fearful reputation which has attached to them as a result of the fact that, as one of the noblest German tribes, they have been so continually disparaged that their name has become an insult. This has been, by the way, a masterpiece of anti-German propaganda for two thousand years.

It is clear, therefore, that the role of the General Government in the overall pattern of the drive to the east is a world-historical one. We are the gate through which one returns to Germany from the east . . .

The deterioration in Germany's position during the winter of 1942 forced a reappraisal of policy towards the General Government and produced conflicting responses from the various Reich departments involved. On 14 December 1942, Frank described the problems this caused for his government to an audience of political leaders of the NSDAP in the General Government:

684

. . . The first problem which always concerns us is that of the ethnic aliens. The ethnic aliens have a tremendous numerical superiority over the Germans here. You know that it is beginning to become a serious problem for the Reich to know what to do about the ethnic aliens whom we rule. We are concerned in the first instance about the Poles and secondarily about the Ukrainians. You know that within the Party the line which is generally adopted is that our Polish policy consists of the deportation of the Poles, their destruction, or their treatment as a mere source of labour. You are also aware that that policy has been largely put into practice. Now, however, things are becoming tremendously complicated in this sphere. The problem arises above all from the fact that the Reich is being forced to transfer large sections of industry from the areas threatened by air attack to the General Government[24]. On the other hand, there is a necessity to ensure the supply of local labour for the plants which are already in the General Government at all costs, to maintain the transport system and the whole administrative apparatus, and to ensure the harvest etc. As a result of this situation, there is a sudden awareness that one cannot simultaneously destroy the Poles and, on the other hand, make calculations about the Polish labour force.

We are at the moment faced with this transitional problem. The demands for labour made upon us by the Reich are the least of our worries. You know that we have sent over 940,000 Polish workers to the Reich. In this the General Government is in both absolute and relative terms at the top of the list of all the European countries involved. This is a tremendous achievement and has been recognized as such by Gauleiter Sauckel.

The fact that we are now faced with the problem of what line should be taken in future towards the Poles is not the result of any immediate cause. It would be desirable if the Reich ministries, the Party agencies and the territorial authorities could finally decide on a course of action. It simply will not do for some people to say all Poles of whatever sort will be exterminated, and for others to say all Poles of whatever kind, if they are fit for work, must be put to work. There is a complete contradiction here. One could say: we will keep all the Poles who are in work, and all Poles who are not in work will be exterminated. There is, however, a major problem there in that the extermination of millions of human beings is dependent on preconditions which at the moment cannot be fulfilled.

It would naturally be best if this Polish policy could be carried out by us, the authorities in the General Government, completely independently . . . On the one hand, people say: we don't need to feed the Poles at all, we should let them starve or else bring them into the Reich; on the other hand, a Reich department says: if the Poles are working for the Germans then they must be given just the same rations as the Poles in the Reich. That is completely contradictory. One side in the Reich says: all Poles capable of work must be transported to the Reich—the other side says: all Poles who are in the country and capable of work must stay there so that we have a labour reservoir for the armaments' plants, for transport, for industry etc. Such totally contradictory and completely incompatible views on Polish policy are raining down on my desk. Often two arrive on the same day from departments which are both armed with equal powers from the Führer, for example, from Party

---

[24] The value of armaments delivered from the General Government increased from 277.3 million RM in 1941 to 629.1 million RM in 1943. See *Deutschland im Zweiten Weltkrieg, op. cit.*, Bd. 4, p. 185.

comrade Speer and Party comrade Sauckel. Then, I have to negotiate, provide information, and find out what line the Reich is taking, Should we exterminate or build things up, should the work be created here or in the Reich, should we give up workers or keep them here, should we let the Poles starve or feed them? . . .

The German reverses in Russia (Stalingrad) and North Africa (El Alemain and 'Torch') in winter 1942 prompted a general reappraisal of policy towards the occupied territories which found expression in Goebbels's directive of 15 February 1943.[25] This directive was warmly welcomed by Frank at a press conference on 23 February. It was, he said,

685

a really revolutionary statement. A great change of course has begun. We are breaking with the previous system of extermination, and discrimination. At last the Reich has recognised that a system based on force cannot be permanent, for force is simply the exploitation of a temporary advantage in weapons.

However, the obstacles to the development and implementation of a coherent and effective policy in the General Government remained. It was impossible to disguise the fact that the new softer line was merely a product of *Realpolitik*. It was adopted only half-heartedly by the German authorities and barely penetrated the SS-police. The ideological prejudices, which had determined the treatment of the Poles hitherto, remained intact, and the Nazi leadership took its cue from Hitler who merely condoned rather than supported energetically the new line.

As the man responsible for maintaining order in and delivering the goods from the General Government, Frank had become the main advocate of a somewhat softer line towards the Poles, for example in a long memorandum to Hitler of 19 June 1943, which criticised past German policy and pressed for improved treatment for the Poles.

686

. . . In the course of time, a series of measures, or of consequences of German rule have let to a substantial deterioration in the attitude of the entire Polish people to the General Government. These measures have affected either individual professions or the entire population and frequently also—often with crushing severity—the fate of individuals.
Among these are in particular:

[25] See above pp. 917–8.

(1) The entirely insufficient nourishment of the population, mainly of the working classes in the cities, the majority of which are working for German interests.

Until the war of 1939 their food supplies, though not varied, were sufficient and were generally assured owing to the agrarian surplus of the former Polish state and in spite of the negligence on the part of their former political leadership.

(2) The confiscation of a great part of the Polish estates, expropriation without compensation, and evacuation of Polish peasants from military training areas and from German settlements.

(3) Encroachments and confiscations in industry, in commerce and trade, and in the field of private property.

(4) Mass arrests and shootings by the German police who applied the system of collective responsibility.

(5) The rigorous method of recruiting workers.

(6) The extensive paralysing of cultural life.

(7) The closing of high schools, colleges, and universities.

(8) The limitation, indeed the complete elimination, of Polish influence from all spheres of state administration.

(9) Curtailment of the influence of the Catholic Church, limiting its extensive influence—an undoubtedly necessary move—and, in addition, until quite recently, often at the shortest notice, the closing and confiscation of monasteries, schools, and charitable institutions.

In contrast with the treatment of the Poles in the General Government, other national groups and minorities were considerably better off. The Ukrainians, Gorelians, White Russians, Caucasians, and Tatars were in general exempt from attacks on their persons and property. In addition, they were allowed, of course under German supervision, to engage in national cultural and educational activities. To some extent they were also more favourably treated in the matter of food supplies. The religious communities of these groups, the Greek-Catholic and Greek-Orthodox churches, and the Muslim religious bodies, were encouraged by the German authorities in contrast with their treatment in the former Polish state.

As a result of the markedly better treatment of the non-Polish groups in the General Government, they have shown from the beginning general sympathy with German aims and particularly with German war needs . . .

The Poles, by contrast, have been constantly made aware of the different treatment of particular population groups in the General Government, particularly in regard to the measures taken by the German Labour Offices which led to restrictions on or threats to the life of individual Poles. In consequence, the great mass of the Poles have gradually and increasingly shown more and more inclination to oppose German rule passively and even actively . . .

As a result of the long series and measures taken during the past years against the Poles their attitude has grown steadily more hostile . . .

The discovery of the mass graves near Katyn now provides the opportunity to introduce a fundamental change in the treatment of the Poles without this alteration in the policy of the German leadership being able to be interpreted as weakness.[26]

---

[26] In April 1943 Berlin Radio announced the discovery of 4,500 corpses in the forest of Katyń near Smolensk and accused the Russians of the atrocity (eds).

However, our propaganda will on its own be incapable of securing an appreciable change in mood. If crucial aspects of the German–Polish relationship do not change then this favourable opportunity for incorporating the indigenous population of the General Government in the anti-Bolshevik front will be lost.

If the Polish people is to adopt the war aims of the Axis powers in Europe's fateful struggle, in fact if it is even to comprehend them, then a declaration on the future of the Polish nation within the new Europe can hardly be postponed any longer. The struggle against Bolshevism will appear all the more justified and necessary to every alien nation the more strongly and the more strikingly the German leadership and the prospects for the individuals living under it differ from the Bolshevik rule of force and from Bolshevik economic forms and ways of life.

Thus the exploitation of the Katyn atrocities will depend on the precondition that such massacres do not occur under German rule. The alien people must gradually come to feel that the Germans are introducing a brighter and better principle for Europe in place of the Bolshevik world. Unfortunately, at the moment Polish public opinion, and not simply the often prejudiced intelligentsia, compares Katyn to the mass deaths in the German concentration camps and the shootings of men, women and even of children and old people in the escalating reprisal measures in partisan areas. It is unnecessary to point out that these reprisals normally do not hit the real guilty ones. Those affected are in may cases not even beneficiaries of the partisan activities, since in view of their inadequate protection and their lack of weapons they are at the mercy of the arbitrary actions of the bands, and therefore only give them support under the compulsion of terror, against which in present circumstances the German authorities cannot unfortunately protect them.

I would like to emphasize once more at this point that I do not wish to see an improvement in German–Polish relations out of emotional sympathy but from rational calculation. In view of the incredible demands on all our resources made by the war, it is necessary ruthlessly to exploit all the available war potential. It is vital to incorporate the Polish people in the front against Bolshevism at a time when the shortage of German reserves is making itself felt more and more in every sphere. In the present strained circumstances the Reich will not benefit from useless ideologies and false notions of overlordship . . .

1. The great mass of the Polish population is completely inadequately clothed and fed . . .

2. The almost complete discontinuation of the possibilities for participation in the cultural field has led, even amongst the lowest classes of the Polish people, to considerable discontent. The Polish middle and upper classes have a great need for self-expression. Experience shows that the possibility of cultural activity would at the same time mean a diversion from the political questions of the day. German propaganda frequently comes across the objection, on the part of Poles, that the restriction of cultural activity enforced by the German authorities not only prevents a contrast being made with Bolshevik lack of culture, but also shows that Polish cultural activity falls far below the degree of culture allowed to Soviet citizens . . .

3. The closing of colleges, high schools, and secondary schools is on the same level. Its well-considered purpose is without doubt the lowering of Polish educational standards. The realization of this goal appears, from the point of view of the

necessities of war, not always beneficial to German interests. As the war goes on the German interest in the mobilization of able foreign replacements in the various fields of knowledge increases. But more important than that is the fact that the crippling of the school system and the severe hampering of cultural activities foster the growth of a Polish national body, led by the intelligentsia, to conspire against Germany. *What was not possible during the course of Polish national history, what even the first years of German dominion could not bring about, namely, the achievement of national unity in a common purpose to hold together through thick and thin, now threatens to become a reality, slowly but surely, because of the German measures.* The German leadership cannot allow this process of unifying the individual classes of the Polish population to pass unheeded in the face of the growing power of resistance of the Poles. The German leadership should promote class distinction by certain cultural concessions and should be able to play one class off against the other.

4. The recruiting of labour and the methods employed, even though often exercised under the unavoidable pressure of circumstances, have, with the aid of clever Bolshevist agitation, evoked a strong feeling of hatred among all classes. The workers thus obtained often come to work with firm resolve to engage in positive resistance, even active sabotage. Improvement of recruiting methods, together with the continued effort to arrest the abuses still practised in the treatment of Polish workers in the Reich, and lastly, some provision, however meagre it may be, for the families left behind, would cause a rise in morale, and the result would be an increased desire to work and increased production in the German interest.

5. When the German administration was set up at the beginning of the war the Polish element was removed from all important positions. The available German staff had always been inadequate in quantity and quality. Besides, during the past year, a considerable number of German personnel have had to be transferred to meet the replacement needs of the armed forces. Already an increased amount of non-German manpower has had to be obtained compulsorily. An essential change in the treatment would enable the administration, while exercising all necessary precautions, to induce a greater number of Poles to collaborate. Without this, the administration, in view of the present amount of personnel—not to mention future transfers—cannot continue to function. The increased participation of Poles would further help to raise morale itself.

Apart from the positive changes referred to in these proposals, there are a number of methods which have been used hitherto in the treatment of the Poles which need altering or ought to be halted altogther, at least for the duration of the European war.

1. I have already reported in special despatches that the confiscation of and expulsions from agricultural land have caused substantial and irreparable damage to agricultural production. No less significant is the damage to morale caused by such actions. . . . The expulsion of Polish peasants from military areas, which was undoubtedly necessary for military reasons, already had an unfavourable impact on the opinions and attitude of many peasants. But at least this expulsion was fairly limited in extent. It was also carried out after careful preparation by the authorities and avoided unnecessary hardship. However, the expulsion of Polish peasants in the district of Lublin with the aim of replacing them with ethnic German settlers,

which was considered necessary by the Reich Commissioner for the Strengthening of German Nationality, was far more significant in terms of its scope.[27] Moreover, as I have already reported in a separate despatch, it was carried out at a speed and with methods which have created completely immeasurable bitterness among the population. Families were torn apart at very short notice; those capable of work were deported to the Reich, while the old people and children were consigned to empty Jewish ghettos. This occurred in the middle of the winter of 1942–3 which resulted in considerable losses among the expelled population, particularly among the latter group referred to. The expulsion involved the complete expropriation of both the movable and fixed assets of the peasants. The whole population came to believe that the expulsion was the beginning of a total expulsion of the Poles from the General Government. In general the opinion was expressed that the Poles would suffer the same fate as the Jews. . . . As a result, large sections of the population in the areas involved in the expulsions, but also in those which were not affected, fled into the forests and provided the partisan bands with a considerable number of recruits. The result was a tremendous deterioration in the security situation. These people who have been driven to despair are being misused by clever agents for the systematic destruction of agricultural and industrial production . . .

My Führer, I beg you to understand my comments as dictated by the burning desire to provide the German people with valuable assistance in the most difficult phase of its fight for existence. I have not referred in my comments to the long-term goals which the German leadership will realize in the east after the successful conclusion of its life and death struggle. It seems to me, however, that damage has been done in particular through the attempt to realize long-range and short-term goals either simultaneously or without adequate coordination and without a sober calculation of the actual possibilities.

Please be reassured, however, that I do not wish to carry out the measures I have proposed with a fanfare or in a way which could be interpreted by the Poles in terms of the weakness of the German leadership. On the contrary, I would carry out these measures very prudently, carefully, and cautiously in accordance with the needs of the time. However, the supreme principle of my actions in these extremely difficult questions will always be devoted and unswerving loyalty to you and your epoch-making work.

Hail to you, my Führer

However, Frank's position had already been undermined by his public opposition in July 1942 to the erosion of the legal order by the growth of the 'SS state', opposition which had led to his dismissal in August from his posts as leader of the National Socialist Lawyers' League and President of the Academy of German Law.[28] Hitler merely listened to his arguments

---

[27] See below pp. 979–982

[28] Hitler declined to accept his resignation as Governor General on 'diplomatic grounds'. See *Das Diensttagebuch des deutschen Generalgouverneurs in Polen 1939–1945* eds. W. Prăg and W. Jacobmeyer (Stuttgart 1975) p. 27.

with apparent benevolence but did little or nothing to rein in the SS-police. Hitler was no doubt aware that obstacles to a new relationship between Germans and Poles were by now built in to the situation. Germany's need to exploit Polish resources of labour and foodstuffs was becoming more urgent than ever. Frank could not refuse these requests from Sauckel, Speer and others for fear of appearing a 'a friend of the Poles'. Indeed, from the autumn of 1942 onwards, the General Government's administration functioned increasingly as merely the executive arm of the central agencies in Berlin. Yet the increasing exploitation of Polish resources was bound to exacerbate the situation. The problem was that there was simply no time to secure Polish cooperation through a conciliatory policy even if such a line had been more systematically pursued. The chance, if it ever existed, had already been missed, and with Germany's strategic situation steadily deteriorating the Poles had little incentive to respond. Indeed they were increasingly encouraged to resist, thereby provoking German reprisals in a vicious cycle of terror and resistance. Nevertheless, Frank continued to urge the need for a new policy towards the Poles as in the following statement to Cracow District leaders on 14 January 1944:

687

When we have won the war then, as far as I am concerned, we can make mincemeat out of the Poles and the Ukrainians and all the other people hanging around here. But, at this moment, the only thing that matters is whether or not we can succeed in keeping almost 15 million members of an enemy nation, which is organizing itself against us, in peace, order, work, and disciplined. If we don't succeed then I may be able to crow that I have killed two million Polacks. But whether the trains will keep running to the eastern front, whether the plants will keep on producing 500,000 litres of Vodka and so many million cigarettes each month, whether food supplies and agriculture can be secured, which has supplied 450,000 tons of wheat alone to the Reich—that is another matter . . .

Politics is more than force. Force is a ridiculously elementary matter. Statesmanship begins where force ends. If I have to give up three police battalions from this area which are urgently needed to fill gaps in the front—today I received just such an urgent request for aid—then that means that I have three police battalions fewer with which to cover this territory. I can only do that if I can so to speak rely to some extent on the population. If I can no longer give the 150,000 Poles who operate the Eastern Railway anything to eat, if I can no longer clothe them, can no longer guarantee their security, the 5,000 Germans whom I employ on the Eastern Railway will be unable to move a single train. I am not even mentioning the factories. Don't you not know that we make 1.5 billion Złoty worth of the most valuable additional armaments and munitions for the Reich per year?

One cannot achieve that by saying: I command it. I want it and if he won't do it I'll shoot him. That's nonsense! I can shoot anyone. There's no skill in that. I am not a friend of the Poles, but I am responsible for ensuring that no rebellion occurs in this area in the rear of the eastern front. If I give the Poles something to eat, if I leave them their churches and give them schools, I do it not as a friend of the Poles but as the politician responsible for this area and I strongly resent anyone poking their nose in. People who don't bear the responsibility can easily shoot their mouths off . . .

The attitude of the SS-Police was very different and they posed the biggest single threat to Frank's more conciliatory policy and to his control over the General Government.

(b) The role of the SS-police.

Whereas the Nazi Party more or less dominated affairs in the incorporated territories through the Reich Governor-Gauleiters, in the General Government the SS-police succeeded in establishing a virtual state within the state to a greater extent than anywhere else in German-occupied Europe. Under the Higher SS and Police Leader in Cracow and the SS and Police Leaders in the four (later five) Districts, it managed to build up an apparatus which operated largely independently of the administration of the General Government, one which took its orders from Himmler and the RSHA in Berlin rather than from Governor General Frank in the Wawel in Cracow. Frank had tried to insist that, under Hitler's decree of 12 October 1939,[29] the Higher SS and Police Leader must be subordinate to his State Secretary, Dr Bühler, and that, correspondingly, the SS and Police Leaders in the districts must be subordinated to the district governors. However, Hitler conspicuously failed to confirm this opinion and the SS insisted that their men were 'assigned' (*zugeteilt*) rather than 'subordinated' (*unterstellt*) to the governors. The Higher SS and Police Leader in Cracow from 1939–43, SS *Obergruppenführer* Friedrich-Wilhelm Krüger, was a coldly efficient bureaucrat who cleverly exploited the weak points in Frank's armour. Thus, in the spring of 1942 Frank and one or two of his senior officials were accused by the SS of corruption. In order to cover up the affair, on 14 March Frank reached an agreement with Himmler which was then embodied in a Führer decree of 7 May 1942. Under it Frank was obliged to accept Krüger's appointment to the new post of 'State Secretary for Security Matters', which placed him on a par with Bühler in the formal hierarchy of the General Government. Although Krüger was still formally subordinate to Frank as Governor General, in practice the new appointment underscored his effective independence since Himmler retained the right to give him 'direct instructions'.

[29] See above p. 926–7.

The key to the power of the SS in the General Government was its police role in a territory where, as a result of the racial imperialist mentality of the Nazi occupiers, security matters were bound to figure prominently. The power which flowed from its police functions was reinforced by its role in the racial policies pursued in this area—the 'Reinhard Action' against the Jews[30] and the resettlement programme involving the displacement of Poles by ethnic Germans.

Soon after the invasion of Poland, the SS was able to exploit the exceptional situation to persuade Frank to issue the following Decree for the Combating of Violent Acts in the General Government, dated 31 October 1939:

688

§ 1. Anyone who commits a violent act against the German Reich or the German sovereign authority in the General Government will receive the death penalty.

§ 2. Anyone who wilfully damages equipment belonging to the German authorities, objects which serve the work of the authorities, or installations which are for the benefit of the public will receive the death penalty.

§ 3. Anyone who encourages or incites disobedience to the decrees or regulations issued by the German authorities will receive the death penalty.

§ 4. Anyone who commits a violent act against a German because of his membership of the German nation will receive the death penalty.

§ 5. Anyone who wilfully commits arson and thereby damages the property of a German will receive the death penalty.

§ 6. Those who incite or aid such acts will be punished in the same way as the persons who commit them. Attempted acts will be punished in the same way as those which have been committed . . .

§ 8. Anyone who conspires to commit a crime such as those contined in §§ 1–5, enters into serious discussion of such crimes, offers to commit such a crime, or anyone who accepts such an offer will receive the death penalty.

§ 9. Anyone who receives information about the intention to commit a crime such as those contained in §§ 1-5 and fails to report it to the authorities, or to the person who is threatened at once, or in time for the crime to be prevented, will receive the death penalty.

§ 10 . . .

(2) Anyone who receives information about the unauthorized possession of a weapon by another person and fails to inform the authorities immediately will receive the death penalty.

This enabled the SS to operate its own courts martial to deal with the cases under this decree independently of the normal judicial process. The police could also arrest people and consign them to concentration camps either

[30] See below pp. 1143–1173.

in the Reich or in Poland, such as the new one which opened in Upper Silesia in the summer of 1940—Auschwitz.

However, the SS resented the continuing application of normal judicial procedures in the case of many criminal offences committed by Poles and insisted that cases involving 'ethnic aliens' were essentially a police rather than a judicial matter, for which responsibility should, therefore, be transferred to the police. The Reich Justice Ministry managed to stall on such proposals for a time. While prepared to see new draconian punishments introduced for Poles, it defended its responsibility for a unified judicial system. However, with the appointment of the hard-line Nazi and former President of the People's Court, Otto Thierack, as Reich Minister of Justice on 20 August 1942, an agreement was rapidly reached on 5 September. The details were passed on to the various SS-police offices by SS *Gruppenführer* Bruno Streckenbach of the RSHA in a circular dated 5 November 1942 'Re: Criminal law procedure vis-à-vis Poles and members of the Eastern Nations':

689

I. The *Reichsführer* SS has agreed with Reich Minister of Justice, Thierack, that the judiciary will abandon normal criminal law procedures vis-à-vis Poles and members of the eastern nations. These ethnically alien persons are in future to be handed over to the police. The same treatment is to be accorded to Jews and Gypsies. The agreement has been approved by the Führer.

Regulations for the implementation of the agreement, which will if possible come into effect on 1 January 1943, are at present being worked out between the RSHA and the Reich Ministry of Justice.

II. This agreement is based on the following considerations. Poles and members of the eastern nations are ethnically alien and racially inferior people who live in the territory of the German Reich. Considerable threats to the German national order arise from this situation, which inevitably lead to the need to place the ethnic aliens under a different criminal law from Germans. Insufficient account has been taken of this requirement hitherto. Only the Poles have received special treatment in the sphere of the criminal law through the Decree concerning Criminal Law Procedure vis-à-vis Poles and Jews in the Incorporated Eastern Territories of 4 December 1941[31].

[31] This decree introduced draconian punishments, e.g. the death sentence for 'vicious and rabble-rousing activity' or 'anti-German remarks'. It included so-called 'rubber clauses' capable of wide interpretation such as that which made punishable anything which 'is detrimental to the sovereignty and prestige of the German Reich'. It also introduced the option 'of transfers to the Gestapo' i.e. a concentration camp, as a punishment, thereby formally giving them for the first time an official role in Reich penal procedure. Hitherto those held by the Gestapo and in concentration camps were in 'protective custody' under § 2 of the Decree for the Protection of the People and State of 28 February 1933. (See Vol. 1. p. 142.)

However, even this special regulation does not contain a fundamental solution of the issues which arise from the fact of Poles and Germans living side by side. It merely increased the punishments and introduced a partially simplified penal procedure for Poles. It ignores the real issue, namely the fact that for political reasons ethnic aliens must be treated completely differently from Germans, since, despite the increase in punishments, it still applies the essential elements of German criminal procedure to Poles.

Thus, in judging an offence committed by a Pole, basically the same principles are applied as those which are decisive in judging a German: i.e. the judge concentrates on the personality of the offender and, taking full account of his personal motives, endeavours to find a form of atonement which is appropriate to the interests of the national community.

These considerations, which may be correct for the judgment of an offence committed by a German, are, however, incorrect for the judgment of an offence by an ethnic alien. In the case of an offence by an ethnic alien, the personal motives of the offender are completely irrelevant. The decisive point must be the fact that his deed threatened the German national order and, therefore, steps must be taken to prevent further such threats. In other words, the deed of an ethnic alien must not be seen from the standpoint of judicial atonement but from the point of view of police action to avert threats. For this reason, criminal law procedure with regard to ethnic aliens must be removed from the judiciary and placed in the hands of the police . . .

Apart from its role in the extermination of the Jews in Poland (the 'Reinhard Action'), the SS had far-reaching plans for the resettlement of ethnic Germans in the General Government: the germanization of 'racially desirable' Poles and the deportation or extermination of the remainder. The years 1940–42 saw feverish activity on the part of the RSHA, the Race and Settlement Main Office (Ru.SHA), the office of the Reich Commissioner for the Strengthening of German Nationhood (RKFDV), and other agencies who put forward plans for the future of the 'living space' in the east which Germany had conquered. One such plan was the so-called 'General Plan East' which was worked out by Amt IIIB (SD *Inland*) of the RSHA at the end of 1941. The desk officer for racial matters in the Reich Ministry for the Eastern Territories, Dr Erhard Wetzel, a lawyer by training and former official of the Ru.SHA, commented on the plan in a memorandum of 27 April 1942 from which the following is an extract:

690

. . . Re: the Solution of the Polish Question

(a) The Poles.

Their numbers must be estimated at between 20–24 million. They are the most anti-German, numerically the strongest, and therefore the most dangerous of all the alien ethnic groups which the Plan envisages for resettlement . . .

From a racial standpoint the Poles contain essentially almost the same racial strains as the Germans, although the proportions of the individual races are different. The nordic-phalian racial type is certainly fairly strongly present, in particular in the north-western parts of the former Poland and is hardly any weaker there than among the surrounding German population. That is the result of the strong strain of German blood which the Polish population of this area have received through the Polonization (*Verpolung*) of the Germans. As a result, the Polish population in Litzmannstadt [Łódź] were in part racially superior to the ethnic Germans because the nordic strain among the German people seems to be the most suitable for changing nationality. According to my reckoning, the leadership corps of the Polish resistance consisted largely of Polonized Germans who had nordic blood to a greater or lesser extent. On the other hand, the eastern Balt racial strain is present in the Polish population to a far greater degree than in the German population. Moreover, in addition to dinaric, *westisch* and *ostisch* strains, there are also some fairly primitive *ostisch* types about whom one must have grave doubts as to whether they can be regarded as identical to the Homo alpinus of the *ostisch* race in Günther's sense[32]. There is in my view some justification for the Polish anthropologist, Ozechanowski, to term these groups 'Lapponoids'. In addition, there are individual cases in Poland of Mongolian blood strains which manifest themselves in slit eyes, Mongolian wrinkles, cheek bones and such like. Whether these alien racial strains derive from cross-breeding with racially alien members of the Tsarist army or from older cross-breeding has not yet been investigated.

The Plan envisages the deportation of 80–85 per cent of the Poles. 16–20.4 million Poles will be deported, while 3–4.8 million are to remain in the German area of settlement. These figures given by the Reich Security Main Office differ from those provided by the Reich Commissioner for the Strengthening of German Nationhood of the percentage of those racially desirables Poles who are considered capable of germanization. On the basis of his analysis so far of the rural population of the *Gaue* Danzig–West Prussia and the Wartheland, the Reich Commissioner for the Strengthening of German Nationhood reckons that three per cent of the population are capable of germanization.† If one used this figure as the basis for calculation, then over 19-23 million Poles would be eligible for deportation. In my view the racial criteria established by the Reich Commissioner are too strict. It is significant that a [NSDAP] district leader in the *Altreich* reports that the Poles who have been sent to him for germanization are the most racially superior section of his population. The figures mentioned by the Reich Security Main Office are perfectly justified in racial terms, whether they are politically advisable is a question which is closely connected with the solution to the problem of where the other Poles are going to go to . . .

We in the Ministry of the Eastern Territories are particularly interested in the question of where the racially undesirable Poles are to go. If twenty million Poles

† The latest information of the SS on those capable of germanization has produced a figure of twenty per cent for the district of Wollstein.

32 Professor Hans Günther had been appointed Professor of Racial Science at the University of Jena in 1930 by the Nazi government in the state of Thuringia. He wrote a large number of works on race using this terminology (eds).

are compulsorily settled in Western Siberia it will undoubtedly represent a permanent threat to the Siberian area, a source of continual unrest against German rule . . .

I can well believe that the large and spacious Siberian steppes with their black earth districts could take far more than twenty million people in more or less concentrated settlements, provided that the resettlement is properly planned . . . If one estimates a period of thirty years, as the Plan does, then there will be approximately 700,000–800,000 settlers [per annum] so that the transportation of these masses of people would require 700–800 trainloads per year and several hundred more for the transportation of equipment and possibly farm animals. That would mean that approximately 100–120 trains per year would be required solely for the Polish transports. However, in a reasonably peaceful period that ought to be technically feasible.

It should be obvious that one cannot solve the Polish problem by liquidating the Poles in the same way as the Jews. Such a solution of the Polish problem would burden the German people with guilt for years to come and lose us the sympathies of people everywhere, particularly since our neighbours would be bound to reckon that they would be treated in the same way when the time came. In my view, a solution of the Polish question must be found which reduces the political dangers referred to above to the absolute minimum. As long ago as March 1941, the undersigned put forward the view in a memorandum that the Polish question could be solved in part by more or less voluntary emigration overseas . . . Brazil with its capacity for one thousand two hundred million people urgently needs people . . .

Although the German defeat ensured that these resettlement plans remained theoretical, there was one particular programme which for some time had been a pet project of Himmler's and was partially realised: the resettlement of the Lublin district to form a German bastion in south-east Poland. On 20 July 1941, Himmler had ordered the SS and Police Leader in Lublin, SS *Gruppenführer* Odilo Globocnik to begin with the 'germanization' of the district of Zamość, a fertile area seventy kilometres south-east of Lublin, and to establish 'strongpoints' there. According to a report from Lublin for the Ru.SHA dated 15 October 1941, Himmler's aim was:

691

Starting with part of the area, to carry out the settlement of the whole district of Lublin with Germans and then beyond that (final objective!) to link the Baltic countries which are nordic or German with the Siebenbürgen, which has also been settled with Germans, via the district of Lublin. [This will enable] the Poles in the territory lying in between [the incorporated Polish territories and the new settlement of Lublin] to be surrounded and gradually crushed both economically and biologically.

In November 1941 Globocnik began the process by evacuating eight villages in the district of Zamość and transferring the inhabitants to a former camp for Soviet prisoners of war. The crisis which developed on the eastern front forced a postponement of the action, but in March 1941 Himmler returned to his pet project. The Main Department of the Interior in the General Government reported on Himmler's plans in a minute dated 27 March:

692

During his stay [in Cracow] the *Reichsführer* SS explained his resettlement plans for the East to the Governor General in my presence. He made it clear at the same time that he was very anxious.
(*a*) that the historic German town centre of Lublin should be completely restored as soon as possible, and be put at the disposal of the German officials in Lublin,
(*b*) that the same should be done to the market place of Zamość. Here, too, dwellings should be placed at the disposal of German officials and other German families in Zamość.

In addition, German peasant families from Transnistria should be settled immediately in the Zamość district. In order not to disturb the resident population, particularly the peasant population, and thereby endanger the harvest, these German peasant families should only be settled on country estates and large holdings. Apart from the peasants from Transnistria, the moving of small but suitable landowners from the German area near Petrikau to the district of Zamość should also be considered. As there already are some villages in the district whose inhabitants are certainly of German origin, a German bastion could in this way be made in the Zamość district.

If it were at all possible these three undertakings in Lublin, Zamość town, and Zamość district should be completed this year.

And again in the following report, dated 30 March 1942:

693

1. The *Reichsführer* SS spoke at the time of his presence on 13 and 14 March in Cracow in detail about the plans of settlement for the next few years and about the planned germanization. Among other things, he took the view that the Gorales, Lemkes, and Hutzules whose Germanic origin, or at least Germanic mixture, is in his opinion indubitable, should be germanized in due course. For this purpose he recommended beginning in the schools of the territory in question by establishing the number of blond and blue-eyed pupils in proportion to the total number of pupils. Then, one should begin to grant them gradually more favourable living conditions, on condition, however, that they make their children learn the German

language and get acquainted with German cultural values. Eventually, one could settle other Germans in the territory of these three peoples later on.

In this connexion, the possibility of some day transferring the Germans from Zips in Slovakia to the General Government should be considered. The *Reichsführer* SS then expounded a further train of thought to the effect that in the first five-year plan of resettlement after the war, once the new German Eastern territories were filled, consideration should be given to providing at any rate a German upper class for the Crimea and the Baltic countries. In the General Government it might be advisable to plan more islands of German settlers from European countries. An exact decision on this point had not, however, yet been made public. In any case, the first thing to be done was to establish a strong settlement along the San and the Bug so as to encircle the alien parts of Poland. Hitherto this kind of encirclement had always been the quickest method of achieving the nationalisation desired.

On 20 July 1942, without informing the Governor General, Himmler instructed Krüger and Globocnik to initiate the first phase of the resettlement of the Zamość district. Plans were drawn up which divided the Poles who were to be expelled into three main groups: II those eligible for germanization; III those to be employed in forced labour; and IV those under 16 and over 65 and 'criminals' and 'asocials'. On 31 October, the Gestapo chief, Muller, sent the following telex to Himmler:

694

Those members of Group III capable of work will be sent to work in the Reich without their dependents who are incapable of work. In agreement with the Plenipotentiary for Labour Mobilization [Sauckel] they will be used to replace Jews who are still employed in important war work. The members of Group IV between 14 and 60 years of age will be transferred to Auschwitz concentration camp. [Those under 16 and over 65 were to be transferred to so-called 'pensioners' villages'.]

The plan was to resettle 27,000 ethnic Germans, who were still in transit camps because no home had yet been found for them, together with 'new arrivals' from Bosnia, Croatia, and Transnistria. A further 70,000 ethnic German settlers were planned for the second phase. On 26 November 1942, the SS and police, with support from Luftwaffe and army units, began to carry out the action. Over the next nine months, some 100,000 people were expelled from over 300 villages in the Zamość district. Of the first 10,000, 300 were placed in Group II for germanization, 2,700 were allocated as 'farm hands' to the German settlers, 2,600 were recruited as forced labour in the General Government or the *Altreich*. 3,300 children and old people were assigned to 'pensioners' villages, and 1,000 were sent to

Auschwitz. The action produced panic among the Polish population of an area which had hitherto been quiet. The Poles who were being resettled thought that they would share the same fate as the Jews of the area who had been rounded up and exterminated only a few months before. They fled into the forests forming bands which then attacked the new ethnic German settlements.

The Zamość affair had serious repercussions for German security in the General Government and Himmler was forced to shelve any further resettlement plans. Probably under the influence of the deteriorating situation, which had strengthened Frank's hand, in the autumn of 1943 Himmler made a truce with Frank and in November replaced his aggressive Higher SS and Police Leader, Krüger, with a more conciliatory figure, SS *Obergruppenführer* Wilhelm Koppe. However, the basic tension between the purely security-oriented approach of the SS-police and the more politically aware attitude of the civilian administration continued to the very end, as is clear from the following excerpt from the minutes of a meeting in Cracow on 9 December 1944 dealing with security matters:

695

State Secretary Koppe points out that if the police intervened too vigorously either the presidents of the Main Departments or the Governor opposed this and considered that such action was not correct. Take, for example, a village in which 20–30 bandits were holding out. If the whole village was giving assistance to the bandits and the SS wanted to carry out a clean sweep then complaints would come in from all sides: how could you burn down a whole village? The food situation, the administration, our prestige etc. will all suffer in consequence. You may be convinced that if the police had an absolutely free hand it would use the toughest methods. One can only defeat the Polish resistance movement if one not only shoots as many of its members as possible but also introduces a system of taking family members hostage and if one acts ruthlessly and shoots 50 Poles a day in Cracow, sixty per cent of whom have been convicted of some criminal act.

The Governor General decidedly opposes this view and is of the opinion that the exact opposite would happen. He states officially that the State Secretary's opinion is completely untenable . . .

(c) Aspects of Polish life under German occupation

Apart from its use as a dumping ground for racial undesirables, the General Government was seen by the Nazis above all as a reservoir of labour. Polish seasonal workers had played an important part in the agrarian economy of eastern Germany since the last decades of the nineteenth century. The years 1936–9 had seen a growing shortage of labour in

Germany, which was particularly acute in agriculture,[33] and the German government tried to meet the problem by recruiting labour from abroad, including Poland. A quota of 60,000 Polish workers was fixed with the Polish government for 1938 and this was raised to 90,000 in 1939. However, in practice an even large number of unemployed Polish agricultural workers sought work in Germany before the outbreak of war.

The Germans had initiated plans to use Polish prisoners of war as labour as early as 1937. However, at that stage it was not envisaged that vast numbers of Poles would come to the Reich, to which indeed there were ideological objections. Soon after the conquest of Poland, the German authorities introduced labour conscription. On 28 October 1939 Frank issued the following decree:

696

By virtue of § 5 (1) of the decree of the Führer and Reich Chancellor concerning the administration of the occupied Polish territories issued on 12 October 1939,[34] I hereby order:

§ 1. (1) All Polish inhabitants of the General Government between the ages of 18 and 60 years shall be subject to compulsory public labour with immediate effect.

(2) A special decree will be issued with regard to Jews.[35]

§ 2. Persons who can prove they are permanently employed in work of public benefit shall not be called upon to perform public labour service.

§ 3. Compulsory public labour shall comprise, in particular, work in agricultural undertakings, the construction and maintenance of public buildings, the construction of roads, waterways, and railways, the regulation of rivers, and work on land improvements.

§ 4. (1) the payment of persons subject to compulsory labour shall be made at equitable rates.

(2) The welfare of persons subject to compulsory labour and their families shall be protected as far as possible.

§ 5. The regulations required for the execution of the present decree shall be issued by the Director of the Department of Labour in the Office of the General Government.

At that stage, the assumption was that the overwhelming majority of Poles would work in the General Government itself. However, at the same time, efforts were made to recruit unemployed Polish agricultural workers for

---

[33] See Vol. 2. pp. 360 ff.

[34] See pp. 926–7.

[35] See p. 1059 below.

work in the Reich to augment the Polish prisoners of war who were already being employed on German farms. Initially, this recruitment drive had some success, since the prospects of a job in Germany appeared more attractive than unemployment in occupied Poland with all its privations. However, the German authorities rapidly came to the conclusion that the shortage of labour in Germany, which had been drastically accentuated by the call-up of large numbers of workers into the armed forces, required a massive recruitment of Polish workers. In his directive of 25 January 1940 Göring mentioned a figure of one million Polish workers who were required.[36]

It was clear that such large numbers could not be secured quickly by the voluntary methods practised hitherto and so the authorities began to introduce compulsion. On 24 April 1940 Frank announced that Poles could be conscripted for work in Germany. Then, as increasing numbers of Poles tried to avoid being deported for forced labour in Germany, so the methods of the Germans became increasingly repressive, turning into veritable manhunts in which cinemas and churches were suddenly surrounded and whole districts cordoned off and those fit for work press-ganged to Germany.

One reason for the increasing unwillingness of Poles to work in Germany was news of the discrimination and poor conditions which faced them there. The SS were determined to prevent the danger of the German people being contaminated by contact with such large numbers of 'ethnic aliens' of an inferior race and so, on 8 March 1940, the RSHA issued a series of directives dealing, on the one hand, with the treatment of Polish workers by employers and the German people and, on the other with the behaviour of Polish workers in Germany. German employers were informed that 'all social contact between these civilian workers and Germans is forbidden . . . Germans who jeopardize the success of these measures, e.g. by collecting money and clothing for Poles, who post letters or buy tickets, who visit inns which are open to Poles while they are present etc. will be called to account. Sexual intercourse between Germans and Polish civilian workers of both sexes will be punished most severely.' Pay for Polish agricultural workers was 'on principle lower than that of German workers'.[37]

The following regulations were issued for Polish workers:

[36] See p. 961 above.

[37] Nüremberg Documents 70-EC.

697

The Greater German Reich provides each and every worker of Polish nationality with work, bread, and pay. It demands in return that everyone carries out conscientiously the work allotted to him and that everyone complies carefully with the laws and orders in force. The following special regulations apply to Polish male and female workers:

1. It is strictly forbidden to leave the place of residence.
2. It is also forbidden to leave the billets during the time of curfew ordered by the police.
3. Public conveyances, such as railways, may be used only after special consent has been obtained from the local police authority.
4. Every Polish male and female worker must always wear visibly the badge issued to him or her.[38] It should be worn on the right breast of every piece of clothing The badge is to be sewn on the clothing.
5. Anyone who shirks his work, strikes, incites other workers, arbitrarily absents himself from the place of employment, etc., will be transferred to a concentration camp for forced labour. Sabotage and other serious offences against work-discipline will be punished severely, at least by transfer to a labour camp for several years.
6. All social contact with the German people is forbidden; especially visits to theatres, cinemas, dances, bars and churches in the company of Germans. Dancing and drinking is only permitted in inns specifically allocated to Polish workers.
7. Anyone who has sexual intercourse with a German man or woman, or approaches them in any other improper manner will receive the death penalty.
8. Any offence against the orders and regulations issued for civilian workers of Polish nationality will be punished in Germany. Nobody will be sent back to Poland . . .

The cases of Poles caught having sexual relations with Germans were referred to the 'racial assessors' of the RuSHA. If the Polish males or females were assessed as 'ineligible for Germanization' then the Polish males were executed and, if they were pregnant, the German or Polish females had their pregnancies terminated. Those found eligible were transferred to a concentration camp for a short sentence. On 26 February 1942, the Chief of the Race Office in the RuSHA sent the following letter to the SS officials responsible for racial assessments and to the RuSHA branch offices:

[38] On 17 September 1940 Himmler issued an order that Poles in the Reich and the incorporated territories must wear on their breasts a violet letter P on a yellow background six centimetres square (eds).

698

According to a directive of the *Reichsführer* SS of 12 December 1941, in cases where the Polish father is assessed as ineligible for Germanization the pregnancy may be terminated. The final decision will be made by the *Reichsführer* SS on the advice of the Reich Security Main Office. The following regulations are to come into operation immediately:

1. Racial assessments of Polish POWs and civilian workers who are scheduled to receive special treatment for illegal sexual intercourse must only be made in accordance with the enclosed specimen form.

2. The large R-cards will continue to be used as the basis for these assessments and must be forwarded to the RuS Main Office together with copies of the assessment. Only those terms used in the R-cards for describing personal characteristics may be used in the assessment.

3. In the column 'Overall Assessment', in addition to the racial assessment, there must also be a short description of the overall impression along the lines of:
(*a*) makes an open, honest impression, has a self-assured bearing and manner
(*b*) is withdrawn, shy, hard to make out
(*c*) makes a sly, underhand impression
etc.

4. The provision of photographs, which must be enclosed with each file, is a matter for the Gestapo offices.

5. In view of the possible necessity for the termination of a pregnancy, the assessments must be made with despatch and handed over to the responsible Higher SS and Police Leader.

[The enclosed specimen form read as follows:]

The Chief of the Race and Settlement Main Office-SS
to the Higher SS and Police Leader . . .

Re: Special treatment—Polish national (Christian name, Surname, date of birth)

The racial assessment of the Polish national (Christian name, Surname, date of birth, last place of residence produced the following result:

Height	Type of hair
Build	Extent of body hair
Shape of head	Colour of hair
Cheek bones	Colour of skin
Shape of eyes	Colour of eyes

Peculiar characteristics

Overall assessment: Grade:

Formula:

Your attention is drawn to the enclosed photographs.

In consequence, the above-mentioned person fulfils the requirements which must be made of ethnic aliens eligible for Germanization. He is considered eligible for Germanization.

Accordingly, the above-named person is eligible for Germanization subject to a positive assessment of his family.

A specimen form was enclosed which was identical, except for the last sentence which concluded that 'the above-named person *does not* fulfil the requirements which must be made of ethnic aliens eligible for Germanization. He is therefore *not considered* eligible for Germanization'. Such persons were then executed, often in public as a warning to others.

The total number of Poles deported to the Reich for forced labour was between 1.3 and 1.5 million, of whom around half were women, and including approximately 400,000 Ukrainians. However, this figure does not include the 400–480,000 Polish prisoners of war who were used as workers or those sent to concentration camps.[39] The General Government suffered proportionately more from the forced labour programme than any other occupied country as is clear from the following figures:

699

Civilian Foreign Workers Employed in the Reich as of 15 November 1943

Country	*Percentage of total population†*
General Government	7.3
Holland	3.4
Bohemia and Moravia	3.0
Belgium	2.7
France	1.7
USSR	1.2
Yugoslavia	0.7

† The number of POWs released for work in the Reich is not included. If it had been the percentages for the USSR and the General Government would increase most significantly.

In their determination to reduce the Poles to a helot population, the Nazis concentrated right from the start on destroying Polish culture, a process which took various forms. There was the ruthless destruction and looting of Polish cultural monuments and intellectual centres. Statues of

[39] See J. T. Gross *Polish Society under German Occupation 1939–1944* (Princeton 1979) p. 78.

Polish national heroes were systematically destroyed, including that of Frederick Chopin in Warsaw. The royal castle in Warsaw was destroyed and its furnishings looted. Churches, museums, libraries, private art collections, scientific laboratories were confiscated and plundered by special teams of German academics.

Secondly, the Nazis endeavoured to destroy the Polish intelligentisa. On 2 October 1940 Hitler told Hans Frank:

700

The Führer must emphasize once again that the Poles may only have one master—a German. Two masters cannot and must not exist side by side; and that is why all the representatives of the Polish intelligentsia must be murdered. That sounds cruel but it is the law of life. The General Government is a Polish reservation, a great Polish labour camp.

It has been estimated that some 10,000 members of the intelligentsia had been murdered in Warsaw alone before the Uprising in July–August 1944. One in six of the academic staff of the pre-war Warsaw institutions of higher education and one in twenty of Warsaw elementary school teachers lost their lives. One in eight of the priests and one in twelve of the members of religious orders in the Diocese of Warsaw were killed.[40]

By closing universities and high schools the Nazis hoped to prevent the intellectual development of the next generation. However, an active underground system of education developed which also provided some employment for professionals who had been systematically deprived of their means of livelihood by the closure of educational institutions, Polish courts, an independent Polish press, book publishing and other cultural activities. Nazi policy towards Polish culture was laid down in a circular of the Department of Popular Enlightenment and Propaganda of the General Government:

701

. . . It is obvious that no German department is to encourage Polish cultural life in any way . . . [However, it is necessary to satisfy] a primitive need for entertainment and amusement:

Theatre. Operettas, revues, and light comedy may be performed by Polish actors for Poles . . . The performance of serious theatre and opera is forbidden for

[40] See T. Szarota *Warschau unter dem Hakenkreuz* (Paderborn 1985) p. 49 ff.

Poles . . . *Cabaret* . . . In the case of performances by Polish artists there is no objection to triviality and eroticism in the programme. All performances which portray the Polish nation must be banned. *Film* . . . Only films released by the Department for Popular Enlightenment and Propaganda may be shown in Polish cinemas . . . *Literature*. Steps will be taken to ensure that only light novels, short stories etc. will be permitted . . . the Poles must be kept away from German books, above all from all ideological works . . . *Painting*. Pictures may be allowed to be sold in the street, in bookshops, cafés etc., provided they do not give the appearance of being part of an exhibition. Pictures with motifs dealing with Polish nationalism, the German and former Polish armies, destroyed houses etc. must be forbidden. *Music*. Performances of Polish music are to be permitted provided they are only for entertainment. Concerts which are intended to offer audiences an artistic experience through a high quality programme must be banned. Polish marches, folk and patriotic songs and all classical pieces must be banned.

The titles of theatre productions in Warsaw during the occupation indicate the level which was being aimed at. They included: *Happy Harem*, *Under a Fig Leaf*, *Your Wife, My Wife*, *From Nipple to Glass*, *Drinks and Kisses*, etc.[41]

However, although the Poles in the General Government suffered labour conscription and serious cultural deprivation during these years, they undoubtedly felt the impact of the German occupation most acutely in their stomachs, particularly the urban population. Early in 1940, Frank introduced a system of food rationing which differentiated between different groups, which he explained to a meeting attended by Herbert Backe, the State Secretary and by now dominant figure in the Reich Ministry of Agriculture, on 23 April 1940:

702

. . . As far as the differential treatment of the various population groups is concerned, the first problem is the members of the ethnic German community who must in future receive the same rations as the Reich Germans. They must not be treated differently. Until now we have taken the view that the ethnic Germans must gradually adjust to the German standard. But today, on the Führer's birthday, I have received them into the German national community.

I am not interested in the Jews. Whether or not they get any fodder to eat (*füttern*) is the last thing I'm concerned about.

The second category is made up of the Poles in so far as I can make use of them. I shall feed these Poles with what is left over and what we can spare. Otherwise, I will tell the Poles to look after themselves—we were not to blame for the war.

[41] J. T. Gross *op. cit.* p. 77.

I am only interested in the Poles in so far as I see in them a reservoir of labour, but not to the extent that I feel it is a governmental responsibility to give them a guarantee that they will get a specific amount to eat. We are not talking of rations for Poles but only of the possibilities of feeding them.

Now we are getting to the real issue of food supplies and in this respect things are not too bad. We have three categories of population in the General Government: the Ukrainians, whom we must treat fairly well. They make up about 600,000 or 700,000 people. In so far as they are not self-sufficient, we will guarantee their food supplies to a certain extent since that is in line with our Polish policy. Then comes the next category whose food supplies we must guarantee—those Poles whom we are employing in the administrative apparatus: Polish civil servants, employees of plants, police, railways, post office etc. We must also look after the agricultural workers to some extent in order to maintain the split within the Polish people. We will say to them: if you work, you will get enough to live on, sufficient in terms of Polish living standards, i.e. in terms of what is available.

Now we are coming to the German sphere. Within this group, i.e. those Poles for whom we guarantee food supplies, the first group is once again the most important, namely the Poles employed in the armaments plants. . . . Then come the Germans, to start with the category of ethnic Germans, of whom there are some 100,000 in the General Government, of whom 30,000 live east of the Vistula. The next category is that of the *Wehrmacht* and the civil servants. . . . There are seven categories in all, therefore 'The Jews are on the bottom rung, the military and civil servants on the top. The majority of the Polish people will still be treated significantly better than the Jews. We have no interest in the Jews.

The following figures give the calorie content of food rations for Poles during 1940–41:

703

	1940		*1941*	
Quarter	*Poles*	*Jews*	*Poles*	*Jews*
I	609	503	611	237
II	704	449	553	219
III	698	331	531	198
IV	938	369	981	360
Yearly average	737	413	669	253

The minimum requirement for physical health is 2,400 calories per day. In 1932, an average Polish worker received 2,602, an unemployed worker 2,087 calories per day. In Warsaw in 1941 the German population was allocated 2,613 calories per day.[42] The extent to which the food rations for Poles in occupied Warsaw met the various nutritional requirements is contained in the following figures in percentage terms:

704

Year	*Protein*	*Fats*	*Carbohydrates*	*Calories*
1940	20.9	4.3	35.8	27.9
1941	25.6	8.0	37.7	29.7
1942	22.2	3.2	32.9	25.8
1943	23.1	2.4	37.2	28.6
1944	27.8	2.5	43.3	38.5
Average	23.9	4.1	37.3	30.1

On 25 January 1943, the State Secretary for Security in the General Government, SS *Obergruppenführer* Friedrich-Wilhelm Krüger, reported to a Police conference:

705

In practice the Poles do not receive the food to which they are entitled. In fact, they only get bread and potatoes. We are not in a position to supply them with any other kind of food to which they are entitled such as meat, fats, jam, ersatz coffee etc. We are aware that the work performance of the ethnic aliens is declining day by day. It is not enough for us to improve their wages or wage scales. In the final analysis, people need a full stomach to work properly. They can only work if one can give them something to eat. The currency situation in the General Government is not normal. An ethnic alien in the General Government can hardly buy anything at all for the 300 Złoty or so which he earns.

The impact of the German occupation on the standard of living of the Polish population in the General Government varied to a considerable extent between the urban and rural population and over the period of the occupation. The urban population suffered worst. Wages and salaries were

[42] See. T. S. Szarota, *op. cit.* p. 113.

fixed according to scales laid down by the German authorities and fell rapidly behind the rising cost of living. The following figures show the increase in wages of an average Warsaw worker compared with the increased cost of living over the period 1939–1941:

706

Month and year	*Hourly Wage*	*Cost of Living*
VII 1939	100	100
VII 1940	132.6	435.2
X 1940	131.3	371.8
XI 1940	136.6	402
XII 1940	135.7	410.9
I 1941	132.7	440.8
II 1941	133.1	425.1
III 1941	137.6	468.3
IV 1941	141.6	558.0
V 1941	142.4	916.4
VI 1941	143.4	1,616.3
VII 1941	153.4	1,294.4
VIII 1941	153.2	1,104.6
XI 1941	156.3	1,211.5

The following figures are for a Warsaw worker with a four person household:

707

Month	*Weekly cost of living in Złoty*	*Weekly expenditure on food in Złoty*
I 1941	117	88
V 1941	310	274
VI 1941	489	435
VII 1941	454	296
VIII 1941	284	234
IX 1941	314	260
X 1941	307	253
XI 1941	303	253
XII 1941	265	213

By the turn of the year 1943–44, the real wages of Polish workers had declined to eight per cent of their pre-war level.

By contrast, the rural population did relatively well out of the occupation, particularly in the early years when debts to Jews were cancelled, taxes were not collected, and the delivery of quotas of foodstuffs was not strictly enforced. Later the Germans adopted a tougher policy of quota enforcement, as is clear from the following figures.

708

Total Grain Quotas in the General Government
(In Tons)

	Quota	
Year	*Assigned*	*Collected*
1940–1941	1,000,000	383,000
1941–1942	770,000	685,000
1942–1943	1,400,000	1,230,000
1943–1944	1,600,000	1,500,000
1944–1945	425,000	

709

Deliveries of Agricultural products sent to Germany from the General Government
(In Tons)

Year	*Grain*	*Potatoes*	*Cattle*	*Fats*	*Sugar*
1940–1941	40,000	121,000	7,510	800	4,500
1941–1942	58,000	134,000	21,498	900	4,465
1942–1943	633,470	434,350	54,272	7,235	28,666
1943–1944	571,682	387,741	53,768	7,700	27,546

The rural population were increasingly alienated by these forced requisitions and also by the SS-police actions in connection with resettlement and the recruitment of forced labour for the Reich. As a result, the aim of driving a wedge between the different sections of the Polish population, a policy which might have had some prospect of success, particularly among the rural population of the southern part of Poland formerly belonging to Austria, was frustrated. Instead, a cycle of resistance and terror was set in motion as is clear from the following figures of Poles killed in the countryside:

710

Year	*No. killed in pacifications and executions*	*No. murdered*
1940	15	699
1941	20	397
1942	122	3,207
1943	308	7,383

Fortunately for the Polish population an element of flexibility was built into the system of repression as a result of the widespread corruption within the German occupation authorities; the black market was a semi-tolerated institution. In the entry for 13 February 1940 in his 'Chronicle of the Occupation', Ludwik Landaus wrote:

711

The corruption among the Germans is indescribable. For money one can get a foreign passport, be excused from work and even from wearing the armbands prescribed for Jews; for money one can get news about the fate of people who have been arrested. Gestapo agents who have been given the task of fighting the black marketeers do business with them and so on and so on virtually without end.

A member of the Polish Underground intelligence network commented on the German occupation officials:

712

They came to Poland out of a desire to rule, to advance their careers, to make their mark, and to avoid being sent to the front. The General Government, in particular Warsaw, offered the Germans undreamt of opportunities. They suddenly found themselves transferred from low-level mainly provincial posts to senior positions in the conquered land, which provided them with responsibilities and privileges which they could never have dreamt of having in the Reich. Above all, they set about enjoying life. They had elegant flats with foreign furniture, amusements, alcohol and girl friends, and for their wives and families in the Reich there were packing cases and parcels full of stuff which one could procure on the spot. They discovered a source of private profit which never dried up—first simple plunder and later bribes. Here in Warsaw they were somebody, a life without restrictions lay open to them.

This picture is not simply a prejudiced view from the standpoint of the Poles as is clear from the following SD report from Leipzig concerning the general mood of the population in the area, dated 6 May 1942:

713

People are hearing more and more about the catastrophically corrupt conditions in Poland. Eye-witnesses report on the economic and moral degeneration which unfortunately is also to be found within the administration and among Party circles. The national comrades believe that while they are overwhelmed with work here, the 'bureaucrats' (*Bonzen*) are enjoying a life of pleasure and plenty in Poland. That creates bitterness and leads to remarks such as: 'so that's what the members of our ruling class are like!'

A report sent by the Polish underground to London in autumn 1942 commented on relations between Germans and Poles as follows:

714

Polish-German relations are based on mutual contempt. The Poles despise the Germans as robbers, bandits, primitive people, louts, cheats and liers; the Germans despise the Poles as bad soldiers, hopeless organisers, as people who live in wretched circumstances, have little to eat and now no longer have their own state.

As a result of the corruptibility, greed for profit, venality, and corruption of the administrative apparatus, they [the Germans] have completely destroyed the earlier legend of German law-abidingness, the German sense of order and honesty, German talent for organization. The Polish population does not allow itself to be in the least impressed by the mendacious German propaganda about 'the model administration in the East' since it knows only too well from its daily experience what the morality, the honesty, and the justice of this whole apparatus, with which we in the occupied territories have been saddled, is worth.

(d) The Warsaw Uprising of July–October 1944.

In the summer of 1944 the Polish tragedy culminated in the Warsaw Uprising which began on 1 August and ended on 2 October with the capitulation of the Polish insurgents. With the support of Frank and the Foreign Ministry, the *Wehrmacht* leadership had decided to grant the Poles an honourable surrender and full prisoner of war status under the Geneva convention in the hope of thereby creating a favourable impression on the Polish people. However, the Security Police soon nullified any remote prospects of such an effect by transporting some 160,000 citizens of Warsaw to forced labour in the *Altreich*, including 60,000 to concentration camps. German casualties in the Uprising had been 17,000 dead and missing and 9,000 injured. The Polish Home Army had lost 16,000 dead and missing and 6,000 were injured. 200,000 civilians were killed in the Uprising and ninety per cent of the city was destroyed. On 21 September 1944, Himmler gave his views on the Uprising to an audience of commanders of the military districts in Jägerhöhe:

715

. . . For the past five weeks we have been fighting for Warsaw. I have appointed SS *Obergruppenführer* von dem Bach[43] as my commander there. It is the hardest battle we have fought since the beginning of the war. It is comparable with the house-to-house fighting in Stalingrad. It is just as tough. This General Bor was betrayed by the Russians—for they have not relieved him; now they are pretending they would like to. And he was egged on and set up by the English. The English set off this uprising and at a very unfortunate moment for us. When I heard the news of the Polish Uprising I went at once to see the Führer. I am telling you about it as an example of how one must react to such news with utter calmness. I said: 'My Führer the timing is unfortunate. But from a historical point of view it is a blessing that the Poles are doing that. We'll get through the four and five weeks [it will take] and then Warsaw, the capital city, the brain, the intelligence of this 16–17 million-strong Polish nation will have been obliterated, this nation which has blocked our path to the east for seven hundred years and since the first battle of Tannenberg, has always been in the way. Then the historic problem will no longer be a major one for our children, for all those who come after us, and for us too.

Moreover, I simultaneously gave orders for Warsaw to be totally destroyed. You may think I am a fearful barbarian. If you like I am one, if I have to be. My orders were to burn down and blow up every block of houses. As a result, one of the biggest abscesses on the eastern front has been removed.

Yet despite the appalling suffering of the Poles and also of the Russians, both of whom were regarded and treated as sub-humans (*Untermenschen*) within the Nazi empire, they were not yet at any rate subjected to systematic extermination. That was, however, the fate of three groups at the hands of Nazi racial imperialism: the mentally sick and handicapped, the Jews, and the Gypsies.[44]

[43] Erich von dem Bach-Zelewski had been put in charge of anti-partisan operations in Russia at the end of October 1942 (eds).

[44] Unfortunately shortage of space prevents the documentation of the Nazi extermination of some 500,000 European Gypsies.

CHAPTER 36

*The 'Euthanasia' Programme 1939–1945**

(i) The Weimar Background

In current parlance the term *euthanasia* refers to the practice of so-called 'mercy killing', that is of painlessly ending the life of a person who is terminally ill at his or her request or, if they are no longer capable of making such a request, then with the consent of their relatives. It is a highly controversial issue, but it should not be confused with the Nazi 'euthanasia' policy. For, although the Nazis used the term to describe their own programme of killing over one hundred thousand mentally sick and handicapped persons from 1939 to 1945, their practice had little in common with the term as it is normally understood. In the first place, the decision to terminate the life of a patient under the Nazi programme was taken not by the individual concerned or by his or her relatives but by an official body. Secondly, the criterion for the 'mercy killing' was not the welfare of the individual patient but whether or not the patient's life was judged to be of 'value' or 'worth', and of value not to the individual concerned (although the Nazis sometimes used this as an additional justification) but to the community.

The concept of the 'destruction of worthless life' was not invented by the Nazis. It had already gained currency in the 1920s, in particular through the publication in 1920 of a book with the title *Permission for the Destruction of Worthless Life, its Extent and Form*, written by Professor Karl

---

*This chapter owes much to the superbly documented book by Ernst Klee, "*Euthanasie" im NS-Staat. Die "Vernichtung lebensunwerten Lebens*" (Frankfurt a.M 1983).

Binding, a former president of the *Reichsgericht*, the highest court, and by Professor Alfred Hoche, Professor of Psychiatry at Freiburg University. Binding and Hoche were primarily motivated by the belief that, because of the war and the alleged expansion in the numbers of mental defectives as a result of an 'exaggerated humanitarianism', Germany had become intolerably lumbered with 'living burdens' (*Ballastexistenzen*), who were absorbing a disproportionate amount of resources which ought to be devoted instead to a national revival. First, Binding asked:

716

Are there humans who have lost their human characteristics to such an extent that their continued existence has lost all value both for themselves and for society? One only needs to pose the question and a feeling of anxiety stirs in anyone who is used to assessing the value of individual lives both to the people themselves and to the community. He is painfully aware of how wasteful we are with the most valuable and self-sufficient lives which are full of energy and vigour and what labour, patience and resources are squandered simply in order to try and sustain worthless lives until nature—often cruelly tardy—removes the last possibility of their continuation. If, at the same time, one thinks of a battlefield covered with thousands of young corpses, or of a mine in which hundreds of hard-working miners have been buried, and if one compares them with our institutions for idiots, with the care which is devoted to their inmates—one is deeply shocked by the sharp discrepancy between, on the one hand, the sacrifice of man's most precious resource and, on the other, the tremendous care devoted to creatures which are not only completely worthless but are of negative value.

It cannot be doubted that there are people for whom death would come as a release and, at the same time, for society and the state in particular would represent liberation from a burden which, apart from being an example of great self-sacrifice, is not of the slightest use . . .

. . . However, I am firmly of the opinion that rational calculation should not be the sole basis on which to answer this question; the reply must win approval through a deep sense of its correctness. Every killing which is permitted must be felt, at least by the person concerned, as a release; otherwise such permission must be ruled out.

It follows from this, however, that is is obsolutely vital to respect completely *everybody's will to live, even that of the most sick, tortured or useless people*.

The legal order can never be allowed to operate as a murderer and a killer forcibly breaking the will to live of its victims. Naturally, there can be no question of permitting the killing of the feeble-minded person who feels happy with his life . . .

Binding suggested that three groups should be permitted to be killed: i) Those who as a result of their illness or injury were 'irretrievably lost', were in full possession of their mental faculties, and had expressed an urgent wish to die, e.g. cancer patients.

717

The second group consists of the incurable lunatics—irrespective of whether they were born as such or whether they are paralytics in the final stage of their condition. They have neither the will to live nor to die. Thus, they are unable to approve their killing; on the other hand, it will not clash with any will to live which would have to be broken. Their life is completely useless, but they do not find it intolerable. They represent a terribly heavy burden for their relatives as well as for society. Their death would not have the slightest impact except perhaps on the feelings of their mothers or their loyal nurses. Since they require a lot of care, they prompt the emergence of a profession which consists simply of maintaining absolutely worthless life for years and decades. It cannot be denied that this is completely absurd, a misuse of human energy for ends unworthy of it.

Again, I can find no reason, either from a legal, or from a social, or from a moral, or from a religious standpoint for not giving permission for the killing of these people who represent the fearful counter-image of real human beings and arouse horror in almost everybody who encounters them—but naturally not to just anybody ! In periods of a higher morality—in ours all heroism has been lost—these poor people would probably have been released from their afflictions by the authorities. But who in our unnerved times would dare to profess this necessity, this justification?

The third category referred to by Binding comprised mentally healthy persons who, through some event—for example, a war wound—had either permanently lost consciousness or, if they regained it, 'would awaken to a nameless misery'. Since, as Binding put it, 'the present state [i.e. Weimar] could never take the initiative for such killings', it would have to lie with the sick people themselves, or their doctors or relatives. He suggested that they should have to apply to a new state authority, composed of a doctor specialising in physical illnesses, a psychiatrist, and a lawyer, which would establish whether the criteria had been met for permission to be given. Even if a mistake was made, Binding maintained,

718

. . . then mankind would be one fewer. But after successfully overcoming this catastrophe [i.e. the illness], this life might have become very expensive to maintain; in most cases its value would have been hardly more than mediocre. The relatives would of course feel the loss badly. But mankind loses so many of its members through mistakes that one more or less hardly matters.

In his section of the book Hoche stressed the enormous financial cost involved in maintaining 'idiots', particularly in terms of the nursing staff who are wasted. And he continued:

The question of whether the resources of all kinds devoted to these living burdens is justified was not an urgent one in the prosperous days gone by; but now things are different and we must deal with it seriously. Our position is like that of participants in an arduous expedition in which the greatest efficiency of everybody is the precondition for the success of the enterprise and where there is no place for people operating with only a half, a quarter, or an eighth of their strength. The task before us Germans for many years to come will be to achieve the most intense concentration of our potential and to liberate every capacity at our disposal in order to advance our goals. The fulfilment of this task runs counter to the modern concern to preserve as far as possible even the weaklings of every kind and to devote increasing care and protection to those who, while not mentally dead, are congenitally inferior elements. These efforts have had such an influence that up to now no attempt has been possible, indeed no serious attempt has even been made to prevent these defective persons from procreating . . . Viewed from the standpoint of a higher state morality, it cannot be doubted that the endeavour to sustain worthless life at all costs has been taken to excess. We have got out of the habit of regarding the state organism as a whole, with its own laws and requirements like, for example, a self-contained human organism which, as we doctors know, abandons and rejects individual parts which have become worthless or damaging.

A review of the series of human burdens outlined above and a brief consideration demonstrates that the majority of them are not suitable for a conscious rejection, i.e. elimination. Even in the times of crisis which we face we shall never wish to cease looking after physical defectives and the infirm so long as they are not mentally dead; we shall never cease treating the physically and mentally ill as best we can so long as there remains any prospect of an improvement in their condition; but one day we may reach the mature opinion that *the elimination of those who are mentally completely dead is not a crime, not an immoral act, not brutal, but a permissible and beneficial act.*

This raises the question of which characteristics and effects are associated with mental death. As far as the external aspects are concerned, we can recognise without difficulty: the alien character of the mentally dead within the context of human society, the lack of any productive achievements, a condition of complete helplessness with the necessity of being looked after by others . . .

Despite all this, only a very slow process of change and reorientation will be possible with regard to this new question. The consciousness of the unimportance of the individual compared with the interests of the whole, the sense of an absolute duty to concentrate all available energies and the rejection of all unnecessary tasks, the sense of being highly responsible participants in a difficult and painful enterprise will have to be become far more widespread than today before the view expressed here can win complete recognition . . .

There was a time which we regard as barbaric, in which the elimination of those who were born or became unviable was regarded as natural. Then came the phase we are in now, in which finally the maintenance of any, even the most worthless, existence was considered to be the highest moral duty; a new period will come which, on the basis of a higher morality, will cease continually implementing the demands of an exaggerated concept of humanity and an exaggerated view of the value of human life at great cost. I know that nowadays these views will by no means receive a positive response in all quarters or even be met with understanding; but this must not be allowed to silence someone who, after a decade of medical service to man, can claim the right to be heard in matters affecting mankind.

Binding's and Hoche's book was highly controversial. However, although their proposals for the destruction of 'worthless life' did not win widespread assent, the mentality which underlay them was much more generally shared. The idea that the worth of a human being is not intrinsic but depends on his or her contribution to a collective—the community, the nation, the state or whatever; the idea that the individual has to justify his existence to some outside authority: these ideas were shared by many Germans. Liberal values, with their emphasis on the importance of the individual and his rights—never very strong in Germany—had been steadily eroded by collectivist pressures of various kinds over the previous half century and, in particular, by a nationalism now made even more virulent by defeat. Moreover, as a result of the growing influence of eugenics among medical, welfare, and penal circles, various forms of social deviance—prostitution, alcoholism, juvenile delinquency and other 'asocial' behaviour—were increasingly coming to be seen as indications of a 'degeneracy' which was, to some extent at least, congenital. In such an intellectual atmosphere the concept of 'worthless life' was capable of radical extension to embrace much broader categories than those proposed by Binding and Hoche. Last but not least, at a time when resources were scarce, there was a temptation to adopt a narrowly materialistic perspective for the establishment of priorities and to seek savings through short cuts at the expense of those who were weak and less able to defend themselves.

(ii) The Impact of the Nazi Take-over

With the Nazi take-over in 1933 this mentality received official endorsement in its most extreme form. Under the Nazis collectivism was sanctified in the concept of the 'national community' to which the individual was totally subordinated. Despite the pseudo-mysticism of Nazi rituals and the routine disparagement of Western materialism in comparison with German spirituality, in homage to the German nationalist tradition, the regime in fact soon established itself on the basis of a biological materialism governed by Social Darwinist criteria. Since human life was a struggle for the survival of the fittest, then 'performance' had to be an essential requirement for all its citizens. The value of a 'national comrade' was to be measured primarily in terms of his contribution to the 'national community' in the most concrete form of his labour. Moreover, an extreme version of eugenics, already part of the Nazi *Weltanschauung*, now became official policy. Hitler had already made his views clear in a speech to the Nuremberg Party Rally on 5 August 1929:

719

If Germany was to get a million children a year and was to remove 700–800,000 of the weakest people then the final result might even be an increase in strength. The most dangerous thing is for us to cut off the natural process of selection and thereby gradually rob ourselves of the possibility of acquiring able people . . . As a result of our modern sentimental humanitarianism we are trying to maintain the weak at the expense of the healthy. It goes so far that a sense of charity, which calls itself socially responsible, is concerned to ensure that even cretins are able to procreate while more healthy people refrain from doing so, and all that is considered perfectly understandable. Criminals have the opportunity of procreating, degenerates are raised artificially and with difficulty. And in this way we are gradually breeding the weak and killing off the strong.

After 1933, positive eugenics found expression in discriminatory welfare benefits to promote births and in favour of the eugenically 'fit'; negative eugenics was implemented in the Sterilization Law of 14 July 1933, which introduced compulsory sterilization for certain categories of 'inferiors',[1] and also in the Law amending the Sterilization Law of 25 June 1935 which permitted abortions in cases where those deemed suitable for sterilization were already pregnant. Thus, it is against this background that one must see the Nazi 'euthanasia' programme, a programme which illuminates the nature of Nazism in a particularly clear light.

During the first years of the Third Reich, the focus of policy for dealing with the mentally handicapped and mentally ill was on sterilization. An essential aspect of this was a propaganda campaign designed to persuade Germans that this group of people were worthless and should be prevented from having offspring who would only represent a further burden on the community. However, although initially designed to remove inhibitions against compulsory sterilization, the logic of such a campaign was to encourage the idea that if these people were a useless burden then they should be eliminated altogether rather than simply prevented from procreating. Before long this theme became explicit as in the following article in the SS journal *Das Schwarze Korps*, which appeared on 18 March 1937:

[1] See vol. 2 pp. 455–459.

720

Re: the topic of mercy deaths:

In response to our article in the previous issue, a reader writes to us as follows:

I have a relative, the mother of five children. Four of them are completely healthy as are the parents. There have been no cases of hereditary illness in the families. The fifth child, now two years old, is an idiot. According to the doctors, the mother carried the child too long. When the parents noted, soon after the birth, that the child was not responding to anything, they took it to the best children's doctor in the area. He transferred it to a hospital. There the professors declared that the child was incurable. It is now in an asylum which brings up idiotic children and cripples at great expense.

The parents pay 100 RM per month. The child has cost thousands already. This money is not only lost to the four healthy children, the heavy burden must also prevent the parents from having any more children. The family and the national community not only have to bring up an idiot, they must also lose further births because it is allegedly a humane duty to keep the idiot alive artificially and allow him as far as possible to reach a biblical age. I think there ought to be a law whereby such children could be killed with the agreement of their parents.

We have already commented on the case of that peasant who was recently sentenced in Weimar to 3 years imprisonment because he killed his grown-up son and heir who had become incurably mentally ill. The man broke the law and had to be punished because he carried out an act which the national community is not yet prepared to do for him, and because he took on a responsibility which legally the state ought to take on. The case described by our reader is even simpler.

If an adult becomes mentally ill, he at least had a personality and has lived consciously. To eliminate him requires a difficult decision, although it will be a release for him and all those involved. A child which is born an idiot has no personality. It would hardly last a year if it were not kept alive artificially. It is even less conscious of its existence than an animal. One does not remove anything from it if one snuffs it out.

If people say that human beings have no right to kill them then one must reply that humans have a hundred times less right to interfere with nature and keep something alive which was not born to live. That has nothing whatever to do with Christian love of one's neighbour. For, under the term 'neighbour', we can only understand our fellow human beings who are capable of responding to the love which we give them. Anyone who has the courage to carry these considerations to their logical conclusion will make the same demand as our reader.

A law should be passed which would give nature its due. Nature would let this unviable creature starve to death. We can be more humane and give it a painless mercy death. That is the only humane act which is appropriate in such cases and it is a hundred times more noble, decent and humane than that cowardice which hides behind a sentimental humanitarianism and imposes the burden of its existence on the poor creature, on its family and on the national community.

Those who proclaim themselves as the defenders of humanity are usually people who themselves do nothing for the maintenance of the nation's strength and for whom a baptised idiot is preferable to a healthy heathen. No sane person will interpret the biblical saying 'Blessed are the poor in spirit' in terms of earthly rights for idiots. No one is denying them the other rights. Let them go to heaven.

Such Nazi attitudes soon began to have an impact on the treatment of mental patients, as one psychiatrist, who was the director of an asylum, recalled after the war:

721

I left the service at the beginning of 1939. Euthanasia was on the horizon. It had not yet arrived. But I was convinced that it would come. There was a progressive deterioration in the care of the mentally ill. Their treatment was governed by the motto: we must save. In those years, the first years of National Socialism, that was more or less the official position. But then the trend went further. The meat rations were cut. The ratio of doctors to patients was reduced; the aim was a ratio of 1:300. There was a progressive deterioration in the medical and personal care; serious cases of neglect of patients went unpunished because the view was: Oh well, they're mental patients. As a result, there was a decline in the sense of duty which I did not think I could put up with. Then my influence over the appointment of staff and doctors was largely removed; only SS doctors were appointed. At the end of 1936, I was told: in future you will only be getting SS doctors: they know how to use injections.

In 1935, Hitler had told the then Reich Doctors' Leader, Dr Wagner, that 'in the event of a war he would take up the question of euthanasia and enforce it' because 'he was of the opinion that such a problem could be more easily solved in war-time, since opposition which could be expected from the churches would not play so significant a role in the context of war as at other times', and therefore 'in the event of war, he intended to solve the problem of the asylums in a radical way'.[2] However, by 1938–9, the regime was sufficiently secure both at home and abroad for such inhibitions both in this sphere and over the Jewish question to have been substantially removed.

[2] Cf. L. Gruchmann, 'Euthanasie und Justiz im Dritten Reich' in *Vierteljahrshefte für Zeitgeschichte* (1972) p. 228.

(iii) The Children's 'Euthanasia' Programme

The programme was finally precipitated by the case of a handicapped child, which occurred in the winter of 1938–9, as Hitler's physician Dr Brandt recalled at Nuremberg after the war:

722

It concerned a father of a deformed child who wrote to the Führer and asked for this child, or this creature, to be put down. Hitler assigned this case to me and ordered me to go to Leipzig at once . . . The child had been born blind, appeared to be an idiot and was also lacking a leg and part of an arm.

He had ordered me to speak with the doctors who were dealing with this child in order to find out whether the father's statements were correct. In the event of their being correct, I was to inform the doctors in his name that they could carry out euthanasia . . . I was also instructed to say that in the event of these doctors becoming involved in a court case as a result of this measure, Hitler would ensure that it would be thrown out. Martin Bormann was instructed to inform the Minister of Justice, Gürtner, of this Leipzig case . . .

The petition to the Führer from the Knauer baby's father had gone to the 'Chancellery of the Führer of the NSDAP' (KdF), an office established by Hitler in 1933 for processing all appeals addressed to him as Führer of the Party. Its head was Philipp Bouhler, the former secretary of the Party. A leading figure in the KdF was Dr Hans Hefelmann who in a post-war trial described what happened next:

723

The Knauer case prompted Hitler to authorize Brandt and Bouhler to deal with similar cases in the same way as with the Knauer child. I cannot say whether or not this authorization was given orally or in writing. In any event, Brandt did not show us a written authorization. This authorization must have been given when Brandt reported to Hitler about the conclusion of the Knauer case. Brandt told me personally that this authorization was given in this form. At the same time, Hitler ordered that all petitions of this kind which were directed to the Reich Ministry of the Interior or to the Presidential Chancellery should be made the sole responsibility of the 'KdF'. In accordance with this instruction, the Reich Interior Ministry and the Presidential Chancellery were requested to send such petitions to the 'KdF' for further processing. It was in this fashion that *Ministerialrat* Dr Linden of the Reich Interior Ministry was involved for the first time, as far as I know, with these measures. The matter was treated as top secret right from the start.[3] When, shortly afterwards, Professor Brandt instructed me to establish an advisory body it had to be set up on the basis that it was dealing with a state secret. The result was that only those doctors etc. were selected of whom it was known that they were 'positively' disposed. A further reason for their selection according to this principle was also the fact that Hitler had ordered that his office, i.e. the 'KdF', must not appear in public as the authority responsible for these things.

Prompted by Hitler's instruction, an *ad hoc* group, composed of officials from the KdF and the Reich Interior Ministry and doctors recruited on the basis of their 'positive' attitude, began with the planning. In order both to disguise the role of the KdF and the unpleasant reality of what was involved, namely child murder, it was necessary to establish a front organization, set up on 18 August 1939, which was given the impressively scientific-sounding title of 'The Reich Committee for the Scientific Registration of Serious Hereditarily- and Congenitally-based Illnesses' (*Reichsauschuss zur wissenschaftlichen Erfassung von erb- und anlagebedingten schweren Leiden*), usually shortened to 'Reich Committee'.

On 18 August 1939, the Reich Interior Ministry issued the following 'highly confidential' circular to the state governments:

724

Re: The duty to report deformed births etc.

1. In order to clarify scientific questions in the field of congenital deformities and intellectual under-development, it is necessary to register the relevant cases as soon as possible.

2. I therefore instruct that the midwife who has assisted at the birth of a child—even in cases where a doctor has been called to the confinement—must make a report to the Health Office nearest to the birth place on the enclosed form, which is available from Health Offices, in the event of the new-born child being suspected of suffering from the following congenital defects:

(i) Idiocy and Mongolism (particularly cases which involve blindness and deafness).

(ii) Microcephalie [an abnormally small skull].

(iii) Hydrocephalus of a serious or progressive nature [abnormally large skull caused by excessive fluid].

(iv) Deformities of every kind, in particular the absence of limbs, spina bifida etc.

(v) Paralysis including Little's disease [Spastics].

[3] *Geheime Reichssache*—the highest category of secrecy (eds).

3. In addition, all doctors must report children who are suffering from one of the complaints in (i–v) and have not reached their third birthday in the event of the doctors becoming aware of such children in the course of their professional duties.

4. The midwife will receive a fee of 2 RM in return for her trouble. The sum will be paid by the Health Office . . .

These forms were returned to the 'Reich Committee', which in fact meant the KdF, from where they were then sent to three paediatricians who acted as assessors: Professor Hans Heinze (Director of the asylum at Brandenburg-Görden), Professor Werner Catel (Director of the University Paediatrics Clinic in Leipzig), and Dr Ernst Wentzler, (a paediatrician and director of a small private clinic in Berlin). Each assessor marked the form either with a + if the child was to die or a − if it was to be allowed to survive and then sent it on to the next one. At no stage were the children actually examined by the assessors. Those children who were to die were then transferred to special 'paediatric clinics', of which eventually there were some thirty established in hospitals throughout the Reich. Here the children were either effectively starved to death, often dying of diseases provoked by malnutrition, or given lethal injections or doses. Their parents were persuaded to agree to have them transferred on the grounds that these special child clinics would be able to provide them with the optimum treatment. In theory it was possible to refuse. Thus, on 17 May 1943, one asylum director complained to the *Landrat* of Kehlheim in Bavaria:

725

The parents, who are evidently besotted with their idiotic child, can take it home any time—however, against medical advice and on their own responsibility.

Such parents had to sign a declaration committing themselves to supervise and care for the child. And it was still possible for the authorities to remove custody over the child from the parents. In the later stages of the war mothers would often be conscripted for war work, making it impossible for them to fulfil their obligations to the child. Thus, a Dr Eidam reported:

726

Recently, the Reich Committee has even sent letters to particular labour offices in order to get the mothers of such children conscripted for labour so that they then have to give up their children. And vice versa, in the case of demands for the asylums to discharge children, the asylums are requested to demand a certificate from the labour office giving them permission to take the children home.

The following passage is a post-war description of one of the more notorious of these child clinics in the asylum of Egelfing-Haar near Munich. The visit took place on 16 February 1940:

727

About forty visitors in uniforms of the most varied hues, from the dark grey of the Wehrmacht via the bright brown of the cadre officials of the Nazi Party to the jet black of the SS gathered round Dr Pfannmüller.[4]

After some brief introductory remarks Dr Pfannmüller approached one of the fifteen cots which flanked the central passage to right and left.

'We have here children aged from one to five', he pontificated. 'All these creatures represent for me as a National Socialist "living burdens" (*Ballastexistenzen*) . . . a burden for our nation . . . In this sense, the Fuhrer's action to free the national community from this overburdening is quite simply a national deed, whose greatness non-medical men will only be able to assess after a period of years if not decades. We do not carry out the action with poison, injections or other measures which can be recognised . . . for then the foreign press and certain circles in Paris or London would only have new opportunities for propaganda against us . . . No, our method is much simpler.'

With these words he pulled a child out of its cot. While this fat, gross man displayed the whimpering skeletal little person like a hare which he had just caught, he coolly remarked: 'Naturally we don't stop their food straight away. That would cause too much fuss. We gradually reduce their portions. Nature then takes care of the rest . . . This one won't last more than two or three more days'.

A number of paediatricians and psychiatrists welcomed the concentration of these handicapped children in special clinics since they provided excellent opportunities for research. For example, a leading role in this research was played by Dr Carl Schneider, Professor of Psychiatry and Neurology at Heidelberg University, who in autumn 1942, launched a research project in a mental hospital in Wiesloch near Heidelberg. Schneider was aware that experiments on the children provided by the 'Reich Committee' would not be limited by ethical considerations and that their deaths could be engineered to suit the experiment, with the subsequent autopsy providing the evidence. As he himself put it in his research plan of 12 March 1942:

---

4 *Obermedizinalrat* Dr Hermann Pfannmüller, director of the asylum in Eglfing-Haar near Munich, one of the leading figures in the children's 'euthanasia' programme (eds).

728

. . . reaching far beyond other scientific discussion and research in the field of psychiatry, at last the most practical and immediate questions affecting the health of the nation can be most comprehensively resolved because thanks to the programme [i.e. 'euthanasia'] a rapid anatomical and histological clarification can be achieved.

On 15 October 1942 Schneider wrote to his colleague Professor Nitsche: 'We have found a lot of "nice" idiots in the Hirt asylum in Strasbourg.[5] Requests for transfers will follow.'

Richard von Hegener, the desk officer in the KdF responsible for the 'Reich Committee', estimated that out of 100,000 cases which he processed some 5,200 children were killed. However, this figure is by no means the whole story. For, although the age range of those children covered by the children's 'euthanasia' programme was later increased to sixteen, the majority of older children—an unknown but considerable number—were included in the adult 'euthanasia' programme which had its own distinct organization and history.

(iv) The Adult 'Euthanasia' Programme

In June or July 1939—the exact date is uncertain—Hitler instructed Dr Leonardo Conti to organize a 'euthanasia' programme for adults. As the state secretary in the Reich Interior Ministry responsible for health matters, Reich Doctors' Leader, and head of the Nazi Party's Department of National Health, Conti was a kind of medical supremo. However, when news of the appointment reached Victor Brack, head of Department II in the KdF and Bouhler's deputy, he pressed his chief to assert the KdF's claim to run the new programme. Bouhler, who was always eager to extend the range of responsibilities of the Führer's Chancellery, which was overshadowed by the Reich Chancellery under Lammers and the Staff of the Führer's Deputy under Hess/Bormann, needed little encouragement. Hitler was evidently soon persuaded of the advantage of having the adult operation run by the office which had already begun planning the children's programme and transferred the responsibility fron Conti to Bouhler. He told Bouhler that he wanted a completely unbureaucratic solution to this problem because he did not want a department such as the Interior Ministry, which was stuck in a rut taking on such a 'difficult assignment.'[6] During

[5] Cf. L. Gruchmann, *op.cit.* p. 241.

[6] Cf. K. Novak, *'Euthanasie' und Sterilisation im 'Dritten Reich'. Die Konfrontation mit dem Gesetz zur Verhütung erbkranken Nachwuchses und der 'Euthanasie-Aktion'* (Göttingen 1978) p. 190.

the following months, the KdF—in conjunction with Dr Herbert Linden of the Public Health section (Department IV) of the Reich Interior Ministry—set up the administrative machinery for implementing the new programme. To begin with, at the end of July, a number of senior medical men were invited to Berlin to be initiated into the programme. They included among others Professors of Psychiatry from the Universities of Berlin (de Crinis), Heidelberg (Schneider), Jena (Kihn), Würzburg (Heyde), as well as those involved in the children's programme. Bouhler justified the programme to his audience on the basis of the need for hospital space in view of the coming war and promised protection against legal proceedings. He explained the lack of legislation covering the programme in terms of Hitler's concern about negative repercussions abroad, but assured them that it had his full support. With the exception of Max de Crinis, all those present agreed to participate. De Crinis simply excused himself on the grounds of being overburdened with work, but approved the programme. An SD agent and friend of Heydrich, de Crinis remained intimately involved with it.

The two key questions facing those organising the 'euthanasia' programme were who? and how? They were discussed at a meeting of the 'steering group' on 9 October 1939, chaired by Brack and attended by the following: Blankenburg, Hefelmann, Vorberg, Dr Bohne (all KdF), Professor Heyde, Professor Nitsche, Dr Linden (Reich Interior Ministry), Dr Werner (Reich Criminal Police Department), Hermine Wolf as secretary (KdF). The following is an extract from the minutes:

729

Brack: Today's meeting is concerned with the final clarification of the questions: who ? and how ? Both questions belong together. Dr Linden will report on the first.
Linden: Today forms are being sent to all asylums together with a circular from the Reich Interior Ministry . . . It is anticipated that the forms will be returned within three weeks since a deadline of 1 November has been given. In reply to a question from party comrade Blankenburg: No suspicions can arise as to the real purpose of the forms because the reason given for them in the circular is rationalisation.
Brack: Thanks Party Comrade Linden and comments on the number of anticipated cases. The number is arrived at through a calculation on the basis of a ratio of 1000:10:5:1. That means out of 1,000 people 10 require psychiatric treatment; of these 5 in residential form. And, of these, one patient will come under the programme. If one applies this to the population of the Greater German Reich, then one must reckon with 65–75,000 cases. With this statement the question of 'who?' can be regarded as settled.
Heyde: Commented on the question of 'how?' The number referred to by Party

comrade Brack also tallies with his own estimation. It makes the proposed method of injections put forward by Professor Nitsche unviable. For the same reason, the use of doses of medicine is also impossible.
Nitsche: Disagrees.
Werner: The question has been discussed with the director of the Reich Criminal Police Department, Nebe. We are in agreement with him that CO (Carbon Monoxide) is the best method.

Meanwhile, however, having worked out a global figure it was necessary to establish which individual patients were to die. Department IV of the Reich Interior Ministry had already issued a circular on 21 September 1939 requiring the registration 'of all asylums and clinics in the Reich in which the mentally ill, epileptics, and the feeble minded are cared for on a long-term basis'. Nearly three weeks later, on 9 October, a further circular was issued by the Interior Ministry to the directors of all such asylums and clinics enclosing forms to be filled in for each patient and then returned. This was the one referred to in the meeting of the 'steering group'. The justification given for this exercise was 'the necessity for the rational and economic utilization of asylums'. The enclosed forms read as follows:

730

Form 1

No,

Name of the asylum.......

Address....

Christian and surnames of the patient (for women maiden name).....

Birthplace....

Citizenship and race...*

Diagnosis....

Detailed statement of the nature of employment....

Since when in asylums....

As a criminal mental patient...

Offences...

Address of next of kin...

Does the patient receive regular visitors?..

Are there relatives?..

Address of legal guardian...

Person responsible for payment of asylum costs...

This space is to be left blank

signature of chief doctor
or his deputy

* German or related blood, Jew, Jewish Mischling I or II degree, Negro, Negro Mischling, Gypsy Mischling etc.

The following instructions were enclosed for filling in the forms:

731

All patients must be reported who

1. Suffer from the following illnesses and cannot be employed in the asylum except in mechanical tasks (e.g. plucking etc.): Schizophrenia, epilepsy (if exogenic give the cause e.g. war wound), senile illnesses, paralysis not responsive to therapy and other Lues illnesses, feeble-mindedness of all kinds, encephalitis, Huntington's Chorea and other terminal neurological disorders.
2. have been in asylums continuously for at least five years or
3. are confined as criminal lunatics or
4. do not possess German nationality—or are not of German or related blood—give details of race and nationality.

The forms are to be filled in for each patient individually and given consecutive numbers . . .

In view of the large number of completed forms which began arriving at the end of October and which continued to arrive over the next eighteen months, it was necessary to recruit doctors to act as junior assessors under the supervision of a senior assessor: first Dr Linden, then Professor Werner Heyde, recently promoted a full professor at Würzburg University, and finally Professor Paul Nitsche, a leading psychiatrist from Saxony. After the war, one of these doctors who was recruited as an assessor reported on his experience:

732

Herr Brack then requested us or rather asked us whether we were prepared to act as assessors in the programme. The criteria were drawn up so that war veterans, or rather those war disabled who had suffered some kind of mental damage from their war disablement, were excluded on principle. The assessment, which was based on the state of the particular patient, was drawn up according to criteria of whether the patient—on the basis of the details in the form—had deteriorated so much mentally and physically that he came into the category of worthless life . . . On principle, patients whose constitution was such that they could perform work, useful work, were to be excluded from this action. It is difficult to draw the line as to what work is useful and what is not. He only used the term: capable of work—in terms of the asylum's therapy. The comments he made were not precise. As far as I know, he did not elucidate the concept of capacity for work more closely. He gave examples, e.g. a patient who can sole shoes in a workshop is performing useful work. People who had had a stroke and had become mentally defective were excluded on principle.

Herr Brack gave a general instruction that the assessments were to be drawn up so that in cases of doubt or in marginal cases the person should be included in the programme, i.e. he went beyond the bounds of medically justifiable criteria. In this context he asserted that now, especially during the war, in which so many healthy people were forced to lose their lives, these mentally sick people, who in any case were of no use to the national community, did not matter, and that in view of the bad food situation at least these people would be removed from the food sector. He emphasized further that numerous healthy people were having to lose their lives, and so it was not surprising that the State should adopt these measures and remove these sick people, who in any case did not represent proper life. He kept speaking of the leadership of the State. A written instruction was never given . . .
. . . Then we were asked whether we were prepared to cooperate as secondary assessors along these lines. People were not asked individually, but rather the whole matter was dealt with in the group in which we sat, more in open colloquium . . . The conclusion of this colloquium was that under these circumstances we would be prepared to cooperate with and support these measures. No objections were raised . . .

It was perfectly possible for doctors to decline to participate in the programme and, provided they remained silent about it, they did not suffer in consequence. One such doctor wrote to Dr Pfannmüller, the director of the Eglfing-Haar asylum on 20 August, declining to become involved in the children's programme:

733

My dear Director, 20 August 1940

. . . I am very grateful for you willingly insisting that I should take time to think things over. The new measures are so convincing that I had hoped to be able to discard all personal considerations. But it is one thing to approve state measures with conviction and another to carry them out yourself down to their last consequences.

I am thinking of the difference between a judge and an executioner. For this reason, despite my intellectual understanding and good will, I cannot help stating that I am temperamentally not fitted for this. As eager as I often am to correct the natural course of events, it is just as repugnant to me to do so systematically, after cold-blooded consideration, according to the objective principles of science, without being affected by a doctor's feeling for his patient. It has not been scientific interest that has made work in a children's home worthwhile for me, but a doctor's hope, amidst our so often fruitless work, to provide aid in many cases and at least bring about some improvement. Psychological assessment and therapeutic-pedagogic treatment were always much closer to my heart than anatomical curiosities, however interesting. And thus, while I can be completely objective in the assessment process, . . . I feel emotionally tied to the children as their medical guardian, and I think that this emotional contact is not necessarily a weakness from the point of view of a National Socialist doctor. It prevents me, however, from adding this new task to the one I have performed up to today.

If this leads you to put the children's home in other hands it would mean a painful loss for me. However, I prefer to see clearly and to recognize that I am too gentle for this work than to disappoint you later. I know that your offer is a mark of special confidence and can honour it only by absolute honesty and frankness.

Heil Hitler!

Directors of asylums could also decline to cooperate in filling in the forms. However, in this event a commission of doctors was sent to the asylum to carry out the selection on the spot, as in the following case:

734

Bavarian State Ministry of the Interior 2 September 1940
to the
Director of the Neuendettelsau Asylum

Re: Registration of Asylums.
The Reich Interior Ministry has informed us that owing to personnel shortages, you are unable to complete the forms sent by him by the deadline.

Since other institutions have also been unable to keep to the deadline, the Reich Interior Ministry has provided a commission of doctors which will take over the completion of the forms. This commission will arrive at your institution on 3 September and will start its work—also in the branch institutions. You are requested to provide board and, if possible, lodging.

After the commission had left the asylum, its director, Dr Rudolf Boeckh, sent the following letter of complaint to the Reich Interior Ministry dated 7 November:

735

As the senior doctor responsible for the Neuendettelsau asylum, I have already made a personal protest to my superiors, the Bavarian State Interior Ministry in Munich, concerning the working methods of this commission. I now hereby reiterate this protest for the following reasons:

The composition of the commission provided no guarantee whatsoever for the proper completion of the forms in accordance with the facts. Contrary to the instructions of the Bavarian State Ministry, the commission completed several hundred of these forms and sent them off to Berlin without the presence of the senior doctor responsible for the asylums . . . The commission did not examine a single one of the 1,800 patients. The majority of the patients are not in Neuendettelsau but in branch asylums distributed all over northern Bavaria. Thus, the commission was incapable of forming its own judgment of the situation . . . Only the nurses were questioned . . . and their objections were largely ignored. Indeed, it was even observed that the opposite of the true statements of the nursing personnel were recorded on the forms. The staff who composed the commission cannot really be blamed since the majority were medical students and typists who were completely incapable of properly assessing the statements of the nursing staff. The senior doctor on the commission, who worked in a separate room on his own, received the forms which had been completed by the assistants and then gave his judgment without any personal knowledge of the individual cases and without looking at the medical records.

As the doctor responsible for the asylums I protest against this unprofessional method of working by the commission which goes against all the traditions of the medical profession . . . In view of the fact that the public is aware of the ultimate objective of this registration of the patients, I have been burdened with a grave responsibility as the senior doctor responsible for these institutions.

Those doctors who agreed to participate did so for a number reasons. Some were primarily careerists like Professor Heyde who gained a chair. There were opportunities for rapid promotion in the psychiatric field—for example, to directorships of asylums—for those prepared to cooperate. For others, such as Professor Nitsche, professional concerns were as or more important. Nitsche had long been one of the most 'progressive' psychiatrists in Germany, advocating a policy of active therapy for the mentally ill, such as electric shock or insulin treatment, instead of the traditional passive policy of simply putting them under restraint and letting them vegetate. He also advocated a policy of release into community care. Nitsche and others who thought like him believed that if the hopeless cases were removed then more effort and resources could be devoted to curing those who responded to therapy. Dr Hefelmann reported after the war on a meeting in the KdF at the start of the 'euthanasia' programme at which this whole issue was discussed:

736

(*a*) Right at the start of the asylum operation in the Second World War, general agreement was reached that personnel who were no longer needed as a result of the euthanasia programme, as well as the medicines and therapeutic facilities which were thereby made available, should be redeployed for the benefit of the remaining eighty per cent of the asylum inmates. For this purpose Professor Schneider of

Heidelberg University accepted an invitation to join the Reich Association [of Asylums] in order to expand the development of therapy and research. This fact underlined the moral justification for the implementation of euthansia measures. Following the appointment of Professor Schneider, we visited the therapy department of the Eglfing-Haar asylum, which at the time was under the direction of Professor Braunmühl. Professor Braunmühl had achieved pioneering therapeutic results in the field of electric shock and insulin therapy, which it was hoped would be passed on to other institutions via Professor Schneider's research department. (*b*) The asylum directors also pointed out that during the First World War there had been a terrible death rate [among mental patients]. It was far higher than the number of those very serious incurable cases who were envisaged for the euthanasia measures. (As far as I remember Nitsche had figures on the death rate in the First World War which proved this). At that time, many doctors and orderlies had been withdrawn. Provisions and drugs had become very scarce so that mortality had reached high levels, since what was available had to be distributed equally among both the curable and the incurable . . . In this context it was pointed out by a doctor that with the serious cases a nursing ratio of 1 orderly to 3–4 patients was required, whereas with the other cases one of only 1 to 8–10 was necessary. Thus, euthanasia for the most serious cases would ensure that, despite the departure of orderlies for military service, a peace-time level of therapy for the less serious cases could be maintained through the release of a relatively large number of orderlies within the asylum. The doctors emphasized at this meeting that the numerous deaths, confirmed on all sides, which had occurred after the even greater suffering in the First World War, would largely justify the euthanasia measures . . . They used what seemed to them a favourable opportunity to demand that more ought to be done for therapy. As far as I remember, schizophrenia in particular was mentioned in this connection. This request from the psychiatrists was probably responsible for Brandt prompting Brack to establish a special department in T4[7] under Professor Schneider which was intended to work for an improvement in therapy going hand in hand [with the 'euthanasia' programme].

The assessors were sent photocopies of the completed forms which, as in the case of those used in the children's programme, had to be marked in the space 'to be left blank' with a red + if the patient was to die, a blue – if he or she was to live and a ? or later a Z in the event of uncertainty. The criteria for assessment were eventually formalized and periodically adjusted. The final set before the official ending of the programme was agreed at a meeting on 10 March 1941:

737

1. Elimination of all those who are incapable, even in asylums, of performing productive work, i.e. not only those who are mentally dead.

[7] See below p. 1021.

2. Those war veterans who either distinguished themselves at the front or who were wounded or who were decorated are not to be included. Herr Jennerwein[8] will make the assessment of what constitutes distinguished service at the front, especially decorations. Relevant cases which come to our asylums [i.e. the extermination centres] are to be held back there until Herr Jennerwein has reached a decision after studying the file. War service in itself does not protect people against inclusion in the programme.

3. Extreme caution in cases of senility. Only urgent cases e.g. criminals or asocials are to be included. In the last two cases the files must be looked at and excerpts from the files included with the photocopies.
This reference to senile patients does not apply to aged patients with psychoses, such as schizophrenia, epilepsy etc. who are basically included in the programme. Special senile cases should be referred to Herr Jennerwein.

4. Only Reich Germans are to be included in the programme. It is envisaged that all the Poles will be collected together in purely Polish asylums in the eastern Gaus . . .

Enemy aliens too must not be included. Only those stateless persons of whom it can be shown that no one has bothered with them for a long time . . .
Otherwise, as before, selection on the basis of a strict interpretation.

In fact, since the forms had to be dealt with at great speed by the assessors, the whole assessment process was largely spurious and functioned to a large extent as a means of alleviating consciences. Indeed, the assessors were paid on a piece-work basis according to the numbers of forms dealt with in a specific period as is clear from a minute of 6 December 1940 signed by Heyde and 'Jennerwein'.

The 'euthanasia' planners had solved the problem of 'who?' In order to solve the second vital question of 'how?', Brack had approached Arthur Nebe, the head of the Reich Criminal Police Office, an obvious source of useful advice for those planning to commit murder on a large scale. Nebe passed him on to the head of the chemical section of the Criminal Technical Institute (KTI), Dr Albert Widmann. According to the judgement on Widman at his post-war trial:

738

Nebe informed the accused already in the planning stage that euthanasia had been decided upon and that the KTI was to have an advisory role. Nebe replied to the accused's question as to whether humans or animals were to be killed by saying

[8] Code name for Brack see below p. 1020.

that neither humans nor animals but 'animals in human form' were to be killed. In reply to a query by the accused, Nebe pointed out that he would not bear the responsibility and that the whole thing would be legalised by a law. Shortly afterwards, the accused was summoned to the Führer's Chancellery and initiated into the euthanasia programme by Brack, probably in the company of Dr Hefelmann, von Hegener and Nebe, and was asked for his opinion as a chemist about the means which might be employed and what kind of dose would be lethal. Under discussion were morphium, scopolamine, prussic acid and carbon monoxide gas. Since the accused had already been heavily involved in a case of carbon monoxide poisoning as regards its effects and provability and had written a report on it which went to all the forensic institutes in the Reich, he advocated the use of pure carbon monoxide gas for killing the mental patients. In order to carry it out he advocated introducing it into the dormitories at night and thereby putting the mental patients to sleep . . .

After unsuccessful tests with injections which proved too slow, on 4 January 1940, a successful gassing took place in the asylum at Brandenburg not far from Berlin. Dr August Becker, one of the chemists in the KTI reported after the war as follows:

739

I was ordered by Brack to attend the first euthanasia experiment in the Brandenburg asylum near Berlin. I went to the asylum in the first half of January 1940. Additional building work had been carried out especially for the purpose. There was a room similar to a shower room which was approximately 3 metres by 5 metres and 3 metres high and tiled. There were benches round the room and a water pipe about 1″ in diameter ran along the wall about 10 cm off the floor. There were small holes in this pipe from which the carbon monoxide gas poured out. The gas cylinders stood outside this room and were already connected up to the pipe. The work on this installation had been carried out by the SS Main Building Office in Berlin . . . There were already two mobile crematoria in the asylum with which to burn the corpses. There was a rectangular peephole in the entrance door, which was constructed like an air raid shelter door, through which the delinquents [!] could be observed. The first gassing was carried out by Dr Widmann personally. He turned the gas tap and regulated the amount of gas. At the same time, he instructed the asylum doctors, Dr Eberl and Dr Baumhardt, who later took over the extermination in Grafeneck and Hadamar. As far as I can remember, among the prominent personalities who were there were: the doctors already mentioned, Professor Dr Brandt, the Führer's personal physician, and a detective, Wirth, at that time head of the homicide branch in the Stuttgart police department and later head of the Hartheim asylum near Linz. For this first gassing about 18–20 people were led into this 'shower room' by the nursing staff. These men had to undress in an anteroom until they were completely naked. The doors were shut behind them. These people went quietly into the room and showed no signs of being upset.

Dr Widmann operated the gas. I could see through the peephole that after about a minute the people had collapsed or lay on the benches. There were no scenes and no disorder. After a further five minutes the room was ventilated. Specially assigned SS people collected the dead on special stretchers and took them to the crematoria. When I say special stretchers I mean stretchers specially constructed for this purpose. They could be placed directly on the ovens and the corpses could be pushed into the oven mechanically by means of a device without the people carrying them coming into contact with the corpse. These ovens and the stretchers were also constructed in Brack's department . . . Following this successful test, Brack—who was naturally also present and whom I forgot to mention—said a few words. He expressed satisfaction with the test and emphasized once again that this action must only be carried out by doctors according to the motto—'syringes are a matter for doctors'. Finally, Dr Brandt spoke and reiterated that doctors alone should carry out this gassing. With that, the start in Brandenburg was considered a success and the thing continued under Dr Eberl.

Apart from the asylum at Brandenburg, the first gassings were carried out at Grafeneck. Grafeneck had been a hospital for cripples run by a Protestant welfare organization. It was a former palace of the Dukes of Württemberg and conveniently situated on the top of an isolated hill in a rural area (Kreis Münsingen). The cripples had been transferred elsewhere, the hospital taken over by the state, and the necessary construction work for its new use was already nearing completion.

Meanwhile, however, even before the start of the official 'euthanasia' programme, a series of actions were already under way in the East. On 29 September 1939, Polish mental patients in the district of Bromberg began to be murdered by shooting. By 1 November, nearly four thousand had been killed. Then, during October 1939, the Gauleiter and Oberpräsident of Pomerania, Franz Schwede-Coburg, ordered the evacuation of mental asylums in his province so that they could be handed over to the SS and the Wehrmacht. Thus, he offered the asylum in Stralsund to the SS Death's Head units as a barracks. The SS reciprocated by providing an execution squad to murder the inmates. They were transported to Neustadt in West Prussia and shot in a forest. Finally, during December 1939 and January 1940, hundreds of patients from Polish asylums were murdered by the SS Special Commando Lange. This was a unit containing 15 members of the Security Police and around sixty members of the paramilitary *Schutzpolizei* and led by SS *Obersturmbannführer* Herbert Lange. The mental patients were locked into a van similar to a furniture van which had a sign 'Kaiser's Coffee' on the side. Carbon monoxide gas was fed into the van from a canister carried in the front cab.

These actions, however, were distinct from the official 'euthanasia' programme which, during the autumn of 1939, acquired an elaborate organization. At the centre was Department II of the Fuhrer's Chancellery (KdF).

Indeed, the whole operation was code-named 'T4' after the address in Berlin from which Department II operated—Tiergartenstrasse 4, a villa acquired from Jews through a forced sale. Department II of the KdF worked closely with Department IV of the Reich Interior Ministry from which Dr Linden and Dr Gerhard Bohne had been effectively seconded to the programme. Dr Bohne was appointed to head a front organization, 'The Reich Association of Asylums' (*Reichsarbeitsgemeinschaft für Heil- und Pflegeanstalten*) which was effectively just a cover name and address for T4 intended to conceal the role of the KdF. Another front organization was established to handle the legal details of the operation such as employment contracts of the personnel and property contracts—the 'Community Foundation for the Encouragement of Asylums' (*Gemeinnützige Stiftung für Anstaltspflege*). Several of the leading figures involved used cover names: Brack, for example, called himself 'Jennerwein' after a notorious poacher in nineteenth-century Bavaria.

The organizers soon came to the conclusion that such an elaborate programme of mass murder, which could come to involve numerous bodies (the courts, local government agencies, religious organizations, insurance companies etc.) required some formal authorization at the highest level. Some time in October 1939, Hitler was persuaded to sign the following document which was written on his personal notepaper rather than as an official document and dated 1 September:

740

Reichsleiter Bouhler and Dr med. Brandt are charged with responsibility to extend the powers of specific doctors in such a way that, after the most careful assessment of their condition, those suffering from illnesses deemed to be incurable may be granted a mercy death.

Just as Hitler preferred to have the programme carried out by his personal chancellery rather than by government bodies, so he preferred this informal authorization to a formal decree or law. Significantly, in future, he resisted all attempts to persuade him to sign a euthanasia law. Such a law was in fact drafted in the Interior Ministry and those involved in the programme—particularly the doctors—were clearly anxious formally to legitimize their actions. However, according to Lammers, the head of the Reich Chancellery, a law 'which would have had to be put to all the Reich Ministries for discussion was unwelcome to Hitler for political reasons.'[9] The back dating

[9] See A. Mitscherlich and F. Mielke eds. *Medizin ohne Menschlichkeit Dokumente des Nürnberger Ärzteprozesses* (Frankfurt a.M. 1960) p. 187.

of the document to 1 September presumably reflected Hitler's sense that the outbreak of war was an appropriate moment from which to date such an extreme measure and such a dramatic new initiative towards realizing his ideological goals.

Once the patients had been selected for 'euthanasia', the method of killing them had been devised, and the sites at which they were to be killed prepared, it only remained to transport them from their existing asylums to the extermination centres. To organize this a new front organization was established by the KdF—the 'Community Patients Transport Service Ltd' (*Gemeinnützige Kranken Transport GmbH.* or Gekrat) under Reinhold Vorberg, a cousin of Brack's, who adopted the code name 'Hintertal'. Gekrat acquired from the Reich Post Office bus service a number of buses which were based at the extermination centres. Letters such as the following were then sent to asylum directors informing them of the impending transfer of patients:

741

The Minister of the Interior Karlsruhe, 29 November 1939
Secret!

Re: Transfer of asylum inmates in the context of special measures for rationalisation.

The present situation necessitates the transfer of a large number of patients in asylums and institutions of a similar nature. In cooperation with the Commissioner for Evacuation, I shall order the transfers which become necessary from time to time. The patients will be transferred together with their medical records in group transports. The asylum from which they are transported will not be liable for any costs. The medical records will be returned to the asylum after perusal by the receiving institution. The relatives will be informed about the transfer by the receiving asylum. Those responsible for financing the patients' stay in the asylum are to be informed that further payments should cease from the date of transfer until they are requested by the receiving asylum.

Then came the actual announcement of a transport as in the following case:

742

Community Patient Transport Service Ltd Berlin W9,14 May 1940
Potsdamer Platz 1

Brandenburg State Asylum Neurüppin Personal
Herr Obermedizinalrat Dr Petsch

Dear Dr Petsch,

I have been requested by the Reich Defence Commissioner to collect 50 women from your asylum on 20.5.1940. I enclose three copies of a transport list. The transport list contains 69 names. However only 50 patients will be collected so that a measure of flexibility exists for people who have been moved, died etc. I would be grateful if you would prepare the personal and medical records as well as any valuables and cash belonging to the patients who are to be transferred. In order to identify the patients you should write their names on plasters and then stick them on their backs.

Heil Hitler!

The sending of a list containing more names than those required was a subtle move introduced shortly after the first transports in response to the resentment of asylum directors at having no choice over which patients would be transferred. Allowing a degree of flexibility not only helped alleviate this frustration it also in effect made the directors accomplices in the programme.

The following is an account of one of the first transports by a nurse in the district asylum of Jestetten in Württemberg:

743

The vehicles . . . were like Post omnibuses, only the windows had been painted so that one could neither see in nor out. The transport leader was in a motor car. He was in civilian clothes not in uniform. The accompanying personnel, consisting of both men and women, did not wear uniforms but civilian clothes, namely white coats. They all made a rough and off-putting impression, the women even more than the men . . . The transport leader declared that he had been authorized by the Reich Interior Ministry to collect 75 patients and immediately took over the medical and personal records.

Dr Lichtenberger immediately asked what the destination of the transport was . . . However, the transport leader refused to reveal the destination and insisted that he had a duty of secrecy just like Dr L. He stuck to this despite the repeated insistence of Dr L. that he could not let his patients go off to an unknown destination. He was very angry and upset and ran like an angry bull backwards and forwards when he simply could not extract the information he desired from the transport leader. As regards informing the relatives, we were simply told that that would be done by the new asylum.

Dr L. was not there for the actual loading because he was called away urgently to a birth. While up to this point we had accepted the affair in good faith as more or less harmless and were prepared to accept the transport leader's refusal to give the destination as a war-time measure, we became dubious when the loading began. The senior sister introduced the patients by name. But the transport leader replied that they did not operate on the basis of names but numbers. And in fact the patients who were to be transported then had numbers written in ink on their wrists which had been previously dampened with a sponge. In other words, the people were transported not as human beings but as cattle, though without any maltreatment. Nevertheless, everybody eagerly boarded the bus and looked forward to the journey, innocent as they are. Only Albert A (a schizophrenic) on saying goodbye to Dr L. announced: 'We shall not leave these vehicles alive'.

The following is an account of what happened when the patients arrived at the extermination centres, in this case Hartheim near Linz, which began to operate in May 1940. The author begins by explaining how he came to be employed as a 'burner' (*Brenner*) in the crematorium:

744

In 1939 I worked for Lell & Co. in Freindorf near Ansfelden and earned 25 RM per week. This was hardly enough to feed my wife and children. So I was always on the look out for ways to earn more money. At this point, my brother had returned from the Reich to Linz as an SA brigade leader. I asked him if he could find me a better job. Finally, in April 1939 [*sic*!] he called me to his office . . . I was asked how much I earned. They laughed when they heard that I was only getting 25 RM. I and the others were then told that we were going to Hartheim and would earn more there. I began work at Hartheim on 2 April 1940 . . .

About a fortnight later, Captain Wirth called us together—there were mainly men present — and made a speech:

'Comrades, I have called you together to explain to you what is going to happen in the palace.[10] I have been ordered by the Reich Chancellery [*sic*!] to take charge here in the palace. I, as Captain, am in overall command. We have got to build a crematorium here in order to burn the mentally ill from the *Ostmark* [Austria]. Five doctors have been assigned to examine the mentally ill in order to establish who is capable of being saved and who is not. Those who aren't will be put in the crematorium and burnt. The mentally ill are a burden on the state. Some men will be assigned to work in the crematorium. Above all, you will have to keep quiet about this or face the death penalty. Anyone who doesn't keep quiet will go to a concentration camp or be shot.

A short time after Captain Wirth's speech, work was started on the crematorium. I and others were given the job of 'burner'. I must emphasize that I did not apply for this job myself. For the job of burner I was promised an additional payment of 35 RM a month which was later paid. In addition, I got a bonus of 35 RM (for silence). This sum was to be paid later.

About six weeks after the 2 April 1940, the preparations and the buildings were ready and the plant began to operate. The mentally ill were, as far as I know, brought from the various asylums by train and bus to Hartheim at very different times of the day. Sometimes the numbers arriving were large, sometimes small.

[10] Hartheim was a former renaissance palace of the Prince of Starhemberg (eds).

The numbers arriving varied between 40 and 150. First, they were taken to the undressing room. There they—men and women in different sections—had to undress or were undressed. Their clothes and luggage were put in a pile, labelled, registered and numbered. The people who had undressed then went along a passage into the so-called reception room. In this room there was a large table. A doctor was there together with a staff of 3–4 assistants. The doctor on duty there was either Dr Lonauer or Dr Renno. As far as I can judge as a layman, the doctors did not examine these people but only checked their files. Someone then stamped them. An orderly had to stamp them individually on the shoulder or the chest with a consecutive number. The number was approximately 3–4 cm in size. Those people who had gold teeth or a gold bridge were marked with a cross on their backs. After this procedure, the people were led into a nearby room and photographed. Then the people were led out of the photography room through a second exit back into the reception room and from there through a steel door into the gas chamber. The gas chamber had a very bare interior. It had a wooden floor and there were wooden benches in the chamber. Later, the floor was concreted and finally it and the walls were tiled. The ceiling and the other parts of the walls were painted with oil. The whole room was designed to give the impression that it was a bathroom. Three showers were fixed in the ceiling. The room was aired by ventilators. A window in the gas chamber was covered with a grill. A second steel door led into the room where the gassing apparatus was installed.

When the whole transport had been dealt with, i.e. when the registration had been carried out, the photographs taken, people's numbers stamped on them, and those with gold teeth marked, they all went into the bath-gas room. The steel doors were shut and the doctor on duty fed gas into the gas chamber. After a short time the people in the gas chamber were dead. After around an hour and a half, the gas chamber was ventilated. At this point, we burners had to start work.

Before I deal with that, I would like to make a few more statements about the feeding of the gas into the gas chamber. Next to the gas chamber there was a small room in which there were a number of steel canisters. I cannot say what kind of gas was in these canisters or where it came from. The contents of these canisters was fed through a rubber pipe into a steel pipe. On the canister there was a pressure gauge. When the gas chamber was full the doctor went to the canisters, opened the tap and the gas poured through a 15–20 mm iron pipe into the gas chamber. As I have stated already, between the gas chamber and the gas canister room there was a steel door. A third door led from the gas chamber into the yard. These doors had a brick surround and there was a peephole into the gas chamber. Through this peephole one could see what went on in the gas chamber.

Once the room had been aired, we burners—we always had twelve hour shifts—had to get the corpses out of the gas chamber and bring them into the mortuary. The mortuary was next to the gas canister room. Getting the corpses out of the gas chamber into the mortuary was a difficult and nerve-racking task. It was not easy to disentangle the corpses, which were locked together, and drag them into the mortuary. This task was made even more difficult initially by the fact that the floor was uneven and when the floor was concreted it was rough. This made dragging the corpses into the mortuary difficult. Later when the floor was tiled we put water down. That made moving the dead much easier. The corpses were piled up in the mortuary. Next to the mortuary was the crematorium. The crematorium was equipped with a so-called pan which could be taken out of the oven. The dead were laid on this pan and were pushed in and left there just like with a baking oven. Depending on the number of corpses, we burnt 2–8 at a time. The oven was coke-fired. The work went on night and day as required. Before the corpses were burnt the burners pulled out the gold teeth of those who had been marked with a cross. They were taken to the administration. Because I cannot feel properly with my right hand because of the partial paralysis of my right side, I was unable to pull the teeth. Once I tried it and the gold tooth slipped down the dead person's gorge. Since I could no longer find the tooth, I was bawled out by Captain Wirth. After that I ceased to pull teeth. After the corpses had been burnt, the remnants of the bones which had fallen through the grid would be put into a bone mill and ground to powder. This bonemeal was then sent to the grieving relatives as the remains of their dead. We estimated roughly 3 kg of such meal for each corpse.

Since the work was very exhausting and, as I said, nerve-racking, we got about 1/4 liter of schnaps per day. I reckon that we burnt about 20,000 mentally ill people in this way.

In 1944 we also burnt concentration camp prisoners. In my opinion they were mostly people with serious illnesses but not mentally sick. Sick eastern workers were also burnt by us in Hartheim. By my reckoning in all about 30,000 people must have been killed.

Before Christmas 1944, the community [!] plant was stopped and the oven dismantled. From this point on, no one else was burnt in Hartheim.

Now I will give a few more details of things which I can remember. On one occasion 150 people were gassed at one time. The gas chamber was so full that the people in there could hardly fall down and got so tangled together that we could hardly pull the corpses apart. Since gassings had already taken place, the mortuary was so full that the corpses at the bottom were already beginning to decay by the time we came to burn them. On another occasion, a transport came with women infected with typhus. On the orders of Captain Wirth four women were brought into the red room and shot in the back of the neck there by Captain Wirth. While I am on the subject of women, I would like to mention that they burnt more easily than the men. I think this was because they have more fat than men. They also have a lighter bone structure. The remains of the incineration were at first thrown into the Danube and then later on were buried. As far as the personality of Captain Wirth is concerned, I only want to say that he was a beast. He threatened everybody at every opportunity with concentration camp or with shooting. Now I think I have said all I know. I still suffer from bad dreams. On these occasions all the dead people appear to me in spirit and I sometimes think I will go mad.

Some participants in the programme such as Wirth were totally cynical and hard-bitten. The following incident occurred at Hadamar, an extermination centre in Hesse, and was recorded after the war by a former employee there:

745

Dr Berner announced at lunch that the ten thousandth corpse would be burnt that day and that all personnel must assemble for it. That evening we all met in the hall in the right-hand wing, where everybody was given a bottle of beer and from where we then went down to the cellar. There a naked male corpse with an enlarged head was laid out on a bier. I must emphasize that it was definitely a real corpse and not a cardboard one. The ‘burner’ then placed it on a sort of bier and pushed it into the crematorium. Then M who had dressed up like a clergyman gave a ‘funeral address’ . . . I recall that this incident took place in August [1941].

Others, however, were not so hard-bitten and according to one participant:

746

In order to relieve our consciences we were given lots of talks in which an attempt was made through statistics, examples etc., to make clear the necessity for this programme. Economic statistics played a particularly important part in the talks. For example, it was demonstrated how many houses could be built for the sums spent on looking after the mentally ill or how many orphans or deprived children could be trained for this money etc. They tried to convince us that the method of elimination was the most humane imaginable, for the patients would simply fall asleep under the gas and feel nothing more.

In fact the death was far from painless as was reported by an employee who witnessed a gassing at Hadamar.

747

I . . . looked through the peephole in the side wall. Through it I saw 40–45 men who were pressed together in the next room and were now slowly dying. Some lay on the ground, others had slumped down, many had their mouths open as if they could not get any more air. The form of death was so painful that one cannot talk of a humane killing, especially since many of the dead men may have had moments of clarity. I watched the process for about 2–3 minutes and then left because I could no longer bear to look and felt sick.

Meanwhile, relatives had been informed officially that the patient had been transferred. Before long, the practice had been introduced of sending patients initially to temporary locations, asylums from where they were then transferred to the extermination centres a week or so later. This was partly for administrative convenience and partly to make it more difficult for relatives to trace the patients: The following letter was sent from the extermination centre at Bernburg/Saxony on 15 June 1941:

748

We beg to inform you that . . . has been transferred to our institution on the basis of a ministerial instruction in accordance with a directive of the Reich Defence Commissioner and has arrived safely.

Visits cannot be permitted at present for reasons connected with the defence of the Reich and, for the same reason, information cannot be given over the telephone. You will be immediately informed of any change in the health of the patient or in the ban on visits.

The shortage of personnel as a result of the war situation and the resultant increase in the work load obliges us to request you politely to refrain from making further enquiries.

Then, a week or two later, a letter along the lines of the following would be sent to the patient's relatives from the 'euthanasia' centre. This particular one came from Brandenburg:

749

Dear Herr . . .

As you are no doubt aware, your daughter Fräulein . . . was transferred to our institution on ministerial orders. It is our sad duty to have to inform you that she died here on . . . of influenza in conjunction with an abscess on the lung. All attempts by the doctors to keep the patient alive were unfortunately unsuccessful.

We wish to express our most heartfelt condolences for your loss and hope that you will find comfort in the knowledge that the death of your daughter has released her from her great and incurable suffering.

In accordance with police instructions we were obliged to cremate the corpse immediately. This measure is designed to protect the country from the spread of infectious diseases which represent a serious threat in war time and we must strictly abide by it.

If you wish the urn to be sent to your there—without cost—then please inform us and send a declaration of approval from the cemeteries' administration. In the event of our not having heard from you within fourteen days we will undertake the burial of the urn elsewhere. Enclosed you will find two death certificates to present to the authorities, which we request you to look after carefully.

These so-called 'letters of condolence' were prepared by an office within the 'euthanasia' centre and care was taken to try and invent plausible causes of death. A further attempt to ensure concealment was the establishment of a separate registry office within the centre itself so that suspicion was not aroused by the numerous death certificates which would have otherwise had to have been issued by the local registry offices in the districts where the centres were based.

Nevertheless, despite these various attempts to conceal what was going on, inevitably news soon began to filter out. The Nazi Party district leader in Ansbach/Bavaria sent the following report to his Gau headquarters in Nuremberg on 12 June 1940:

750

The transfer of patients from the asylums, lunatic asylums etc. to other areas naturally could not be concealed from the public.

It appears that the commission involved have worked too fast, have not always been skilful and that some mistakes have been made. It cannot be avoided that individual instances become known and talked about:

The following cases should not of course have been allowed to happen:

1. A family received two urns by mistake.
2. A death notice gave the cause of death as appendicitis. But the appendix had been removed ten years before.
3. Another cause of death was spinal disease. But the relatives had visited the man only eight days earlier when he was completely healthy.
4. A family received a death notice when the woman is still living in the asylum and is in the best of health.

Not long ago a relative published a death notice in the local *Fränkische Zeitung:* ' . . . was torn from us by a tragic fate'.

In the case of these extremely delicate measures it is very difficult to make suggestions as to how one can counteract the spreading of facts or of rumours which derive from them or are invented.

News of what was happening soon reached the asylums themselves and their patients. The following are just two examples of numerous moving documents of these tragedies which have survived: The first is the statement by a nursing sister in an asylum in Stetten/Württemberg made at a post-war trial:

751

One evening an epileptic, who always knew what was going on, came into the dormitory and reported: 'The buses are coming again in two days time'. M.G. who was already in bed in the other dormitory overheard it: she got up in great agitation, ran in distress to her nurse and expressed her anxiety. On the day on which she had to go, her nurse called her into her room to tell her. She took the words out of her mouth: 'Klara I know that I have got to go. That's why I was so upset, I was so frightened'. She cried piteously and begged to be forgiven for all her faults. While she was being led across the courtyard she cried out in anguish and gave moving expression to the injustice being done to her and her fellow sufferers: 'How can I help being as I am and that people are doing this to me ?' Paralysed with terror, she got into the bus from which she looked back in a final despairing glance at her nurse.

The following letter is from a patient in the asylum of Liebenau/ Württemberg:

752

Beloved father,

Sadly it had to be. And so today I must send you my words of farewell from this earthly life as I go to my eternal home. It will make you and my other loved ones very very sad. But think that I can die as a martyr which cannot happen without the will of my Redeemer for whom I have longed for years. But father, dear father, I do not want to leave this life without once more begging your forgiveness and that of all my brothers and sisters for what I have failed you in throughout my life. May God accept my illness and this sacrifice as an expiation for it. Dearest father, please do not hold anything against your child who loved you so deeply and think always that I am going to heaven, where we all meet again with God and our loved ones who have died. Father, dear father, I am going with strong courage and faith in God and never doubt His goodness to me, though here on earth we unfortunately do not understand it. We will have our reward on the Day of Judgment. God has commanded it. Please tell my dear brothers and sisters not to be sorrowful but rather to rejoice. I am giving you this little picture to remember me by. And so your child goes to meet her Saviour, embraces you in true love and with the firm promise, which I gave you at our last farewell, that I would endure bravely.

Your child

Helene

Please pray for my soul. Farewell good father till we meet in heaven.

Her brother later explained the circumstances of her death:

753

My sister had been in Liebenau asylum for a long time. She was mentally normal and only suffered from epileptic fits. She could write letters which were censored. She twice succeeded in smuggling letters out. The first of these two letters basically stated the following: she was in continual fear of being fetched away and killed. Vehicles often came and collected inmates of the asylum. Relatives of the inmates had said that they had been killed. She asked my father to help her and to ensure that the same thing did not happen to her. Since my father had a heart problem I established contact with the Health Office in Stuttgart. I spoke with a man there who was a doctor, whose name I cannot remember. He was the desk officer for the asylums. He did not answer my direct question as to whether my sister's suspicion was correct . . . After I had reported this conversation to my father he himself contacted the Health Office. Subsequently, the desk officer gave him positive assurances. My father returned from each meeting ever more optimistic. His written request had allegedly been sent on to Berlin. Just when my father was very hopeful the farewell letter from my sister arrived . . . We at once contacted the asylum at Liebenau and established that my sister had been transferred. Despite all our efforts we could not establish where she had been sent. After four weeks (approximately) of waiting a letter came from the state asylum in Brandenburg to my father. This letter expressed regret that his daughter Helene, who as he was aware (!) had been admitted some time previously, had died of suffocation after a particularly severe attack . . . Soon after the arrival of this message came the authorization from Berlin via the Health Office in Stuttgart that my sister was to be spared from the transfer.

(v) Opposition to 'euthanasia' and Hitler's 'halt' order of 24 August 1941

Meanwhile, the judicial authorities had become involved since a number of mentally ill patients were wards of court; also other legal guardians and relatives turned to the courts for guidance and redress. Since the 'euthanasia' programme had not been officially legalised, the courts were uncertain how to respond. The Reich Minister of Justice, Hans Gürtner, a Conservative, disapproved of the programme and wrote to Bouhler on 24 July 1940 expressing his misgivings. However, Bouhler responded on 27 August by showing him Hitler's authorization and thenceforward Gürtner contented himself with passing on complaints to the Reich Interior Ministry and the Reich Chancellery. Only one judge, Dr Lothar Kreyssig of Brandenburg, who was responsible for guardianship matters in his area, had the courage to file an official complaint about the programme with the Reich Justice Ministry. Indeed, he then went further and filed an official accusation of murder against Bouhler with the Public Prosecutor's Office. Kreyssig was summoned to the Reich Justice Ministry, where he was shown a copy of the Führer's authorization. When he declared that he could not regard it as legally binding, Gürtner replied that if Kreyssig was unable to recognize that the declared will of the Führer created law then he could do nothing for him in the matter. Kreyssig was later retired, but significantly not on the grounds of this particular incident which had no direct repercussions for him.

Gürtner had at least expressed his misgivings about the programme and clearly disapproved of it. The man who took over on his death, on 29 January 1941, as acting Minister, State Secretary Franz Schlegelberger, showed no such qualms. Schlegelberger, a career civil servant, clearly hoped to succeed Gürtner and gave his full cooperation to the KdF. On 23 and 24 April 1941, he invited Brack to address a conference of the senior court presidents (*Oberlandesgerichtspräsidenten*) and public prosecutors to explain the programme. In his introductory speech Schlegelberger gave his views on the question of the independence of the judiciary:

754

. . . Prejudices which the legal system still comes up against so frequently are associated with the often misunderstood concept of the independence of the judiciary. The nation is firmly convinced that independence from instructions is a self-evident and indispensable attribute of a judge. The Führer already emphasized in his first speech as Chancellor that the law can only be declared by judges who are independent in this sense. Judges must know that in preparation of their judgments they are free from any instructions. The judge must establish the law freely and independently and—that is the significance of the symbol of the sword—must commit himself to this right with courage. This freedom from instructions must be paired with true i.e. inward independence. That is a matter of character. The true judge must carry an immunity against outside influence within himself and must not wish, as a substitute for it, anxiously to shut himself off from the opinions of outsiders. The person who is totally independent is he who, in full awareness of all the available opinions about the case, decides with an inward freedom based on his expertise.

At the same time, the following is also true. The nation demands the exercise of justice by judges whom it trusts. It is well aware that the professional judiciary as an institution is only the consequence of the ever-increasing complexity of life and therefore of the legal system, but that the learned judge has to be a part of the national community just like the lay judges of past times. If a judge does not feel bound to his nation with all his heart then he cannot fulfil the task given to him by the nation, through the Führer, of establishing the law. The judge should declare the law in the name of the people. If the world view of his nation has changed so fundamentally and decisively, as in Germany after the victory of the Movement, then a judge can only be true to his office if he is thoroughly permeated with the new world view. There can be no doubt that from now onwards every norm of the law must be interpreted and applied with reference to the morality and world view reflected in the Party programme and, in addition, with reference to the decisive expressions of will of its creator and most qualified exponent. Anyone who wished to deny this by referring to his judicial independence would misjudge the extent of the limitation which the state imposes on him as well. It is the self-evident duty of every judge to keep within these limitations. He is responsible to the Führer from whom he derives his authority to declare the law . . .

Gentlemen, it is my most urgent task to ensure that all officials in the Reich judicial system increasingly fit into the National Socialist state along these lines. You, gentlemen, must be the means by which, or even better the source from which, a knowledge of this need to fit in flows directly and ruthlessly to your subordinates (*Gefolgschaft*) in every sphere. From this there derives for me the duty of making you aware of all the decisions of the Führer which are of importance for your official actions. You must not only be aware of rumours but also know the facts. If this does not occur then it is inevitable that judges and prosecutors will act against measures which they in good faith but erroneously consider to be illegal and so will innocently put themselves in conflict with the will of the Führer to the serious detriment of justice and of the state. Gentlemen, in your oral and written reports you continually express doubts concerning the question of the destruction of worthless life. You report about incredible rumours going round among the people and you complain that you are not in a position to enlighten people because you lack information about these matters. This complaint is justified. I have, therefore, soon after taking over the Ministry, sought an opportunity to clarify the matter for myself and, at this point, I would like to thank the chief of the Führer's Chancellery, *Reichsleiter* and Party Comrade Bouhler for the detailed explanation. I am even more grateful to him for agreeing to allow his leading experts to provide this conference with the information necessary for the Senior State Court Presidents [*Oberlandesgerichtspräsidenten*] and General State Prosecutors to carry out their duties. I would like to welcome Herr Brack and Herr Professor Heide [Heyde] and ask them to take the floor.

According to notes made at the time by the Senior State Court President of Cologne, Brack began by mentioning Hitler's authorization and then continued:

755

Not a task for a state body. New problem, no experience, therefore prior sounding necessary before a law is introduced. A state body unsuitable for such a task which from the outside appears illegal.
Not a matter of the destruction of worthless life, but the carrying out of an act of release for people who are suffering and for their relatives.
Law re: terminal medical assistance

1. At their own request in the case of incurably sick (shortening of death agony).

2. Painless ending of life in the case of incurably mentally ill without their approval.

[Then, after describing the programme itself, Brack continued:]

Value of the action–not simply pecuniary. Care of these patients ties up a lot of valuable personnel . . .

[Brack concluded:]

Patient dies of a fictitious cause. Reason: Führer's insistence on secrecy. Death certificate. Date and cause of death both incorrect. A proper register is kept at the same time. Now we keep a proper record of the estate which is what the relatives are most concerned about. In 80% of cases the relatives are in agreement, 10% protest, 10% are indifferent.

None of these senior judges and public prosecutors protested; some asked questions about matters of legal procedure raised by the programme. The mood of those present was summed up by one prosecutor from the People's Court:

756

I know from two or three private conversations with Public Prosecutors, which I had following the briefing, that these colleagues had misgivings about the measures envisaged. The view was expressed that one would have to wait and see how things turned out. There might be cases in which mental patients were completely incurable and then one could consider killing them to be justifiable. I would say that there was a mood of wait and see . . . In the view of the older lawyers an unpublished directive of Hitler's could never become law. However, according to the official view it was the case that the Führer directives had the force of law. But the lawyers of the old school had misgivings 'in their heart of hearts'.

Apart from the judiciary, the other institution most closely concerned with the effects of the 'euthanasia' programme was the Church. The two Churches controlled some of the asylums and many of the nursing personnel; they had to bury the urns of those who had been cremated and comfort their relatives. In general, the response of the Churches was slow and hesitant; above all, they were anxious to avoid a confrontation with the state. A number of Church asylums even participated in the programme by becoming 'intermediate stations' on the way to the extermination centres.

There were a few individual instances of great moral courage. The most striking on the Protestant side was that of Pastor Braune, the director of the Hoffnungstal Institutions and Vice President of the Central Committee of the *Innere Mission,* the main Protestant welfare organization. On 9 July 1940, Braune wrote a long memorandum to Hitler which he delivered personally to the Reich Chancellery. In it he set out his assessment of what was happening and made a strong protest. On 12 August, he was arrested by the Gestapo, although his interrogators denied that this had anything to do with his memorandum; they were anxious not to admit to the existence of the programme.

However, as Braune himself put it later: 'The official Church remained completely silent, the official *Innere Mission* also did not dare do anything . . . When I was released, the treasurer of the *Innere Mission* reproached me for having gone out on a limb over this matter. One mustn't do that.' Indeed, the president of the *Innere Mission*, Constantin Frick, adopted a much more conciliatory position and, when informed of the Führer's authorization, allowed himself to be convinced of the programme's legitimacy.

The Roman Catholic Church adopted a similar line. Although protests were made by individual bishops, which culminated in a protest on 11 August 1940 by the Fulda Bishops' Conference, the senior body of the Church, all these protests were behind the scenes and through official channels. Moreover, the Church tended to try and seek a compromise with the state and special favours—for example, by trying to get priests excluded from the programme and to secure agreement for the provision of sacraments for those to be killed. Had they been implemented, such measures would have given the appearance that the Church condoned the programme. Fortunately, however, at this juncture, the Vatican intervened with the following statement by the Holy Office on 2 December 1940:

757

The direct killing of an innocent person because of mental or physical defects is not allowed. With the decree of 2 December 1940 the Holy Office replies to the following

Question: Whether it is permissable on the basis of an order by the state authority directly to kill those who, although they have not committed a crime worthy of death, nevertheless cannot be of any further use to the nation and are rather a burden for the nation and an hindrance to its energy and strength.

Answer: No, since it is against the natural and positive law of God. His Holiness Pope Pius XII has approved and confirmed this decision of the cardinals in his audience on 1 December and ordered its publication.

However, even this statement was not made the basis for a vigorous and uncompromising campaign by the Church against 'euthanasia'. Above all, no attempt was made to mobilize the faithful by a specific and detailed condemnation of the programme. Instead, public pronouncements by the Church on the matter tended to be restrained assertions of the sanctity of human life.

Finally, however, on 3 August 1941, the Bishop of Münster, Cardinal August Count von Galen, decided to make a public stand, prompted by the removal of mental patients from his diocese. Galen, an ultra-Conservative who had been close to the circle of the former Vice-Chancellor von Papen, had been informed about the 'euthanasia' programme as early as July 1940. At the time, he had expressed his misgivings in a letter to the Chairman of the Fulda Bishops' Conference, Bishop Bertram. However, Bertram and his officials had advised that 'precipitate action could have far-reaching repercussions for pastoral and ecclesiastical concerns and in general have very serious effects'.[11] Now, on 3 August 1941, Galen preached a sermon in the Lamberti church in Münster from which the following extracts are taken:

758

Fellow Christians! In the pastoral letter of the German bishops of 26 June 1941, which was read out in all the Catholic churches in Germany on 6 July 1941, it states among other things: It is true that there are definite commandments in Catholic moral doctrine which are no longer applicable if their fulfilment involves too many difficulties. However, there are sacred obligations of conscience from which no one has the power to release us and which we must fulfil even if it costs us our lives. Never under any circumstances may a human being kill an innocent person apart from war and legitimate self-defence. On 6 July, I already had cause to add to the pastoral letter the following explanation: for some months we have been hearing reports that, on the orders of Berlin, patients from mental asylums who have been ill for a long time and may appear incurable, are being compulsorily removed. Then, after a short time, the relatives are regularly informed that the corpse has been burnt and the ashes can be delivered. There is a general suspicion verging on certainty, that these numerous unexpected deaths of mentally ill people do not occur of themselves but are deliberately brought about, that the doctrine is being followed, according to which one may destroy so-called 'worthless life', that is kill innocent people if one considers that their lives are of no further value for the nation and the state.

I am reliably informed that lists are also being drawn up in the asylums of the province of Westphalia as well of those patients who are to be taken away as

[11] Cf. Martin Höllen, *Heinrich Wienken, der 'unpolitische' Kirchenpolitiker. Eine Biographie aus drei Epochen des deutschen Katholizismus* (Mainz 1981) p. 93.

so-called 'unproductive national comrades' and shortly to be killed. The first transport left the Marienthal institutuion near Münster during this past week.

German men and women §211 of the Reich Penal Code is still valid. It states: 'he who deliberately kills another person will be punished by death for murder if the killing is premeditated.'

Those patients who are destined to be killed are transported away from home to a distant asylum presumably in order to protect those who deliberately kill those poor people, members of our families, from this legal punishment. Some illness is then given as the cause of death. Since the corpse has been burnt straight away the relatives and also the criminal police are unable to establish whether the illness really occurred and what the cause of death was. However, I have been assured that the Reich Interior Ministry and the office of the Reich Doctors' Leader, Dr. Conti, make no bones about the fact that in reality a large number of mentally ill people in Germany have been deliberately killed and more will be killed in the future.

The Penal Code lays down in §139: 'He who receives credible information concerning the intention to commit a crime against life and neglects to alert the authorities or the person who is threatened in time . . . will be punished'. When I learnt of the intention to transport patients from Marienthal in order to kill them, I brought a formal charge at the State Court in Münster and with the Police President in Münster by means of a registered letter which read as follows: 'According to information which I have received, in the course of this week a large number of patients from the Marienthal Provincal Asylum near Münster are to be transported to the Eichberg asylum as so-called "unproductive national comrades" and will then soon be deliberately killed, as is generally believed has occurred with such transports from other asylums. Since such an action is not only contrary to the moral laws of God and Nature but also is punishable with death as murder under §211 of the Penal Code, I hereby bring a charge in accordance with my duty under §139 of the Penal Code, and request you to provide immediate protection for the national comrades threatened in this way by taking action against those agencies who are intending their removal and murder, and that you inform me of the steps that have been taken'. I have received no news concerning intervention by the Prosecutor's Office or by the police.

. . . Thus we must assume that the poor helpless patients will soon be killed. For what reason? Not because they have committed a crime worthy of death. Not because they attacked their nurses or orderlies so that the latter had no other choice but to use legitimate force to defend their lives against their attackers. Those are cases where, in addition to the killing of an armed enemy in a just war, the use of force to the point of killing is allowed and is often required. No, it is not for such reasons that these unfortunate patients must die but rather because, in the opinion of some department, on the testimony of some commission, they have become 'worthless life' because according to this testimony they are 'unproductive national comrades'. The argument goes: they can no longer produce commodities, they are like an old machine that no longer works, they are like an old horse which has become incurably lame, they are like a cow which no longer gives milk. What does one do with such an old machine? It is thrown on the scrap heap. What does one do with a lame horse, with such an unproductive cow? No, I do not want to continue the comparison to the end—however fearful the justification for it and the symbolic force of it are. We are not dealing with machines, horses and cows whose only function is to serve mankind, to produce goods for man. One may smash them, one may slaughter them as soon as they no longer fulfil this function. No, we are dealing with human beings, our fellow human beings, our brothers and sisters. With poor people, sick people, if you like unproductive people. But have they for that reason forfeited the right to life? Have you, have I the right to live only so long as we are productive, so long as we are recognised by others as productive? If you establish and apply the principle that you can kill 'unproductive' fellow human beings then woe betide us all when we become old and frail! If one is allowed to kill the unproductive people then woe betide the invalids who have used up, sacrificed and lost their health and strength in the productive process. If one is allowed forcibly to remove one's unproductive fellow human beings then woe betide loyal soldiers who return to the homeland seriously disabled, as cripples, as invalids. If it is once accepted that people have the right to kill 'unproductive' fellow humans—and even if initially it only affects the poor defenceless mentally ill—then as a *matter of principle* murder is permitted for all unproductive people, in other words for the incurably sick, the people who have become invalids through labour and war, for us all when we become old, frail and therefore unproductive.

Then, it is only necessary for some secret edict to order that the method developed for the mentally ill should be extended to other 'unproductive' people, that it should be applied to those suffering from incurable lung disease, to the elderly who are frail or invalids, to the severely disabled soldiers. Then none of our lives will be safe any more. Some commission can put us on the list of the 'unproductive', who in their opinion have become worthless life. And no police force will protect us and no court will investigate our murder and give the murderer the punishment he deserves. Who will be able to trust his doctor any more? He may report his patient as 'unproductive' and receive instructions to kill him. It is impossible to imagine the degree of moral depravity, of general mistrust that would then spread even through families if this dreadful doctrine is tolerated, accepted and followed. Woe to mankind, woe to our German nation if God's holy commandment 'Thou shalt not kill', which God proclaimed on Mount Sinai amidst thunder and lightning, which God our Creator inscribed in the conscience of mankind from the very beginning, is not only broken, but if this transgression is actually tolerated and permitted to go unpunished.

I'll give you an example of what is going on. In Marienthal there was a man of about 55, a peasant from a rural parish in the Münster area—I could give you his name—who for some years had been suffering from mental disturbance and who had therefore been put in the care of the Marienthal asylum. He was not really mentally ill, he could receive visitors and was very pleased whenever his relatives came to see him. Only a fortnight ago, he received a visit from his wife and from one of his sons who is a soldier at the front and had home leave. So the farewell was a sad one: who knows if the soldier will return, will see his father again, for after all he may die in the struggle on behalf of his national comrades. The son, the soldier, will almost certainly never see his father again here on earth because since then he has been put on the list of the 'unproductive'. A relative who wanted to visit the father in Marienthal last week was turned away with the news that the patient had been transported away from here on the orders of the Ministerial Council for the Defence of the Reich. Nobody could say where to; the relatives would be informed in a few days time. What will the news be? Will it be the same as in other cases? That the person has died, that the corpse has been burnt, that the ashes can be delivered after payment of a fee? In that case, the soldier who is at the front risking his life for his German national comrades, will not see his father again here on earth because German national comrades at home have killed him . . .

Galen's sermon came as a bombshell. Thousands of copies were printed and circulated. The Nazi leadership were furious but helpless. Walter Tiessler, an official in the Party Chancellery responsible for propaganda matters, expressed this sense of frustration in a minute to Bormann on 13 August 1941:

759

After the ministerial conference Dr G[oebbels] spoke to me about the sermon of the Bishop of Münster. He did not know what one could effectively do at the moment. I explained to him that in my opinion there could be only one effective measure, namely to hang the Bishop, and that I had already informed Reichsleiter Bormann accordingly.

Dr Goebbels thereupon said that this was a measure on which the Führer alone could decide. He was, however, afraid that if any action was taken against the bishop the population of Münster could be written off for the duration of the war, and for that matter the whole of Westphalia.

. . . He maintained that it would be better in wartime to preserve appearances where the Church was concerned. To attack an opponent is permissible, always provided that one is in a position to reply adequately to the opponent's decisive counter attack. But in the case of the Church's counter attack in wartime this was extraordinarily difficult, indeed next to impossible. Revenge should not be indulged in with heat but taken coldly. In politics one should know how to wait.

Galen's sermon was only the most dramatic event in a growing wave of discontent about the 'euthanasia' programme which had found expression in letters of complaint from other bishops of both denominations and even from senior party figures. On 13 August 1941 the Roman Catholic Bishop of Limburg wrote to the Reich Minister of Justice complaining about goings-on in Hadamar which was in his diocese:

760

Buses arrive in Hadamar several times a week with a large number of these victims. School children in the neighbourhood know these vehicles and say: 'Here comes the murder wagon'. After the arrival of such vehicles the citizens of Hadamar then see the smoke coming from the chimney and are upset by constant thoughts about the poor victims especially when, depending on the direction of the wind, they have to put up with the revolting smell. The consequence of the principles being practised here is that children, when quarrelling with one another make remarks like: 'You are thick, you'll be put in the oven in Hadamar'. People who do not want to get married or who do not get the opportunity say: 'Get married? No fear. Put children into the world who then end up going through the rack'. Old people are saying 'on no account will I go into a state hospital! After the feeble-minded, the old will be next in line as useless mouths to feed'.

There had even been minor public demonstrations when patients were being transported from particular asylums. One witness, a doctor involved in the programme, testified after the war that Hitler himself was subjected to a hostile demonstration while his train was waiting in a station in Bavaria while simultaneously a group of mentally handicapped children were being transported. On 24 August 1941, therefore, under the pressure of these events, Hitler issued an order to halt the programme. Hefelmann recalled after the war:

761

Hitler [had] . . . ordered the immediate termination of the 'T4 operation' because of the episcopal protests against it. Brandt came to see Brack one day (it was 24 August 1941) and informed him in my presence that Hitler had ordered that the 'euthanasia measures' should be terminated at once. It is possible that Brandt may have said 'provisionally' terminated. It is certain that the order passed on by Brandt was a general one and did not permit exceptions. I asked therefore whether the 'Reich Committee' (cover name for the child killings) had to stop its activities. Brandt could not give me an answer, but then having consulted Hitler, informed me that the work of the 'Reich Committee' could continue . . . However, I was aware that the T4 office continued to operate. I did not learn what tasks were being carried out there.

A statistician from T4 produced the following figures for those killed under the programme:

762

Up to 1 September 1941, 70,273 persons have been disinfected.[12] Distributed among the individual institutions for the years 1940 and 1941 this figure breaks down as follows:

[12] i.e. killed (eds).

	1940	*1941*	*Total*
A (Grafeneck)	9,839		9,839
B (Brandenburg)	9,772		9,772
Be (Bernburg)		8,601	8,601
C (Linz) [Hartheim]	9,670	8,599	18,269
D (Sonnenstein)	5,943	7,777	13,720
E (Hadamar)		10,072	10,072
	35,224	35,049	70,273

A post-war court case in Tübingen subsequently established the number of those killed in Grafeneck as 10,654, which makes a revised total of 71,088.

Dr Eduard Brandt, a T4 statistician, then worked out the savings made as a result of the programme:

763

On the assumption that the level of nutrition of the inmates of asylums will remain the same as at present even after the end of the war, the savings in foodstuffs in the case of 70,273 disinfected persons with an average life expectancy of ten years would be as follows:

Type of foodstuff	*kg*
Potatoes	189,737,160
Meat and sausage products	13,492,440
Bread	59,029,320
Flour	12,649,200
Butter	4,216,440
Butter fat	421,680
Margarine	3,794,760
Bacon	531,240
Quark	1,054,080
Cheese	1,054,080
Special foods	1,686,600
Pastry products	1,475,766
Sago, etc.	421,608
Coffee substitute	3,373,080
Jam	5,902,920
Sugar	7,589,520
Eggs	33,731,040 items
Vegetables	88,544,040
Pulses	4,216,440
Salt and spice substitutes	1,054,080
Total	400,244,520 kg
	= 141,775,573.80 RM

On the basis of an average daily cost [per patient] of RM 3.50 there will be:

1. a daily saving of RM	245,955.50
2. a yearly saving of RM	88,543,980.00
3. with a life expectancy of ten years RM	885,439,800.00

in words: eight hundred and eighty-five million four hundred and thirty-five thousand and eight hundred Reich marks

i.e. this sum will be or has been saved up to 1 September 1941 through the disinfection of 70,273 persons carried out so far.

The maths problem devised for school children in 1935 had become reality.[13] In fact, since the figure of those 'disinfected' used by T4 as the basis for the above calculations applied only to those gassed, and did not include those killed by injections and deliberate malnutrition, it underestimated the total involved. A further statistic at the end of 1941 gave a figure of 93,251 beds which had been released as a result of the programme, almost exactly one third of the 282,696 beds available for mental patients. In other words, the original target for the 'euthanasia' programme had already been achieved when Hitler issued his order to halt it.

(vi) The 14 f13 programme and 'wild' 'euthanasia' 1941–45

Although, 'euthanasia' had been officially stopped by Hitler's 'halt' order of 24 August 1941, in practice this only applied to the large-scale gassing of mental patients. The programme in fact continued, though in a somewhat different form.

Initially, the focus shifted towards the liquidation of concentration camp prisoners who were sick and incapable of work under an agreement reached between Bouhler and Himmler. This scheme, which had already begun in the spring of 1941, was code-named 14 f 13. 14 f was the code number of the Inspectorate of Concentration camps and the following number referred to the cause of death in the camps. Thus 1 referred to death from natural causes, 2 to suicide, 3 to shot while trying to escape. 13 referred to 'the special treatment of sick and frail prisoners'. 'Special treatment' was the official SS euphemism for liquidation. Lists of sick prisoners were prepared in the camps; sometimes prisoners were invited to apply for transfer to a 'sanatorium'. Then forms were prepared for the prisoners on the lists. These forms were then processed by roving commissions of T4 doctors visiting the camps to make the final selection of those prisoners who were to be transferred to one of the remaining gassing centres—Sonnenstein, Hartheim or Bernburg. The lists included Jewish prisoners who were neither mentally nor physically sick but who were selected simply on the grounds of their race.

The senior Dachau camp doctor, Dr Muthig, reported after the war:

[13] see vol. 2 p. 439.

764

In the autumn of 1941 . . . I was informed that shortly a commission consisting of four doctors under the direction of Professor Heyde would visit the Dachau concentration camp. The task of this commission was to register concentration camp inmates, who were unfit for work, for transfer to Mauthausen concentration camp for the purpose of euthanasia. The commission arrived shortly after this . . . It consisted of four psychiatrists and was led by Professor Heyde, who was himself present. I myself and other camp doctors of Dachau had nothing to do with the commission or its work. I saw, however, how these four doctors sat at separate tables between two barracks and several hundred prisoners were lined up in front of them. There, the individual prisoners were examined on the basis of their fitness for work and their political files and selected accordingly . . . I know that this commission only spent a few days in Dachau and that it was impossible for it to give such large numbers of prisoners a medical examination in such a short time. The examination consisted simply of a perusal of files in the presence of the individual prisoners conerned.

The mentality of the members of these commissions and their methods of operation are further illuminated by the private correspondence of one of the doctors, Dr Mennecke, which has survived. The following letter of 19 November was sent from Ravensbrück women's concentration camp:

765

My dearest Mummy,

It is 17.45. I have finished my day's work and am once more sitting in my hotel. The result of my day's work is 95 forms completed . . . The work speeds along thanks to the fact that the headings have already been typed and I only have to write in the diagnosis, main symptoms etc. I don't want to write about the patients in this letter. I'll tell you more later . . . Everything is going perfectly. I am having my meals in the camp: for lunch in the mess there was lentil soup with bacon and omelette for pudding. I finished at 17.00 and had my supper in the mess: 3 sorts of sausage, butter, bread, beer. I sleep marvellously in my bed, it is just like in Hilmershausen . . . I hope you are as well as I am. I feel perfect.

The following day he wrote to his wife:

The work speeds along . . . Dr. Sonntag sits in with me and comments on their behaviour in the camp, an [SS] *Scharführer* brings in the patients—it all works perfectly . . . 22.50 hours. The people in Berlin (Jennerwein) simply say we have to do 2,000—whether or not so many people come under the basic criteria doesn't bother them.

[Then, a letter from Buchenwald concentration camp to his wife on 28 November 1941:]

7.40 Off I go happy hunting. This morning I got a terrific lot done, in the two hours from 9–11 I got through 70 forms. Dr Muller did 56 so another 126 are finished.

[Then, again from Ravensbrück to his wife on 2 December 1941:]

I worked fast up to 11.15 and got 80 forms finished. So, counting yesterday and today that makes 320 forms which I'm sure Dr Muller could not have done in 2 full days. He who works fast saves time.

[The comments made on the photographs of those selected for 'euthanasia' by Dr Mennecke are also illuminating:]

Capell, Charlotte Sara, 4.10.93 Breslau, divorced. *Catholic Jewess* 740 Ravensbrück Nurse. Persistent miscegany (*Rassenschande*). Hid her Jewish origin behind Catholicism, hung a Christian cross round her neck.

. . . Alfred Israel, 14.11.06 Dusseldorf, married. Jewish. Businessman. Diagnosis: Fanatical Germanophobe and asocial psychopath. Main symptoms: Hard-bitten Communist, unworthy to bear arms, penitentiary sentence for high treason: six years.

Schönhoff Egon Israel, Lawyer, 9.4.80 Vienna. Dachau 1938, 6069.
Communist lawyer. Member of Red Aid. 1927 in Russia. Major Germanophobe. Agitator. In the camp: presumptuous, impertinent, lazy, obstructive.
Since 1901 1st Lieutenant in the Austro-Hungarian army. Lieutenant of the Reserve. Front-line service from start of World War till May 1915; then Russian POW. Promoted to 1st Lieutenant at the front, to Captain while a POW.

On 27 April 1943, Himmler issued an order restricting the application of the 14 f 13 programme to prisoners who were mentally ill, probably because of the need to maintain the concentration camp labour force which had become increasingly important to the SS and the war economy. As a result, Bernburg and Sonnenstein were closed down. However, on 11 April 1944, the programme was restarted and a considerable number of prisoners from Mauthausen and its sub-camp, Gusen, were gassed in Hartheim.

The statistics on those killed under the 14 f 13 programme are incomplete. However, the numbers were clearly considerable. Nearly 5,000 prisoners from Mauthausen and Gusen and 3,225 from Dachau were gassed in Hartheim between 1941–5, and at least 834 prisoners from Buchenwald were gassed in Sonnenstein and 400 in Bernburg by the end of March 1942.

The second major trend in the 'euthanasia' programme after the 'halt' was for gassing to be replaced as the main method of killing mental patients—though it continued in Hartheim until the end of 1944—by deliberate malnutrition and lethal injections and doses. Also patients were now killed in their existing institutions or after being transferred to a number of new 'euthanasia' centres such as Meseritz-Obrawalde in the East, Eichberg in the West, and Kaufbeuren in the South. Hadamar started up again in August 1942, replacing gas with injections.

On 30 November 1942, the following circular was sent by the Bavarian Interior Ministry to the asylums throughout the state:

766

In view of the war-time food situation and the health requirements of those inmates who are working, it is no longer justifiable for all inmates of asylums to receive the same sustenance irrespective of whether, on the one hand, they are performing productive work or are undergoing therapy, or on the other, are simply being cared for in the asylums without performing any notably useful work. With immediate effect, therefore, those inmates of asylums who perform useful work or are undergoing therapy, as well as those children who are educable, the war-disabled, and those suffering from senile dementia will receive superior rations both quantitively and qualitatively at the expense of the other inmates . . .

This directive was evidently prompted by an instruction from Berlin and the new practice was not confined to Bavaria. Throughout Germany, large numbers of mental patients were put on a diet consisting largely of boiled cabbage, nettles, dandelion leaves, and potato peelings and containing virtually no fat. The result was described by a doctor in a post-war statement:

767

One could hardly bear to look at the pale, yellowish-looking figures in the wards. Some of the patients were no longer capable of lifting themselves up, and when one visited the wards one could hardly resist the begging for bread. Until then, even in war—and I was a front-line soldier—I had never seen so many tears shed as during this time.

The combination of malnutrition and the cold—mental asylums were provided with totally inadequate supplies of coal for heating—ensured that thousands of patients died of 'natural causes'. This proved a more acceptable form of 'euthanasia' for many asylum directors than the gassing process about which most had qualms. However, this method was not fast enough for those responsible for the programme, particularly towards the end of the war when the pressure on hospital space increased.

On 17 August 1943, asylum directors were summoned to a meeting in Berlin by Professor Nitsche, the medical chief of T4, at which they were authorized by Dr Brandt to kill patients at their own discretion. In 1940 Professor Nitsche had devised a technique of progressive overdosing with Luminal, which ensured death within a few days from congestion of the lungs. Morphine and Scopolamine were also extensively used. Large quantities of these drugs were supplied to asylums throughout the Reich by the T4 organization.

The main criterion for the selection of patients to die remained their usefulness, in this case to the institution concerned, and the extent to which they caused difficulties. Decisions were arbitrary and often based on personal prejudice as is clear from the following comments on the medical records of patients transferred from the Hamburg asylum, Langenhorn, to the 'euthanasia' centre at Meseritz:

768

'Unpleasant patient; not popular; once again planning to escape; homosexually active; masturbates a lot; grumbles.'

[And in the case of a group of patients transported to Hadamar:]

'Doesn't achieve much; inactive; works without enthusiasm; wants to go home; talks too much; very erotic; makes a lot of demands; often shouts: 'Heil Moscow'.

Relatives were now told that the patients were being transferred from areas threatened by air raids for their own safety. Those who made a fuss were liable to receive short shrift as in the following case of a father who complained about the deterioration of his formerly healthy son after his transfer to the Eichberg asylum in the Rheingau. The director of the asylum Dr Walter Schmidt replied:

769

The tone and content of your letter of 5 June 1944 prompt me to contemplate having you psychiatrically examined. I therefore feel obliged to inform you that if you continue to annoy us with your letters I will be compelled to have you examined by the Medical Officer of Health.

The same Dr Schmidt developed the practice of stopping beside the beds of patients on his evening rounds and saying 'I don't like him/her any more'— a signal to the nursing staff for the patient's liquidation.

It is impossible to estimate how many died in the second, post- 'halt' phase of the 'euthanasia' programme, though it was clearly tens of thousands. For, apart from the mentally ill and sick concentration camp inmates, the programme also included other groups—sick slave workers from Poland and Russia, *Mischling* children from reform schools, old people, particularly from institutions for the poor. Moreover, it is clear that, had Germany won the war, the categories of those regarded as 'worthless life' would have been extended to include all those regarded as eugenically 'unfit' or in the Nazi jargon of the time, *Gemeinschaftsfremden* or 'community aliens'. Many of them would have been worked to death in concentration camps or liquidated by gas or injection.

The 'euthanasia' programme had initiated systematic mass murder by the Nazis. T4 had selected the personnel and developed the techniques for the murder of thousands of human beings with maximum efficiency. With Hitler's 'halt' order of 24 August 1941, many of those personnel and their techniques were transferred to deal with an even larger problem: the murder not of thousands but of millions—the 'final solution of the Jewish question'.

CHAPTER 37

The Persecution of the Jews 1939–41

The outbreak of war represented a watershed in Nazi policies towards the Jews. Hitler blamed the Jews for the war. This was partly no doubt for propaganda purposes, but he also seems to have believed it through a form of psychological projection. In a major speech to the Reichstag on 30 January 1939, the anniversary of his appointment as Reich Chancellor, he had made a chilling prophecy:

770

. . . Europe cannot find peace until the Jewish question has been solved. It may well be that sooner or later an agreement may be reached in Europe itself between nations who otherwise would not find it so easy to arrive at an understanding. There still exists sufficient available land on this globe . . .

One thing I should like to say on this day which may be memorable for others as well as for us Germans. In the course of my life I have very often been a prophet, and have usually been ridiculed for it. During the time of my struggle for power it was in the first instance only the Jewish race that received my prophecies with laughter when I said that I would one day take over the leadership of the State, and with it that of the whole nation, and that I would then among other things settle the Jewish problem. Their laughter was uproarious, but I think that for some time now they have been laughing on the other side of their face. Today I will once more be a prophet: if the international Jewish financiers in and outside Europe should succeed in plunging the nations once more into a world war, then the result will not be the Bolshevizing of the earth, and thus the victory of Jewry, but the annihilation of the Jewish race in Europe!

There is no evidence that Hitler had any idea at this stage how or when he would carry out this threat. Indeed, some historians have seen it as pure rhetoric designed to intimidate those engaged in anti-German activities abroad by using the Jews as hostages. Nevertheless, there does seem to have been a widespread view among the Nazi leadership that war would bring about an intensification of Nazi persecution. Thus, at the conference on the Jews held on 12 November 1938, Göring had insisted 'that if the German Reich becomes involved in a diplomatic conflict in the foreseeable future, then it is only natural that we in Germany should also contemplate a major reckoning with the Jews'.[1] Moreover, with the outbreak of war Hitler's paranoia was intensified by a deep-rooted fear. The defeat of Germany and the revolution in November 1918 had had a traumatic effect on him and he associated that defeat with the machinations of the Jews. He asserted again and again during these years that November 1918 would not be repeated, and to guarantee this he was determined to eliminate the Jews one way or the other.

Apart from intensifying Nazi paranoia about the Jews, the outbreak of war also created a new context for dealing with the Jewish problem. It simultaneously created the extreme conditions in which an extreme solution came to appear more acceptable and appropriate and removed the need to take account of world opinion. Secondly, the war vastly increased the numbers of Jews who came under German control, while at the same time largely preventing the main method used for their elimination before the war, namely emigration. This problem was most serious with regard to Poland.

(i) Poland 1939–40: (a) Deportations and the Plan for a Jewish Reservation

According to the official census of 1931, there were 3,115,000 Jews in Poland of whom 1,901,000 (61 per cent) were in the territory occupied by Germany, namely:

1,269,000 (41 per cent) in the 'General Government'.
632,000 (20 per cent) in the areas incorporated into the Reich.
1,214,000 (39 per cent) in the territory occupied by the Soviet Union.

During the Polish campaign, Jews fell victim to persecutions carried out by the five Security Police *Einsatzgruppen* (task forces), which operated behind the German front-line troops; they were beaten, humiliated, and in some cases murdered. In mid-September, a 'task force for special purposes' under SS *Obergruppenführer* v. Woyrsch was despatched to carry

[1] Cf. I.M.T. Vol. XXVIII, p. 539.

out more systematic mass shootings of Jews in the Katowice area of Upper Silesia with the aim of driving the Jews out of this territory, which was incorporated into the Reich, and into the neighbouring Russian-occupied area. This large-scale brutality provoked protests from the *Wehrmacht* which brought a temporary halt to these measures.[2]

On 21 September, Heydrich issued the following instructions to the chiefs of the *Einsatzgruppen* 're: the Jewish question in the occupied territory' of Poland:

771

With reference to the meeting which took place today in Berlin, I would like to emphasize once again that the *overall measures envisaged* (i.e. the final goal) must be kept strictly secret.

A distinction must be made between.

1. the final goal (which will require a lengthy period) and
2. the stages towards the achievement of this final goal (which can be carried out on a short-term basis).

The measures envisaged require the most thorough preparation both in the technical and in the economic sense.

It is obvious that the tasks which are desirable cannot be defined in every detail from here. The following instructions and directives serve simultaneously the purpose of encouraging the chiefs of the *Einsatzgruppen* to reflect on the practical issues.

I. The first preliminary measure for achieving the final goal is the concentration of the Jews from the countryside in the larger cities. It must be speedily implemented.

A distinction must be made:

1. Between the territories of Danzig and West Prussia, Posen, eastern Upper Silesia and
2. The other occupied territories.

If possible, the areas referred to under 1. are to be liberated from Jews, or at least the aim must be to establish only a few cities as concentration points.

In the areas referred to under 2. as few concentration points as possible should be established so that the later measures are facilitated. In this connexion you should ensure that only those cities are designated which are either railway junctions or at least lie on a railway line.

As a matter of principle, Jewish communities of under 500 are to be dissolved and transferred to the nearest concentration city.

This directive does not apply to the territory of *Einsatzgruppe* I, which lies roughly east of Cracow and is bounded by Polanice, Jaroslav, the new demarcation line [with the Russian-occupied part of Poland], and the previous Slovakian-Polish

[2] See above pp. 938–940.

border. Within this area only a summary census of Jews should be made. . . .[3]
II. Councils of Jewish Elders.
1. A Council of Jewish Elders is to be established in every Jewish community, which as far as possible is to be created from the leading persons and rabbis. Up to 24 male Jews (depending on the size of the Jewish community) are to belong to the Council of Elders.

It is to be made entirely responsible, within the meaning of the word, for the exact and prompt fulfilment of all instructions which have been or will be given.
2. The councils are to be informed that the toughest measures will be taken in the event of the sabotage of such directives . . .
4. . . . The reason to be given for the concentration of the Jews in the cities is that Jews have played a major part in ambushes and plundering.
5. . . . The concentration of the Jews in the cities will probably necessitate, for general considerations of security, regulations banning the Jews from certain parts of the city, forbidding them to leave the ghetto—though always bearing economic considerations in mind, forbidding them to go out after a certain hour in the evening etc. . . .
III. As a matter of principle all necessary measures should be taken in the closest agreement and cooperation with the German civil administration and the locally responsible military authorities.

It must be ensured that the economic exploitation of the occupied territories does not suffer as a result of these measures.
1. Above all, consideration must be given to the needs of the Army, e.g. it will hardly be possible to avoid leaving commercial Jews behind here and there, who will have to remain behind to ensure the provisioning of the troops in view of the lack of alternatives. However, in these cases, the attempt must be made, in agreement with the locally responsible German administrative authorities, to aryanize these businesses as soon as possible and to catch up on the emigration of these Jews.
2. Jewish branches of industry and businesses, which are vital for the war or for the Four Year Plan, must obviously remain in operation in order to maintain German economic interests in the occupied territories.

Early aryanization is also desirable in these cases as is the emigration of the Jews . . .
V. To achieve these goals I expect the absolute commitment of all forces of the Security Police and the Security Service . . .

On the following day, Heydrich mentioned to the Commander-in-Chief of the Army, v. Brauchitsch, a plan 'to establish a Jewish state under German administration near Cracow, into which other undesirable elements could also be admitted'.[4] Brauchitsch protested and Himmler

---

[3] This was the area destined for transfer to the Soviet Union, though this did not in fact occur (eds).

[4] See S. Goschen, 'Eichmann und die Nisko-Aktion in Oktober 1939' in *Vierteljahrshefte für Zeitgeschichte*, 29.1.1981, p. 79.

intervened to explain that Heydrich's order should be interpreted in terms of large-scale preparations and that its execution in the fullest sense of the word should be postponed to a later date.[5]

The following are excerpts from the minutes of a meeting of Heydrich with his department heads in the RSHA and the task force leaders on 27 September 1939:

772

. . . The deportation of the Jews to the foreign Gau [the General Government], their removal across the demarcation line has been approved by the Führer. However, the whole process is to take place over a period of one year . . .

The Jews are to be brought together in ghettos in the cities in order to ensure a better chance of controlling them and later of removing them. The most pressing matter is for the Jews to disappear from the countryside as small traders. This action must have been completed within the next three to four weeks. Insofar as the Jews are traders in the countryside, it must be sorted out with the Wehrmacht how far these Jewish traders must remain *in situ* in order to secure the provisioning of the troops. The following comprehensive directive was issued:
1. Jews into the towns as quickly as possible.
2. Jews out of the Reich into Poland.
The remaining Gypsies also to Poland.
4. The systematic evacuation of the Jews from German territory via goods trains . . .

The exact destination of the Jews who were to be sent to the General Government (Heydrich's 'final goal') remained somewhat vague until the final borders of Poland had been settled with the Russians. This occurred with the Russo-German border agreement of 28 September. The Russians agreed to let the Germans have the district of Lublin in the South-East of Poland and the Nazis now focused on this area for a Jewish reservation. On 29 September Hitler informed Rosenberg that he wanted to move 'all the Jews, including those from the Reich, as well as all elements who were in the least unreliable, to the area between the Vistula and the Bug'. And on the same day, according to the minutes of a RSHA heads of department meeting, Heydrich reported that 'in the area between Warsaw and Lublin a "nature reserve" or "Reich ghetto" is going to be established in which all the Polish and Jewish elements to be resettled from the future German

---

[5] See H. Krausnick, 'The Persecution of the Jews' in H. Buchheim *et. al.* *Anatomy of the SS State* (London 1968) p. 70.

Gaus i.e. Danzig–West Prussia and the Wartheland will have to be accommodated.'[6] In fact, the implementation of these plans was delayed for a time, partly in order to await the Allied response to Hitler's peace offer made on 6 October, and partly because of *Wehrmacht* opposition to radical resettlement policies in Poland, where military government was still in place.

However, one SD official, dazzled by the perspectives opened up by these plans, saw no reason to wait—Adolf Eichmann. Eichmann had already gained a reputation for himself as the ruthless organizer of the emigration of Austrian Jewry after the *Anschluss*. Following the take-over of Czechoslovakia in March 1939, he had also been appointed to carry out the same task in Prague. However, with the outbreak of war Eichmann found that the possibilities of Jewish emigration had been drastically curtailed. Now, the plans being discussed in the RSHA for a Jewish reservation near Lublin encouraged him to demonstrate his initiative to his superiors within the Gestapo where he had been assigned to Desk IV D4 (Emigration and Evacuation) in October 1939, later being transferred to IVB4 (Jewish Affairs-Evacuation Affairs).

During October 1939, Eichmann organized transports of Jews from Vienna, Upper Silesia, and the Reich Protectorate (Bohemia and Moravia) to the General Government. They were sent to a rural area near Nisko on the River San, part of the district of Lublin which had just been vacated by the Russians. Eichmann variously claimed to have been authorized to carry out these deportations by his own chief, Müller, by Heydrich, Himmler, and even Hitler. In fact, it appears he had no such authorization and was clearly hoping to win laurels by laying the foundations for the Jewish reservation envisaged by his superiors. Beginning on 18 October, several train loads of Jews from Vienna, Kattowitz and Ostrau were sent to Nisko. The majority did not stay in the makeshift camp, which they were forced to erect near the village of Zarzecze, but were simply driven into the countryside and literally ordered to get lost; those who returned were shot. However, within a few days, complaints from the local German civil and *Wehrmacht* authorities about the chaos being produced by these actions prompted the RSHA to call a halt to the transports which stopped on 26 October. Of the several thousand Jews transported to Nisko, a few hundred had managed to escape over the border into the Russian-occupied part of Poland. Some 500 had actually remained in the Zarzecze camp and returned home in April 1940, only to be transported east again later; the remainder had perished. Despite its failure, the Nisko operation had provided useful experience for subsequent deportations.

---

[6] S. Goschen, *op. cit.*, p. 80.

One reason for halting the Nisko operation was that Himmler had his own priorities for Jewish expulsions. On 25 October 1939, Hitler ended the military government of Poland, thereby giving a free hand to the SS. Five days later, on the 30th, Himmler ordered the 'resettlement' of all Jews from the Polish territories which had been incorporated into the Reich to be carried out between the beginning of November 1939 and the end of February 1940.[7] They were to be expelled to the area south of Warsaw and round Lublin. Unlike Eichmann's Nisko operation this one was agreed with the German civil authorities. However, this did little to improve the lot of those Jews who were expelled. Thus, at a meeting of German officials in the district of Radom on 25 November 1939, the Governor of the General Government, Hans Frank, made clear his views about the function of this expulsion programme:

773

. . . We won't waste much time on the Jews. It's great to get to grips with the Jewish race at last. The more that die the better; hitting them represents a victory for our Reich. The Jews should feel that we've arrived. We want to put ½ to ¾ of all Jews east of the Vistula. We will crush these Jews wherever we can. Everything is at stake. Get the Jews out of the Reich, Vienna, everywhere. We have no use for Jews in the Reich. Probably the line of the Vistula, behind this line no more. We are the most important people here . . .

The Nazi leadership was anxious to deport the German Jews as well to the General Government. The only question was whether or not a Jewish reservation as such should be created. This issue was discussed on 19 December 1939 at a meeting of department heads of the RSHA on 'The Final Solution of the German Jewish Question': for which the following notes were prepared either for or by Heydrich:

774

I. Jewish reservation in Poland.

The question arises whether a Jewish reservation should be created in Poland or whether the Jews should be accomodated in the future Gouvernement Poland [General Government].

If the creation of a reservation is envisaged, it would be necessary to examine whether it should be administered by Jews or by Reich Germans. A Jewish adminis-

[7] See *Faschismus–Getto–Massenmord. Dokumentation über Ausrottung und Widerstand der Juden in Polen während des Zweiten Weltkrieges* (Frankfurt a.M n.d.) pp. 42–3.

tration would be more advantageous, since it would result in a saving of German officials. Only the top posts would have to be staffed with Germans. Further, one would have to decide to whom the administration should be subordinated.

In my view, it would be appropriate to leave the administration under the leadership of the Security Police until the resettlement of the Jews from the Reich territory, the *Ostmark* [Austria] and Bohemia/Moravia has been carried out.

II. In this connection, a final decision would have to be taken on whether Jewish emigration should continue in the light of the creation of the reservation. Moreover, a reservation would represent a good means of diplomatic pressure against the Western Powers. Perhaps this could lead to the raising of the question of the world solution at the end of the war.

A further meeting was held in the RSHA on 30 January 1940 under Heydrich's chairmanship to discuss the deportation of Poles, Jewish Poles, Germans, and Gypsies, from the minutes of which the following extracts are taken:

775

1. *Gruppenführer* Heydrich announces that the present meeting has been called on the instructions of the *Reichsführer* SS in order to ensure a uniform line among all those agencies participating in the resettlement tasks ordered by the Führer. The deportations carried out so far involved roughly 87,000 Poles and Jews from the Warthegau who provided space for the Baltic Germans who were to be settled there. In addition, there was so-called illegal emigration which was not controlled . . .

3. Following the two mass evacuations
(*a*) of 40,000 Poles and Jews for the sake of the Baltic Germans and
(*b*) of roughly 120,000 Poles for the sake of the Wolhynian Germans, the last mass evacuation will be of all Jews from the new eastern Gaue and 30,000 Gypsies from the Reich territory into the General Government. After it has been established that the evacuation of 120,000 will only begin in March 1940, the evacuation of Jews and Gypsies will have to be postponed until the conclusion of the actions mentioned above. However, the distribution ratio has been announced by the General Government so that planning can begin.

SS *Gruppenführer* Heydrich announces that a fairly large number of training areas will be required in the General Government for the *Wehrmacht*, *Luftwaffe* and SS, which will require a resettlement of roughly 100,000 to 120,000 people in the General Government. It would, therefore, be desirable if, in order to avoid a second resettlement, evacuations to the General Government could take this into account. SS *Gruppenführer* Heydrich commented that the construction of the wall[8]

[8] For a brief period a scheme was envisaged of building a defensive line in south-east Poland (eds).

and other projects in the East will presumably provide the opportunity for bringing together several hundred thousand Jews in forced labour camps, whose families could then be allocated to the other Jewish families already living in the Government, which would solve this problem . . .

In mid-February 1940, 1,000 Jews from Stettin [Pomerania], whose dwellings are urgently required for war purposes, will be evacuated and also deported to the General Government . . .

Finally, SS *Gruppenführer* Heydrich emphasized that it was particularly important that persons to be evacuated, in particular the urban population, should be promptly reported to the responsible Trusteeship Offices so that their property can be secured.

In his January report, dated 19 February 1940, the chief of the Cracow district, SS *Gruppenführer*, Dr Karl Wächter, described the resettlement of the Warthegau Jews in his area as follows:

776

Attention must be drawn to the large number of evacuees from Posen and the Warthegau who are incapable of work. Further difficulties have been created by the uncoordinated direction of the trains. Thus, train-loads of Jews and townspeople were directed to rural districts, whereas transports with peasants arrived in the town . . .

Thus, transports of women and children were placed in overcrowded and unheated cattle trucks without the minimum provisions necessary. As a result, there were many deaths during the journeys and a large number of physical injuries and cases of frostbite . . .

The Joint Polish-Jewish Aid Commission reported on the plight of transports of Jews from Pomerania in Germany, referred to by Heydrich at the RSHA meeting on 30 January:

777

. . . On 12 March 1940, the 160 Jews of Schneidemühl were deported in box-cars to the region of Lublin. Other convoys are expected there. The deportees had to abandon all their possessions. They were not even allowed to take suitcases; the women had to leave their purses. Some deportees had their coats taken away, especially those who had tried to put on several to protect themselves better against the cold. They were not able to take any money, not even the twenty złotys granted to the Stettin deportees. Nor were they able to take either food, bedding, or dishes.

They arrived at Lublin owning only what they were wearing on their backs.

The deportees have been sent to the villages of Piaski, Glusk, and Belcyka, twenty-five to thirty kilometres from Lublin. There they found the deportees from Stettin, or those of them who were still alive. Men, women and children have had to walk to these villages on roads covered with deep snow in a temperature of −22°(centigrade). Of the 1,200 deportees from Stettin, 72 died during a march that lasted more than fourteen hours. The majority died from exposure.

Among others, a mother who was carrying a three-year-old child in her arms, trying to protect him from the cold with her own clothes, was found dead, frozen in this position. The half-frozen body of a five-year-old girl was found wearing around her neck a cardboard sign with the words, 'Renate Alexander, from Hammerstein, Pomerania'. This child was visiting relatives in Stettin and was included in the deportation; her mother and father stayed in Germany. Her hands and feet had to be amputated at the Lublin hospital. The bodies of the deportees who had died of exposure were piled on sleds and buried in the Jewish cemeteries at Piask and Lublin.

The General Government (district governor Zörner) has declined all responsibility for these occurrences and for their consequences. Marshal Göring has been informed of the situation.

The administrative difficulties caused by the mass resettlement of Poles and Jews in the General Government prompted Frank to appeal to Göring, who still officially had overall responsibility for the Jewish question, to halt the deportations. Göring was receptive to such arguments because of his growing concern at the economic disruption they caused. On 12 February, therefore, he announced at a conference at his country house, Karinhall, that all deportations should be cleared with Frank in order not to reduce the labour force and disrupt the economy of the Polish territories. However, evidently this declaration did not have the desired effect, for, on 24 March 1940, Göring issued the following directive which, for the next nine months or so, virtually put an end to the deportation of Jews to the General Government and to the idea of establishing a Jewish reservation there:

778

The Governor General for the occupied Polish territories has complained that deportations of Jews from the Reich into the General Government are still taking place although the facilities for receiving them are at present not available. I hereby forbid further such deportations without my permission and without proof of the prior agreement of the Governor General. I will not accept excuses to the effect that such 'migrations' are being carried out by subordinate agencies.

(ii) Poland 1939–40: (b) Forced Labour and the Creation of the Ghettos

During 1939–40, the Jews of Poland were subjected to a whole series of repressive measures. On 26 October 1939, Governor Frank issued the following Decree concerning the Introduction of Compulsory Labour for the Jewish Population of the General Government:

779

§ 1. Compulsory labour for the Jews domiciled in the General Government shall be introduced with immediate effect. The Jews shall for this purpose be formed into forced labour detachments.
§ 2. The directives required for the implementation of the present decree shall be issued by the Higher SS and Police Leader. He may define the territories east of the Vistula in which the implementation of the present decree shall be waived.

This was followed, on 11 December, by the first supplementary regulation which prevented all Jews from changing their abode without permission and imposed a curfew from 9 p.m. to 5 a.m. The following day, §1 of the second supplementary regulation laid down: 'all Jewish inhabitants of the General Government are subject to compulsory labour from the end of their 14th to the end of their 60th year. This compulsory labour will normally last for two years; it will be extended if the educational aims have not been achieved within this period'.[9] Many Jews were organized in labour camps away from their families and forced to work on various construction projects for the German authorities. The following excerpts from a report of the Labour Camp desk of the Jewish labour battalion in Warsaw describe the inhuman conditions in these camps: The report dates from the end of 1940:

780

V. *Nature of the work*:
The work in the camps is mostly very heavy physical labour. In the vast majority of camps melioration work is carried out: the regulation of large and small rivers . . . strengthening the banks with willows, planting the banks, digging canals, erecting dams.

[9] See *Faschismus–Getto–Massenmord, op. cit.* pp. 205–6.

The workers employed on these tasks did not receive suitable clothing for this work or special boots for their work in the water. With this kind of work they had to spend 8–10 hours a day standing up to their knees in water; they had no opportunity to dry their wet clothing so they had to remain in it, since the shortage of suits and underwear made it impossible to change. Working in the water without shoes and leg-coverings, people found leeches a particular nuisance; they bit terrible wounds in people's legs.

In other camps road works were carried out: the collection and unloading of material (stones, cement, gravel), the breaking-up of stones, the laying of road surfaces. Here too, the work was done with very primitive tools or by hand, although the distribution of a sufficient number of suitable tools would have greatly increased productivity.

The easiest work was in the camps in which other construction work was carried out (the digging of ditches and earth walls).

All the work required great effort by the workers; they were employed for 8–10 hours a day or longer. The working conditions were very unfavourable; they had to work in water or stand in marshy fields and walk long distances to their places of work which were 4–6, sometimes even up to 12km distance from the camps.

The following excerpt is from a report of a visit by doctors to the Belzec group of labour camps in South-East Poland in the middle of September 1940:

781

Conditions of accommodation:
In general awful, worst in the north. The rooms are completely unsuitable for accommodating so many people. They are dark and dirty. There is serious lice infestation. Roughly thirty per cent of the workers have no shoes, trousers or shirts. All sleep on the floor without straw. The roofs are damaged, the windows have no glass; it is fearfully cramped in there. For example, 75 people sleep in a room measuring 5 × 6 metres, lying on top of each other on the floor. Of course there can be no question of undressing under these conditions. Moreover, there is no soap and it is even difficult to get hold of water. The sick lie and sleep together with the healthy. At night, they are not allowed to leave the barracks and so must relieve themselves on the spot. It is, therefore, not suprising that in these circumstances many people fall ill. It is very difficult to get excused from work even for a day. So the sick have to go off to work as well . . .

Meanwhile, on 23 November 1939, the following Decree concerning Distinguishing Marks for Jews and Jewesses in the General Government had been issued:

782

From 1 December 1939
§ 1. All Jews and Jewesses resident in the General Government and more than ten years old must wear on the right sleeve of their clothes and outer garments a white strip at least 10 cm wide with a star of David upon it.
§ 2. Jews and Jewesses must obtain this armlet themselves and provide it with the appropriate sign.
§ 3. Infractions will be punished with imprisonment and a fine up to an unlimited amount or with one or other of these penalties.
(2) The special courts have jurisdiction in this matter . . .

Similar regulations had already been issued by Nazi officials in the incorporated territories.

The ending of the deportations to the General Government and the abortion of the plan for a Jewish reservation in the Lublin area posed the question of what was to be done about the Jews. In his first directive to the *Einsatzgruppen* in Poland of 21 September Heydrich had referred to the need to concentrate the Jews in ghettos. This process of ghettoization began to be implemented during 1940. The first Jewish ghetto was established in April 1940 in Łódź, the second largest city in Poland, which was now in the Warthegau. Łódź was a major centre of textile production in which the Jews played a predominant role. On 10 December 1939, the *Regierungspräsident* of Kalisch, Friedrich Uebelhoer, sent the following circular to the local party and police authorities and economic organizations:

783

Construction of a Ghetto in the city of Łódź

Secret
Strictly Confidential

I estimate that *c.* 320,000 Jews are now living in the city of Łódź. Their immediate evacuation is impossible. Detailed investigations by all the relevant bodies have shown that the concentration of all Jews in a closed ghetto is feasible. The Jewish question in the city of Łódź must be provisionally solved as follows:

1. Those Jews living north of the line Listopada (Novemberstrasse, Freiheitsplatz, Pomorska) Pommerschestrasse are to be accommodated in a closed ghetto so that, on the one hand, the space required for the construction of a German bastion round the Freiheitsplatz is cleared of Jews and, on the other hand, the northern part of the city, which is almost exclusively inhabited by Jews, is included in this ghetto.

2. The remaining Jews living in the city of Łódź who are fit for work are to be concentrated into labour gangs, accommodated in barrack blocks and kept under guard.

The preparations for and implementation of this plan are to be carried out by a working party to which the following bodies or agencies are to send representatives. 1. NSDAP. 2. Łódź district office of the *Regierungspräsident* in Kalisch. 3. City administration of the city of Łódź (Housing Department, Building Department, Health Department, Food Department etc.) 4. Order police. 5. Security police. 6. Death's Head Formation. 7. Chamber of Industry and Commerce. 8. Finance Office . . .

After these preparations have been completed and after the provision of sufficient guards, the ghetto will be established suddenly on a day to be chosen by me, i.e. at a certain time the boundaries of the ghetto, which have been fixed, will be manned by the guard units envisaged for this purpose and the streets will be blocked off by barbed wire barricades and other barriers. At the same time, the walling-up or barricading of the house fronts will start being carried out by Jewish workers who will be recruited from the ghetto. In the ghetto itself a Jewish administration will be instituted immediately which will consist of the Jewish elders and a considerably enlarged council. This Council of the Elders of the ghetto will have the following tasks to fulfil:

1. *Food Department*: Establishment and maintenance of communal kitchens. Utilization of the food supplies available in the ghetto and those delivered by the city administration.
2. *Health Department*: Deployment of the available doctors. Supervision of pharmacists. The establishment of one or more hospitals as well as epidemic centres, provision of drinking water, lavatories and sewage disposal, burial arrangements.
3. *Finance Department*: The financing of food supplies.
4. *Security Department*: The establishment of a police force. The establishment of a fire service,
5. *Accommodation Department*: Distribution of the available rooms. Erection of barracks. The provision of beds for the ghetto inhabitants.
6. *Registration Department*: Registration of all persons in the ghetto and control over those moving to and from it.

The Food Office of the city of Łódź will transport the requisite foodstuffs and heating materials to specified points in the ghetto and transfer them to the representative of the Jewish administration for distribution. The basic principle will be that foodstuffs and heating materials cannot be paid for with barter goods such as textiles etc. We ought thereby to succeed in getting out all the valuables which have been hoarded and concealed by the Jews.

At the same time, or shortly after the creation of the ghetto, those Jews who are living outside the ghetto and are incapable of work are to be deported into the ghetto. Those dwellings in the other part of the city which become vacant as a result of this deportation are to be secured against unauthorised entry. The toughest measures are to be taken against Jews who inflict malicious damage on being driven out of their dwellings . . .

In the process of combing the other parts of the city for Jews who are incapable of work and who are to be deported to the ghetto at the time of its creation or shortly afterwards, those Jews living there who are capable of work must also be secured. They should be concentrated in labour gangs and accommodated in barrack blocks previously designated by the city administration and the security police. These Jews are to be assigned to labour gangs en bloc. This work will initially consist of these labour gangs clearing away those houses in the city centre which are ripe for demolition . . .

The creation of the ghetto is of course only a provisional measure. I reserve for myself the decision as to the point in time and the means by which the ghetto and thereby the city of Łódź will be cleared of Jews. The final goal, at any rate, must be to lance this festering boil.

On 30 April 1940, the *Oberbürgermeister* of Łódź issued a ban on Jews leaving the ghetto and delegated to the senior Jewish elder, Chaim Rumkovski, the responsibility for maintaining 'an orderly community life' in the ghetto.[10] He was given *carte blanche* to impose the necessary measures for achieving that end, including the conscription of all Jews for unpaid labour. As a result, Rumkovski established himself as the effective dictator of the ghetto, suffering in the process from delusions of grandeur in which he referred to 'my Jews'.

The Łódź ghetto, which initially contained 155,000 Jews out of a total city population of 600,000, was of considerable economic importance to the German war machine. As a result, although it underwent periodic selections of Jews for deportation to the nearby death camp of Chełmno,[11] it survived until August 1944, when the remaining 60,000 Jews were shipped to Auschwitz.

The largest Jewish ghetto established by the Nazis in Poland was in Warsaw. A report on the history of its creation by Waldemar Schön, director of the Resettlement Department attached to the governor of the Warsaw District, dated 20 January 1941, gives a good insight into the development of German policy towards the Jews in Poland during the first year of occupation:

784

. . . The idea of creating a Jewish residential district in Warsaw emerged as early as February 1940, shortly after the establishment of the Resettlement Department, and the first preparations were begun. The Governor originally planned to turn that part of the city which is bordered on the Eastern side by the Vistula into a

[10] See *Faschismus–Getto–Massenmord, op. cit.* p. 84.

[11] See below p. 1138.

Jewish district. The head of the Resettlement Department was given the task of carrying it out.

It was clear that, in view of the special and extremely complex conditions in the city of Warsaw, this idea was bound initially to appear unfeasible. Objections came from various quarters, in particular from the city administration. The point was made that the creation of a ghetto would cause considerable disruption to industry and business. Since eighty per cent of the artisans were Jews, one could not place them under siege for they were indispensable. Finally, the objection was made that the Jews could not be provisioned if they were concentrated in a closed district.

A meeting on 8 March 1940 came to the conclusion that the plan for the creation of a ghetto would be postponed. At about the same time, the idea was mooted within the General Government that the district of Lublin should be made into a catchment area for all the Jews in the General Government and, in particular, for the Jewish evacuees and refugees who were arriving.

Illegal Jewish evacuations and unauthorized border crossings by Jews were increasing at this time, particularly on the borders of the districts of Lovicz and Skiernievice. As a result of this illegal Jewish immigration, conditions in the city of Lovicz were becoming alarming from the point of view of both health and security. The head of the district of Lovicz justifiably felt the need to ward off these dangers by creating Jewish residential districts in Lovicz and Glovno [May 1940]. The experience which was gained by the creation of the Jewish districts in Lovicz and Glovno has shown that these methods are the only correct ones for removing all the threats which emanate from the Jewish sphere.

At the beginning of April, the Higher SS and Police Leader in Cracow informed us that it was not intended to concentrate the Jews in the district of Lublin. Thereupon, the Department for Resettlement resumed the preparations for the creation of Jewish districts in the District of Warsaw. The Governor gave instructions for the creation of the Jewish districts to begin in time for the resettlement to be completed before the onset of winter.

The plan now proposed by the Resettlement Department aimed at the creation of two ghettos on the outskirts of the city, namely embracing the district of Kolo and Wola in the west of the city and the district of Grochow in the East. This idea was based on the awareness that these ghettos on the edge of the city would cause the least disruption and damage to business, industry, and transport in the city of Warsaw. The deadline for the beginning of these actions was fixed for 1 July 1940 so that the most essential measures would have been carried out by the beginning of winter.

Then, as early as the first phase of the preparations, a directive came from Cracow to gear all activities to the fact that, according to the Führer's plan, after the end of the war all the Jews in Europe were to be sent to Madagascar and thus it would effectively be illusory to create a ghetto. Whereupon the preparations of the Resettlement Department were once more halted.

At the end of August 1940, the creation of a ghetto was once more encouraged by the Health Department in order to protect the German Army and population, particularly in view of the increasing concentrations of troops in the area of the Warsaw District. On 20 August 1940, the Department of Internal Administration in the office of the General Governor confirmed the necessity for the creation of

Jewish residential districts. However, hermetically sealed Jewish ghettos should not be created, but rather Jewish residential districts which permitted economic links with the surrounding Aryan area, which would be vital to the survival of the Jewish residential district.

Time had by now moved on fast. The creation of a ghetto at the edge of the city would have taken four to five months in view of the need to regroup nearly 600,000 people. However, the resettlement measures had to be completed by 15 November, at the latest by the end of November. This was particularly stressed by the chief doctor for the District, since experience showed that the winter months saw an increase in epidemics to which the resettlement measures would have given an alarming boost.

Thus, the plan for a ghetto on the outskirts of the city was abandoned. The area chosen for the creation of a Jewish residential district was the one which had been placed under restriction because of the danger of epidemics and which in its existing state had hitherto been unable to provide a secure protection against epidemics.

After extensive preliminary discussions, negotiations, inspections and preparatory work, it was possible to present the Governor with a promising plan.

On 2 October 1940, the head of the Warsaw District sent a general directive to all *Kreishauptleute*[12] and to his representative for the city of Warsaw ordering them to initiate and carry out the resettlement necessary for the creation of Jewish residential districts by 15 November 1940. It was clear that one would have to deal with this problem all along the line if one was going to be certain of success. On the same day, the Governor issued the regulation No. 50/40, concerning the creation of a Jewish residential district in the city of Warsaw, and delegated the carrying out of the whole resettlement operation to the head of the Resettlement Department . . .

Apart from general ethnic requirements, the reasons which have led to the creation of Jewish residential districts are as follows:

1. The German Army and population must at all costs be protected from the immune bacillus-carrier of the plagues—the Jew.
2. The separation of the Jews from the rest of the population is politically and morally desirable. Jewish ideas and modes of behaviour had hitherto held the population of the East in their thrall. The beneficial effects of the removal of the influence of Jewry are already becoming apparent. If the German work of reconstruction is to be crowned with any success, then it must prevent the Jew from having a free hand in this area.
3. A further reason arises from the necessity of securing the implementation of measures required for the war economy and securing food supplies through the prevention of the black market and price increases.

The Course of the Resettlement Actions in Warsaw

The resettlement actions started at the beginning of October, Initially, a deadline of 31.10.1940 was set for their completion . . .

Overall a total of 113,000 Poles and 138,000 Jews were resettled. Since the Jews who were outside the Jewish residential district normally possessed large apart-

[12] The German District administrative chiefs (eds).

ments, the exchange could be accomplished with the minimum of disruption, since the large apartments could be occupied by several Polish families. 11,567 Aryan apartments were given up in the Jewish district and approximately 13,000 Jewish apartments outside the Jewish district were taken over . . .

According to the position on 30 October 1940, 8,600 apartments had been voluntarily exchanged, so that counting both sides together around 65,000 people had moved. The remainder moved after the Governor extended the deadline to 15 November 1940 . . .

It is astonishing that the resettlement actions, involving around 250,000 people in the relatively short period of not quite six weeks, should have been carried out without spilling any blood and only in the last phase with the help of police pressure. It was achieved through the mobilization of the Polish mayor on the one hand and the Jewish Council on the other.

A major police action was launched on 16 November 1940 under the direction of the head of the Resettlement Department which once again combed all the sections of the city where Jews were living and in the process caught 11,130 Jews who were compulsorily brought to the Jewish residential district. On the same day, 1,170 grocers and 2,600 other Jewish businesses were sealed by the police and taken over and cleared by the appropriate departments and organizations . . .

The External Appearance of the Jewish Residential District

The Jewish residential district is approximately 403 hectares in size. According to statements by the Jewish Council, who claim to have carried out a census, there are around 410,000 Jews living in this area, but according to our own observations and various other estimates there are around 470–590,000 Jews.

On the basis of the statistics given us by the Jewish Council, and excluding the open spaces and cemeteries, there are 1,108 people living in each hectare of built-up area i.e., 110,880 persons per square kilometre. The population density of the city of Warsaw is 14,000 people per square km of the total area and 38,000 per square km of built-up and inhabitable space.

One should mention that this total will increase as a result of a new resettlement action which has become necessary involving 72,000 Jews from the western part of the District of Warsaw. Space has to be created for 62,000 Poles who have been evacuated.

In the Jewish residential district there are around 27,000 apartments with an average of 2½ rooms each. This produces an occupation density of 15.1 persons per apartment and 6–7 persons per room.

The Jewish residential district is separated off from the rest of the city by the utilization of existing walls and by walling up streets, windows, doors and gaps between buildings. The walls are three metres high and are raised a further metre by barbed wire placed on top. They are also guarded by motorized and mounted police patrols.

Initially, twenty-two gaps were left in the wall for the necessary pedestrian traffic; these have meanwhile been reduced to fifteen. To start with, strong German police forces were posted at the entrances, but these were later replaced by Polish police forces, while the German police concentrated on supervision . . .

Passes are issued for passage in and out of the ghetto for essential purposes—yellow cards for Reich Germans, ethnic Germans, and Poles, yellow cards with a blue oblique stripe for Jews. The passes are only valid in conjunction with an identity card containing a photograph . . .

(iii) Poland 1940–42: Life in the Ghettos

The inhabitants of the Warsaw ghetto had to survive on an official food allocation of 300 calories per day compared with 634 calories for the Poles and 2,310 for the Germans. On average, a person was allocated half a pound of sugar and four pounds of bread per month. Heating materials were extremely short. In the winter of 1941–2, 718 out of the 780 flats that were investigated were unheated. Those who did not have access to the black market trade which flourished with the 'Aryan' sector of the city, either because they lacked any resources to start with, as was the case with the Jews deported to the city from the surrounding areas, or because they could not work, could not survive long under these conditions. The vast majority steadily deteriorated in health and strength. The situation within the Warsaw ghetto was paralleled by that in the other ghettos which were established in towns and cities throughout Poland during 1940.

The following is a description of life in the Warsaw ghetto from the diary of a visitor, Stanislav Rozycki:

785

. . . The majority are nightmare figures, ghosts of former human beings, miserable destitutes, pathetic remnants of former humanity. One is most affected by the characteristic change which one sees in their faces: as a result of misery, poor nourishment, the lack of vitamins, fresh air and exercise, the numerous cares, worries, anticipated misfortunes, suffering and sickness, their faces have taken on a skeletal appearance. The prominent bones around their eye sockets, the yellow facial colour, the slack pendulous skin, the alarming emaciation and sickliness. And, in addition, this miserable, frightened, restless, apathetic and resigned expression like that of a hunted animal. I pass my closest friends without recognising them and guessing their fate. Many of them recognise me, come up to me and ask curiously how things are 'over there' behind the walls—there where there is enough bread, fresh air, freedom to move around, and above all freedom . . .

On the streets children are crying in vain, children who are dying of hunger. They howl, beg, sing, moan, shiver with cold, without underwear, without clothing, without shoes, in rags, sacks, flannel which are bound in strips round the emaciated skeletons, children swollen with hunger, disfigured, half conscious, already completely grown-up at the age of five, gloomy and weary of life. They are like old people and are only conscious of one thing: 'I'm cold'.'I'm hungry'. They have become aware of the most important things in life that quickly. Through their innocent sacrifice and their frightening helplessness the thousands upon thousands of these little beggars level the main accusation against the proud civilization of today. Ten per cent of the new generation have already perished: every day and every night hundreds of these children die and there is no hope that anybody will put a stop to it.

There are not only children. Young and old people, men and women, bourgeois and proletarians, intelligentsia and business people are all being declassed and degraded . . . They are being gobbled up by the streets on to which they are brutally and ruthlessly thrown. They beg for one month, for two months, for three months—but they all go down-hill and die on the street or in hospitals from cold, or hunger, or sickness, or depression. Former human beings whom no one needs fall by the wayside: former citizens, former 'useful members of human society'.

I no longer look at people; when I hear groaning and sobbing I go over to the other side of the road; when I see something wrapped in rags shivering with cold, stretched out on the ground I turn away and do not want to look . . . I can't. It's become too much for me. And yet only an hour has passed . . .

For various reasons standards of hygiene are terribly poor. Above all, the fearful population density in the streets with which nowhere in Europe can be remotely compared. The fatal over-population is particularly apparent in the streets: people literally rub against each other, it is impossible to pass unhindered through the streets. And then the lack of light, gas, and heating materials. Water consumption is also much reduced; people wash themselves much less and do not have baths or hot water. There are no green spaces, gardens, parks: no clumps of trees and no lawns to be seen. For a year no one has seen a village, a wood, a field, a river or a mountain: no one has breathed slightly better air for even a few days this year. Bedding and clothing are changed very rarely because of the lack of soap. To speak of food hygiene would be a provocation and would be regarded as mockery. People eat what is available, however much is available and when it is available. Other principles of nutrition are unknown here. Having said all this, one can easily draw one's own conclusions as to the consequences: stomach typhus and typhus, dysentery, tuberculosis, pneumonia, influenza, metabolic disturbances, the most common digestive illnesses, lack of vitamins and all other illnesses associated with the lack of bread, fresh air, clothing, and heating materials. Typhus is systematically and continually destroying the population. There are victims in every family. On average up to a thousand people are dying each month. In the early morning the corpses of beggars, children, old people, young people and women are lying in every street—the victims of the hunger and the cold. The hospitals are so terribly overcrowded that there are 2–3 patients lying in every bed. Those who do not find a place in a bed lie on the floor in rooms and corridors. The shortage of the necessary medicines in sufficient quantities makes it impossible to treat the sick. Moreover, there is a shortage of food for the sick. There is only soup and tea . . .

While this cruel struggle for a little bit of bread, for a few metres of living space, for the maintenance of health, energy and life is going on, people are incapable of devoting much energy and strength to intellectual matters. In any case, there are German restrictions and bans. Nothing can be printed, taught or learnt. People are not allowed to organize themselves or exchange cultural possessions. We are cut off from the world and from books. It is not permitted to open libraries and sort out books from other printed materials. We are not allowed to print anything, neither books nor newspapers; schools, academic institutions etc. are not permitted to open. There are no cinemas, radio, no contacts with world culture. Nothing reaches us, no products of the human spirit reach us. We have to smuggle in not only food stuffs and manufactured goods, but also cultural products. For that reason everything which we achieve in this respect is worthy of recognition irrespective of how much there is or what it consists of . . .

In fact, the Jews in the Warsaw ghetto made remarkable efforts not only to sustain life itself but also to maintain educational and cultural activities.

The Nazi organisation 'Strength through Joy'[13] organized coach tours to the Warsaw ghetto. A report issued by the Polish government in exile in May 1942 contained the following description:

786

Every day large coaches come to the ghetto; they take soldiers through as if it was a zoo. It is the thing to do to provoke the wild animals. Often soldiers strike out at passers-by with long whips as they drive through. They go to the cemetery where they take pictures. They compel the families of the dead and the rabbis to interrupt the funeral and to pose in front of their lenses. They set up genre pictures (old Jew above the corpse of a young girl).

Official films of the ghetto were also made for propaganda purposes. One famous visitor was Alfred Rosenberg who reported to the Reich press department as follows:

787

. . . Large ghettos have been established in the cities which function reasonably well but cannot represent the final solution of the Jewish question. I had the opportunity to get to know the ghetto in Lublin and the one in Warsaw. The sights are so appalling and probably also so well-known to the editorial staffs that a description is presumably superfluous. If there are any people left who still somehow have sympathy with the Jews then they ought to be recommended to have a look at such a ghetto. Seeing this race en masse, which is decaying, decomposing, and rotten to the core will banish any sentimental humanitarianism. In the Warsaw ghetto there are at present fifty typhus cases a month and one cannot ascertain how many are not reported. Seven hundred Jewish doctors have been put in the ghetto who live there and have to concentrate on fighting typhus. Seventy thousand Jews have been deported to Warsaw from the Warthegau. It is the 'Reich rubbish

[13] See vol. 2, pp. 346 ff.

dump' according to the desk officer responsible. The Warsaw ghetto contains 500,000 Jews of whom 5–6,000 die each month. In reply to my question as to whether it was reckoned that in ten years time the Jews would be finished through having died off, Dr Frank said that he did not want to wait such a long time. The Jews would have to be deported before then to reservations in deepest Russia (the Urals). The view that the District of Lublin would become a Jewish reservation was wrong since the fertile areas of this district were far too good for the Jews . . .

The following are the monthly death figures for the Jewish ghetto in Warsaw:

788

	1941	1942
January	898	5,123
February	1,023	4,618
March	1,608	4,951
April	2,061	4,432
May	3,821	3,636
June	4,290	3,356
July	5,550	
August	5,560	
September	4,545	
October	4,716	
November	4,801	
December	4,239	

In their propaganda the Nazis ruthlessly linked the Jews with typhus, aiming to underline their stereotype of the Jews as bacilli; typhus is a disease associated with poor hygiene and malnutrition.

On 15 October 1941, the following decree, issued by Hans Frank, introduced the death penalty for Jews who left their ghettos and for those who assisted them in doing so:

789

. . . § 4b (1) Jews who leave the residential district assigned to them without permission will be punished by death. The same punishment will be meted out to

persons who wilfully give refuge to such Jews.
(2) Those who encourage and assist such persons will receive the same punishment as those who carry out the deed. Attempted deeds will receive the same punishment as those carried out.
(3) Sentencing will be carried out by the special courts. . .

The decree was rigorously enforced as is clear from the following documents:

790

Ghetto Police Station 6 — Litzmannstadt [Łódź] 1.12.1941
Re: Use of firearms.
On 1 December 1941 I was at Checkpoint 4 in the Hohensteinerstrasse between 14.00 and 16.00. At 15.00 I saw a woman climbing onto the ghetto fence, stick her head through it and attempt to steal a turnip from a passing lorry. I used my firearm. The Jewess was killed with two shots. Type of weapon: Carbine 98. Munition expended: 2 bullets.

Signed: Naumann
Constable of the Reserve Security Police
1 Comp Bl. Batt. Ghetto

On 8 April 1942, the *Kreishauptmann* in Tomaschow reported to his superiors as follows:

791

The Jews remain determined to escape starvation and to live on the outside. In the past month *c.* thirty Jews who had left the ghetto without permission and wanted to flee were shot . . .

It has been estimated that some 500–600,000 Polish Jews, about one fifth of the total, died in ghettos and labour camps.

(iv) The Jews in Germany 1939–1940

Meanwhile, German Jews had found that the outbreak of war had given a new impetus to discriminatory measures against them. During the first weeks such measures were often initiated by local officials such as mayors who imposed curfews on Jews or banned them from certain areas. Soon, however, they were being applied more comprehensively and systematically. A leading role in this process was played by Joseph Goebbels. On 23 September 1939, the Gestapo ordered the confiscation of all radios from Jews and on 20 November, instructions were given to prevent them from acquiring new ones. On 2 December, Goebbels encouraged the Reich Food Ministry to issue the following directive, which was passed on to the *Landräte* by the state economics ministries, in this case the Württemberg Economics Ministry:

792

The Reich Minister for Food and Agriculture has sent a telex on 2 December 1939 forbidding the sale of chocolate products (chocolate bars, chocolates, and other cocoa products) and cakes of all kinds to Jews with immediate effect.

You are requested to instruct the local authorities to inform the retailers of this at once. A public announcement should not be made.

Goebbels and the Staff of the Führer's Deputy also prompted the imposition of restrictions on the provision of clothing for Jews as defined in the following letter from the Minister of Finance and Economics in Baden to the Prime Minister of Baden, dated 1 February 1940:

793

The serious situation as regards the supply of textiles and shoes, coupled with the excessive hoarding in Jewish families, makes it appear desirable—as in the case of foodstuffs—to issue the following special regulations for Jews:

1. Jews will not receive a Reich clothing card.
2. As a matter of principle, Jews are not to be issued with coupons for textiles, shoes and material for soling shoes.
3. The provision of textiles and shoes for Jews will be carried out by the Reich Association of Jews in Germany on the basis of mutual assistance. Jewish applicants should therefore be referred to this organization. In addition they may acquire second-hand goods without coupons.

On 11 March 1940, the Reich Minister of Food and Agriculture issued the following directive concerning 'food supplies for the Jews'.

794

1. Rations for normal consumers and special groups of consumers. Jews will receive the same normal rations as other consumers unless it has been determined otherwise for the Reich as a whole.

The regulations for sick and frail persons, expectant and nursing mothers and women in child bed also apply to Jews.

Since the food bonuses for heavy, very heavy, and night workers and those working exceptionally long hours are based on the nature of the activity, Jews can also receive the bonus coupons in so far as their employment in this particular activity is necessary for the war effort.

2. Special allocations.

Jews are excluded from special allocations of foodstuffs on principle . . .

4. Unrationed foodstuffs.

Jews are not subject to any restrictions on the acquisition of foodstuffs which are not rationed. However, in so far as customer lists have been introduced for poultry, small game, fish, smoked meats, and skimmed milk, or other sale restrictions have been imposed, Jews are excluded from the acquisition of these foodstuffs.

5. The identification and cancelling of ration cards.

To facilitate the implementation of these regulations the food ration cards should be clearly stamped with a J before being handed out to the Jews.

Jews were also subjected to local restrictions on shopping hours which ensured that they were served last, as in the following ordinance issued by the Police President of Berlin on 4 July 1940:

795

§ 1. The shopping hours are fixed for Jews as 16.00–17.00. This applies to all public places of sale, all public and private markets, including market halls and street sales.

§ 2. Jews within the meaning of this police ordinance are those persons whose ration cards are marked with a J or the word 'Jew'.

§ 3. When requested, shopkeepers must place a notice which refers to the restriction of shopping hours for Jews to 16.00–17.00 in all public places of sale, on all public and private market stalls, and on street stalls.

The process of excluding Jews from the normal rights of German citizens continued in other spheres, as in the following judgement by the Cologne Labour Court dated 21 January 1941 which denied the claim of Jewish employees to a vacation:

796

1. The precondition for the claim to a vacation—membership of the plant community—does not exist. A Jew cannot be a member of the plant community on account of his whole racial tendency which is geared to forwarding his personal interests and securing economic advantages. His disposition precludes him from fitting in as a member of this community and gearing his thoughts and actions to the idea of the community.
2. Plant and wage regulations only apply to Jews in so far as they deal with the work performed by the Jew. Thus Jews have a right to a return for the work they have performed; no more and no less. That exhausts the employer's duties arising from his working relationship vis-à-vis Jews. The wage is a remuneration for work. A vacation is not a remuneration for work. The view that the claim to a vacation is a form of remuneration, which was dominant in the liberal epoch, has been finally exploded.
3. The claim to a vacation is a product of the duty of loyalty and care. However the duty of loyalty and care only exists in the relationship between the employer and national comrades. Jews have no particular duties arising from any relationship of loyalty vis-a-vis employers. Employers equally have no particular duty to care for Jews.

As a result, Jews have no claim to a vacation in the national socialist state.

(iv) Jewish Emigration and Deportations April 1940–September 1941 and the 'Madagascar Plan'

Although the outbreak of war had greatly complicated the problem of Jewish emigration, the German authorities continued to encourage it as far as possible as is clear from the following directive of the RSHA dated 24 April 1940:

797

1. The Jewish emigration from Reich territory is to be encouraged as before even during the war.

The Chief of the Security Police and SD has informed Minister-President Field Marshal Göring, with whose express approval the emigration of Jews is being continued, that Jews who are capable of bearing arms or of work are as far as possible not being permitted to emigrate to European countries and definitely not to European enemy states.

In this connection, I would like to say that each emigration case, in so far as the person is not going overseas, should be examined in the light of the above principles and decided on your own responsibility.

2. A marked increase in emigration to Palestine is undesirable for diplomatic reasons. In order to deal with all the difficulties arising from this, I have reserved

for myself the right to approve transports . . .

I request that no Jews from the individual districts should be permitted to participate in such special group transports to Palestine before my express permission for such a transport has been given. Attention must be paid to ensuring that, as far as possible, Jews in their prime are excluded . . .

Approved travel agents who deal with the emigration of Jewish individuals are not to be hindered in their activities.

3. Emigration cannot be considered for the time being for Jews of Polish or former Polish nationality who are at present interned in concentration camps.

Jewish women and children, male Jews over sixty years old, cripples etc. who possessed Polish nationality can be permitted to emigrate.

4. I have noticed that rumours keep occurring concerning official permission for the deportation of Jews from Reich territory into the General Government. In this connection, I can say that for the time being the deportation of Jews irrespective of their nationality, from the Reich to the General Government will not take place. Also, all voluntary emigration of Jews into the General Government is forbidden.

Any attempt by anybody to deport Jews on their own initiative to the General Government, whatever their nationality or whether or not they are stateless, which becomes known, is to be reported to me immediately by express telex.

With the defeat of France in June 1940, the prospect of a new solution to the Jewish question opened up—the Madagascar plan. In December 1938, Georges Bonnet, the French Foreign Minister had told Ribbentrop of a French plan to get rid of 10,000 Jews to Madagascar. This idea had then surfaced in the German press in 1939. Now it was taken up again by Franz Rademacher, an official in the German Foreign Ministry's Department for Internal German Affairs (D III). On 3 July 1940, Rademacher produced the following memorandum on 'The Jewish Question in the Peace Treaty':

798

The imminent victory gives Germany the possibility, and in my opinion also the duty, of solving the Jewish question in Europe. The desirable solution is: All Jews out of Europe. The task of the Foreign Ministry in this is:

(*a*) to anchor this demand in the peace treaty and to put through the same demand by means of separate negotiations with the European countries not affected by the peace treaty;

(*b*) to assure in the peace treaty the necessary territory for settling the Jews and to determine the principles for the cooperation of the enemy countries in this problem:

(*c*) to determine the position of the new Jewish overseas settlement area under international law;

(*d*) as preparatory work:

1. clarification of the wishes and plans of the interested party, Government, and scientific offices inside Germany and to harmonize these plans with the wishes of the Foreign Minister; for this the following is also necessary:
2. preparation of a survey of the objective data available at various places (number of Jews in the different countries); making use of their assets through an international bank,
3. taking up of negotiations with our ally Italy on these questions.

With regard to beginning the preparatory work, *Referat* D III has already approached the Foreign Minister with suggestions via the Department for German Internal Affairs, and has been instructed by him to institute this preparatory work at once. There have already been discussions with the office of the *Reichsführer* SS in the Ministry of the Interior and with a number of party offices. These offices approve the following plan of *Referat* D III:

Referat D III suggests as a solution to the Jewish question: In the peace treaty France must make the island Madagascar available for the solution of the Jewish question, and must resettle the approximately 25,000 French people living there and compensate them. The island will be transferred to Germany as a mandate. The strategically important Diégo Suarez Bay, as well as the harbor of Antsirane, will be German naval bases (if the Navy should so desire perhaps these naval bases could also be expanded to include the harbours—open roadsteads—of Tamatave, Andevorante, Mananjary, etc.). In addition to these naval bases, suitable portions of the country will be detached from the Jewish territory for construction of air bases. The portion of the island not needed for military purposes will be placed under the administration of a German police governor, who will be under the control of the *Reichsführer* SS. In this territory the Jews will otherwise have self-administration: their own mayors, police, postal and railroad administrations, etc. The Jews will be jointly liable for the value of the island. Their former European assets will be transferred for liquidation to a European bank to be set up for the purpose. In so far as these assets are insufficient to pay for the land which they get and for the necessary purchase of commodities in Europe needed for developing the island, bank credits will be made available to the Jews by the same bank.

Since Madagascar will be only a mandate, the Jews who live there will not acquire German citizenship. On the other hand, all Jews deported to Madagascar will from the time of deportation be denied the citizenship of the various European countries by these countries. Instead they will be citizens of the mandate of Madagascar.

This arrangement will prevent the possible establishment of a Vatican State of their own in Palestine by the Jews, thus preventing them from using for their own purposes the symbolic value which Jerusalem has for the Christian and Mohammedan portions of the world. Moreover, the Jews will remain in German hands as a pledge for the future good conduct of the members of their race in America.

We can utilize for propaganda purposes the generosity which Germany shows the Jews by granting them self-government in the fields of culture, economics, administration, and justice, and can stress that our German sense of responsiblity to the world does not permit us to give a race that has not had national independence for thousands of years an independent state immediately; for this they must still prove themselves to history.

This plan was taken up with enthusiasm by the SS and by Hitler himself. Indeed, Hitler had evidently already contemplated the idea since, according to his interpreter Paul Schmidt, he had suggested to Mussolini on 18 June that 'one could establish a Jewish state in Madagascar'.[14] At the beginning of August, Hitler told Otto Abetz, the German ambassador in France, that 'he intended to evacuate all Jews from Europe after the war'.[15] Eichmann's office began working out the concrete steps necessary for implementing the project, which were laid down in the following RSHA memorandum sent to Rademacher on 15 August 1940:

799

The following piece of work represents the outcome of the preparations which have been carried out so far by the Security Police for the project to settle around 4,000,000 Jews on Madagascar.

To prevent lasting contact between the Jews and other nations a solution in terms of an overseas island is superior to all others . . .

3. *Preparations*.

(*a*) All agencies charged with carrying out the project must first conduct a detailed examination of all the Jews in their area. They are responsible for ordering and arranging all the preparatory work necessary for Jewish emigration such as the procuring of documents for the individual Jews, the registration and utilization of property as well as the assignment of the Jews to transports. The first transports are to consist mainly of farmers, building workers, artisans and labourer's families up to the age of 45, as well as doctors. These will then be sent ahead as pioneers so to speak in order to prepare accomodation for the masses coming after.

(*b*) The Jews will be allowed to take up to 200 kg of non-bulky baggage per person. Jewish farmers, artisans, doctors etc. must take all the equipment which they may have in their possession necessary for the exercise of their trade. The relevant regulations apply for the taking of cash and precious metals.

(*c*) The property left behind by the evacuees must be reported to the 'Trustee Offices for Jewish Property' which will be established in each country. The total amount which remains after the sale of the immovable property will be passed on to a central evacuation fund which will be established and which will be set up along the lines of the emigration funds in Vienna and the emigration funds in Bohemia and Moravia and will use this fund and further funds deriving from other countries as its basis . . .

As part of the Madagascar plan, the Jews of Alsace and Lorraine were deported to southern France. The Gauleiters of the Gaus into which the two former French provinces were incorporated (Baden and the Saar-

[14] Cf. P. Schmidt, *Statist auf Diplomatischer Bühne 1923–45* (Bonn 1949) p. 485.

[15] U. D. Adam, *Judenpolitik im Dritten Reich* (Düsseldorf 1972) p. 256 fn.66.

Palatinate respectively) seized this opportunity to deport their own German Jews as well, having gained Hitler's approval for this measure which was carried out on 22–23 October 1940. The following is an excerpt from the instruction sheet provided for the officials carrying out the deportation of the Jews from the Rhineland Palatinate:

800

1. Only full Jews are to be deported. *Mischlinge*, partners of mixed marriages, and foreign Jews, insofar as they are not nationals of enemy states and of the territories occupied by us, are to be excluded from the action. Stateless Jews will be arrested as a matter of principle. Every Jew is considered eligible for transportation; the only Jews excluded are those who are actually bed-ridden.

2. Assembly points have been established in Ludwigshafen, Kaiserslautern and Landau for the collection of the Jews. Those arrested will be brought there in buses. A detective will be appointed as transport leader for each bus. He will be assigned uniformed police or detectives as required.

3. Every transport leader will be provided with a list at the assembly point from which he will be able to ascertain the bus and officers assigned to him and the names and addresses of the persons who are to be arrested . . .

5. After the officials involved have been notified of the personal details of the Jews, they will proceed to the dwellings of those affected. They will then inform them that they have been arrested for the purpose of deportation and will add that they must be ready to move within two hours. Any queries are to be referred to the person in charge of the assembly point who will clarify them; postponement of the preparations is not permitted.

6. Those arrested should if possible take with them the following:
(*a*) for each Jew a suitcase or bag with pieces of equipment; adults are permitted to take up to 50kg., children up to 30kg.
(*b*) a complete set of clothing.
(*c*) a woollen blanket for each Jew.
(*d*) provisions for several days.
(*e*) crockery and cutlery.
(*f*) up to 100 RM in cash per person.
(*g*) passports, identity cards or other means of identification which, however, should not be packed but carried on their persons.

7. The following items must not be taken: savings books, stocks and shares, jewellery, and amounts of cash over the limit of 100 RM . . .

9. Before leaving their dwellings they must carry out the following:
(*a*) Farm animals and other live animals (dogs, cats, pet birds) must be handed over to the chairman of the parish council, the branch leader, the local peasant leader or some other appropriate person in return for a receipt.
(*b*) perishable foodstuffs must be put at the disposal of the NSV.
(*c*) open fires must be extinguished.
(*d*) water and gas must be turned off.

(*e*) electric fuses must be unscrewed.
(*f*) the keys of the dwelling must be tied together and labelled with the owner's name, town or village, street, and house number.
(*g*) those arrested must as far as possible be searched for weapons, ammunition, explosives, poison, foreign exchange, jewellery etc. before departure . . .
13. It is essential that the Jews are properly treated at the time of their arrest. Mob violence must be prevented at all costs.

The following is an excerpt from a letter from Heydrich to Martin Luther, Under State Secretary in the Foreign Ministry who dealt with Jewish matters, dated 29 October 1940:

801

The Führer ordered the deportation of the Jews from Baden via Alsace and the Jews of the Palatinate via Lorraine. Following the action, I can inform you that seven trains left Baden on 22 and 23.10.1940 and two trains left the Palatinate on 22.10.1940 with a total of 6,504 Jews and, in liaison with the local agencies of the *Wehrmacht* but without prior notice to the French authorities, travelled to the unoccupied zone of France via Châlon-sur-Saône.

The deportation of the Jews was carried out smoothly and without incident throughout Baden and the Palatinate. The population was hardly aware of the action taking place.

The collection of the Jewish property and its administration and utilization is being carried out by the responsible *Regierungspräsidenten*.

The following excerpt from a 'report on the deportation of Jews of German nationality to southern France', drawn up in Karlsruhe on 30 October 1940, describes the deportation:

802

The deportation of the Jews from Baden and the Palatinate was carried out in such a way that, according to the Gauleiters' orders, 'all persons of Jewish race' must be deported 'in so far as they are fit to travel', without regard to age or sex. Only the partners of existing mixed marriages were excluded. Even men who had participated in the World War of 1914–1918 on the German side as front soldiers and, in some cases, as officers of the old *Wehrmacht* had to be sent off. The old people's homes in Mannheim, Karlsruhe, Ludwigshafen etc. were evacuated. Men and women who were incapable of walking were ordered to be transported to the trains on stretchers. The oldest person deported was a ninety-seven-year-old man from Karlsruhe. The time limit given to those being deported to get ready varied from a quarter of an hour to two hours depending on the locality. A number of men and women used this time to escape deportation by committing suicide. In Mannheim alone there had been eight suicides by Tuesday morning, in Karlsruhe three. *Wehrmacht* vehicles were made available to transport people from remote places to the assembly points. Those deported were obliged to leave behind their belongings, capital and real estate. It is being held in trust until the Gauleiters have reached a final decision about it. Since in many cases the emigration did not take place according to the rules, i.e. without having fulfilled the legal provisions, e.g. payment of the Reich emigration [lit. 'flight'] tax, the property has been impounded. Sums of cash of between 10 and 100 RM could be taken and were changed into French francs. The dwellings were sealed by the police.

According to available reports, the transports consisting of twelve sealed trains have arrived in concentration camps in the south of France at the foot of the Pyranees after a journey of several days. Since there is a shortage of food and suitable accomodation for the deportees, who consist mainly of old men and women, it is believed here that the French government is intending to send them on to Madagascar as soon as the sea routes have been reopened.

Conditions in the Gurs camp near the Pyranees were appalling and over the next few months many of the Jews succumbed to the effects of malnutrition and disease.

The RSHA tried as far as possible to restrict the voluntary emigration of Jews overseas to those from 'Greater Germany'. Thus, on 25 October 1940 it issued the following directive for the General Government:

803

Since the emigration of Jews from the General Government would significantly decrease what are in any case shrinking opportunities for the emigration of Jews from the old Reich, the Ostmark [Austria], and the Protectorate of Bohemia and Moravia, contrary to the wishes of Reich Marshal Göring, I request that you refrain from contemplating such emigration.

The progressive emigration of eastern Jews represents a continuing regeneration of world Jewry, since—on account of their religious orthodoxy—the eastern Jews provide in the main a large proportion of the rabbis, Talmud teachers etc., who are much sought after by the Jewish organizations active in the USA according to their own admission. Moreover, as far as these Jewish organizations in the USA are concerned, each orthodox eastern Jew represents a valuable addition to their continuing attempts at the spiritual regeneration and concentration of American Jewry. With the help of the immigrant Jews, particularly those from eastern Europe, American Jewry in particular is bent on creating a new platform from which it plans to step up its struggle, especially against Germany.

For this reason it can be assumed that after a few emigration permits have been granted, i.e. after the creation of precedents for Jews from the General Government, a large proportion of the immigration permits, mainly for the USA, would in future only be granted to eastern Jews.

However, despite all the efforts of the RSHA, emigration of Jews from 'Greater Germany' was only in the form of a trickle. Hitler clearly remained torn between, on the one hand, his desire to rid 'Greater Germany' of Jews and his sympathy for Gauleiters who were pressing for their Gaus to be 'cleansed' of Jews, and, on the other hand, his awareness of the problems involved in deporting more Jews to France, which would alienate the Vichy government, or to the General Government, where the authorities were already complaining that they had too many Jews. On 2 October 1940, the Gauleiter of Vienna, Baldur von Schirach, urged Hitler to agree to the deportation of the Viennese Jews to the General Government. On 20 November, Bormann informed Lammers, the head of the Reich Chancellery, that Hitler had told Gauleiter Bürckel of the Saar-Palatinate and Lorraine and Gauleiter Robert Wagner of Baden and Alsace.

804

that in ten years time there was only one report he would want to have from the Gauleiters, namely that their areas were German and by that he meant completely German. He would not ask questions about the methods they had used to make the areas German and could not care less if sometime in the future it was established that the methods used to gain the territories had been unpleasant or not absolutely legal.

On 3 December 1940, Lammers sent the following letter to Schirach:

805

Reichsleiter Bormann has informed me that, in response to a report submitted by you, the Führer has decided that the deportation of 60,000 Jews still living in the Reich Gau Vienna to the General Government is to be accelerated, i.e. to take place during the war, on account of the housing shortage. I have informed the General Governor in Cracow and the *Reichsfüher* SS of the Führer's decision and request you to take note of it as well.

This deportation of the Viennese Jews was part of a new programme of deportations to the General Government which was agreed at a meeting in the RSHA on 8 January 1941. For, while Madagascar had replaced the

Lublin reservation idea as the 'long term' plan, the RSHA was obliged to continue to implement the various phases of its 'short-term plan'. The following is an extract from a report of the meeting of 8 January by SS *Obergruppenführer* Friedrich-Wilhelm Krüger, the Higher SS and Police Leader in the General Government:

806

SS *Gruppenführer* Heydrich who chaired the meeting explained that the Reich needed to deport Poles and Jews from the eastern incorporated territory as rapidly as possible so that the settlement of the ethnic Germans from Wolhynien, Lithuania etc. could at last be carried out. According to a calculation presented by *Gruppenführer* Heydrich, the total number of evacuees would be 831,000. Apart from that, it was necessary to resettle around 200,000 people within the General Government on account of the military training areas being established, so that in all one arrived at a figure of one million people being moved within one year . . .

The detailed figures for resettlement up to 1 May this year are: 30,000 from East Prussia, 24,000 from Silesia, 40,000 from Danzig–West Prussia, 90,000 from the Warthegau—184,000 people in all. In the context of the evacuation of the proposed military training areas on behalf of the *Wehrmacht* the following numbers would be resettled: 8,500 from East Prussia, 10,000 from Silesia, 27,000 from Danzig–West Prussia, 19,000 from the Warthegau—64,500 in all. The Wehrmacht intended to retain 2,000 workers with their families—10,000 people in all—for work on the military training areas. Thus, in the context of the so-called 3. short term plan 184,000 + 54,500 or 238,500 people in all would have to be evacuated by 1 May 1941, to which the 10,000 Jews to be evacuated from Vienna would then be added . . .

State Secretary Dr Bühler [General Government] declared that he considered it impossible to distribute one million people throughout the General Government in the way envisaged. The strain in terms of problems of security, transport, the prevention of epidemics, and food supplies would be so great that unrest could not be avoided in the long run. He proposed the initiation of major work projects and the accommodation of the evacuees in labour camps.

The Governor General replied that unrest would be dealt with by the toughest measures. The Reich would have to assist with problems of food supply. He would return to the question of work projects.

. . . At a time when the General Government was carrying on under the most unusual and difficult economic, political, and military conditions, the absorption of hundreds of thousands of aliens from a foreign territory into the area of the General Government represented a burden which was barely supportable. These people were being expropriated in Germany and arriving here without possessions, coming to an area in which they could see no chance of rebuilding their lives in any way. However, in viewing the whole question one must not adopt any position other than that of the best interests of the Reich . . .

All criticism of such measures on the basis of vestiges of humanitarian views or utilitarian considerations must be completely excluded. The settlement must take place; the General Government must absorb these people, since it is one of the great tasks which the Führer has set the General Government.

The Führer had told the Governor General both on 4 November and at a later meeting in December that the settlement of Poles in the General Government was part of his policy and that the measures necessary for this settlement must be implemented during the war because after the war they would involve international difficulties.

On 17 January 1941, Bühler informed the officials of the General Government that from 1 February until 1 May 1941 two trains a day, each containing up to 1,000 Jews, would arrive in the General Government from the so-called incorporated eastern territories. In addition, during February and March some 7,000 Austrian Jews arrived in the General Government. However, the military build-up in Poland, in preparation for the attack on Russia, caused transport problems. These appear to have prompted a halt to the resettlement programme which was reported to a meeting of the senior officials of the General Government on 25 March 1941:

807

The Higher SS and Police Leader, SS *Obergruppenführer* Krüger announces that the resettlement of Poles and Jews in the General Government has been stopped for the time being. The resettlement within the General Government for the purpose of preparing the way for military training areas is continuing.

Governor General Reich Minister Frank announces that the Führer informed him at the meeting on 17 March that in future the settlement of the General Government would be made dependent on the facilities of this territory. In addition, the Führer promised that, in recognition of his performance, the General Government would be the first territory to be freed from Jews. Moreover, one should bear in mind that the extent to which the General Government was being made use of for resettlement was not the result of the hostile intentions of the agencies involved but derived inevitably from the need to repatriate Germans from the East . . . [i.e. who replaced the Poles and Jews evacuated from the incorporated territories].

Meanwhile, frustrated by the slow progess in getting rid of the Jews from the Warthegau, its Gauleiter, Greiser, had offered to supply 42,187 male and 30,936 female Jews to the Reich as a labour force. Göring was increasingly concerned at the growing shortage of labour. On 18 February 1941, he instructed the Gauleiters in their capacity as Reich Governors and Reich Defence Commissioners to remove obstacles to the employment of Jews deriving from racial objections and, on 14 March, the Reich Minister of Labour instructed the State labour offices to undertake the necessary preparations for the employment of Jews from the East.

However, Hitler was bent on ridding the Reich of Jews and, however useful they might have been as a labour force, he was not prepared to compromise on this issue. On 22 April 1941, the delegate of the Reich Minister for Armaments and Munitions in Military District V issued the following directive 'concerning the ban on the employment of Jews from the East on Reich territory':

808

Following a directive from the Führer, which has arrived in the meantime, there should be no attempt to transfer Jews from the east to the Reich for use as labour.

It is thus no longer possible to contemplate using Jews as replacements for labour which has been withdrawn, particularly from the building sector and from textile plants.

However, even at this late stage, the emigration of Jews from Reich territory overseas was encouraged where possible as is clear from the following edict of the RSHA of 20 May 1941 concerning 'the emigration of Jews':

809

According to information from the Reich Marshal of the Greater German Reich, the emigration of Jews from Reich territory, including the Protectorate of Bohemia and Moravia, is to be stepped up even during the war within the bounds of the available opportunities and while observing the regulations laid down for Jewish emigration. Since, at the moment, there are insufficient opportunities for the Jews to emigrate from the Reich, mainly via Spain and Portugal, the emigration of Jews from France and Belgium would represent a further reduction in such opportunities. In view of these facts and of the final solution of the Jewish question which is doubtless pending, the emigration of Jews from France and Belgium must be prevented . . .

As far as the emigration of Jews from Reich territory, including the Protectorate of Bohemia and Moravia into unoccupied France is concerned, in general it may be permitted in special cases, e.g. the resettlement of penniless Jews to relatives in unoccupied France, provided the security police raise no objections and after presentation of an immigration permit from the French government. The decisive factor in this connection is that an advantage accrues to the German Reich from the granting of permission for the emigration of Jews to unoccupied France even if it is only the fact that a Jew has left German territory . . .

The immigration of Jews from the other occupied territories of Europe into unoccupied France is not desirable, although it cannot always be prevented.

The immigration of Jews into the territories occupied by us is to be prevented in the light of the final solution of the Jewish question which is doubtless pending.

In so far as the RSHA had anything specific in mind at this stage, the final solution of the Jewish question to which it referred was probably still the Madagascar plan. However, the attack on Russia in June 1941 was to create an entirely new situation. By removing the prospect of an early end to the war, it undermined the whole basis of the Madagascar solution to the Jewish question. Moreover, the invasion of Russia threatened to complicate the position. For the German armies moved into the Baltic States, White Russia, and the Ukraine, territories containing further millions of Jews. Above all, the war in Russia fostered both a mentality and conditions on the ground which encouraged the most extreme solution of the Jewish question. With the actions of the SS *Einsatzgruppen* the persecution of the Jews was transformed into systematic extermination.

CHAPTER 38

The Transition to the Systematic Extermination of the Jews 1941–42

(i) The Role of the SS Einsatzgruppen in Russia and the Mass Shootings of the Russian Jews

With the invasion of the Soviet Union on 22 June 1941 Hitler had embarked on an ideological war against 'Jewish Bolshevism' and Nazi Jewish policy entered a new phase involving the systematic extermination of Russian Jews. On 30 March 1941, Hitler outlined what would be involved in a war with Russia at a conference with his military leaders. General Halder recorded Hitler's comments in his diary:

810

Struggle between two Weltanschauungen. Devastating assessment of Bolshevism: it is the equivalent of social delinquency. Communism is a tremendous danger for the future. We must get away from the standpoint of soldierly comradeship. The Communist is from first to last no comrade. It is a war of extermination. If we do not regard it as such, we may defeat the enemy, but in thirty years' time we will again be confronted by the communist enemy. We are not fighting a war in order to conserve the enemy.

Future State structure: North Russia belongs to Finland. Protectorates for the Baltic States, Ukraine, White Russia.

Fight against Russia: destruction of the Bolshevik commissars and the Communist intelligentsia.[1] The new states must be socialist states, but without their own intelligentsia. A new intelligentsia must be prevented from emerging. A primitive Socialist intelligentsia is sufficient there. The struggle must be fought against the poison of subversion. It is not a question of court martials. The leaders of the troops must know what is involved. They must take the lead in the struggle. The troops must defend themselves with the methods with which they are attacked. Commissars and the GPU people are criminals and must be treated as such. That does not mean that the troops need get out of hand. The leader must draw up his orders in accordance with the sentiment of his troops.

The struggle will be very different from that in the west. In the east toughness now means mildness in the future. The leaders must make the sacrifice of overcoming their scruples.

Two weeks earlier, on 13 March, OKW had drawn up 'Directives for Special Areas concerning Directive No. 21 (Barbarossa)', in which on Hitler's instructions the *Reichsführer* SS had been assigned a special role:

811

. . .

2. As soon as military operations are concluded the *Russian territory* which is to be occupied is to be divided up into individual states with *governments of their own* in accordance with special instructions:
From this follows:

(*a*) *The area of operations* created by the advance of the Army beyond the frontiers of the Reich and the neighbouring countries is to be limited in depth as far as possible. The Commander-in-Chief of the Army has the right to exercise executive power in this area and may delegate his authority to the Supreme Commanders of the Army groups and armies.

(*b*) In the Army's area of operations the *Reichsführer* SS is entrusted on behalf of the Führer with *special tasks* for the preparation of the *political administration*, tasks which result from the necessity of finally resolving the conflict between two opposing political systems. Within the framework of these tasks the *Reichsführer*

[1] On 6 June 1941, OKW issued special 'guidelines for the treatment of political commissars'. These laid down that 'the commissars are the initiators of barbaric, asiatic methods of combat. Thus the toughest action must be taken against them at once and without further ado. If encountered in combat or engaged in resistance they must be shot at once on principle. Those taken prisoner will not be recognised as soldiers; the protection of POWs guaranteed by international law will not be accorded to them. After being separated from the others, they must be finished off'. Significantly this order was only issued in writing to Army commanders. They were then obliged to pass it on orally down the chain of command. See G. R. Ueberschär/W Wette, eds., *'Unternehmen Barbarossa'. Der deutsche Überfall auf die Sowjetunion 1941*. (Paderborn 1984) pp. 313–14.

will act independently and on his own responsibility. The executive power vested in the Commander-in-Chief of the Army (OKH) and the agencies to which it may be delegated by him will not however be affected by this. It is the responsibility of the *Reichsführer SS* to ensure that military operations are not affected by measures taken in the discharge of this task. Details will be settled directly between the OKH and the *Reichsführer SS*.

(*c*) As soon as the area of operations has reached sufficient depth, it is to be *limited in the rear*. The newly occupied territory in the rear of the area of operations is to be given its own *political administration*. For the present it is to be divided, according to it's ethnic basis and the positions of the Army groups into North (Baltic countries), Centre (White Russia) and South (Ukraine). In these territories the political administration is to be taken over by *Commissioners of the Reich* who receive their orders from the Führer . . .

On 26 March, following discussions with Heydrich, the Quartermaster General, Eduard Wagner, who incidentally had opposed *Einsatzgruppen* actions in Poland, prepared an OKH draft directive 'On Cooperation with the Security Police and SD in the Eastern War which is envisaged' which, with a few grammatical corrections, was accepted by Heydrich and issued as an order by the Commander-in-Chief of the Army, Field Marshal Von Brauchitsch, on 28 April 1941:

812

Re: the regulation of the deployment of the Security Police and SD within the context of army operations:

The deployment of special commandos of the Security Police (SD) in the area of operations is necessary in order to carry out special security police tasks *outside the ambit* of the military forces.

With the agreement of the Chief of the Security Police and SD the deployment of the Security Police and SD in the area of operations will be regulated as follows:
1. *Tasks*:

(*a*) *In Army rear areas*:
Prior to the start of operations the listing of certain designated objects (material, archives, card index files of anti-German and anti-state organizations, associations, groups etc.), as well as particularly important individuals (leading emigrés, saboteurs, terrorists etc.) The Commander-in-Chief of the Army can exclude the deployment of the special commandos in parts of the military area where disruption could be caused.

(*b*) *In the Army Group rear areas*.
To investigate and combat anti-German and anti-state activities in so far as they are not carried out by the enemy's armed forces, as well as to keep the commander of the Army Group rear areas informed of the political situation.
2. *Cooperation between the special commandos and the military command in the Army rear areas* (re: 1a)

The special commandos of the Security Police and SD carry out their tasks on their own responsibility. They are subordinated to the armies as far as movement, rations and billets are concerned. This does not affect their subordination to the Chief of the Security Police and SD in matters of discipline and jurisdiction. They receive the functional instructions for carrying out their tasks from the Chief of the Security Police and SD and may be subject to restrictions by the Army (viz: 1a).

A representative of the Chief of the Security Police and SD will be assigned to each Army to control these commandos. He is obliged to inform the Army commander in good time of the instructions which he has received from the Chief of the Security Police and SD. The military commander is entitled to give the representative directives which may be required to prevent the disruption of operations; they have priority over all other directives.

The representatives are required to maintain continuous and close cooperation with the Ic.[2] The Army commander can request the assignment of a liason officer from the representative to the Ic. The Ic has the responsibility of coordinating the tasks of the special commandos with those of military intelligence and the Secret Field Police and with operational requirements.

The special commandos are entitled within the framework of their assignment to take executive measures vis-à-vis the civilian population on their own responsibility. They are required to cooperate closely with military intelligence in these matters. Measures which affect operations require the approval of the Army commander . . .

4. *The delimitation of responsibilities between the Special Commandos, Einsatzkdos and Einsatzgruppen and GFP* [Secret Field Police]:

The police intelligence tasks within the military sphere and the immediate protection of the troops remain the sole responsibility of the GFP. All matters of this kind are to be referred by the Special Commandos and *Einsatzgruppen-* and *kommandos* to the Secret Field Police at once, just as vice versa they must refer all those matters which fall within the sphere of competence of the special commandos immediately to them. . .

These directives contained no specific mention of the Jews. Significantly, however, the directives drawn up for the *Einsatzgruppe* which was to go into Yugoslavia during the Balkans campaign, which were issued on 2 April 1941, while closely following those for the Russian campaign, included 'Jews and Communists' in the category of persons mentioned under 1(*a*) to be 'arrested'. Moreover, on 19 May 1941, OKW issued the following 'Directives for the behaviour of the troops in Russia', of which the following is an extract:

[2] The Ic was the Intelligence officer (eds).

813

I

1. *Bolshevism is the deadly enemy of the National Socialist German people. Germany's struggle is directed against this subversive ideology and its functionaries.*
2. This struggle requires ruthless and energetic action against Bolshevik agitators, guerillas, saboteurs, and Jews, and the total elimination of all active or passive resistance.

II

3. The members of the Red Army—including prisoners—must be treated with extreme reserve and the greatest caution since one must reckon with devious methods of combat. The asiatic soldiers of the Red Army in particular are devious, cunning, and without feeling.
4. When taking units prisoner *the leader must be separated* from the other ranks *at once*.

III

5. In the Soviet Union the German soldier is not confronted with a unified population. The USSR is a state which unites a multiplicity of Slav, Caucasian, and asiatic peoples which are held together by the Bolshevik rulers by force. Jewry is strongly represented in the USSR. . .

The Army's acceptance of the role of the SS *Einsatzgruppen* in Russia and its close cooperation with them contrasts sharply with its attitude during the Polish campaign of 1939. To some extent, this reflected its loss of self-confidence vis-à-vis the regime as a result of the brilliantly successful campaigns of 1940. They had confounded the initial doubts of the military and seemed to confirm that Hitler was indeed a man of destiny as the Nazis had always proclaimed. The generals had happily accepted the promotions and decorations which Hitler had showered on them. Even more important, however, was the fact that many *Wehrmacht* officers shared the Nazi view of the Soviet Union as the centre of 'Jewish Bolshevism'. This association of the Jews with Bolshevism had become widely current among the European upper and middle classes after the Bolshevik Revolution. The fact that, as an educated and persecuted minority, Jews were prominently represented among the leading Bolsheviks appeared to confirm traditional antisemitic beliefs about the subversive nature of the Jews. Moreover, in Germany after 1933, this identification of the Jews with Bolshevism had become part of the official ideology and, therefore, of the political indoctrination of the armed forces. To many upper-and middle-class Germans, including non-Nazis, the image of the Soviet Union was of a country in which hordes of culturally if not racially inferior Slavs and 'asiatics' were led by a group of Jewish Bolsheviks bent on subverting the holiest values of Western civilization. This view was apparently confirmed by horrific stories about the barbaric activities of the OGPU (NKVD), culminating in the great purges of the 1930s.

Four *Einsatzgruppen* were established for operations in Russia:

1. *Einsatzgruppe* A for the Baltic States. Led by SS *Brigadeführer* and Police General Dr Walther Stahlecker, it comprised Special Commandos 1a and 1b and Einsatzkommandos 2 and 3.
2. *Einsatzgruppe B* for White Russia. Led by SS *Brigadeführer* and Police General Arthur Nebe, the head of the Criminal Police, it comprised Special Commandos 7a and 7b and *Einsatzkommandos* 8 and 9 as well as *Vorkommando* Moscow (from February 1942 Special Commando 7c).
3. *Einsatzgruppe* C for the north and central Ukraine. Led by SS *Brigadeführer* and Police General Dr Otto Rasch, the Inspector of Security Police and SD in Königsberg, it comprised Special Commandos 4a and 4b and *Einsatzkommandos* 5 and 6.
4. *Einsatzgruppe* D for Bessarabia, the southern Ukraine, the Crimea, and the Caucusus. Led by Otto Ohlendorf head of Amt III (SD-Inland) of the RSHA, it comprised Special Commandos 10a and 10b and *Einsatzkommandos* 11a, 11b and 12.

Each *Einsatzgruppe* contained between 600 and 1,000 men and was fully motorized. The lower ranks were made up of Gestapo, criminal police, order police, Waffen SS and a number of specialists (for example interpreters, communications experts etc.). Most had been hurriedly seconded from the various police departments. The leaders, however, were carefully selected, came largely from the SD, and most had middle class professional backgrounds and included many law graduates.

The *Einsatzgruppen* advanced into Russia on 23 June 1941 directly behind the invading German troops. On 2 July, Heydrich issued written instructions to the four Higher SS and Police Leaders, who had been appointed to Russia, concerning the operations of the *Einsatzgruppen*, of which the following is an excerpt:

814

. . .

4. EXECUTIONS. The following will be executed:
All officials of the Comintern (most of these will certainly be career politicians);
Officials of senior and middle rank and 'extremists' in the Party, the Central Committee, and the provincial and district committees;
The People's Commissars;
Jews in the service of the Party or the State;
Other extremist elements (saboteurs, propagandists, snipers, assassins, agitators, etc.); in so far as in individual cases they are not required, or are no longer required,

for political intelligence of special importance, for future security police measures, or for the economic rehabilitation of the occupied territories. . . No steps will be taken to interfere with any purges that may be initiated by anti-Communist or anti-Jewish elements in the newly occupied territories. On the contrary, these are to be secretly encouraged. At the same time every precaution must be taken to ensure that those who engage in 'self-defence' actions are not subsequently able to plead that they were acting under orders or had been promised political protection. Special care must be taken in regard to the shooting of doctors and others engaged in medical practice. . .

In this directive Heydrich refers only to the execution of 'Jews in the service of the Party or the State'. However, according to one witness, he had already given an order for the extermination of all Russian Jews when he addressed the *Einsatzgruppen* commanders in Berlin on 17 June. Thus, the more restrictive order may have been designed to reassure outside agencies such as the *Wehrmacht* which might have been shocked by such a blanket extermination instruction. On the other hand, there is evidence that during the first few weeks, women and children were not generally included in the extermination and it may be that the instructions were left deliberately vague. In any case, in the course of their operations all the *Einsatzgruppen* soon came to interpret their task as the extermination of all Jews including women and children. The actions were justified in the reports of the *Einsatzgruppen* on the grounds that the Jews were saboteurs, partisans, or criminals, or as 'retaliations'. An attempt was made to prompt the indigenous population to carry out progroms against the Jews, as is clear from the following account of the operations of *Einsatzgruppe* A which covered the Baltic States, dated 15 October 1941. This report also indicates that the Commander of *Einsatzgruppe* A at least was clear about his role vis à vis the 'Jewish question' at a very early stage.

815

. . . Similarly, native antisemitic forces were induced to start pogroms against Jews during the first hours of the invasion, though this proved to be very difficult. Carrying out orders, the Security Police were determined to solve the Jewish question with all possible means and most decisively. But it was desirable that the Security Police should not put in an immediate appearance, at least at the beginning, since the extraordinarily harsh measures were apt to cause a stir even in German circles. It had to be shown to the world that the inhabitants themselves took the first measures by way of natural reaction against the repression by the Jews over several decades and against the terror exercised by the Communists during the preceding period . . . It was anticipated from the beginning that the Jewish problem in the *Ostland* [Baltic] would not be solved solely through progoms. On the other hand, in accordance with basic orders, the cleansing operation of the Security police had the goal of the most comprehensive elimination possible of the Jews. Extensive executions were thus carried out by special units in the cities and the plains.

Although the Germans were relatively unsuccessful in provoking 'spontaneous' pogroms, the auxiliary forces recruited from the indigenous populations of the Baltic States and the Ukraine played a key role in the extermination programme as is clear from the following reports. The first is by Dr Rudolf Lange responsible for operations in Latvia and dated January 1942:

816

At the time of the German invasion there were around 70,000 Jews in Latvia. At the time of the Bolsheviks considerably more Jews lived in Latvia, however a large number fled with the Bolsheviks.

The aim of *Einsatzkommando* 2 from the beginning was a radical solution of the Jewish problem through the execution of all Jews. For this purpose comprehensive purges were carried out in the whole area of our operations by special commandos with the help of selected forces from the Latvian auxiliary police (mainly relatives of Latvians who had been abducted or murdered by the Bolsheviks). Around the beginning of October, the number of Jews executed in the Commando's sphere of operations was about 30,000. In addition, there are a few thousand Jews who have been eliminated by the self-defence formations off their own bat after they had been given suitable encouragement.

It was impossible to achieve the complete elimination of Jews from Latvia in view of the economic factors and, in particular, the demands of the Wehrmacht. Jewish craftsmen were also used for the reconstruction of towns which had been destroyed . . . Where Latvian specialists were not available the required craftsmen and specialists were therefore provisionally excluded. However, by the end of October the rural areas of Latvia at least had been completely purged.

In order to exclude Jews who were needed for labour as far as possible from local life, they were concentrated in ghettos which were established in Riga, Dünaburg, and Libau. At the same time, Jews were ordered to identify themselves by wearing the Jewish star . . .

At the beginning of November 1941, there were only around 30,000 Jews in the Riga ghetto, in Libau around 4,300 and in Dünaberg around 7,000. From this point on around 4–5,000 Jews were executed as a result of prosecutions for failure to wear the Jewish star, black market activities, theft, fraud etc. In addition, the ghettos were purged of Jews, who were not fully fit for work and no longer required, in major actions. Thus, on 9 November 1941 11,034 Jews in Dünaberg and, at the beginning of December 1941, 27,800 Jews in Riga were executed in a major action ordered and directed by the Higher SS and Police Leader, and in mid-December 2,350 Jews were executed in Libau at the request of the Reich Commissioner. The remaining Jews (2,500 in Riga, 950 in Dünaburg and 300 in Libau) were excluded from this action because they were good skilled workers whose labour is still indispensable for the maintenance of the economy, especially the war economy.

The next report is by Karl Jäger, the head of *Einsatzkommando* 3 which operated in Lithuania, dated 1 December 1941:

817

I can now state that the aim of solving the Jewish problem for Lithuania has been achieved by *Einsatzkommando* 3. There are no more Jews in Lithuania apart from the work-Jews and their families. These include:

in Scaulen	*c*. 4,500
in Kauen	*c*. 15,000
in Vilna	*c*. 15,000

I wanted to bump off these work-Jews and their families but this brought me smack up against the civil administration (the Reich Commissioner) and the Wehrmacht and prompted a ban on the shooting of these Jews and their families.

The aim of freeing Lithuania from Jews could only be achieved by setting up a special unit with selected men under the leadership of SS-*Obersturmführer* Hamann who adopted my aims unconditionally and was capable of cooperating with the Lithuanian partisans and the responsible civil authorities.

The carrying out of such actions is first and foremost a matter of organization. The decision to clear each district systematically of Jews required a thorough preparation of every single action and the investigation of the conditions in the particular district. The Jews had to be concentrated in one place or in several places. The place for the pits which were required had to be found and dug out to suit the numbers involved. The distance from the place where the Jews were concentrated to the pits was on average 4–5km. The Jews were transported to the place of execution in groups of up to 500 with gaps of at least 2km . . .

The action in Kauen itself can be regarded as a model shooting (*Paradeschiessen*) compared with the incredible difficulties which often had to be overcome outside.

All leaders and men of my commando in Kauen have taken an active part in the major actions in Kauen. Only one official of the records department was excused participation on grounds of sickness.

I consider that the Jewish actions are basically concluded as far as the EK 3 is concerned. The remaining work-Jews and -Jewesses are urgently required and I can imagine that after the winter these workers will still be urgently needed.

The following report by *Einsatzgruppe* C operating in the Ukraine, dated 3 November 1941, is particularly illuminating:

818

. . .

B. *Operations*

As far as the actual executive actions are concerned, the Commandos of the *Einsatzgruppe* have liquidated around 80,000 persons up to now. Among them are around 8,000 persons who, on the basis of investigations, were proved to have taken part in anti-German or Bolshevist activity. The remainder was dealt with on the basis of retaliatory measures.

Several retaliatory measures were carried out in the context of major operations. The largest of these actions took place immediately after the capture of Kiev; Jews with their whole families were utilised (*sic*!) (*verwandt*) exclusively.

The difficulties arising from such a major operation—above all as regards getting hold of them—were overcome in Kiev by putting up wall posters inviting the Jews to be resettled. Although initially we only expected about 5–6,000 Jews would report, 30,000 Jews turned up who, as a result of a very clever piece of organisation, still believed they were going to be resettled until just before their execution.

Although up to now around 75,000 Jews have been liquidated in this fashion, it must surely be clear that it does not provide a feasible solution of the Jewish problem. It is true that we have succeeded in achieving a total solution of the Jewish question, above all in the smaller towns and in the villages. However, in the larger towns we continually find that, although all the Jews have disappeared after such an execution, if a commando returns after a certain interval, it keeps finding Jews in numbers which considerably exceed those who have been executed.

C. *Cooperation with the Wehrmacht and GFP*

As far as the relations between the *Einsatzgruppe* and its Commandos and other agencies and authorities are concerned, our relations with the Wehrmacht deserve special mention. From the first day onwards, the *Einsatzgruppe* has succeeded in establishing an excellent understanding with all sections of the *Wehrmacht*. As a result, from the very beginning of its operations, the *Einsatzgruppe* has never kept to the Army's rear areas, on the contrary, the *Wehrmacht* has repeatedly requested that the *Einsatzkommandos* should operate as far forward as possible. In numerous cases the fighting troops have requested assistance from the *Einsatzkommandos*. In every major military action advance units of the *Einsatzgruppe* have invariably moved into newly-conquered places with the fighting troops. In all such cases it has received the greatest possible support. . .

The successful work of the *Einsatzgruppe* has ensured that the Security Police enjoys a high reputation, particularly among the *Wehrmacht* staff officers. The liaison officers appointed to the AOKs are locally kept informed about all military operations and, in addition, are given the widest possible support. The Commander of the AOK 6, Field-Marshal von Reichenau, has also repeatedly praised the work of the *Einsatzkommandos* and represented the interests of the SD vis-à-vis his staff officers in an appropriate fashion . . .

It was only as regards the Jewish question that until recently there was a lack of understanding on the part of lower level *Wehrmacht* HQs. This had an impact, in particular, on the process of combing through the POW camps. An especially crass example is worth mentioning, namely the attitude of a camp commandant in Vinnitsa who totally disapproved of his deputy handing over 362 Jewish POWs and even began court martial proceedings against him as well as against two other officers. Only too often the *Einsatzkommandos* have had to put up with more or less veiled reproaches about their rigorous stance on the Jewish question. An OKH decree forbidding the SD to set foot in the Dulags [POW camps] provided an additional complication. These difficulties ought to have been removed by a new OKW decree in which it is clearly stated that the *Wehrmacht* too must make its contribution to the solution of these problems and which, above all, provides the SD with a very wide sphere of competence. Although in the past few days, we have become aware that this fundamental decree has still not penetrated down to the lower level HQs. As far as the area of the AOK 6 is concerned, in future we can anticipate further support and readiness to assist from the *Wehrmacht* HQs. For, Field-Marshal von Reichenau has issued an order on 10 October 1941, which clearly lays down that the Russian soldier must be regarded on principle as a representative of Bolshevism and be treated accordingly by the Wehrmacht . . .

The following is an excerpt from the order issued by Field-Marshal von Reichenau to AOK 6 on 10 October 1941 referred to in the *Einsatzgruppe* C report:

819

There is still a lot of uncertainty regarding the behaviour of the troops towards the bolshevist system. . .

The main aim of the campaign against the Jewish-bolshevist system is the complete destruction of its forces and the extermination of the asiatic influence in the sphere of European culture. As a result, the troops have to take on tasks which go beyond the conventional purely military ones. In the eastern sphere the soldier is not simply a fighter according to the rules of war, but the supporter of a ruthless racial (*völkisch*) ideology and the avenger of all the bestialities which have been inflicted on the German nation and those ethnic groups related to it.

For this reason soldiers must show full understanding for the necessity for the severe but just atonement being required of the Jewish subhumans. It also has the further purpose of nipping in the bud uprisings in the rear of the *Wehrmacht* which experience shows are invariably instigated by Jews . . .

Apart from any political considerations affecting the future, the soldier has two duties to perform:

1. the complete destruction of the Bolshevik heresy, of the Soviet state and its armed forces.
2. the merciless extermination of degenerate treachery and cruelty, thereby ensuring the security of the *Wehrmacht* in Russia.

Only in this way will we fulfil our historic duty of liberating the German people once and for all from the Asiatic-Jewish threat.

On 12 October, the commander of Army Group South, Field-Marshal von Rundstedt, sent Reichenau's order to his other Army Commands (AOK 11,17 and Pz.A.O.K I) with a covering letter in which he declared that he was 'in full agreement with its contents' and suggested that the Army commanders should issue appropriate directives since 'in view of the impending need to go into winter quarters and the limited forces in the rear areas, the laxity and softness after the actual fighting, which one still frequently encounters, are intolerable.[3] On 28 October, following Hitler's description of Reichenau's order as 'excellent', OKH made it a model for all military commands who were instructed to issue orders along the same lines. Many issued the Reichenau order with additional explanations.[4]

The issue of exempting Jews from extermination for the purposes of labour produced considerable friction between the civilian authorities (Reich Commissioners) and the *Wehrmacht* on the one hand and the SS on the other. For example, on October 1941, Lohse, the Reich Commissioner for the Baltic States intervened to stop the execution of some Jews, thereby prompting a complaint by the SS to his superiors in the Reich Ministry for the Eastern Territories in Berlin. Lohse replied to their request for an explanation on 15 November as follows:

820

I have forbidden the indiscriminate executions of Jews in Lepaya because they were not carried out in a justifiable manner.

I should like to be informed whether your inquiry of 31 October is to be regarded as a directive to liquidate all Jews in the east. Is this to take place without regard to age and sex and their usefulness to the economy (for instance skilled workers in the armament industry working for the *Wehrmacht*).
(*note in different handwriting*: Of course the cleansing of the east of Jews is a necessary task; its solution, however, must be harmonized with the necessities of war production).

So far I have not been able to find such a directive either in the regulations regarding the Jewish question in the 'Brown Portfolio'[5] or in other decrees.

The Ministry's reply, dated 18 December, was sent by Dr Otto Bräutigam, head of its political department:

---

[3] See G. R. Ueberschär/W. Wette *Op. cit.*, p. 340.
[4] Ibid.
[5] The 'Brown Portfolio' contained directives drawn up by the Four Year Plan for the economic exploitation of the east (eds).

821

The Jewish question has probably been clarified by now through verbal discussions. Economic considerations are to be regarded as fundamentally irrelevant in the settlement of the problem. Moreover, you are requested to settle questions which arise directly with the Senior SS and Police Leaders.

This was a statement of fundamental importance establishing the principle of the irrelevance of economic considerations for the solution of the Jewish problem. However, in practice, a compromise was struck between the SS and the *Wehrmacht* and economic agencies, whereby a number of Jews in Russia were provisionally exempted from extermination for labour purposes. However, over the next two years the ghettos in the east were progressively liquidated, sometimes through piecemeal selections of those no longer capable of work, sometimes more comprehensively, particularly during the so-called 'second sweep' during the summer of 1942. The following is an account of the liquidation of the ghetto in Borissov in Byleorussia in October 1941 given to the Soviet authorities in 1948 by its organiser, David Ehof. He had been appointed by the SD to head the local Russian Security Police. Ehof had mobilized around 200 police, mainly Latvians, for the purpose:

822

For two days and two nights they were placed under the influence of alcohol and ideologically prepared to inflict atrocities on innocent people. For this purpose I organized a party with a banquet in a restaurant in the town for the participants during which the policemen had the opportunity of imbibing alcoholic drinks to excess. The following were guests of honour: *Obersturmführer* Kraffe [Rudolf Grave], the mayor of the Borissov district, Stankewitsch, as well as officials of the Gestapo and the Secret Field Police (GFP).

I was the first to speak at the banquet. In my speech I congratulated those present on the victories won by Germany, praised the fascist German army and urged them to wage a merciless fight against anti-German activities. In order to stimulate a hatred of Jews among those present, I tried to justify the Nazi policy of exterminating the Jews in my speech and urged the policemen not to express any feelings of compassion and humanity towards either the adult Jews or the children. Similar speeches, which served to prepare the police ideologically for mass terror, were held by the GFP official of the town of Borissov [Steiler], the mayor of Borissov, Stankewitsch, the local garrison commander of Borissov as well as other senior officials . . .

– On Kraffe's instructions, I sealed off the ghetto during the night of 8–9 November [19-20 October] with additional guards. By this time, three graves had been dug near the airfield about 2km. from Borissov by prisoners of war under the direction of the Secret Field Police. They were about 400 metres long, 3 metres wide and up to 2 metres deep and were intended for burying the corpses.

Early in the morning of the 9 November [19 October], we assembled the police, who were not yet sober, in front of the security administration building and explained to them that we were now going to begin shooting all the Jews in the ghetto. I also announced that I had been put in charge of shooting the Jews. I then once again called for a merciless reckoning with the Jews.

I then ordered my deputy Kowalski [*sic*!] and the police platoon leader, Pipin, to organize the transport of the Jews to the place of execution and ensure that they were guarded. After the number of guards round the ghetto had been increased we sent the police in groups into the ghetto and sent in lorries to carry away the Jewish population which had been condemned to be shot. The police broke into the Jewish houses, chased the people to the square in the centre of the ghetto, drove them into the vehicles by force and transported them to the place of execution. There was no mercy shown either to old people, children, pregnant women, or the sick. Anyone who offered resistance was shot on the spot on my orders—in the square, in the houses, on the trip to the place of execution—or they were beaten half to death.

The condemned people were not only brought in lorries but also on foot in groups of 70 or 80 persons and were mercilessly beaten in the process.

The people who had been brought to the place of execution were placed about fifty metres from the graves and guarded until it was their turn to be shot. Twenty or twenty-five people at a time were led to the place of execution, to the graves. At the graves they were undressed; they even had their good quality underclothes torn from their bodies. Having been completely undressed they were driven to the graves and were forced to lie face down. The police and Germans shot them with rifles and automatic weapons. In this way more and more groups were driven to the graves and shot. They too were made to lie face down on the corpses of those who had been previously shot.

At the place of execution there were snacks and schnaps. The police drank schnaps and had a snack in the intervals between shooting the groups of Jews and then got back to their bloody work in a state of intoxication.

I arrived at the place of execution at about 11 o'clock in the morning and saw an indescribably horrific sight—the place of execution was filled with groans and cries and the continual shrieks of horror of the women and children.

The dehumanized and drunken policemen beat those who offered resistance, who did not step to the edge of the grave, with rifle butts and kicked them. The children were thrown into the graves and shot there.

During the first few minutes this horrific picture even shook me although by then I had shot hundreds of people. I was roused from this mood of uncertainty and depression, which had gripped me against my will under the impression of what I had seen, by the official of the Minsk SD, Kraffe [*sic*!] who accused me of sympathising with the Jews.

The police who had been egged on by me, Kraffe, and the other SD officials exterminated no fewer than 7,000 people on the first day of the mass shooting. On the third day, i.e. on 10 November 1941 [21 October] we continued with the 'cleansing' of the ghetto of Jews. On my orders, the police searched all the houses and other buildings, arrested all the Jews hiding there and brought them to the place of execution. On this day another one thousand people approximately were discovered and shot in the same way.

These mass executions were so numerous and widespread throughout the Soviet Union that they were often observed by members of the *Wehrmacht* or civilians, both Russian and German. The most moving account of such a massacre, which took place during the 'second sweep', was given to the Nuremberg tribunal by a German builder, Hermann Graebe:

823

From September 1941 until January 1944, I was the manager and chief engineer of a branch of the construction firm, Josef Jung of Solingen with its headquarters in Sdolbunow, Ukraine. In this capacity I had to visit the firm's building sites. The firm was contracted by an Army construction office to build grain silos on the former air field near Dubno in the Ukraine.

When I visited the site office on 5 October 1942 my foreman, Hubert Moennikes of Hamburg–Harburg, Aussenmühlenweg 21, told me that Jews from Dubno had been shot near the site in three large ditches which were about thirty metres long and three metres deep. Approximately 1,500 people a day had been killed. All of the approximately 5,000 Jews who had been living in Dubno up to the action were going to be killed. Since the shootings had taken place in his presence he was still very upset.

Whereupon I accompanied Moennikes to the building site and near it saw large mounds of earth about thirty metres long and two metres high. A few lorries were parked in front of the mounds from which people were being driven by armed Ukrainian militia under the supervision of an SS man. The militia provided the guards on the lorries and drove them to and from the ditch. All these people wore the prescribed yellow patches on the front and back of their clothing so that they were identifiable as Jews.

Moennikes and I went straight to the ditches. We were not prevented from doing so. I could now hear a series of rifle shots from behind the mounds. The people who had got off the lorries—men, women, and children of all ages—had to undress on the orders of an SS man who was carrying a riding or dog whip in his hand. They had to place their clothing on separate piles for shoes, clothing and underwear. I saw a pile of shoes containing approximately 800–1,000 pairs, and great heaps of underwear and clothing.

Without weeping or crying out these people undressed and stood together in family groups, embracing each other and saying good-bye while waiting for a sign from another SS man who stood on the edge of the ditch and also had a whip. During the quarter of an hour in which I stood near the ditch, I did not hear a single complaint or a plea for mercy. I watched a family of about eight, a man and a woman, both about fifty-years-old with their children of about one, eight, and ten, as well as two grown-up daughters of about twenty and twenty-four. An old woman with snow-white hair held a one year old child in her arms singing to it and tickling it. The child squeaked with delight. The married couple looked on with tears in their eyes. The father held the ten-year-old boy by the hand speaking softly to him. The boy was struggling to hold back his tears. The father pointed a finger to the sky and stroked his head and seemed to be explaining something to him. At this moment, the SS man near the ditch called out something to his comrade. The latter counted off some about twenty people and ordered them behind the mound. The family of which I have just spoken was among them. I can still remember how a girl, slender and dark, pointed at herself as she went past me saying 'twenty three'.

I walked round the mound and stood in front of the huge grave. The bodies were lying so tightly packed together that only their heads showed, from almost all of which blood ran down over their shoulders. Some were still moving. Others raised their hands and turned their heads to show they were still alive. The ditch was already three quarters full. I estimate that it already held about a thousand bodies. I turned my eyes towards the man doing the shooting. He was an SS man; he sat, legs swinging, on the edge of the ditch. He had an automatic rifle resting on his knees and was smoking a cigarette. The people, completely naked, climbed down steps which had been cut into the clay wall of the ditch, stumbled over the heads of those lying there and stopped at the spot indicated by the SS man. They lay down on top of the dead or wounded; some stroked those still living and spoke quietly to them. Then I heard a series of rifle shots. I looked into the ditch and saw the bodies contorting or, the heads already inert, sinking on the corpses beneath. Blood flowed from the nape of their necks. I was surprised not to be ordered away, but I noticed three postmen in uniform standing nearby. Then the next batch came up, climbed down into the ditch, laid themselves next to the previous victims and were shot.

On the way back, as I rounded the mound, I saw another lorry load of people which had just arrived. This one included the sick and infirm. An old and very emaciated woman with frightfully thin legs was being undressed by others, already naked. She was being supported by two people and seemed paralysed. The naked people carried the woman round the mound. I left the place with Moennikes and went back to Dubno by car.

The next morning, returning to the building site, I saw some thirty naked bodies lying thirty to fifty metres from the ditch. Some were still alive; they stared into space with a fixed gaze and seemed not to feel the coolness of the morning nor be aware of the workers from my firm standing around. A girl of about twenty spoke to me and asked for clothes and to help her escape. At that moment, we heard the sound of a car approaching at speed; I saw that it was an SS Commando. I went back to my building site. Ten minutes later, we heard rifle shots coming from the ditch. The Jews who were still alive had been ordered to throw the bodies into the ditch; then they had to lie down themselves to receive a bullet in the back of the neck.

I am making the above statement in Wiesbaden, Germany on 10 November 1945. I swear to God that it is the whole truth.

Fred. Gräbe

The numbers of those killed in the course of the *Einsatzgruppen* operations in the Soviet Union can only be estimated. During the 'first sweep' from June 1941 to April 1942 it has been estimated that some 700–750,000 Jews were murdered. This includes the victims of the four *Einsatzgruppen* themselves—*Einsatzgruppe* A alone claimed to have murdered 240,410 (of whom 229,052 were Jews) by the end of January 1942—Gestapo units from Tilsit, *Einsatzkommandos* from the General Government and units of the Higher SS and Police Leaders. In the second and more comprehensive sweep during 1942–3 an estimated further 1.5 million Jews were murdered in the Soviet Union, making a sum total of around 2.2 million.[6]

(ii) The decision to exterminate the European Jews

With the *Einsatzgruppen* operations in Russia in the summer of 1941 Nazi Jewish policy had entered a new phase. The maltreatment of Jews practised hitherto through discrimination, deportation, ghettoization, and forced labour had been replaced by their systematic extermination, with only skilled workers temporarily exempted; a Rubicon had been crossed. At first, this new policy of extermination was confined to the Jews in the Soviet Union. Within a few months, however, it was being extended to include all European Jews who fell within Germany's sphere of influence.

The decision to exterminate the Jews almost certainly emerged gradually as what its perpetrators came to regard as the most appropriate solution to a pressing problem, namely what to do with the millions of Jews in Greater Germany and its occupied territories and sattelites. During 1940–41, Hitler had encouraged his Gauleiters to purge their territories of Jews and declared his lack of interest in how they did it, thereby virtually launching a competition to see who could make his Gau 'clean of Jews' the fastest. The question remained, however, of what to do with them since deportation to Madagascar was no longer an option and Poland was already full of Jews. Indeed, the most pressing problem was the three million Polish Jews now concentrated in ghettos infested with typhus. Forced to live in subhuman conditions, their deteriorating physical appearance and environment began to approximate to the sub-human stereotype of Nazi anti-Jewish propaganda. To German administrators and police, for whom hygiene and orderliness were the hallmarks of civilization, the Jews appeared an affront, a source of disease, moral corruption and political subversion, a kind of pestilence. The systematic dehumanization of the Jews by the Nazis since 1933, culminating in the Polish ghettos, helped to remove the moral inhibitions which would otherwise have prevented the

---

[6] Cf. H. Krausnick and H. H. Wilhelm, *op. cit*. p. 621. This section owes much to this work.

contemplation let alone the implementation of a policy of extermination. In addition there was a widespread mentality of 'professionalism' in which the efficient performance of a professional function became the overriding consideration and moral criteria were reduced to secondary virtues such as duty and loyalty.

In the summer of 1941, SS officials on the ground were already speculating about the best method for dealing with problem. On 16 July 1941, SS *Sturmbannführer* Höppner based in Posen sent the following minute to Adolf Eichmann in the Reich Security Main Office:

824

I enclose a minute in which the contents of various discussions in the Reich Governor's office here are summarized. I would be grateful for your comments in due course. Parts of it sound incredible but would in my view be perfectly feasible.

. . . The issue of the solution of the Jewish question in the Reich Gau Wartheland has been raised by various agencies at meetings in the Reich Governor's [Greiser's] office. The following solution is being proposed:

1. All Jews in the Warthegau will be put in a camp for 300,000 Jews which will be constructed in the form of barracks as close as possible to the coal depot and will contain workshops for tailors, shoemakers etc.
2. All the Jews in the Warthegau will be brought to this camp. Jews capable of work can be placed in labour gangs as required and deployed outside the camp.
3. In the opinion of SS *Brigadeführer* Albert such a camp requires far fewer police to guard it than is the case at present. Moreover, the continual threat of epidemics to the population round Litzmannstadt [Łódź] and other ghettos is reduced to a minimum.
4. This winter there is a danger that not all the Jews will be able to be fed. Serious consideration must be given as to whether the most humane solution might not be to finish off those Jews who are incapable of work with some quick-acting preparation. At all events, this would be more pleasant than letting them starve.
5. Furthermore, it was proposed to sterilize all those Jewesses who are still fertile so that the Jewish problem would be finally solved with the present generation.
6. The Reich Governor has not yet commented on this matter. People have the impression that *Regierungspräsident* Ubelhör does not want the Litzmannstadt ghetto to disappear since he seems to earn a lot from it. As an example of what one can earn from Jews, I was told that the Reich Labour Ministry pays 6 RM [per day] from a special account for every Jew employed, while the actual cost of the Jew is only 80 pf.

On 31 July 1941, Göring, who was still officially responsible for the Jewish question, signed the following document in response to a request from Heydrich's office which had drafted it:

825

To supplement the task that was assigned to you on 24 January 1939, which dealt with the solution of the Jewish problem by emigration and evacuation in the most suitable way, I hereby charge you with making all necessary preparations with regard to organizational, technical and material matters for bringing about a complete solution of the Jewish question within the German sphere of influence in Europe.

Wherever other governmental agencies are involved, these are to cooperate with you.

I request you further to send me, in the near future, an overall plan covering the organizational, technical and material measures necessary for the accomplishment of the final solution of the Jewish question which we desire.

It is still not clear whether or not this document initiated the policy of comprehensive extermination of the Jews. For example, it has been argued that it simply represented an extension of Himmler's responsibility for the Jewish question beyond Germany's borders and an authorization to prepare the next phase of Jewish policy and coordinate the actions of the various departments involved i.e. that it was simply one more stage in the SS's struggle to extend its sphere of competence. However, in practice the SS already had far-reaching authority to carry out deportations and even exterminations and indeed had already done so on a large scale. Thus, it seems more likely that this initiative involved something much more far-reaching than that.

One possible explanation is that, in the light of the victorious advances of the German forces into Russia in July 1941 and the systematic extermination of the Jews there by the *Einsatzgruppen*, Hitler may have been carried away by the prospect of a final settling of accounts with his ideological enemies, above all the Jews. At the same time, Himmler may have brought to his attention the problems posed by the Jews in Poland and elsewhere. Then Hitler may have authorized Himmler to produce a comprehensive solution of the Jewish problem 'one way or the other', without enquiring too closely into what would be involved. Both men were presumably aware of the practical alternatives: a slow death through forced labour in inhuman conditions, probably in the Soviet Union, or a more speedy method. The SS was then left to work out its own scheme. However, since the elaborate logistics involved in any 'complete solution of the Jewish question' required the participation of numerous state agencies, some form of formal authorization at a very high level would be necessary. But, in view of his experience of the problems involved with the 'euthanasia' programme, Hitler may have been even more anxious to avoid associating himself with such a controversial matter as the extermination of the Jews which might adversely affect his charisma. Thus, he was not even prepared to grant Himmler the kind of semi-official authorization which he had given Bouhler in 1939 to cover the 'euthanasia' programme.[7] Instead, he left it to Göring and Himmler to sort it out between them having given them the go-ahead in general terms.

Although the above scenario is speculation, evidence that Hitler did in fact take a fundamental decision around this time is provided by the following statement by Eichmann to an Israeli interrogator in 1960:

826

I think the war against the Soviet Union started in June 1941. And I think it must have been two months later, it could have been three months later, that Heydrich ordered me to come and see him. I went and he said to me: 'About the emigration, the Führer' . . . With a little speech beforehand: 'The Führer has ordered the physical extermination of the Jews.' He said this sentence to me and then, quite contrary to his habit, paused for a long time as if he wanted to test the effect of his words on me. At first I could not grasp the implications because he chose his words carefully. But then I understood and said nothing further because there was nothing more I could say . . .

The reliability of this statement is somewhat undermined by the fact that Eichmann goes on to describe a visit to an extermination camp in the process of construction which he claims was Treblinka[8] and which he alleges took place immediately after this conversation. There can be little doubt that such a visit took place. However, since the construction of Treblinka did not begin until the spring of 1942, it could hardly have taken place in August or September 1941 as he claimed.

A further piece of evidence supporting a decision by Hitler to exterminate the Jews at this time is provided by the following excerpt from an affidavit by Rudolf Hoess, the first commandant of Auschwitz, which he wrote in 1946:

827

In the summer of 1941, I cannot remember the exact date, I was suddenly summoned to the Reichsführer SS, directly by his adjutant's office. Contrary to his usual custom, Himmler received me without his adjutant being present and said to me in effect:

---

[7] See above p. 1021. My interpretation owes much to Professor Browning's work.

[8] On Treblinka see below pp. 1153 ff.

'The Führer has ordered that the Jewish question be solved once and for all and we, the SS, are to implement that order.

'The existing extermination centres in the East are not in a position to carry out the large actions which are anticipated. I have therefore earmarked Auschwitz for this purpose. . . .'[9]

Nevertheless, the fact that a decision appears to have been taken in the summer of 1941 to seek a comprehensive solution of the Jewish question involving their extermination did not mean that the Nazi authorities had a clear idea of how to proceed. The systematic extermination of a whole race, consisting of millions of men, women, and children, was unprecedented; there were no guidelines to follow. This helps to explain the confusion of the following months during which different approaches were followed and different methods applied by the various individuals and agencies involved as they grappled with the particular problems facing them in their areas.

During this transitional period of 1941–2 three main methods of liquidation were applied: mass shootings by *Einsatzgruppen* in an extension to German, Austrian, and Czech Jews, who were deported to Russia, of the programme already directed against Russian Jews; the deployment of special gassing vans which were a modified version of those which had already been used in the 'euthanasia' campaign in East Prussia and Poland in 1940;[10] and, finally, the use of gas chambers which were a modified version of those used in the main 'euthanasia' programme in Germany during 1940–41. By the late spring of 1942, extermination by means of gas had emerged as the most appropriate solution to the 'Jewish problem', given the prevailing mentality among the German authorities responsible for dealing with it. Proven techniques and trained personnel already existed and, since the official ending of the 'euthanasia' campaign in August 1941, the Führer's Chancellery (KdF) was eager to redeploy its unemployed T4 personnel.[11] However, there were constraints on the speed with which an extermination programme could be implemented, constraints imposed both by the logistical—particularly transport—problems involved and by the extent to which Jewish labour had acquired a significant role in parts of the German war economy. For a time, therefore, a distinction was made, though by no means always adhered to, between those Jews who were fit and those who were unfit for labour, with the former being provisionally

[9] For the full statement see below p. 1175 ff.

[10] See above p. 1020.

[11] See above p. 1020.

spared. However, the principle already laid down, according to which economic considerations were irrelevant to the problem,[12] was rigorously enforced by Himmler, and it was clear all along that those Jews who were temporarily spared for forced labour would die sooner rather than later 'one way or the other'.

(iii) The Fate of the German Jews 1941–5

The radicalization of Nazi policy towards the Jews, which had occurred in the war against Russia during the summer of 1941, began to have an impact on German Jews in the early autumn. The first of a new wave of repressive measures concerned the wearing of a mark of identification. As early as 1938, at the conference on the Jews held on 12 November in the aftermath of the 'Night of Broken Glass', Heydrich had urged that Jews should be forced to wear some mark of identification. However, at that stage Hitler had vetoed the proposal. Then, after its introduction in Poland on 23 November 1939, Gauleiter Mutschmann of Saxony had advocated it in the spring of 1940. But his proposal too was turned down by the Reich Interior Ministry with reference to Hitler's previous veto. Then, in April 1941, Goebbels took the matter up again and, after being stalled by the Interior Ministry, approached Hitler directly on 20 August. Significantly this time Hitler agreed 'to the identification of Jews in Germany as a preparation for all further measures'.[13] However, the RSHA managed to insist on its responsibility for the Jewish question and, on 1 September 1941, Heydrich issued the following police decree:

828

I (1) Jews over six years of age are prohibited from appearing in public without wearing a Jewish star.

(2) The Jewish star is a yellow piece of cloth with a black border, in the form of a six-pointed star the size of the palm of the hand. The inscription reads 'JEW' in black letters. It shall be worn visibly, sewn on the left chest side of the garment.

II Jews are forbidden:

(*a*) to leave their area of residence without written permission of the local police, carried on their person.

(*b*) to wear medals, decorations or other insignia.

III Articles I and II shall not apply:

(*a*) to a Jewish husband living in a mixed marriage if there are children born of this marriage who are not considered Jews. This also applies if the marriage is

[12] See above p. 1098.

[13] See U. D. Adam, *Judenpolitik im Dritten Reich* (Dusseldorf 1972) p. 336.

dissolved or if the only son was killed in the present war.

(*b*) to a Jewish wife in a childless mixed marriage for the duration of the marriage.

IV (1) Anyone who violates articles I and II deliberately or negligently will be punished with a fine of up to 150 RM or with imprisonment not exceeding six weeks . . .

The concessions to those living in mixed marriages were included at the request of the Interior Ministry.

As Hitler had recognised, by ensuring that Jews could be instantly identified, this law facilitated the implementation of all the other restrictions on Jews of which a new wave now ocurred. Thus, on 18 September 1941, the Reich Transport Minister issued the following instruction to the states:

829

Re: The use of transport by Jews:

In order to execute the Police Decree concerning the Identification of Jews of 1 September 1941 and to regulate the use by Jews of the railways, road transport, inland water and sea transport, the following regulations are introduced in agreement with the Reich Minister of the Interior:

A. *General Matters*

I. *Journeys beyond the local community*

For journeys beyond their local community Jews must carry with them a written police permit such as the enclosed specimen A, allowing them to leave their community and use transport. In special cases joint permission can be given.

II. *Journeys within the local community*

Jews may use transport within their local community, but in order to use taxis, hired cars and steamers they require a police permit like the enclosed specimen B or, in the case of a closed group transport e.g. to work etc., a written police permit which must be secured by their employer.

III. *Police Permits*

1) The police permits are issued by the local police authorities (for Reich Gau Vienna the Central Office for Jewish Emigrés in Vienna), in special cases by the Secret State Police or the Chief of the Security Police and SD (Central Office for Jewish Emigration, Berlin).

2) The police permit and an official passport with photograph must be produced on the purchase of a ticket—at the latest on commencing the journey—and must be produced when the tickets are inspected without being requested.

3) Where possible, the issuing of a ticket or the use of transport should be confirmed by making a note on, or stamping the back, of the police permit at the time when the ticket is issued or on the commencement of the journey.

B. *Particular Matters*

I *Exclusion from transportation*

1) Jews are not permitted to use sleeping cars and restaurants or excursion vehicles

or ships either within or outside their communities.
2) Jews are not permitted to enter trams, buses, steamers and local trains if there is a large crowd wanting to get on.
II *Limits on the use of classes and seats.*
1) Jews may only use the third class on the railways and the lowest class in other forms of transport.
2) As a matter of principle, Jews may only sit down when these seats are not required by other travellers.
III *Use of waiting rooms and other facilities.*

Regardless of restrictions going even further, Jews may only use waiting rooms, buffets, and other facilities of the transport services if they have a police permit to leave their local community and to use transport.[14]

C. *Further regulations*
Further regulations, in particular concerning particular times, means of transport, and lines may be issued. Provisionally, they require the approval of the Reich Transport Minister.

The effect of such restrictions and of having to wear the yellow star is clear from the following post-war account by a Stuttgart Jewess:

830

Wearing the yellow star, with which we were branded from 1941 onwards as if we were criminals, was a form of torture. Every day when I went out in the street I had to struggle to maintain my composure.

I had some bitter disappointments with acquaintances and colleagues. I was treated very badly by a doctor. I learnt then what it meant to be at the mercy of someone without compassion.

In 1943 I took a tram from Sillenbuch to my place of work and on the platform—it was forbidden for Jews to go inside the vehicle even if one had the travel permit issued by the Gestapo—I found myself among a group of teenage school children. They shouted: 'Throw the Jewess off'. They recognised that I was Jewish because of the yellow star. Throughout the journey through the Sillenbücher forest I could feel them pressing against my back. The pupils behind me (both boys and girls) shouted and abused me. Some boys were standing in front of me and I looked at them very calmly and seriously. They looked away in embarrassment and did not move. And then the others quietened down and nothing happened.

During the following months, a stream of regulations subjected German Jews to increasing restrictions on their lives and reductions in the quantity and quality of food rations and other essentials. For example, on 30 September 1941, the Reich office for the industrial provision of fats sent the following circular to the Reich Governors, *Oberpräsidenten* etc.:

[14] Even this was banned on 6 June 1942 (eds).

831

Re: The provision of soap for Jews:
The Reich Minister of Economics, in agreement with the Reich Minister of the Interior and the Führer's Party Chancellery, has reached the following decision in relation to the provision of soap for Jews:
1) Jewish children will only be allocated quality soap up to the end of their first year. However, the additional amounts received by children from 2–8 years of age will continue to be allocated (i.e. 500 gr. of washing (soap) powder per month).
2) The allocation of shaving soap to male Jews will cease in future.

Jews were also subjected to petty humiliations of various kinds. For example, on 10 January 1942, the Reich Ministry of Justice instructed judicial officials throughout the Reich that it was inappropriate to call Jews 'Herr' [Mr].

On 15 May 1942, the following notice appeared in the Jewish Newsletter (*Jüdisches Nachrichtenblatt*):

832

The Reich Association of the Jews in Germany hereby announces the following directive from its supervisory authority [i.e. the Gestapo]:
1. Jews who are required to wear the badge and those persons living with them are forbidden to possess household pets (dogs, cats, birds) with immediate effect.
2. Jews who possess household pets at the time of the publication of this directive are required to report to the Jewish Cultural Association in their district or to the district office of the Reich Association of the Jews in Germany by 20.5.1942 under the reference 'household pets' what pets they own.
3. The owners of animals (viz.para.2) will receive instructions from their local Jewish Cultural Association of the Jews in Germany concerning the handing over or collection of the pets.
4. The removal of the pets to another place, in particular into the care of third parties is not permitted.
5. Contraventions of these instructions will be dealt with by the State Police.
6. This directive does not apply to Jews of foreign nationality unless they are obliged to wear the badge.

While some Germans were actively hostile to the Jews, the majority were either indifferent or felt too intimidated to help them, let alone protest. A few, however, courageously showed humanity as is clear from the account by the Stuttgart Jewess quoted from earlier:

833

1939—My mother and I are forced to leave our flat. The beginning of the war—further restrictions and bans. However, these bans are not always respected by non-Jewish fellow-citizens. When the foodstuffs allocated to us begin to get scarce, a woman who is a complete stranger gives my mother a quarter of a pound of butter as she passes her in the street. Now and then we find a basket of vegetables, fruit and eggs in front of our door. Those are in short supply particularly for us. Sometimes such things are brought to us in our flat by loyal people, to a flat which non-Jews should not have entered. But these are only glimpses of light in this gloomy hopelessness.

The Gestapo took steps to prevent such gestures of humanity. On 24 October 1941, its chief, Heinrich Müller, issued the following instruction to all its branches:

834

Re; Behaviour of persons of German blood towards Jews:

It has repeatedly come to our notice recently that persons of German blood continue to maintain friendly relations with Jews and appear with them in public in a blatant fashion. Since such persons of German blood apparently even now still show a lack of understanding of the most elementary and basic principles of National Socialism and since their behaviour must be regarded as a flouting of official measures, my orders are that in such cases the person of German blood concerned is to be taken into protective custody for educational purposes or in serious cases to be transferred to a concentration camp, Grade I. The Jewish participant is invariably to be taken into protective custody and transferred to a concentration camp for the time being.

Requests for such action should be made to the RSHA Ref. IV C 2.

Ironically, but, given the paranoid nature of Nazi antisemitism, characteristically, the increasing flood of restrictions on the Jews which poured out from September 1941 onwards was rapidly rendered superfluous by the disappearance of their target. In August 1941, Hitler had vetoed a proposal by Heydrich to deport the German Jews, possibly on the grounds of lack of transportation.[15] For, in the same month, he had told Goebbels that the Jews would have to go east as soon as transport was available: 'Then they will have to live in a much harsher climate'. Then, in the autumn of 1941, the deportation of German Jews to the east, halted in March, was resumed and this time on a much larger scale on Hitler's orders.

[15] For the following see U. D. Adam *op. cit.* pp. 308–9.

In the early autumn of 1941, the assumption still appears to have been that many Jews, including those from Germany, would eventually be deported to occupied Russian territory. It was presumably in the late summer or early autumn of 1941 that the following undated guidelines for the 'treatment of the Jewish question in the occupied territories of the USSR 'were issued by the RSHA. They clearly assumed that, despite the activities of the *Einsatzgruppen*, a considerable number of Jews would remain in German-occupied Russia for the time being:

835

1. The responsibility of the Chief of the Security Police and the SD, who has been charged with the solution of the Jewish question, also covers the occupied eastern territories. . . . All measures concerning the Jewish question in the occupied territories must be taken on the basis of the standpoint that the Jewish question will be completely solved for the whole of Europe at the latest after the war. They are, therefore, to be imposed as preparatory and partial measures and need to be coordinated with the other decisions adopted in this sphere. This applies in particular to the creation of at least temporary possibilities for accommodating Jews from the Reich.

Actions by the local civilian population against the Jews are not to be hindered in so far as they are compatible with the need to maintain order and security in the rear of the troops engaged in combat. . .

2. Definition of the concept of a 'Jew'.

The satisfactory solution of the Jewish question presupposes in the first instance the definition of who in the occupied eastern territories is to be regarded as a Jew. In view of the final solution of the European Jewish question . . . it appears necessary both from the political as well as from the racial [*völkisch*] standpoint, in order to avoid a subsequent revival of Jewry, for the concept of the Jew to be defined as widely as possible. Thus, a Jew is anyone who is or has been a member of the Jewish religion or otherwise declares himself to be a Jew or has done so or whose membership of the Jewish race is apparent from other circumstances. Anyone who has one parent who is a Jew within the meaning of the previous sentence is also regarded as a Jew.[16]

3. Registration, Marking, Removal of freedom of movement, and Segregation.

One of the first and crucial objectives of the German measures must be to segregate the Jews from the rest of the population. A precondition for this is the comprehensive registration of the Jewish population by requiring them to report to the authorities and other appropriate measures . . .

Then they must be marked without delay by being made to wear a yellow Jewish star at all times and the freedom of movement of all Jews must be prevented. The

[16] This goes beyond the definition of a Jew contained in the First Supplementary Decree of the Reich Citizenship Law of 14 November 1935. See Vol. 2 pp. 538–9.

aim must be to transfer them to ghettos while at the same time separating the sexes. The presence of a large number of more or less closed Jewish communities in White Russia and the Ukraine will facilitate this task. Moreover, places for such ghettos must be selected which provide opportunities for work in order to facilitate the complete exploitation of the Jews' labour capacity. These ghettos can be placed under the supervision of a Jewish authority with a Jewish police force. However, the guarding of the frontiers between the ghetto and the outside world is a matter for the police. . . .

4. Removal of Jewish influence in the political, economic, cultural, and social spheres.

At the same time as the measures for the outward separation of the Jews from the rest of the population, everything possible must be done to exclude any Jewish influence on the Russian population. This must be carried out at once in the political and cultural spheres, while in all other cases care must be taken to ensure that no significant damage is done to our overall objectives. In view of the primacy of the economic tasks in the east as a result of the war, this must be borne in mind with all measures which affect the economy. . . . All Jewish property must be registered, confiscated and requisitioned apart from what is necessary to ensure a minimum standard of living. In this context, the Jews' control over their property must be removed as soon as possible by a decree of the provisional administration and by other measures in so far as general economic conditions permit.

Jews will be completely banned from any cultural activity. This includes a ban on the Jewish press, the Jewish theatre and Jewish schools. Ritual slaughter must also be prevented.

In September 1941, Himmler sent Eichmann to Poland to assess the situation as far as accommodating Jews was concerned. On 18 September, Himmler informed Greiser, Gauleiter of the Wartheland:

836

It is the Führer's wish that the *Altreich* and the Protectorate should be emptied of and liberated from the Jews from west to east as soon as possible. I am thus endeavouring to ensure that the deportation of the Jews from the *Altreich* and the Protectorate to the territories incorporated into the Reich during the past two years is completed during this year as a first step preparatory to their being sent further east in the spring. During the winter, I intend to send some sixty thousand Jews from the *Altreich* and the Protectorate to the Litzmannstadt ghetto which, as I understand is just able to accommodate them . .

On 16 October 1941, the first train load of German Jews arrived in Łódź. Protests from the German authorities in Łódź about their inability to absorb so many Jews had led to reduction in the numbers deported there. When the transports ceased on 4 November, twenty thousand Jews had arrived in the Łódź ghetto: 5,000 from Vienna, 5,000 from Prague, 4,200 from Berlin, 2,000 from Cologne, 1,000 from Frankfurt, 1,000 from Hamburg, 1,000 from Düsseldorf, and 500 from occupied Luxembourg. In addition 5,000 Gypsies had arrived. For the time being all were absorbed into the ghetto, though Greiser was desperate to be rid of the unproductive ones.

Poland, however, was not the only destination for German Jews in the winter of 1941. On 11 October, Franz Stahlecker, the commander of *Einsatzgruppe* A, told Dr Otto Drechsler, the General Commissioner in Latvia, that in accordance with a 'wish of the Führer', a 'big concentration camp' was to be established near Riga for Jews from Germany and the Protectorate.[17] And, ten days later, on 21 October, *Sturmbannführer* Lange, chief of the *Einsatzkommando* in Latvia, telephoned Dreschler to report that a camp was to be established for 25,000 Jews some fourteen miles from Riga. In addition, Minsk in Byelorussia was scheduled to receive a further 25,000 Jews from Germany and the Protectorate.

On 24 October 1941, *Obergruppenführer* Kurt Daluege, the chief of the order police (*Ordnungspolizei*) signed the first deportation orders for Riga and Minsk and, during November and December, some 25,000 Jews from Germany, Austria and the Protectorate arrived in Riga and around 7,000 in Minsk.

On the previous day, the RSHA had issued a very significant edict:

837

The *Reichsführer* SS and Chief of the German Police has ordered that the emigration of Jews is to be prevented with immediate effect. (Existing regulations concerning deportations will remain in force.)

Only in exceptional cases, e.g. in the event of the Reich securing a positive advantage therefrom, can the emigration of individual Jews be permitted after securing prior permission from the Reich Security Main Office.

Among the German Jews arriving in Riga in December 1941 was a transport from Stuttgart. On 18 November, the Gestapo branch office in Stuttgart had sent the following directive to the *Landräte* and police chiefs in Württemberg, in this case to the *Landrat's* office in Biberach. It referred to 'the deportation of Jews to the *Reichskommissariat Ostland*' and was marked 'very urgent!':

[17] See Raul Hilberg, *The Destruction of the European Jews* (New York 1973) p. 232. This was Salaspils camp. See below pp. 1121–2.

838

I. Within the framework of the de-jewifying [*Entjudung*] of the whole of Europe, railway transports containing 1,000 Jews each are at present regularly leaving from Germany, the *Ostmark*, and the Protectorate of Bohemia and Moravia for the *Reichskommissariat Ostland*. Württemberg and Hohenzollern are participating initially with a transport of 1,000 Jews which will leave Stuttgart on 1 December 1941.
II. Those Jews involved have already been selected and registered here. They were selected in accordance with § 5 of the first supplementary decree of the Reich Citizenship Law of 14 November 1935. . .[18] The following were exempted:
1. Jews living in German-Jewish mixed marriages.
2. Jews of foreign nationality.
3. Jews over 65 years of age.

However, these criteria were breached in individual cases.
Those Jews scheduled for evacuation from your area are listed in appendix 1. You will be kept informed of alterations which are unavoidable as a result of the resettlement of the remaining Jews in Württemberg, which is continuing simultaneously, and on account of special circumstances, illness etc. I must emphasize that on no account may the number scheduled for your area be deviated from either upwards or downwards. Surplus Jews must be sent back to their previous locations. Absentees (through suicide etc.) must be reported immediately.
III. The train scheduled for transporting the Jews is timetabled to leave Stuttgart on 1 December 1941 between 8 and 9 o'clock.
The Jews who are to be evacuated from Stuttgart itself as well as from the country areas will be concentrated in a transit camp in the grounds of the former Reich Garden Show (Killesberg) in Stuttgart from 27 November onwards.
IV. Each person may take with them:
(*a*) Money up to 50 RM in Reich credit notes. This money will be supplied from here so in practice the Jews should not bring any money with them on their journey here.
(*b*) 1 or 2 cases (no bulky goods). This luggage must not weigh more than 50 kg.
(*c*) Bedding, consisting of 1–2 blankets, 2 sheets and 1 mattress for two people (but without a bolster).
(*d*) A complete set of clothing (particularly warm underwear and decent shoes).
(*e*) Food for 1-2 days. We have already seen to the further adequate provisioning of all participants in the transport.
(*f*) Crockery (a plate or pot with a spoon).
The following must not be taken: bonds, foreign exchange, saving books, etc. and valuables of all kinds (gold, silver, platinum with the exception of wedding rings), livestock.
Those ration books valid for the period after 1 December 1941 must be handed in to the local Food Office in return for a receipt. This receipt must be presented in the transit camp.

[18] See vol. 2 p. 539.

Work books must be withdrawn and handed over to the local Labour Office.

V. Before the groups which have been assembled for transportation in the various districts are handed over, the local police authority must carry out a thorough search for weapons, ammunition, explosives, poison, foreign exchange, jewellery etc. Any property seized must be listed and handed over to the local finance office (see further § VI)

VI. To prevent fraudulent transfers, the entire property of the Jews being deported will be confiscated by the police. I request that this measure is implemented. The Jews have already been sent, via the Jewish Cultural Association, the enclosed property declaration form in which they are obliged to provide a complete declaration of their assets and present the list to their town hall by 25.11.1941 at the latest. The mayors must carry out sample inspections of the declarations and send them to the local Finance Office.

The entire assets of these Jews will be confiscated. The confiscation orders will be handed over to individuals in the transit camp. The liquidation will be carried out by the President of the Finance Office in Württemberg through the local Finance Offices. You are requested to liaise with them in connection with the sealing of the [Jews'] dwellings and other measures.

VII. Those Jews being evacuated have been informed of my orders today in the enclosed circular. This was done through the Jewish Cultural Association for the sake of administrative convenience and uniformity. In this communication every one of those Jews has been given a transport number which corresponds with the enclosed list. For the sake of convenience, therefore, I suggest that in the event of any queries, and when collecting the group together for transportation, these numbers should be used.

In view of the restricted number of available goods waggons, I request that you pay particular attention to ensuring that the amount of individuals' luggage is kept strictly within the allowance.

I have engaged the firm of Barr, Moering & Co. of Stuttgart to collect the rest of the luggage, some of which is heavy, for the whole area of Württemberg and Hohenzollern. In cooperation with the local authorities, it is responsible for collecting the luggage from the individual districts and transporting it to the station of departure. A representative of this firm will visit you shortly to discuss the procedure in detail.

In addition, I request that you ensure, possibly by employing a Jewish middle man, that a sufficient quantity of building equipment, tools, kitchen equipment for communal feeding, e.g. cauldrons, stoves, buckets, and first aid boxes are provided. For this purpose, the following rough proportions should be adhered to: one bucket for ten persons, one shovel or spade for ten persons, one pickaxe for ten persons, a sharp hatchet or axe for twenty persons, a saw for twenty persons, a stove with chimney and a tray for fifty persons, and a first aid box, a cauldron and a sewing machine for a hundred persons, a large tool box for twenty persons. However, these materials should not be bought new.

VIII. Your task, therefore, is to collect the Jews together at the proper time, to secure their property in cooperation with the financial authorities, to seal their dwellings and if necessary appoint caretakers, search the Jews' persons and their luggage and, deploying an appropriate number of officials, to deliver the Jews on

27 or 28 November 1941 to the camp in Stuttgart (special instructions will be given concerning the exact time for their delivery to the camp). If the numbers of those involved in the transport to Stuttgart require special railway carriages you must ensure their provision. The transport leader (official) must present a detailed list in quadruplicate containing the transport numbers, the personal details, and the identity numbers.
Any costs arising will be met by the Jewish Cultural Association in Stuttgart and paid from a special fund.
In the event of any queries please ring 29741 . . .

On 17 November 1941, the Jewish Cultural Association of Württemberg sent the following circular to those Jews who had been selected for 'evacuation':

839

Re: Evacuation.

On the orders of the Secret State Police regional headquarters in Stuttgart we are obliged to inform you that you and the children mentioned above have been assigned to an evacuation transport to the East. At the same time, you, together with the above-mentioned children who have been assigned to the transport, are hereby obliged to hold yourselves in readiness from Wednesday 26 November 1941 onwards in your present abode and not to leave it even temporarily without the express permission of the authorities.

Employment, even in important plants, does not provide exemption from the evacuation. Any attempt to resist the evacuation or to avoid it is pointless and may have serious repercussions for the person concerned.

The enclosed declarations of assets must be filled in carefully for each member of the family involved, including each child, and delivered to the local police authority within three days.

Enclosed is a list of the most essential items to be brought with you. Each participant in the transport is entitled to take with them up to 50kg of luggage whether in the form of suitcases, rucksacks or shoulder bags. You are recommended to carry a large part of the luggage in a rucksack. It must be assumed that the members of the transport will have to carry their own luggage for part of the time. Suitcases, rucksacks, and travel rugs should be marked with the transport number noted above without fail; in addition, you are strongly advised to add your full name. If possible use indelible ink, otherwise use fixed tags.

In addition, you are advised to put on warm underwear, warm clothing, the strongest possible boots and shoes, galoshes, coats and caps rather than hats.

Apart from hand luggage, it will probably be possible to take with you in addition mattresses, some bedding, some kitchen equipment—but without kitchen furniture—cooking materials, tins of food, first aid materials, sewing equipment, needles, all tools and gardening equipment. Some stoves with chimneys and sewing machines, preferably portable ones, will probably be able to be taken. Spades, shovels and such like as well as building tools are particularly important.

We request that you get such objects ready in your flat and if possible pack them up, with sharp tools covered with protective packing, and mark these things clearly too, particularly matresses, with the transport number, if necessary with a cardboard label. These objects should be mentioned on the form but with a note 'are being taken with me'.

With the delivery of this letter you have been officially banned from disposing of your property. Thus you are no longer permitted to sell, give away, lend, pawn or in any way dispose of any of your property.

Every member of the transport will receive RM 50 in Reich credit notes and two food parcels worth RM 7.65, of which one contains food for consuming on the journey, while the second parcel with flour, pulses etc, will be carried as luggage.

You should pay the required sum of RM 57.65 per person immediately to the Jewish Cultural Association of Württemberg, Stuttgart, Hospitalstraße 36 or to the special W account of the Württemberg branch of the Reich Association of German Jews at the Gymnasialstraße branch of the Deutsche Bank.

If you are unable to pay the amount, inform the Jewish Cultural Association immediately . . .

Prior to your departure, you must return your ration cards for the period after 1 December to the local office in return for a receipt.

Finally, we ask you not to delay; the efforts of our members, particularly in the employment field, entitle us to hope that this new and most difficult task can be mastered as well.

Jewish Cultural Association Württemberg

Ernst Israel Moos   Theodor Israel Rothschild   Alfred Israel Fackenheim

There followed a long list of clothing and other items which it was suggested that people should bring with them.

On 25 November 1941, the eleventh supplementary decree to the Reich Citizenship Law was issued. This enabled the authorities to confiscate the property of all those Jews who had been deported by claiming that they had lost their German nationality since they had transferred their normal residence abroad (!):

840

§ 1. A Jew who has his normal residence abroad cannot be a German national. The term normal residence abroad applies when a Jew remains abroad under circumstances which indicate that he is not staying there temporarily.

§ 2. A Jew loses his German nationality with the coming into effect of this decree:

(*a*) If, on the coming into effect of this decree, he already has his normal residence abroad.

(*b*) With the removal of his normal residence abroad if he takes up his normal residence abroad after the decree has come into effect.

§ 3.(1) The property of a Jew who loses his German nationality on account of this decree is forfeited to the Reich on the loss of nationality. The property of those

Jews who are stateless on the coming into effect of this decree, and who previously possessed German nationality, is also forfeited to the Reich if they have their normal residence abroad or take it up there.

(2) The forfeited property will be used to further all aims associated with the solution of the Jewish question.

§ 4.(1) Persons whose property is forfeited to the Reich under § 3 cannot inherit anything from a German citizen on death.

(2) Gifts by German citizens to persons whose property is forfeited to the Reich under § 3 are forbidden. Anyone who makes or promises a gift contrary to this ban will be punished with imprisonment of up to two years and with a fine or with one or other of these punishments. . .

The Nazis were not content with confiscating the Jews' property after their departure, the Jews were even obliged to pay for their own deportation as is clear from the following circular from the Reich Associations of Jews in Germany to the Jewish Cultural Associations and the branches of the Reich Association, dated 3 December 1941.

841

The following regulation is being introduced for the raising of funds in connection with evacuation transports on the orders of our supervisory authority [i.e. the Gestapo].

1. Every participant in the evacuation transports is obliged to pay an appropriate portion of his liquid assets (excluding bonds) to the Reich Association. It should be made clear that the amount paid should not be less than 25 per cent of his liquid assets (excluding bonds).

2. This payment represents a donation the necessity for which should be made clear to the donors in a suitable fashion. It can be pointed out that the donations are intended, in the first instance, for the sums of money which are being given to those being evacuated as well as for the provision of food, equipment etc. Any surplus will go towards financing the tasks of the Reich Association, in particular the care of its members.

3. If the task of collecting the asset declarations of those assigned to an evacuation transport has been transferred to the Cultural Association or a branch of it by the State Police (regional) office, it would be convenient to link the collection of the funds with the collection of the lists.

Where this is not the case, the participants in the transport must be requested to make the donations immediately after the lists have been handed over, in so far as this is possible, preferably through a personal request, alternatively through a circular to the participants in the transport. In the case of any future transports, the local State Police (regional office) should be requested to facilitate the donations by prompt disclosure of the transport lists . . .

5. Those cultural associations and district offices which are responsible for preparing evacuations must open a special W account at their bank. All monies

coming in should be transferred to this W account. All expenditure connected with the evacuation transport must be carried out through this W account. Where money coming into this account is insufficient, particularly for the initial expenditure, requests for appropriate funds to be transferred to this account should be made to the financial department of the Reich Association . . .

One of the many unpleasant aspects of this whole deportation procedure was the way in which the Gestapo used the Jewish organizations to do much of their dirty work for them. Most cooperated in the hope of easing the situation for their fellow Jews, but in the process found themselves turned into tools of the Gestapo.

The amount and types of equipment carried by these Jews from Württemberg suggest that the Gestapo was anxious to reassure them about their fate, leading them to believe that they were simply being resettled, and thereby ensure a smooth deportation. Equally, however, it suggests an assumption that they were to be kept alive for some time, rather than immediately exterminated. For it would have been perfectly feasible to allow the Jews to take their personal belongings, but inform them that adequate facilities had already been prepared at their destination—had the intention been to exterminate them on arrival.

In fact, developments in the east from November 1941 onwards suggest that, while the ultimate fate of the Jews was never in doubt, the actual timing and form of the extermination was determined in a largely *ad hoc* fashion with the members of each transport having different experiences depending on where and when they arrived. Thus, on 25 and 29 November 1941, five transports of German Jews from Munich, Berlin, Frankfurt, Vienna, and Breslau were massacred in Fort IX in Kovno Lithuania soon after their arrival and without prior screening to select those fit for labour. The same thing happened in Riga on 30 November 1941. Fourteen thousand Jews from Riga itself were massacred, as well as one thousand Jews who had arrived from Berlin the night before and were taken straight from the train to pits dug in the Rumbuli forest outside Riga where they were shot. At 1.30 p.m on that day, Himmler telephoned Heydrich from Hitler's headquarters in East Prussia ordering that the Berlin transport to Riga should not be liquidated. The reason for Himmler's action is unclear, but it certainly referred only to this one particular transport. It is possible that it contained Jews over sixty-five years of age or with war decorations who should have been exempted. In any case, Himmler's order came too late and, moreover, the extermination was to continue: on 8 December, another 13,000 Jews were massacred outside Riga.

In fact, Himmler had given orders for the extermination of all the Jews in the Baltic States to SS *Obergruppenführer* Friedrich Jeckeln on his appointment as Higher SS and Police Leader in the *Ostland* (Baltic States and White Russia). Jeckeln told a post-war Russian interrogator:

842

On 10th or 11th of November 1941, I was summoned by Himmler to the Gestapo building in the Prinz-Albrecht-Straße in Berlin to discuss my appointment as Higher SS and Police Leader. Himmler told me that I would have to carry out all his orders and advised me to make use of the police organs already in existence in the *Ostland*, which consisted of Latvians, Lithuanians and Estonians. Himmler also said that I should discuss all official matters affecting the SS and police with Reich Commissioner Lohse. In the course of this meeting, Himmler delegated very wide powers to me and ordered me to act in his name and to intervene in the event that his, i.e. Himmler's orders were not being carried out.

Himmler told me that I must organize my work in the *Ostland* in such a way as to ensure that absolute peace and order reigned throughout the whole territory of the *Ostland* and White Russia [*sic*!] and that all the Jews in the *Ostland* must be exterminated right down to the very last one . . .

Himmler told me that the Jewish question in the *Ostland* had been solved. Only in Riga had a ghetto survived which had not been liquidated and I should carry out this liquidation. Himmler said that my predecessor, Adolf Prützmann . . . had said that Lohse was opposed to the liquidation of this ghetto. Himmler said I should discuss this with Lohse and, even if he were opposed, the Riga ghetto should still be liquidated. 'Tell Lohse that these are my orders which also correspond to the Führer's wish'.

A few days after my arrival in Riga, I visited Reich Commissioner Lohse and told him that Himmler had demanded that the ghetto in Riga be liquidated. 'Are you agreeable to that?' Lohse replied that he had nothing against it and I could regard his agreement as an order. After a little time, I gave the order to liquidate all the Jews from the Riga ghetto . . .

On my arrival in Riga in November 1941 there were 20–25,000 Jews in the Riga ghetto. Apart from Jews from the *Ostland*, there were also Jews here who had arrived with transports from the Reich . . .

All the Jews from the Riga ghetto were shot at the end of November or the beginning of December in the course of one week. They were shot in a little wood three kilometres outside Riga on the left hand side of the road between the road and the railway line . . .

I reported to Himmler by telephone that the Riga ghetto had been liquidated and when I visited Himmler in December 1941 in Lötzen (East Prussia), I also reported to him directly. Himmler was content and said that further Jewish transports would arrive in the *Ostland* which I must also exterminate . . .

At the end of January 1942, I visited Himmler in Lötzen to discuss matters to do with the organisation of the Latvian SS legion. There Himmler told me that further transports would arrive in the Salaspils concentration camp from the Reich and other countries. Himmler said that he had not yet decided how they were to be exterminated, whether to shoot them in Salaspils or to chase them off into the marshes somewhere . . .

I pointed out that from my point of view shooting would would be a simpler and quicker form of death. Himmler said he would think about it and give me orders later via Heydrich . . .

Jews were brought to the Salaspils camp from Germany, France, Belgium, Holland, Czechoslovakia and other occupied countries. It is difficult to give an exact figure for the Jews who were in Salaspils, but all the Jews in this camp were exterminated . . .

I can give you a rough estimate. The first Jewish transports arrived in Salaspils already in November 1941. In the first half of 1942 the transports came in regular succession. I think no more than three transports arrived in November 1941 but during the next seven months, from December 1941 to June 1942, 8–12 transports arrived each month. If one reckons on 1,000 persons for each transport, then 55–87,000 Jews were exterminated who had come to Salaspils from the Reich and other countries . . .

Thousands of Jews arriving in Riga from Germany and elsewhere over the next few months were transferred to camps, notably Salaspils camp near the town. Here the vast majority either died in the poor conditions or were liquidated in periodic selections. This is what happened to those Jews who had left Stuttgart on 1 December 1941. Dr Otto Schulz-Du Bois, a captain in the Engineer Reserve, wrote to his wife in January 1942:

843

. . . I also saw concentration camps filled with German Jews. Four thousand from Württemberg were kept on a single farm, Camp Jungfernhof, Riga; poorly fed and penned up in barns; naturally they dropped like flies. It was strange suddenly to be surrounded by Swabian accents. Many of the children were wearing warm ski outfits, and everyone bore up quite adequately under the circumstances. In what used to be the local ghetto, on the other hand, one could hear Berlin accents. I recently saw children standing at the barbed wire, all of them well clothed, begging the Jews who worked in the city: 'Ah Uncle, a piece of bread, ah Uncle!' But in the meantime even this, I am told, has been stopped! How long will it be until these Jews, too, are 'resettled' to the pine forest, where I recently saw mounds of earth heaped up over five large pits, sharply sagging in the middle, and despite the cold a sickly, sweet odour lingered in the air.

In Minsk some 7,300 Jews from Berlin, Hamburg, the Rhineland, Frankfurt, Vienna and Brünn had arrived during November 1941. They were housed in the former ghetto, whose previous inhabitants had been 'liquidated' to make room for them. 1,425 of these Jews were employed locally in a hospital, a Luftwaffe warehouse, a shoe-making workshop etc., receiving one Reichsmark per day in wages each, from which all the expenses of the camp including the food had to be paid. One of the nine survivors of the Jews deported to Minsk, Karl Loewenstein, reported after the war on the food situation as follows:

844

. . . For lunch we had five grams of buckwheat boiled in 300 grams of water per head. There was no fat and for months no salt. For further nourishment we received 150 grams of bread per day. This bread was baked from buckwheat flour and tasted awful. And yet, while the horses refused to eat it, we hungered for it. Often, only too often, the SS who brought us the bread stole it in order to exchange it later for watches, brooches, rings, and gold. There was no tea or coffee. Unfortunately, it was not only the SS who stole the bread. [Jewish] Officials too, i.e. fellow-sufferers, took this sad road in order to enrich themselves at the expense of the suffering of their own comrades. It was not surprising that within a few weeks 700 people had died of debilitation and from the camp sickness, which is what we called diarrhoea. The incredible loss of warmth through the lack of fat and the harsh winter of 1941/2 helped to rob people of their powers of resistance. In addition, there was the mental suffering.

In the harsh Russian winter we suffered particularly from the cold because we had soon used up all the combustible material in the camp and had no more wood. What could we do? There was a block of houses which had been completely destroyed adjacent to the camp where we went and ripped out any remaining wood in order to get heating materials. Anybody caught doing it was shot dead by the pistol of an SS man or a policeman. But that did not prevent anyone from continuing to get wood. Because a quick death was better than starving or freezing.

The majority of the German and Austrian Jews in Minsk were killed between 28–30 July 1942, and the remainder on 8 May 1943, apart from seventy employed in the General Commissioner's office. All these Jews owed their temporary reprieve largely to the intervention of the General Commissioner for White Russia and former Gauleiter of Kurmark, Wilhelm Kube. Kube was shocked by the SS policy of subjecting 'civilized' German Jews, many of whom had fought in the First World War and been decorated, to the same fate as the eastern Jews. In a letter to his old comrade and superior Hinrich Lohse, the Reich Commissioner in the Baltic States, dated, 16 December 1941, he wrote: 'I am certainly tough and prepared to do my bit towards the solution of the Jewish question, but people from our own cultural sphere are rather different from the brutalised hordes living here.'[19]

[19] See H. Heiber, 'Aus den Akten des Gauleiters Kube' in *Vierteljahrshefte für Zeitgeschichte* 1956. 4. p: 75.

On the 25 July 1943, the Commander of the Security Police and SD in Minsk, SS *Obersturmbannführer* Dr Eduard Strauch wrote to SS *Obergruppenführer* von dem Bach-Zelewsky, who was in charge of anti-partisan operations, complaining about Kube's activities:

845

. . . On 1.3.1942, an operation was scheduled against the ghetto in Minsk. The General Commissioner had been informed beforehand. The operation was to be disguised by informing the Council of Elders that 5,000 Jews from the Minsk ghetto were to be resettled. They were to be selected and got ready by the Council of Elders. Each Jew could take five kg. of luggage with him.

The real intentions of the Security Police were intentionally betrayed by the General Commissioner's Office . . .

The Gauleiter had learnt that a German Jew had received a box on the ears from a police officer. Kube questioned the police officer in the presence of the Jew and shouted at him asking whether he had won the Iron Cross like the Jew had. Fortunately, the officer was able to reply in the affirmative.

On 2.12.1941, the senior Elder of the Jews from the *Altreich* declared that he had gained the impression from visits to the Gauleiter that he wished to see the Jews from the Reich rather less harshly treated than the Russian Jews who simply could not be compared with them.

On 2.2.1942, the Commander of the Security Police in Minsk was informed in confidence that the Jewish barber employed by the General Commissioner in Minsk, who shaves him every day, had declared that all the Jews employed in the office of the General Commissioner were under his personal protection . . .

On 20 July 1943, Strauch had reported to his superiors as follows:

846

On Tuesday 20 July, following orders, I arrested the seventy Jews employed by the General Commissioner for White Russia at 7.00 and took them for special treatment.

On the same day at 10.00, I received a telephone call from the General Commissioner's Office that the General Commissioner wished to speak to me at once.

In his outward appearance the General Commissioner made a calm impression, while I could tell from the way he spoke that he was in a state of great agitation. He asked me why I had arrested the Jews employed by him. I declared that I had a strict order to carry out this operation . . .

I emphasized that I could not understand how Germans could quarrel over a few Jews. I said that people kept accusing me and my men of barbarism and sadism, while I was only doing my duty. Even the fact that those Jews who were to be specially treated had had their gold teeth removed by qualified doctors in accordance with instructions was being talked about. Kube replied that this way of carrying on was unworthy of a German or of the Germany of Kant and Goethe. The fact that Germany's reputation was declining all over the world was our fault. Moreover, he said it was quite true that my men would really enjoy these executions. I protested vigorously against these comments and said that it was regrettable that in addition to having to carry out this unpleasant work we were also subjected to mudslinging.

(iv) The Wannsee Conference of 20 January 1942 concerning the 'Final Solution of the Jewish Problem'

Meanwhile, having launched the deportation process somewhat precipitately in the autumn of 1941, the RSHA soon found itself confronted with the practical problem of defining criteria for those to be transported. Were specific categories of Jews to be exempted—for example, Jews employed in the war economy, foreign Jews, those in mixed marriages or over a certain age? What was to be the position of the *Mischlinge*—the half- and quarter-Jews? Moreover, the process of removing thousands of people almost overnight from their homes and employment, transporting them hundreds of miles in the middle of wartime, and then dealing with them when they arrived in occupied territory—all this produced massive organisational problems within Germany itself. These problems involved the police, finance, labour, economics, and railway departments, as well as local government, while outside Germany both the Foreign Ministry and the occupation authorities were closely concerned. Careful coordination was required, which was after all the task which had been assigned to Heydrich by Göring in his commission of 31 July 1941.

On 29 November, therefore, Heydrich invited a number of senior officials to a conference to discuss the matter. The following invitation was addressed to SS *Gruppenführer* Hofman of the SS Race and Settlement Office in Berlin:

847

On 31.7.1941, the Reich Marshal of the Greater German Reich charged me, in cooperation with all the other relevant central agencies, to make all the necessary preparations with regard to organisational, technical and material measures for a complete solution of the Jewish question in Europe and to present him shortly with a complete draft proposal on this matter. I enclose a photocopy of this commission.

In view of the extraordinary importance which must be accorded to these questions, and in the interest of securing a uniform view among the relevant central agencies of the further tasks concerned with the remaining work on this final solution, I propose to make these problems the subject of a general discussion. This is particularly necessary since from 10 October onwards the Jews have been being evacuated from Reich territory, including the Protectorate, to the East in a continuous series of transports.

I therefore invite you to a discussion followed by luncheon on 9 December 1941 at 12.00 in the office of the International Criminal Police Commission, Berlin, Am grossen Wannsee, Nr. 56/58.

I have sent similar invitations to Governor General Dr Frank, Gauleiter Dr Meyer [Ministry of the Eastern Territories], State Secretaries Stuckart [Interior], Dr Schlegelberger [Justice], Hütterer [?], and Neumann [4 Year Plan] as well as *Reichsamtsleiter* Dr Leibrandt [Ministry of the Eastern Territories], Under State Secretary Luther [Foreign Ministry], SS *Obergruppenführer* Krüger [General Government], SS *Gruppenführer* Greifelt [Staff Main Office of the Reich Commissioner for the strengthening of German Nationality], SS *Oberführer* Klopfer [Party Chancellery], and *Ministerialdirektor* Kritzinger [Reich Chancellery].

On learning of the scheduled conference in Berlin, Dr Frank, the Governor General, was so anxious to know what was being envisaged for the Jews that he sent his State Secretary, Dr Bühler, to see Heydrich to find out. On 16 December, Frank reported to a meeting of the senior officials of the General Government on the Jewish question as follows:

848

As for the Jews—I will be quite open with you—they will have to be finished off one way or the other. The Führer said once: if the whole of Jewry once again succeeds in unleasing a world war, then peoples who have been hounded into this war will not be the only ones to shed their blood because the Jews in Europe will meet their end. I know that many of the measures now being taken against the Jews in the Reich are criticised. It is clear from the reports on popular opinion that there are accusations of cruelty and harshness. Before I continue, I would like you to agree with me on the following principle: we are only prepared to show compassion towards the German people and to no one else on earth. The others did not show compassion towards us. As an old National Socialist, I must state that if the Jewish clan were to survive the war in Europe, while we had sacrificed our best blood in the defence of Europe, then this war would only represent a partial success. With respect to the Jews, therefore, I will only operate on the assumption that they will disappear. They must go. I have begun negotiations with the aim of deporting them to the East. In January there is to be a big meeting in Berlin on this question to which I will send State Secretary Dr Bühler. This meeting is to take place in the Reich Security Main Office under SS *Obergruppenführer* Heydrich's chairmanship. In any event a big Jewish migration will begin.

But what will happen to the Jews? Do you imagine that they will actually be settled in the *Ostland* in villages? People said to us in Berlin: why do we go to all this trouble? We in the *Ostland* or in the *Reichskommissariat* [Ukraine] do not know what to do with them either. Liquidate them yourselves! Gentlemen, I must ask you to arm yourselves against any feelings of compassion. We must exterminate the Jews wherever we find them and whenever it is possible to do so in order to maintain the whole structure of the Reich here. That will of course occur through methods other than those to which division chief, Dr Hummel, has just referred.[20] The judges of the special courts cannot be blamed either, for the point is that that does not come within the framework of the legal process. One cannot apply views held up to now to such gigantic and unique events. At all events, we must find a way which achieves the goal and I have my own thoughts about that.

The Jews are also extremely harmful to us through the amount of food they gorge. We have an estimated 2.5 million Jews in the General Government; if one includes those married to them and all their dependents, perhaps 3.5 million. We cannot shoot these 3.5 million Jews, we cannot poison them, but we must be able to intervene in a way which somehow achieves a successful extermination and do so in the context of the major measures to be discussed in relation to the Reich. The General Government must be just as free of Jews as the Reich is. Where and how that occurs is a matter for the agencies [*Instanzen*] which we must establish and deploy here and I will inform you of how they will work in good time.

The Wannsee conference had in fact been postponed to 20 January 1942 and the actual participants were as follows: Reinhard Heydrich, Dr Alfred Meyer, Dr Georg Leibbrandt, Dr Wilhelm Stuckart, Erich Neumann, Dr Roland Freisler [Justice Ministry], State Secretary Dr Josef Bühler [General Government], Martin Luther, Dr Gerhard Klopfer, Dr Wilhelm Kritzinger, Otto Hofmann, SS *Gruppenführer* Heinrich Müller [RSHA], SS *Obersturmbannführer* Adolf Eichmann [RSHA], SS *Oberführer* Karl Schoengarth [Commander of the Security Police and SD in the General Government], SS *Sturmbannführer* Dr Otto Lange [Commander of the Security Police and SD in Latvia]. The following are the minutes prepared by Eichmann:

849

. . . II. The Chief of the Security Police and SD, SS *Obergruppenführer* Heydrich, began by announcing his appointment by the Reich Marshal as the person responsible for the preparation of the final solution of the European Jewish question and

[20] Dr Herbert Hummel, the Chief of Staff in the Warsaw District had reported on the problems of carrying out death sentences on Jews convicted of leaving their ghettos because of the need to go through the appeal procedures: 'The process leading to liquidation was too time-consuming; it was burdened with too many formalities and must be simplified.' See W. Präg and W. Jacobmeyer eds. *Das Diensttagebuch des deutschen Generalgouverneurs 1939–1945* (Stuttgart 1975) pp. 456–7.

pointed out that this meeting was being held to achieve clarity in basic questions. The Reich Marshal's wish that he should be sent a draft on the organizational, technical, and material matters regarding the final solution of the European Jewish question made it necessary that all central authorities directly concerned with these questions should deal with them together in advance so as to ensure the coordination of the lines to be taken.

The supervision of the final solution was, regardless of geographical boundaries, centralized in the hands of the *Reichsführer SS* and Chief of the German Police (Chief of the Security Police and SD).

The Chief of the Security Police and SD then gave a brief review of the struggle which had been waged hitherto against these opponents. The basic elements were

(*a*) the exclusion of the Jews from the individual spheres of German life,

(*b*) the exclusion of the Jews from the living space of the German people.

In pursuit of these efforts, the acceleration of the emigration of Jews from the Reich territory was increased and systematically adopted as provisionally the only feasible solution.

In January 1939, on the orders of the Reich Marshal, a Reich Central Office for Jewish emigration was established and the Chief of the Security Police and SD was appointed to head it. Its main tasks were

(*a*) to take all measures necessary to *prepare* for an increase in emigration.

(*b*) to *direct* the flow of emigration

(*c*) to speed up the implementation of emigration in particular cases.

The objective was to purge Germany's living space of Jews in a legal fashion.

The disadvantages of such a policy of forced emigration were clear to all the authorities involved. However, they had to be tolerated in view of the lack of alternative solutions.

Subsequently, coping with emigration was not simply a German problem but also a problem with which the countries to which the Jews were emigrating also had to deal. The financial difficulties, such as those caused by the increase in the visa and landing fees by the various foreign governments, the lack of berths on ships, growing restrictions on immigration or even total bans greatly complicated the efforts to emigrate. Despite these difficulties, during the period from the takeover of power (30.1.1933) to 31 October 1941 a total of around 537,000 Jews have been persuaded to emigrate:

From 30 January 1933 from Germany	*c.* 360,000
From 15 March 1938 from the *Ostmark*	*c.* 147,000
From 15 March 1939 from the Protectorate of Bohemia and Moravia	*c.* 30,000

The financing of the emigration was undertaken by the Jews or rather Jewish political organizations themselves. To avoid the proletarianized Jews remaining behind, the principle was followed that the wealthy Jews had to finance the emigration of the propertyless Jews; an appropriate emigration fee was laid down, graded according to wealth, which was used to pay for the financial costs of the emigration of propertyless Jews.

In addition to the Reichsmark agreement, foreign exchange was necessary to pay for the visa and landing fees. In order to protect the German foreign exchange reserves, foreign Jewish financial institutions were requested by our domestic Jewish organizations to ensure the provision of sufficient foreign exchange. Around

9,500,000 dollars had been donated by these foreign Jews up to 30 October 1941.

Meanwhile, in view of the dangers involved in emigration during the war, and in view of the opportunities provided by the east, the *Reichsführer SS* and Chief of the German Police has banned emigration.

III. The evacuation of the Jews to the east has now emerged, with the prior permission of the Führer, as a further possible solution instead of emigration.

These actions, however, must be regarded only as an alternative solution. But already the practical experience is being gathered which is of great importance to the coming final solution of the Jewish question.

Around 11 million Jews come into consideration for this final solution of the European Jewish question who are distributed among the individual countries as follows:

	Country	Number
A.	Altreich [Germany pre-1938]	131,800
	Ostmark [Austria]	43,700
	Eastern territories [incorporated from Poland]	420,000
	General Government	2,284,000
	Bialystok [White Russia]	400,000
	Protectorate of Bohemia and Moravia	74,200
	ESTONIA—Free of Jews	
	Latvia	3,500
	Lithuania	34,000
	Belgium	43,000
	Denmark	5,600
	France, occupied territory	165,000
	unoccupied territory	700,000
	Greece	69,600
	Netherlands	160,000
	Norway	1,300
B.	Bulgaria	48,000
	England	330,000
	Finland	2,300
	Ireland	4,000
	Italy, including Sardinia	58,000
	Albania	200
	Croatia	40,000
	Portugal	3,000
	Romania. incl. Bessarabia	342,000
	Sweden	8,000
	Switzerland	18,000
	Serbia	10,000
	Slovakia	88,000
	Spain	6,000
	Turkey (europ. part)	55,500
	Hungary	742,800
	USSR	5,000,000
	Ukraine	2,994,684
	White Russia. excl. Bialystok	446,484
		Total: over 11,000,000

However, the numbers of Jews in the various countries refer only to those of Jewish faith, since the definition of Jews according to racial principles does not exist in some of them. Certain difficulties will be met in dealing with the problem in the individual countries in view of the general behaviour and attitude towards it, particularly in Hungary and Romania. Thus, for example, a Jew in Romania can still pay for documents which will officially confirm he is a foreign national.

The influence of the Jews in all spheres of the Soviet Union is well-known. There are some 5 million living in the European part, in the Asiatic part just under ½ million Jews.

The employment structure of the Jews living in the territory of the USSR was roughly as follows:

in agriculture	9.1%
as urban workers	14.8%
in commerce	20.0%
employed as state workers	23.4%
in the private professions—medicine, the press, theatre etc.	32.7%

In pursuance of the final solution, the Jews will be conscripted for labour in the east under appropriate supervision. Large labour gangs will be formed from those fit for work, with the sexes separated, which will be sent to these areas for road construction and undoubtedly a large number of them will drop out through natural wastage. The remainder who survive—and they will certainly be those who have the greatest powers of endurance—will have to be dealt with accordingly. For, if released, they would, as a natural selection of the fittest, form a germ cell from which the Jewish race could regenerate itself. (That is the lesson of history.)

In the process of carrying out the final solution, Europe will be combed through from west to east. The Reich territory, including the Protectorate of Bohemia and Moravia, will have to be dealt with first, if only because of the accommodation problem and other socio-political requirements.

The evacuated Jews will initially be brought in stages to so-called transit ghettos in order to be transported from there further east.

An important precondition for carrying out the evacuation was, SS *Obergruppenführer* Heydrich continued, the precise definition of the group of persons involved.

It is intended not to evacuate Jews over 65 years of age, but to transfer them to an old people's ghetto—Theresienstadt is envisaged.

In addition to this age group—of those roughly 280,000 Jews remaining in the *Altreich* and the *Ostmark* on 31 October 1941 around 30 per cent are over 65 years old—the war-disabled Jews and Jews with war decorations (Iron Cross First Class) will also be admitted to the Jewish old people's ghettos. This expedient solution will put an end to the numerous interventions at one stroke.

The timing for the start of the individual large-scale evacuation actions will be largely dependent on military developments. As far as dealing with the final solution in those European territories occupied or influenced by us is concerned, it was suggested that the desk officers of the Foreign Minister would liaise with the desk officers of the Security Police and SD.

In Slovakia and Croatia the matter is no longer all that difficult since the vital core issues in this respect have already been resolved there. In Romania the government has meanwhile also appointed someone to be responsible for Jewish affairs. In order to deal with the question in Hungary, it will shortly be necessary to impose an adviser for Jewish questions on the Hungarian government.

With regard to the initiation of preparations for dealing with the problem in Italy SS *Obergruppenführer* Heydrich considers liaison with the Police Chief over these matters to be appropriate.

In occupied and unoccupied France the registration of the Jews for evacuation will probably go ahead without too great difficulties.

Under-State Secretary Luther comments that if this problem is dealt with thoroughly then difficulties will arise in some countries, for example in the nordic countries, and it would therefore be advisable to exclude these countries for the time being. In view of the small numbers of Jews involved there, this postponement would not in any case represent a significant restriction. On the other hand, the Foreign Ministry does not envisage any great difficulties with the south-east and west of Europe.

SS *Gruppenführer* Hofmann intends to send a representative of the Race and Settlement Main Office to Hungary for the purpose of general orientation when things are set in motion there by the Chief of the Security Police and SD. It was agreed that this representative of the Race and Settlement Main Office, who should not play an active role, would be provisionally officially assigned to the police attaché as an aide.

IV. The Nuremberg Laws would form, so to speak, the basis for carrying out the final solution project and the solving of the mixed marriages and *Mischling* questions is a precondition for the comprehensive resolution of this problem.

The Chief of the Security Police and SD discusses with reference to a letter from the Chief of the Reich Chancellery, to begin with hypothetically, the following points:

1. Treatment of the Mischlinge 1. degree.

Mischlinge 1. degree are to be treated as Jews for the purpose of the final solution. The following will be excluded from this treatment.

(*a*) *Mischlinge* 1. degree married to persons of German blood from whose marriage children (Mischlinge 2. degree) have been born. These *Mischlinge* 2. degree will essentially be treated as Germans.

(*b*) *Mischlinge* 1. degree who have been granted exemptions in certain spheres of life by the highest organs of the Party and State. Each individual case must be carefully examined and the possibility that the decision may this time go against the *Mischling* cannot be excluded.

The precondition for an exemption must always be the fundamental personal merits of the *Mischling* in question (not the merits of the parent of German blood or the marriage partner).

The *Mischlinge* 1. degree who are exempted from evacuation will be sterilised in order to forestall any offspring and to resolve finally the *Mischling* problem. The sterilisation will be voluntary. It will, however, be a precondition for remaining in the Reich. The sterilised *Mischling* will then be freed from all restrictions to which he has hitherto been subjected.

2. Treatment of Mischlinge 2. degree.

The *Mischlinge* 2. degree will be treated as Germans as a matter of principle with the exception of the following cases in which the *Mischlinge* 2. degree will be placed on a par with the Jews.

(*a*) If the *Mischling* 2. degree is the offspring of a bastard marriage (both partners *Mischlinge*).

(*b*) A particularly unfavourable racial appearance of the *Mischling* 2. degree which gives him the outward appearance of a Jew.

(*c*) A particularly poor police and political assessment of the *Mischling* 2. degree which makes it clear that he feels and behaves like a Jew.

In these cases, however, exceptions should not be made even if the *Mischling* 2. degree is married to a person of German blood.

3. Marriages between full Jews and persons of German blood.

The decision on whether the Jewish partner should be evacuated or sent to an old people's ghetto must be decided from case to case depending on the effects of such a measure on the German relatives of this mixed marriage.

4. Marriages between Mischlinge 1. degree and persons of German blood

(*a*) Without children.

If the marriage has not produced any children, the *Mischling* 1. degree will be evacuated or transferred to an old people's ghetto. (Same treatment as with marriages between full Jews and persons of German blood. Point 3)

(*b*) With children.

If the marriage has produced children (*Mischlinge* 2. degree), in the event of their being treated as Jews they will be evacuated together with the Mischling 1. degree or transferred to a ghetto. In the event of these children being treated as persons of German blood (normal case), they are to be exempted from the evacuation as is the *Mischling* 1. degree as well.

5. Marriages between Mischlinge 1. degree or Mischlinge 2. degree and Jews.

In the case of these marriages, all parties, including the children, will be treated as Jews and therefore evacuated or transferred to a ghetto.

6. Marriages between Mischlinge 1. degree and Mischlinge 2. degree.

Both partners will be evacuated or transferred to an old people's ghetto irrespective of whether or not there are children, since such children generally display a stronger Jewish element than the Jewish *Mischlinge* 2. degree

SS *Gruppenführer* Hofmann maintains that extensive use must be made of sterilization, particularly since if the *Mischling* is offered the choice of evacuation or sterilization he will prefer to undergo sterilization.

State Secretary Stuckart argues that the proposed solution for resolving the mixed marriage and *Mischling* problems, if implemented in practice in this form, would produce endless administrative work. On the other hand, in order to take the biological factors into account, State Secretary Stuckart proposed the adoption of compulsory sterilisation [i.e. instead of evacuation for these cases].

In order to simplify the *Mischling* problem one ought also to contemplate ways by which the legislator might say, for example: 'these marriages are dissolved'.

With respect to the impact of the Jewish evacuation on economic life, State Secretary Neumann stated that those Jews who were working in plants essential to the war effort could not be evacuated so long as replacements were not available.

SS *Obergruppenführer* Heydrich pointed out that, according to the guidelines for the current evacuation actions approved by him, these Jews were not being evacuated.

State Secretary Dr Bühler stated that the General Government would welcome it if the final solution of this question could begin in the General Government because the transport problem did not play a pre-eminent role here and labour factors would not hinder this operation. Jews should be removed from the territory of the General Government as quickly as possible because here in particular the

Jew represented a significant threat as a carrier of epidemics and also, through systematic black market activities, was continually bringing the economic structure of the country into disorder. Moreover, the majority of the roughly two and a half million Jews in question were incapable of work.

State Secretary Bühler stated further that the Chief of the Security Police and SD was directly responsible for the solution of the Jewish question in the General Government and his work would be supported by the authorities of the General Government. He only had one request—that the Jewish question in this area should be solved as soon as possible.

In conclusion, various types of solutions were discussed and both Gauleiter Dr Meyer and State Secretary Dr Bühler expressed the view that certain preparatory work for the final solution should be carried out within the relevant territories themselves, though without upsetting the population.

After a request from the Chief of the Security Police and SD to the participants to provide him with appropriate support in carrying out the solution, the meeting was closed.

The minutes of the Wannsee conference were euphemistically circumscribed since they would have a relatively wide circulation—30 copies were circulated to government departments and SS head offices. However, those attending the conference could have had no doubt about the fact that the 'final solution' involved the 'evacuation' of the Jews to the east and then their extermination, one way or the other. Most of the fit would be worked to death in 'labour gangs', with those who survived being 'dealt with accordingly', i.e. liquidated; the fate of the unfit was not mentioned directly, but the implication was clear: they were to be massacred straight away.

On the question of the numbers and locations of European Jewry, Eichmann's office in the RSHA, IV B 4 had clearly done its homework and already formed a fairly clear idea of the political feasibility of such a programme within the various countries involved, with the Foreign Ministry eagerly offering advice.

On the question of the criteria for defining the group to be deported, and this was clearly of particular importance to Heydrich, final decisions were not reached. Further inconclusive conferences were held on the question of those in mixed marriages and the *Mischlinge*, and the outcome of this failure to reach a decision was that the overwhelming majority of the *Mischlinge* and Jews in mixed marriages were not deported. The *Mischlinge* were saved because officials in the Reich Interior Ministry managed to stall the issue and Hitler declined to support the SS and the Party Chancellery. This was almost certainly because he did not think pursuing the matter was worth the discontent it would cause among the Aryan relatives of those involved. Unfortunately, the saving of the *Mischlinge* simply made it easier to deport the Jews; they had no lobby to support them either in the bureaucracy or within the German population.

A total of 139,654 'privileged' Jews were sent to the 'old people's ghetto, which was created in Theresienstadt in Czechoslovakia, of whom 73,608 came from the Protectorate, 42,832 from Germany, and 15,254 from Austria. Most of the remainder came from Holland, Slovakia, and Denmark. By the end of the war only 17,320 were left. The vast majority had either been shipped to Auschwitz for extermination or had died in the camp where conditions were poor.[21]

At the end of the conference the question of 'various types of solution' were discussed. No doubt Dr Lange, the chief of the *Einsatzkommando* operations in Latvia contributed his own experiences. Under interrogation by the Israelis in 1960, Eichmann was rather franker about this aspect of the conference than he was in his minutes:

850

What I know is that the gentlemen sat together, and then in very blunt terms—not in the language that I had to use in the minutes, but in very blunt terms—they talked about the matter without any circumlocution. I certainly could not have remembered that if I had not recalled saying to myself at the time: look, just look at Stuckart, who was always regarded as a legal pedant, punctilious and fussy, and now what a different tone! The language being used here was very unlegalistic. I should say that this is the only thing from all this that has still stuck clearly in my mind.

Presiding Judge: What did he say on this matter?
Answer: In particular, Mr President, I would like to . . .
Question: Not in particular—in general!
Answer: The talk was of killing, elimination, and annihilation.

On 30 January 1942, in the course of his annual major address to the Reichstag on the anniversary of his appointment as Reich Chancellor, Hitler made the following statement:

851

We are clear about the fact that the war can only end either in the extermination of the Aryan nations or in the disappearance of Jewry from Europe. On 1 September 1939,[22] I already announced in the German Reichstag—and I avoid making prema-

[21] See R. Hilberg, *op. cit.* pp. 283 ff.

[22] Hitler actually made this statement on 30 January 1939 but significantly post-dates it here to the outbreak of war. See above p. 1049 (eds).

ture prophecies—that this would not end as the Jews imagined, namely with the extermination of the European-Aryan nations, but rather that the war will result in the destruction of Jewry. This time, for the first time, the old and typical Jewish law will be applied 'An eye for an eye, a tooth for a tooth'.

And the more the fighting spreads, the more—and world Jewry should take note of it—antisemitism will spread. It will find nourishment in every prisoner of war camp, in every family which becomes aware of the reason why it has had to make its sacrifice. And the hour will come when *the most evil enemy of the world of all time* will for at least a thousand years have played his last role.

The process by which total extermination replaced resettlement in Madagascar or 'the East' as the so-called 'final solution of the Jewish question' remains unclear. No written order by Hitler for the extermination of the Jews has been discovered and the evidence of an oral order is only indirect. The chronology of the development of the extermination programme is also confused. The first phase is characterised by apparently haphazard initiatives by various individuals and offices suggesting a large measure of improvisation rather than the implementation of a coherent plan. The only element of coordination appears to have come from Eichmann's office in the RSHA (IV B 4) which was primarily concerned with the deportation process. Not until the spring of 1942 had the extermination programme been turned into a quasi-industrial process for the most efficient destruction and disposal of human beings on a mass scale. Nevertheless, the fact that a number of different extermination initiatives emerged more or less simultaneously in the second half of 1941 suggests that a green light was coming from the highest level for extermination as the final solution of the Jewish question. We have already considered one of these initiatives—the extension of the *Einsatzgruppen* massacres from Russian to German and Austrian Jews. It remains to consider the other three: the setting up of Chełmno (Kulmhof) extermination camp in the Warthegau, the establishment of the 'Reinhard Action' death camps in the General Government, and the development of Auschwitz–Birkenau in Upper Silesia as an extermination camp.

CHAPTER 39

The Extermination Camps

Although the massacre of Jews by shooting proved highly effective in terms of the large numbers killed, it had distinct disadvantages as a method of mass murder. First, such executions were difficult to conceal and were witnessed by large numbers of unauthorized persons; they sometimes produced complaints from the military, not so much out of sympathy with the Jews as from concern about the morale of the troops. The massacres of German Jews in Riga and Kovno, for example, had caused a stir. Secondly, such massacres produced considerable psychological stress among the participants, which could not always be overcome by the consumption of large amounts of alcohol which was the normal method. What was needed was a method of execution which could liquidate large numbers of people quickly, discreetly, and as anonymously as possible.

Himmler was well aware of this situation; indeed, he himself had nearly fainted when he had insisted on witnessing a mass execution near Minsk in August 1941 and had commented that mass shooting was evidently not the most rational or 'humane' method of exterminating hundreds of thousands of Jews. He asked Artur Nebe, the head of the Reich Criminal Police Department and currently chief of *Einsatzgruppe* B, which had carried out the execution, whether explosives or gas might not be more effective.[1]

[1] See H. Krausnick and H. H. Wilhelm, *op. cit.* p. 543.

(i) The Gas Vans and Chełmno (Kulmhof) Extermination Camp

Gas was indeed to prove the most effective method. It began, however, with a rather crude process involving the use of so-called 'gas vans'. Gas vans had already been used in the course of the 'euthanasia' programme in 1940 in Poland. However, the process had involved the use of cylinders of carbon monoxide and now the transport of these over the long distances and often difficult terrain of the Soviet Union was considered to raise insuperable problems. Some other method was required. The post-war judgment of a Stuttgart court in the trial of Dr Albert Widmann of the RSHA's Criminal Technical Institute (KTI) described how this new method was initiated:

852

. . . After only a brief period, the commandos of the *Einsatzgruppen* got into considerable difficulties. The members of the *Einsatz-* and special commandos, some of whom were themselves fathers, were in the long run not up to the mental strain caused by the mass shootings, particularly when women and children were involved. There were disputes, refusals to obey orders, drunken orgies, but also serious psychological illnesses. Himmler, who was not unaware of the situation, was looking for a way of reducing the nervous psychological strain on the men involved in the shooting. Thus, in discussions with Heydrich and other leading figures the plan emerged of utilising gas vans for this purpose, which were to be used for the liquidation of women and children in particular . . . In September or October 1941, the head of Department IID in the RSHA, SS *Obersturmbannführer* [Walter] Rauff was ordered by Heydrich to build gas vans . . . After abortive attempts by [Friedrich] Pradel [the head of the transport department IID 3a] to acquire such vehicles, five Saurer vans were secured, probably by Rauff himself. Following various preliminary discussions, the vehicles were sent to Gaubschat & Co. of Berlin to be converted. To start with, they used one vehicle as a prototype and built an airtight van frame about two metres wide and five metres long following the exact measurements provided by Pradel and Wentritt [the foreman of Pradel's workshop] . . . Inside, the van frame was coated with galvanised tin and provided with light fittings in the top corners protected by iron grilles. A wooden grid was placed on the floor. The driver's cabin was separated from the van but connected through a small observation window. Outside, the vehicle was painted battle grey . . . After completion, Wentritt collected the prototype van and, following instructions, used his own technical expertise to make the following alterations: He cut the exhaust pipe behind the engine and inserted a T-joint into it. Then, he bored a hole in the floor of the van about 50–60 mm wide through which he introduced a nozzle into the inside of the van. The nozzle was welded in place and a U-shaped pipe was joined on to it inside the van. This pipe was perforated at regular intervals. When required, all that was now necessary was to establish a connection between the T-joint in the exhaust and the nozzle in the floor of the van, both of which had a thread, by means of a hose which could be screwed on, and to close the exhaust with a cap. Then, without any difficulty, one could feed the exhaust fumes, which were produced by running the motor, through the nozzle into the pipe and from there into the interior of the van. The grid on the floor both concealed the gas supply and facilitated the rapid cleaning of the vehicle after use. Wentritt reported the completion of the prototype to his superior Pradel, who ordered him to drive the van personally to the KTI and report there in order for air samples to be taken . . . Some time later, Dr Heeß ordered his colleagues, Dr Leidig and Dr Hoffmann to participate in the testing of this first vehicle in Sachsenhausen concentration camp . . .

In fact, the van was first tested on Russian prisoners of war in Sachsenhausen in the autumn of 1941.

The first gas van was deployed in Russia in December 1941 and over the next three years some fifteen were used by the *Einsatzgruppen* in the Soviet Union. Although many thousands of Jews and Russians fell victim to them, in fact they were not popular with SS personnel since they proved if anything even more unpleasant to operate than mass executions by shooting, which remained the main method of liquidating the Jews in the Soviet Union.

Gas vans were, however, used in the first extermination centre which was established by the Germans in the village of Chełmno (renamed Kulmhof) in the Warthegau. Chełmno had a population of some 250, mainly Poles, and was situated on the river Ner, a tributary of the Warthe, some fifty-five kilometres from Łódź. The centre appears to have been established in response to pressure from Artur Greiser, Gauleiter of the Warthegau, to clear his Gau of Jews, pressure which had intensified as a result of the deportation of 20,000 German Jews and 5,000 Gypsies to the Łódź ghetto between 14 October and 5 November 1941. Himmler had initially assumed the Łódź ghetto would be a transit camp for the German Jews on their way 'to the east'. However, he evidently soon gave up this idea and agreed to a more drastic measure, which had already been mooted in the Warthegau in the summer.[2]

At the end of October/beginning of November, the first unit of a special commando under SS *Hauptsturmführer* Herbert Lange arrived in Chełmno. Lange had been in charge of the 'euthanasia' gas vans of 1940 and so had the requisite experience. The commando took over a mansion in the village as the extermination centre, and a large clearing in the forest, some four kilometres from the village with easy access to the road, as the site for the mass graves.

[2] See above p. 1113.

By the beginning of December, they were ready for the first transport of Jews which arrived in lorries on 5 December 1941. By now the commando consisted of some fifteen Security Police and around eighty order police who had been transferred from the police battalion in Łódź and who carried out guard duties. In a post-war statement, Kurt Möbius, a member of the 'Special Commando Kulmhof' described what happened to the Jews when they arrived:

853

When the Jews had been driven in lorries into the mansion area, they waited for a time in the yard. Here they listened to a speech by Plate or me. They were told that they were going to a large camp in Austria where they would have to work. But beforehand, they were told, they would have to take a bath and their clothes be disinfected. These speeches were held by Plate and me so that the Jews remained uncertain about the fate that was in store for them and so that they would calmly obey instructions. After this address the Jewish people (men, women and children) were led into the ground floor of the mansion . . . The Jews went via a flight of steps into a straight passage at the end of which was a door which led into two inter-connecting rooms. Here the Jewish people undressed—they were not separated into sexes—under my supervision. They had already had to give up their valuables; these were collected in baskets by the Polish workers. There was a door in the passage which led to the cellar. On it was a sign: 'To the bath'. A group of 35–40 persons at a time was led into the gas vans. From the door in the passage a staircase led down to the cellar where there was a passage which at first went straight ahead but then, after a few metres, was cut off by another passage at right angles to it. Here the people had to turn right and go up a ramp where the gas vans parked with their doors open. The ramp was tightly enclosed with a wooden fence up to the doors of the gas van. Usually, the Jewish people went quickly and obediently into the gas van trusting the promises which had been made to them. The Polish workers accompanied the people. They carried leather whips with which they hit any Jews who had become mistrustful and hesitated to go in.

There were three vans, two of which were permanently in action and one occasionally. After the war, Gustav Laabs, who was employed to drive one of the vans, described his first experience of the extermination process:

854

. . . After [Hans] Bothmann had ended his speech, the people were led into the mansion—to the ground floor. I cannot say what rooms there were on the ground floor because I never went inside the mansion. I forgot to mention that Bothmann said in his speech that the people would have to undress inside the mansion. Shortly afterwards, Bürstinger came over to me and ordered me to back the van which had been assigned to me up to a ramp which was on the side of the mansion looking out towards the park. This ramp led down into a cellar passage of the mansion. On two sides it was protected from view and secured by a 2.5 metre high wooden fence. The open side was closed off by the van which I had to drive up to the ramp . . . After the rear doors had been opened there was a completely enclosed space on the ramp which could not be looked into and from which no one could escape either. I stayed in the cab of the van which Bothmann had assigned to me. Bürstinger left the ramp through the cellar passage. I now sat in the cab of the van racking my brians as to what was going to happen next. But I couldn't make head or tail of it. After Bothmann's speech I assumed that Hering and I were going to drive the people to bathe, but I was sceptical because I had not seen any bathing place in the village. I talked to Hering about it but we couldn't work out what was going to happen to the people. After about half and hour I heard loud shouts from the cellar passage and then I saw in the van mirror that people in bare feet were running up the ramp into my van. I couldn't see the people themselves but I could see the naked feet running through a gap between the right door of my van and the ramp. From this I assumed that the people were naked. I gathered that they had entered my van from the fact that it shook. When the inside was full of people, the rear doors were evidently shut by Bürstinger and locked with a padlock since he then hung the key up in the cab. I then saw Bürstinger order a Polish civilian to bend down under the van and do something there. At that point I didn't know what it was.

Then Bothmann, who had also come through the cellar passage, came up to me and ordered me to start the engine and let it run for ten minutes. I carried out this order and after about a minute I heard terrible cries and groans from inside the van. I got scared and leapt from the cab. Now I understood that the exhaust fumes had been fed into the inside of the van to kill the people. Bothmann then snapped at me asking if I'd gone mad. He ordered me to get behind the steering wheel again. I sat behind the wheel again and waited. I didn't dare do anything because I was afraid of Bothmann. After a few minutes the cries and groans of the people gradually died away. After about ten minutes when a police officer had sat down next to me, Bothmann ordered me to drive off . . .

As I said, I then drove off with the van on Bothmann's orders. The policeman sitting beside me told me where I had to go. After about three kilometres we drove into a clearing in a forest which stretched alongside the road to Warthebrücken. Having arrived at the clearing the policeman ordered me to stop at a mass grave at which a work detail composed of Jewish people was working. There were also some policemen who were spread out in a circle and evidently on guard. The policeman who was in charge of the work detail ordered me to back up to the mass grave. I do not know who this policeman was any more. Then, the policeman who had travelled with me opened the padlock securing the doors. Some of the members of the work detail were then ordered to open the rear doors. After this had been done 8–10 bodies fell out of the van onto the ground. The remaining bodies were then thrown out of the inside of the van. After the van had been emptied, I drove back to the mansion in Kulmhof. On the way I met Hering with his van which evidently also contained a considerable number of bodies. I can say that in the gas van—afterwards this was the usual term—driven by me about fifty people had been gassed. Hering's van would probably have contained the same number of people. Having returned to the mansion, some Jews who presumably belonged to the work detail in the mansion, had to clean the inside of the vehicle with water and disinfectant. For this purpose they also had to take out the wooden grids from the floor of the van . . . After the van had been cleaned and the grids put back, the police official named Heinl, whom I've already mentioned, ordered me to drive to the ramp again. The same process which I have just described in detail was repeated.

Between 5 December 1941 and mid-January 1942, Jews from the surrounding district in the Warthegau were rounded up and transported to Chełmno. From 16 January until the end of May 1942 at least 55,000 Jews from the nearby Łódź ghetto were gassed as well as 5,000 Gypsies. Greiser's aim was to concentrate all those Jews who were fit for work in the so-called 'Gau ghetto' in Łódź, while all those from Łódź and the Warthegau who were considered unfit for work were to be sent to Chełmno. This is clear from the following report of the Gestapo in Łódź of 9 June 1942:

855

As regard the Jews, the work of the state police was focused on the Gau ghetto which, on the instructions of the Gauleiter, was to be created in Litzmannstadt [Łódź]. On the instructions of the Gauleiter, all Jews not fit for work were to be evacuated and all those fit for work in the whole Gau were to be concentrated in the Litzmannstadt ghetto. Then, large numbers of Jews would be sent out from here to carry out various jobs (rail and road building) and, after completing the work, would be returned to the ghetto. Those Jews remaining in the ghetto would all be put to work there. In the process of constructing the Gau ghetto, it first proved necessary to create space for those Jews who were to be brought in. For this purpose a large number of Jews who were unfit for work were evacuated from the ghetto and transferred to the special commando [i.e. Chełmno]. Of the Polish Jews 44,152 have been evacuated since 16.1.42. Of those 19,848 Jews from Germany Austria, and the Protectorate who were assigned to the ghetto here in October [1941], 10,993 have been evacuated so that now space had been created in the ghetto for c. 55,000 Jews. Following on from this, the focus shifted to clearing the country districts . . . As a provisional conclusion to the clearing of the country districts, the town of Pabianice has been cleared of Jews. Around 3,200 Jews were evacuated, the remaining 4,000 Jews were transferred to the ghetto here.

Early in 1943, the gassing in Chełmno stopped and in March the mansion was dynamited and, at the beginning of April, the special commando left Chełmno. Early in 1944, however, it was decided to liquidate the remnant of the Łódź ghetto and, in April 1944, Bothmann returned with his commando which had been specially reassembled for the purpose. New barracks and a crematorium were constructed in the forest camp and the same extermination process began again. From 23 June–mid-July 1944 ten transports of Jews arrived from Łódź and were gassed despite an intervention by Speer who wanted to retain valuable Jewish armaments workers. From August onwards, however, the few remaining Jews from the Warthegau were sent to Auschwitz and, on 17–18 January, the remaining members of the Jewish work detail were shot. It has been estimated that during the first phase from 5 December 1941–early January 1943 some 145,301 Jews, Gypsies, Poles, and Russians were gassed, the vast majority being Jews. In the second phase from 23 June–14 July 1944 some 7,176 were gassed in Chełmno.

(ii) The 'Reinhard Action'

(a) The Death Camps—Belzec, Sobibor and Treblinka

The Chełmno extermination centre had been geared to liquidating the Jews in the Warthegau. However, the vast majority of Polish Jews, including many who had been deported or fled from the Warthegau in the years 1939–41, were in the General Government—a total of around 2.3 million.

At the Wannsee conference in January 1942, Dr Bühler had requested that the final solution of the Jewish question should begin in the General Government. In fact, preparations were already being made to achieve this goal. Such a massive undertaking, however, required elaborate organization as well as effective machinery for mass murder. As far as the latter was concerned, a pool of expertise lay ready to hand in the personnel of the 'euthanasia' programme, most of whom had been transferred to other duties since the official ending of the programme in August 1941. Brack was clearly anxious to secure a new role for the T4 organization and, in the autumn of 1941, he had offered to help with setting up a programme for gassing Jews in the Soviet Union. On 25 October, Dr Wetzel, the Advisor on Jewish Affairs with the Reich Ministry for Eastern Territories drafted the following letter from his minister, Alfred Rosenberg, to Hinrich Lohse, the Reich Commissioner of *Ostland* 're: the solution of the Jewish question':

856

With reference to my letter of 18 October 1941, I wish to inform you that *Oberdienstleiter* Brack of the Führer's Chancellery has agreed to assist in the construction of the necessary buildings and gassing apparatus. At the moment, the suitable apparatus is not available in sufficient quantity and so it must first be built. Brack considers that since construction of the apparatus within the Reich would create far more difficulties than production on site, the most appropriate course of action is for him to send his people straight to Riga, in particular his chemist, Dr Kallmeyer, who will set things in motion from there. *Oberdienstleiter* Brack points out that the method envisaged is not without danger and thus special safety precautions will be required. In these circumstances I would ask you to contact *Oberdienstleiter* Brack in the Führer's Chancellery through your Higher SS and Police Leader and request the secondment of the chemist Dr Kallmeyer, and such other assistants as you may require. Furthermore, I would like to point out that *Sturmbannführer* Eichmann, the desk officer for Jewish Affairs in the Reich Security Main Office, is in complete agreement with this procedure. According to *Sturmbannführer* Eichmann, camps for Jews will be set up in Riga and in Minsk, to which Jews from Germany [the *Altreich*] may also be sent. At the moment Jews are being evacuated from Germany to Litzmannstadt [Łódź] and other camps from where those fit for work will be transferred for use as labour in the East. In the present situation, there are no objections to getting rid of Jews who are unable to work with the Brack remedy. Incidents such as those that took place during the shootings of Jews in Vilna, according to a report I have received, can hardly be tolerated, in view of the fact that the executions took place in public, and the new procedures will ensure that such incidents will no longer be possible.[3] On the other hand, Jews who are fit for work will be transported further east for use as labour. It is clear that men and women in this latter group must be kept apart from one another. Please report to me about any further measures you may take.

In fact, there is no evidence that any such gassing programme was implemented in the Soviet Union other than the gas vans already referred to. The problems of transporting large numbers of Jews to Russia and dealing with them when they arrived soon made themselves felt. Those responsible for the Jewish question rapidly came to the conclusion that it made more sense to transport German and other Jews to Poland and to liquidate the Polish Jews on the spot rather than to send them further East to an area which was after all adjacent to a battle zone. After the war, Brack made the following statement:

[3] During July 1941, thousands of Jews had been slaughtered in Vilna by Lithuanian auxiliaries (eds).

857

In 1941 I received the order to halt the euthanasia programme. In order to keep the personnel employed, and also in the light of the need for an EP after the war, Bouhler ordered me—I think it was after a conference with Himmler—to send the personnel to Lublin and place it under the supervision of SS *Brigadeführer* Globocnik.

The Odilo Globocnik referred to by Brack was the SS and Police Leader in Lublin. Himmler had a high regard for 'Globus's' abilities and had placed him in his debt by appointing him to the Lublin post in November 1939 after his dismissal as Gauleiter of Vienna for currency offences. Sometime in the early autumn of 1941, Himmler ordered Globocnik to organize the extermination of Jews in the General Government, an operation which later became known as the 'Reinhard Action' in honour of Reinhard Heydrich who was assassinated by Czech partisans on 27 May 1942.[4]

The first task facing Globocnik was to find appropriate sites and a suitable technique for extermination. Initially, it appears that the aim was to exterminate those Polish Jews in the Lublin area who were unfit for work, thereby making room for Jews deported from Germany and elsewhere. These too would then be selected into the fit and the unfit. The unfit would be exterminated at once like their Polish fellows, while the fit would be exploited and would gradually be eliminated through 'natural wastage' and periodic selections for extermination. That this was the initial policy, one which was in line with Heydrich's statement at the Wannsee Conference, is suggested by the following document. It contains excerpts from a minute written by Fritz Reuter, the desk officer responsible for population matters in the office of the governor of the district of Lublin, concerning a conversation with SS *Hauptsturmführer* Hans Höfle, Globocnik's chief of staff. It is dated 17 March 1942:

858

. . . I arranged a meeting with Hstuf Höfle for Monday 16 March 1942 at 17.30. In the course of our conversation Hstuf Höfle made the following points:

1. It would be a good idea to divide the Jewish transports arriving in the district of Lublin into those Jews who are fit for work and those who are not and to do so at the station of departure. If this separation is not possible at the station of departure, then one might have to start dividing the transport in Lublin in accordance with the above criteria.

[4] Heydrich died on 4 June 1942.

2. Jews who are not fit for work will all go to Belzec, the furthest frontier station in the district of Zamość.

3. Hstuf Höfle is in the process of building a large camp in which Jews who are fit for work can be registered on a card index file and requested from there[5] . . .

Finally, he declared that he could take 4–5 transports of 1,000 Jews each per day with Belzec as the destination. These Jews would cross the frontier and would never return to the General Government.

Belzec was the site chosen for the first extermination camp. It was a small town in the south-east of the district of Lublin on the railway line Zamość–Rawa–Ruska–Lemberg-[Lvov]. After the war, a Pole, Stanisław Kozak described its beginnings as follows:

859

In October 1941, three SS men arrived in Belzec and demanded twenty workers from Belzec council. The council detailed twenty workers from the inhabitants of Belzec of whom I was one. The Germans selected the area south-east of the railway station and which was adjacent to a siding. It is on the line to Lemberg [Lvov]. We began work on 1 November by building barracks on the piece of land adjacent to the siding . . . After we had built the three barracks which I have described, the Germans dismissed us Poles on 22 December 1941.

The camp was situated five hundred metres from the station on a siding. The south side was two hundred metres long, the three other sides were each two hundred and fifty metres in length. It was divided into two parts: Camp I on the north-west side contained the reception area with two barracks—one for undressing and where the women had their hair shorn and the other one for storing clothes and luggage. Camp II contained the gas chambers and mass graves on the east and north-east side and two barracks for the Jewish work details, one as living quarters and one containing a kitchen. The gas chambers were surrounded by trees and had camouflage nets on the roof. Camps I and II were separated by a wire fence in which there was a gate which was guarded. The barrack for undressing and the gas chambers were linked by a path two metres wide and fifty–seventy metres long, known as the 'tube', which was bordered on both sides by a wire fence into which fir branches were woven. The Jews were herded along this path from the undressing barrack in Camp I to the gas chambers in Camp II. The whole camp was surrounded by a wire fence

[5] This probably refers to Majdanek see below pp. 1189 ff. (eds).

topped with barbed wire and concealed with newly planted conifers. There were four watch towers, two on the east side, one on the south-west side, and one in the centre near the gas chambers. These towers were manned with armed Ukrainian guards, of whom there were around eighty in the camp. These Ukrainians had been trained at Travniki, a special camp near Lublin set up in Autumn 1941 to prepare Ukrainians and ethnic Germans for their role in the Reinhard Action.

During December 1941, Christian Wirth arrived in Belzec to take up the post of commandant of the new camp, together with a group of about ten other 'euthanasia' specialists, including the notorious chemist, Dr Kallmeyer. Their job was to construct the gassing facility and then operate it. Whereas the design of the gas chambers was similar to those used in the 'euthanasia' centres in Germany, the gassing technique was different. Instead of cylinders of carbon monoxide gas, a 250 hp diesel engine from a tank was installed outside the chambers into which the exhaust fumes from the engine were fed. This new technique was both cheaper and avoided the need for a constant supply of CO gas to a remote corner of Poland. It may well have originated from an experiment which had been carried out in September 1941 by Dr Widmann of the KTI in the mental asylum in Mogidew in the Soviet Union. A number of inmates had been gassed there by feeding the exhaust fumes from a police lorry into a hermetically sealed room. This experiment had been carried out in direct reponse to Himmler's request for an alternative method of execution to mass shooting.

The Belzec extermination camp began its operations on 17 March 1942 with a transport of 40–60 goods waggons containing Jews from Lublin. Between then and the end of April, thousands of Jews from the Lublin and Lemberg [Lvov] districts had been exterminated in Belzec. At the end of April or beginning of May, Wirth and the SS personnel suddenly left Belzec and returned to Berlin without informing Globocnik. Then, early in May, Brack visited Globocnik in Lublin. On 23 June 1942, Brack wrote to Himmler as follows:

860

Some time ago, on the instructions of *Reichsleiter* Bouhler, I placed some of my men at the disposal of *Brigadeführer* Globocnik. Following a further request from him, I have transferred additional personnel. *Brigadeführer* Globocnik took the opportunity of expressing the opinion that the whole Jewish action should be carried out as quickly as possible to avoid the danger of one day finding ourselves stuck in the middle of it in the event of difficulties forcing us to halt the action. You yourself, *Reichsführer*, some time ago expressed to me the opinion that we should work as fast as possible if only for reasons of concealment. In my opinion, both views, which after all lead to the same result, are more than justified. Nevertheless, in this context I would be grateful to be permitted to make the following observation: I think there must easily be 2–3 million men and women among the ten million European Jews who are very well capable of working. In view of the extraordinary difficulties which the labour question poses for us, in my opinion we should definitely preserve and make use of these 2–3 million. However, that will only be possible if they are simultaneously sterilised. I already reported to you about a year ago that people working for me have concluded the necessary experiments for this purpose. I would like to remind you of these facts. The kind of sterilization normally carried out on the hereditarily sick is not ˜easible in this instance because it would take up too much time and be too expensive. However, a castration by means of X-rays is not only relatively cheap, but also could be carried out on thousands in a very short time. I think the fact that those affected may become aware that they have been sterilised after a few weeks or months has now become irrelevant.

If, *Reichsführer*, you decide to follow this course of acton in the interests of preserving labour material, then *Reichsleiter* Bouhler is prepared to provide you with the doctors and other personnel required to carry out this work. He has also instructed me to inform you that I will then order the requisite apparatus as soon as possible.

However, Himmler was not primarily interested in Brack's expertise in sterilisation but above all in his T4 personnel's experience in 'euthanasia'.

Wirth returned with his 'euthanasia' personnel in the middle of May and the gassings resumed. From then until the middle of June, thousands of Jews from Cracow were exterminated. In the meantime, however, Wirth had realised that the wooden gas chambers were inadequate and, in the middle of June, he stopped the gassings while the three old chambers were replaced by six new ones doubling the gassing capacity of the camp. After the war, the sole survivor of Belzec, Rudolf Reder, described the new gas chambers as follows:

861

The building was low, long and wide. It was made of grey concrete with a flat felt roof on top of which was netting covered with branches. Three steps without a railing led into the building. They were approximately one metre wide. In front of the building was a large tub with colourful flowers and a clearly visible sign: 'Bathing and inhalation rooms'. The steps led into a dark empty corridor which was very long but only fifteen metres wide. To the left and right of it were the doors to the gas chambers. They were wooden doors one metre wide . . . The corridor and the chambers were lower than normal rooms, no higher then two metres. On the opposite wall of each chamber was a removable door where the bodies of those who had been gassed were thrown out. Outside the building was a shed 2 × 2 metres in size, in which the gas machine was installed. The chambers were 1.5 metres off the ground . . .

In August 1942 one of the gassings at Belzec was witnessed by a young SS officer, Kurt Gerstein. Gerstein was opposed to the regime and had secured the position of the head of the department of health technology in the SS with responsibility for disinfection services in order to investigate the extermination programme and do what he could to sabotage it. He was ordered to visit Belzec to deal with the problem of disinfecting the clothing left by the dead Jews. On 26 May 1945, shortly before committing suicide, he wrote the following account of his experiences during his visit:

862

On 8 June 1942 I received a visit from SS *Sturmführer* Günther of the Reich Security Main Office who was hitherto unknown to me. Günther was wearing civilian clothes. He instructed me to secure 100 kg. of prussic acid for a highly secret Reich operation and to take it in my car to an unknown destination, which was known only to the driver . . . We were accompanied—more or less by chance—by Professor Dr med. Pfannenstiel, SS *Obersturmbannführer* and Professor of Hygiene at the University of Marburg . . .

We then took the car to Lublin where SS Gruppenführer Globocnek [*sic*!] was expecting us . . . Globocnek told us: 'This whole affair is one of the most secret matters there is at the moment, in fact one can say the most secret. Anyone who talks about it will be shot on the spot. Only yesterday two people who gossiped were shot.' Then he explained to us:

'At the moment—that was on 17 August 1942—we have three installations in operation, namely

1. Belzec, on the road and railway line between Lublin and Lemberg (Lvov) and on the edge of the previous [Demarcation] line with Russia. Maximum performance per day: 15,000 persons.[6]
2. Treblinka, 120 kilometres north east of Warsaw. Maximum performance: 25,000 persons per day.
3. Sobibor, also in Poland, I do not know where: 20,000 persons maximum performance per day.
4. Then under construction—Maidanek near Lublin.

I have personally conducted a thorough inspection of Belzec, Treblinka, and Maidanek together with the head of these institutions, Police Captain Wirth.'

[6] This and the subsequent figures are somewhat exaggerated (eds).

Globocnek then turned to me and said: 'Your particular task is disinfecting the large amount of textiles. The whole clothing collection[7] has been carried out to provide an explanation for the origins of the clothing given to the eastern workers etc. and to present it as the result of the self-sacrifice of the German people. In reality, the amount produced by our institutions is 10–20 times that of the whole clothing collection . . .

Your other and far more important task is the conversion of our gas chambers, which at present operate with diesel exhaust gases, to something better and quicker. I am thinking above all of prussic acid. The day before yesterday the Führer and Himmler were here[8] and, on their instructions, I must take you there personally. I am not supposed to give anyone written permits.'

Pfannenstiel then asked: 'What did the Führer say?' Globocnek: 'Speed things up, carry out the whole operation quicker'. His companion, *Ministerialrat* Dr Lindner [Linden][9] then asked: 'Herr Globocnek, do you consider it right and proper to bury all the corpses instead of burning them. A generation might come after us which does not appreciate the whole thing'.

Globocnek replied: 'Gentlemen, if there is ever a generation after us which is so wet and weak-kneed that it does not understand our great task then the whole of National Socialism will have been in vain. On the contrary, in my view bronze tablets ought to be buried, on which is recorded that we had the courage to carry out this great work which is so vital.

The Führer then said: 'You're right, Globocnek, that is my view too!'

Later on, the other view came to be accepted. The corpses were then placed on large pyres, which were improvised with the use of railway lines, and burnt with the help of petrol and diesel oil.

The following day we travelled to Belzec. A small special station had been erected for this purpose on a hill just north of the Lublin–Lemberg (Lvóv) road in the left hand corner of the Demarcation line. South of the road there were some houses with a sign up: 'Special Commando Belzec of the Waffen SS'. Since the real boss of the whole killing installations, Police Captain Wirth, was not yet there, Globocnek introduced me to SS *Hauptsturmführer* Obermeyer [Oberhauser][10] (from Pirmasens). That afternoon he only let me see what he absolutely had to show me. I did not see any dead people that day. However, the smell which hung over the whole area on a hot August day was pestilential and millions of flies were everywhere.

Just next to the small station with two platforms there was a large barrack, the so-called 'Cloak Room', with a large counter for valuables. Then came a room

---

[7] This clothing collection had been organized in Germany in December 1941.to provide warm clothing for the German forces in Russia (eds).

[8] There is no other evidence that Hitler visited Lublin at this time and Globocnik's statements should be treated with extreme scepticism (eds).

[9] Dr Linden was the liaison official between the Reich Interior Ministry and the T4 organization. See above pp. 1010 ff. (eds).

[10] SS *Obersturmführer* Josef Oberhauser was Wirth's second-in-command in Belzec and later, on his appointment as Inspector of the death camps in August 1942, became his adjutant (eds).

with about one hundred chairs, the hairdressing room. Then a small path in the open air under birch trees, enclosed by a double fence of barbed wire to right and left with signs up: 'To the inhalation and bath rooms'.

In front of us a kind of bath house with geraniums, then a little staircase, and then, to left and right, three rooms on each side 5 × 5 metres × 1.9 metres high with wooden doors like garages. On the far wall, not clearly visible in the darkness, large wooden stage-type doors. On the roof, as a little practical joke the Star of David!! In front of the building a sign: Heckenholt Foundation! I was not able to see any more that afternoon.

Next morning, shortly before seven, I was told: 'the first transport will arrive in ten minutes.' And, in fact, after a few minutes, the first train arrived from the direction of Lemberg (Lvov). 45 waggons with 6,700 people, of whom 1,450 were already dead on arrival. Behind the barred hatches stared the horribly pale and frightened faces of children, their eyes full of the fear of death. Men and women were there too.

The train arrives: 200 Ukrainians fling open the doors and chase the people out of the waggons with their leather whips. Instructions come from a large loudspeaker: Undress completely, including artificial limbs, spectacles etc. Give your valuables up at the counter without receiving a ticket or a receipt. Tie your shoes together carefully (for the clothing collection), because otherwise in the twenty-five metre high pile of shoes no one can sort out which shoes belong together. Then, the women and girls have to go to the hairdressers who, with two or three snips of the scissors, cut off all their hair and put it in potato sacks. 'That is for some special purpose to do with U Boats, for insulation or something like that', the SS *Unterscharführer* on duty told me.

Then the procession starts to move. They all go along the path with a very pretty girl in front, all naked, men, women, and children, cripples without their artificial limbs. I myself am standing with Captain Wirth up on the ramp between the chambers. Mothers with their babies at the breast, come up, hesitate, enter the death chambers. On the corner stands a tough SS man who tells the poor people in a pastoral voice: 'Nothing is going to happen to you. Just breathe in deeply in the chambers. It will strengthen your lungs. This inhalation is necessary because of all the sickness and epidemics.' In reply to the question of what is going to happen to them, he says: 'well, naturally the men will have to work, build houses and roads, but the women won't need to work. Only if they want to, they can do housework or help in the kitchen.' For some of these poor people a ray of hope which suffices to persuade them to walk the few steps to the chambers but the majority understand what is happening, the smell reveals their fate to them. And so they climb the little staircase and then they see it all: mothers with children at the breasts, little naked children, adults, men, women, all naked. They hesitate but they enter the death chambers, driven on by the others behind them or by the leather whips of the SS, the majority without saying a word. A Jewess of about forty, eyes blazing, curses the murderers. She receives five or six lashes with his riding whip from Captain Wirth personally and then disappears into the chamber. Many people pray. I pray with them. I press myself into a corner and cry out to my and their God. How gladly I would go into the chamber with them. They would then find a uniformed SS officer in their chambers: the matter would be regarded and treated as an accident, totally forgotten about. So I must not do it yet. I must first report my experiences here.

The chambers fill up. 'Pack them in'—that is what Captain Wirth has ordered. People are treading on each others' toes. 700–800 in an area of twenty-five square metres, in forty-five cubic metres! The SS push them in as far as possible. The doors shut; in the meantime, the others are waiting outside in the open, naked. 'It is the same in winter', I was told. 'But they could catch their death of cold', I say. 'But that's just what they are there for', replied an SS man in dialect. Now at last I understood why the whole apparatus is called the Heckenholt Foundation. Heckenholt is the driver of the diesel engine, a little technician who constructed the installation. The people are going to be killed by the diesel exhaust gases. But the diesel engine won't start! Captain Wirth arrives. He is clearly embarrassed that this should happen just on the day when I am here. Yes indeed, I can see the whole thing. And I wait. My stop watch faithfully records it all. Fifty minutes, 70 seconds [*sic*!]. Still the diesel won't start. The people wait in their gas chambers. In vain. One can hear them crying, sobbing . . . Captain Wirth hits the Ukrainian who is responsible for helping *Unterscharführer* Heckenholt with the diesel engine twelve or thirteen times in the face with his riding whip. After two hours forty-nine minutes—the stop watch has recorded it all—the engine starts. Up to this moment, the people have been living in these four chambers, four times 750 people in four times forty-five cubic metres. A further twenty-five minutes pass. That's right, many are now dead. One can see through the little peepholes when the electric light illuminates the chambers for a moment. After twenty-eight minutes, only a few are still alive. At last, after thirty-two minutes, they are all dead.

Men from the work detail open the wooden doors from the other side. Even though they are Jews, they have been promised their freedom and a small percentage of all the valuables which are found as a reward for their frightful duty. The dead stand like basalt pillars pressed together in the chambers. There is no room to fall or even to lean over. Even in death one can tell which are the families. They are holding hands in death and it is difficult to tear them apart in order to empty the chambers for the next batch. The corpses are thrown out wet with sweat and urine, smeared with excrement and with menstrual blood on their legs. The corpses of children fly through the air. There is no time. The riding whips of the Ukrainians whistle down on the work details. Two dozen dentists open mouths with hooks and look for gold. Gold to the left no gold to the right. Other dentists tear out the gold teeth and crowns with pincers and hammers.

Captain Wirth is in the thick of it. He is in his element. Some of the workers check genitals and anus for gold, diamonds and valuables. Wirth calls me over. 'Just lift up this tin full of gold teeth, that is only from yesterday and the day before!' In an incredibly vulgar and phoney voice he tells me: 'You have no idea what we find every day in the way of gold and diamonds and dollars. But see for yourself', and then he takes me over to a jeweller who is responsible for looking after all the treasures and shows me everything. I am then shown a former manager of the Kaufhaus des Westens in Berlin[11] and a violinist: he is a captain of the old

---

[11] A leading department store in Berlin (eds).

Imperial Austrian Army, a knight of the Iron Cross I Class, who is now the chief of the Jewish work detail.

The naked corpses are carried on wooden stretchers only a few metres to the ditches which are 100 × 20 × 12 metres in size. After a few days, the corpses swell up and then collapse so that one can throw another layer on top of this one. Then ten centimetres of sand are strewn on the top so that only the occasional heads or arms stick out . . .

Captain Wirth asks me not to suggest any alterations to his apparatus when I return to Berlin and to ask for everything to be left as it is, as it has proved itself most effective. I have the prussic acid buried under my supervision on the grounds that it has allegedly deteriorated.

Gassing ceased in Belzec in December 1942. By then, around 500,000 had been murdered, over ninety per cent of whom were Polish Jews from the General Government, mainly from Lublin, Galicia, and Cracow. Among the remainder, were Jews from France, Holland, Slovakia, Germany, Greece and Theresianstadt. Only one inmate survived the war.

It had soon become clear that Belzec would prove inadequate for the purpose of the 'Reinhard Action' and so, in March 1942, construction of a new camp had begun at Sobibor, a small town on the Chełm–Wlodawa railway line east of Lublin. It was an enlarged and improved version of Belzec but the basic layout and procedure were the same. SS *Hauptsturmführer* Franz Stangl, an Austrian graduate of Hartheim 'euthanasia' centre was appointed commandant.

Mass extermination began in Sobibor at the end of April 1942. It continued until 14 October 1943, when an uprising by Jewish workers, in which nine Germans and two Ukrainians were killed, brought about the closure of the camp, which was in any case already intended. During the period of its operation, some 150–200,000 Jews died in the camp. These included over 34,000 Jews from Holland, 24,000 from Slovakia, at least 10,000 from Germany and Austria, 2,000 from France, and 1,000 from Russia. The remainder were from the General Government. Many of those from outside Poland passed through the ghettos of the Lublin district before arriving in Sobibor. Some thirty Jews who had worked in the camp survived the war, having escaped during the uprising of 14 October 1943.

The third of the death camps in the 'Reinhard Action' was built in the early summer of 1942, 120 km north-east of Warsaw and four kilometres from the station of the village of Treblinka on the Małkinia–Siedlce railway line, from which a spur went to the camp. It was 600 × 400 metres, roughly the same size as Sobibor, and constructed more or less according to the Belzec prototype. Particular efforts were made to reassure the arriving Jews. Thus, the ramp was designed to look as far as possible like a normal station with a clock, a ticket office, and timetables. There was also a large notice at the entrance to the camp:

863

Attention Warsaw Jews!

You are now entering a transit camp from which you will be transported to a labour camp.

To prevent epidemics both clothing and luggage must be handed in for disinfecting. Gold, cash, foreign exchange, and jewellery are to be given up at the cash desk in return for a receipt. They will be later returned on presentation of the receipt. All those arriving must cleanse themselves by taking a bath before continuing their journey.

In the case of some of the Jews coming from the West this ruse appears to have had a measure of success. For example, a member of the Jewish station commando in Sobibor reported after the war.

864

The transports from Germany, Austria, and Czechoslovakia arrived in luxury carriages with all their personal luggage and the people were convinced that they were coming to be resettled. Their naivety was such that some people from the transport turned to us workers of the so-called 'station commando' and offered us tips to help them carry their luggage. I assume that even when they were led naked into the gas chambers they were still convinced that they were going to have a bath.

However, particularly in the case of those transports coming from Poland and eastern Europe, where the Jews were less likely to have the morale or physical energy to resist, the Germans employed terror and speed as the main means of ensuring a smooth killing operation. A witness reported after the war on his arrival in Treblinka:

865

When the train arrived in Treblinka I can remember seeing great piles of clothing. Now we feared that the rumours really had been true. I remember saying to my wife more or less: this is the end.

We were transported in goods waggons. The goods waggons were very overcrowded. We were able to take something to eat with us but got nothing to drink and that was the worst thing. When the train arrived in Treblinka a considerable number of people had already died of exhaustion. I can no longer remember how many there were. I would like to point out that one of the worst things about the transport was the lack of air. There was only a small window covered with a grill and there were no sanitory facilities. Anybody can imagine what that meant.

I can remember the terrible confusion when the doors were pulled open in Treblinka. The Germans and Ukrainians shouted 'get out, out'. The members of the so-called Red Jewish Commando also shouted and yelled. Then the people who had arrived began to scream and complain. I can remember too that whips were used on us. Then, we were told: 'Men to the right, women to the left and get undressed'. My little daughter was with me and then ran to her mother when we were separated. I never saw them again and could not even say good-bye. Then, while I was undressing I was selected by a German to be a so-called work-Jew.

The killing operation began in Treblinka on 23 July 1942. Between then and 28 August a total of 268,000 Jews were gassed, of whom 215,000 came from the Warsaw ghetto, for whose liquidation Treblinka had been primarily designed. However, by the end of August, the system was breaking down. The commandant, SS *Untersturmführer* Dr Irmfried Eberl, formerly of Brandenburg 'euthanasia' centre, was accepting more transports than he could cope with, with the result that large numbers of bodies were lying around the camp unburied. Eberl was replaced as commandant by Franz Stangl, the commandant of Sobibor, who built new chambers alongside the old ones. Whereas the old ones had a total capacity of 600, the new ones could kill around 4,000 at a time. At the end of the 'tube' the Jews now found themselves facing a flight of five steps, decorated with flower tubs, which led up to a door on the gable above which was fixed a Star of David. Then, at the entrance to the corridor leading to the gas chambers, was a heavy dark curtain from a synagogue with an inscription written in Hebrew: 'This is the gate through which the righteous enter'. As in the other camps, those Jews who were too sick or frail to make their way to the gas chamber were taken to the 'hospital'—a shed next to a pit—where they were shot in the back of the neck.

Under Stangl the killing operation ran smoothly. According to a colleague: 'I think what he really cared about was to have the place run like clockwork.'[12] The first transport arrived around 8.00 a.m. and by 11.00 a.m. it would have been 'dealt with'. Around twelve thousand a day were being gassed after the construction of the new chambers. From spring 1943 onwards, following a practice already introduced in the other two camps, the bodies were burnt on large pyres constructed by laying railway lines on concrete blocks with a fire permanently burning underneath. Moreover, all those corpses which had been buried in mass graves were now exhumed and burnt in order to avoid leaving incriminating evidence.

Gassing went on in Treblinka until 19 August 1943. An uprising of Jewish prisoners on 2 August had accelerated a closure which was already intended. On 17 November 1943, the last group of Jewish prisoners who

[12] See G. Sereny, *Into that darkness. An Examination of Conscience* (London 1974) p. 202.

had been involved in dismantling the camp were shot. Estimates of those killed between 23 July 1942 and 19 August 1943 range from 900,000 to 1.2 million. They included 339,000 Jews from the Warsaw ghetto, virtually all the Jews from the district of Radom, thousands of Jews from other Polish ghettos and Jews from many other countries including Germany, the Protectorate, Bulgaria, Yugoslavia, Greece, and Austria. They also included a group of Gypsies. There were some sixty to seventy survivors of Treblinka, mainly from the uprising.

(b) The Clearing of the Ghettos 1942–43

The 'Reinhard Action' had involved not only the planning, construction, and operation of the three extermination camps, but also the organization of the deportations to the camps within Poland and the collection and storing of the personal property left by those who had been killed. The whole operation was carried out by a group of 450 Germans, of whom 92 belonged to the T4 organization. These key T4 personnel were still subordinate to and paid by the KdF in Berlin and, as the role of Captain Wirth makes clear, they operated with a measure of autonomy. In August 1942, Wirth was appointed 'Inspector of the SS Special Commando for the Reinhard Action' covering the three camps, with his own headquarters in Lublin which operated largely independently of Globocnik. Nevertheless, the T4 personnel received their general instructions for the 'Reinhard Action' from Globocnik, who in turn was answerable to Himmler personally. All the Germans were given grey SS uniforms and those who were not already members of the SS were given SS ranks equivalent to those they held in other organizations. In addition to the Germans, there were several hundred Ukrainians and ethnic Germans who had been trained at the Travniki camp. They acted as guards in the camps and provided much of the 'muscle' for clearing the ghettos.

Responsibility for clearing the ghettos and for organizing the transportation of the Jews to the death camps within Poland, in liaison with the railway authorities of the *Ostbahn*, lay with SS *Hauptsturmführer* Höfle, Globocnik's chief of staff. The largest operation of this kind was the clearing of the Warsaw ghetto and the transportation of its inhabitants to Treblinka. The first and major phase of this operation began on 22 July 1942 and continued until 3 October 1942. During this period 310,322 Jews were deported from Warsaw to Treblinka. On 22 July 1942, Höfle issued the following announcement to the Jewish Council in Warsaw:

866

The Jewish Council is hereby informed of the following:

1. All Jewish persons irrespective of age or sex who live in Warsaw will be resettled to the east.

2. The following are excluded from the resettlement:
(*a*) all Jewish persons who are employed by the German authorities or by German agencies and can provide proof of it.
(*b*) all Jewish persons who belong to the Jewish Council and are employees of the Jewish Council. (The qualifying date is the date of publication of the order).
(*c*) all Jewish persons who are employed by German firms and can provide proof of it.
(*d*) all Jews capable of work who have not hitherto been employed. They are to be placed in barracks in the ghetto.
(*e*) all Jewish persons who are members of the personnel of the Jewish hospitals. Similarly, the members of the Jewish disinfection troops.
(*f*) all Jewish persons who belong to the Jewish police force.
(*g*) all Jewish persons who are close relatives of the persons referred to in (*a*)–(*f*). Such relatives are restricted to wives and children.
(*h*) all Jewish persons who on the first day of the resettlement are in one of the Jewish hospitals and are not capable of being released. The fitness for release will be decided by a doctor to be designated by the Jewish Council.

3. Every Jewish person being resettled may take 15 kg. of his property as personal luggage. All valuables may be taken: gold, jewellery, cash etc.
Food for three days should be taken.

4. The resettlement begins on 22 July 1942 at 11 o'clock . . .

II. The Jewish Council is responsible for providing the daily quota of Jews for transportation. To carry out this task the Jewish council will use the Jewish police force (100 men). The Jewish Council will ensure that every day from 22 July onwards, by 16.00 at the latest, 6,000 Jews are assembled at the collecting point. The collecting point for the whole period of the evacuation will be the Jewish hospital in Stawki street. On 22 July, the 6,000 Jews will be assembled directly on the loading platform near the transfer office. To start with, the Jewish Council may take the quotas of Jews from the whole population. Later, the Jewish Council will receive special instructions according to which particular streets and blocks of flats are to be cleared . . .

VIII. Punishments:
(*a*) Any Jewish person who leaves the ghetto at the start of the resettlement without belonging to the categories of persons spelled out in 2(*a*) and (*c*), and in so far as they were not hitherto entitled to do so, will be shot.
(*b*) Any Jewish person who undertakes an act which is calculated to evade or disturb the resettlement measures will be shot.
(*c*) Any Jewish person who assists in an act which is calculated to evade or disturb the resettlement measures will be shot.

(*d*) All Jews who, on completion of the resettlement, are encountered in Warsaw and do not belong to the categories referred to in 2(*a*)–(*h*) will be shot.

The Jewish council is hereby informed that, in the event that the orders and instructions are not carried out 100%, an appropriate number of the hostages who have been taken in the meantime will be shot . . .

In a desperate attempt to pacify the Germans by proving their efficiency, the leader of the Jewish police force issued the following announcement to the inhabitants of the ghetto on 29 July 1942:

867

I hereby announce that all persons who are liable for resettlement in accordance with the orders of the authorities and who present themselves for departure voluntarily on 29,30, and 31 July will receive 3 kg. of bread and 1 kg. of jam per person.

The collecting point and distribution point: Stawki square on the corner of Wild Street.

The Germans had almost certainly arranged the quota system and the large number of exemptions in order to divide the ghetto and give its more active and authoritative members the illusion that they were to be exempt. However, as the deportations continued so they increasingly ignored their own criteria and began to deport more and more indiscriminately. On 7 August 1942, dissatisfied with the arrangement for the quota system, Höfle sent in his uniformed thugs to conduct the kind of manhunt which was the normal method for clearing other Polish ghettos under the 'Reinhard Action'. Among those driven out in this way were the 200 children of the Janusz-Korczak orphanage. The scene was described in the following statement by the writer, Jehoszua Perle:

868

Once again I must repeat here the banal words that there is no pen in existence which can describe this fearful scene. The fascist child murderers were gripped with a frenzied rage; they kept on shooting. Two hundred children stood there frightened to death. Soon they would be shot right down to the very last one. And then something extraordinary happened. These two hundred children did not scream, two hundred innocent creatures did not cry, not one of them ran away, none of them hid. Like sick swallows they snuggled up to their teacher and educator, their father and brother, to Janusz Korczak, looking to him to care for them and protect them.

He stood in the front row. He shielded the children with his weak, emaciated body. The Hitler beasts showed no consideration. With a pistol in one hand and a whip in the other, they bawled out:

'March'

Woe to the eyes which were forced to witness this fearful scene.

Janusz Korczak, bare-headed, with a leather belt round his coat, with tall boots, bent, held the youngest child by the hand and went on ahead. He was followed by some nuns in white aprons and then came the two hundred freshly combed children.

The children were surrounded on all sides by German, Ukrainian, and Jewish policemen.

Meanwhile, in the Jewish Council they had learnt what was happening at No. 16 Sienna Street. Telephone calls were made, people rushed backwards and forwards wanting to help. But who did the Jewish Council want to save? Janusz Korczak. He gratefully declined the offer of the gentlemen of the Jewish Council, who had sacrificed all the Jews of Warsaw, and strode on at the head of his children to the loading place.

The stones wept as they saw this procession. But the fascist murders drove the children on with whips and kept on shooting.

To the present day there is no trace of what has happened to Janusz Korczak with the two hundred children. All the signs suggest that there is nothing left of them. May these few words be the introduction to that blood-filled chronicle which bears the name 'Janusz Korczak and his two hundred children'. It is the tribute of a simple ghetto Jew, a tribute to Korczak's deed.

Although the policy laid down by Heydrich at the Wannsee conference envisaged a separation of the Jews into those fit and those unfit for work, and although this distinction appears to have been made in the initial stages of the 'Reinhard Action; there was a growing tendency during 1942 for it to be ignored and for Jews to be exterminated more or less indiscriminately. A major reason for this was undoubtedly convenience, combined with a general and undiscriminating contempt for all Jews among the personnel involved. However, another crucial factor was pressure from the top—from Himmler and perhaps also from Hitler—for a speedy solution to the Jewish question. On 19 July 1942, for example, Himmler wrote to SS *Obergruppenführer* Friedrich-Wilhelm Krüger, the Higher SS and Police Leader in the General Government and as such the senior SS officer there, as follows:

869

I hereby order that the resettlment of the whole Jewish population of the General Government be carried out and completed by 31 December 1942.

After 31 December 1942 no persons of Jewish descent will be permitted to reside in the General Government unless they are living in the camps in Warsaw, Cracow,

Czestochowa, Radom, Lublin. All other undertakings which employ Jews must have ceased by then or, if this proves impossible, then they must be transferred to one of the camps.

These measures are necessary if the ethnic separation of races and peoples envisaged in the New Order in Europe is to be achieved and the security and purity of the German Reich and its sphere of interest. Any relaxation of this ruling would represent a threat to the peace and stability of the whole German sphere of interest, a focus for the resistance movement, and a source of contagion both morally and physically.

For all these reasons, a comprehensive clearing out is necessary and must therefore be achieved. Foreseeable delays in meeting the deadline must be reported to me in good time so that remedial action can be taken. All requests from other agencies for alterations or exceptions to the programme are to be referred to me personally.

A week later, on 28 July 1942 Himmler wrote to SS *Obergruppenführer* Gottlob Berger, the Chief of the SS Main Office as follows:

870

1. I urgently request that no decree concerning the definition of 'a Jew' should be published. We only tie our hands with these stupid commitments.

The occupied Eastern territories will be made free of Jews. The Führer has placed the implementation of this very difficult order on my shoulders. Nobody can remove the responsibility from me. Therefore, I forbid all discussion . . .

However, as German war production suffered increasingly severe bottlenecks in the supply of labour in 1942–3, so the contribution of Jews to the economy grew in importance. The destruction of the Jewish ghettos in Poland had a serious impact on industrial production there. At the end of the first phase of the Warsaw deportation in October 1942, for example, textile production in Warsaw was halved. Since more and more Poles were being deported to Germany, the civilian and military authorities responsible for overseeing production in the occupied territories became advocates of retaining at least those Jews who were engaged in war production. However, they received little support from OKW, which issued an order on 5 September, signed by Keitel, that all Jewish labour was to be replaced with Poles at once. On 18 September 1942, the Military Commander in the General Government, General von Gienanth, responded with a memorandum stressing the necessity of provisionally leaving Jewish workers in the armaments' factories:

871

I. To date the following regulations have been implemented in the General Government:

1) Polish and Ukrainian workers are being replaced by Jewish workers to free them for transfer to the Reich. For this purpose Jewish camps have been constructed near the factories affected.

2) Plants employing Jews wholly or in part will be established so that Jewish labour may be fully utilised in the war effort.

The resettlement of the Jews, which took place without most of the *Wehrmacht* offices receiving prior notification, has caused considerable redeployment difficulties as well as delays in production directly geared to the war effort. Work for SS-priority and for priority code 'Winter' cannot be completed on schedule . . .

III. According to figures provided by the Labour Department, the total number of workers employed in industry is slightly more than a million, of whom 300,000 are Jews. Among these are roughly 100,000 skilled workers.

In the individual plants working for the *Wehrmacht* the number of Jews among the skilled workers varies between twenty-five and one hundred per cent; it is one hundred per cent in the textile plants producing winter clothing. In other plants, for example, in the important vehicle plant producing the 'Fuhramm' and 'Pleskau' models, the majority of platers and wheelwrights are Jewish. The harness makers with few exceptions are all Jews.

In private firms involved in repairing uniforms there are at present 227,000 workers employed, of whom 222,000 (97%) are Jews, and of whom 16,000 are skilled (textile and leather workers).

A purely Jewish firm with 168 workers is making harnesses. On it depends the entire harness production in the General Government, in the Ukraine, and to some extent in the Reich.

IV. The immediate withdrawal of the Jews would have the effect of considerably reducing the war potential of the Reich, and the provisioning of the front as well as of the troops in the General Government would be held up at least temporarily.

1) A serious drop in production would occur in the armaments industry of between 25 and 100 per cent.

2) There would be a twenty-five per cent reduction in the performance of the motor vehicle repair workshops, i.e. on average 2,500 fewer motor vehicles per month would be repaired.

3) Replacement units would have to be brought in to ensure the supply of provisions.

V. If important war work is not to suffer, the Jews should only be released after substitutes have been trained, i.e. in stages. This task can only be carried out locally, but must be centrally coordinated from one place in cooperation with Higher SS and Police Leader.

I request permission to implement such a scheme. The guiding principle should be the exclusion of the Jews as quickly as possible, without thereby damaging important war work.

VI. As has now been established, important war contracts of the highest priority, above all for winter requirements, are being placed in the General Government by various *Wehrmacht* offices without the knowledge of the Armaments Inspectorate or of the Military Commander. The scheduled completion of this work is being rendered impossible by the deportation of the Jews.

It will require some time to produce a systematic registration of all such plants. I request that the deportation of those Jews employed in industrial plants should be postponed until then.

Himmler was unimpressed and responded on 9 October 1942 as follows:

872

My reply to the letter of the Military Commander in the General Government to the High Command of the *Wehrmacht* is as follows:

1. I have given instructions that all the so-called armament workers who merely work in tailors', furriers' and shoemakers' workshops should be brought together by SS *Obergruppenführer* Krüger and *Obergruppenführer* Pohl'[13] on the spot, i.e. in Warsaw and Lublin, and put in concentration camps. The *Wehrmacht* must transfer its outstanding orders to us and we will guarantee the continuation of the deliveries of the clothing it requires. However, I have given instructions to proceed mercilessly against all those who take it upon themselves to cause difficulties by putting forward alleged armaments interests, but who in reality merely wish to protect the Jews and their own business affairs.
2. The Jews who are in real armaments plants, i.e. workshops making weapons, motor vehicle workshops etc. are to be removed in stages. As the first stage, they are to be concentrated in particular sections. In the second stage of this process the work forces of these particular sections should be concentrated in secure plants through an exchange of personnel so that we will then simply have a few secure concentration camps in the General Government.
3. We will then endeavour to replace these Jewish workers with Poles and amalgamate the majority of these Jewish concentration camp plants into a few large Jewish concentration camp enterprises, ideally in the east of the General Government.

However, one day the Jews must disappear from there too in accordance with the Führer's wishes.

OKW was also unsympathetic to the problems of its officers who were responsible for armaments production and on 10 October 1942 sent the following telex:

[13] Oswald Pohl was the chief of the Economic-Administrative Main Office (*Wirtschafts und Verwaltungshauptamt*—WVHA) of the SS in charge of concentration camps and SS business enterprises (eds).

873

OKW is completely in agreement with the principle established by the *Reichsführer* SS that all Jews employed by the armed forces in auxiliary military services and in the armaments industries are to be replaced at once by Aryan workers.

Significantly, the senior SS officials in the General Government shared the concern of the military. This was partly because the SS was itself becoming a considerable employer of Jewish labour. This is clear from the following minute by the commander of the order police (*Orpo*) in the General Government, General Becker, of 14 November 1942:

874

. . . In mid-October, on a Sunday afternoon (I think it was the 17.10) the Higher SS and Police Leader [Krüger] invited the Commander of the Security Police and me to a discussion. On this occasion, the Commander of the Security Police said that if he was ordered to dismiss his Jews immediately he would of course do so, but then he would at the same time have to report that his plant, in particular the motor vehicle plant, would have to close as a result. I too made the point that the immediate dismissal of all the Jews from the plants of the order police would cause considerable difficulties. The *Obergruppenführer* [Krüger] commented on this as follows: He was aware of the situation and he too was dubious as to whether the deadlines set by the *Reichsführer* could be met. He intended to put this to the *Reichsführer* SS once again. Apart from that, the situation was that above all the *Reichsführer* did not want the Jews running around freely and not under control. If they were confined in guarded camps and taken to work as a group this would satisfy one of the main demands of the *Reichsführer* SS. Thus, he did not object to the employment of Jews, who were confined in camps, in the police plants for a transitional period. However, the *Obergruppenführer* concluded by emphasizing that he could only agree to such measures provided the principle was adhered to that the SS and police should set an example to everybody else and release its Jews for resettlement as soon as possible.

The SS in the General Government, therefore, now set about concentrating the Jews who were fit or skilled workers and had been left behind by the dissolution of the ghettos into central labour camps such as the Plaszow labour camp established near Cracow early in 1943. From there the Jews were hired out to firms for cash on a daily basis, returning to the camps at night. However, the living conditions in these camps and the working conditions in many of the plants were such that many Jews succumbed to them.[14]

The local SS officials continued to assume that they would be able to retain a substantial number of Jews as a crucial labour force from which after all the SS now acquired a considerable income. Thus, on 19 February 1943, a discussion was held at the office of the Commander of the Security Police in the Białystok district concerning the Białystok ghetto. The following is an excerpt from the minutes:

875

The representative of the Commander of the Security Police announced at this meeting that a further deportation of the Jews was not expected for the time being. 30,000 Jews were expected to remain in the ghetto until the end of the war. The economic implications of this fact must be taken into account from now onwards, since the RSHA is expected to agree with this view of the situation. This creates a new situation for the supply of labour and the maintenance of economic strength.

1) The ghetto will remain with new boundaries but essentially with the same size.

2) Factories which are in the ghetto will continue to operate but with a Jewish work force.

3) Irrespective of the future peace-time tasks of the city, the political goal and that of the Security Police must be that in the foreseeable future the 4,000 Jews outside the ghetto disappear and from then on only work in the ghetto.

The local security police intend to maintain the ghetto at its present size for the time being. However, the issue is to be finally decided by the RSHA in the course of this month.

Himmler, however, remained generally unimpressed with the concerns of his subordinates. On 10 May 1943, in a minute concerning, among other things, the General Government, he noted:

876

. . . (*e*) I will not halt the evacuations of the roughly 300,000 Jews remaining in the General Government but rather continue them with the greatest speed. However much the Jewish evacuations may cause upheaval while they are being carried through, they will be that much more the precondition for the fundamental pacification of the area after their completion.

---

[14] For a powerful and moving account of this process as it affected one group of workers in the Plaszow camp see Thomas Keneally, *Schindler's Ark* (London, 1983.).

Three weeks later, however, on 31 May, the Higher SS and Police Leader, Krüger, commented on the stance of the *Reichsführer* SS at a cabinet meeting of the General Government as follows:

877

Recently he was once again ordered to carry out the elimination of the Jews [*Entjudung*] in a very short time. He was compelled to remove the Jews from the armaments industry and from plants of military importance as well, unless they were exclusively employed in important war work. The Jews were then concentrated in large camps and were being released from there each day for work in these armaments factories.

However, the *Reichsführer* SS wishes that the employment of these Jews too should cease. He [Krüger] has discussed this question at length with Lieutenant General Schindler[15] and considers that in the final analysis this wish of the *Reichsführer* SS probably cannot be fulfilled. Among the Jewish workers there are skilled workers, precision mechanics and other qualified craftsmen whom one could not easily replace with Poles. He therefore requests SS *Obergruppenführer* Dr Kaltenbrunner[16] to explain the situation to the *Reichsführer* SS and ask him to refrain from removing these Jewish workers.

In the meantime, however, the ghettos continued to be dissolved and their inhabitants either exterminated or deported to labour camps. By this time, however, the Jews were fully aware of what was in store for them and many of the physically weaker ones—the old and mothers with children—had already been deported leaving behind those who were not only fit for work but also more capable of resistance. A resistance organization had been formed in a number of ghettos and a few weapons were acquired through the Polish resistance, the black market, and by making them secretly in the ghetto workshops.

The Germans had already tried to liquidate the remnants of the Warsaw ghetto on 19 January 1943 but had met with organized resistance and had given up the attempt on the 22nd. They returned on 19 April much better prepared. However, the Jews had also had time to prepare an elaborate network of bunkers and underground passages. They had no illusions about the final outcome but were determined to make a stand and assert their dignity as human beings and as Jews. The following is a telex report on the first day's action by SS *Brigadeführer* Jürgen Stroop, the SS and Police

[15] The Armaments Inspector in the General Government (eds).

[16] Ernst Kaltenbrunner had replaced Heydrich as Chief of the Security Police and SD and head of the RSHA after the latter's assassination (eds).

Leader in the Warsaw district and commander of the German forces, to Krüger:

878

The course of the action in the ghetto on 19.4.43:

Ghetto was sealed off at 3.00. At 6.00 the Waffen SS in a strength of 16/850[17] was sent out to comb through the remainder of the ghetto. Immediately after the launching of the units, they came under strong coordinated attack with firearms by the Jews and bandits. The tank and the two armoured reconnaissance vehicles were attacked with Molotov cocktails (incendiary bottles). Tank set on fire twice. This attack by the enemy initially prompted a withdrawal by the units in action. Losses in the first attack: 12 men (6 SS men, 6 Travnicki men). About 8.00 second attack by the units under the command of the undersigned. Despite a small amount of enemy fire, this attack achieved the success of enabling the block of buildings to be systematically combed through. We succeeded in forcing the enemy to retire from the roofs and upper strong points into the cellars, bunkers, and sewers. The search produced only 200 Jews. Following on from this, special combat units were deployed against known bunkers with the task of forcing out those inside and destroying the bunkers. Appoximately 380 Jews were captured in this operation. It was discovered that the Jews were in the sewers. The sewers were completely flooded to prevent them from remaining there. Around 17.30 machine gun fire was used against very strong resistance from a group of houses. A special combat unit crushed the enemy and forced a way into the houses without, however, being able to capture the enemy. The Jews and criminals defended each strongpoint and then escaped at the last minute through attics and underground tunnels. Around 20.00 the barricades round the ghetto were strengthened. All units were withdrawn from the ghetto and dismissed to their quarters. The barricades were strengthened by 250 members of the Waffen SS.

The action will be continued on 20.4.43

Forces at my disposal:

SS Panzer-Grenadier Btl.	6/400	Sappers	2/16
SS Cavalry Reserve	10/450	First aid unit	1/1
Orpo	6/165	3 flak 2.28 cm.	2/24
SD	2/48	1 French tank of the Waffen SS	
Trawniki men	1/150	2 Armoured personnel carriers	
1 10 cm. howitzer	1/7	of the Waffen SS	
1 flame thrower	1		

During the next four weeks, through the sheer weight of their fire power and by systematically burning down buildings and dynamiting and smoking out bunkers, the SS gradually won the upper hand. On 8 May 1943, Stroop reported in his daily telex to Krüger:

[17] i.e 16 officers and 850 men (eds).

879

Today, the whole area of the former Jewish ghetto was searched by special units looking for bunkers and Jews. As already reported a few days ago, the sub-humans, bandits and terrorists are at the moment holding out in bunkers in which, because of the fires, the heat has become intolerable. These creatures know only too well that there is only one thing left for them to do, either to hide as long as they can, or to come to the surface and then attempt to wound or kill the men of the Waffen SS who are closing in on them.

The discovery of the bunker of the so-called inner 'party leadership' reported in yesterday's telex was followed up today. We succeeded in opening up the bunker of the party leadership and in getting our hands on around 60 bandits who were heavily armed. We succeeded in capturing and liquidating the deputy head of the Jewish military organization 'ZWZ'[18] and his so-called chief of staff. Around 200 Jews were housed in this bunker, 60 of them were caught, 140 of them destroyed through the effects of smoke candles and by planting high explosives in various places. Numerous deaths of Jews from the effects of smoke candles have been reported. If the struggle against the Jews and bandits in the first six days was difficult, then it must be said that the Jews and Jewesses who organized the struggle then have been caught. No bunker is now opened up without the Jews inside offering resistance with the weapons at their disposal, light machine guns, pistols and hand grenades. Today, once again a whole lot of Jewesses were caught who had loaded and cocked pistols in their knickers.

According to statements which have been made, there are still 3–4,000 Jews hiding in the underground holes, sewers and bunkers. The undersigned is determined not to complete this major action until the last Jew has been destroyed.

In all we caught 1,091 Jews in bunkers today, 280 Jews were shot, innumerable Jews destroyed in the 43 bunkers which were blown up. The total number of Jews caught so far has increased to 49,712. The buildings which have not yet been destroyed by fire have been set alight today and we discovered that there are still Jews hiding somewhere in the walls or under staircases . . .

On 16 May, Stroop declared major operations at an end and, after dynamiting the great Tlomacki synagogue in the Aryan sector of the city, he withdrew his troops. Small pockets of resistance, however, continued for several more weeks. 56,065 Jews had surrendered and were either shot on the spot or transported to death and labour camps; several thousand were buried in the rubble.

Despite the expectations expressed by the Commander of the Security Police in February that the Białystok ghetto would remain until the end of the war, it too was liquidated in the second half of August. As in Warsaw

---

[18] Mordechai Anielewicz (eds).

this provoked the resistance of its inhabitants, though it proved much less effective. Finally in November 1943, 40,000 Jews remaining in labour camps in the Lublin area were slaughtered in 'Operation Harvest Festival'(!).

(c) The End of the 'Reinhard Action' and the Stocktaking

Although Jews continued to be gassed in Sobibor until 14 October 1943, Globocnik's appointment to the post of Higher SS and Police Leader in Istria at the end of August 1943 marked the effective end of the 'Reinhard Action', particularly since he took with him the key T4 personnel, including Wirth and Stangl. The intention appears to have been that they should set up an extermination centre for Jews in the former Italian sphere of influence who, until the fall of Mussolini, had been more or less unmolested.

By the end of November 1943, the three 'Reinhard Action' camps had been dismantled and the remaining work-Jews shot. On 4 November, Globocnik wrote to Himmler as follows:

880

On 19 October 1943 I concluded the Reinhard Action which I have been carrying out in the General Government and dissolved all the camps . . .

As a final report I have taken the liberty of sending you the enclosed file, *Reichsführer*. My observations in Lublin have shown that there was a particular source of infection [*Ausstrahlungsherd*] in the General Government, but particularly in the district of Lublin and so I endeavoured to produce a graphic record of these threats. It may prove useful in future to be able to draw attention to this threat. On the other hand, I have attempted to provide a description of the work involved from which one can see not only the amount of work but also with how few Germans this major action could be carried out. At any rate, it has now increased to such an extent that renowned industries are showing an interest in it.[19] In the meantime, I have handed over these camps to SS *Obergruppenführer* Pohl.

I would be grateful, *Reichsführer*, if you would peruse this file.

During a visit, *Reichsführer*, you indicated to me that, after the conclusion of the work, some Iron Crosses could be awarded for the particular achievements involved in this difficult task. I would be grateful if you could let me know if I may put forward recommendations.

I would like to take the liberty of pointing out that such awards were made to the forces of the SS and Police Leader who was involved in the Warsaw operation which represented a relatively small part of the whole project.

I would be grateful to you, Reichsführer, for a positive decision in this matter since I like to see the hard work of my men rewarded.

---

[19] This refers to the take-over of Jewish plant (eds).

Himmler replied on 30 November 1943:

881

Dear Globus,

I confirm receipt of your letter of 4 November 1943 and your report of the conclusion of the 'Reinhard Action'. I also am grateful to you for sending me the file.

I would like to express to you my thanks and appreciation for the great and unique service which you have performed for the whole German people by carrying out the 'Reinhard Action'.

The 'Reinhard Action' was not only a programme of mass murder on a gigantic scale but also a vast plunder operation. On 5 January 1944, Globocnik sent a report detailing the amount of plunder which had been secured, from which the following are extracts:

882

Provisional final financial report on the Reinhard Action of 15 December 1943:

In the course of the 'Reinhard Action', Lublin, during the period 1942 until 15 December 1943 inclusive, the Greater German Reich received the following cash and material assets . . .

Total:

Cash in ZL[oty] and RM notes	RM 73,852,080.74
Precious metals	8,973,651.60
Foreign exchange in notes	4,521,224.13
Foreign exchange in gold coinage	1,736,554.12
Jewels and other assets	43,662,450.00
Textiles	46,000,000.00

The textiles consisted of 1,901 railway waggon loads of clothing, bed linen, feather bedding and rags with an estimated value of RM 26,000,000. The remaining 20,000,000 worth was stored in the 'old airport' in Lublin. The total figure excluded the valuables stolen by the SS personnel directly involved and above all the vast amount of plant and moveable assets confiscated from the Jews and transferred to the SS combine, *Ostindustrie* (Osti), in August 1943.

Senior officials of the Reichsbank were fully involved in this plunder as is clear from the following post-war statement by Emil Puhl, a director of the Reichsbank.

883

. . . 2. In the summer of 1942, the Reichsbank President and Reich Economics Minister, Walther Funk, had a conversation with me and with Herr Friedrich Wilhelm, a member of the board of the Reichsbank. Funk told me that he had made arrangements with the *Reichsführer* Himmler to receive gold and jewellery from the SS for safe-keeping. Funk gave instructions to me to make the necessary arrangements with Pohl, who was head of the economic department of the SS and to whom the economic side of the concentration camps was subordinated.

3. I asked Funk where the gold, jewellery and cash and other items which were to be delivered by the SS came from. Funk replied that it was confiscated property from the occupied eastern territories and that I should not ask any further questions. I protested against the Reichsbank taking over these assets. Funk replied that we should make the necessary arrangements for taking over the assets and keep the matter absolutely secret.

4. Thereupon, I made the necessary arrangements for receiving the assets with the officials responsible for the safes and, at its next board meeting, I reported to the board of the Reichsbank about the measures which had been taken. On the same day, Pohl of the Economic Department of the SS rang me up and asked me whether I was informed about the matter. I refused to discuss the matter on the telephone, whereupon he came to see me and said that the SS had some jewellery which it wished to hand over to the Reichsbank for safe-keeping. I made the necessary arrangements with him for the transfer and, from then onwards, deliveries were made from time to time from August 1942 through the following years.

5. Among the items deposited by the SS were jewellery, watches, spectacle frames, gold fillings, and other objects in large quantities which had been removed by the SS from Jews, concentration camp victims, and other persons. We became aware of this when the SS attempted to transform this material into cash and, with Funk's knowledge and approval, made use of Reichsbank personnel for this purpose. Apart from gold, jewellery, and other such items, the SS delivered paper money, foreign exchange, and bonds to the Reichsbank which were dealt with in the legal way usual for such items. As far as the jewellery and gold were concerned, Funk told me that Himmler and the Reich Finance Minister, von Krosigk, had reached an agreement whereby gold and similar items were deposited under the State's account and amounts which were later realised by the sale of these items were credited to the State.

6. In pursuance of my duties, I visited the safes of the Reichsbank from time to time and saw what was stored there. Funk too visited the safes from time to time in the pursuance of his duties.

7. Following Funk's instructions, the Gold Discount Bank established a current account, which finally contained 10–12 million Reich Marks, and which was put at the disposal of the economic administration of the SS for financing the production of material in factories under SS control by workers from concentration camps.

There were other ways of disposing of the plunder as is clear from the following documents. The first is a letter from Pohl to Himmler dated 29 November 1944:

884

Re: Distribution of watches to members of the Waffen SS:

At the moment the following are stored with Amtsgruppe D[20] in Oranienburg:

20,000 pocket watches
4,000 wrist watches
3,000 alarm and ornamental clocks
5,000 fountain pens
24 clocks for the blind
80 stop watches

The watches and fountain pens have been overhauled and are ready to be dispatched. As last year, I have assigned quotas to the Waffen SS divisions in accordance with the enclosed list. These gifts are distributed in your name to those members of the divisions who have proved themselves most worthy to receive them. Because of the short time available I have already approved the list and request your confirmation of it . . .

The following is a letter from the Gau representative of the Winter Aid Programme in the Wartheland to the ghetto administration in Łódź, dated 16 January 1943:

885

Re: Transfer of textile goods to the NSV by the ghetto administration.

In connection with above matter, I refer to the previous discussions between my senior official, Party Comrade Eichehorn and yourself and the later negotiations between you and my official, Party comrade, Koalick, according to which it was agreed that the NSV should be donated suits, dresses, and linen which had been cleaned and were fit to wear, in return for reimbursement of the costs of cleaning and refurbishment.

The first consignment of 1,500 suits sent to the *Kreis* Office of Litzmannstadt-Land corresponds in no way to the textiles which were viewed earlier while lying in store in Kulmhof at the disposal of your ghetto administration. The suits delivered by you are so poor in quality that the majority cannot be used for our welfare

[20] An office of the WVHA (eds).

purposes. Moreover, your consignment does not contain complete suits but only unmatched jackets and pairs of trousers. A large number of the pieces of clothing are covered in spots and some are stained with dirt and blood. The collars of most of the jackets are so fatty that further thorough cleaning is required.

Since the cases were sent on by the *Kreis* Office in Litzmannstadt-Land to other *Kreis* offices in the Gau unopened, it only became clear later when the cases were opened, for example in a consignment to the *Kreis* Office of Posen-City, that *in the case of 51 jackets out of 200 the Jewish stars had not been removed*! Since in the district camps we mainly have to employ Polish labour camp workers, there is the danger that the returnees [i.e. immigrant ethnic Germans] who are to be looked after by the Winter Aid Programme [WHW] will discover the origins of the goods and, as a result, the WHW will be discredited . . .

I hope that you understand my complaints and appreciate that we cannot donate such poor pieces of clothing to our returnees but only good ones.

If you can find a satisfactory solution to my requests, then you will be simultaneously assisting the WHW in its great welfare task.

The ghetto administration replied six weeks later acknowledging the return of 2,750 suits and 1,000 dresses, but insisting that the stains were not blood but rust! The ghetto administration then had second thoughts and decided it would need the suits after all. However, it insisted that 'even if it proves impossible to remove the rust stains, the Jewish stars, which in some cases are still on the suits, must be removed.'

It was not just the property of the Jews which was confiscated and exploited by the SS as is clear from the following document which provides a particularly revealing insight into the mentality of the SS. It is a letter from SS *Gruppenführer* Richard Gluecks, Chief of *Amtsgruppe* D in the SS Economic Administration Main Office to the Commandants of the Concentration camps, dated 6 August 1942:

886

Re: the utilization of cut hair.

In response to a report, the Chief of the SS Economic Administration Main Office, SS *Obergruppenführer* Pohl, has ordered that all human hair cut off in concentration camps should be utilized. Human hair will be processed for industrial felt and spun into thread. Female hair which has been cut and combed out will be used as thread to make socks for U-boat crews and felt stockings for the railways.

You are instructed, therefore, to store the hair of female prisoners after it has been disinfected. Cut hair from male prisoners can only be utilized if it is at least 20 mm. in length.

SS *Ogruf*. Pohl, therefore, agrees that, initially for a trial period, the hair of male prisoners should only be cut when it has reached a length of 20 mm. In order to prevent ease of escape, which will arise from the increased length of hair, where the commandants consider it necessary, the prisoners should be identified by cutting a swathe of hair down the centre of their heads with a small pair of hair clippers.

It is intended to utilize the hair which accumulates in all the camps by setting up a processing plant in a concentration camp. Further instructions concerning the delivery of the hair which has been collected will follow.

The amounts of hair collected each month, separated into female and male hair, must be reported on the 5th of each month to this office, beginning with the 5th September 1942.

The majority of the three million Polish Jews were killed during 1942, and most of them were murdered in the three death camps of the 'Reinhard Action' and in Chełmno. However, in the meantime, two further camps had become involved in the extermination of the Jews. In 1943 one of them became the largest killing centre of all, a huge plant for the destruction of human life—Auschwitz–Birkenau.

(iii) Auschwitz and Majdanek

By the end of 1939, the prisons in Upper Silesia were becoming crowded with Polish civilians arrested by the German occupiers. In December, SS *Oberführer* Arpad Wigand, the Inspector of the Security Police and SD in the South-East district, requested that a concentration camp should be set up in the former Austrian barracks near the town of Auschwitz (Oświęcim). He argued that the site was relatively isolated and had good rail communications to Austria, Czechoslavakia, and the General Government. After an inspection of the site, this proposal was initially rejected. However, following a second inspection, on 21 February 1940, Richard Gluecks, the head of *Amt* D in the WHVA, proposed to Himmler the establishment of a 'quarantine camp' in which Polish prisoners would be held prior to their transfer to concentration camps further West. After a visit by a third SS committee of inspection, which included the then commandant of Sachsenhausen concentration camp, Rudolf Hoess, on 27 April 1940, Himmler gave the go-ahead for the construction of a concentration camp in Auschwitz.

On 4 May 1940, Hoess was appointed commandant of the new camp. He immediately began the building work with three hundred local Jews and a number of Poles. On 20 May, thirty specially selected hard core German criminals were brought in from Sachsenhausen to act as overseers within the camp and given the prisoner numbers 1–30. On 14 June, 728 Polish men were transferred to Auschwitz from the prison in Tarnów in the General Government.

The SS now began to develop increasingly ambitious plans for the new camp. Five days after the arrival of the first Polish prisoners, what was to become a massive resettlement programme began, eventually involving the eviction of thousands of Poles. For, ultimately, the Auschwitz complex was to cover a vast area of nearly eighteen square miles and to become a special government district (*Amtsbezirk*). In November 1940, Himmler decided to construct a home farm round the camp in which experiments in animal breeding, crop growing, and fish farming could be carried out. Then, at the end of December, Heydrich decided to set up a second concentration camp in Auschwitz. On 2 January 1941, he allocated Auschwitz I to the category I concentration camps for 'less serious prisoners definitely capable of rehabilitation' and Auschwitz II, which did not yet exist, to Category II for 'serious prisoners who are, however, still capable of rehabilitation and re-education'.

Meanwhile, the big German chemical combine of IG Farben, which was looking for a site for a new plant for making artificial rubber (Buna) had begun negotiations with the SS for the use of labour from the new camp at Auschwitz. On 6 February 1941, the first meeting was held and, four weeks later, on 4 March, Carl Krauch, simultaneously the supremo for chemical production in the Four Year Plan and chairman of the supervisory board of IG Farben, wrote to Otto Ambros, a member of the board as follows:

887

At my request, and on the instructions of the Reich Marshal, the *Reichsführer* SS has given the following orders.

1. The Jews in Auschwitz must be expelled as soon as possible, their dwellings must be vacated and secured for the workers who are to build the Buna works.
2. Poles in the Auschwitz district who may be eligible as workers or building workers for the Buna works may not be expelled.
3. The Inspector of the Concentration Camps and Chief of the Economic and Administrative Main Office has been instructed to establish contact at once with the building manager of the Buna works and to give all possible assistance to the building project through the provision of prisoners from the concentration camp.

Two days earlier, on his first visit to Auschwitz on 1 March 1941, Himmler informed Hoess of his goals for the camp as the latter recalled after the war:

888

After Himmler had inspected the camp in 1941, I received the order to build it up as a large concentration camp for the east, to employ the prisoners in particular in agriculture, which was to be expanded as much as possible, thereby utilizing the whole area beside the Vistula which was boggy and subject to flooding. Furthermore, he instructed that 8–10,000 prisoners should be made available for the construction of the new IG Farben Buna plant. At the same time, he ordered that a prisoner of war camp for 100,000 Russian prisoners of war should be constructed on the land round Birkenau [the Polish village of Brzezinka].

At the time of Himmler's visit, Auschwitz contained 10,900 prisoners, most of whom were Poles. The draft plans for the extension of the original camp (*Stammlager*), or Auschwitz I as it came to be known, were ready by June 1941 and work began at once on the construction of two large complexes, divided by a big parade ground, to contain a planned total of seventy-eight one-storey barracks. Building went on until the autumn of 1944 and, although the plan was only partially realised, it is clear that Auschwitz I was envisaged as a major concentration camp built to last.

Himmler's statement to Hoess in March suggests that he had substituted the plan for a Russian POW camp for Heydrich's second concentration camp in the light of the planning for Barbarossa, which was a major preoccupation in the first months of 1941. However, both plans for the Birkenau area were soon rendered obsolete by a new one as Hoess recalled after the war:

889

In the summer of 1941—I can no longer remember the exact date—I was suddenly summoned to the *Reichsführer* SS in Berlin directly by his adjutant's office. Contrary to his normal practice, he received me without his adjutant being present and told me in effect:

'The Führer has ordered the final solution of the Jewish question and we—the SS—have to carry out this order. The existing extermination centres in the east are not in a position to carry out the major operations which are envisaged. I have, therefore, earmarked Auschwitz for this task both because of its favourable communications and because the area envisaged can be easily sealed off and camouflaged. Initially, I selected a senior SS leader for this task but changed my mind to avoid disputes over competencies and you must now carry out this task. It will be onerous and difficult and will require your full personal commitment without regard for any difficulties that may arise. You will be given further details by *Sturmbannführer* Eichmann of the RSHA who will call on you shortly. I will inform the departments involved in due course.

You will maintain the strictest silence concerning this order even vis-à-vis your superiors. After your meeting with Eichmann send me the plans for the proposed installations at once. The Jews are the eternal enemies of the German people and must be exterminated. Every Jew we can lay our hands on must be exterminated during the war without exception. If we now fail to destroy the biological basis of Jewry then one day the Jews will destroy the German people.'

On receiving this grave order, I returned at once to Auschwitz without reporting to my superiors in Oranienburg.

Shortly afterwards, Eichmann came to see me in Auschwitz. He initiated me into the plans for the actions in the various countries concerned. I can no longer remember the exact order in which they were to take place. To start with, Auschwitz was expected to deal with the eastern part of Upper Silesia and the adjacent parts of the General Government, then, depending on circumstances, simultaneously the Jews from Germany, Czechoslovakia, and finally, the Jews from the West—France, Belgium, and Holland. He mentioned to me the rough figures of the transports which could be expected, but I can no longer remember them. In addition, we discussed how the extermination was to be carried out. Gas was the only feasible method, since it would be impossible too liquidate by shooting the large numbers envisaged and shooting would place too heavy a burden on the SS men who had to carry it out, particularly in view of the women and children involved.

Eichmann informed me of the method of killing by exhaust fumes from vans, which had been implemented in the east hitherto. However, it was out of the question to use it in Auschwitz on the mass transports which were envisaged. The method of killing by means of carbon monoxide gas through showers in a bath room, which was being used for the destruction of the mentally ill in various places in the Reich, would require too many buildings; it would also be very difficult to secure gas for such large numbers. We failed to reach a decision on this matter. Eichmann decided to look for a gas which would be easy to obtain and would not require special installations and then report back to me. We drove through the area to select a suitable place. We decided that the farmstead in the north-west corner of what later became the Building Sector III at Birkenau was suitable. It was isolated, screened by the surrounding woodlands and hedges and not too far from the railway. The corpses could be accommodated in long deep pits in the adjacent meadow. At that point we did not think of cremation. We estimated that we could kill approximately eight hundred people simultaneously with gas in the available premises after they had been made gastight. This estimate was later borne out in practice.

Eichmann travelled back to Berlin in order to report to the *Reichsführer* SS on our discussions. A few days later, I sent the *Reichsführer* SS by courier a detailed plan of the camp and an exact description of the installation. I never received a reply or a decision. I heard later from Eichmann that the *Reichsführer* SS had approved it.

At the end of November, there was a meeting at Eichmann's office in Berlin of the whole Jewish section to which I was also summoned. Eichmann's representatives in the various countries reported on the state of the operation and on the difficulties to be encountered in implementing it, such as the accommodation of those arrested, the provision of trains for the transports, the planning of timetables etc. I could not find out when the actions were due to begin. And Eichmann had not yet managed to get hold of a suitable gas.

In the autumn of 1941, a special secret order was issued for the Russian *politruks*, commissars, and special political functionaries to be weeded out of the prisoner of war camps by the Gestapo and to be taken to the nearest concentration camp for liquidation. Small transports of such people were continually arriving in Auschwitz and they were shot either in the gravel pit near the Monopoly buildings[21] or in the courtyard of Block 11. While I was away on official business, my deputy, *Hauptsturmführer* Fritsch, on his own initiative, used gas to exterminate these Russian prisoners of war. He crammed the individual cells in the cellar with Russians and, protected by gas masks, hurled Cyclon B into the cells which caused death immediately. The Cyclon B gas was supplied by the firm of Tesch and Stabenow and regularly used in Auschwitz for the purpose of pest control, and so the administration always had a supply of cannisters of this gas. Initially, this poison gas, a preparation of Prussic acid, was only used by the firm of Tesch and Stabenow under strict safety precautions, but later some members of the medical service were trained by the firm in its use and they then used the gas for disinfection and pest control. During Eichmann's next visit I reported to him about this use of Cyclon B and we decided to employ this gas for the future mass extermination operation . . .

According to Hoess, this gassing of Russian POWs took place on 3 September 1941. Confirmation of this is provided by the statement of the Czech prisoner, Josef Vacek, made on 8 May 1945:

890

At the beginning of September, Soviet prisoners of war were brought into the camp. There were more than 500 of them. 196 sick prisoners who were selected by the SS doctor, Jungen, were added and were gassed together with the Russian prisoners of war in the gas chamber in Block 11. We nursing orderlies who brought them there were told that they were being taken away on a transport . . . The following night, when everyone was asleep and nobody was allowed to leave the block, I was summoned, together with thirty other orderlies, and for three nights we brought the gassed corpses to the crematorium.

Soon afterwards, a room next to the crematorium known as the 'mortuary' was converted into a gas chamber as Hoess reported:

[21] These were buildings in Auschwitz I which stored clothing and equipment for the SS (eds).

891

I have an even clearer memory of the gassing of nine hundred Russians which occurred shortly afterwards. This took place in the old crematorium, since Block 11 involved too many complications. While they were being unloaded, several holes were drilled in the earth and concrete roof of the mortuary. The Russians had to undress in the ante-room and then went quite calmly into the mortuary since they were told that they would be fumigated. The whole transport just managed to fit inside the mortuary. The doors were locked and the gas was poured in through the openings. I do not know how long this killing took. But the buzzing noise could be heard for quite a time. When the gas was thrown in some people shouted: 'gas' and then there was a lot of shouting and they pressed against both the doors. But they withstood the pressure.

The first transports of Jews arrived early in 1942 from Upper Silesia. To start with they were gassed in the 'mortuary', but the difficulty of coping with the numbers involved—the crematorium could only burn around 340 corpses a day, and it was difficult to preserve secrecy—prompted Hoess to shift the gassing to Birkenau, to the site which he had already selected on his tour of inspection with Eichmann in the previous autumn. The construction of the camp in Birkenau (Auschwitz II), three kilometres from the main camp, had begun in October 1941 and was carried out by prisoners from the main camp at great speed because the transfer of 10,000 Russian prisoners of war to Auschwitz had increased the number of inmates to over 20,000 causing overcrowding. After the war, SS *Rottenführer* Pery Broad described the first gassing installations in Birkenau:

892

At some distance from the Birkenau camp, which was expanding at a tremendous rate, in the middle of a charming landscape, were two pretty and well-kept-looking farm houses separated from one another by a small wood. They were white-washed, had nice thatched roofs, and were surrounded by homely fruit trees . . . The first thing to strike a careful observer of these houses would be notices in various languages stating: 'To the disinfection [room]'. Then, he would notice that the houses had no windows and an unusual number of remarkably strong doors with rubber seals and screwtype hinges, with little wooden flaps next to them, and that near-by there were large stable-type barracks like those which served as accommodation for the prisoners in the Birkenau camp, which did not fit in with the houses . . .

These two houses were, in the jargon of the camp, Bunkers 1 and 2. Bunker 1, which began operations early in 1942, had two gas chambers with only one door each and two undressing rooms; it was dismantled in December 1942. Bunker 2 began operations in the summer of 1942, when the Jewish transports began to build up. It contained three gas chambers and three undressing barracks and could accommodate 1,200 people at a time, compared with 800 in Bunker 1. It continued in operation on and off until autumn 1944.

The transports arrived at the platform or ramp of the goods station at Auschwitz, located half-way between Auschwitz I and II. From July 1942 onwards, those arriving were selected by an SS doctor into those who were considered fit—mainly young men and women, who were taken to Auschwitz I, and those considered unfit—the old, sick, and mothers with young children—who were taken straight to the bunkers in Birkenau. The numbers in each category fluctuated to some extent. This fluctuation depended more on the labour demands of Auschwitz I and its later branch camps, notably Monowitz, which supplied the labour for the IG Farben Buna plant, than it did on the actual physical health of those arriving. For the selection process was extremely crude and the tendency was to declare people unfit for work where possible—much to the annoyance of the SS personnel in Berlin, who were responsible for maintaining the supply of labour. On average, however, up to thirty per cent of each transport was declared fit for work. After the war, Broad described the arrival of a transport at Auschwitz as follows:

893

A long train made up of closed goods waggons is standing at a side platform of the marshalling yard. The sliding doors are sealed with barbed wire. The squad of troops has taken up position around the train and the ramp . . . The SS men of the inmate control section [*Schutzhaftlagerführung*] ensure that the prisoners leave the train. There is chaos and confusion on the ramp . . . To start with the men and women are separated. There are heart-breaking scenes. Married couples separate. Mothers wave good-bye to their sons for the last time. The two columns stand in ranks of five several metres apart from one another on the ramp. Anyone who is overcome with grief and tries to rush over to embrace his or her loved one once more and give them words of comfort is hurled back by a blow from one of the SS men. Now the SS doctor begins to select those fit for work from those who, in his opinion, are unfit for work. Mothers with small children are on principle unfit for work as are all those who convey the impression of being frail or sick. Portable step ladders are placed on the backs of lorries and those who have been selected by the SS doctor as unfit must climb up. The SS men of the reception department count each person who climbs these steps . . .

The French doctor, André Lettich, who at one time was assigned to the Jewish 'special commando' responsible for removing the bodies from the gas chambers, recorded after the war what happened when those designated unfit for work reached the 'bunkers':

894

Until the end of January 1943, there were no crematoria in Birkenau. In the middle of a small birch forest, about two kilometres from the camp, was a peaceful looking house, where a Polish family had once lived before it had been either murdered or expelled. This cottage had been equipped as a gas chamber for a long time.

More than five hundred metres further on were two barracks: the men stood on one side, the women on the other. They were addressed in a very polite and friendly way: 'You have been on a journey. You are dirty. You will take a bath. Get undressed quickly.' Towels and soap were handed out, and then suddenly the brutes woke up and showed their true faces: this horde of people, these men and women were driven outside with hard blows and forced both summer and winter to go the few hundred metres to the 'Shower Room'. Above the entry door was the word 'Shower'. One could even see shower heads on the ceiling which were cemented in but never had water flowing through them.

These poor innocents were crammed together, pressed against each other. Then panic broke out, for at last they realised the fate in store for them. But blows with rifle butts and revolver shots soon restored order and finally they all entered the death chamber. The doors were shut and, ten minutes later, the temperature was high enough to facilitate the condensation of the hydrogen cyanide, for the condemned were gassed with hydrogen cyanide. This was the so-called 'Zyklon B', gravel pellets saturated with twenty per cent of hydrogen cyanide which was used by the German barbarians.

Then, SS *Unterscharführer* Moll threw the gas in through a little vent. One could hear fearful screams, but a few moments later there was complete silence. Twenty to twenty-five minutes later, the doors and windows were opened to ventilate the rooms and the corpses were thrown at once into pits to be burnt. But, beforehand the dentists had searched every mouth to pull out the gold teeth. The women were also searched to see if they had not hidden jewellery in the intimate parts of their bodies, and their hair was cut off and methodically placed in sacks for industrial purposes.

The increase in the number of Jewish transports during the summer of 1942 prompted the SS not only to open Bunker 2, but also to initiate the construction of four large crematoria complexes in Birkenau. This was carried out in collaboration with a number of German firms: Topf and Sons of Erfurt, specialists for crematoria, and the building firms of W. Riedel and Son of Bielitz, Robert Köhler in Myslowitz, and Josef Kluge in Gleiwitz. In a post-war statement Hoess described the new crematoria as follows:

895

The two large crematoria, Nos. I and II, were built during the winter of 1942–43 and began operating in the spring of 1943. They each had five three-retort ovens and each could cremate *c.* 2,000 corpses within twenty-four hours . . . Crematoria I and II both had underground undressing and gassing rooms which could be completely ventilated. The corpses were brought up to the ovens on the floor above by lift. The gas chambers could hold *c.* 3,000 people, but this figure was never achieved since the individual transports were never as large as that.

The firm of Topf had calculated that the two smaller crematoria, III and IV, would each be able to cremate 1,500 corpses within twenty-four hours. However, owing to the wartime shortage of materials, the builders were obliged to economise and so the undressing rooms and gassing rooms were built above ground and the ovens were of a less solid construction. But it soon became apparent that the flimsy construction of these two four-retort ovens was not up to the demands made on it. No. III ceased operating altogether after a short time and later was no longer used. No. IV had to be repeatedly shut down since after a short period in operation of 4–6 weeks, the ovens and chimneys had burnt out. The victims of the gassing were mainly burnt in pits behind crematorium IV.

The largest number of people gassed and cremated within twenty-four hours was somewhat over 9,000. This figure was achieved in the summer of 1944 during the action in Hungary and involved using all the installations except No. III. On that day, owing to delays on the railways, five trains arrived instead of three as expected, and, moreover, the waggons were more crowded than usual.

In addition to the construction of the new gassing complexes, a railway line was laid to enable the transports to be brought directly into the Birkenau camp where the ramp was now situated; it was finished in mid-May 1944. A French doctor, Sigismund Bendel, who for a time was attached to the Jewish special commando in Birkenau, reported after the war as follows:

896

Two railway tracks brought the deportees directly to the door of the twin crematoria I and II. With their spacious rooms equipped with telephones and radio, with their ultra-modern dissecting room and their museum of anatomical specimens, these installations were, as an SS man unashamedly told me, ‘the best of their kind which have every been built . . .’

The procession of those condemned to death was directed down a broad stone staircase into a large underground room which served as an undressing room. The rubric was that everyone should take a bath and then go and be disinfected. Everyone bundled their clothing together and—the culmination of the illusion—

hung it up on a numbered peg. From there they went stark naked via a small passage into the actual gas chambers (there were two of them). The gas chambers were made of reinforced concrete and the ceiling was so low that on entering one had the feeling that they would fall on one's head. In the middle of these chambers there were two [vertical] pipes covered with a grill with vents to the outside which were used for throwing in the gas. The SS could watch the terrible death agonies of these unfortunates through a small peephole in the massive oak double doors. The corpses were then brought out by the men of the commando and taken up to the ground floor in a lift where the sixteen ovens were situated. Their total cremation capacity was roughtly 2,000 corpses in twenty-four hours. The twin crematoria III and IV, which were generally known as 'forest cremas' (for they were situated in an attractive clearing) had more modest dimensions with their eight ovens and a capacity of 1,000 corpses per twenty-four hours.

One day, in June 1944 at six o'clock in the morning, I join the day shift (150 men) of crematorium IV. . . At eleven o'clock, a member of the political section appears on a motor cycle and reports that a transport is on its way. It is mid-day, when a long line of women, children, and old people enter the yard of the crematorium, people from the Lódź ghetto. One can see that they are exhausted and anxious. The senior official in charge of the crematorium, Herr *Hauptscharführer* Mohl . . . climbs on a bench to tell them that they are going to have a bath and that afterwards they will get a drink of hot coffee. There is applause . . . They all undress in the yard. The doors of the crematorium open and they enter the large room which in winter serves as an undressing room. Pressed together like sardines, they realize they have fallen into a trap out of which there is no longer any escape. Nevertheless, they continue to hope since a normal brain is incapable of grasping the terrible death which awaits them. Finally, everything is ready. The doors are opened and an indescribable jostling begins. The first people to enter the gas chamber begin to draw back. They sense the death which awaits them. The SS men put an end to this pushing and shoving with blows from their rifle butts beating the heads of the horrified women who are desperately hugging their children. The massive oak double doors are shut. For two endless minutes one can hear banging on the walls and screams which are no longer human. And then—not a sound . . . Five minutes later the doors are opened. The corpses, squashed together and distorted, fall out like a waterfall . . . The bodies which are still warm pass through the hands of the hairdresser who cuts their hair and the dentist who pulls out their gold teeth . . . One more transport has just been processed through No. IV crematorium.

As Hoess reported, Birkenau achieved its highest murder rate in the summer of 1944 when the Hungarian transports were arriving. This was confirmed by Pery Broad:

897

Auschwitz reached its high point in the spring of 1944. Long trains travelled backwards and forwards between the subsidiary camp of Birkenau and Hungary . . . A triple track railway line leading to the new crematoria enabled a train to be unloaded while the next one was arriving. The percentage of those who were assigned to 'special accommodation'—the term which had been used for some time in place of 'special treatment'—was particularly high in the case of these transports . . . All four crematoria operated at full blast. However, soon the ovens were burnt out as a result of the continuous heavy use and only crematorium No. III was still smoking . . . The special commandos had been increased and worked feverishly to keep emptying the gas chambers. Even one of the white farmhouses was brought back into use . . . It was given the title 'Bunker 5' . . . The last body had hardly been pulled from the gas chambers and dragged across the yard behind the crematorium, which was covered in corpses, to the burning pit, when the next lot were already undressing in the hall ready for gassing.

In these circumstances there were problems with the disposal of the corpses and the maintenance of secrecy as Hoess recalled:

898

Already with the initial cremations in the open air, it became apparent that this could not be continued on a permanent basis. In bad weather or a strong wind the smell of burning spread over several kilometres and caused the whole population of the surrounding area to start talking about the burning of the Jews, despite the counter-propaganda on the part of the Party and the administrative agencies. Although all the members of the SS participating in the extermination programme received very strict instructions to keep silent about the whole procedure, later SS court proceedings showed that the participants did not in fact remain silent. Even severe punishments could not stop people from gossiping.

Furthermore, the air defence authorities complained about the fire at night, which could be clearly seen from the air. However, we had to keep cremating at night in order not to have to halt the incoming transports. The timetabling of the individual actions was firmly fixed by the Reich Transport Ministry in a time-table conference and had to be adhered to in order to avoid clogging up and disorganising the railway lines concerned—particularly for military reasons.

After the transports had arrived, the results of the selections were reported to *Amt* D II of the WVHA headquarters in Oranienburg as in the following document from Auschwitz dated 8 March 1943 and signed *Obersturmführer* [Albert] Schwarz:

899

Re: Transport of Jewish armaments' workers.

On 5 and 7 March, the following transports of Jewish prisoners arrived: (and 96 women). Transport from Berlin. Arrivals 5 March 1943. Total 1,128 Jews. 389 men were selected for work (Buna). 151 men and 492 women and children were given special treatment. Transport from Breslau. Arrival 5 March 1943. Total 1,405 Jews. 406 men and 190 women were selected for work (Buna). 125 men and 684 women and children were given special treatment.

Transport from Berlin. Arrival 7 March 43. Total 690 including 25 prisoners in protective custody. 153 men and 25 prisoners and 65 women were selected for work (Buna). 30 men and 417 women and children were given special treatment.

Those Jews who were not selected for 'special treatment' were either held in Auschwitz itself or were transferred to one of the many branch camps which sprang up between 1942 and 1944. Some Jews were transferred to the original camp (Auschwitz I), where they formed a significant proportion of the prisoner population, of whom the majority, however, were non-Jews from several countries. Here they were employed in workshops (DAW) doing repairs for the *Wehrmacht*, or in the various tasks involved in running the camp: for example, the 'potato commando', which stored and transported the vegetables which formed the main food of the camp—a watery soup made of turnips, potatoes, and peelings.

Some Jews remained in Birkenau (Auschwitz II) which expanded rapidly during 1942–3 and was divided into separate units each containing thirty-two barracks. BIa was the camp for women prisoners, which at the end of 1943 was extended into BIb. BIId was the camp for male prisoners. BIIb became a separate camp for Jews transferred from Theresienstadt, of whom some 11,000 passed through before being eventually gassed. BIIe became a camp for Gypsy families. Between 26 February 1943 and 21 July 1944 some 20,967 Gypsy men, women and children were accommodated there until it was liquidated on 2 August 1944 and the remaining 2,897 were gassed. In June 1944, BIIc and BIII were established as a transit camp for female Jews, mainly from Hungary. At the end of September 1944, some 40,000 of these Jewesses were gassed over a period of ten days, leaving 17,202 still alive.

Finally, other Jews selected for work were transferred to one of the forty-odd branch camps which sprang up between 1942 and 1944, most of which were situated within a radius of one hundred kilometres of Auschwitz. Of these, twenty-eight were situated near industrial plants which were working directly or indirectly for the armaments industry: nine near iron, steel, and metal-working plants, six near coal mines, six near chemical plants, three near light industrial factories, two near power stations under construction, one near a building firm, and one near a food factory. In 1942 there were 6,000 Auschwitz prisoners working in industrial plants; in 1943 this had risen to 17,000 and, by the end of 1944, to 41,000, though many of these were non-Jews. These camps were supplying labour for some of the most established German firms: Krupp, Siemens-Schuckert, Rheinmetall, Borsig etc. The most important of these links between Auschwitz and German industry was that with IG Farben. Early in 1941, the SS had reached an agreement with IG Farben to supply workers from Auschwitz for the new Buna plant which the firm had decided to build nearby at Dwory. On 12 April 1941, Otto Ambros, the deputy-director of the main Ludwigshafen plant of IG Farben, wrote to Dr Fritz Ter Meer, the chairman of the key Technical Committee (TEA), and the Secretary, Dr Ernst Struss, as follows:

900

I am enclosing the reports about our discussions concerning construction, which are taking place on a regular weekly basis under my chairmanship. From them you will be able to follow the organisational arrangements which have been made concerning our activities in the east and above all the date on which they start.

In the meantime, the inaugural meeting has taken place in Kattowitz which in general went smoothly. Certain objections from petty bureaucrats were quickly overcome.

Dr Eckell proved very valuable in this connexion and also our new friendship with the SS had a very beneficial effect.

On the occasion of a dinner given in our honour by the leadership of the concentration camp, we reached agreement on the measures concerning the intervention of the truly superb management of the concentration camp on behalf of the Buna works.

Building work began on the Buna plant in Dwory near Auschwitz in April 1941. Before long, the problems involved in transporting the workers the seven kilometres from Auschwitz to Dwory prompted IG Farben and the SS to build a camp near the plant in the village of Monowice (Monowitz), from which the Polish inhabitants had been previously expelled.

Conditions in all the camps were appalling. *Schutzhaftlagerführer* Fritsch greeted new arrivals in the main camp with the words: ‘You have not come to a sanatorium but to a German concentration camp from which there is no exit other than up the chimney of the crematorium’.[22] Prisoners had to

[22] Cf. *Auschwitz. Geschichte und Wirklichkeit des Vernichtungslagers* (Reinbek 1980) p. 27. This section owes much to this book.

work at a murderous tempo and were subject to brutal physical punishments, including flogging, for the slightest breach of regulations or at the whim of the SS guards or the prisoner-overseers (Kapos and *Lagerälteste*), who in many cases were hardened criminals. It was up to the prisoner himself to learn what to do since there were no official rules as such. And, if he was to survive he had to learn fast. After the war, a Polish doctor, Czeław Jaworski, who had been sent to Auschwitz on suspicion of being a member of an illegal organization, recounted an illuminating incident:

901

On the stairs I saw a noticeboard in the corridor with various announcements in German. I was looking for rules which applied to us in the camp on the assumption that they would take the form of official regulations and be made generally known. Suddenly, I saw the Block clerk and so I turned to him. 'Excuse me, sir, are there any rules for prisoners in this camp? I would like to get to know them in order to avoid any unpleasantness'. He looked at me as if I was mad, hit me in the face, and said: 'There are your rules, Herr Ministerial Councillor!' This explanation cost me two teeth.

The employers and foremen of the German firms, for which the prisoners in the branch camps worked, adopted the methods and mentality of the SS and the prisoners were effectively worked to death. In 1944, a group of prisoners arriving in Monowitz were told that they were now in a concentration camp of IG Farben and had come not to live there but to 'perish in concrete', a reference to the practice of throwing the corpses of prisoners who died on the job into the trenches dug for cables which were then concreted over.[23] Of the 35,000 inmates who passed through Monowitz, not all of whom were Jews, at least 25,000 died. Their life expectancy was three months or, if they were in one of the IG Farben coal mines near-by, a month.

Prisoners were also subject to continual selections which were carried out not only in Auschwitz main camp and in Birkenau, but also in the branch camps. Here the SS had a direct financial interest in replacing unfit prisoners with fit ones, since the firms employing them only paid for work actually performed. After the war, a former prisoner, Franciszek Stryf recalled the procedure:

[23] Cf. R. Hilberg, *The Destruction of the European Jews* (New York 1973) p. 595.

902

Selections in the sick bays were an every day occurrence, but every prisoner was gripped with fear when, after the evening roll call, a camp curfew was imposed and a group of SS men, with the camp leader, Baer, the work leader, SS *Untersturmführer* Sell, and *Rapportführer* Kaduk in the lead, walked into the bath house. On a sign from the Block leader, we began to run past them in single file so that the SS men could just about recognize us as individuals. We had to be very careful because the wooden grill under the showers was very uneven and so one could easily sprain one's leg and fall down. That was enough to put oneself among those condemned to death. The SS people gazed at us greedily. They were looking for victims. The more the merrier. After the inspection, when we had run right across the bath house, all the prisoners assembled in the birch avenue along the wire fence. The block leader counted us again. Six men from our block had stayed behind to be gassed or given a phenol injection. It was an awful time. Some people were completely exhausted by it; others were exhilarated. Adolf, for example, after returning to the block, couldn't believe that he had withstood the baptism of fire. He tried to run through the barrack at the same speed as he had just run through the bath house and stumbled on the even floor. He touched his swollen feet, stroked them gently, and kept repeating: 'My God, dear God, how did I do it?' Then, he marched naked through the room as if he wanted to reassure himself that he was still among the living. He was as pleased as a child and showed off to everybody as if he looked like a young god. In October that same year we had to go through another such test of strength and nerves. Adolf did not return with us that time . . .

Prisoners were also used for medical experiments; indeed, some had been expressly selected for that purpose. Himmler was concerned both to restrict the birth rate of those ethnic groups which he considered racially inferior and to increase that of the German people. *Obersturmbannführer* Rudolf Brandt, Himmler's personal secretary, reported after the war as follows:

903

Himmler was extremely interested in developing a cheap and rapid method of sterilization which could be used on enemies of the German Reich such as Russians Poles, and Jews. The hope was that in this way one could not only conquer the enemy but also destroy him. The labour power of those who were sterilised could be utilised by Germany, while their procreative capabilities would be destroyed. Mass sterilization was part of Himmler's racial theory and so a great deal of time and effort was devoted to the sterilization experiments.

Professor Carl Clauberg concentrated on the sterilization of women by blocking the uterus through injections of an irritant fluid, experiments which were extremely painful and produced infertility. His colleague, Dr Horst Schumann, concentrated on sterilization by means of large doses of X-rays on both men and women which produced radiation burns and effective castration. Dr Josef Mengele, who supervised most of the selections on the ramp in Auschwitz, was attached to the prestigious Kaiser-Wilhelm Institute in Berlin. He was interested in genetics, with the aim of improving the quality and quantity of German births. His main focus of research was identical twins and he preferred children for his experiments. Apart from experiments on live children, he also took advantage of the otherwise rare opportunity of studying the organs of twins who had died simultaneously, by killing them after he had concluded his experiments.

Hoess controlled the whole Auschwitz complex directly through *Schutzhaftlagerführer* in the various camps. However, on 11 November 1943, he was transferred to the WVHA headquarters and replaced as commandant of Auschwitz by the previous head of *Amt* DI in the WVHA, SS *Obersturmbannführer* Arthur Liebehenschel, who remained until his transfer to Majdanek on 11 May 1944. Pohl now ordered a re-organization of Auschwitz, which Liebehenschel implemented by an order of 22 November 1943, dividing the camp into three separate sections:

Concentration camp I— Original camp (*Stammlager*)
Concentration camp II—Birkenau
Concentration camp III—Outside camps (Monowitz and nine other camps).

Liebehenschel was commandant of Camp I and the commandants of Camp II (Fritz Harfenstein) and Camp III (Heinrich Schwarz) were subordinate to him.

The number of those held in Auschwitz and its various camps, of whom from 1942 onwards Jews formed a significant but varying proportion, were subject to considerable fluctuation, as a result of the high death rate and the irregularity of the arrival of transports. On 20 January 1944, there were 80,839 male and female prisoners. 18,437 were held in Auschwitz I, 49,114 in Auschwitz II (male camp 22,061, female camp 27,053) and 13,288 in Auschwitz III, of whom 6,571 were in Monowitz itself. A month later, the figure had dropped to 73,669, but by 22 August 1944, it had climbed to 105,168. This was only the figure of those registered in the camp files. In addition, there were some 50,000 unregistered male and female Jewish prisoners held as so-called 'deposit' in the BIIc, BIIe, and BIII (Mexico) compounds in Birkenau. From then onwards, the camp began to be run down under the growing threat of the advancing Russians. Prisoners were transferred to other concentration camps or gassed. The last recorded Jewish transport reached Auschwitz on 3 November 1944. On 25

November, Birkenau was merged into Auschwitz I and Auschwitz III was renamed Monowitz. The following day, Himmler ordered the destruction of the crematoria to conceal the incriminating evidence of the Holocaust. The exception to the run-down was Monowitz which, by December 1944, contained 35,000 prisoners, including 2,000 women. Here, the Nazis desperately squeezed the last ounce of productivity out of their labour slaves.

At the last roll call in Auschwitz on 17 January 1945, there were 67,012 male and female prisoners, over half of them in Monowitz. The following day, the Nazis began hurriedly evacuating the camp. Most of the surviving prisoners were transferred to other camps further west, a frightful journey partly on foot in the depths of winter which many did not survive. When Russian troops reached the camp on 27 January they found some 7,000 prisoners alive. The camp records contained the names of 400,000 prisoners who had been registered as having passed through Auschwitz. Of these, some 60,000 survived the war. This figure of 400,000 excluded those Jews who had never been registered, since they had either been gassed on arrival in Birkenau or after having been held as 'deposit' for a few weeks or months. In a post-war statement Hoess gave the following estimate of the numbers of Jews killed in Auschwitz, figures which most scholars now regard as a reasonably accurate estimate:

904

I can only remember the numbers involved in the larger actions which were repeated to me by Eichmann or one of his representatives.

From Upper Silesia and the General Government	250,000
Germany and Theresienstadt	100,000
Holland	95,000
Belgium	20,000
France	110,000
Greece	65,000
Hungary	400,000
Slovakia	90,000

I can no longer recall the figures for the smaller actions. However, they were insignificant by comparison with those above.

The Majdanek camp in Lublin originated as part of Himmler's schemes for the racial reorganization of Eastern Europe. On 20–21 July 1941, Himmler ordered the construction of a major SS base in Lublin which was intended to function as the core of a racial barrier stretching north to East

Prussia and south to Galicia. The territory would be cleared of 'racially undesirable elements' (Poles and Jews) and settled with Germans, an extension of the process which had already taken place in the Warthegau. As part of this plan, Himmler envisaged a large concentration camp in Lublin which could provide the necessary labour for his construction plans. In September 1941, plans were developed for a camp which was eventually envisaged as housing 125,000 prisoners. The *Wehrmacht* had promised up to 100,000 Soviet prisoners of war. However, the refusal of the *Reichsbahn* to provide sufficient transport, difficulties in obtaining supplies of building materials, and the demand for Soviet prisoners' labour elsewhere ensured that Majdanek never reached more than half its planned size.

Although Majdanek was in Lublin, it was not properly part of the 'Reinhard Action'. Like Auschwitz, it was directly subordinate to the WVHA in Oranienburg and not to Globocnik. Its personnel, including its second commandant, the notorious Karl Koch, were largely drawn from Buchenwald not from T4. It was primarily a forced labour camp for Poles and Russian prisoners of war, who worked in the SS plants in the Lublin area. However, it also contained at various times a substantial number of Jews, mainly from Poland, but also from Slovakia and elsewhere. The numbers fluctuated from, for example, 20–25,000 in September 1942 to 6,000 in December 1943.

Of the roughly 200,000 who died there, some 60,000 were Jews. In September–October 1942, three gas chambers were constructed in which both carbon monoxide in cylinders and Zyklon B gas were used. Of those killed in Majdanek around twenty-five per cent were gassed, sixty per cent died of sickness, malnutrition, and over-work, and the remainder were shot or beaten to death. Early in November 1943, the remaining Jews in Majdanek numbering several thousand were all shot, part of a total of some 40,000 Jews in labour camps in the Lublin area who were shot over a period of a few days in an operation which carried the code name 'Harvest festival' (*Erntedankfest*).

(iv) The Deportation of the Jews of Western and Southern Europe 1942–1944

While the vast majority of Polish Jewry died in the death camps in the General Government and the Russian Jews were killed by the *Einsatzgruppen* in the Soviet Union, most of the Jews of Western and Southern Europe who were deported, including many Germans, died in Auschwitz. The arrangements for the deportation of Jews to Auschwitz were handled by Department IV B4 of the RSHA under its head, Adolf Eichmann. It worked in liaison with the Foreign Ministry and the German railways. A special department within the Foreign Ministry, first under Martin Luther, a hard-line Nazi and protégé of Ribbentrop and his deputy, Rademacher, and then, from 1943, under Horst Wagner and his deputy, von Thadden, was responsible for handling the Jewish question. It played an active role in pressing Germany's allies and satellites to introduce anti-semitic measures and then to release their Jews for deportation. Officials of Eichmann's department were attached to German embassies and missions abroad.

Eichmann's department had begun preparations for the deportation of the Jews in western and southern Europe immediately after Heydrich had received his commission from Göring to prepare for the final solution of the Jewish question at the end of July 1941. They were aware of the political and diplomatic problems that would be involved. In dealing with allies and satellites, Germany was obliged to move cautiously, particularly since her position was deteriorating from 1943 onwards. Some of these governments, such as Slovakia and Croatia, which were in fact German creations, cooperated with more or less enthusiasm. Romania even killed over a hundred thousand of its own Jews in the eastern provinces of Bukovina and Bessarabia, recovered from the Russians in 1941. However, it then had second thoughts, as a result of the developing war situation, and declined to deport the 300,000 Jews of Old Romania. Other allies, such as Italy and Hungary, resisted the deportation of their Jews until they were taken over by the Germans in September 1943 and March 1944 respectively. However, whereas in Italy the deportations were largely frustrated, even after the German takeover, by the lack of cooperation by the Italian authorities and the active and passive resistance of the Italian people, in Hungary the cooperation of the new puppet Hungarian government of Sztojay ensured that the majority of the Hungarian Jews died in Auschwitz. Only Finland among the German allies and satellites succeeded in protecting its few Jews completely, partly because of its remoteness, partly because of its political sensitivity, and partly because of the uncompromising stance of the Finnish government.

In the case of the occupied territories, the Jew-hunters of IV B4 had, on the face of it, an easier time. However, even here much depended on the extent of German control over a particular territory and on the attitude of the local government authorities and population. Where the German grip was tight, as in Holland, the majority of the Jews perished, where it was relatively loose and where the local authorities and population strongly resisted Nazi anti-semitic policy, as in Denmark, most of the Jews survived, escaping in this case to Sweden.

In a post-war statement, SS *Hauptsturmführer* Dieter Wisliceny, a friend and subordinate of Eichmann's, gave an account of the deportation process in which his own role was somewhat whitewashed:

905

. . . Responsibility for carrying out the deportations to the Auschwitz and Lublin camps was assigned to the Central Office in Vienna and the Central Department in Prague. In the Reich the local Gestapo offices and in Poland the SS and Police Leaders were responsible. In the occupied territories Eichmann normally sent in his own commandos, which were organizationally attached to the commanders of the Sipo [*Sicherheitspolizei* = Security Police] and the SD. With the deportations from the occupied territories and the countries allied to Germany, Eichmann operated on the basis of the existing political realities and initially he avoided exerting political pressure. This approach also reflected the attempt to make the operation run as unobtrusively and secretly as possible. It was only later, in 1943–44, that he departed from this principle. The correctness of this observation is best demonstrated by a comparison of the events in Slovakia and in Romania.

The deportations from the European countries began simultaneously in France, Holland, Belgium and Slovakia in March/April 1942. In all these countries Eichmann made particular efforts to get hold of the Jews who were fit for work first, since the extermination camps in Auschwitz and Lublin were still being set up. In France the Jewish emigrés were the first to be caught up in the action, while the Vichy government only agreed to the deportation of French citizens at a later date. The situation was similar in Holland and Belgium. In Slovakia the then Slovakian government made a clear-cut offer to deport Jewish workers and then their families. Just how cautiously Eichmann moved in this case, which involved the first country which was not occupied, is clear from the fact that he demanded the removal of their citizenship and the payment of a 'resettlement contribution' [from the Slovakian goverment]. He did not subsequently make such a demand of any other country. The fact that the Slovakian goverment agreed to Eichmann's demand indicates that it had an interest in the deportation. Had it not made such a voluntary offer, Slovakia would probably not have been included in the deportation programme until 1944, since Eichmann initially postponed action in Hungary and Romania for political reasons. In Romania the 'advisor' and police attaché there, on Eichmann's orders, tried to persuade the Romanian government to deport its Jews to Poland. However, Antonescu rejected this and carried out an action of his own, deporting the Jews into the Russian territory occupied by Romania, in particular the area round Odessa. In fact, no Jews were transported from Romania to the extermination camps, despite all Eichmann's efforts in this direction. During the summer and autumn of 1942, actions were being carried out in France, Holland, Belgium, and Slovakia. As far as I know, there was only one transport from Croatia, from Agram; the other Jews had fled, either to the Italian-occupied part or to the partisans.

At the end of the summer of 1942, a general halt to the deportations began. Resistance to the deportations had increased in every country. That had much to do with the true facts becoming widely known. Until the autumn of 1942, Eichmann kept the final solution secret even from his colleagues. This was all the more easy to achieve in that they only came to Berlin rarely when summoned by Eichmann. It was only in November 1942, at a meeting in Berlin, that he informed some of his colleagues about the extermination operation. Eichmann only held such meetings once a year.

In January 1943, Eichmann sent his representative, Günther,[24] to Salonika in order to negotiate with the German military administration there about the Jews in the German zone in northern Greece. The military government was planning to establish a ghetto and to conscript the Jews for labour there under the auspices of the O[rganisation] T[odt]. When I went to Salonika in February 1943, Eichmann gave me this commission, but at the same time he sent Brunner[25] to Salonika with instructions to prepare the deportations. Since the military administration accepted Brunner's proposals, he carried out the deportation from Macedonia from the end of March to the end of May. An attempt by me to secure a postponement of the action, on the grounds of a typhus epidemic and the huge distance involved, failed.

After the conclusion of the deportation in Macedonia, Brunner, who was highly regarded by Eichmann, was sent with his commando to France to set the deportations in motion, since Eichmann accused the commander of the *Sipo* in Paris, Dr Knochen, of sabotaging his measures. Brunner was particularly active in southern France and the previously unoccupied French territory. Transports also began again from Holland and Belgium in the spring of 1943. Simultaneously with the action in Macedonia, a number of transports left Bulgaria from the previously Greek territory of Thrace. These were organized by Dannecker,[26] who was operating under Eichmann's instructions on secondment to the police attaché in Sofia. After the Italian surrender in September 1943, Dannecker was sent by Eichmann to Rome. Despite various efforts by Himmler to persuade Mussolini, the Italian government had not joined in the deportation programme and, in the case of Salonika, had even repatriated its Jewish citizens to Italy. Dannecker, and from 1944 onwards, Bosshammer, deported some transports from Italy. However, the majority of Italian Jews could not be caught because of the rapid development of events there and the partisan activities. In September 1943, Eichmann sent me to Athens with instructions to deport the Jews from southern Greece at once. Since I did not carry out this order, although it would have been possible to do so, I was relieved and Burger[27] was sent to Athens. He organized some transports in the early summer of 1944. In the spring of 1944, Eichmann's representative went to Copenhagen with a commando in order to deport the Danish Jews. However, since the action became known beforehand, the majority of them managed to escape to Sweden. Only a few were arrested and these were sent not to Auschwitz but to Theresienstadt. They owed this to the courageous intervention of the Danish king.

Thus, up to the spring of 1944, deportations had occurred in almost all the countries which were under German influence. However, the actions had not been completed everywhere or had occurred very unevenly. Only two countries had been hitherto spared: Hungary and Romania. Romania did not join in the deportations to Poland right up to the end of the war, while it was Hungary's turn in

[24] SS *Sturmbannführer* Rolf Günther, Eichmann's deputy in IV B4 (eds).

[25] SS *Hauptsturmführer* Alois Brunner (eds).

[26] SS *Hauptsturmführer* Theodor Dannecker (eds).

[27] SS *Obersturmführer* Anton Burger (eds).

March 1944. The more the war went on, and the more it became clear that a German victory was inconceivable, the more Eichmann pressed for the comprehensive implementation of the deportations and the extermination programme. For this reason, he went to Budapest himself with a commando to which he assigned most of his colleagues. Only Brunner remained in France and Bosshammer in Italy. During his stay in Budapest, Rolf Günther stood in for him in Berlin. The police forces stationed in Hungary and Eichmann's commando would not in fact have been sufficient to carry out the deportation of the Hungarian Jews. However, Eichmann secured the total support of the State Secretaries, Endre and Bakyin of the Hungarian Interior Ministry, who made full use of the Hungarian gendarmerie. Eichmann's aim was to carry out a 'lightning action' and did in fact succeed in this. The only thing he failed to achieve was the deportation of the Jews from Budapest, since this action, which had been prepared with particular secrecy, was betrayed in time and, following the intervention of neutral diplomats, Horthy banned the action . . . The efforts of representatives of the 'Joint Distribution Committee', which had been going on in Budapest since spring 1944, then led in October 1944 to an order from Himmler which cancelled the 'final solution'.[28] The last action which Eichmann carried out, although he was aware of the state of the negotiations with Himmler, was the deportation of the remainder of the Jews from Slovakia. Brunner, who had returned from France, was sent in September 1944 to Bratislava and deported at great speed all the Jews he could lay his hands on. But even after Himmler's edict of October 1944, Eichmann was not yet content. The edict banned the extermination of the Jews and so he endeavoured to recruit Jews from Budapest as workers for the concentration camps and for the defences of Vienna. In December 1944, he had to stop even this activity since Budapest was surrounded by Russian forces. From February 1945 onwards Eichmann's department was in complete dissolution . . .

The process of deportation involved a series of stages which were based on experience dating back to the deportations from Austria in 1938. First, a definition of a 'Jew' had to be worked out, with governments being encouraged to adopt that contained in the first supplementary decree to the Reich Citizenship Law of 15 November 1935 as a minimum.[29] Then, Jews were registered, dismissed from government service and the professions, and Jewish businesses were 'aryanized'. Next, a Jewish organization was established through which the Nazis could implement their measures and thereby reduce their own direct involvement to a minimum. Then, Jews were obliged to wear a yellow star, were recruited for forced labour,

[28] This refers to a committee of Zionists, originally formed to help Jews escaping to Hungary from Slovakia, Poland, and the Reich. With the Nazi take-over of Hungary in 1944, the Committee tried to bargain directly with the Germans to get permission for Hungarian Jews to emigrate. In fact, Himmler only ordered a halt to the extermination programme and the dismantling of the killing centres on 25 November 1944 on the grounds that the Final Solution was effectively complete (eds).

[29] See Vol. 2 pp. 538–9.

and concentrated in camps, such as Drancy in France, Malines in Belgium, and Westerbork in Holland. And then, finally, they were transported to Auschwitz or to one of the other death camps.

In the case of France, the situation was complicated by the existence of the occupied part under a German military government and—until 1943—the unoccupied part with its semi-independent government based in Vichy to which many Jews fled. However, the French right-wing tradition represented by the Vichy government had a strong anti-semitic strain, dating back to the late nineteenth century (Dreyfus Affair). This had been stimulated by the influx of large numbers of emigré Jews from Germany and Austria during the 1930s. Thus, Vichy was happy to cooperate with the Germans in introducing measures to eliminate Jewish economic and political influence and, on 29 March 1941, agreed to set up a special French Jewish commissariat under a notorious antisemite, Xavier Vallet. However, the antisemitism of the French Conservatives was essentially religious and economic rather than racial. And the Vichy government regarded those Jews who had become assimilated into French life and who had possessed French citizenship before the Nationality Law of 10 August 1927 in a different light from the emigré Jews. Thus, while it agreed to the deportation of foreign Jews, it resisted German attempts to deport French Jews. It was assisted in this by the lack of cooperation which the SS received from the German military authorities under the anti-Nazi military commander in Paris, Karl-Heinrich von Stülpnagel. As a result, the number of Jews deported to Germany was restricted to around 65,000–100,000 out of the well over three hundred thousand who were living in France at the time of the German invasion in 1940.

The following two documents convey something of the flavour of the bureaucratic side of the deportation programme. The first is a report by SS *Hauptsturmführer* Theodor Dannecker, the head of the Jewish department in the office of the Security Police and SD in France, 'concerning the organizational and ideological preparations for the deportation' dated 22 February 1942.

906

1. Task of the *Sipo* [Security Police] and the SD in France.

The responsibility of the Paris office [of the Sipo and SD] for the combating of anti-German activities on the part of Jewry has been defined by various directives of the OKW, OKH, and the Military Commander in France.

Viewed in the context of Europe as a whole, on the basis of the Reich Marshal's commission of 31 July 1941, the Chief of the Security Police and SD is in practice the 'Jewish Commissar for Europe'. While the regulation issued by the military had a fairly limited application, at the same time more had to be achieved in the interests of the European final solution.

However, gradually, and after the removal of numerous difficulties caused by the agencies of the Military Commander (conflicts over competence) the following successes have been achieved:

(*a*) Jewish file.

As a result of pressure from this office, an exemplary card index file has been prepared in a department of the Prefect of Police in Paris which is arranged as follows: I. purely alphabetically. II. according to street addresses. III. according to profession. IV. according to nationality. Thus, preparatory work is already under way which will be essential for a subsequent deportation programme or a change in employment patterns . . .

(*b*) A French Jewish commissariat.

It would be desirable in the context of the final solution of the Jewish question if in France too only French agencies were involved. However, it is impossible to achieve that one hundred per cent for the time being, owing to the existence of two legislative authorities (Military Commander and the French government). Nevertheless, as early as the beginning of 1941, following a suggestion from this office, the German embassy indicated to the deputy French Prime Minister the necessity of establishing a French Jewish commissioner. On 8 March 1941, the French Cabinet adopted the proposal and the Jewish commissioner was appointed on 29 March.

Although the Jewish commissioner (Vallat) is for various reasons a controversial figure (Vallat is about to be sacked at Germany's request), nevertheless it must be said that the presence of a Jewish commissioner has activated and speeded up anti-Jewish legislation . . .[30]

(*d*) Actions.

Up to now three major actions have been initiated against the Paris Jews. On each occasion this office was responsible both for the selection of the Jews to be arrested and for the technical side of the operation. The card index file referred to above proved a great help in all these actions.

(*e*) Anti-Jewish Institute.

Naturally, the coordination and dissemination of all opposition currents had to be resisted. The establishment of an anti-Jewish institute was set in motion on the principle that the European solution of the Jewish question will be carried out by National Socialism and therefore from Germany. On 11 May 1941, the 'Institute d'Étude des questions Juives' was established in Paris. The Institute made its mark in the last four months of 1941 with a major exhibition 'The Jew and France' and has become widely known . . .

In response to our suggestion, the responsible offices of the RSHA have agreed to the provision of assistance to the Institute by the official Party Jewish Institute in Frankfurt (*Reichsleiter* Rosenberg). A representative from Frankfurt has been in Paris since December 1941. For some weeks he has had a written commission from *Reichsleiter* Rosenberg.

(*f*) Jewish compulsory association.

---

[30] Vallat was replaced on 6 May 1942 by Louis Dasquier de Pellepoix who proved an obedient servant of the Germans (eds).

Experience in Germany and in the Protectorate of Bohemia and Moravia has shown that with the progressive exclusion of the Jews from the various spheres of life it becomes essential to establish a 'Jewish compulsory association' (viz. the Reich Association of Jews in Germany).

On 29 November 1941, the French law concerning the 'Union générale des Israelites de France' finally appeared. Separate administrative councils are envisaged for the occupied and the unoccupied territory. However, because of the resistance of the Jewish Commissioner which is still continuing, this institution must be regarded as still embryonic.

The following document is the minutes of a meeting in IVB4 between Eichmann and Dannecker 'in connexion with the impending evacuation from France' dated 1 July 1942:

907

After discussing the particular issues which are pending, the problem was then reviewed as a whole. The following points emerge as relevant to the work on the final solution of the Jewish question in France.

(*a*) Implementation in the occupied part: smooth and clear-cut.

(*b*) Preparatory work of a political nature in connexion with the practical implementation of the programme in the unoccupied part has not yet been completed since the French Government is increasingly creating difficulties.

In view of the RF SS's order (sent to department IVB4 via the department chief of IV [Müller] on 23.6.42), according to which all Jews resident in France should be deported as soon as possible, it unavoidably follows that the acceleration of the operation will require appropriate pressure on the French Government. It is clear that practical results cannot be achieved straight away. However, in the meantime the transports from the occupied territory are available so that, in view of the difficulties in the unoccupied part, the RF SS's order can nevertheless be pushed through completely at the present time.

This was also the basis of the negotiations with the commander of the Security Police and the SD in Paris, SS *Standartenführer* Dr Knochen.

It was clearly and definitely agreed with SS *Hauptsturmführer* Dannecker that the Jews who are transferred to their final destinations are to be regarded as stateless the moment they cross into Reich territory and, in addition, their property arrangements are to be settled in every respect. The office must push forward the creation of the necessary legislative basis for this since, in the event of failure in this sphere, considerable diplomatic complications can be anticipated, which must be avoided at all costs in carrying out the RF SS's order.

Finally, it was established that the rate envisaged so far (3 transports of 1,000 Jews each per week) must soon be significantly increased with the aim of making France completely free of Jews. The creation of the necessary preconditions for this in the transport sphere is currently being dealt with from Berlin.

The Paris office must ensure that the current rate referred to is maintained in the interests of the smooth running of the final solution of the Jewish question.

(v) Mentalities

Participation in the cold-blooded mass murder of human beings required a suspension of the moral inhibitions which would normally have prevented civilized people from carrying out such atrocities. The ground had been prepared by the progressive dehumanization of the Jews through Nazi propaganda and legislation since 1933, a campaign which could exploit existing anti-semitic feelings among large sections of the German population which, though largely latent, were often deep-rooted. By 1939, the Jews in Germany had been stripped of their rights as citizens and of their dignity as human beings. They had been pushed to the margins of German society so that their subsequent disappearance caused little surprise in a community preoocupied with the problems and anxieties of war.

The occupation of Poland and Russia, the homelands of the overwhelming majority of European Jews, reinforced in the minds of many German officials the Nazi propaganda image of the Jews as profoundly alien. For here most Jews had not been assimilated into their host communities but lived more or less apart and followed strict orthodox rules on matters of dress and other customs. They appeared to conform to the stereotype of the 'eastern Jew' who was already associated in the minds of much of the European middle class with Bolshevism and 'Asia' and who had become a mythical figure embodying all the forces which appeared to threaten the social order and traditional values. When their alien quality was combined with the deterioration of the Jewish community, as a result of the German policies of ghettoization, forced labour, and starvation, the Jews began increasingly to approximate to the Nazi propaganda images of them as 'vermin', a 'bacillus', carriers of disease and corruption, particularly in the eyes of Germans for whom 'cleanliness' was a supreme virtue and mark of civilization.

For the senior SS and SD officials, many of whom were highly educated, the combination of ideological bigotry, a ruthless professionalism, and personal ambition in varying proportions sufficed to suspend normal human inhibitions. Above all, the quintessentially modern cult of professionalism enabled them to make a sharp distinction between public and private morality and reduce the former to the virtue of the efficient performance of a duty imposed by a superior. Through this form of tunnel vision they were able, to some extent at any rate, to overlook the inhumanity of their actions distancing themselves from the horrors through the extensive use of euphemisms and thereby retain a sense of moral integrity. The often fairly primitive low-ranking SS men, on the other hand, were quickly corrupted by being given the power of life and death over people whom they were officially encouraged to regard as sub-human, even though they were aware that in practice many were of superior social background and culture to themselves.

The following documents illuminate the mentalities of those involved in the extermination programme at various levels. The first is an excerpt from a speech by Himmler to SS leaders on 4 October 1943 in Posen:

908

. . . I also want to talk to you quite frankly about a very grave matter. We can talk about it quite frankly among ourselves and yet we will never speak of it publicly. Just as we did not hesitate on 30 June 1934[31] to do our duty as we were bidden, and to stand comrades who had lapsed up against the wall and shoot them, so we have never spoken about it and will never speak of it. It was that tact which is a matter of course, and which I am glad to say is inherent in us, that made us never discuss it among ourselves, never speak of it. It appalled everyone, and yet everyone was certain that he would do it the next time if such orders should be issued and it should be necessary.

I am referring to the Jewish evacuation programme, the extermination of the Jewish people. It is one of those things which are easy to talk about. 'The Jewish people will be exterminated', says every party comrade, 'It's clear, it's in our programme. Elimination of the Jews, extermination and we'll do it.' And then they come along, the worthy eighty million Germans, and each one of them produces his decent Jew. It's clear the others are swine, but this one is a fine Jew. Not one of those who talk like that has watched it happening, not one of them has been through it. Most of you will know what it means when a hundred corpses are lying side by side, or five hundred or a thousand are lying there. To have stuck it out and—apart from a few exceptions due to human weakness—to have remained decent, that is what has made us tough. This is a glorious page in our history and one that has never been written and can never be written. For we know how difficult we would have made it for ourselves if, on top of the bombing raids, the burdens and the deprivations of war, we still had Jews today in every town as secret saboteurs, agitators and troublemakers. We would now probably have reached the 1916–17 stage when the Jews were still part of the body of the German nation.

We have taken from them what wealth they had. I have issued a strict order, which SS *Obergruppenführer* Pohl has carried out, that this wealth should, as a matter of course, be handed over to the Reich without reserve. We have taken none of it for ourselves. Individual men who have lapsed will be punished in accordance with an order I issued at the beginning which gave this warning: Whoever takes so much as a mark of it is a dead man. A number of SS men—there are not very many of them—have fallen short, and they will die, without mercy.

---

[31] i.e. during the Röhm 'putsch' affair—see vol. 1, pp. 167 ff.

We had the moral right, we had the duty to our people, to destroy this people which wanted to destroy us. But we have not the right to enrich ourselves with so much as a fur, a watch, a mark, a cigarette or anything else. We have exterminated a bacterium because we do not want in the end to be infected by the bacterium and die of it. I will not see so much as a small area of sepsis appear here or gain a hold. Wherever it may form, we will cauterize it. All in all, we can say that we have fulfilled this most difficult duty for the love of our people. And our spirit, our soul, our character has not suffered injury from it. . . .

Himmler told a meeting of generals in Sonthofen on 5 May 1944:

909

There is one thing you can be sure of: if we had not removed the Jews from Germany, it would have been impossible for us to get through the bombing campaign, despite the decency of the German people. I am convinced of that. The Führer announced to the Jews at the beginning of the war or before the war: 'If you once again incite the European nations to wage war on each other, then the result will be not the extermination of the German people but the extermination of the Jews.' The Jewish question has been solved within Germany itself and in general within the countries occupied by Germany. It was solved in an uncompromising fashion in accordance with the life and death struggle of our nation in which the existence of our blood is at stake. I tell you that as comrades in arms. For, whatever uniform we may wear we are all soldiers. You can understand how difficult it was for me to carry out this military (*soldatisch*) order which I was given and which I implemented out of a sense of obedience and absolute conviction. If you say: 'we can understand as far as the men are concerned but not about the children', then I must remind you of what I said at the beginning. In this confrontation with Asia we must get used to condemning to oblivion those rules and customs of past wars which we have got used to and prefer. In my view, we as Germans, however deeply we may feel in our hearts, are not entitled to allow a generation of avengers filled with hatred to grow up with whom our children and grandchildren will have to deal because we, too weak and cowardly, left it to them.

The following document is an extract from a speech by Hans Frank, the Governor of the General Government, to a *Wehrmacht* audience on 19 December 1940 in Cracow:

910

. . . And a few days ago the Führer told me something else with great seriousness, namely that the old Japanese saying will be proved right which goes: 'After victory tighten your helmet, comrades, never again will we be a weak Reich. The

Wehrmacht will be the culmination of our programme of education for the community. Just as the National Socialist German Workers' Party will be the culmination of the social, political, and ideological leadership, so the *Wehrmacht* will also be the very epitome of defence training, of the proud and clean attitude of our people. And you will be able to say that you were there as soldiers. I am delighted by this *Wehrmacht* hour for it unites us all. Some of you have a mother or parents, others have wives, fiancées or children at home. They will be thinking of you during all these weeks and will be saying to themselves: My God, he is over there in Poland where there are lice and Jews. Perhaps he is cold and hungry. Perhaps he doesn't dare to write . . . It might be rather nice if we were to send the loved ones at home a picture and were to tell them: Well, things in the General Government have changed and got better. Of course, I couldn't get rid of all the lice and all the Jews in only one year (Laughter!). But in the course of time and above all if you will all help me, it can be achieved. It's not necessary to do everything in one year, to do it at once, otherwise what will those who come after us have to do?

The mentality of those involved in the massacres carried out by the *Einsatzkommandos* is illustrated by the following letters from a young German police sergeant, Jacob, to an acquaintance from his home district, SS *Obergruppenführer* and Police General Rudolf Querner. Jacob was operating in Kamenetz-Podolsk in the south-west Ukraine. His first letter is dated 5 May 1942:

911

I have been here at Kamenetz-Podolsk for a month. The territory I administer with twenty-three men and 500 Ukrainian police, is as big as a German *Regierungsbezirk*. Most of the work is done for me by the police, the good-for-nothings. No surprise. Yesterday half-Bolsheviks and today wearing the honourable police uniform. There are some hard-working chaps among them but the percentage is low. As commanding officer, I am simultaneously prosecuting council, judge, executioner etc.

Naturally, we are cleaning up considerably, especially among the Jews. But the population has to be kept firmly in check too. One has to keep one's eyes open. We act fast. Well, we shall be able to get home all the sooner. My family is very unhappy. I have been away for two years.

I have a cosy flat in a former children's home (Asylum). One bedroom and a living room with all amenities. Nothing is missing. Apart of course from my wife and children. You will understand me. My Dieter and my litle Liese write often in their own way. Sometimes I could weep. It is not good to love one's children as I do. I hope that the war will soon be over and with it the period of service in the East . . .

Querner replied on 10 June with a reproof: 'I can understand that you miss your wife and children. But in war we men must be hard, above all with ourselves.' Jacob replied to Querner on 21 June 1942:

912

I am replying to your letter of the 10th immediately . . . I am grateful for your reprimand. You are right. We men of the new Germany must be strict with ourselves even if it means a long period of separation from our family. For we must finish matters once and for all and finally settle accounts with the war criminals, in order to create a better and eternal Germany for our heirs. We are not sleeping here. There are three or four operations a week. Sometimes Gypsies, another time Jews, partisans and all sorts of trash . . . We are not carrying on a lawless regime here, but when an action requires immediate atonement we contact the SD and justice takes its course. If the official judicial system were operating, it would be impossible to exterminate a whole family when only the father is guilty.

I do not know if you Herr *Obergruppenführer* ever saw such frightful kinds of Jews in Poland. I am grateful for having been allowed to see this bastard race close up. If fate permits, I shall have something to tell my children. Syphilitics, cripples, idiots were typical of them. One thing was clear: they were materialists to the end. They were saying things like: 'We are skilled workers, you are not going to shoot us'. They were not men but monkeys in human form.

Ah well, there is only a small percentage of the 24,000 Jews of Kamenetz-Podolsk left. The yids in the surrounding area are also clients of ours. We are ruthlessly making a clean sweep with a clear conscience and then '. . . the waves close over, the world has peace.'

On 5 June 1942, Willy Just, a welder in Pradel's RSHA transport department, replied to complaints about the inadequacies of the gas vans in a minute prepared for *Obersturmbannführer* Walter Rauff, the man responsible for technical matters in Amt VI. Its use of language and coldly technocratic approach illuminate the mentality of those involved in the Reinhard programme:

913

Re: Technical alterations to the special vehicles already in operation and those in production.

Since December 1941, for example, 97,000 have been processed (verarbeitet) using three vans without any faults developing in the vehicles. The well-known explosion in Kulmhof must be treated as a special case. It was caused by faulty practice. Special instructions have been given to the relevant offices in order to avoid such accidents. The instructions were such as to ensure a considerable increase in the degree of security.

Further operational experience hitherto indicates that the following technical alterations are appropriate.

. . .

2) The vans are normally loaded with 9–10 people per square metre. With the large Saurer special vans this is not possible because although they do not become overloaded their manoeuvrability is much impaired. A reduction in the load area appears desirable. It can be achieved by reducing the size of the van by c.1 metre. The difficulty referred to cannot be overcome by reducing the numbers (*Stückzahl*) of the load. For a reduction in the numbers will necessitate a longer period of operation because the free spaces will have to be filled with CO. By contrast, a smaller load area which is completely full requires a much shorter period of operation since there are no free spaces.

In a discussion with the firm which makes the vans, they pointed out that a reduction in the size of the van would produce an unfavourable weight distribution. It was emphasized that the front axle would be overloaded. In fact, however a compensation in the weight distribution occurs automatically through the fact that in the course of the operation the cargo, in pressing towards the back door, is always primarily concentrated there. As a result, there is no additional burden on the front axle.

3) The connecting hoses between the exhaust and the van frequently rust through because they are corroded inside by the liquids which fall on them. To prevent this the connecting piece must be moved so that the gas is fed from the top downwards. This will prevent liquids flowing in.

4) To facilitate the cleaning of the vehicle a draining hole should be inserted in the middle of the floor which can be tightly closed. The drain cover with a diameter of about 200–300mm. should have a syphon so that thin liquid can drain away during the operation. To prevent blockages, the syphon should be covered with a sieve. Lumps of dirt can be flushed out through the large drain opening when the van is cleaned. The floor of the vehicle should be inclined slightly towards the drain opening. The aim is to ensure that all liquids flow directly towards the centre. This will largely prevent the liquids seeping into the pipes . . .

6) The lighting must be better protected against damage than hitherto. The iron grill must be arched over the lights so that damage to the covers is no longer possible. It has been suggested by those involved that the lights should be dispensed with since they are allegedly never used. However, experience shows that when the rear door is closed and therefore when it goes dark, the cargo (*Ladung*) presses hard towards the door. This is explained by the fact that when darkness comes the cargo presses towards the light. It makes it difficult to latch the door. Furthermore, it has been observed that the noise always begins when the doors are shut presumably because of fear brought on by the darkness. It is, therefore, desirable for the lighting to be switched on before and during the first few minutes of the operation. The lighting is also useful for night operations and for cleaning the inside of the vehicle . . .

The following document contains excerpts from the diary of SS *Hauptsturmführer* Dr Johann Kremer, Professor of Medicine at the University of Münster, who was assigned to Auschwitz as a doctor from 29 August to 18 November 1942:

914

2.IX.1942. This morning at three o'clock I attended a special action for the first time. Dante's hell seemed like a comedy in comparison. Not for nothing is Auschwitz called an extermination camp.

5.IX.1942. I was present this afternoon at a special action applied to prisoners in the female camp, the worst I have ever seen. Dr Thilo was right this morning in telling me that we are in the *anus mundi*. Tonight, about eight, I was present at a special action on the Dutch. All the men are anxious to take part in these actions because of the special rations they get on such occasions, consisting of one-fifth of a litre of schnapps, 5 cigarettes, 100 grams of sausage and bread.

6–7.IX.1942. Sunday, an excellent lunch: tomato soup, half a chicken with potatoes and red cabbage, petits fours, a marvellous vanilla ice cream. After lunch I was introduced to . . . (illegible word). Left at eight in the evening for a special action, for the fourth time.

23.IX.1942. Present last night at the sixth and seventh special actions. In the morning, *Obergruppenführer* Pohl arrived with his staff at the Waffen SS house. The sentry at the door saluted me first. In the evening, at eight o'clock, dinner in the commandant's house, with *Obergruppenführer* Pohl, a real banquet. We had apple pie, as much as we wanted, good coffee, excellent beer, and cakes.

7.X.1942. Present at the ninth special action. Foreigners and women.

11.X.1942. Today, Sunday, rabbit, a good leg, for lunch, with red cabbage and pudding all for 1.25 RM.

12.X.1942. Innoculation for typhus. Following this, feverish in the evening; still, went to a special action that night (1,600 Dutch). Terrible scenes near the last bunker. The tenth special action.

The following documents are excerpts from post-war West German court judgments against SS guards in the Polish death camps. The first is from the Sobibor trial:

915

. . . The Jewish workers were at the complete mercy of the German camp guards who were the lords of the camp. Most of them had a very limited education, were completely under the influence of the major [Nazi] figures and their anti-semitic ideology and in most cases their moral sense had been totally blunted by their activity in the euthanasia centres. Their relations with the prisoners who—as they knew—were nothing but work slaves, who were living on borrowed time, but who were often far more highly educated than themselves, generated among a number of them a sense of superiority and primitive cravings for power and domination. Guards such as these—and they were in the majority—gave vent to their moods at the expense of their 'slaves' and used them as objects for their lowest instincts. They were assisted in overcoming the remnants of inhibitions by their knowledge that all the Jews would be killed and the witnesses of their behaviour would therefore be eliminated. Witness C was not alone in reporting that, on going from Camp III to his lodging, Kurt B was regularly accompanied by his St. Bernhard dog, Barry, of which the prisoners were terrified. On one such occasion. . . C had heard B say to his dog: 'Man get the dog, He's not working' or 'he's not running'. The animal then leapt at the worker concerned and often bit him badly . . .

. . . The witness, Stanislav Sz, a goldsmith by trade, who arrived in Sobibor on 12 May 1942, had a particularly privileged position. At the selection, he had claimed that his four young relatives who arrived with him were also goldsmiths and, together with them, he was assigned by W to a small barrack. Sz. had a suitcase containing his tools with him. Together with his relatives, he was obliged to set up a goldsmithy. It was disguised as a plumber's work shop and, after Reichleitner[32] took over from Stangl as commandant in autumn 1942, it was always called that. The workshop did actually do plumbing but only as a sideline. Among other things, the five young prisoners had to make tricycles for the children of the German guards out of prams which had arrived with the transports. The five boys also received from W the commission to make rings for all the German camp personnel which were decorated with SS runes in gold inlay. The witness Sz made the credible statement that he found difficulty in getting on with the work because each of the guards kept expressing particular wishes. For example, he had to make a monogram in silver for B. And he had to fix a valuable gold coin on the pommel of B's whip.

The following document contains excerpts from the Treblinka trial:

916

. . . The camp showed a completely different face when it came to 'leisure-time activities'. The German camp leadership had the approval of Christian Wirth in trying to provide its personnel with entertainment which would encourage their work performance. While in the upper camp there was only a small band consisting of three or four men, in the lower camp there was an orchestra which consisted of ten professional musicians and was conducted by Arthur Gold, a well-known conductor in Poland. This orchestra had time set aside for rehearsal. The musicians were freed from all work during these rehearsal sessions. They were later even provided with their own uniform in white and blue silk similar to a tail coat.

In the first weeks of the camp's operation the orchestra played operetta melodies next to the tube in order to drown the cries of the victims in the gas chambers. Later, that was stopped. The orchestra then played mostly marches and Polish and yiddish folk songs at the evening roll call. Also, in 1943, the orchestra appeared at major events (boxing fights, the performances of short plays, dances and such

[32] SS *Obersturmführer* Franz Reichleitner, like Globocnik, Stangl and several leading T4 personnel, was Austrian (eds).

like). Those were macabre scenes, for, during these events the flames of the pyres were flaring up to the sky high above the camp. Such entertainments for the German camp personnel were mostly organised by the accused, Franz.[33] During the period in 1943, when the transports were declining, there were even several ritual marriages arranged between male and female prisoners and these were encouraged through special allocations of food and drink by the German camp guards who found great enjoyment in watching the proceedings.

The German camp personnel received special supplies, in particular a lot of alcohol. Many of the German SS people were thus often drunk. Their food was also excellent, since the deported Jews brought fresh and preserved food with them which they had to give up before being gassed . . . In the camps the German SS people had numerous privileges. Their rooms were cleaned by female prisoners. Their shoes were cleaned. Their uniforms were brushed and ironed. Their dirty washing was washed in the laundry. Every special requirement could be fulfilled thanks to the workshops in the camp, in which tailors, shoemakers, furriers, shirt-makers, locksmiths and so on also worked. Thus, for example, every German SS man had the right to a free hand-made civilian suit and a made-to-measure civilian coat. Plenty of quality cloth which had been taken from the victims was available. Furthermore, the German SS men in the camp received a special bonus on top of their normal pay.

There were two horses for riding . . . However, only the accused, Franz, made use of the opportunity to ride. The horses were looked after by the prisoners just as carefully as the dog, Barry.[34] The animals in the camp zoo (in particular foxes, deer and other animals native to Poland) were carefully tended. The zoo was turned into a little ornament of the camp which the German SS people could enjoy . . .

(vi) The statistics of the 'Final Solution'

The total number of Jews who died in the Nazi extermination programme can never be known exactly since we lack detailed figures even for those who were gassed, let alone for those who were massacred by the *Einsatzgruppen* or who died from disease, malnutrition, overwork, and maltreatment as a direct result of Nazi policies. Although some statistics were prepared by a professional SS statistician, they do not cover the last phases during 1944–5. Clearly, the single most authoritative source was the man in charge of Jewish affairs in the Reich Security Main Office, Adolf Eichmann. The following statement was made after the war by Wilhelm Hoettl, a member of Amt VI (Foreign Intelligence) in the RSHA:

[33] SS *Obersturmführer* Kurt Franz replaced Stangl as commandant in August 1943 (eds).

[34] Barry moved to Treblinka from Sobibor with Stangl on his transfer (eds).

917

. . . At the end of August 1944, I had a conversation with SS *Obersturmbannführer* Adolf Eichmann, whom I had known since 1938. The conversation took place in my flat in Budapest.

At this time, according to my information, Eichmann was a section chief in Amt IV (Gestapo) of the Reich Security Main Office and, in addition, had been commissioned by Himmler to get hold of the Jews throughout Europe and transport them to Germany. At that time, Eichmann was very much affected by Romania's withdrawal from the war, which had occurred then. It was for this reason that he had visited me in order to enquire about the military situation, of which I received daily news from the Hungarian Honved (War) Ministry and from the Commander of the Waffen SS in Hungary. He expressed his conviction that Germany had lost the war and that he saw no future for himself. He knew that he was regarded by the United Nations as one of the main war criminals because he had millions of Jews on his conscience. I asked him how many there were, to which he replied that, although the number was a great Reich secret, he would tell me since, as a historian, I must be interested and since he would probably not return from his commando's operation in Romania. He had recently prepared a report for Himmler, since he had wanted to know the exact number of Jews who had been killed. On the basis of the information at his disposal, he had arrived at the following result:

Around four million Jews had been killed in the various extermination camps, while two million had died by other means, of whom the majority had been shot by the *Einsatzkommandos* of the Security Police during the campaign against Russia.

Himmler was not satisfied with the report, since in his view the number of Jews who had been killed must be larger than six million. Himmler declared that he would send a man from his statistical office to Eichmann so that he could produce a new report on the basis of Eichmann's material in which the exact number could be worked out.

I must assume that the information which Eichmann gave me is accurate since of all the people involved he definitely had the best over-view of the number of Jews murdered. First, with his special commandos he 'delivered' the Jews so to speak to the extermination centres and therefore knew this number exactly; and, secondly, as the section chief in *Amt* IV of the RSHA, who was responsible for Jewish affairs, he certainly knew best the number of those Jews who had died from other causes.

In addition, there is the fact that, as a result of events, Eichmann was at that point in such a state of mind that he had no intention of telling me anything that was untrue.

I myself can remember the details of this conversation so well because, understandably, it affected me very much and, even before the German collapse, I gave details of it to an American agency in a neutral country with which I was in contact at that time.

I swear that I made the above statement of my own free will and without being compelled to do so and that, according to my best information and conscience, the above statement corresponds to the truth.

The following figures are estimates of the numbers of Jews who died in the Holocaust, divided according to nationality:

918

Country	Previous number of Jews	Losses: Lowest estimate	Losses: Highest estimate
1 Poland	3,300,000	2,350,000	2,900,000 = 88%
2 USSR	2,100,000[35]	700,000	1,000,000 = 48%
3 Romania	850,000	200,000	420,000 = 49%
4 Czechoslovakia	360,000	233,000	300,000 = 83%
5 Germany	240,000	160,000	200,000 = 83%
6 Hungary	403,000	180,000	200,000 = 50%
7 Lithuania	155,000	—	135,000 = 87%
8 France	300,000	60,000	130,000 = 43%
9 Holland	150,000	104,000	120,000 = 80%
10 Latvia	95,000	—	85,000 = 89%
11 Yugoslavia	75,000	55,000	65,000 = 87%
12 Greece	75,000	57,000	60,000 = 80%
13 Austria	60,000	—	40,000 = 67%
14 Belgium	100,000	25,000	40,000 = 48%
15 Italy	75,000	8,500	15,000 = 26%
16 Bulgaria	50,000	—	7,000 = 14%
17 Denmark	—	(less than 100)	— —
18 Luxembourg	—	3,000	3,000 —
19 Norway	—	700	1,000 —
Total		4,194,200	app. 5,721,000 = 68%

[35] Subsequent research has revised the estimate of the number of Jews in the Soviet Union in the summer of 1941 to 4.7 million of whom an estimated 2.2 million were killed by the Germans or their allies. Cf. H. Krausnick and H. H. Wilhelm *Die Truppe des Weltanschauungskrieges. Die Einsatzgruppen der Sicherheitspolizei und des SD 1938–1942* (Stuttgart 1981) pp. 618 ff.

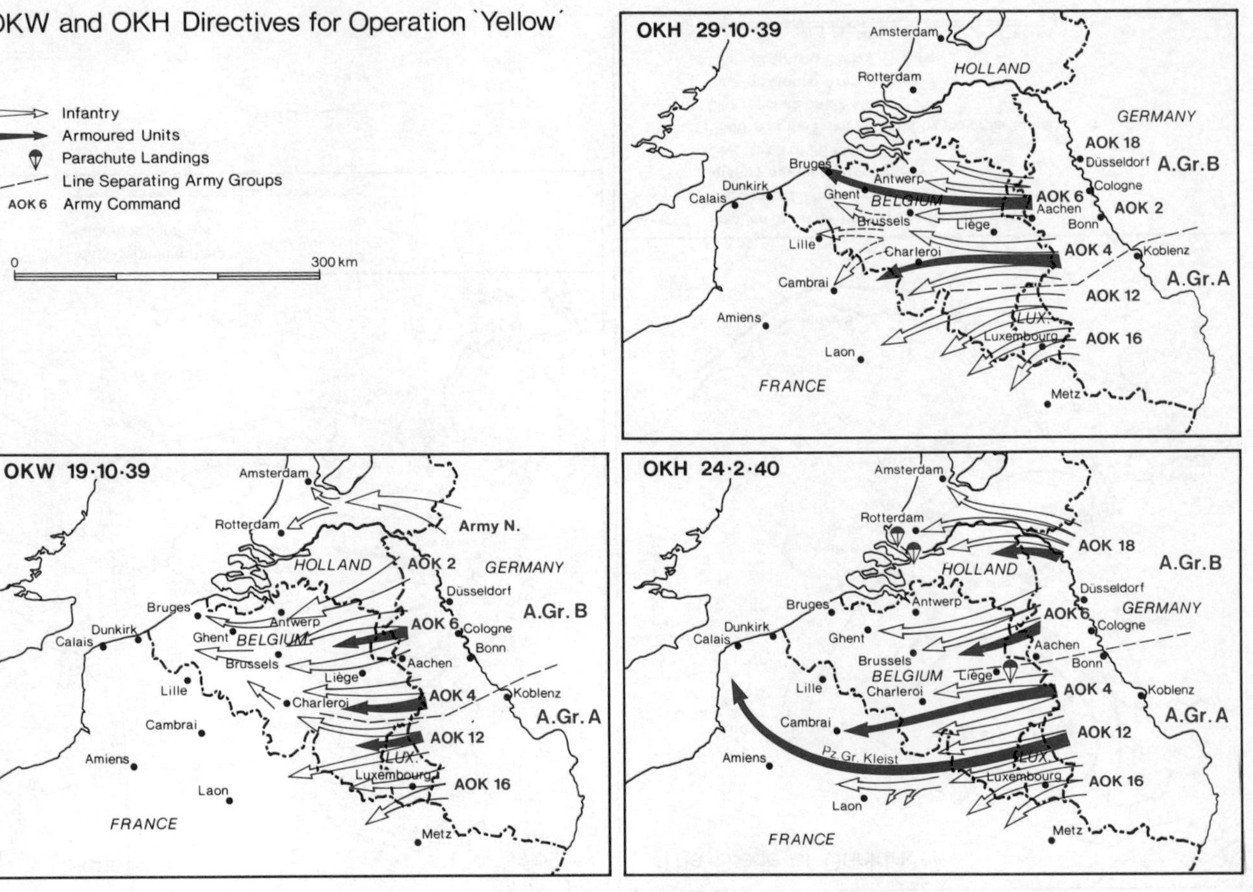
OKW and OKH Directives for Operation 'Yellow'
Infantry
Armoured Units
Parachute Landings
Line Separating Army Groups
AOK 6 Army Command
0
300 km
OKH 29·10·39
Amsterdam
Rotterdam
HOLLAND
GERMANY
AOK 18
Düsseldorf
A.Gr.B
Bruges
Antwerp
Dunkirk
Calais
Ghent
BELGIUM
AOK 6
Aachen
Cologne
AOK 2
Brussels
Liège
Bonn
Lille
Charleroi
AOK 4
Koblenz
Cambrai
A.Gr.A
AOK 12
Amiens
LUX.
Luxembourg
AOK 16
Laon
FRANCE
Metz
OKW 19·10·39
Amsterdam
Rotterdam
Army N.
HOLLAND
AOK 2
GERMANY
Düsseldorf
Bruges
A.Gr. B
Dunkirk
Antwerp
AOK 6
Cologne
Calais
Ghent
BELGIUM
Bonn
Brussels
Aachen
Lille
Liège
AOK 4
Koblenz
Charleroi
Cambrai
A.Gr. A
AOK 12
Amiens
LUX.
Luxembourg
AOK 16
Laon
FRANCE
Metz
OKH 24·2·40
Amsterdam
Rotterdam
AOK 18
HOLLAND
A.Gr.B
Düsseldorf
Bruges
Antwerp
AOK 6
GERMANY
Dunkirk
Cologne
Calais
Ghent
Aachen
Brussels
Bonn
BELGIUM
Liège
Lille
Charleroi
AOK 4
Koblenz
Cambrai
AOK 12
A.Gr.A
Pz Gr. Kleist
Amiens
LUX.
Luxembourg
AOK 16
Laon
FRANCE
Metz

Map 1

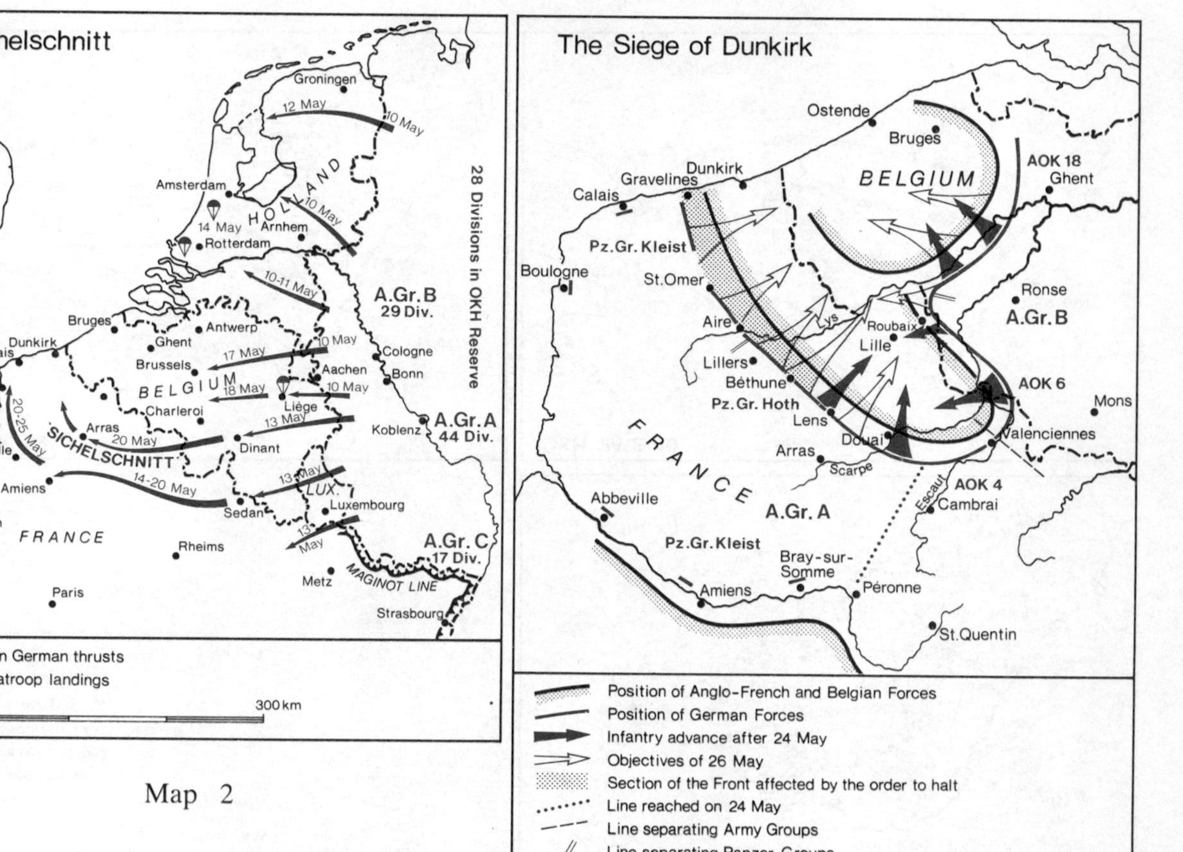
Sichelschnitt
28 Divisions in OKH Reserve
A.Gr. B
29 Div.
A.Gr. A
44 Div.
A.Gr. C
17 Div.
HOLLAND
BELGIUM
FRANCE
LUX.
SICHELSCHNITT
MAGINOT LINE
Groningen
Amsterdam
Rotterdam
Arnhem
Antwerp
Ghent
Bruges
Brussels
Charleroi
Aachen
Liège
Cologne
Bonn
Koblenz
Dinant
Luxembourg
Sedan
Metz
Strasbourg
Rheims
Paris
Rouen
Amiens
Abbeville
Arras
Boulogne
Calais
Dunkirk
10 May
12 May
14 May
10-11 May
17 May
18 May
13 May
20 May
14-20 May
20-25 May
Main German thrusts
Paratroop landings
0
300 km
The Siege of Dunkirk
AOK 18
A.Gr. B
AOK 6
AOK 4
A.Gr. A
Pz.Gr. Kleist
Pz.Gr. Hoth
BELGIUM
FRANCE
Ostende
Bruges
Ghent
Ronse
Mons
Valenciennes
Cambrai
St.Quentin
Roubaix
Lille
Douai
Lens
Arras
Béthune
Lillers
Aire
St.Omer
Dunkirk
Gravelines
Calais
Boulogne
Abbeville
Amiens
Bray-sur-Somme
Péronne
Escaut
Scarpe
Lys
Position of Anglo-French and Belgian Forces
Position of German Forces
Infantry advance after 24 May
Objectives of 26 May
Section of the Front affected by the order to halt
Line reached on 24 May
Line separating Army Groups
Line separating Panzer Groups
0
50
100 km

Map 2

Map 3

Plan for Operation Barbarossa
Boundary before September 1939
0
300 km
Helsinki
Stockholm
Leningrad
Tallinn
Narva
Estonia
Luga
Pärnu
Valga
Ostrov
Riga
Latvia
Cholm
Kalinin
Volga
Liepaja
Opočka
BALTIC SEA
Velikie Luki
Šiauliai
Dvina
Ržev
Moscow
Lithuania
Polock
18 A
Pz.Gr.4
16 A
Postavy
Kaunas
Vjaz'ma
Danzig
Kaluga
A.Gr.North
Vilna
Suwalki
Olsztyn
Pz.Gr.3
Roslavl
9 A
Minsk
Vistula
Grodno
Bialystok
Brjansk
A.Gr.Centre
Sluck
Orel
Warsaw
Pz.Gr.2
Pinsk
Pripjat
4 A
Desna
Kursk
Lublin
Kovel
Černigov
6 A
Kielce
Černobyl
Konotop
Pz.Gr.1
A.Gr.South
Luck
Korosten
Crakov
17 A
Žitomir
Kiev
Rava Russkija
Karkov
Rzeszów
Mirgorod
Lvov
Tarnopol
Čerkassy
SLOVAKIA
Dnepr
Dnestr
Uman
Tisza
Kirovograd
Dnepropetrovsk
Budapest
Prut
Debrecen
Balta
HUNGARY
11 A
Kišinev
Cluj
Nikolaev
Melitopol
Piatra Neamt
Odessa
Timişoara
Braşov
Crimea
Kerč
ROMANIA
Danube
BLACK SEA
Belgrade
Sevastapol
Bucharest

Map 4

Front line and OKH and OKW alternative operational plans July - August 1941

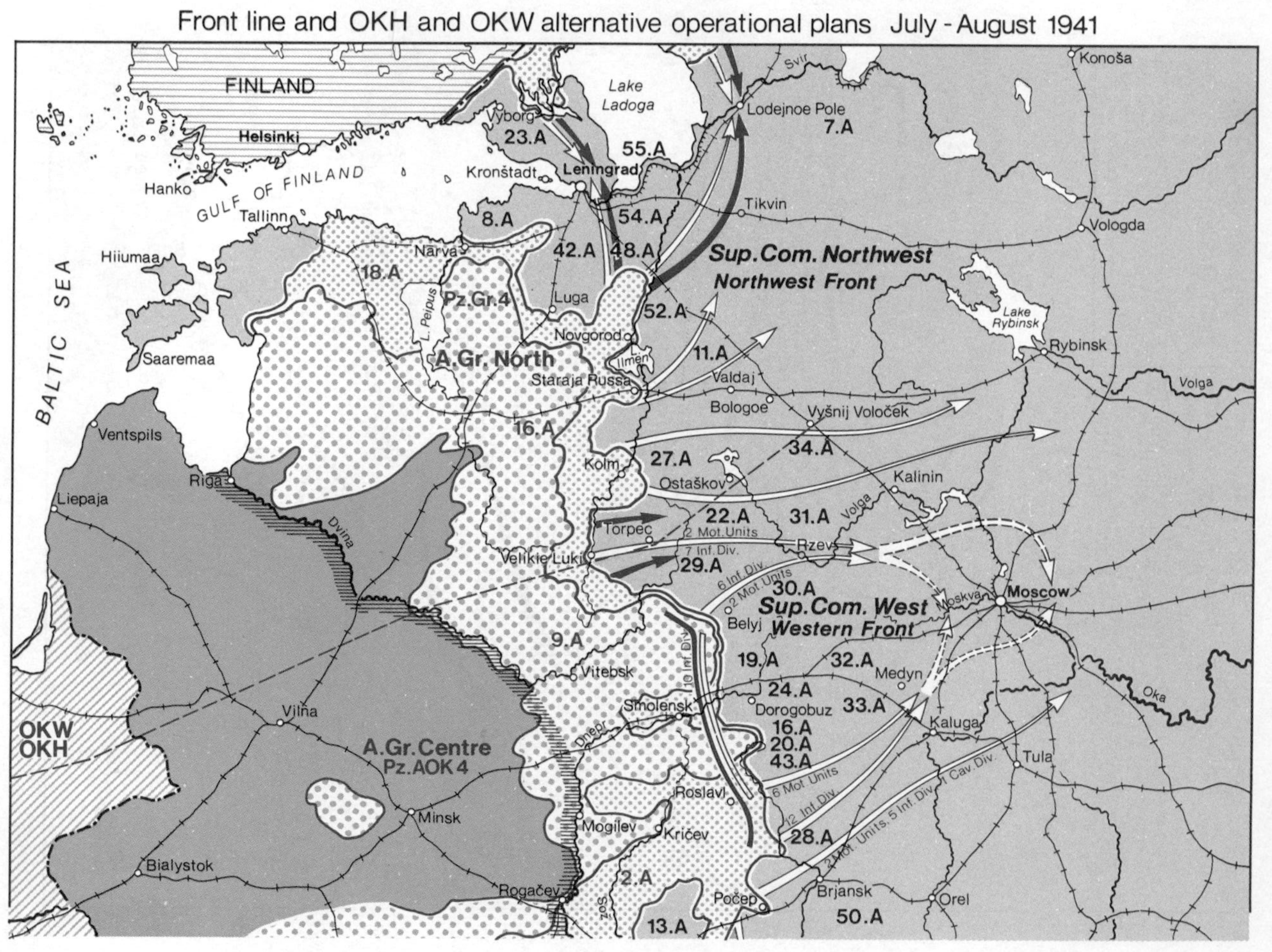

"Dnepr - Dvina Line"
Front line and occupied area on 5·7·41
Front line and occupied area on 23·7·41
Front line and occupied area on 18·8·41
OKH plan of operations of 18·8·41
OKH plan of operations of 18·8·41 – still provisional
Hitler's own plan decided on 21·8·41
Territory still in Soviet hands on 18·8·41
37.A
Soviet Commands and Armies
0
100
200
300 km
Brjansk Front
Sup. Com. Southwest
Southwest Front
Southern Front
A.Gr.South
Pz.Gr.1
13.A
3.A
21.A
40.A
5.A
37.A
26.A
38.A
6.A
17.A
12.A
18.A
9.A
51.A
11.A
Rom.3.A
Rom.4.A
Crimea
SEA OF AZOV
BLACK SEA
HUNGARY
ROMANIA
Voronež
Don
Kursk
Karkov
Rostov
Taganrog
Mariupol
Melitopol
Kerč
Sevastopol
Perekop
Nikolaev
Odessa
Dnepropetrovsk
Kremenčug
Čerkassy
Kanev
Kiev
Romny
Konotop
Glukov
Novgorod Severski
Starodub
Novozybkov
Gomel
Černigov
Desna
Rečica
Mozyr
Černobyl
Ovruč
Korosten
Berdičev
Vinnica
Uman
Balta
Južny Bug
Dnestr
Prut
Dubno
Lvov
Lublin
Bug
Vistula
Pripjat
Dnepr
Severski Donec

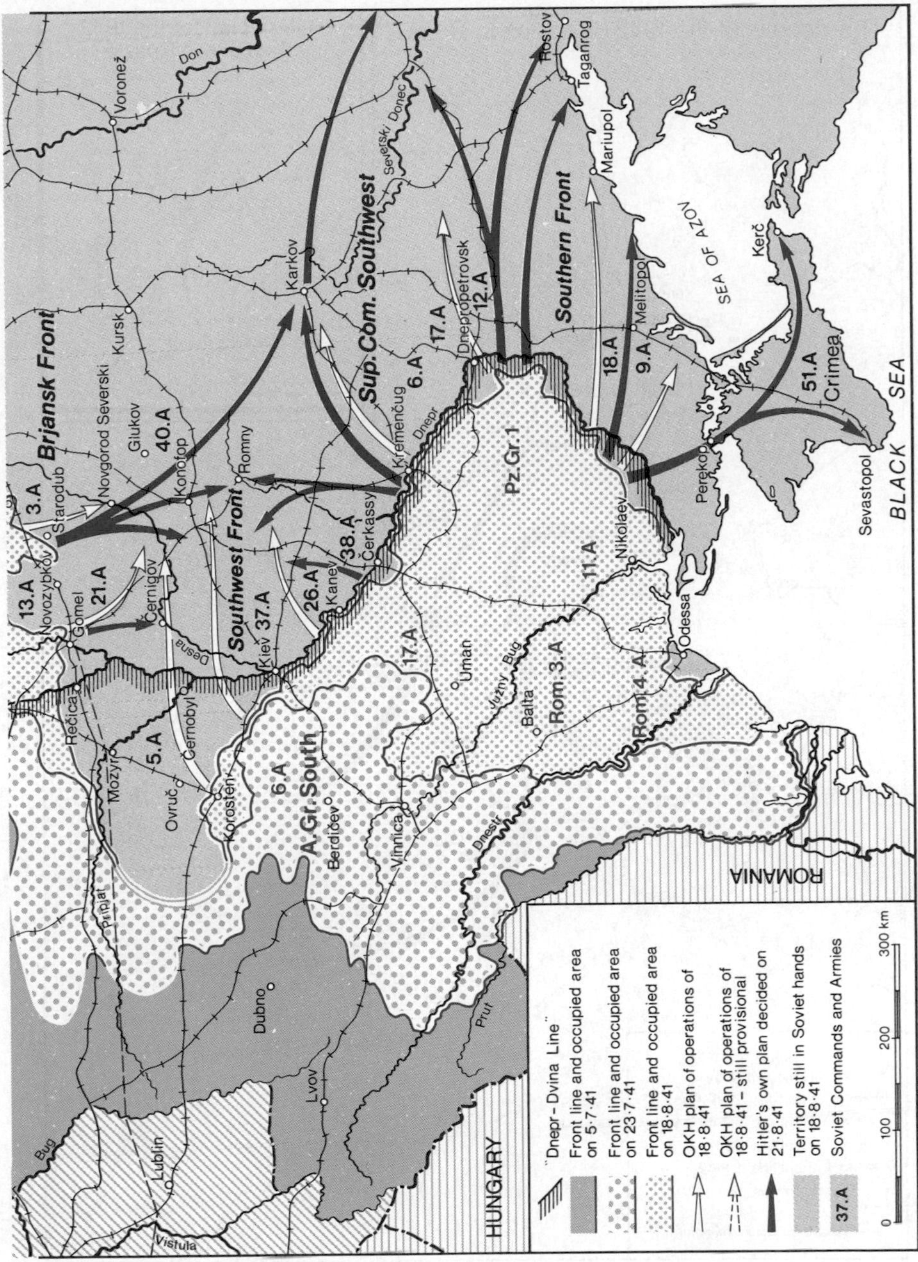

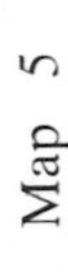

Map 5

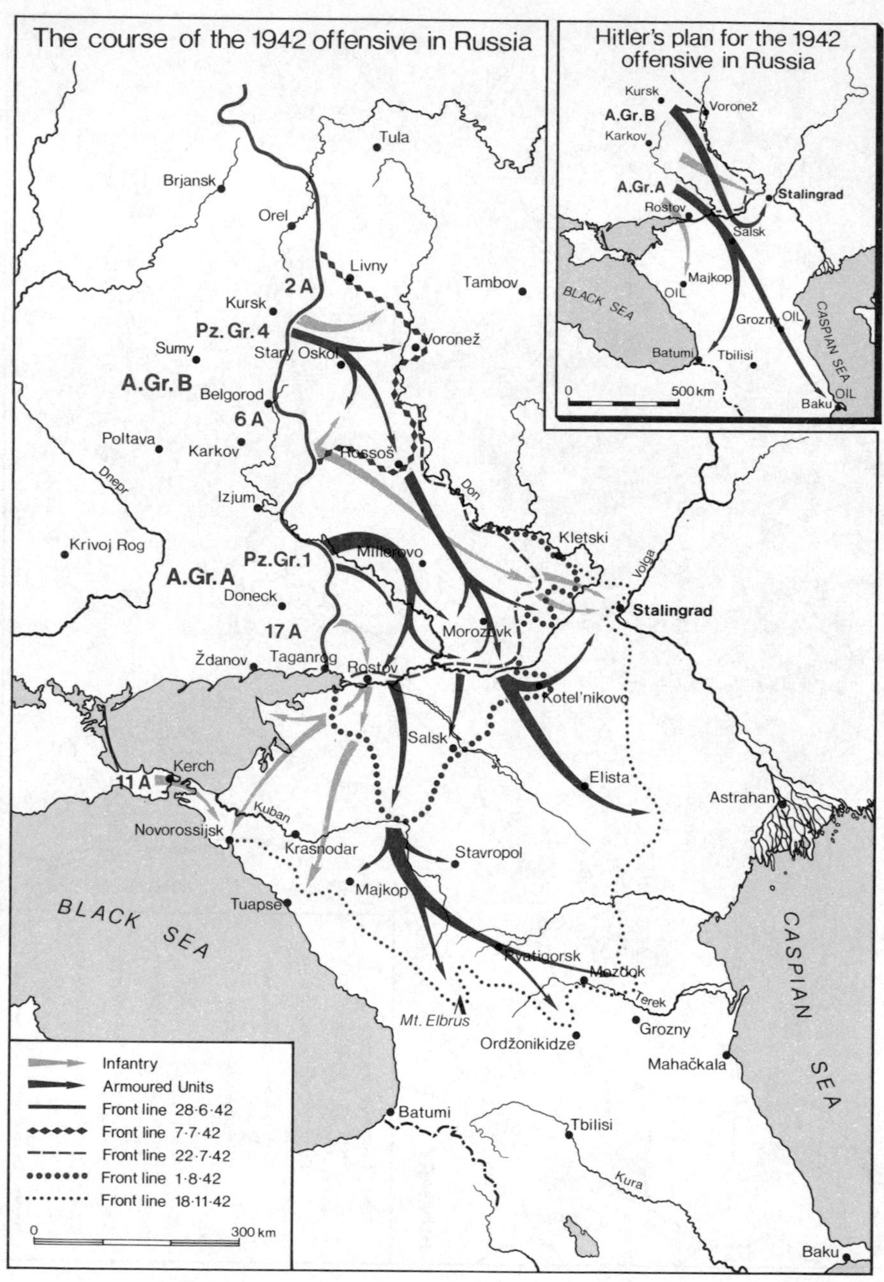
The course of the 1942 offensive in Russia
Hitler's plan for the 1942 offensive in Russia
Kursk
A.Gr.B
Voronež
Karkov
A.Gr.A
Stalingrad
Rostov
Salsk
Majkop
OIL
BLACK SEA
Grozny
CASPIAN SEA
Batumi
Tbilisi
0
500 km
Baku
Tula
Brjansk
Orel
Livny
2 A
Tambov
Kursk
Pz.Gr.4
Voronež
Sumy
Stary Oskol
A.Gr.B
Belgorod
6 A
Poltava
Karkov
Rossoš
Dnepr
Don
Izjum
Kletski
Krivoj Rog
Millerovo
Pz.Gr.1
A.Gr.A
Volga
Doneck
Stalingrad
17 A
Morozovk
Ždanov
Taganrog
Rostov
Kotel'nikovo
Salsk
Kerch
11 A
Elista
Astrahan
Kuban
Novorossijsk
Krasnodar
Stavropol
Majkop
Tuapse
BLACK SEA
CASPIAN SEA
Pyatigorsk
Mozdok
Terek
Mt. Elbrus
Grozny
Ordžonikidze
Mahačkala
Infantry
Armoured Units
Front line 28·6·42
Front line 7·7·42
Front line 22·7·42
Front line 1·8·42
Front line 18·11·42
0
300 km
Batumi
Tbilisi
Kura
Baku

Map 6

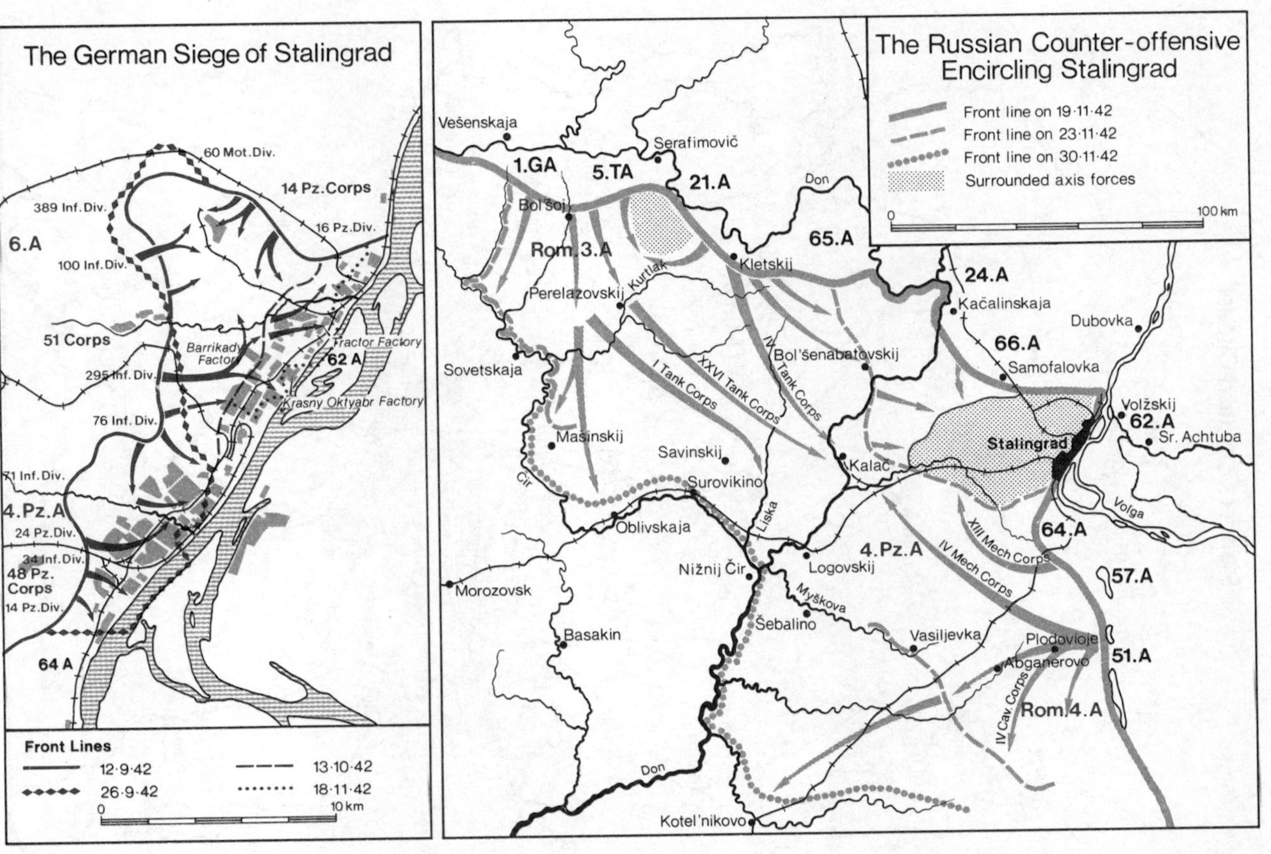

The German Siege of Stalingrad
60 Mot.Div.
14 Pz.Corps
389 Inf.Div.
16 Pz.Div.
6.A
100 Inf.Div.
51 Corps
Barrikady Factory
Tractor Factory
62 A
295 Inf.Div.
Krasny Oktyabr Factory
76 Inf.Div.
71 Inf.Div.
4.Pz.A
24 Pz.Div.
34 Inf.Div.
48 Pz. Corps
14 Pz.Div.
64 A
Front Lines
12·9·42
26·9·42
13·10·42
18·11·42
0
10 km
The Russian Counter-offensive Encircling Stalingrad
Front line on 19·11·42
Front line on 23·11·42
Front line on 30·11·42
Surrounded axis forces
0
100 km
Vešenskaja
Serafimovič
1.GA
5.TA
21.A
Don
Bol'šoj
Rom.3.A
65.A
Kletskij
Kurtlak
24.A
Perelazovskij
Kačalinskaja
Dubovka
66.A
Sovetskaja
Bol'šenabatovskij
IV Tank Corps
XXVI Tank Corps
I Tank Corps
Samofalovka
Volžskij
62.A
Sr. Achtuba
Mašinskij
Savinskij
Kalač
Stalingrad
Čir
Surovikino
Oblivskaja
Liska
Volga
4.Pz.A
XIII Mech Corps
IV Mech Corps
64.A
Nižnij Čir
Logovskij
57.A
Morozovsk
Myškova
Šebalino
Basakin
Vasiljevka
Plodovitoje
Abganerovo
51.A
IV Cav. Corps
Rom.4.A
Don
Kotel'nikovo

Map 7

Map 8

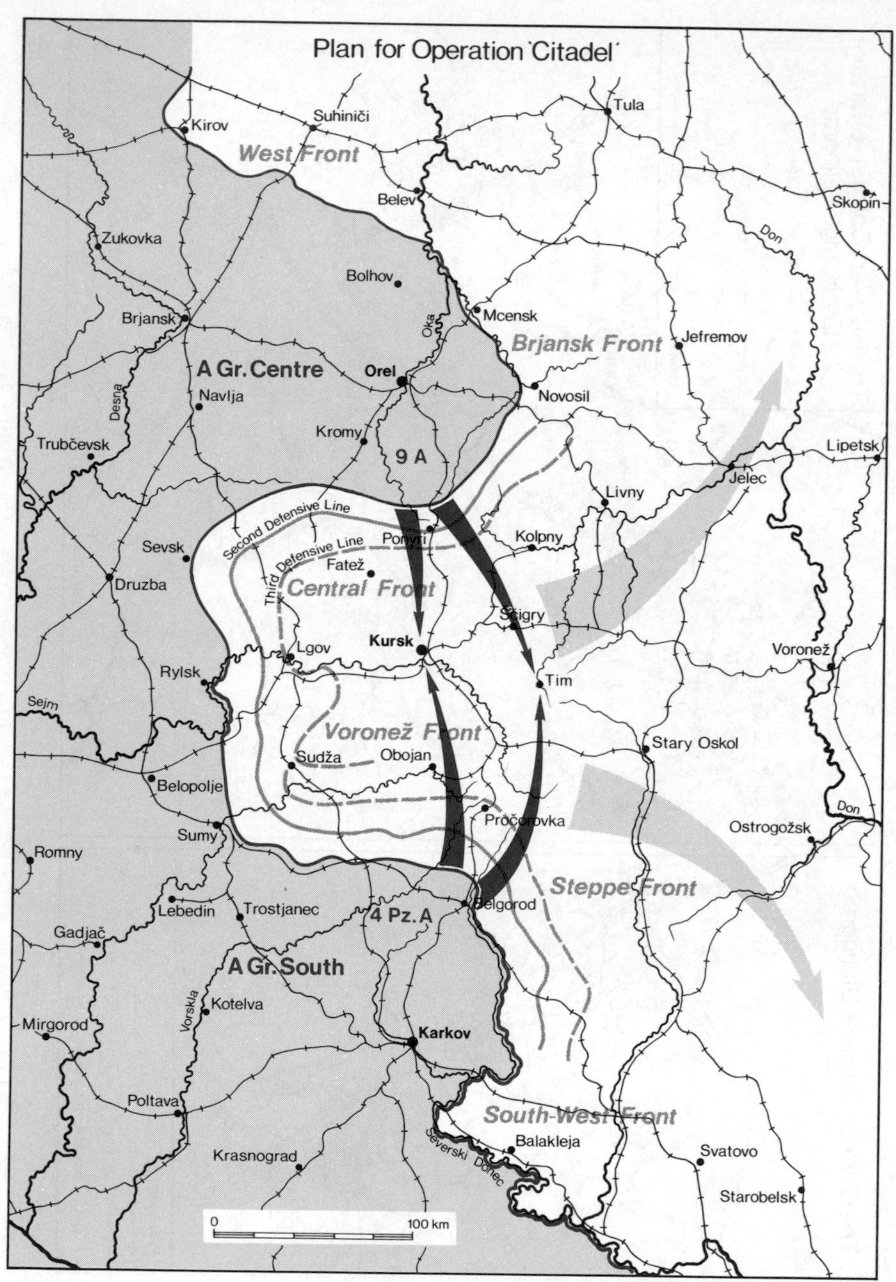
Plan for Operation 'Citadel'
Tula
Suhiniči
Kirov
West Front
Belev
Skopin
Don
Zukovka
Bolhov
Mcensk
Oka
Brjansk
Brjansk Front
Jefremov
A Gr. Centre
Orel
Novosil
Desna
Navlja
Kromy
Trubčevsk
9 A
Lipetsk
Jelec
Livny
Second Defensive Line
Ponyri
Kolpny
Sevsk
Third Defensive Line
Fatež
Druzba
Central Front
Ščigry
Kursk
Lgov
Voronež
Rylsk
Tim
Sejm
Voronež Front
Stary Oskol
Sudža
Obojan
Belopolje
Don
Pročorovka
Ostrogožsk
Sumy
Romny
Steppe Front
Lebedin
Trostjanec
Belgorod
4 Pz. A
Gadjač
A Gr. South
Vorskla
Kotelva
Mirgorod
Karkov
Poltava
South-West Front
Balakleja
Severski Donec
Svatovo
Krasnograd
Starobelsk
0
100 km

Map 9

The German Offensives on the Northern and Southern Flanks of the Salient

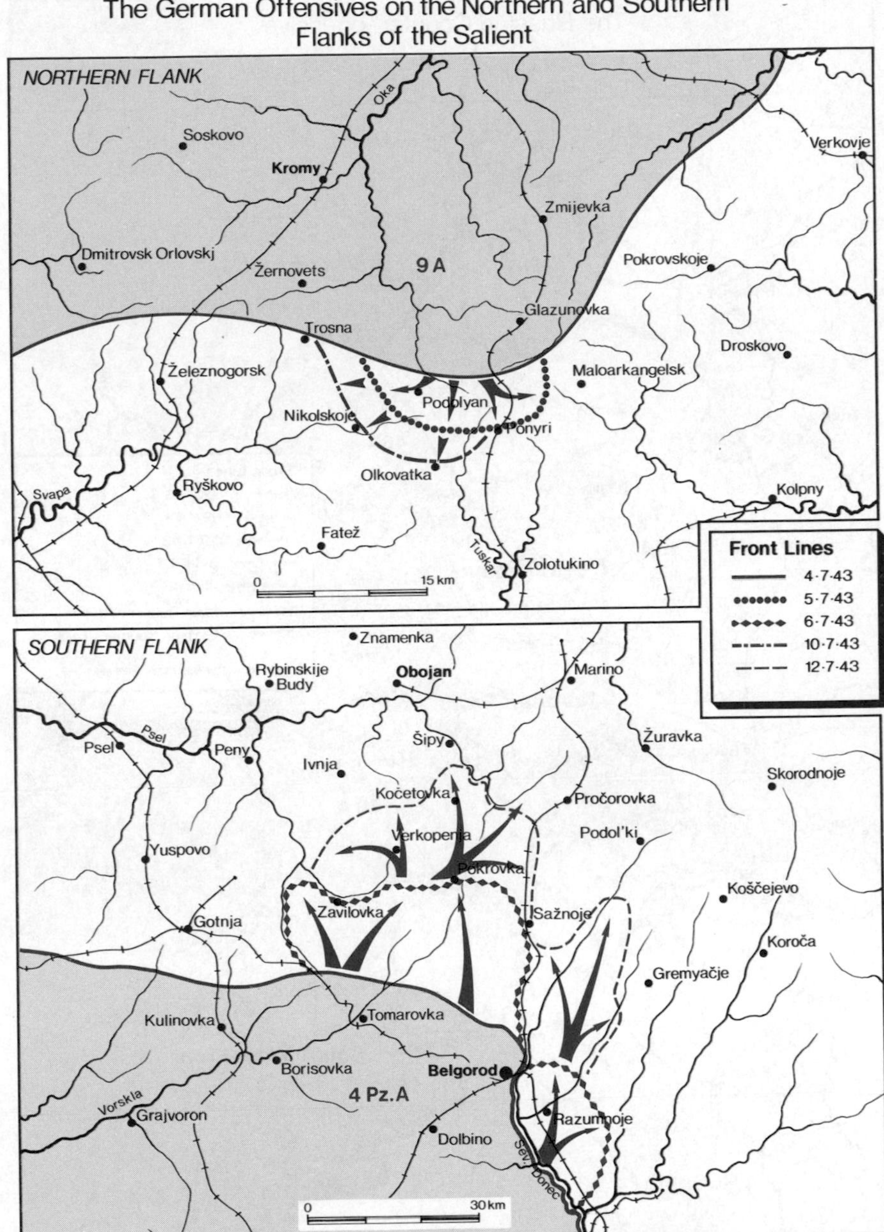

Map 10

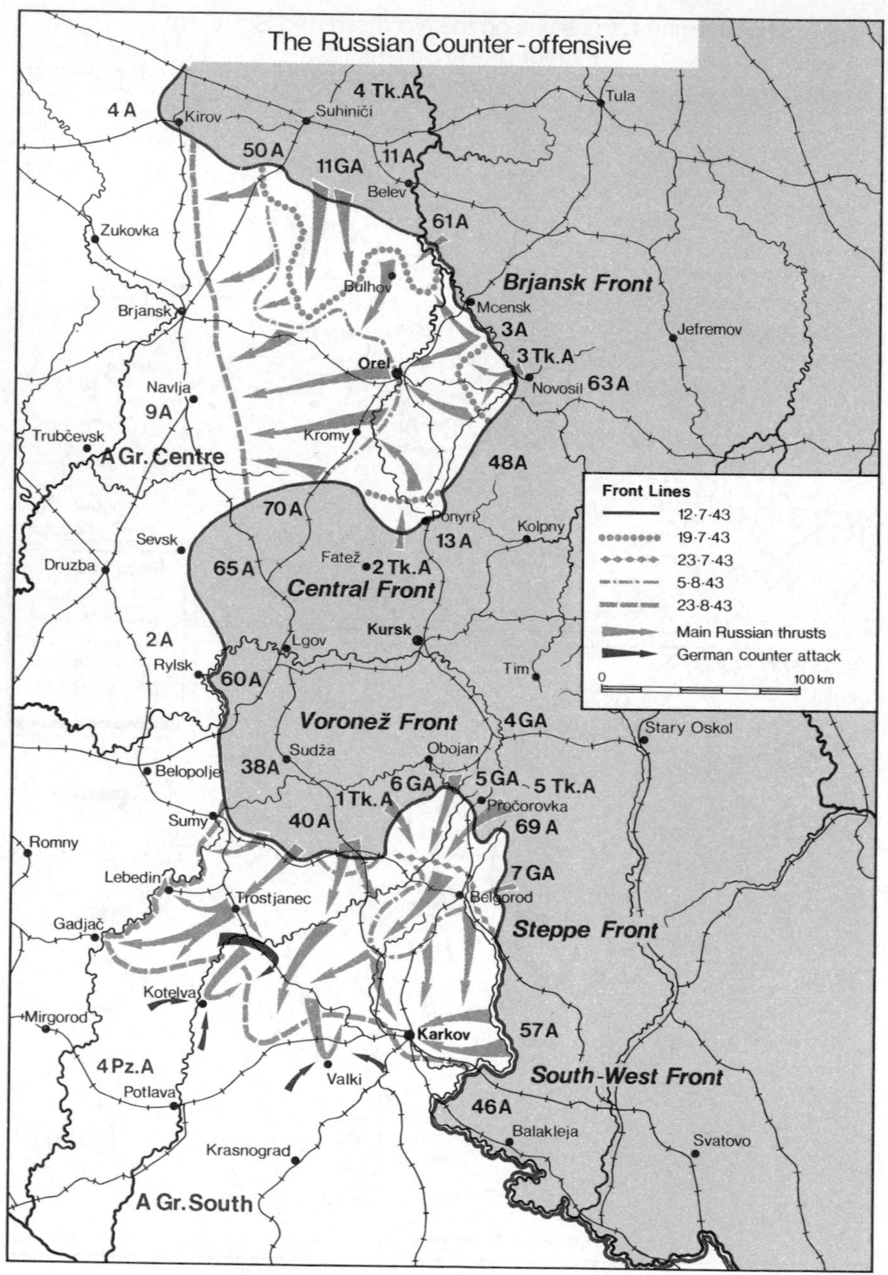
The Russian Counter-offensive
4 Tk.A
4 A
Kirov
Suhiniči
Tula
50 A
11GA
11 A
Belev
Zukovka
61A
Bulhov
Brjansk Front
Brjansk
Mcensk
3A
Jefremov
3 Tk.A
Orel
Novosil
63 A
Navlja
9A
Kromy
Trubčevsk
A Gr. Centre
48A
70 A
Ponyri
Kolpny
Sevsk
13 A
Fatež
2 Tk.A
Druzba
65 A
Central Front
Kursk
2 A
Lgov
Rylsk
Tim
60A
Voronež Front
4GA
Stary Oskol
Sudža
Obojan
Belopolje
38A
6 GA
5 GA
5 Tk.A
1 Tk.A
Pročorovka
Sumy
40 A
69 A
Romny
7 GA
Lebedin
Trostjanec
Belgorod
Gadjač
Steppe Front
Kotelva
Mirgorod
Karkov
57 A
4 Pz.A
Valki
South-West Front
Potlava
46A
Balakleja
Svatovo
Krasnograd
A Gr. South
Front Lines
12·7·43
19·7·43
23·7·43
5·8·43
23·8·43
Main Russian thrusts
German counter attack
0
100 km

Map 11

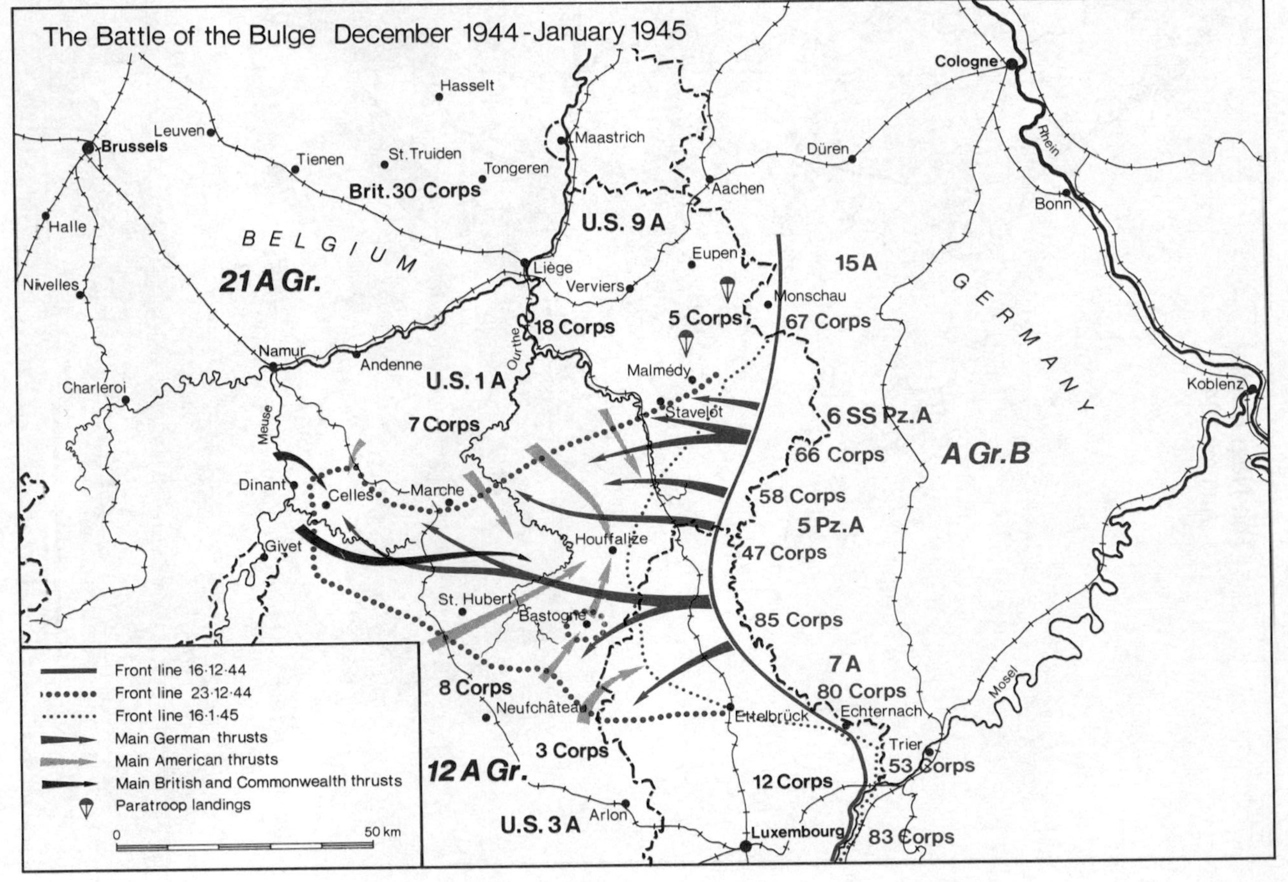
The Battle of the Bulge December 1944 - January 1945
Hasselt
Maastrich
Leuven
Brussels
Tienen
St. Truiden
Tongeren
Brit. 30 Corps
Halle
BELGIUM
21 A Gr.
Nivelles
Liège
Verviers
U.S. 9 A
Aachen
Düren
Cologne
Rhein
Bonn
Eupen
15 A
GERMANY
Monschau
5 Corps
67 Corps
18 Corps
Ourthe
Namur
Andenne
Charleroi
U.S. 1 A
Malmédy
Stavelot
6 SS Pz.A
Koblenz
7 Corps
Meuse
66 Corps
A Gr. B
Dinant
Celles
Marche
58 Corps
5 Pz. A
Houffalize
47 Corps
Givet
St. Hubert
Bastogne
85 Corps
7 A
80 Corps
8 Corps
Neufchâteau
Ettelbrück
Echternach
Mosel
Trier
53 Corps
3 Corps
12 A Gr.
12 Corps
U.S. 3 A
Arlon
Luxembourg
83 Corps
Front line 16·12·44
Front line 23·12·44
Front line 16·1·45
Main German thrusts
Main American thrusts
Main British and Commonwealth thrusts
Paratroop landings
0
50 km

Map 12

The Nazi Empire
Autumn 1942
NORWAY
SWEDEN
Oslo
Stockholm
Helsinki
DENMARK
Copenhagen
Baltic Sea
London
Amsterdam
1
Berlin
Brussels
2
Bonn
GREATER GERMANY
Paris
Luxembourg
Prague
3
GENERAL
GOVERNMENT
Danube
4
FRANCE
Vichy
6
Vienna
Budapest
HUNGARY
PORTUGAL
SPAIN
Madrid
Lisbon
CROATIA
Belgrade
SERBIA
5
Sofia
ITALY
CORSICA
Rome
SARDINIA
ALBANIA
GREECE
Tangier
Mediterranean Sea
Algiers
MOROCCO
ALGERIA
Tunis
TUNISIA
Tripoli
0
1000 km
LIBYA

Map 13

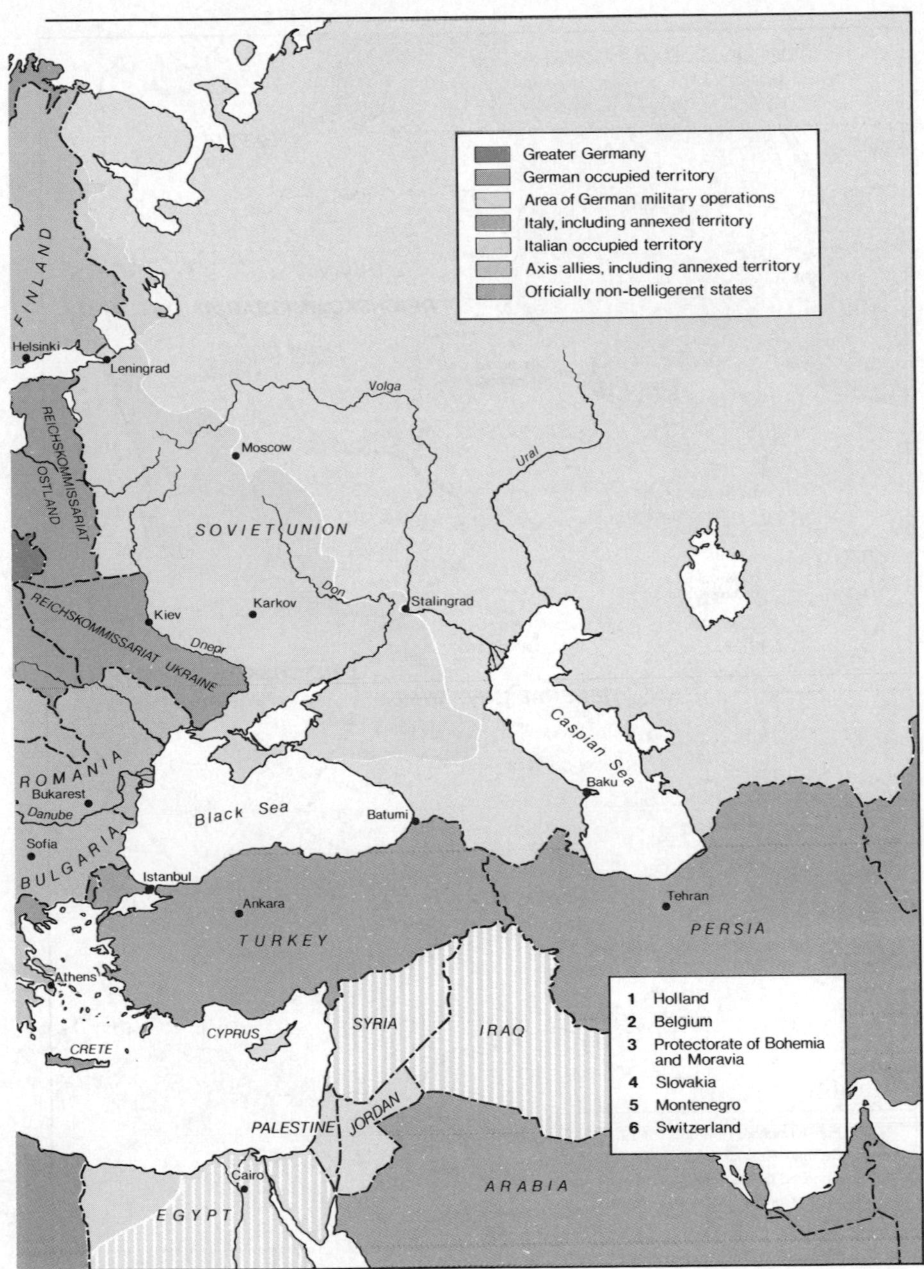
Greater Germany
German occupied territory
Area of German military operations
Italy, including annexed territory
Italian occupied territory
Axis allies, including annexed territory
Officially non-belligerent states
FINLAND
Helsinki
Leningrad
REICHSKOMMISSARIAT OSTLAND
Moscow
Volga
Ural
SOVIET UNION
Don
Stalingrad
Kiev
Karkov
Dnepr
REICHSKOMMISSARIAT UKRAINE
Caspian Sea
ROMANIA
Bukarest
Danube
Black Sea
Batumi
Baku
Sofia
BULGARIA
Istanbul
Ankara
TURKEY
Tehran
PERSIA
Athens
CYPRUS
SYRIA
IRAQ
CRETE
PALESTINE
JORDAN
Cairo
EGYPT
ARABIA
1 Holland
2 Belgium
3 Protectorate of Bohemia and Moravia
4 Slovakia
5 Montenegro
6 Switzerland

Map 13

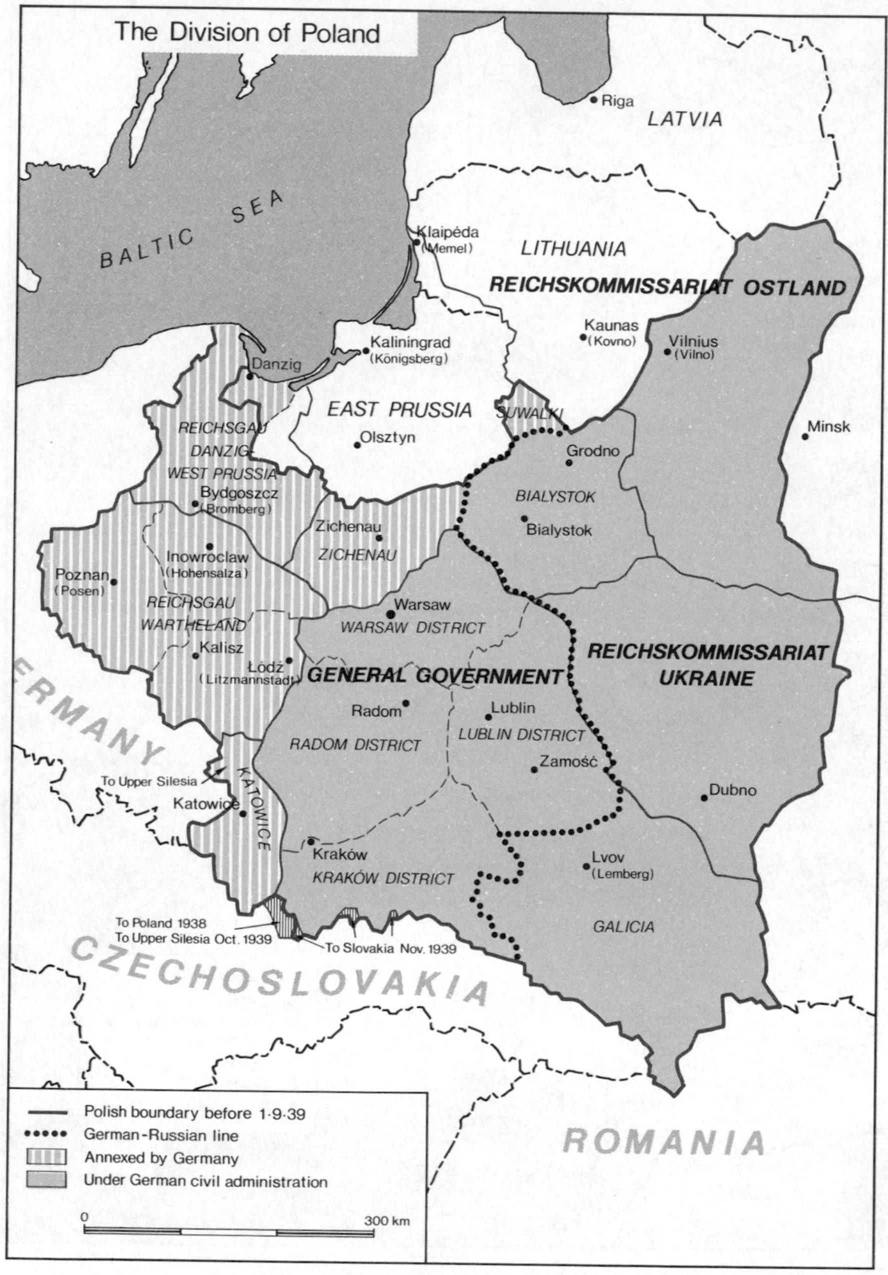

The Division of Poland
BALTIC SEA
Riga
LATVIA
LITHUANIA
Klaipėda (Memel)
REICHSKOMMISSARIAT OSTLAND
Kaunas (Kovno)
Vilnius (Vilno)
Kaliningrad (Königsberg)
Danzig
EAST PRUSSIA
SUWALKI
Olsztyn
Minsk
REICHSGAU DANZIG-WEST PRUSSIA
Grodno
BIALYSTOK
Bialystok
Bydgoszcz (Bromberg)
Zichenau
ZICHENAU
Inowroclaw (Hohensalza)
Poznan (Posen)
REICHSGAU WARTHELAND
Warsaw
WARSAW DISTRICT
Kalisz
Łódź (Litzmannstadt)
GENERAL GOVERNMENT
REICHSKOMMISSARIAT UKRAINE
GERMANY
Radom
RADOM DISTRICT
Lublin
LUBLIN DISTRICT
Zamość
Dubno
To Upper Silesia
KATOWICE
Katowice
Kraków
KRAKÓW DISTRICT
Lvov (Lemberg)
GALICIA
To Poland 1938
To Upper Silesia Oct. 1939
To Slovakia Nov. 1939
CZECHOSLOVAKIA
ROMANIA
Polish boundary before 1·9·39
German-Russian line
Annexed by Germany
Under German civil administration
0
300 km

Map 14

Concentration and Extermination Camps and Major 'Euthanasia' Centres
NORTH SEA
BALTIC SEA
SOVIET UNION
GERMANY
POLAND
CZECHOSLOVAKIA
AUSTRIA
HUNGA
SWITZ
ANCE
Königsberg
Danzig
Stutthof
Kiel
Hamburg
Neuengamme
Bremen
Elbe
Ravensbrück
Bydgoszcz
Treblinka
Bug
Bergen-Belsen
Sachsenhausen
Meseritz-Obrawalde
Vistula
Amsterdam
Wesser
Hannover
Berlin
Poznan
Warsaw
Magdeburg
Brandenburg
Kulmhof
Oder
Łódź
Sobibor
Bernburg
Lublin
Majdanek
Ruhr
Leipzig
Cologne
Dresden
Gross-Rosen
Breslau
Buchenwald
Erfurt
Sonnenstein
Belzec
Rhein
Hadamar
Limberg
Katowice
Frankfurt
Kraków
Lvov
Main
Eichberg
Prague
Auschwitz
Luxembourg
Nürnberg
Brno
Strasbourg
Stuttgart
Danube
Natzweiler
Ulm
Grafeneck
Dachau
Munich
Hartheim
Mauthausen
Vienna
Eglfing-Haar
Salzburg
Zürich
Inn
Budapest
Bern
'Euthanasia' centres
Concentration camps
Extermination camps
Combined Concentration and Extermination camps
0
300 km

Map 15

List of Sources

467. (*a*) R. Phelps, 'Hitler als Parteiredner'. Dokument Nr. 1. *Vierteljahrshefte für Zeitgeschichte* 11 (1963), p. 290.
(*b*) E. Deuerlein, 'Hitlers Eintritt in die Politik und die Reichswehr'. Dokument Nr. 16. *Vierteljahrshefte für Zeitgeschichte* 7 (1959), p. 209.
468. A. Hitler, *Mein Kampf* (London1969) (modified translation) pp. 120ff., 587ff.
469. T. Vogelsang, 'Hitler's Brief an Reichenau vom 4 Dezember 1932'. *Vierteljahrshefte für Zeitgeschichte* 2 (1954), pp. 434–7.
470. E. Röhricht, *Pflicht und Gewissen. Erinnerungen eines deutschen Generals 1932–1944* (Stuttgart 1956) pp. 42–3.
471. T. Vogelsang, 'Neue Dokumente zur Geschichte der Reichswehr 1930–1933'. Document Nr. 6. *Vierteljahrshefte für Zeitgeschichte* 2 (1954), pp.432–4.
472. *Ibid.*, Nr. 7.
473. H-J. Rautenberg, 'Drei Dokumente zur Planung eines 300,000 Mann-Friedensheeres aus dem Dezember 1933'. *Militärgeschichtliche Mitteilungen* 2 (1977), pp. 119ff.
474. M. Domarus, ed., *Hitler. Reden 1932 bis 1945* (Wiesbaden 1973), pp. 355–6.
475. K-J. Müller, *Das Heer und Hitler. Armee und nationalsozialistisches Regime 1933–1940* (Stuttgart 1969), pp. 599–600.
476. *Ibid.*, p. 606.
477. H. Foertsch, *Schuld und Verhängnis. Die Fritsch-Krise im Frühjahr 1938 als Wendepunkt der NS-Zeit* (Stuttgart 1951), p. 57.
478. M. Messerschmidt, *Werden und Prägung des preussischen Offizierskorps—Ein Überblick*, in: *Offiziere im Bild von Dokumenten aus drei Jahrhunderten* Vol. 6, (Stuttgart 1964), p. 254.
479. K-J. Müller, *op. cit.*, p. 603.
480. M. Messerschmidt, *op. cit.*, pp. 225–6.
481. K-J. Müller, *op. cit.*, p. 255–6.
482. *Ibid.*, p. 592.
483. *Reichsgesetzblatt* I, (1935), p. 558.
484. M. Messerschmidt, *op. cit.*, p. 263.
485. K-J. Müller, *op. cit.*, p. 621.
486. M. Messerschmidt, *Die Wehrmacht im NS-Staat* (Hamburg 1969), pp. 64–5.
487. F. Hossbach, *Zwischen Wehrmacht und Hitler 1934–1938* (Wolfenbüttel-Hanover 1965), pp. 68ff.
488. P. Krüger and E. J. C. Hahn, 'Der Loyalitätskonflikt des Staatssekretärs Bernhard Wilhelm von Bülow im Frühjahr 1933'. *Vierteljahrshefte für Zeitgeschichte* 20, (1972), p. 396.

489. *Ibid.*, pp. 387–8.
490. W. Michalka, ed., *Das Dritte Reich*. Vol. 1 *Volksgemeinschaft und Grossmachtpolitik* (Munich 1985), pp. 216ff.
491. N. H. Baynes, ed., *The Speeches of Adolf Hitler 1922–1939* Vol. II (Oxford 1942), pp. 1046–8.
492. *Documents on British Foreign Policy 1919–1939* 2nd Series, Vol. VI pp. 152–3.
493. *Die polnisch-deutschen und polnisch-sowjetischen Beziehungen im Zeitraum von 1933 bis 1939. Dokumente und Urkunden zum Kriegsausbruch September 1939* (Basel 1940) pp. 20ff.
494. Documents on German Foriegn Policy (DGFP), Series C, Vol. 111, pp. 329–30.
495. *Ibid.*
496. DGFP Series C, Vol. III, pp. 1043ff.
497. Nuremberg Document (ND) 46-TC.
498. *Royal Institute of International Affairs, Documents on International Affairs 1936* (Oxford 1937), pp. 345–6.
499. W. Michalka, *Ribbentrop und die deutsche Weltpolitik 1933–1940* (Munich 1980), p. 155.
500. Bundesarchiv Koblenz (BAK) Z.Slg. 101 Nr. 32.
501. K-J. Müller, *General Ludwig Beck. Studien und Dokumente zur politisch-militärischen Vorstellungswelt und Tätigkeit des Generalstabschefs des deutschen Heers 1933–1938*, (Boppard 1980), pp. 469ff.
502. J. Dülffer, *Weimar, Hitler und die Marine. Reichspolitik und Flottenbau 1920–1939* (Düsseldorf 1973), p. 447.
503. DGFP, Series D, Vol. I, pp. 29–38.
504. F. Hossbach, *op. cit.*, p. 191.
505. DGFP Series D, Vol. I, pp. 55ff.
506. ND 175-C, DGFP, Series D, Vol. III, pp. 635–7.
507. W. Michalka, ed. *Das Dritte Reich op. cit.*, pp. 241ff.
508. *Ibid.*, pp. 245–6.
509. R. Absolon, *Die Wehrmacht im Dritten Reich. Aufbau, Gliederung, Recht, Verwaltung* (Boppard 1975), p. 500.
510. DGFP Series D, vol .I, pp. 513–14.
511. *Ibid.*, p. 548.
512. *Ibid.*, p. 576.
513. ND 102-C.
514. ND 2949-PS.
515. *Ibid.*
516. DGFP, Series D, Vol. I, pp. 240ff.
517. DGFP, Series D, Vol. II, p. 198.
518. *Ibid.*, p. 242.
519. *Ibid.*, p. 300–2.
520. F. Wiedemann, *Der Mann der Feldherr werden wollte* (Kettwig 1964), pp. 127–8.
521. K-J. Müller, *General Ludwig Beck*, *op. cit.*, pp. 512ff.
522. ND 1780-PS.
523. DGFP Series D, Vol. II, p. 358.
524. *Ibid.*, p. 608.
525. *Ibid.*, pp. 863–4.
526. I. Kirkpatrick, *The Inner Circle* (London 1959), pp. 114–18.
527. DGFP Series D, Vol. II, pp. 1014–16.
528. *Die Weizsäcker-Papiere 1933–1950* ed. L. E. Hill (Frankfurt–Berlin–Vienna 1974), p. 145.
529. W. Treue, ed. 'Rede Hitlers vor der deutschen Presse (10 November 1938)'. *Viertel-jahrshefte für Zeitgeschichte* 6 (1958), pp. 175–191.

530. DGFP, Series D, Vol. IV, p. 99.
531. W. Michalka, ed., *Das Dritte Reich op. cit.*, pp. 224–5.
532. DGFP, Series D, Vol. IV, pp. 244–45.
533. *Ibid.*, p. 266.
534. *Ibid.*, p. 270.
535. J. Dülffer, *op. cit.*, p. 502.
536. ND 028-EC.
537. DGFP, Series D, Vol. V, pp. 153ff.
538. DGFP Series D, Vol. VI, pp. 224–5.
539. *Ibid.*, pp. 575ff.
540. C. J. Burckhardt, *Meine Danziger Mission* 1937–1939, (Munich 1962) p. 272.
541. DGFP, Series D, Vol. VII, pp. 200–4.
542. *Ibid.*, pp. 205–6.
543. *Ibid.*, pp. 245–7.
544. DBFP Third Series, Vol. VII, pp. 228–9.
545. DGFP Series D, Vol. VII, pp. 280–81.
546. DBFP Third Series, Vol. VII, pp. 432–3.
547. DGFP, Series D, Vol. VII, pp. 477–8.
548. M. Domarus, *Hitler. Reden op. cit.* , pp. 1316–7.
549. Paul Schmidt, *Hitler's Interpreter* (New York 1950), pp. 157–8.
550. *Das Deutsche Reich und der Weltkrieg*. Vol. 2.*Die Errichtung der Hegemonie auf dem europäischen Kontinent* eds, A. Maier *et al.* (Stuttgart 1979), p. 111.
551. *Ibid.*, p. 133.
552. *Das politishe Tagebuch Alfred Rosenbergs 1934/35 und 1939/40* (Munich 1964), pp. 103–4.
553. H-A. Jacobsen, ed., *Dokumente zur Vorgeschichte des Westfeldzuges 1939–1940* (Göttingen 1956), pp. 5ff.
554. ND 789-PS
555. G. Wagner ed., *Lagevorträge des Oberbefehlshabers der Kriegsmarine vor Hitler 1939–1945* Munich 1972, pp. 20–21.
556. *Das Deutsche Reich und der Zweite Weltkrieg* Vol. 2, *op. cit.*, p. 162.
557. DGFP, Series D, Vol. VIII, pp. 831–2.
558. H-A. Jacobsen, *Dokumente zur Vorgeschichte des Westfeldzuges op. cit.*, pp. 46–49.
559. *Ibid.*, pp. 155–6.
560. *Ibid.*, pp. 64–5.
561. *Das Deutsche Reich und der Zweite Weltkrieg* Vol. 2 *op. cit.* p. 282.
562. (*a*) H-A. Jacobsen, *1939–1945: Der Zweite Weltkrieg in Chronik und Dokumenten* (Darmstadt 1962) pp. 146–147.
(*b*) *Ibid.*
563. F. Halder, *Generaloberst Halder. Kriegstagebuch. Tägliche Aufzeichnungen des Chefs des Generalstabes des Heeres 1939–1942 (Halder Tagebuch)*, Vol. 1, p. 319.
564. *Das Deutsche Reich und der Zweite Weltkrieg* Vol. 2, *op. cit.*, p. 296.
565. *Ciano's Diary 1939–43* (London 1947), pp. 266–7.
566. *Deutschland im Zweiten Weltkrieg* Vol. 1. *Vorbereitung, Entfesselung und Verlauf des Krieges bis zum 22 Juni 1941* eds, W. Schumann and G. Hass (East Berlin 1975), p. 332.
567. BAK Z.Slg. 101 Nr. 36. pp. 51–2.
568. DGFP Series D, Vol. VIII, pp. 875–7.
569. *Halder Tagebuch*, Vol. 2, p. 20.
570. DGFP, Series D, Vol. X, pp. 226–8.
571. M. Domarus, *op. cit.*, p. 1558.
572. *Halder Tagebuch*, Vol. 2, pp. 30–1.
573. *Ibid.*, pp. 43–4.

574. *Halder Tagebuch*, Vol. II, pp. 46ff.
575. *Lagevorträge des Oberbefehshabers der Kriegsmarine vor Hitler 1939–1945 op. cit.*, pp. 143–4.
576. DGFP Series D, Vol. XI, pp. 204–5.
577. *Ibid.*, pp. 248–9.
578. DGFP Series D, Vol. XI, pp. 527–30.
579. *Ibid.*, pp. 544ff.
580. *Ibid.*, pp. 554ff.
581. *Ibid.*, pp. 567ff.
582. BAK Z.Slg. 101 N. 37. pp. 277–9.
583. DGFP Series D, Vol. XI, p. 52.
584. W. Michalka, ed., *Das Dritte Reich*, Vol. 2, *Weltmachtanspruch und nationaler Zusammenbruch 1939–1945* (Munich 1985), pp. 50–1.
585. *Ibid.*, pp. 57–9.
586. DGFP, Series D, Vol. XII, pp. 1066ff.
587. *Halder Tagebuch*, Vol. III, pp. 38–9.
588. *Ibid.*, p. 170.
589. *OKW Kriegstagebuch* (Frankfurt/M 1961–65) Vol. II, pp. 1052ff.
590. *Ibid.*, pp. 1063.
591. H-A. Jacobsen, *1939–1945: Der Zweite Weltkrieg op. cit.*, pp. 354–5.
592. *Heeresadjutant bei Hitler 1938–1943. Aufzeichnungen des Majors Engel* ed. H. Von (Stuttgart 1974), pp. 114–16.
593. H-A, Jacobsen, *1939–1945: Der Zweite Weltkrieg op. cit.*, pp. 281–2.
594. W. Michalka, ed. *Das Dritte Reich* Vol. 2, op. cit., pp. 66–7.
595. H-A. Jacobsen ed. *Der Weg zur Teilung der Welt. Politik und Strategie 1939–1945* (Koblenz/Bonn 1977), pp. 138–9.
596. M. Domarus, *op. cit.*, pp. 1803ff.
597. DGFP, Series D, Vol. XIII, pp. 999–1000.
598. W. Michalka, ed. *Das Dritte Reich* Vol. 2, *op. cit.*, p. 65.
599. *Ibid.*, pp. 67–70.
600. *Ciano's Diary*, *op. cit.*
601. W. Michalka, ed., *Das Dritte Reich*, *vol. 2 op. cit.*, pp. 75–6.
602. M. Domarus, *op. cit.*, pp. 1937–8.
603. J. Hohlfeld, ed. *Dokumente der deutschen Politik von 1848 bis zur Gegenwart*, Vol. 6, (Berlin/Munich undated), pp. 387–91.
604. *Deutschland im Zweiten Weltkrieg*, Vol. 3, ed., W. Schumann (East Berlin 1982), p. 103.
605. *Ibid.*, p. 128.
606. *Ibid.*, p. 131.
607. *Ibid.*, pp. 136–7.
608. S. W. Roskill, *The War at Sea*, Vol. I, (London 1954), pp. 599ff, 614, Vol. II (London 1956), pp. 467ff., 475, Vol. III Part 1 (London 1960), pp. 364ff.
609. M. Salewski, *Die deutsche Seekriegsleitung, 1935–1945*, Vol. III, *Denkschriften und Lagebetrachtungen 1938–1944* (Frankfurt 1973), p. 342.
610. *Deutschland im Zweiten Weltkrieg*, Vol. 3, *op. cit.*, pp. 411–13.
611. W. Michalka, *Das Dritte Reich*, Vol. 2, *op. cit.*, p. 154.
612. *Der Zweite Weltkrieg. Dokumente* eds., G. Förster and O. Groehler (East Berlin 1974), pp. 207ff.
613. *Hitler's Weisungen für die Kriegführung* ed. W. Hubatsch (Munich 1965), pp. 270ff.
614. A. Hillgruber, *Staatsmänner und Diplomaten bei Hitler*, Vol. II, (Frankfurt 1967), p. 350f.
615. *Ibid.*, pp. 418ff.
616. H.-A. Jacobsen, ed., *1939–1945: Der Zweite Weltkrieg op. cit.*, p. 474.

617. *Deutschland im Zweiten Weltkrieg*, Vol. 6, eds, W. Schumann and O. Groehler (East Berlin 1985), p. 783.
618. ND 862–PS.
619. *Royal Institute of International Affairs, Documents on International Affairs 1939–46*, Vol. II *Hitler's Europe*, ed., M. Carlyle (London 1954), pp. 220–1.
620. BAK Z.Slg.101 Nr.36 pp. 39–40.
621. W. Michalka, ed., *Das Dritte Reich*, Vol. 2, *op. cit.*, pp. 127–8.
622. DGFP, Series D, Vol. IX, pp. 496ff.
623. *Deutschland im Zweiten Weltkrieg*, Vol. 1, *op. cit.*, p. 389.
624. *Ibid.*, pp. 391–2.
625. *Anatomie der Aggression. Neue Dokumente zu den Kriegszielen des faschistischen deutschen Imperialismus im zweiten Weltkrieg*, eds, G. Hass and W. Schumann (East Berlin 1972), pp. 80–1.
626. *Ibid.*, pp. 81–2.
627. *Anatomie des Krieges. Neue Dokumente über die Rolle des deutschen Monopolkapitals bei der Vorbereitung und Durchführung des zweiten Weltkrieges*, eds, D. Eicholtz and W. Schumann (East Berlin 1969), pp. 275ff.
628. *Ibid.*, pp. 286–7.
629. *Ibid.*, pp. 289ff.
630. DGFP, Series D, Vol. XIII, pp. 149–56.
631. H.-A. Jacobsen, ed., *Der Zweite Weltkrieg. Grundzüge der Politik und Strategie in Dokumenten* (Frankfurt 1965), p. 181.
632. W. Runge and W. Schumann, eds, *Dokumente zur Deutschen Geschichte 1939–1942* (Frankfurt 1973), pp. 54–55.
633. W. Michalka, *Das Dritte Reich*, Vol. 2, *op. cit.*, pp. 174–5.
634. L. Poliakov and J. Wulf, eds, *Das Dritte Reich und seine Deiener* (Frankfurt/Berlin/Vienna 1983), pp. 197–8.
635. *Deutschland im Zweiten Weltkrieg*, Vol. 6, *op. cit.*, p. 394.
636. *Ibid.*
637. *Survey of International Affairs 1939–1946. Hitler's Europe*, Vol. I (London 1954), pp. 197–8.
638. E. L. Homze, *Foreign Labour in Nazi Germany* (Princeton 1967), pp. 195, 235.
639. *(a)* A. S. Milward, *War, Economy and Society 1939–1945* (London 1977), p. 262.
(b) L. Burchardt, 'Die Auswirkungen der Kreigswirtschaft auf die deutsche Zivilibevölkerung im Ersten und im Zweiten Weltkrieg'. *Militärgeschlichtliche Mitteilungen* 15 (1974), p. 79.
(c) Ibid., p. 75.
640. ND 294–PS.
641. W. Michalka, ed., *Das Dritte Reich*, Vol. 2, *op. cit.*, pp. 212–3.
642. ND 1919–PS.
643. *Reichsgesetzblatt* (1939) I, p. 2042.
644. *Ibid.*, p. 2077.
645. *Das Politische Testament Alfred Rosenbergs aus den Jahren 1934/35 und 1939/40* ed. H-G. Seraphim (Munich 1964), pp. 98–100.
646. ND 789-PS.
647. K. Pätzold, ed., *Verfolgung, Vertreibung, Vernichtung. Dokumente des faschistischen Antisemitismus 1933 bis 1942* (Leipzig 1984), p. 234.
648. *Ibid.*, pp. 239–40.
649. ND 686–PS.
650. M. B roszat, *Zweihundert Jahre deutsche Polenpolitik* (Frankfurt 1972), p. 288.
651. W. Michalka, *Das Dritte Reich* Vol. 2, *op. cit.*, pp. 163–6.
652. *The German New Order in Poland* (London undated, 1942?), pp. 421–2.

653. K. Pätzold, *op. cit.*, 245–6.
654. *The German New Order in Poland, op. cit.*, pp. 181–2.
655. H-A. Jacobsen, ed., *1939–1944. Der Zweite Weltkrieg, op. cit.*, pp. 606–9.
656. *Heeresadjutant bei Hitler 1938–1943, op. cit.*, pp. 67–8.
657. L. Poliakov and J. Wulf eds., *op. cit.*, pp. 385–6.
658. M. Haman, 'Erwünscht und unerwünscht. Die rassenpsychologische Selektion der Ausländer' in *Herrenmensch und Arbeitsvölker. Ausländische Arbeiter und Deutsche 1939–1945* eds G. Aly *et. al.* (Berlin 1986), pp. 145–7.
659. *Ibid.*
660. *Ibid.*, pp. 164–5.
661. *Documents on International Affairs 1939–1946* Vol. II *Hitler's Europe op. cit.*, p. 246.
662. M. Broszat, *Nationalsozialistische Polenpolitik 1939–1945* (Stuttgart 1961), p. 127 f.n. 3.
663. *Ibid.*, p. 129 f.n. 2.
664. *Ibid.*, p. 130 f.n. 1.
665. *Ibid.*, f.n. 3.
666. A. Hohenstein, *Wartheländisches Tagebuch 1941/42* (Munich 1963), p. 193 f.n. 1.
667. *Ibid.*, p. 31 f.n. 1.
668. *The German New Order in Poland, op. cit.*, pp. 410–11.
669. *Ibid.*, p. 420.
670. *Reichgesetzblatt* (1940) I, p. 1270.
671. *The German New Order in Poland, op. cit.*, p. 262.
672. *Ibid.*, pp. 408–9.
673. M. Broszat, *Nationalsozialistische Polenpolitik, op. cit.*, p. 169.
674. *Ibid.*, p. 174.
675. A. Hohenstein, *op. cit.*, pp. 183–4.
676. ND 410–EC.
677. *Das Diensttagebuch des deutschen Generalgouverneurs in Polen 1939–1945* eds W. Präg and W. Jacobmeyer (Stuttgart 1975), pp. 91, 94.
678. *The German New Order in Poland, op. cit.*, pp.289ff.
679. *Das Diensttagebuch, op. cit.*, p. 117.
680. *Ibid.*, pp. 127–8.
681. *Ibid.*, pp. 209–10.
682. *Ibid.*, pp. 210ff.
683. *Ibid.*, p. 458–9.
684. *Ibid.*, pp. 590–1.
685. *Ibid.*, p. 625.
686. ND 437–PS.
687. *Das Diensttagebuch, op. cit.*, p. 772.
688. T. Tsarota, *Warschau unter dem Hakenkreuz* (Paderborn 1985), pp. 21–2.
689. *Aus Deutschen Urkunden 1935–1945* (undated *c.*1945), pp. 127–8.
690. H. Heiber, 'Der Generalplan Ost' in *Vierteljahrshefte für Zeitgeschichte* 6 (1958), pp. 305–8.
691. ND 910–PS.
692. *Documents on International Affairs 1939–1946*, Vol. II, *op. cit.*, p. 254.
693. *Ibid.*, p. 255.
694. *Deutschland im zweiten Weltkrieg* Vol. 2, *op. cit.*, p. 445.
695. *Das Diensttagebuch, op. cit.*, pp. 934–5.
696. R. Lemkin, *Axis Rule in Occupied Europe* (Washington DC 1944), p. 542.
697. ND 70–EC.
698. L. Poliakov and J. Wulf, eds, *Das Dritte Reich und seine Diener* (Frankfurt 1983), pp. 299ff.
699. J. T. Gross, *Polish Society under German Occupation 1939–1944* (Princeton 1979), p. 81.

700. T. Szarota, *op. cit.*, p. 49.
701. *Ibid.*, pp. 178–9 and *The German New Order in Poland*, *op. cit.*, pp. 490–2.
702. *Das Diensttagebuch*, *op. cit*, pp. 186–8.
703. T. Szarota, *op. cit.*, p. 113.
704. *Ibid.*, p. 114.
705. *Ibid.*, p. 113.
706. *Ibid.*, p. 80.
707. *Ibid.*, p. 81.
708. J. T. Gross, *op. cit.*, p. 106.
709. *Ibid.*
710. J. T. Gross, *op. cit.*, p. 107.
711. T. Szarota, *op. cit.*, p. 241.
712. *Ibid.*, p. 235.
713. *Aus deutschen Urkunden*, *op. cit.*, p. 254.
714.. T. Szarota, *op. cit.*, p. 294.
715. *Himmler. Geheimreden 1933 bis 1945* eds, B. F. Smith and A. F. Peterson (Frankfurt 1974), p. 242.
716. K. Binding and A. Hoche, *Die Freigabe der Vernichtung lebensunwerten Lebens. Ihr Mass und ihre Form* (Leipzig 1920), pp. 27ff.
717. *Ibid.*
718. *Ibid.*, pp. 40, 55ff.
719. *Völkischer Beobachter*, 7.8.1929.
720. J. Tuchel, ed., *'Kein Recht auf Leben'. Beiträge und Dokumente zur Entrechtung und Vernichtung 'lebensunwerten Lebens' im Nationalsozialismus* (Berlin 1984), pp. 48–9.
721. E. Klee, ed., *Dokumente zur 'Euthanasie'* (Frankfurt 1985), p. 63.
722. E. Klee, *'Euthanasie' im NS-Staat. Die Vernichtung 'lebensunwerten Lebens'* (Frankfurt 1983), p. 78.
723. *Ibid.*, pp. 78–9.
724. *Ibid.*, p. 80.
725. F. K. Kaul, *Die Psychiatrie im Strudel der 'Euthanasie'* (Frankfurt 1979), p. 41.
726. *Ibid.*, p. 42.
727. *Ibid.*, p. 33.
728. G. Aly, 'Der saubere und der schmutzige Fortschritt' in G. Aly, ed., *Reform und Gewissen. 'Euthanasie'im Dienst des Fortschritts* (Berlin 1985), p. 60.
729. F. K. Kaul, *op. cit.* p. 63ff.
730. E. Klee, *'Euthanasie' im NS-Staat*, *op. cit.*, p. 92.
731. *Ibid.*, p. 93.
732. *Ibid.*, p. 118.
733. E. Klee, ed., *Dokumente*, *op. cit.*, pp. 246–7.
734. E. Klee, *'Euthanasie' im NS-Staat*, *op. cit.*, p. 244.
735. *Ibid.*, p. 246.
736. *(a)* G. Aly, *op. cit.*, p. 50.
 (b) Ibid., pp. 9–10.
737. J. Tuchel, *op. cit.*, pp. 64–5.
738. E. Klee, *'Euthanasie' im NS-Staat*, *op. cit.*, pp. 84–5.
739. *Ibid.*, pp. 110–12.
740. E. Klee, ed., *Dokumente*, *op. cit.*, p. 89.
741. E. Klee, *'Euthanasie' im NS-Staat*, *op. cit.*, p. 104.
742. E. Klee, ed., *Dokumente*, *op. cit.*, p. 108.
743. E. Klee, *'Euthanasie' im NS-Staat*, *op. cit.*, pp. 179–80.
744. E. Klee, ed., *Dokumente*, *op. cit.*, pp. 124ff.
745. E. Klee, *'Euthanasie' im NS-Staat*, *op. cit.*, p. 336.

746. *Ibid.*, p. 159.
747. *Ibid.*, p. 148.
748. E. Kogon, *et. al.*, *Nationalsozialistische Massentötungen durch Giftgas* (Frankfurt 1983), p. 44.
749. *Ibid.*, pp. 50–1.
750. E. Klee, *'Euthanasie' im NS-Staat*, *op. cit.*, p. 251.
751. *Ibid.*, p. 186.
752. *Ibid.*, p.184.
753. *Ibid.*, p. 185.
754. E. Klee, ed., *Dokumente*, *op. cit.*, pp.216–18.
755. E. Klee, *'Euthanasie' im NS-Staat*, *op. cit.*, p. 332.
756. *Ibid.*, p. 333.
757. *Ibid.*, p. 288.
758. ND 3701–PS.
759. ND 615–PS.
760. *Ibid.*
761. E. Kogon, *op. cit.*, p. 62.
762. E. Klee, *Dokumente*, *op. cit.*, p. 232.
763. J. Tuchel, *op. cit.*, pp. 94–5.
764. *Medizin ohne Menschlichkeit. Dokumente des Nürnberger Ärzteprozesses*, eds A. Mitscherlich and F. Mielke (Frankfurt 1960), p. 217.
765. E. Kogon, *op. cit.*, pp. 67–70, E. Klee, *'Euthanasie' im NS-Staat*, *op. cit.*, p. 346.
766. E. Klee, *'Euthanasie' im NS-Staat*, *op. cit.*, p. 430.
767. *Ibid.*, p. 431.
768. *Ibid.*, p. 435.
769. *Ibid.*, p. 439.
770. M. Domarus, *op. cit.* pp. 1057–8.
771. *Faschismus-Getto-Massenmord. Dokumentation über Ausrottung und Widerstand der Juden in Polen während des zweiten Weltkrieges*, eds, T. Berenstein *et. al.* (Frankfurt n.d. 1960?), pp. 37–41.
772. K. Pätzold, ed., *Verfolgung, Vertreibung, Vernichtung. Dokumente des faschistischen Antisemitismus* (Leipzig 1984), pp. 239–40.
773. *Faschismus*, *op. cit.*, p. 46.
774. K. Pätzold, *op. cit.*, p. 253.
775. *Faschismus*, *op. cit.*, pp. 50–2.
776. *Ibid.*, pp. 52–3.
777. L. Poliakov, *Harvest of Hate* (London 1954), pp. 48–9.
778. K. Pätzold, *op. cit.*, p. 262.
779. *Faschismus*, *op. cit.*, p. 203.
780. *Ibid.*, pp. 219–20.
781. *Ibid.*, p. 221.
782. *The German New Order in Poland*, *op. cit.*, pp. 560–61.
783. *Faschismus*, *op. cit.*, pp. 78–81.
784. *Ibid.*, pp. 108–13.
785. *Ibid.*, pp. 152–3.
786. T. Szarota, *op. cit.*, p. 46.
787. BA Z.Slg. 101 Nr.41, pp. 55–7.
788. *Faschismus*, *op. cit.*, p. 138.
789. *Ibid.*, pp. 128–9.
790. L. Poliakov and J. Wulf, eds, *Das Dritte Reich und die Juden* (Frankfurt 1983), p. 201.
791. *Faschismus*, *op. cit.*, p. 133.
792. *Dokumente über die Verfolgung der jüdischen Bürger in Baden-Württemberg durch das*

nationalsozialistische Regime 1933–1945, ed. P. Sauer, Vol. II (Stuttgart 1966), p. 189.
793. *Ibid.*, p. 190.
794. K. Pätzold, *op. cit.*, p. 261–2.
795. *Ibid.*, pp. 266–7.
796. *Völkischer Beobachter*, 21.1.1941.
797. K. Pätzold, *op. cit.*, pp. 262–3.
798. DGFP Series D, Vol. X, pp. 111–13.
799. K. Pätzold, *op. cit.*, pp. 269–70.
800. P. Sauer, *Dokumente*, *op. cit.*, pp. 236–9.
801. *Ibid.*, p. 241.
802. K. Pätzold, *op. cit.*, pp. 274–5.
803. *Faschismus*, *op. cit.*, p. 59.
804. NO–251.
805. K. Pätzold, *op. cit.*, p. 279.
806. *Faschismus*, *op. cit.*, pp. 60–1.
807. *Ibid.*, p. 64.
808. K. Pätzold, p. 286.
809. *Ibid.*, p. 288.
810. *Halder Tagebuch*, II, *op. cit.*, p. 337.
811. G. R. Übershär and W. Wette, eds., *"Unternehmen Barbarossa", Der deutsche Überfall auf die Sowjetunion 1941* (Paderborn 1984), pp. 300–1.
812. *Ibid.*, p. 288.
813. *Ibid.*, p. 312.
814. H. Buchheim, M. Broszat, H. Krausnick, H-A. Jacobsen, *Anatomy of the SS State* (London 1968), ppl. 62–3.
815. ND 180–L.
816. H. Krausnick and H. H. Wilhelm, *Die Truppe des Weltanschauungskrieges. Die Einsatzgruppen der Sicherheitspolizei und des SD 1938–1942* (Stuttgart 1981), pp. 534–5.
817. *Ibid.*, pp. 536–7.
818. G. R. Übershär and W. Wette, eds, *op. cit.*, pp. 373–4.
819. *Ibid.*, pp. 339–40.
820. ND PS–3663.
821. ND PS–3666.
822. H. Krausnick and H. H. Wilhelm, *op. cit.*, pp. 578–9.
823. ND PS–2992.
824. K. Pätzold, *op. cit.*, p. 295.
825. *Ibid.*, p. 298.
826. J. von Lang, ed., *Das Eichmann-Protokoll. Tonbandaufzeichnungen der israelischen Verhöre* (Berlin 1982), p. 69.
827. *Faschismus*, *op. cit.*, p. 374.
828. K. Pätzold, *op. cit.*, pp. 306–7.
829. P. Sauer, ed. *Dokumente*, *op. cit.*, p. 270.
830. M. Zelzer, *Weg und Schicksal der Stuttgarter Juden. Ein Gedenkbuch* (Stuttgart 1964), p. 231ff.
831. P. Sauer, *Dokumente*, *op. cit.*, p. 220.
832. L. Poliakov and J. Wulf, eds, *Das Dritte Reich und seine Diener*, *op. cit.*, pp. 218–19.
833. M. Zelzer, *op. cit.*, p. 232.
834. K. Pätzold, *op. cit.*, pp. 311–12.
835. *Ibid.*, pp. 328–30.
836. Institut für Zeitgeschichte (IfZ) MA 3/9, folder 94.
837. K. Pätzold, *op. cit.*, p. 306 (wrongly dated).
838. P. Sauer, *op. cit.*, pp. 277ff.

839. *Ibid.*, pp. 278ff.
840. K. Pätzold, *op. cit.*, pp. 320–1.
841. P. Sauer, *op. cit.*, pp. 306–7.
842. H. Krausnick and H. H. Wilhelm, *op. cit.*, pp. 566–9.
843. G. Fleming, *Hitler and the Final Solution* (London 1985), pp. 85–6.
844. K. Loewenstein, *Minsk. Im Lager der deutschen Juden* (Bonn 1961), p. 22.
845. H. Heiber, 'Aus den Akten des Gauleiters Kube' *Vierteljahrshefte für Zeitgeschichte* 1956.4, pp. 87, 90–1.
846. *Ibid.*, pp. 78–9.
847. ND PS–709.
848. *Das Diensttagebuch*, *op. cit.*, pp. 457–8.
849. L. Poliakov and J. Wulf, *Das Dritte Reich und die Juden*, *op. cit.*, pp. 119–26.
850. G. Fleming, *op. cit.*, pp. 91–2.
851. M. Domarus, *op. cit.*, pp. 1828–29.
852. H. Krausnick and H. H. Wilhelm, *op. cit.*, p. 551.
853. E. Kogon, *et al.*, *op. cit.*, pp. 122–3.
854. *Ibid.*, pp. 126–8.
855. *Faschismus*, *op. cit.*, pp. 285–6.
856. J. von Lang, *op. cit.*, Appendix. (NO–365).
857. NO–205.
858. *Faschismus*, *op. cit.*, pp. 269–70.
859. E. Kogon, *et al.*, *op. cit.*, p. 152.
860. *Faschismus*, *op. cit.*, pp. 295–6.
861. E. Kogon, *et al.*, *op. cit.*, p. 183.
862. L. Poliakov and J. Wulf, *Das Dritte Reich und die Juden*, *op. cit.*, pp. 103–8.
863. A. Rückerl, ed., *NS Vernichtungslager im Spiegel der deutscher Strafprozesse. Belzec, Sobibor, Treblinka, Chełmno* (Munich 1977), p. 219.
864. *Ibid.*, pp. 174–5.
865. *Ibid.*, p. 218.
866. *Faschismus*, *op. cit.*, pp. 305–7.
867. *Ibid.*, p. 307.
868. *Ibid.*, pp. 313–14.
869. *Ibid.*, p. 303.
870. NO–626.
871. *Faschismus*, *op. cit.*, pp. 444–6.
872. *Ibid.*, pp. 446–7.
873. NOKW–134.
874. *Faschismus*, *op. cit.*, p. 447.
875. *Ibid.*, p. 449.
876. *Ibid.*, p. 355.
877. *Ibid.*, pp. 450–1.
878. *Ibid.*, p. 510.
879. *Ibid.*, pp. 538–9.
880. L. Poliakov and J. Wulf, *Das Dritte Reich und die Juden*, *op. cit.*, pp. 44–5.
881. *Ibid.*, p. 45.
882. *Faschismus*, *op. cit.*, pp. 421–2.
883. L. Poliakov and J. Wulf, *Das Dritte Reich und die Juden*, *op. cit.*, pp. 65–6.
884. *Ibid.*, pp. 54–5.
885. *Ibid.*, pp. 58–9.
886. *Faschismus*, *op. cit.*, p. 402.
887. *Anatomie des Krieges*, *op. cit.*, p. 320.

888. Y. Bauer, 'Auschwitz' in E. Jäckel and J. Rohwer, eds, *Der Mord an den Juden im Zweiten Weltkrieg* (Stuttgart 1985), p. 165.
889. *Faschismus*, *op. cit.*, pp. 374ff.
890. Y. Bauer, *op. cit.*, p. 167.
891. E. Kogon, *et al.*, *op. cit.*, p. 205.
892. *Ibid.*, p. 207.
893. *Ibid.*, p. 213.
894. *Ibid.*, pp. 210–11.
895. *Ibid.*, pp. 224–5.
896. *Ibid.*, pp. 227–8.
897. *Ibid.*, pp. 235–6.
898. *Ibid.*, pp. 234–5.
899. L. Poliakov and J. Wulf, eds, *Das Dritte Reich und die Juden*, *op. cit.*, p. 198.
900. *Ibid.*, p. 67.
901. *Auschwitz. Geschichte und Wirklichkeit des Vernichtungslagers* (Reinbek 1980), p. 103.
902. *Ibid.*, pp. 130–1.
903. *Ibid.*, pp. 135–6.
904. *Faschismus*, *op. cit.*, pp. 376–7.
905. L. Poliakov and J. Wulf, *Das Dritte Reich und die Juden*, *op. cit.*, pp. 95–7.
906. K. Pätzold, *op. cit.*, pp. 343–5.
907. L. Poliakov and J. Wulf, *Das Dritte Reich und die Juden*, *op. cit.*, pp. 223–4.
908. ND PS–1919.
909. B. F. Smith and A. Peterson, eds, *Heinrich Himmler. Geheimreden 1933 bis 1945* (Frankfurt 1974), p. 202.
910. L. Poliakov and J. Wulf, eds, *Das Dritte Reich und die Juden*, *op. cit.*, p. 179.
911. L. Poliakov and J. Wulf, *Das Dritte Reich und seine Diener*, *op. cit.*, pp. 378ff.
912. *Ibid.*.
913. E. Kogon, *et. al.*, *op. cit.*, pp. 333ff.
914. K. Smolen, ed., *Auschwitz in den Augen des SS* (Auschwitz 1973), pp. 212ff.
915. A. Rückerl, ed., *op. cit.*, pp. 187–8, 192–3.
916. *Ibid.*, pp. 215–16.
917. *Faschismus*, *op. cit.*, pp. 381–3.
918. H-A. Jacobsen, *Der Zweite Weltkrieg: Grundzüge der Politik und Strategie in Dokumenten* (Frankfurt 1965), p. 186.

A Selective Bibliography

G. Aly et al., *Cleansing the Fatherland. Nazi Medicine and Racial Hygiene* (Baltimore 1994).

Y. Arad, *Belzec, Sobibor, Treblinka: The Operation of the Reinhard Death Camps* (Bloomington/Indiana 1987).

P. Baldwin, ed., *Reworking the Past: Hitler, the Holocaust and the Historians' Debate* (Boston 1990).

D. Bankier, *The Germans and the Final Solution* (Chapel Hill 1995).

O. Bartov, *The Eastern Front, 1941–45, German Troops and the Barbarization of Warfare* (London 1985).

O. Bartov, *Hitler's Army. Soldiers, Nazis and War in the Third Reich* (Oxford 1991).

A. Barkai, *From Boycott to Annihilation. The Economic Struggle of German Jews 1933–1943* (London 1989).

Y. Bauer, *A History of the Holocaust* (New York 1982).

Y. Bauer, *Jews for Sale? Nazi–Jewish Negotiations 1933–1945* (New Haven 1990).

R. Bessel, *Life in the Third Reich* (London 1987).

P.R. Black, *Ernst Kaltenbrunner. Ideological Soldier of the Third Reich* (Princeton 1984).

M. Bloch, *Ribbentrop* (London 1993).

R. Breitman, *The Architect of Genocide. Himmler and the Final Solution* (London 1991).

M. Broszat, 'Hitler and the Genesis of the "Final Solution": An Assessment of David Irving's Theses' in H.W. Koch, ed., *Aspects of the Third Reich* (London 1985).

C.R. Browning, *The Final Solution and the German Foreign Office* (New York 1978).

C.R. Browning, *Fateful Months: Essays on the Emergence of the Final Solution, 1941–42* (New York 1985).

C.R. Browning, *Path to Genocide. Essays on the Launching of the Final Solution* (London 1992).

C.R. Browning, *Ordinary Men* (London 1993).

A. Bullock, 'Hitler and the Origins of the Second World War' in E.M. Robertson, ed., *The Origins of the Second World War* (London 1971).

M. Burleigh & W. Wippermann, *The Racial State. Germany 1933–1945* (London 1992).

M. Burleigh, *Death and Deliverance* (London 1994).

P. Burrin, *Hitler and the Jews: The Genesis of the Holocaust* (London 1994).

W. Carr, *Arms, Autarky, and Aggression. A Study in German Foreign Policy 1933–1939* (London, 2nd ed., 1979).

W. Carr, *Hitler. A Study in Personality and Politics* (London 1978).

W. Carr, *Poland to Pearl Harbor. The Making of the Second World War* (London 1985).

B.A. Carroll, *Design for Total War* (The Hague 1968).
F.L. Carsten, *The Reichswehr and Politics 1918–33* (London, 2nd ed., 1973).
D. Cesarani, ed., *The Final Solution. Origins and Implementation* (London 1994).
T. Childers & J. Caplan, eds, *Reevaluating the Third Reich* (New York 1993).
M. Cooper, *The German Army 1933–45* (London 1978).
M. van Crefeld, *Hitler's Strategy 1940–41* (London 1973).
D. Crew, ed., *Nazism and German Society 1933–1945* (London 1994).
A. Dallin, *German Rule in Russia 1941–45. A Study in Occupation Policies* (London, 2nd ed., 1981).
L. Dawidowicz, *The War Against the Jews, 1933–45* (London 1979).
W. Deakin, *The Brutal Friendship: Mussolini, Hitler and the Fall of Italian Fascism* (London 1962).
W. Deist, *The Wehrmacht and German Rearmament* (London 1981).
W. Deist, *The German Military in the Age of Total War* (London 1985).
J. Erickson, *The Road to Stalingrad* (London 1975).
J. Erickson, *The Road to Berlin* (London 1984).
G. Fleming, *Hitler and the Final Solution* (London 1985).
H. Friedlander & S. Milton, eds, *The Holocaust. Ideology, Bureaucracy, and Genocide* (Milwood, New York 1980).
H. Friedlander, *The Origins of Nazi Genocide. From Euthanasia to the Final Solution* (Chapel Hill 1995).
M. Geyer, 'Professionals and Junkers: German Rearmament and Politics in the Weimar Republic' in R. Bessel & E.J. Feuchtwanger, eds, *Social Change and Political Development in Weimar Germany* (London 1981).
M. Geyer, 'Etudes in Political History: Reichswehr, NSDAP and Seizure of Power' in P.D. Stachura, ed., *The Nazi Machtergreifung* (London 1983).
M. Gilbert, *Auschwitz and the Allies* (London 1981).
M. Gilbert, *Atlas of the Holocaust* (London 1982).
M. Gilbert, *The Holocaust. The Jewish Tragedy* (London 1986).
M. Gilbert, *The Dent Atlas of the Holocaust* (London 1993).
D.J. Goldhagen, *Hitler's Willing Executioners. Ordinary Germans and the Holocaust* (London/New York 1996).
J.T. Gross, *Polish Society under German Occupation. The Generalgouvernement 1939–44* (Princeton NJ. 1979).
L. Gross, *The Last Jews in Berlin* (London 1983).
Y. Gutman, *The Jews of Warsaw 1939–1943: Ghetto, Underground Revolt* (Bloomington/Indiana 1989).
P. Hayes, ed., *Lessons and Legacies: the Meaning of the Holocaust in a Changing World* (Evanston, Ill. 1991).
J.L. Heinemann, *Hitler's First Foreign Minister. Constantin Freiherr von Neurath* (Berkeley 1979).
U. Herbert, *A History of Foreign Labor in Germany 1880–1980* (Ann Arbor 1990).
J. Hiden, *Germany and Europe 1919–1939* (London 1977).
R. Hilberg, *The Destruction of the European Jews* (New York, 2nd ed., 1983).
K. Hildebrand, *The Foreign Policy of the Third Reich* (London 1973).
G. Hirschfeld, ed., *The Policies of Genocide. Jews and Soviet Prisoners of War in Nazi Germany* (London 1986).
A. Hitler, *Mein Kampf* (London 1969).
A. Hitler, *Hitler's Second Book* (London 1962).
A. Hitler, *Hitler's Secret Conversations* (New York 1961).
H. Höhne, *The Order of the Death's Head* (London 1969).
R. Hoess, *Commandant of Auschwitz* (London 1959).

E.L. Homze, *Foreign Labor in Nazi Germany* (Princeton NJ. 1967).
D. Irving, *Hitler's War* (London 1977).
E. Jäckel, *Hitler's Weltanschauung*.
E. Jäckel, *Hitler in History* (Hanover/London 1984).
M. Kater, *Doctors under Hitler* (Chapel Hill 1989).
I. Kershaw, *The Nazi Dictatorship. Problems and Perspectives of Interpretation* (London 1994).
I. Kershaw, *The 'Hitler Myth'. Image and Reality in the Third Reich* (Oxford 1986).
E. Klee, *'The Good Old Days': The Holocaust as seen by its Perpetrators and Bystanders* (London 1991).
R.L. Koehl, *RKFDV: German Resettlement and Population Policy 1939–1945* (Cambridge, Mass. 1957).
R.L. Koehl, *The Black Order. The Structure and Power Struggles of the Nazi SS* (Wisconsin 1983).
H. Krausnick et al., *Anatomy of the SS State* (London 1968).
A.B. Leach, *German Strategy against Russia 1939–41* (London 1973).
R.J. Lifton, *The Nazi Doctors. Medical Killing and the Psychology of Genocide* (New York 1986).
R.C. Lucas, *Forgotten Holocaust. The Poles under German Occupation 1939–1944* (Kentucky 1986).
M. Marrus, *The Holocaust in History* (London 1988).
M. Marrus & R.O. Paxton, *Vichy France and the Jews* (New York 1981).
T.W. Mason, *Social Policy in the Third Reich* (London 1993).
S. Milton, ed., *The Stroop-Report. The Jewish Quarter of Warsaw is no more* (London 1979).
W. Michalka, 'From the Anti-Comintern Pact to the Euro-Asiatic Bloc: Ribbentrop's Alternative Concept to Hitler's Foreign Policy Programme' in H.W. Koch, ed., *Aspects of the Third Reich* (London 1985).
A. Milward, *The German Economy at War* (London 1965).
A. Milward, *The New Order and the French Economy* (London 1970).
A. Milward, *The Fascist Economy in Norway* (London 1972).
A. Milward, *War, Economy and Society* (London, 2nd ed., 1987).
H. Mommsen, *From Weimar to Auschwitz* (London 1991).
The Nazi Decision to Commit Mass Murder. Three Interpretations in *German Studies Review* XVII.3.October 1994)
R.J. O'Neill, *The German Army and the Nazi Party 1933–39* (London 1966).
R. Overy, *Göring. The 'Iron Man'* (London 1984).
R. Overy, 'Germany, "Domestic Crisis" and War in 1939' *Past and Present* 116, August 1987.
R. Overy, *War and Economy in the Third Reich* (Oxford 1994).
N. Rich, *Hitler's War Aims* 2 vols (New York 1973, 1974).
E.M. Robertson, ed., *The Origins of the Second World War* (London 1971).
T. Schulte, *The German Army and Nazi Policies in Occupied Russia* (Oxford 1989).
A. Seaton, *The German Army 1933–45* (London 1982).
G. Sereny, *Into that Darkness. From Mercy Killing to Mass Murder* (London 1974).
W.D. Smith, *The Ideological Origins of Nazi Imperialism* (Oxford 1986).
J. Steinberg, *All or Nothing. The Axis and the Holocaust 1941–43* (London 1990).
G. Stoakes, *Hitler and the Quest for World Domination: Nazi Ideology and Policy in the 1920s* (Leamington 1986).
C.W. Sydnor, *Soldiers of Destruction* (Princeton NJ. 1977).
E.M. Robertson, ed., *The Origins of the Second World War* (London 1971).
A.J.P. Taylor, *The Origins of the Second World War* (London 1963).
C.S. Thomas, *The German Navy in the Nazi Era* (London 1990).

H.R. Trevor-Roper, 'Hitler's War Aims' in H.W. Koch, ed., *Aspects of the Third Reich* (London 1985).
I. Trunk, *Judenrat: The Jewish Councils in Eastern Europe under Nazi Occupation* (London 1977).
D.C. Watt, *How War Came* (London 1989).
B. Wegner, *The Waffen SS: Ideology, Organization and Function* (Oxford 1990).
G.L. Weinberg, *The Foreign Policy of Hitler's Germany* 2 vols (Chicago 1970, 1980).
G.L. Weinberg, *A World at Arms. A Global History of World War II* (Cambridge 1994).
J. Wright & P. Stafford, 'Hitler and the Hossbach Memorandum' in *History Today* 38, 1988.
L. Yahil, *The Holocaust. The Fate of European Jewry 1932–1945* (New York/Oxford 1990).